CITIES OF WORDS

STANLEY CAVELL

CAVELL

CITIES OF WORDS

PEDAGOGICAL LETTERS ON A REGISTER OF THE MORAL LIFE

THE BELKNAP PRESS OF
HARVARD UNIVERSITY PRESS
CAMBRIDGE, MASSACHUSETTS
LONDON, ENGLAND
2004

Library of Congress Cataloging-in-Publication Data
Cavell, Stanley, 1926–
Cities of words : pedagogical letters on a register of the moral life / Stanley Cavell.
p. cm.
Includes bibliographical references and index.
ISBN 0-674-01336-0 (alk. paper)
1. Perfection—Moral and ethical aspects. 2. Conduct of life. 3. Ethics. I. Title.
B945.C273C58 2004
171′.3—dc22   2003067677

To the Teaching Fellows in Moral Reasoning 34

CONTENTS

The book of letters you have before you follows the course of a course of lectures called Moral Perfectionism, which I gave a number of times over the last decade and a half. The book differs from the lectures most notably in the circumstance that the secrets of its ending and the mysteries of its beginning are here fixed, for you and for me. It is the same man saying "I" here as said "I" there, but the you, whom I address here, unlike the students and friends in the classroom, are free to walk away from any sentence or paragraph of it without embarrassment to either of us, and indeed to drop the course at any time without any penalty other than its own loss.

I lectured twice a week. The Tuesday lectures concerned central texts of moral philosophy, early and late (Plato, Aristotle, Locke, Kant, Mill, Nietzsche, Rawls) or literary texts presenting moral issues bearing on perfectionist preoccupations (Shakespeare, Ibsen, George Bernard Shaw), or philosophical presentations of texts by writers not usually considered by professional philosophers to be moral thinkers (Emerson and Freud). Thursdays were devoted to masterpieces (according to me) of American film from the so-called Golden Age of the Hollywood talkie (the earliest dating from 1934, the latest from 1949).

The idea of the book is to keep in the published chapters something of the sound of the original classroom lectures, as distinguished from the sound of a presentation to a scholarly organization or a formal talk to a general public, for several reasons. First, I am not (I know of no one who is) a scholar in all the fields touched upon in this book: ancient and modern philosophy, moral and aesthetic philosophy, literature, psychoanalysis, American transcendentalism, and the aesthetics and history of film. If teachers confined themselves to ideas and texts about which they considered themselves experts, some of the best courses I ever took would not have been given. Second, I love the sound of interesting, which means interested, academic lecturing. Third, I have had in mind, in writing about my experience of the course, an audience that extends to those past their college lives who have retained, or returned to, an interest in a college classroom.

Because, when the suggestion came from Lindsay Waters of Harvard University Press to think about publishing a version of my Moral Perfectionism lectures, some four years had passed since I last gave the course at Harvard, to get back into the spirit of the course I accepted an invitation to commute to the University of Chicago to present it in a format that beneficially doubled the period of time allotted to each lecture and that stretched the span of the lectures over a full academic year. When I confided to the class gathered at Chicago that for my Tuesday lectures (on works of philosophy or of literature) I proposed to read them texts that would, if things worked out, become part of a book, they were encouraging, and even interested in the idea that what I wanted to arrive at was not simply a transcription, smoothed out, of lecture notes but some kind of written equivalent of the experience of *giving* the course. For the Thursday lectures I would write out less material in advance in order to leave time for discussion, which itself would variously be incorporated into chapters.

As I sat in Boston, more precisely in Brookline, one street from the Boston city limits, within earshot of Fenway Park, which mattered in October and would matter again in April and May, writing out documents of a certain intimacy to be delivered, a day or two after I completed them, to a shifting audience living a two-hour plane ride away, I came to think of these documents as a sequence of pedagogical letters, although I do not insist on referring to them that way in the book (since the idea of a chapter, as marking a segment of a life, is an equally apt and interesting concept). Speaking of the segments as letters invokes an illustrious precursor in the line of moral perfectionism, Friedrich Schiller's "series of letters" *On the Aesthetic Education of Man*—although Schiller's views of perfectibility and of the authority of philosophy and, for that matter, the nature of morality and of aesthetics are at variance with those advanced here.

In the Introduction I say more about the difference between attending a course of lectures and following its progress in a book. Here I anticipate an immediate difference. The Introduction, though it goes over some material that would occur in the opening lecture of a course, is more detailed than the orientations and confusions and general nervousness of a first day in a new class would allow. If you do not like reading introductions, or prefer postponing them—I confess I never skip them—a book frees you to turn at once to Chapter 1, or, for that matter, to any other.

I know that the world I converse with in the cities and in the farms, is not the world I *think*.

        —*Emerson*

Furthermore, the idea of a pure intelligible world as a whole of all intelligences to which we ourselves belong as rational beings (though on the other side we are at the same time members of the world of sense) is always a useful and permissible idea for the purposes of a rational faith.

        —*Kant*

—The man of sense . . . will avoid both public and private honors which he believes will destroy the existing condition of his soul.
—He will not then, he said, if that is his concern, be willing to go into politics.
—Yes, by the dog, he will, I said, at least in his own kind of city, but not in his fatherland perhaps, unless divine good luck should be his.
—I understand, he said, you mean in the city which we were founding and described, our city of words, for I do not believe it exists anywhere on earth.
—Perhaps, I said, it is a model laid up in heaven, for him who wishes to look upon, and as he looks, set up the government of his soul. It makes no difference whether it exists anywhere or will exist. He would take part in the public affairs of that city only, not of any other.
—That is probable, he said.

        —*Plato*

In every work of genius we recognize our own rejected thoughts; they come back to us with a certain alienated majesty.

        —*Emerson*

Try to be one of the people on whom nothing is lost.

—*Henry James*

In our times, from the highest class of society down to the lowest, everyone lives as under the eye of a hostile and dreaded censorship. Not only in what concerns others, but in what concerns only themselves, the individual or the family do not ask themselves, what do I prefer? Or, what would suit my character and disposition? Or, what would allow the best and highest in me to have fair play and enable it to grow and thrive? They ask themselves, what is suitable to my position? . . . It does not occur to them to have any inclination except for what is customary . . . conformity is the first thing thought of . . . until by dint of not following their own nature they have no nature to follow: they become incapable of any strong wishes or native pleasures, and are generally without either opinions or feelings of home growth, or properly their own. Now is this, or is it not, the desirable condition of human nature?

—*J. S. Mill*

The mass of men lead lives of quiet desperation.

—*Thoreau*

But even if Protestantism was not the true solution, it did pose the problem correctly. It was now no longer a question of the struggle of the layman with the priest outside himself, but rather of his struggle with his own inner priest, with his priestly nature.

—*Marx*

There are nowadays professors of philosophy, but not philosophers. Yet it is admirable to profess because it was once admirable to live.

—*Thoreau*

If you can't stand the coldness of my sort of life, and the strain of it, go back to the gutter . . . Oh, it's a fine life, the life of the gutter . . . you can taste it and smell it without any training or any work. Not like Science and Literature and Classical Music and Philosophy and Art.

—*G. B. Shaw's Professor Higgins*

So far I have said very little about the principle of perfection . . . There are two variants: in the first it is the sole principle of a teleological theory directing society to arrange institutions and to define the duties and obligations of individuals so as to maximize the achievement of human excellence in art, science, and culture.

—*John Rawls*

This revolution is to be wrought by the gradual domestication of the idea of Culture. The main enterprise of the world for splendor, for extent, is the upbuilding of a man. Here are the materials strewn along the ground.

—*Emerson*

For the question is this: how can your life, the individual life, receive the highest value, the deepest significance? How can it be least squandered? Certainly only by your living for the good of the rarest and most valuable exemplars, and not for the good of the majority, that is to say those who, taken individually, are the least valuable exemplars . . . for culture is the child of each individual's self-knowledge and dissatisfaction with himself. Anyone who believes in culture is thereby saying: "I see above me something higher and more human than I am; let everyone help me to attain it, as I will help everyone who knows and suffers as I do."

—*Nietzsche*

Every Man being . . . naturally free, and nothing being able to put him into subjection to any Earthly Power, but his own Consent; it is to be considered, what shall be understood to be a sufficient Declaration of a Man's Consent.

—*Locke*

He who marries, intends as little to conspire his own ruin as he that swears allegiance; and as a whole people is in proportion to an ill government, so is one man to an ill marriage . . . For no effect of tyranny can sit more heavy on the commonwealth than this household unhappiness of the family. And farewell all hope of true reformation in the state, while such an evil as this lies undiscerned or unregarded in the house: on the redress whereof depends not only the spiritful and orderly life of our grown men, but the willing and careful education of our children.

—*John Milton*

What marriage may be in the case of two persons of cultivated faculties, identical in opinions and purposes, between whom there exists that best kind of equality, similarity of powers and capacities with reciprocal superiority in them—so that each can enjoy the luxury of looking up to the other, and can have alternately the pleasure of leading and of being led in the path of development—I will not attempt to describe.

—*J. S. Mill*

Helmer: Nora—can't I ever be anything more than a stranger to you?
Nora (picking up her bag): Oh, Torvald—there would have to be the greatest miracle of all.
Helmer: What would that be—the greatest miracle of all?
Nora: Both of us would have to be so changed that . . . our life together could be a real marriage. Good-bye.

—*Ibsen*

The finding of an object is in fact the refinding of it.

—*Freud*

Moreover, friendship would seem to hold cities together, and legislators would seem to be more concerned about it than about justice. For concord would seem to be similar to friendship and they aim at concord above all, while they try above all to expel civil conflict, which is enmity. Further, if people are friends, they have no need of justice, but if they are just they need friendship in addition; and the justice that is most just seems to belong to friendship.

—*Aristotle*

The untold want by life and land ne'er granted,
Now voyager sail thou forth to seek and find.

—*Walt Whitman*

In the Place of the Classroom

The first of the epigraphs I have placed as guardians or guides at the entrance to this book—"I know that the world I converse with in the cities and in the farms, is not the world I *think*"—opens the concluding paragraph of Emerson's "Experience." It captures one of Kant's summary images of his colossal *Critiques,* epitomized in the *Groundwork of the Metaphysics of Morals,* namely that of the human being as regarding his existence from two standpoints, from one of which he counts himself as belonging to the world of sense (the province of the knowledge of objects and their causal laws, presided over by the human understanding), and from the other of which he counts himself as belonging to the intelligible world (the province of freedom and of the moral law, presided over by reason, transcending the human powers of knowing). But each of the thinkers and artists we will encounter in the following pages may be said to respond to some such insight of a split in the human self, of human nature as divided or double.

Emerson's variation of the insight (not unlike John Stuart Mill's) is to transfigure Kant's metaphysical division of worlds into a rather empirical (or political) division of the world, in which the way we now hold the world in bondage is contrasted with, reformed into, a future way we could help it to become (this is not exactly foreign to Kant). Plato's variation—or rather Plato's vision of which Kant's is a variation—is that the world of sense is a degraded scene or shadow of an intelligible world which can be entered only by those fit to govern the world perfectly, that is, with perfect justice. Locke's vision is between a world of nature ruled by power and violence and a world of the political created by common human consent. Ibsen's division, in *A Doll's House,* is between an incomprehensibly unjust present world and a world of freedom and reciprocity which is almost unthinkable, which only human instinct and risk can begin to divine and describe. Freud's sense of our division shows the details of the private epic in which the world we do not know we know rules the world we imagine we know. Shakespeare's late romance *The Winter's Tale* posits, in its longest act, a pastoral world of song and dance and familiar mischief which is a kind of dream of the actual world, one in which the various roles into which the arbitrariness of birth and accident have cast us—kings, princesses, merchants, clowns, peasants— are occupied by those whose natures exactly fit them for these roles, in which indeed there would be no need for "roles," since all members of such a society would know and receive pleasure and reward from their natural, and naturally modifiable, constellation of positions.

And so forth. Each of these variations provides a position from which the present state of human existence can be judged and a future state achieved, or else the present judged to be better than the cost of changing it. The very conception of a divided self and a doubled world, providing a perspective of judgment upon the world as it is, measured against the world as it may be, tends to express disappointment with the world as it is, as the scene of human activity and prospects, and perhaps to lodge the demand or desire for a reform or transfiguration of the world. So common is this pattern of disappointment and desire, in part or whole, as represented in the philosophical figures to follow here, that I think of it as the moral calling of philosophy, and name it moral perfectionism, a register of the moral life that precedes, or intervenes in, the specification of moral theories which define the particular bases of moral judgments of particular acts or projects or characters as right or wrong, good or bad.

An idea of the moral calling of philosophy as such inspires the American event in philosophy, as philosophy is discovered by Emerson. In putting Emerson first—say this is making the last first, looking back over the history of philosophy from the perspective of that re-beginning—I accordingly wish here to accent that history differently from the way it presents itself to philosophers who begin their sense of philosophy's re-beginning in the modern era with the response, in Bacon and in Descartes and in Locke, to the traumatic event of the New Science of Copernicus and Galileo and Newton, for which the basis of human knowledge of the world rather than of human conduct in that world is primary among philosophical preoccupations. It is familiar to describe modern philosophy as dominated by epistemology, the theory of knowledge, making the fields of moral philosophy and the philosophy of art and of religion secondary, even optional. My claim for Emerson's achievement is not exactly that he reverses this hierarchy but rather that he refuses the breakup of philosophy into separate fields, an eventuality fully institutionalized as philosophy becomes one discipline among others in the modern university. (Such a refusal can be understood to manifest itself in the writing of Wittgenstein and of Heidegger. But in these cases this aspect of the writing is, for reasons yet unarticulated, ignorable at will.) So that Emerson's effort to reclaim or re-begin philosophy as such on these new, perhaps intellectually inhospitable, shores ("these bleak rocks"), is precisely what keeps him from being recognized, either by friends or by enemies, as a philosopher.

The sense of disappointment with the world as a place in which to seek the satisfaction of human desire is not the same as a sense of the world as cursed, perhaps at best to be endured, perhaps as a kind of punishment for being human. This sense of existence cursed requires not merely a philosophical but a religious perspective. I do not, in what follows, take up perfectionisms based on a religious perspective, any more than I regard the perfectionism I do follow out as requiring an imagination of some ultimate human perfection. Emersonian perfectionism, on the contrary, with which I begin and to which I most often recur, specifically sets itself against any idea of ultimate perfection.

But if the world is disappointing and the world is malleable and hence we feel ourselves called upon for change, where does change begin, with the individual (with myself) or with the collection of those who make up my (social, political) world? This question seems to make good sense if we contrast Emerson or Freud with, say, Locke or Marx (who is not featured in these pages but puts in a distinct cameo appearance), but its sense is questioned as we consider what perfectionist encounters look and sound like. I would say, indeed, that it is a principal object of Emerson's thinking to urge a reconsideration of the relation ("the" relation?) of soul and society, especially as regards the sense of priority of one over the other. I take seriously, that is, Emerson's various formulations of the idea that, as he words it in "The American Scholar," "The deeper [the scholar] dives into his privatest, secretest presentiment, to his wonder he finds this is the most acceptable, most public, and universally true." By taking it seriously I mean I find it intuitively valuable enough that I am moved to work with it in making it plainer. It bears directly on what I have called the arrogance of philosophy, its claim to speak universally, to discover the bases of existence as such.

In the Place of the Classroom

In Emerson, as in Wittgenstein's *Investigations,* I encounter the social in my every utterance and in each silence. Sometimes this means that I find in myself nothing but social, dictated thoughts (the condition Emerson opposes as "conformity," what philosophy has forever called the unexamined life); sometimes it means that I find in the social nothing but chaos (Emerson cries out, "Every word they say chagrins us"). What I conceive as the moral calling of philosophy is what I conceive the Freudian intervention in Western culture to have responded to. If I say that philosophy, as influenced by the later Wittgenstein, is therapeutically motivated, this does not mean, as some philosophers have construed it, that we are to be cured of philosophy, but that contemporary philosophy is to understand its continuity with the ancient wish of philosophy to lead the soul, imprisoned and distorted by confusion and darkness, into the freedom of the day. (A condition of philosophy is that the day not absolutely be closed to freedom, by tyranny or by poverty.) Freud perpetually distinguished his work from that of philosophy, recognizing that what he meant by the unconscious of experience and speech challenged philosophy's understanding of consciousness (I take it for granted that philosophy had no systematic understanding of the unconscious). I believe that Freud's stance against what he called philosophy has proved unfortunate both for philosophy and for psychoanalysis. It is my impression that Lacan's way of overcoming that stance only served to harden its prevalence in the United States. Perhaps those days are passing.

The sense of disappointment I find in the origin of the moral calling of philosophy is something that I have derived principally from my reading of Wittgenstein, most particularly his *Philosophical Investigations,* where the human being perpetually attacks its everyday life as intellectually lacking in certainty or fastidiousness or accuracy or immediacy or comprehensiveness and is compelled to search for an order or a system or a language that would secure a human settlement with the world that goes beyond human sense and certainty. Sometimes Wittgenstein describes or pictures this as a search or demand for the absolute, which he more generally names the metaphysical. Wittgenstein's principal contrast with the metaphysical is what he calls the ordinary or the everyday, a perpetual topic in the pages to follow here. Where Wittgenstein describes his effort in philosophy as one of "returning words from their metaphysical to their everyday use," I habitually speak of the task of accepting finitude. The attempt to satisfy the demand for the absolute makes what we say inherently private (as though we withheld the sense of our words even, or especially, from ourselves), a condition in which the good city we would inhabit cannot be constructed, since it exists only in our intelligible encounters with each other. The philosophical outlook of Deweyan pragmatism, considerably more prominent in contemporary American intellectual life, at least in American academic life, than Emersonianism, is equally devoted to discarding empty quests for the absolute. But for my taste pragmatism misses the depth of human restiveness, or say misses the daily, insistent split in the self that being human cannot, without harm to itself (beyond moments of ecstasy) escape, and so pragmatism's encouragement for me, while essential, is limited.

Wittgenstein's disappointment with knowledge is not that it fails to be better than it is (for example, immune to skeptical doubt), but rather that it fails to make us better than we are, or provide us with peace.

The sequence of texts I devote attention to—while just about all of the texts are monsters of fame—is too selective to count as a proposed canon of reading in moral philosophy, even for one register of moral thinking. The severity of selectiveness in limiting the number of principal texts to the number of weeks of the course from which this book derives was itself limited by the hope that each text could receive enough of a consecutive exposition from me to prompt and allow my reader to go on with it alone. Any sensible teacher (myself half the time) will find the pace too fast. But any fewer texts would not, it seems to me, give a sense of the magnitude and variousness of the register of moral thinking I wish to bring to attention.

I have been guided in my specific selection by two main considerations: first, to show the persistence of a family of articulations of the moral life in modern thought (say from the time of Shakespeare and, in the following generations, in the work of Milton and of Locke) that begins most famously in Western culture with the beginning of philosophy marked by Plato and Aristotle; second, to include texts that no serious (or say professional) philosophical discussion of moral reasoning would be likely to neglect, but at the same time to insist upon the pertinence of further (literary) texts that few professional philosophical discussions, or courses, would feel pressured to acknowledge. The inclusion of the films that accompany the discursive texts here is meant to help in exerting such pressure, but no professor of philosophy should be expected to feel that their omission would intellectually be much of a loss, let alone unsafe. Nor would I wish to give the impression that philosophy left to itself requires compensation by revelations within the medium of film. These films are rather to be thought of as differently configuring intellectual and emotional avenues that philosophy is already in exploration of, but which, perhaps, it has cause sometimes to turn from prematurely, particularly in its forms since its professionalization, or academization, from say the time of Kant (the first modern to show that major philosophy can be produced by a professor, namely within a discipline that is one among other university disciplines). The implied claim is that film, the latest of the great arts, shows philosophy to be the often invisible accompaniment of the ordinary lives that film is so apt to capture (even, perhaps particularly, when the lives depicted are historical or elevated or comic or hunted or haunted).

While the wisdom in discussing a text of Emerson's first is something whose fruitfulness can only manifest itself as the sequence develops, there are reasons for it that can be given at the outset. One reason is that the primary body of Hollywood films to be adduced here may be understood as inspired by Emersonian transcendentalism. Another is that Emerson brings to philosophy dimensions of human concern that the field of philosophy, in its Anglo-American academic dispensation, in which I was trained, particularly discouraged, not to say disheartened. Matters have modified themselves to some degree over the decades since I began writing, but Emerson continues to suggest for me, for example, a remarkably apt source of paths between the Anglo-American dispensation of philosophy and the German-French.

The hard division of the philosophical mind between these dispensations has been costly to academic life, hence to intellectual life more generally, if less assessibly, in the humanities and the humanistically interested social studies in these decades. The division has served, for example, to deepen the suspicion between literary studies in America and American pedagogy in philosophy, the former so often hungrily incorporating the primarily French structuralist and post-structuralist theory that began in the late 1960s, the latter equally often holding this material in contempt. It may seem paradoxical, or irrelevant, to understand Emerson as a bridge between these philosophical dispensations since he is not widely accepted as a formidable philosophical thinker in either of them. So it figures that my fascination with Emerson has been a gift whose value I can neither renounce nor easily share.

I came late, as Emerson in his American context came late, to philosophy. This is not particular to me (merely exaggerated, as I spent the years of my life through college as a musician); it is reflected in such facts as that philosophy is not a regular part of an American high school education and that the field of American studies was formed by an association of literary study and historical study, with philosophy left, or leaving itself, out. Emerson's response, in his new world, to his irresistible want of philosophy was to include habitually in his writing any and all of the vocabulary of philosophy—from ideas and degrees of participation in ideas, to impressions as the origin of ideas, to the distinction of accident and necessity, and reason and understanding, and fate and freedom, and possibility and actuality, and theory and practice. But he often introduces terms from this vocabulary in ways that disguise their origin, hence he allows an assessment of these terms by testing whether they hold up under the pressure of ordinary speech.

When he says, in "Fate," "Ideas are in the air," can we doubt that he is invoking Plato's theory of forms at the same time that he is speaking, in 1850, of the absorbing issue of slavery, as if inquiring as to our participation in, call it our stance toward, these ideas? He goes on to follow out the literal consequence that something essential to our lives, the air we breathe, would be fatal to us but for the fact that our lungs are already filled with this air, allowing us to withstand the weight and pressure of air from above by the counterpressure of that air from within ourselves. This becomes, I take it, a parable whose moral is that the issue of slavery is a matter of life and death, for the nation and for the nation's breath, its speech, its power to understand itself, and therewith for philosophy, whose demand for freedom is incompatible with slavery. (This incompatibility may be denied, or repressed. It once helped me to assert a difference between the idea that some people may rightly be made slaves and the idea that some group of people are inherently slaves, something other than exactly human. The former idea is merely hideous. Holders of the latter idea are accursed.) A leaf I take from Emerson's essays is the sense of writing philosophy from belated America as if this locale is the remaining place where one can take philosophy by surprise, I mean with surprise at the fact that there should be such an enterprise that measures the value of our lives. The familiar recognition that famous philosophers have failed to understand their predecessors, or say to do them justice, should perhaps be seen less as a matter of a need to transcend past achievements than as an effort to discover philosophy for oneself, as if philosophy exists only in its discovery.

What impels me to such a course, risking impertinence, is that America (unless I specify otherwise, I use this term as shorthand for the United

States), in refusing Emerson's bid for philosophy, has not to my mind sufficiently joined philosophically in measuring the value of our lives (unless perhaps one conceives that its literary accomplishments are its philosophy). Contemporary American philosophy has dominated the worldwide development of analytical philosophy, for which, in Quine's words, "philosophy of science is philosophy enough." It perhaps also dominates the field of moral philosophy, but with a, perhaps well-deserved, distrust of the rest of philosophy. And pragmatism, in its classical writers and in its contemporary forms, to the extent that I know them, does not, as I have suggested, seem to know what half of my life is, the half that is not subject to superstition or fanaticism or magic thinking (the traditional black beasts stalked by Enlightenment thought), but that is fraught with, let us say, disproportionate invitations to disappointment and chaos, to the sense of the public world as one in which "every word they say chagrins us."

But consider that there are no *other* words to say than the words everyone is saying. Hence each of the words at Emerson's disposal is one that he has found used in a tone or place or out of some inattentiveness or meanness that requires unswerving examination. His language is hence in continuous struggle with itself, as if he is having to translate, in his American idiom, English into English. I think Emerson is thus dramatizing a dissatisfaction with everyday language that philosophers congenitally sense. A persistent philosophical attempt to cure this dissatisfaction with the everyday is to link philosophical language with logic as in the work of Frege and Russell, initiating what has become known as analytical philosophy. When the later Wittgenstein and J. L. Austin, in a counterdevelopment of this dispensation, declare philosophy's reclamation of ordinary language, they are at the same time suggesting that logic provides not a solution to this dissatisfaction but a substitute satisfaction (which may indeed be all that is rationally attainable), and they are undertaking to demonstrate that only ordinary language is powerful enough to overcome its own inherent tendency to succumb to metaphysical denunciations of its apparent vagueness, imprecision, superstition—not overcome this once for all, but in each incidence of our intellectual and spiritual chagrin.

A sense of the struggle of language with itself forces a certain liberation in interpreting texts that seems to some to go beyond the apparent evidence of their words. Here I recall Emerson's repeated idea that serious writers write beyond themselves, or as he also puts the matter, that character (meaning our constitution and our writing) teaches above our will. So that to understand serious writing will precisely require us to question what a text asserts in order to arrive at the conviction that we are covering the ground gained in what its words actually contrive to say.

In what follows, I take my examples of moral issues most systematically from their manifestation in the art of film. A favored way of approaching the field of moral theory is to contrast two major theories: one of them, called deontological, takes the notion of the right as fundamental, independent of the good, and emphasizes the assessment of human action by its responsiveness to obligation and the motive of duty; the other of them, called teleological, takes the notion of the good as fundamental, deriving from it the notion of right, and stresses the consequences or utility of actions rather than their motives, emphasizing the assessment of human action by its responsiveness to the call to maximize the pleasure or happiness at a person's or a group's disposal. The most influential theory of the good is that of utilitarianism, represented most famously by John Stuart Mill in the nineteenth century; the principal theories of the right are associated with the names of Kant and Hegel.

But when I thought about these eminent theories in connection with the lives depicted in the grand movies I had been immersed in, the theories and the depicted lives passed one another by, appeared irrelevant to each other. Yet these lives seemed and seem to me ones pursued by thoughtful, mature people, heavily in conversation with one another about the value of their individual or their joint pursuits. I could not understand my interest in them as unrelated to moral reflection. I claim for these films that they are masterpieces of the art of film, primary instances of America's artistic contribution to world cinema, and that their power is bound up in their exploration of a strain of moral urgency for which film's inherent powers of transfiguration and shock and emotionality and intimacy have a particular affinity.

But if this moral urgency seems, at an early glance, marginal to the interests of the formidable moral theories most favored in courses in moral philosophy, how is one to assess its presence in the moral outlook explored in, to begin with, the writing of Emerson, hence who knows how deeply in the writings of those whom Emerson takes as his instructors—for example, Plato, Montaigne, Shakespeare, Milton, Kant—and in those who acknowledge instruction from him, notably Thoreau and Nietzsche? I came to imagine that offering a course exploring such a question might prove to be an adventure for me that students and friends would be interested to share, ones at any rate prepared to follow out an inkling of curiosity about the interaction of moral reflection, one of the world's oldest subjects of philosophical investigation, with film, the latest of the great worldwide arts.

I call the film comedies in question remarriage comedies. Unlike classical comedies, where the problem of the drama is to get a young pair past the obstacle of an older figure, usually a father, and see them married (as, for example, in *A Midsummer Night's Dream*), these films concern getting a somewhat older pair who are already together past some inner obstacle between them and hence together *again, back* together. This simple difference turns out to generate an unpredictable, open-ended set of features shared by the films. For example, the woman of the principal pair is never a mother and never (with one exception that proves the rule) shown to have a mother; and, as if negating the pattern of classical comedy, her father is always on the side of her desire, not of the law; and the narrative opens in a city and moves at the end to the country, a place of perspective Shakespeare calls the Green World; and the principal man and woman, speaking, sometimes appearing to invent, each other's language, may seem a mystery to the world around them; and, as we shall see, so on.

In each of these comedies some element of melodrama variously makes an appearance without getting to the point of shattering the comedic universe. This fact eventually prompted me to look for a genre of film melodrama that makes explicit and focuses this intrusion into the life that the pair in remarriage comedy aspires to. When I found a form of melodrama that to my mind satisfies this intellectual or moral requirement, it proved to be one that questions the choice to marry as such. I call this genre the melodrama of the unknown woman, naming it after its most renowned instance, Max Ophuls's *Letter from an Unknown Woman*. These films were among many called "women's pictures" by Hollywood in its marketing of them; others called them tear-jerkers. These titles no more recognize, let alone account for, the power and richness of these films than the title "screwball comedies" accounts for, or helps alert one to, the intelligence and depth of remarriage comedy. Such titles, in serving at once to sell and to avoid the films, are prime exhibits in my view of America as tending to overpraise and undervalue its best achievements.

The Hollywood films to which I devote chapters are representative of the best that American film has contributed to the art of world cinema. But the very facts that they are all, especially the comedies, beloved worldwide, and have kept their force for audiences over a major span of the existence of the medium of which they are part, and at the same time that they bear up (or so I claim) under the same critical pressure that one would bring to works in any of the other of the great arts, should suggest some fascination with the question of what film is, or does, that a substantial body of its instances manifest these powers.

It is true that none of the films under discussion in this book concerns front-page moral dilemmas, say the death penalty (as in *Dead Man Walking*) or whistle blowing (as in *The Insider*), or informing (as in *The Front*), or abortion (as in *Cider House Rules*). Yet it is notable that the newspaper figures in all but two of the remarriage comedies, sometimes so prominently that one may wonder whether it is a feature required by the genre, as if the genre is itself about the question of what is and is not news. What is the public's business? How do we come to our knowledge of what bears on the common good of our lives?

What can be said at once is that, if not front-page news, the issues raised in these films concern the difficulty of overcoming a certain moral cynicism, a giving up on the aspiration to a life more coherent and admirable than seems affordable after the obligations and compromises of adulthood begin to obscure the promise and dreams of youth and the rift between public demands and private desires comes to seem unbridgeable. The issues the principal pair in these films confront each other with are formulated less well by questions concerning what they ought to do, what it would be best or right for them to do, than by the question of how they shall live their lives, what kind of persons they aspire to be. This aspect or moment of morality—in which a crisis forces an examination of one's life that calls for a transformation or reorienting of it—is the province of what I emphasize as moral perfectionism. I do not conceive of this as an alternative to Kantianism or utilitarianism (Kant and John Stuart Mill both have deep perfectionist strains in their views) but rather as emphasizing that aspect of moral choice having to do, as it is sometimes put, with being true to oneself, or as Michel Foucault has put the view, caring for the self. That Shakespeare in *Hamlet* gives the line "to thine own self be true" to Polonius alerts us to the ease with which moral perfectionism can be debased (as when someone is glad to *tell* you how to be all you can be, or, in a more recent television advertisement, to promise you fulfillment through day trading on the stock market)—as philosophy can itself be debased, the condition Socrates combated with his life.

There is a passage in an early dialogue of Plato, the *Euthyphro*, where the division of moral questions between those concerning the good and those concerning the right or just (prefiguring the division between what I have called utilitarianism and Kantianism) is explicitly distinguished, and where room is made for a further distinction. Here is Socrates speaking to Euthyphro:

> But what kind of disagreement, my friend, causes hatred and anger? . . . If we were to disagree as to the relative size [or weight] of two things, we should measure [or weigh] them and put an end to the disagreement at once, should we not? . . . Is . . . not the question which would make us . . . enemies if we could not come to a settlement . . . the question of the just and unjust, of the honorable and the dishonorable, of the good and the bad?

(It is not clear, and for my purposes need not be, whether Socrates is differentiating competing segments of a question or different emphases of a question.) It is what Socrates is calling the honorable and the dishonorable that I propose to take as pointing to the issue of perfectionism—not in the sense of conduct expected of high rank and enforceable by others of that rank, but in the sense of conduct confrontable in moral conversation that affects your sense of your own worth and of those who in various ways identify or associate themselves with you. When the Cary Grant character in *The Philadelphia Story*, during an exchange with his former wife, played by Katharine Hepburn, touches on their past together, he rebukes her for her coldness and moralism, instancing her refusal to tolerate his taste for alcohol; and when she replies that that taste made him unattractive, he returns, "Granted [it was my problem]. But you were no help there. You were a scold." He is not accusing her of some misdeed (as lying, stealing, treachery of some kind) but rather describing her as being unworthy of herself, of what she could be.

Such concerns are paramount in the moral thinking of Plato's *Republic*, in which the soul is pictured as on a journey from spiritual slavery to perfectionist enlightenment. From the period since, say, Kant and Hegel, at the turn of the eighteenth into the nineteenth century, my favorite moral perfectionists are Emerson and Thoreau, to my mind the most underrated philosophical minds (however otherwise praised) to have been produced in the United States. In Emerson's and Thoreau's sense of human existence, there is no question of reaching a final state of the soul but only and endlessly taking the next step to what Emerson calls "an unattained but attainable self"—a self that is always and never ours—a step that turns us not from bad to good, or wrong to right, but from confusion and constriction toward self-knowledge and sociability. Plato's idea of a path to one goal (the one sought by the sage) does not exactly fit Emerson's idea of how to live. In both, the idea of philosophy as a way of life plays a role in assessing your life now, but Emerson is less interested in holding up the life of the sage as a model for ours than in reminding us that the power of questioning our lives, in, say, our judgment of what we call their necessities, and their rights and goods, is within the scope of every human being (of those, at any rate, free to talk about their lives and to modify them).

In the period after Kant and Hegel, moral perfectionism is identified less with canonical moral philosophers than with figures who work, let's say, between philosophy and literature, such, beyond Emerson, and indebted to him, as Nietzsche, or with obviously literary figures such as Jane Austen, George Eliot, Matthew Arnold, Ibsen, Bernard Shaw, Oscar Wilde, who look back to such writers as Rousseau, Goethe, and Wordsworth. Partly because of this shift in the division of intellectual labor, perfectionism has not been much esteemed among philosophers in my part of the philosophical forest, a lack of esteem that seems to climax with Rawls's discussion of Nietzsche in *A Theory of Justice*, which identifies moral perfectionism, in its strongest form, with Nietzsche and rules it out as a serious contender among views of the just life (interpreting perfection to regard certain privileged and cultivated styles of life as of intrinsically greater worth, and deserving of greater material rewards, than more vulgar, common lives). My discussion of Nietzsche in Chapter 11, prepared by the discussion of Rawls in Chapter 9, argues that Rawls's judgment in this rejection is based on an uncharacteristically (for him) ungenerous reading, in this case of Nietzsche's admittedly distressed and distressing sound. And since the central passage in question is one in which Nietzsche shows fairly openly his profound indebtedness to Emerson, its dismissal seems to me a continuation of the repression of Emerson's thought in professional American philosophy.

My stake in protecting perfectionism's examination of moments of crisis (perhaps one or other such moment will present itself as boredom), of the sense of a demand that one's life, hence one's relation to the world, is to undergo change, is deepened in recognizing that two of the most influential, if problematic, philosophers working in roughly the central four decades of the twentieth century and alive in contemporary thought, namely Heidegger and Wittgenstein, neither of whom wrote works specifically identified as of ethics, produced defining texts (Heidegger's *Being and Time* and Wittgenstein's *Philosophical Investigations*) that may be seen to advance claims for a way of life, for a transformation of one's life, demanded by philosophy as such and that accordingly may be characterized as what I am calling perfectionist works. Each of these thinkers has left marks on my own work as decisive as those left by any other philosophical writers of the century just past, and while I from time to time note a conjunction of what I am moved to say with themes associated with their obviously different and sometimes strangely similar modes of philosophizing, I am not assuming in the present book a familiarity with their writing. I shall cite them from time to time to intrigue those who have not yet experienced them, and, for those who have, to suggest contexts of their pertinence that may not yet have dawned.

Whether the perfectionist view that will emerge is essentially elitist, or on the contrary whether its imagination of justice is essential to the aspiration of a democratic society, is a guiding question of this book. As I have emphasized elsewhere and will expand upon later in this book, there is no essential or closed list of features that constitute perfectionism. This idea follows from conceiving of perfectionism as an outlook or dimension of thought embodied and developed in a set of texts spanning the range of Western culture, a conception that is odd in linking texts that may otherwise not be thought of together and that is open in two directions: as to whether a text belongs in the set and as to what feature or features in the text constitute its belonging.

My conception of this book, like the course in which it originated, as being in what used to be called the humanities as well as in philosophy, places contradictory demands on your capacities. It asks you to read both very fast and very slow. (Although I cannot here, as I did in the course, assign you to read the works addressed, I hope that many of you will wish to read them—and to view the films. While each chapter is meant to have its autonomy, an irreducible feature of the book's motivation is to lead its readers outside the chapters and into the marvelous works, of literature and philosophy and film, that have inspired them.) Wittgenstein, in *Philosophical Investigations*, declares it to be "of the essence of our investigation that we do not seek to learn anything new by it. We want to *understand* something that is already in plain view. For this is what we seem in some sense not to understand" (§89). This formulation captures the familiar fact that philosophers seem perpetually to be going back over something, something most sane people would feel had already been discussed to death. A more familiar formulation is to say that philosophy does not progress. This depends on who is doing the measuring. What I call slow reading is meant not so much to recommend a pace of reading as to propose a mode of philosophical attention in which you are prepared to be taken by surprise, stopped, thrown back as it were upon the text. When I say that in the humanities more generally you have to be prepared to read fast, the idea is that you have to make yourself not so much go back over a text as go on from it. You respond in a sense oppositely to the same fact as discovered in philosophy, namely that a text worth reading carefully, or perpetually, is inexhaustible. You always leave it prematurely. And a reason for leaving is that the next text may be more apt to illuminate it than another look at the same text. What I try to do in my work is to motivate both gestures of progress, both states of mind, going back and going on.

There is another inflection to the idea of reading fast. It warns not only that you must leave a work prematurely but that there is no given order that we know is the best one in which to read what you are drawn to read. These are both striking differences of a humanities course from a course in science. There are many ways of sequencing the written texts and sequencing the films, as well as of choosing the pairings between films and texts, that appear in the coming chapters. Each way would yield its own accents. The sequences and pairings to follow here (as well as certain choices of instances) are not exactly the solutions I have used in the past—I altered them somewhat each time I gave the course in part to ensure surprises for myself, but also because as new thoughts occur, new arrangements seem better suited to bring them into view. If the idea of reading the assigned films as instances manifesting a dimension of moral thinking traceable throughout Western culture is sound, then any pairing of one of these films with one of the assigned books should produce interesting, surprising results.

In case it seems that marriage is too specialized an issue to bear up under the thinking represented in the texts discussed here, I have a double response. First, marriage is an allegory in these films of what philosophers since Aristotle have thought about under the title of friendship, what it is that gives value to personal relations, and this is a signature topic of

In the Place of the Classroom

15

perfectionism. Second, the idea I want conveyed is that the moral life is not constituted solely by consideration of isolated judgments of striking moral and political problems but is a life whose texture is a weave of cares and commitments in which one is bound to become lost and to need the friendly and credible words of others in order to find one's way, in which at any time a choice may present itself (whether, or when, say, as in *The Lady Eve,* to confess an indiscretion, or whether, as in *The Awful Truth,* to take offense at an indiscretion), in pondering which you will have to decide whose view of you is most valuable to you.

Something more needs to be said about marriage as a specialized moral relationship. The marriages accepted or rejected by the two film genres in question here all conceive the specific relation as between a man and a woman. (A famous case in which the relation promises to be abrogated is the conclusion of Billy Wilder's *Some Like It Hot,* itself evidently not a remarriage comedy.) So many terrible charges can be brought against the institution of modern, or say, bourgeois, marriage, that it can sometimes seem a wonder that sensible people who have a choice in the matter continue to seek its blessings and accept its costs. Remarriage comedies characteristically contain glimpses of cursed or confined marriages, but this never, within this comic structure of assumption, leads the intelligent and engaging couple, with whom we are given to identify, to consider that what is cursed is the institution of marriage itself. Nor is this conclusion reached by me or by most of my friends. My interest in these comedies continues to be aroused, however else, by this persistent faith, or wager.

While the aggressive playfulness and instruction between the principal pair of remarriage comedy involves questions and exchanges of gender roles, the topic of gender, while explicitly not excluded, is not explicitly and systematically explored in the following pages. While same-sex marriages, or unions, have become common enough to force a consciousness, and elaboration, of the economic and legal consequences for partners and for children reared in such marriages, it is too early yet to know (or I am too isolated in my experience to tell) what new shapes such marriages will discover for their investments in imaginativeness, exclusiveness, and equality.

A sensible discussion of such matters would have to take up the history of topics and encounters broached for a couple of centuries now concerning the education of women, from the time these topics were producing revolutionary thoughts, such as that men and women are essential to each other's education, under explicit discussion in Rousseau and in Kant's early writings. While this history is not likely to be work that will fall to my hands, I hope the thoughts represented in these chapters will enter into that work as from a moment in which a certain bargain of public calm on the subject of women's education was forever broken, and a mode of mutuality demonstrated, by the restless conversation in sets of Hollywood films of the 1930s and 1940s.

These films can give the impression of regarding the more outstanding issues of moral perplexity (abortion, euthanasia, poverty, taxation, capital punishment) as matters that will take care of themselves for people of good will. The perpetual moral risk run by the principal pair of these comedies is that of snobbery. This is a reason the narrative of the films inevitably provides each of the pair with a moment of being humbled, or humiliated, hence with an opportunity for self-knowledge.

———————

A text that I have left unmentioned and that bears distinctly on Emersonian perfectionism is William James's still marvelous, brave *Varieties of Religious Experience,* which challenges both philosophy and religion in its faithfulness to human experience. At the conclusion of his book James finds that his testimony yields "a certain uniform deliverance in which religions all appear to meet. It consists of two parts: 1. An uneasiness; and 2. Its solution." And early in chapter 2 James had said: "I am willing to accept almost any name for the personal religion of which I propose to treat. Call it conscience or morality, if you yourselves prefer, and not religion." But I cannot really be indifferent to differences, intellectual and practical, between what we will call religious uneasiness and what we call a moral crisis. James treats the seriousness of the testimonies he cites (explicitly out of deference to the imagined sensibilities of scientists) as hypotheses of the existence of "facts" that cannot actually (by us) be verified. But the existence of divinity, whatever its further intellectual problems, is no more a *hypothesis* than the existence of my neighbor is, though I might deny, or hedge, either. So I say. But I am here leaving my expression of unease in the status of testimony, or intuition. (Wittgenstein pictures a pertinent sense of unease as mortal restlessness.)

Each of the works we will encounter contains some vision of and arguments about the good city—I earlier called it the imagination of justice. Part of the business of each of the works is to demonstrate whether and how this matters to the characters who harbor these visions and engage in these arguments. That this utopian moment in moral thinking is particularly emphasized in the conversations of moral perfectionism is an effect of the estrangement of philosophy from theology. It expresses the sense that a transcendental element is indispensable in the motivation for a moral existence. Emerson, in the opening paragraph of "Self-Reliance," calls this element "the voice of the mind," harking back to an idea that Socrates, in an onset of philosophy, invokes as listening to one's genius (meaning not our virtuosity but something like our receptiveness), which may require self-disobedience.

The necessity of such moments arises from the awful knowledge expressed in Emerson's acknowledgment of the "discrepance" between the world I converse with and the world I think. One may respond that this knowledge is not awful, but simply a well-known fact. Yes, but what is not known is whether there is something undone that it is mine to do, that fits my hands. What I will call debased perfectionisms propose individual cultivation in forms that distract us from this knowledge. That we must have some such distraction from this knowledge, or ignorance, proves its existence. But what kind of distraction? This has been a topic of philosophy since Plato's *Republic*. What I call Emersonian perfectionism I understand to propose that one's quarrel with the world need not be settled, nor cynically set aside as unsettlable. It is a condition in which you can at once want the world and want it to change—even change it, as the apple changes the earth, though we say the apple falls. (Nietzsche's word for the spreading inability to want the world is nihilism.)

It is a characteristic criticism of Emerson to say that he lacks a sense of tragedy; for otherwise how can he seem so persistently to preach cheerfulness? But suppose that what Emerson perceives, when he speaks of his fellow citizens as existing in a state of secret melancholy, is that in a democracy, which depends upon a state of willingness to act for the common good, despair is a political emotion, discouraging both participation and patience. So when Emerson asks of the American Scholar that he and she raise and cheer us, he is asking for a step of political encouragement, one that assures us that we are not alone in our sense of compromise with justice, that our sense of an unattained self is not an escape from, it is rather an index of, our commitment to the unattained city, one within the one we sustain, one we know there is no good reason we perpetually fail to attain.

1

EMERSON

I spoke in the Introduction of moments of humiliation or humbling in remarriage comedy, as a prelude to overcoming the vice of snobbery. It happens that Emerson's "Self-Reliance," at the close of its opening paragraph, describes, and I would say recalls and enacts, a scene of a certain humbling, or chastening, or shaming, in particular of being humbled by the words of someone else, a scene that takes many forms in both the comedies and the melodramas we will consider.

> In every work of genius we recognize our own rejected thoughts; they come back to us with a certain alienated majesty. Great works of art have no more affecting lesson for us than this. They teach us to abide by our spontaneous impression with good-humored inflexibility then most when the whole cry of voices is on the other side. Else tomorrow a stranger will say with masterly good sense precisely what we have thought and felt all the time, and we shall be forced to take with shame our own opinion from another.

In my saying Emerson is here enacting as well as describing a scene of humbling or shaming, I mean that he is to be taken as presenting an instance of a work of genius (but what this means is a matter he will go on to examine, has already, if invisibly, begun examining in his speaking of "abiding by our impression"), in the face of which we are free to test our capacity for shame (or perhaps for congenial company, in case we know ourselves to be clear of his charge). Why has he begun with a little lesson in reading (the opening words of the essay are "I read the other day")? In particular, the idea of words presenting themselves to us with majesty is virtually a definition of the emotion of the sublime, a mode much in favor in the Romanticism which is one source of Emerson's writing, and the theory of which in recent memory was at the forefront of literary theory. (Emerson's insight that this feeling of majesty is alienated and—or because—projected out of being rejected by us, is the kind of insight I have learned to expect of Emerson.) And why does he, or where does he get the confidence to, ask us to let his work teach us, or warn us, to change our ways?

Without trying to answer at once a question that the whole of Emerson's essay is about, I can already ask you to have in mind the question whether the sound of this writing is a sound you would expect from philosophy. Serious theology, or psychoanalysis, would seem more to the point. Here again I shall not try to answer at once—but I can at least say this much by way of anticipation. I myself experienced, especially after writing a little book on Thoreau's *Walden*, a sort of cringe in trying to get back into Emerson, a recoil from what struck me as his perpetual and irritating intertwining of lyricism and cajoling. Yet I was convinced, from my experience with *Walden*, that some such mode of writing may lend itself to a systematic thoughtfulness in a way only the name of philosophy suits. And, since it is obvious that *Walden* is in conversation with Emerson's writing in every page, and since nothing before Emerson in America is philosophically ambitious and original on this scale, it is reasonable to conclude that what we have in these two writers is nothing less than the origins of the American difference in philosophical thought, as this enters into a new well of American literary ambition on these shores. I will make a perhaps smaller, if no clearer, claim for Emerson's "Self-Reliance" than that it is philosophy. I will say it calls for philosophy, intermittently by quoting or parodying undoubted and familiar philosophy. Nothing has nourished my conviction in this matter more than the number and fervor of people who have gone out of their way to deny that Emerson is capable of challenging philosophy.

The question of Emerson's powers as a philosopher has been raised about his work from early in his career and fame, from 1848 when James Russell Lowell in his recounting of American letters to his time referred to Emerson's prose as a "mist" (and because Lowell admired Emerson, he qualified his epithet by describing it as a "golden" mist). And throughout most of the century and a half since, it has continued repeatedly to be called, by admirers and detractors, something like a fog—rather discouraging attempts to read it with trust in its intellectual originality and accuracy. Why should we still be concerned with this question—of philosophicality, let's say? In today's environment, or in some regions of it, it would be acceptable to identify our age as one of post-philosophy and indeed to praise Emerson for his avoidance or transcendence of the question. I think he is to be praised—

though less for avoiding the issue than for facing it in his own way. But again, if we can say that Emerson is a useful, interesting, moving, provocative writer, whose powers increase with increased attention to them, why bother about whether he is called a philosopher or something else, or nothing but a writer?

There are several reasons why it matters. First, it matters to me because I do not want a text to be denied the title of philosophy on the ground that it does not exactly take the form you might expect of philosophy. The denial of the title tends to excuse the tendency to refrain from putting much intellectual pressure on Emerson's words, to refrain from accepting the invitation of those words to get past their appearance, if I can put it so.

Second, it matters to Emerson's idea of himself, of his task, or fate, as a writer. The question whether he speaks with philosophical authority—and if not, with what authority—is an undertone, I find, of his prose throughout, connected, I cannot doubt, with the crisis in his life as a result of giving up the questionable, for him, authority of the pulpit. To give up on the question would be to give up following the way Emerson's prose questions itself. (As when, in the opening of "Self-Reliance," he describes the impressions he inscribes as merely those already rejected by the reader—leaving it open how far his own work of genius is to undo the alienation of the majesty that is the cost of the reception of other such works. The self-questioning is hence simultaneously a questioning of his audience, of those he writes for, taking the form of asking what reading is.) Third, it matters to the idea of moral perfectionism, which is somehow bound up with an idea of a philosophical way or imagination of life. Fourth, I think the ambiguity in whether or not Emerson is to be received as a philosopher may be key in working on another pervasive puzzle in the reception of Emerson, namely that he has endeared himself both to politically radical and to politically conservative temperaments.

These standing issues form a good place from which to approach the text of "Self-Reliance" more intensively, if not more consecutively. It is as familiar an American text as exists, and because for some the text, or its sound, will seem so familiar that it can seem we do not know whether we understand it at all—that it is indeed as unresistant or unsupportive as mist—I have adopted the strategy of isolating a few sentences, in pairs, torn from their contexts in that essay, in order to force us to stop over them. I adopt the strategy also because everyone knows that, but no one finds it easy to say how, the Emersonian sentence is a remarkable achievement, bearing some-how the brunt of what Emerson has to say, or to do, and often making it difficult to see how his paragraphs, let alone what he calls his Essays, hang together. I'm suggesting we don't even know what makes the sentences themselves hang together, what produces that perpetual air of understanding and not understanding, insight and obscurity.

As an introduction to the exemplary yoking of sentences I shall cite in a moment, I repeat ones I have in the past often been glad to invoke. I have in mind Emerson's saying: "The virtue most in request in society is conformity. Self-reliance is its aversion."

Immediately, as with Emerson's allusion to his own writing in speaking of returning rejected thoughts, thoughts we all have had, however bathed in mist (which we might project upon Emerson), here, in saying "Self-reliance is its aversion," he is pretty explicitly naming his own writing, as represented in his essay "Self-Reliance," as saying of itself that it is written in aversion, aversion to conformity. And since the work of the word "conformity" in its sentence is to name a virtue, a contribution to a way of life, the implication is that his writing in self-reliance exhibits or enacts a contribution to a counter way of life. "Aversion" is a striking word, not to be taken lightly as a description of his writing as such. It invokes the preacher's word once familiar to his life, that of conversion, and accordingly should raise the question whether the turning implied in conversion and aversion is to be understood as a turning away from the society that demands conformity more than as a turning toward it, as in a gesture of confrontation.

And which comes first, conformity or its aversion? Is the idea that we experience the demands of conformity, and either obey them or else find that reliance upon oneself demands, and provides in return, ways to confront those who guard and impose conformity? The demand of conformity would accordingly demand that I justify my wayward life (not at this stage criminal, but, say, critical, discomfiting), and the provision of justification, as exemplified by the self-reliance of Emerson's writing, takes the form of making myself intelligible to those concerned. (This is precisely what Thoreau stages himself as attempting to do, as he simultaneously suggests the magnitude of the task, on the opening page of *Walden*: "I . . . require of every writer, first or last, a simple and sincere account of his own life, and not merely what he has heard of other men's lives; some such account as he would send to his kindred from a distant land, for if he has lived sincerely, it must have been in a distant land to me.") Or is it the other way around—that I find myself outside, sensing a lack of justification for my existence, and interpret this as a call for conformity, showing that a rapprochement with others is something I also, other things equal, desire?

Either way, this perplexity seems particularly to mark that fateful moment of each human existence at which, given at least a minimum sense of political freedom and justice in your society, you recognize that you participate in your society's work and profit from it, you understand that you are—as liberal political theory puts the matter—asked to show your *consent* to that society, to recognize the legitimacy of its governing you. We shall see this centrally in Locke's *Second Treatise of Government* and reinterpreted in John Rawls's *A Theory of Justice*. A standing problem with this idea is that it remains unclear what it is that shows or expresses your consent. (This is a burning question for Thoreau, in *Walden* as well as in his deeply influential essay "Civil Disobedience," known to be an inspiration for both Mahatma Gandhi and Martin Luther King Jr.)

Let's put this demand as the expectation of your "taking your place" in society. And let's suppose that you do not see the place, or do not like the places you see. You may of course take on the appearance of accepting the choices, and this may present itself to you as your having adopted a state of fraudulence, a perpetual sense of some false position you have assumed, without anyone's exactly having placed you there. A mark of this stage is a sense of obscurity, to yourself as well as to others, one expression of which is a sense of compromise, of being asked to settle too soon for the world as it is, a perplexity in relating yourself to what you find unacceptable in your world, without knowing what you can be held responsible for. Do I, for example, consent to the degree of injustice we all live with? Do I know how to define my position with respect to it? Since it probably doesn't make sense for me either to assume direct responsibility for it or to deny all indirect responsibility for it, where do I stand?

I am assuming that we can all recognize such moments in our lives. They are not confined to the period between adolescence and the claims of adulthood, though they may be first encountered, and be concentrated, there. I have identified the moment as located and inhabited by the remarriage comedies as one in which moral cynicism threatens, the temptation to give up on a life more coherent and admirable than seems affordable after the compromises of adulthood come to obscure the promise and dreams of youth. The fact that the principal pair in these comedies is somewhat older than the young pairs of classical comedy provides a context in which certain ways of fulfilling earlier dreams have collapsed and a new regime must be formed to which consent can now, on reflection, be won, or wagered.

I have characterized Emerson as perceiving this state as one of my wanting (that is, lacking and desiring) justification, and understood him as perceiving our lacking the means of making ourselves intelligible (to others, to ourselves). And the depth of this crisis (if I do not miss the fact that it is a crisis) is expressed in, and by, Emerson's writing as responding to a time in which I sense as it were a lack in language itself, as if to explain myself I would have to reinvent my words. (Writing, as an allegory of aversion to conformity, to going along, getting along, inevitably raises the question of the direction of aversive turning as turning toward or away, since I crave the words I cringe from—all the words I have.)

I mean this to capture the experience of Emerson's saying, as we shall see in a moment, that conformity makes "most men," meaning most to whom he feels he is responding, "not false in a few particulars, authors of a few lies, but false in all particulars . . . So that every word they say chagrins us and we know not where to begin to set them right." I relate this to Aristotle's famous claim, at the opening of his *Politics,* that it is the gift of language that makes human beings fit for, and fated for, political association, the association that places and measures all the others. Emerson's claim of finding the language of most others depressing, let us say uncommunicative, made against the background of Aristotle's idea, which seems to me its most plausible inspiration, in effect declares that a genuine political association does not exist between him and those others; that, said otherwise, America has not yet been discovered. Then his task as a writer is to discover the terms in which it can be discovered. Then what will constitute its discovery?

I make the following fundamental assumption: What I characterized as making oneself intelligible is the interpretation moral perfectionism gives to the idea of moral reasoning, the demand for providing reasons for one's conduct, for the justification of one's life. Utilitarianism proposes a means of calculation to determine the good of an action. Kantianism proposes a principle of judgment to determine the rightness of an action. Perfectionism proposes confrontation and conversation as the means of determining whether we can live together, accept one another into the aspirations of our lives. This does not mean that perfectionism is an alternative to these other famous positions. Left to itself it may seem to make the ability to converse do too much work—what prevents us from coming to unjust agreements, or intimately talking ourselves into misdeeds? Perfectionism is the province not of those who oppose justice and benevolent calculation, but of those who feel left out of their sway, who feel indeed that most people have been left, or leave themselves out, of their sway. It is a perception, or an intuition, that Emerson articulates as most men living in "secret melancholy" and that Thoreau a few years later transcribes as "the mass of men liv[ing] lives of quiet desperation."

I put matters by contrasting utilitarianism, Kantianism, and perfectionism in terms of providing means of coming to agreement, or establishing conditions of understanding, to align them with Socrates' question to *Euthyphro* that I cited in the Introduction: "What kind of disagreement, my friend, causes hatred and anger?" Some philosophers have taken the fact of moral disagreement to show the inherent irrationality of moral argument—show it to be essentially a matter of which side has the greater power, political, rhetorical, psychological, economic. Heaven knows there are mortal conflicts of such kinds, and they often give themselves out as moral conflicts. Whereas my suggestion is that moral reasoning of the standard sorts—calculation of consequences, interpretation of motives and principles—is to be understood as obeying the moral demand for intelligibility. It is in its meeting of that demand that perfectionism counts as a moral theory (or as a dimension of any moral theory). Everything else is still open. For example, whether there are limits to the obligation to be intelligible, whether everyone isn't entitled to a certain obscurity or sense of confusion, and at some times more than others. Maybe there isn't always something to say; and there is the question of what one is to do about persisting disagreement, how far you must go in trying to resolve it—as Adam Bonner (Spencer Tracy) will put the matter to Amanda Bonner (Katharine Hepburn) in *Adam's Rib*, "I've always tried to see your point of view. But this time you've got me stumped."

Socrates' mode is important. He is clearly in disagreement with Euthyphro, as he is discussing disagreement, and I like the notation of his credibly affirming, in that circumstance, friendship with Euthyphro ("What kind of disagreement, my friend, causes hatred and anger?"). The implication is that there the context for moral argument or reasoning, one in which there is a willingness to understand and to be understood, may be difficult to maintain. A further implication I draw is that hatred and anger are not essentially irrational, but may clearly be called for. To live a moral life should not require that we become Socrateses or Buddhas or Christs, all but unprovokable. But we are asked to make even justified anger and hatred intelligible, and to be responsible for their expression in our lives, and sometimes, not always and everywhere, to put them aside.

One reason for my placing Emerson first, as a figure of the perfectionist, is the clarity and passion with which his writing tests its aspiration to honesty, to expressing all and only what it means. "Self-reliance is [conformity's] aversion" is one of Emerson's many efforts at the self-description of his writing, of the point of every word he writes. Take it this way: "Self-reliance" characterizes the manner in which his writing relates to itself, stands by itself, accounts for itself. "Conformity" characterizes the audience of this writing, the one it seeks to attract; an audience, I said earlier, from which and to which it turns, incessantly (so it is as attracted to that audience, or what it may become, as it is chagrined by it). If he believed that the audience *could not* turn to him, it would be folly for him to write as he does. As it would be folly if he believed that he was not subject to the same failings as they. (Thoreau says it this way: "I never knew . . . a worse man than myself." And "I would not [waste myself in?] preaching to a stone.") This turning is Emerson's picture of thinking, explicit in *The American Scholar*. It is manifest in the way Emerson turns words and sentences—as if you are to read them forward and backward, inside out and outside in.

Emerson's writing, in demonstrating our lack of given means of making ourselves intelligible (to ourselves, to others), details the difficulties in the way of possessing those means, and demonstrates that they are at hand. This thought, implying our need of invention and of transformation, expresses two dominating themes of perfectionism.

The first theme is that the human self—confined by itself, aspiring toward itself—is always becoming, as on a journey, always partially in a further state. This journey is described as education or cultivation. (Thoreau characteristically names his audience the student, and Emerson names it the scholar, but neither of them has in mind simply, or even primarily, people enrolled in what we call a school, but rather an aspect of their conception of the human, of any age.) Since an emphasis on cultivation is an essential feature of perfectionism, the ease with which perfectionism can be debased into a form of aestheticism or preciosity or religiosity is a measure of the ease with which perfectionism can be debased, as philosophy can be, or religion.

The second dominating theme is that the other to whom I can use the words I discover in which to express myself is the Friend—a figure that may occur as the goal of the journey but also as its instigation and accompaniment. Any moral outlook—systematically assessing the value of human existence—will accord weight to the value of friendship. But only perfectionism, as I understand it, places so absolute a value on this relationship. The presence of friendship in the films we will consider (including the sometimes drastic lack of this relation in the melodramas) is of the most specific importance in establishing them as perfectionist narratives.

We come, then, to the four pairs of excerpts from "Self-Reliance." I have arranged them as follows: The first two passages indicate how the *question of philosophy* shows itself as a determining matter of Emerson's writing. The second two suggest the role of *moral paradox* in Emerson. The next two name two narrative figures or characters whom Emerson invokes to measure his claim to authority or authorship (his disdaining of any standing authority is a measure of his claim to philosophy)—said otherwise, these figures occupy *the role of the Friend*. And the final two passages are meant as specimens of how *reading that writing* is to be accomplished.

THE QUESTION OF PHILOSOPHY

Man is timid and apologetic; he is no longer upright; he dares not say "I think," "I am," but quotes some saint or sage.

Most men have bound their eyes with one or another handkerchief, and attached themselves to some one of these communities of opinion. This conformity makes them not false in a few particulars, authors of a few lies, but false in all particulars. Their every truth is not quite true . . . so that every word they say chagrins us and we know not where to begin to set them right.

In the first extract, Emerson is invoking Descartes's fateful idea "Cogito ergo sum," "I think, therefore I am." (Don't be put off by the lack of "therefore" in Emerson's version. Descartes also leaves out the therefore in the most likely place one may encounter his idea, in the second of his six Meditations, where he writes: "*I am, I exist* is necessarily true every time that I pronounce it or conceive it in my mind.") I say Emerson is playful and serious in his repetition of Descartes because what Emerson does, in a passage that identifies quoting with a *fear of saying* ("I dare not say"), is to quote (a sage) and there-fore not exactly, or exactly not, to say the thing for himself. (I do not here invoke the technical philosophical distinction between mentioning and using a signifying phrase. One reason not to do so is that there is an ordinary use of a quotation, irrelevant to logic, in which you introduce it by saying "As so-and-so aptly remarks," thus claiming your acknowledgment of the truth or aptness of the remark without taking responsibility for forming the thought. Another reason is that I take Emerson here to be questioning the flat distinction between saying and quoting. A favorite idea of Emerson's is precisely that, except in those moments when self-reliance, or coming to oneself, has overcome the necessities of conformity, one is incessantly quot-ing, using what Proust calls "public words.")

The implications of Emerson's strategy are various: (1) He shows himself not to have announced his own cogito (not here anyway); accordingly he shows himself to be unable or unwilling to claim and prove his own exis-tence in that moment, hence then and there to be haunting it ("we glide ghost-like"). (2) His inability to assert the most basic facts of existence, for example the inability to name Descartes, to claim the authority of a founder of modern European philosophy, implies that America is unable to inherit and claim philosophy for itself, hence remains haunted by it. (3) If we Amer-icans are to claim philosophy for ourselves, we will have to invent a language for it in which our existence without philosophy, or haunted by philosophy, is itself expressible philosophically. It will require a look and a sound so far unheard of, an originality not expressed in new words, as if we had to speak in tongues; we want the old words, but transfigured by our unprecedented experience of discovery, displacement, and inhabitation, of mad conflicts between the desire for freedom and the immediacy of heaven, and unending disappointment with our failings to become a new world. It will be a lan-guage, or a mode of speech, in which what we say is neither just quoted nor just said, perhaps because it is denied as well as said or because more than one thing is said.

On the second page of his essay "The Poet," Emerson says: "The highest minds of the world have never ceased to explore the double meaning, or, shall I say, the quadruple, or the centuple, or much more manifold meaning, of every sensuous fact." There is some suggestion here, no doubt, that the daring philosopher whom Emerson calls for, taking on directly the assertion of his (and our) existence, will have also to be something of a poet—the ideal of Coleridge and Wordsworth as well as of their contemporary German Romantics such as Schlegel and Tieck (the influential translators of Shakespeare into German). The process of discovering and announcing a fact is something Emerson (in "The American Scholar") calls thinking and describes in a way philosophers of our time will have difficulty recognizing as part of the work they are obliged to do: Emerson writes of a process "by which experience is converted into thought," which is a way of making the meaning of a fact public. A little later he says there is "no fact, no event, in our private history, which shall not, sooner or later, lose its adhesive, inert form, and astonish us by soaring from our body into the empyrean."

This sense of being able to speak philosophically and openly about anything and everything that happens to you is an ideal of thinking that first seemed to me possible in contemporary professional philosophy in the work of the later Wittgenstein and in that of J. L. Austin. It is what their redemption of what they call the ordinary from its rejection in much of philosophy has perhaps most importantly meant to me. Without the sense of liberation that afforded me, I do not know that I would have persisted in attempting to find a place in academic philosophy.

In the second of the two passages quoted a moment ago, Emerson specifies further characteristics of a speech that can incorporate the fatedness to quotation (to America's having come late into the world) and to the absence of a philosophical voice of America's own. (Not that America's relation to philosophy is in all respects unique. Nietzsche had his own conditions for experiencing the loss of a credible language of philosophy.) To be chagrined by every word that most men say is going to put you at odds with those men and make your common sense sound paradoxical. This is the crisis out of which moral perfectionism's aspiration takes its rise, the sense that either you or the world is wrong. For example, Emerson somewhere refers to a *casual* remark or action as a *casualty*. This may be taken as idle, cute, or perverse of him. But consider first that remarks worth calling casual (especially as an excuse) are expressions of thoughtlessness and conformity; and second that what is said is permanent, it can rarely be neutralized by a simple "Pardon me." We understand that the bustling and bumping that the human body is subject to in its daily rounds will cause some unintentional bruises, but purely unintentional words are harder to find or ignore or explain or excuse; and consider further that, unlike your unintentional actions, your as it were unintentional words may endlessly have already been taken up and repeated as they made their way amid the varied interests and accidents of others, the most ordinary perhaps affording, as in Emerson's case, a certain melancholy.

MORAL PARADOXES

I shun father and mother and wife and brother when my genius calls me. I would write on the lintels of the door-post *Whim*. I hope it is somewhat better than whim at last, but we cannot spend the day in explanation.

Do not tell me, as a good man did today, of my obligation to put all poor men in good situations. Are they *my* poor? I tell thee, thou foolish philanthropist, that I grudge the dollar, the dime, the cent I give to such men as do not belong to me and to whom I do not belong.

These two instances of paradoxes are both allusions to, some might say parodies of, words reported in the Gospels as said or heard by Jesus. In the first quotation Emerson is following the injunction not to delay, for example by appealing to the obligation to bury the dead, when the King of Heaven is at hand. Yet where others will claim that this is a private appeal to faith, Emerson suggests writing "Whim" for all to see. One might feel that this shows Emerson's distrust or chagrin in response to so many ready mouthfuls of faith. But then consider that it also shows a dedication of his writing to the work of faith, to transfigured, redemptive words, which means that he cannot, in his finitude, and his distrust of the exchanges of words as they now stand in society, claim more than the existence of his own call to write otherwise. Whether it is more, whether it speaks for the world and to others, is not for him to say.

The second quotation, containing the disturbing question "Are they *my* poor?" has, you may imagine, caused hard looks and words to be sent Emerson's way. But consider that Emerson is alluding, so I claim, to Jesus' famous dismissal, or acceptance, of the poor: "The poor you have always with you." The occasion was, similarly, one in which "a good man" (a good instance of what a man is) had said to Jesus something about helping the poor. It was, namely, the occasion on which Jesus allowed Mary, the sister of Lazarus, to anoint his feet with expensive oil, and the man objecting to this gesture, instructing Jesus in the moral impropriety of this extravagance, was Judas. Does this extravagant allusion on Emerson's part alleviate his apparent harshness, or does it magnify it? Since he claims to have his own poor, and since these must be his way of referring to those for whom he spends his life writing, we will want to know on what basis he places this degree of confidence in the good of his writing, for which he claims no more than whim, betting his life that its good may prove "better than whim at last."

TWO FIGURES OF THE FRIEND

[The true man] measures you and all men and all events. You are constrained to accept his standard.*

The nonchalance of boys who are sure of a dinner, and would disdain as much as a lord to do or say aught to conciliate one, is the healthy attitude of human nature. A boy is in the parlor what the pit is in the playhouse; independent, irresponsible, looking out from his corner on such people and facts as pass by, he tries and sentences them on their merits, in the swift, summary way of boys, as good, bad, interesting, silly, eloquent, troublesome . . . But the man is as it were clapped into jail by his consciousness. As soon as he has once acted or spoken with *éclat* he is a committed person, watched by the sympathy or the hatred of hundreds, whose affections must now enter into his account . . . Ah, that he could pass again into his neutrality! . . . He would utter opinions on all passing affairs, which being seen to be not private but necessary, would sink like darts into the ear of men and put them in fear.

I take both figures, the true man and the boy, to represent what Emerson calls "speaking with necessity," something I relate to Kant's demand that I speak with a "universal voice." Kant introduces the idea in accounting for the aesthetic judgment, but it seems to me to be understood, in his moral philosophy, as alluding to moral judgment, namely the application to one's conduct of the categorical imperative, which may be pictured as the universal voice speaking to me. The boy still in his neutrality is the model of an aspiration of philosophical writing, not on the ground that his judgment is always sound, but on the ground that it is always *his,* and because it concerns the basis for eventually judging usefully, fruitfully, anything and everything that passes through his world. The image of the true man is, I believe, a further development of Kantian ideas, which I will dwell on with more care in Chapter 7. But before leaving this initial sketch of Emerson's

---

* The second sentence here appears in the first edition of Emerson's *Essays* but not in most of the later editions that I have consulted. I regret Emerson's whim in excising this sentence.

ways and means, I want at least to indicate how I see this connection with Kant.

Emerson's true man, whose "standard you are constrained to accept" is a recasting of Kant's idea, mentioned in my Introduction, of the human as having two "standpoints" on his existence, which Kant also pictures as our living in two worlds—the sensuous world in which we are governed by the laws of material things, and the intelligible world in which we are free. The true man's standard is, in short, ours so far as we live adopting the standpoint of the intelligible world. (The justification for linking standard and standpoint involves my claim that "Self-Reliance" as a whole can be taken as an essay on human understanding and being misunderstood. If you take these recurrences of the idea of "standing" to be merely puns, I point to another claim of "Self-Reliance" in which Emerson declares, "I stand here for humanity," where the meaning of "standing for" as both representing something and bearing up under something is, I trust, too plain to deny. But this will come back.)

I note as a companion gesture Emerson's idea of being "constrained" by a standard as a recasting of Kant's idea of the human as "constrained" by a feeling of "ought," expressed as our recognizing and obeying the moral law, the categorical imperative. Kant pictures the origin, or what he would call the "possibility," of this feeling as a function of the human as being neither beast nor angel. This is clearly a relative of the picture of our living in two worlds, neither wholly in the sensuous world nor wholly in the intelligible world. If we lived wholly in the sensuous world, as beasts do, we would not recognize the demand of the moral law; if we lived wholly in the intelligible world, as only angels could, we would have no need of the law. Kant's constraint is that of duty, obligation, as I recognize the power of reason to overcome inclination. Emerson's constraint is that of attraction, recognizing myself as drawn, as it were, beyond my present repertory of inclination, to my unattained but attainable self. Moral reasoning is not to take me from irrational to rational choice (in the distribution of satisfactions, as in the case of moral theories that take the good as fundamental, such as that of John Stuart Mill); nor from a will corrupted by sensuous concerns to one measured and chastened by the demands of the moral law (represented by Kant and in an important sense by John Rawls, who defines an idea of right or justice in independence of a definition of the good); but to take me from confusion to (relative) clarity in seeking a world I can want.

Moral perfectionism challenges ideas of moral motivation, showing (against Kant's law that counters inclination, and against utilitarianism's calculation of benefits) the possibility of my access to experience which gives to my desire for the attaining of a self that is mine to become, the power to act on behalf of an attainable world I can actually desire.

THE NATURE OF READING

Character teaches above our wills.

In every work of genius we recognize our own rejected thoughts; they come back to us with a certain alienated majesty.

The idea of "character" in Emerson always (so far as I recall) refers simultaneously to something about the worth and stamp of an individual's (or human group's) difference from others and to physical traces of writing (or expression more generally). So "Character teaches above our wills" means simultaneously that writing conveys meaning beyond our intention, and quite generally that we express in every gesture more than our will accomplishes or recognizes. "In every work of genius we recognize our rejected thoughts . . . with a certain alienated majesty," as a description of the ambition Emerson harbors for his own writing, links up with Wittgenstein's saying of philosophy that what it seeks is not (as in the case of science) to teach something new and to hunt out new facts to support its claims, but rather to understand what is already before us, too obvious and pervasive to be ordinarily remarked. Wittgenstein uses as the epigraph for *Philosophical Investigations* the following, from Nestroy: "Progress generally looks much greater than it really is." This seems to me to capture (beyond the suggestion that a decisive advance may be produced by a small move) the sense of philosophy as revealing the rejected or undervalued, in which the uncovering of something obvious can create astonishment, like the relation of something casual as yielding casualties, or in Wittgenstein's *Investigations* such a remark as "I am not of the *opinion* that another has a soul." (One might equally say of such cases that progress seems smaller than it really is; in neither case are we assured of its permanence.) Philosophers like to follow Aristotle in saying that philosophy begins in wonder. My impression is that philosophers nowadays tend to associate the experience of wonder with the explanations of science rather than, as in Wittgenstein and Austin, with the recognition of our relation to things as they are, the perception of the extraordinariness of what we find ordinary (for example, beauty), and the ordinariness of what we find extraordinary (for example, violence).

Emerson's very familiarity to Americans makes him in some way the easiest and in some way the hardest to assess of the writers discussed in this book. Because I use Emerson as both a means or touchstone of interpretation and an object of interpretation, there will be many opportunities in later chapters to refine our assessment.

2

The Philadelphia Story

1 The film opens upon a country scene containing a luxurious dwelling where, on a cut to its entrance, we observe C. K. Dexter Haven (Cary Grant) storming, in a silent rage, out of its front door, hat on for travel, carrying a suitcase and a bag of golf clubs to a car waiting under the porte cochère. He turns around to glare back at the entrance, in which Tracy Lord (Katharine Hepburn), in a negligee, is standing, in silent contempt, holding a putter, evidently left out of the bag Grant is holding. She snaps the putter in two over her upraised knee (in those graceful years putters had wooden shafts) and throws the fragments on the ground between her and Grant. He drops his baggage, storms back toward Hepburn, raises his arm to punch her, and instead shoves her back into the house and onto the floor.

2 A title card fills the screen with the line "Two Years Later." Inside the same house, the three Lord women—the mother, Tracy, and her pre-adolescent sister Dinah—are discussing Tracy's impending wedding. Tracy does not expect her father to attend the wedding because of his involvement with an entertainer called Tina Mara. Dinah, out of Tracy's hearing, tells her mother she thinks that stinks. Her mother asks Dinah not to say "stinks," but, if absolutely necessary, "smells"; but she admits that she agrees with Dinah's view of the matter.

3 At the family's stables, Tracy, Dinah, and their neighbor Uncle Willie (Roland Young) await Tracy's fiancé George (John Howard), a rising, wooden man of the people, who upon his arrival displays with his new-bought outfit and his (lack of) horsemanship just how far out of his element he is.

4 In the headquarters of *Spy* magazine, its publisher, Sidney Kidd (Henry Daniell), assigns Macauley Connor, Mike to his friends (James Stewart), and Liz Imbrie (Ruth Hussey) to cover, respectively with words and photos, the wedding of Tracy Lord. Dexter is to get them into the Lord household, which is essentially closed to reporters, as friends of Tracy's absent brother.

5 Dexter introduces Mike and Liz into the house, where they are shown to the south parlor. Mike shows his disapproval of the existence and the taste of the monstrously rich.

6 Mrs. Lord and daughters are in a sunroom in some other latitude of the house when a whistle from outside indicates that Dexter has returned. They remind him that there is a wedding at hand which calls for his absence, and he gets Tracy alone to tell her that he has arranged to have her wedding covered in *Spy* magazine in exchange for Sidney Kidd's agreement not to print a scandalous story about her father and Tina Mara.

7 Tracy puts on a show of welcoming the intruders and learns more about them than they about her.

8 Uncle Willie shows up, and Tracy introduces him to Mike and Liz as her father; then when her father himself unexpectedly arrives, she introduces him as Uncle Willie, blaming him (her father), surreptitiously, for the necessary deceptions.

9 At the town library (which we have learned Dexter's grandfather built), Mike discovers Tracy reading his book of short stories. She tells him she too knows quite a lot about hiding a poetic soul under a tough exterior.

10a Tracy and Mike walk through a large park (the Lord property) to the Lords' swimming pool, where, in adjoining dressing rooms, Tracy offers to let Mike use her summer house as a place to write and Mike refuses.

10b Dexter enters, sets a wrapped object on a table, and engages Tracy in a conversation whose intimacy Mike shrinks from. Asked by Tracy to stay, Mike hears Dexter dress down Tracy for her cold intactness and her intolerance of human frailty, as, for example, of his drinking ("my gorgeous thirst"). She says it made him unattractive; he replies she was no helpmeet there, but a scold.

10c Mike has left; Dexter leaves just before George arrives, as Tracy dives into the pool alone. George says they are late for the party, comes to the edge of the pool, sets down contemptuously the now unwrapped object Dexter brought, and is informed by Tracy that it is a model of the boat he designed and built for Tracy and Dexter's honeymoon. This seems to precipitate Tracy's crying out, in anguish, "Oh, to be useful in the world." George responds by saying he's going to build a castle for her and worship her from afar. "Like fun you are." George knows he's made a misstep, and he departs.

11 The family is gathering for drinks on the terrace. Tracy comes upon her father and mother together and openly accuses her father's philandering of letting them in for the intrusions of the world. Her father dresses her down, saying that she lacks an understanding heart, that she might as well be made of bronze, and, moreover, that she sounds like a jealous woman. She hurriedly tosses down a defensive sequence of martinis.

12   At the party, a glum George disapproves of a Tracy whose giddy behavior, earlier praised by Dexter, is new to him; Mike, also well on his way to giddiness, wants to dance with her; George disapproves further.

13   Mike grabs a bottle of champagne and asks a chauffeur waiting among the limousines to drive him to C. K. Dexter Haven's house, where he awakens Dexter, tells him he (Dexter) doesn't understand Tracy, says "either I'm going to sock you or you're going to sock me," reveals that he knows a story that would ruin Kidd, and agrees to let Dexter use the story as counter-blackmail.

14   Tracy shows up with Liz, who is pressed into service typing up the new story; Tracy drives off with Mike.

15   Beyond the terrace, Tracy and Mike dance around the edge of a fountain, discuss the difference between champagne and whiskey, and run off to the pool.

16   Dexter and Liz return to the Lord house after finishing the counter-blackmail letter.

17a   At the pool, Tracy and Mike contest the difference between heart and mind, between lower and upper classes, and fall into an embrace that they will each have to interpret for themselves.

17b   At the terrace Dexter is looking for Mike when George appears, still glum; Dexter sees evidence that Tracy and Mike are swimming and advises George to leave, but George declines.

17c   Mike arrives singing "Over the Rainbow" and carrying Tracy in his arms like a child. Dexter assures himself that Tracy is not hurt.

17d   After Mike returns from depositing Tracy in her bedroom, George demands an explanation, but Dexter pushes him out of the way and socks Mike (fulfilling Mike's prophecy). George marches away; Dexter and Mike have a friendly exchange; the camera moves up the ivy-covered column of the terrace to show that Dinah has witnessed the whole scene.

18   Tracy, hung over, has, as Dexter has predicted on the basis of a past experience, "drawn a tidy blank" about the events before she fell asleep. Dexter asks her about last night, which starts "getting those eyes open"; Mike fairly completes the task by saying he's lost his watch and identifying as his the watch she found on her bedroom floor.

19   She confesses to Dexter what she concludes must have been her transgression; he asks where he comes into it any longer and tells her to remember

George. She remembers George and phones to ask him to come over right away, before the wedding ceremony.

20 She receives a note from George, written earlier, and reads it aloud to her friends; in it George expresses his dismay at her conduct and suggests that if she has no explanation they had better call off the marriage. George arrives as she is finishing the letter. She confirms that she has no answer; Mike gives the answer, namely that two kisses had happened, and Tracy is moved to say, "I think men are wonderful." Whereupon it is announced that Sidney Kidd has arrived, saying he's licked, and George, appreciating the national importance Kidd lends the occasion, expands himself and proposes to go on with the wedding. Tracy bids him a fond farewell; again he departs.

21 We reach the climactic moment at which Mike asks Tracy to marry him. Tracy sees that that is not where her future lies, and accepts Dexter's suggestion to announce that the assembled guests will now be treated to the wedding ceremony they were deprived of two years earlier when the pair eloped. Except that Liz, asked by Tracy to be the maid of honor, corrects the title to matron of honor, and Dexter is not dressed properly for his role, as if nothing special is going on, or nothing whose importance others are, in his eyes, in a position to judge.

I said of moral perfectionism—in the version I portray of it, and defend, which I call Emersonian perfectionism—that the issues it assesses are typically not front-page news, not, for example, issues like abortion, euthanasia, capital punishment, whistle-blowing, plagiarism, informing, bribery, greed, scapegoating, torture, treason, rape, spousal abuse, child neglect, genital mutilation, and so on. But not every fateful moral choice, every judgment of good and bad or right and wrong, is a matter for public debate. This may already seem contentious. Morality is what applies to all equally, to humans as humans. If abortion and euthanasia and capital punishment are wrong, they are wrong for everybody, for reasons everybody should recognize and accept. Some of these headline issues leave room, for some people, for crises of conscience, but this means that someone feels that he or she has reason, with fear and trembling, to go against a moral consensus of right and wrong, reason to feel that in *this* case, abortion or euthanasia or informing, say, is justified. Some issues do not leave this room, as rape, spousal abuse, and child neglect do not.

But the issues in moral perfectionism are not crises of conscience of this kind. The crises portrayed in the films we will consider are not caused by the temptation or demand to go against a standing moral consensus, but, on something like the contrary, are ones in which it is a question whether a moral issue is to be raised. Their central case is one in which a pair are deciding on divorce, on whether they wish to (continue to) be married. They are deciding on what kinds of lives they wish to live and whether they wish to live them together, to consent to each other, to say yes to their lives and their life together; nothing has happened between them that requires more than their mutual forgiveness. Of course one will feel that in each case of moral conflict, certainly in the moral crises that make the newspapers, persons are deciding what kind of life they wish to lead, what kind of person they mean to be. But that is the point. One might say that in our remarriage comedies and their derived melodramas, this is all that is being decided, that our interest in these relatively privileged couples is their pure enactment of the fact that in each moral decision our lives, our senses of ourselves, and of what, and whom, we are prepared to consent to, are at stake. Emerson will put such an idea variously, for example, in "Self-Reliance," in a remark recorded to different effect (a characteristic potentiality of Emerson's remarks) in the previous chapter, he says: "Character teaches above our wills. Men imagine that they communicate their virtue or vice only by overt actions, and do not see that virtue and vice emit a breath every moment."

The couples of our films all take for granted, accordingly, that divorce is a moral option for them—however careful its moral justification must be. And, I should add, now in the early years of the twenty-first century, they assume that marriage is itself a moral option, I mean a relationship to be ratified by state and, perhaps, by church, something that would have been questioned in an earlier period only by fairly unusual moral and political sensibilities. In my Introduction I said that marriage in these films may, to some arguable degree, be taken to stand for the idea of friendship. This is a matter more important in some moral theories of life than in others; in Plato's *Republic* it is mostly implicit; in Aristotle's *Nichomachean Ethics* it is climactic. But the question of sealing or weaving together the life of romance and of friendship, while clearly taken in the films, almost without exception, as ideal, is rarely made explicit in the pair's conversations to which we are made privy, though it should be seen as pervading them.

The Philadelphia Story

Obviously contesting the simple conclusion that the issues dealt with in the films are private is the plain fact that the antics of the pair typically make the newspapers. The very title of *The Philadelphia Story* is, within the film, the proposed title of the coverage of the pair's wedding in a news magazine, called—in a sense to its credit—*Spy*. Whether and why such a medium should have the right to make this material public is a point of argument within the plot of the film. The proposed bridegroom for Tracy Lord's new marriage is delighted with the idea of that publicity; he observes that it means their marriage is of "national importance." "Importance" is an important word for Tracy's former (and future) husband C. K. Dexter Haven, who applies it, to Tracy's chagrin, to the night she got drunk and danced naked on the roof of the house—it is her saying impatiently to him that he attached too much importance to that silly escapade that prompts him to say to her, "It was immensely important."

I pause to note that importance is also an important word in Wittgenstein's description of his own philosophizing in *Philosophical Investigations,* as when one of his interlocutors, real or imagined, causes him to ask: "Where does our investigation get its importance from, since it seems to destroy everything great and interesting?" (§118) His answer in effect is that it is precisely philosophy's business to question our interests as they stand (as philosophers from Plato to Montaigne and Rousseau and Thoreau have explicitly insisted); it is our distorted sense of what is important—call this our values—that is distorting our lives. That this questioning at first leaves us divested, or devastated, is accordingly inevitable. This is the background against which, in *The Philadelphia Story,* I see the Dexter character as playing the role of a kind of sage. (This role will in turn no doubt cause suspicion of itself.) Speaking of importance, I identify Philadelphia as the site of two of the biggest stories enacted on this continent, the site of the creation of the founding documents of the United States.

The topic of what is essentially public and what is essentially private is established at the beginning of the film as an issue within it. First, at the stables, Tracy picks up Uncle Willie's copy of *Spy* magazine and gives a recitation of its "disgusting" story, written in "that corkscrew English" (a clear enough reference to the prose of *Time* magazine of that period) about a day in the life of a congressman's wife. In the next sequence, which takes place in the offices of *Spy* magazine, Mike and Liz identify Dexter as having broken the cameras of photographers attempting to cover his and Tracy's honeymoon. Nothing short of blackmail would force Tracy to open her house to the invasion of newshounds; and these sympathetic hounds are shown to be kept from following their vocations as writer and painter by the corkscrew demands of bringing back their bones of news. Are we, then, to ask what the relation is of journalism to serious art—for example, ask whether serious art does not itself make public matters private?

Does this film have anything worth saying about such a topic? If nothing, why does virtually every remarriage comedy have moments, and why do some have an entire setting, that features the newspaper? At some point we are bound to consider that these films are asking us to compare our enjoyment of them with our enjoyment of gossip and spying on the particularly lucky or unlucky. Mike says that taking the assignment of getting the story is degrading. How is our getting the results of the story, in the form of a film, less degrading? Liz says they do it "to keep a roof over our heads." Where is the profit for us? And if it is perhaps a degrading pastime, why do we not take the time to think about it?

I call attention to a moment in *The Philadelphia Story* in which the film calls attention to, and questions, the condition of its existence as a film— namely in its two closing images. First, at the click of Sidney Kidd's camera, the image of Mike, Dexter, and Tracy standing together in front of the wedding's official celebrant freezes, as if the three are getting married (it is a kind of wedding photo). Second, that view is then replaced, as an album leaf is turned, by a still of just Dexter and Tracy embracing. The motion picture camera has declared its relation to still photography, hence to the work Liz and Sidney Kidd are doing, one reluctantly, one greedily—questioning what it is we have been doing as witnesses to this work, having passed an hour and a half of our life investing in it. It might suggest that film—as some kind of art, some site of the transmutation of public and private into and out of each other—is peculiarly fit to capture lives as they pass by, without time or space to examine themselves, to examine the magnitude of concepts and forces that are determining them: life passing itself by.

For the moment, let's consider the form the issue of questioning takes in the narrative of *The Philadelphia Story*, or questioning the right to question. Any moral theory will require of itself that it seek the ground of rationality in moral argument, the thing that makes conduct criticizable by reason. Utilitarianism seeks rationality in the maximization of value (it is irrational to achieve less pleasure for fewer persons if you have the choice to achieve more for more). Kantianism seeks rationality in the universality of the principle on which one acts (it is against reason to exempt oneself from the judgment of one's principles). Kantianism focuses on the disruption of principle by the infection of inclination; for example, the value of charity is lessened if it is given out of either a feeling of pity or a swell of benevolence or for the acclaim it will command (in other words, if the left hand knows what the right hand is doing). Perfectionism also focuses on the one acting, but detects irrationality in failing to act on one's desire, or acting in the absence of sufficient desire, in the case where an act has value (positive or negative) essentially as a function of whether one desires it. Dexter says to Tracy about her proposed marriage to George that "it doesn't even make sense"; and when Mike tells her "You can't marry that guy," it turns out that he too means not that it is provably bad or wrong but that it just doesn't fit. Tracy accuses them both of snobbery. What they are both doing is appealing to her to recognize that she does not desire what she protests she desires. They are trying, as Dexter will put it, "to get those eyes open."

This is the aim of moral reasoning in perfectionism, not to assess pluses and minuses of advantage, nor to assess whether the act is recommendable universally, but yet to see to what those two standard theories wish to accomplish, namely that the one in question make himself intelligible, to others and to himself. Perfectionism concentrates on this moment. First, it recognizes difficulties in the moral life that arise not from an ignorance of your duties, or a conflict of duties, but from a confusion over your desires, your attractions and aversions, over whether, for example, you want the duties associated with marriage at all, whether you can bear the sense of failure in another divorce, whether your inability to act on your self-confessed longing to be useful in the world is based on anything more than fear or your vanity in wanting to be perfect, intact, without the need of human company. Second, it proposes that such muddles essentially stand in need of the perception of a friend. Third, it underscores that for one to confront another with her confusion, especially when she has not asked for advice, requires the justification of one's moral standing with her. To whom are reasons owed? Dexter asks Tracy, when she begins to confess to him that she doesn't know what happened between her and Mike, "Why [are you saying this] to me, Red? Where do I come into it any longer?"—not as rhetorical questions, but to get those eyes open to the fact that she continues to regard him as her helpmeet.

The moment of encounter, or challenge, does not exist in utilitarianism, in which, as Rawls remarkably observes, the individual does not exist. Nor does it exist essentially in Kant, where the challenge comes from the moral law alone. (We shall see in Chapter 7 that a condition of the appearance to you of the law, which Kant articulates in his categorical imperative, is that you are, in your life, and your present intention, "stopped," brought to take thought, to think whether you can, let us say, want a world characterized by an act such as you propose. What, among the nests and webs of actions and intentions and distractions in which your life is invested, has, in this instance, here and now, stopped you?)

The general cause of intervention in the films of remarriage comedy—given that the fact of these marriages means that the pair are in conversation—is to educate; to begin with, to respond to the woman's sense of her lack of education, her demand to know something that will change her dissatisfaction with the way things are, or reveal her role in it, or her, after all, greater satisfaction with this way than any other. In *Adam's Rib*, the Hepburn character will not place this demand explicitly until the next-to-last line of the film, in which, as the pair are about to get into bed together, she asks her husband, evidently in all comic seriousness (as it were, as a test of whether to get into bed with him again), what the difference is, or means, if anything much, between men and women. In *The Philadelphia Story*, the demand, to my ear, is placed in that outcry of Tracy's to George, "Oh, to be useful in the world!"

Tracy has, like Portia, three men to choose from; in her case the choice lies in determining who can help her answer that demand, which means, finding whom she can talk to, whom she believes. George on the spot rules himself out by failing to take her demand seriously; one question of the comic plot is to figure out how this news, of the foundering of an engagement to marry, is to break. To believe Dexter is to believe him when, for example, he says, an hour or so earlier, that Tracy was no helpmeet, she was a scold; their conversation had run aground; has it started again? Mike seems to have reached her, after a passionate exchange ending in a kiss, but the result of their reenacting a favorite scene from her earlier life with Dexter—having a midnight swim together after a party—is that she links up again with her desires, as Dexter keeps hoping for and holding up to her, but this time the immediate result is the scene with her and all three men, as Mike is carrying her from the swimming pool to her bedroom. Here she sings out in full giddiness that she has feet of clay, meaning roughly that she is subject to desire. It is here that she describes her condition, in response to Dexter's expression of concern, as that of being "not wounded, Sire, but dead." (This provided a signal moment of confirmation for me in working out the characteristics of remarriage comedy against Northrop Frye's characterization of New and Old Comedy. Frye remarks of Old Comedy that in it the woman undergoes something like death and resurrection and holds the key to the plot.)

The playful dig in Tracy's in effect addressing Dexter as "Sire" is good enough in itself, but it is obvious that Tracy is quoting something. It is only within the past year that, after desultory spurts of unsuccessful rummaging in Kipling and Browning, I am able to report, with some pleasure and relief, that the source is Robert Browning's "Incident at the French Camp," as follows:

> "You're wounded." "Nay," the soldier's pride
> Touched to the quick, he said:
> "I'm killed, Sire!" And his chief beside
> Smiling the boy fell dead.

Of course Tracy Lord would know Robert (and Elizabeth Barrett) Browning. I note that, having re-found her playfulness in response to Dexter's concern, a quality in her he has told her he relished (I am remembering her having described Dexter, to George, as "my lord and master"), and, leaving aside the question of who is the chief who is present "beside" her (it could be George, but the idea that her pride in battle is touched rather suggests that it is Mike), I note further that what has died is specified in Tracy's allusion to herself, via Browning's poem, as a boy, hence she is in effect acknowledging that the "garçonne" quality associated with Katharine Hepburn (fully recognized on film in her playing a boy in *Sylvia Scarlett*, directed by George Cukor in the mid-1930s) is part of why she requires resurrection as a grown woman.

Or is this worth noting? Can this little radiation from Browning's poem have been intended? By whom? These are questions I know will, even should, arise often. My advice is not to ignore them, but also not to let them prevent your imagination from being released by an imaginative work. To deflect the question of intention you have to say something to yourself about how, for example, just this poem by just this poet is alluded to just here in this work. So if you tell yourself it is an accident, then take that idea seriously.

What is the accident? That it is this poem by this poet? That it is said just this way by just this actress playing just this role in the presence of just this set of characters at just this moment in this plot in just this notable posture (the unique time in the film a character says anything while being carried)? This is a conjunction of seven or eight accidents, to go no further. Is it more satisfying intellectually, or as a point of common sense, to attribute this conjunction of events to a set of accidents than to suppose that it was intended that Tracy Lord allude, with understanding, to Browning's line? Why resist it? (I am asking this in all seriousness. Is intention dismissed, or resisted, less in response to the traditional arts than in response to film? Of course the concept of intention is in need of analysis. There is hardly a concept more in philosophical need.)

It may help in the present case to recall that the play from which this screenplay was adapted was written by Philip Barry, a considerable playwright of the period; and that the screenplay was adapted by Donald Ogden Stewart; and that the two writers studied together in a legendary class in playwriting given by George Baker just after the First World War, first at Harvard, then moving with Baker to Yale. It is not as if I am asking you to recognize in-jokes in the film/play, such as that George Kittredge (the very George that Tracy is engaged to as our story opens), bears the same name as the most famous Shakespearean scholar at Harvard at the time Philip Barry and Donald Ogden Stewart would have been there; or such as that, among other allusions to *A Midsummer Night's Dream,* Uncle Willie, characterized by pinching bottoms, says of himself, the morning after the engagement festival, that his head just fell off, the fate more or less suffered by Shakespeare's Bottom as he awakens from his dream of festival; which in turn suggests that you may take Uncle Willie as sharing Shakespeare's given name, especially since it is explicitly and momentarily shifted from one person to another in the course of the film. Here it may perhaps help to note that the director of the film, George Cukor, had before coming to Hollywood directed a fair sample of the corpus of Shakespeare's plays in and around New York.

The period in American culture in which the sensibilities and education were formed of those responsible for such a film as *The Philadelphia Story,* specifically the confidence with which sophisticated exchange and allusion were expected to be understood by a considerable proportion of one's fellow citizens, was, I suppose, not matched before or since. Don't make me seem to say more than I mean. These people were not intellectuals in a European mold; Philip Barry is not Bertolt Brecht; George Cukor is not Jean Cocteau. There are limitations on both sides. I am talking about a culture in which Broadway musical theater was thriving, and the *New Yorker* magazine was in stride, and jazz, still segregated, was meant for everyone who had ears to hear, and Hemingway and Fitzgerald and Dos Passos and Willa Cather were writing bestsellers.

But we were talking about Tracy Lord's education (Katharine Hepburn's education is explicitly referred to in *Adam's Rib*, where Spencer Tracy will poke admiring fun at her "Bryn Mawr accent"). And the genre of remarriage is talking about the woman's demand to be educated, and to educate, that is, to be listened to. Tracy receives lectures from all the men in her life, from Dexter and Mike and her father and George. George's idea is always to constrict her behavior, as when he responds to her wish to be useful by saying that instead he is going to build her an ivory tower; and as when at the party, in response to her tipsy gaiety, he disapprovingly insists that it's time for them to leave. He in effect takes himself out of the running; how the plot manages this is fun to see. (Whether in old or in new comedy, the renewed community at the end is formed at the price of ridding itself of a character of gloom, cursed with an intractable lack of sociability—think of Malvolio in *Twelfth Night*, or, as we shall see, Muggsy in *The Lady Eve*. If the character is unsociable not because of gloom but because of an ungovernable appetite for life, as in Falstaff's case, the society feels lessened that has to refuse him acknowledgment.)

The effect of each of the other three men is to humble or chasten this woman. Early, Dexter tells her she was no helpmeet and is chaste and virginal and will never be a "first-class human being" until she has some regard for human frailty. Before the party, her father accuses her of being as good as made of bronze and tells her she sounds like a jealous woman. After the party, Mike shows her she has feet of clay. What is the fruit of their instruction? It is summarized at almost the last moment, as they are to enter the replaced wedding ceremony which, Tracy announces to the awaiting guests, was denied them the first time around (there is no marriage without remarriage). Tracy's father says to her that she looks like a goddess; Tracy responds that she feels like a human being. She has come down to earth ("very down to earth" is how Dexter describes Mike's collection of short stories; Tracy regards them as poetry). But how does she arrive there?

Calling it off with George on the ground of his impoverished imagination, and seeing that he wouldn't be (and that she has no wish to try to make him) happy, Tracy has also had to see that Mike is not for her. Not for her, partly because, as she says, "Liz wouldn't like it," but partly too because of Liz's knowledge of Mike, expressed by whatever exactly she means in saying that he's not ready for marriage, that "he still has things to learn and I don't want to get in his way." I think of this as Mike's version of being innocent, virginal. (Liz's insistence on being "matron" not "maid" of honor in the wedding ceremony is in contrast both with Tracy's perception of her and with Mike's difference from her, in a sense his ignorance of her.)

I have elsewhere described the thought of Mike's not being ready to put aside his intactness by recurring to the moment—the detour—in Genesis where, just before God creates woman as a helpmeet for the single man, he allows Adam to give names to the animals. (The passage in Genesis about creating a helpmeet will come up emphatically again for us, since it is the classical theological justification, for both Christians and Jews, of marriage, and is featured as such in John Milton's tract on divorce, central to my account of remarriage comedy. Not for nothing do two of the definitive comedies of remarriage feature the names Adam and Eve in their titles.) My midrash on this Adam's (Mike's) "detour" (Freud might call this moment in the development of the human being the period of latency) is that it accomplishes two things: (1) it creates time for the man, a sense of the reality of life as irreversible, consequential, time to come into his own words (Mike is said to be a writer), giving himself language, his names for things, making the shared world his; (2) it allows him to survey the world of living things and to learn that none but the woman will make him feel other than alone in the world, will be a companion, reciprocal. His "not being ready" accordingly means that he is not ready to recognize Liz as his other, not Liz as opposed to all others, but as another to his separateness, to what Emerson calls "the recognition that he exists," the fact Emerson identifies as the Fall of Man (in the wonderful essay "Experience," which will also come up again).

Hence Tracy learns, or has learned, that Dexter is ready, that he is her company, that they exist. It is what she expresses to her father by declaring her feeling that she is a human being. Has she thereupon become what Dexter calls "a first-class human being"? Dexter here is on dangerous moral ground. One way to describe this is to put the remark next to the several remarks in the film on upper and lower classes ("Mac the night watchman is a prince among men; Uncle Willie is a pincher. What has class got to do with it?"). If we are to take Dexter seriously, he cannot mean that being first class means you deserve to command a greater share of the world's goods than others do. (Similarly, the film puts Tracy at risk when, in her first interview with Mike, she responds to his speaking of his early "lack of wherewithal" by saying "But that shouldn't be." Does she know whether she means that this shouldn't be because Mike is talented, or because no one should lack wherewithal?) We would like to take Dexter to mean by "a first class human being" something like being one who makes serious moral demands upon her/himself. (Tracy's mother has said that Tracy sets exceptionally high standards for herself. They evidently do not satisfy Dexter, as though they amount to making an exception of herself.) What counts as serious demands upon oneself, genuine caring for the self, is what perfectionism concerns itself with, after rational calculations have been made and standing obligations have been assessed and met, or found unworthy.

3

LOCKE

I was saying: The laws of the genre of remarriage comedy culminate in the definitive demand of marriage for "a meet and happy conversation," a phrase from Milton's tract on divorce. My claim for the genre is that it participates in the moral outlook (or dimension) of moral perfectionism, one which, in contrast to an emphasis on calculating the good or bad of a course of action, or establishing the morality of a principle announcing the right or wrong of a course of action, focuses instead on the worth of a way of life, of my way of life, which has come to a crossroads demanding self-questioning, a pause or crisis in which I must assess something that has been characterized as my being true to myself, something the romantics (explicitly including Emerson) articulated as the imperative to become the one I am. The claim of this field of concern to the status of morality is that the conversation required to assess my life—playing the role in perfectionism that calculation plays in Utilitarianism or derivation from the moral law plays in Kantianism—is one designed to make myself intelligible (to others, by way of making myself intelligible to myself). One could say that in the more academically established dispensations of morality I must justify myself (offer or refuse reasons on which I am acting) whereas in perfectionism I must reveal myself, sometimes as acting on no more reason than my desire, as if desire might, under certain circumstances, have its own rights. What links the exchanges in these domains is the sense of moral confrontation as one soul's examination of another.

In taking Emerson's essay "Self-Reliance" as exemplary of moral perfectionism, we began uncovering topics which seem essential in discovering the conditions of the genre of remarriage. For example, Emerson insists upon the importance—emphasizing the lack—of shared words ("Every word they say chagrins us"); Tracy Lord notes *Spy* magazine's "corkscrew English"; and C. K. Dexter Haven expresses chagrin when he says to Tracy that in speaking of the man she is engaged to marry she sounds like *Spy* magazine, a sure sign she doesn't know what she is saying. And when he tells her that she was no helpmeet with his thirst for alcohol, he names what she was as a scold, precisely not someone to whom one can say, or from whom one can derive, words that express oneself, words in which to become intelligible. And— a new discovery for me, one, I believe, that comes from a fresh sense of the juxtaposition of "Self-Reliance" with *The Philadelphia Story*—I have cited Emerson's remarking, at the end of his essay's opening paragraph, that words worth saying, words owed another, may leave the other humbled, chastened, ashamed, as when Tracy is humbled in the face of lectures by Dexter and by her father. (Late accusations from her departing fiancé are without effect; which is to say, she discovers that he and she do not speak the same language.) But, since I claim that Emerson is including his essay among those it describes as a "work of genius" marked, as such works universally are, by returning our rejected thoughts to us, which we accordingly receive with shame, I have to ask, taking up Dexter's form of question to Tracy when she says she has to confess something shameful to him ("Why to me, Tracy? Where do I come into it any longer?"): Why shame from Emerson? Where does Emerson begin to come into it? Which is to ask: What is Emerson's standing with us, that it gives him the right to attempt to shame us?

Moral standing is pushed to the center of the stage in perfectionism. Where the morally good is calculated, say in a revised tax code, or where the morally right is derived from Kant's categorical imperative, say in the case of abortion or capital punishment, if an act is bad or wrong, then it is bad or wrong period; that is, no matter who you are. But if you tell me "Neither a borrower nor a lender be" or "To thine own self be true," you had better have some standing with me from which you confront my life, from which my life matters to you, and matters to me that it matters to you. (Laurence Olivier's film of *Hamlet* memorably elaborates this fact of standing in connection with Polonius's speech of advice, staging it so that Laertes, as its recipient, without showing his father disrespect, expresses his impatience with this obligatory, impotent sagacity—the cautions of which he has evidently heard, more or less, many times—by teasing his sister behind his father's back.) When at the close of *Adam's Rib* Amanda says to Adam, "I'm real proud of you" (that is, the negation of ashamed of you), Adam replies, "I'd rather have you say that than anything," which in remarriage lingo means: I'd rather have *you* say that than anyone. They give each other standing.

If we put this moment of my words returning with an alienated majesty, humbling me, next to another moment in "Self-Reliance" that I harped on in the chapter on Emerson, namely my loss of the ability to say what I have to say for my existence, my reduction to quoting some saint or sage, then Emerson shows I have lost, or forgone, my voice. He is claiming no special standing with us, he assumes no particular or personal right. What standing he has we must grant him, by, since we have approached him, finding our voice returned in his. He does say, "I stand for humanity"—meaning both that he represents the human and that he bears up under the pain of it, and the one (representation) because of the other (suffering). His idea is that each of us stands, or may stand, in this position. What he writes amounts to a confession, which for him means something like an autobiography of America.

(So again the question arises: With what authority does he claim to write it? Which is a form of the question: With what right does philosophy claim to speak for others, for the human? It is importantly in their fundamental and original consideration of this question that the works of J. L. Austin and the later Wittgenstein began, and continue, to prove invaluable to me.)

I take the feature of the voice, or the discovery of my voice and its conversation, as the principal bearing of the texts of Locke and of Milton on the development of moral perfectionism. I think of the bearing as a continuation in our time of Aristotle's perception that it is essential to the idea of a polis, to political association, that its members be those who can speak, speak together, an association, accordingly, made for the human. Conversation here means, as I have suggested for philosophy, my speaking for others and my being spoken for by others, not alone speaking to and being spoken to by others. So we shall not be surprised by the urgency of the question: How do you know you are speaking for anyone and being spoken for by someone?

Milton and Locke were revolutionary writers: Milton the theorist of the Puritan Revolution that first overthrew the Stuarts and killed a king (Charles I) in 1649; Locke the theorist who found the way to the bloodless or "glorious" revolution that, after the Restoration of the Stuarts, deposed James II in 1688 in favor of William and Mary. The revolutionary insight that inspired their genius for persuasion was that fundamental public institutions held to be sacred, beyond human judgment (the divine right of kings to rule; the sacrament of marriage), are human interpretations of constructions which, whether devised by God or by man, are meant for human benefit (as Christianity itself is); and that when that benefit is lost, a given dispensation of such institutions (of a marriage, of an entire government) may be rejected and dissolved—a government violently, that is, by revolution, if necessary.

Both revolutionary doctrines depend on a notion of something like a contract or a covenant between those who are to be governed and those who are to govern, or, as in marriage, between those who are to govern each other; hence both depend upon a notion of the consent or agreement to the contract. It is here that the idea of the individual voice comes into play. The idea of my consent is evidently pictured as my giving my voice to the contract. (I will later in this chapter lay heavy stress on Locke's insistence that the consent that establishes or validates the social contract, the contract that establishes the legitimacy of a government, must be *express* consent; what Locke calls—in contrast with express consent—*tacit* consent is insufficient. It is to mark this insistence—a perpetually contested crux in Locke's theory of legitimate government—that I invoke the image of my voice.) And here the institution of government poses an issue that seems precisely to distinguish the ratification of this most public ("universal," Locke says) institution of society from that of marriage, perhaps the most private of institutions within society. Supposing the legitimacy of a government or an institution to be a function of whether it has elicited the approval, the giving, of my voice, Locke is forced to the question of how it is known (by the government, or by me) whether my voice has been given, that is to say, heard; and indeed whether it may have been revoked. Whereas Milton seems to take it as obvious enough that we are able to tell whether our mate is mute and spiritless—without conversation.

Remarriage comedy contests this obviousness. "Mute and spiritless" is meant, we must take it, to point to various degrees and modes of responsiveness. Even in a mate so responsive as Spencer Tracy is to Katharine Hepburn in *Adam's Rib,* there arise moments, small or large crises that begin and drive the narrative, when the woman finds cause to suspect that a point or level has been reached at which the man is no longer responsive to her beliefs and desires. And even when the man accuses his mate of a striking lack of responsiveness—as Dexter Haven accuses Tracy Lord in *The Philadelphia Story*—he does not, or does no longer, take this as a ground for seeking his freedom. Who, outside the marriage, is to judge such matters?

Perhaps Milton takes such matters as obvious because in the way he casts his view it is the husband who appears primarily to require protection against vows to a mute and spiritless mate. But surely Milton can be thought to recognize that, even within this constriction, husbands can abuse the claim to a wish for their freedom. These important questions aside, at least for the moment, I note in Milton's text its stress on the analogy (where Locke stresses the difference) between the state of the parties to the covenant creating a legitimate government and the state of those to a covenant establishing a valid marriage, an analogy that Milton takes to work in both directions. Quoting him: "For no effect of tyranny can sit more heavy on the commonwealth than this household unhappiness on the family. And farewell all hope of true reformation in the state, while such an evil as this lies undiscerned or unregarded in the house: on the redress whereof depends not only the spiritful and orderly life of our grown men, but the willing and careful education of our children." In one direction, the analogy claims that the effects of a bad marriage are like the effects of a tyranny on the commonwealth (depression, disorder, neglect of children). In the other direction, the analogy claims that, as the parties of marriage are entitled to a meet and happy conversation with each other (say mutual responsiveness), so the members of a commonwealth (one, Milton says, that lives in hopes of true reformation) are similarly entitled to responsiveness from one another. (Milton's phrase "undiscerned and unregarded in the house" seems to me to imply a question of the relation of a contract and a conspiracy, a distinction that becomes crucial in Rousseau's version of contract theory.)

It is to capture something of the idea of a mutual criticism of marriage and society at large that I speak of *The Philadelphia Story,* in its rediscovery of marriage, as inviting a conversation with the society of which it is a reflection and upon which it permits perspective, the society it reflects and the principal pair it depicts each being recognizable as embarked upon an adventure, and each valuing itself because of that aspiration. It goes without saying that not all films are capable of providing such perspective. It does not, alas, go without saying that films which do provide it are by that fact revealed as more than symptoms of the wishes or fears of the dominant culture that produces them.

I thereby place two cards on the theoretical table, one claiming that the concept of art remains powerful enough to contest the idea that human artifacts are homogeneously and with no resistance ideological reflections of their culture; and one claiming that works with the power of art were regularly, not of course predominantly, produced within the Hollywood studio system.

Another mode of the mutual examination of marriage and society is manifested, I shall argue, in *Adam's Rib* (the subject of the next chapter), where trouble in a sordid marriage (a wife follows her husband to a tryst and shoots him) is held by the principal woman (Katharine Hepburn as Amanda) to reveal an inequality in the way women and men are treated before the law. We are asked to see that as the more glamorous and free couple incorporate a touch of the squalor of the unhappier, unstylish couple into their lives, society's inequality is revealed as lodged in the cause of the squalor as much as in its response to it. The ironic reflection of the lower- and the higher-class couple in each other is given relatively early when Adam (Spencer Tracy), according to Amanda, "slugs" her; and relatively late when Adam pulls a phony gun on her, reversing the interruption and the act for which they take their marriage to court—that is, allow society to judge their marriage while at the same time they use their days in court to judge or defend society by the state of their and their clients' marriages.

But if a society that lives in the hope of reformation demands for its legitimacy, on Milton's analogy with marriage, a mutual responsiveness among its citizens, what does this willingness for exchange look and sound like? Can happiness, or the expression of happiness, be required of citizens? What would public happiness consist in? Is it expressed most purely in patriotic ritual? In viewing such films as under discussion here?

Let's continue with such questions, unclearly formulated questions, still unformulated questions, by turning to Locke's *Second Treatise of Government*. It is not particularly difficult to read, unless many of its ideas are so famous as almost to make it illegible in its specificity. It is uncontroversial to concede Locke to be the father or the soul of European and American liberalism, namely of the idea that government is a trust, that it is held legitimately only so far as it sustains the freedom of the individual members of society and is answerable to them; in short, that legitimate government is based upon the consent of the governed. So that any contradictions or confusions in Locke's views, notoriously concerning consent and property, have seemed the contradictions and confusions of liberalism itself, which is, and has been, continually under attack from the left and from the right for as long as there have been a left and a right.

To establish his political theory, Locke needed immediately to refute two competing theories: first, the theory of the divine right of kings, and second, less radically, Hobbes's theory, also employing the idea of a social contract, which resulted in giving too absolute a power to the absolute will of the sovereign.

The refutation of the doctrine of divine right is the task of Locke's *First Treatise of Government*, which takes on Sir Robert Filmer's defense of the doctrine in his aptly named *Patriarcha*. The conclusion arrived at in Locke's *First Treatise* is inscribed in the opening of the *Second Treatise* (I quote from the edition of Peter Laslett):

> It is impossible that the Rulers now on earth, should make any benefit, or derive any the least shadow of Authority from that, which is held to be the Fountain of all Power, *Adam's Private Dominion and Paternal Jurisdiction,* so that, he that will not give just occasion, to think that all Government in the World is the product only of Force and Violence, and that Men live together by no other Rules but that of Beasts, where the strongest carries it, and so lay a Foundation for perpetual Disorder and Mischief, Tumult, Sedition and Rebellion (things that the followers of that Hypothesis so loudly cry out against) must of necessity find out another rise of Government, Another Original [Origin] of Political Power, and another way of designing and knowing the Persons that have it, then [than] what Sir Robert F[ilmer] hath taught us.

Locke's positive account can be said to turn on three pivotal concepts: those of property and of consent and that of the state of nature, from which the others can be seen to be shaped. I'm going to force myself not to discuss at any length the fascinating pages on the concept of property, where you get an extraordinary texture of arguments at once commonsensical and mysterious, perhaps a secret of Locke's fantastic influence in the century following his. Take Locke's idea that a thing becomes my property if I mix my labor with it. It seems commonsensical that if I carved a little figure then it is mine, I own it. But suppose I stole the wood or soap from which I carved it. In that case I might now buy the piece of wood, or trade for it, or hire myself out to its owner to pay it off. Then doesn't one or another of *these* actions constitute my ownership? Or take a variant of Locke's example of an apple. If one plants the seed, another harvests it, and a third eats it, who owns it, or owned it? Yet it seems clear that labor establishes some internal relation to an object. But then, adducing examples from Wittgenstein, what makes a sensation, or a limb, *mine?* Evidently not labor. We might conclude that my relation to a sensation or a limb of mine is not one of owning it. We might conclude this in the case of an apple too. And should we say that a doll is mine if I mix my play with it? Perhaps it is mine *for now*.

I say only this in parting from the idea of something's being mine (barely having entered its consideration): Locke's defense of private property, while satisfying his view that such a thing is legitimate (fairly fundamental for the father of classical liberalism), nevertheless compromises the idea, for two reasons. First, to my mind, because the very forced quality of his reasoning suggests that if it takes this much metaphysics to justify and to limit private property, there must be something suspicious or still unspoken in it. Second, because he seems to me to betray a sense that the natural or primary, hence presumably the most just, state of property or ownership is ownership *in common.* He does not find that ownership in common requires any special argumentation. Perhaps this is because the concept comes up in the context of his remarking that God gave the earth to mankind in common. In this case the question does not arise about whether the earth was God's to give. (It might be worth asking why not. Was Locke assuming that God had mixed his labor with his creation? Or that infinite power confers property? Or that, more simply, incontestable power confers property? Or that with a god the question does not arise? In any case it seems that if you already have owner-ship of something you can, in principle, barring some specific obstruction, transfer it.)

What Locke has (also) to argue for, as he puts matters, is how, from the condition of common ownership, individuals can "begin a property." Locke's taking property in common to be as intuitive as private property alerts us to the fact that it is anachronistic to speak of Locke as the father of liberalism. He wrote before liberalism and socialism began their quarrel with one another, and he can be taken to contribute to both.

Since the concepts of both property and consent are, as I put it, shaped by that of the state of nature, let us go into Locke's description of the state of nature, or rather his descriptions. I mention two, which seem not obviously compatible with each other.

One description occurs in his attack on Hobbes in chapter 3, para-graph 19. Hobbes is not mentioned by name, but Locke is obviously allud-ing to him when he refers to "some Men [who] have confounded [the state of nature with a state of war; whereas they are] as far distant as a State of

Peace, Good Will, Mutual Assistance, and Preservation, and a State of Enmity, Malice, Violence and Mutual Destruction." Hobbes gave the most famous of all the classical descriptions of the state of nature of the kind Locke deplores, imagining human life within it as "solitary, poor, nasty, brutish and short." Locke does not *equate* the state of nature with the state of peace, goodwill, and so on; he says only that the state of nature is "as far distant" from a state of war "as a State of Peace" and a "State of Enmity." But the point of Locke's assertion of difference seems to be to picture the state of nature as the precise opposite of war, and if the state of nature is anything like what Locke here appeals to as war's opposite, why do we ever leave it?

The fact is that Locke also has an opposed conception of what life in the state of nature is like. He gives this in chapter 9, paragraph 123:

> Though in the state of Nature, [men have] such a right [of freedom and property], yet the Enjoyment of it is very uncertain, and constantly exposed to the Invasion of others; for all being Kings as much as he, every Man his Equal, and the greater part no strict Observers of Equity and Justice, the enjoyment of the property he has in this state is very unsafe, very unsecure. This makes him willing to quit a Condition which, however free, is full of fears and continual dangers. And 'tis not without reason that he seeks out and is willing to joyn in Society with others.

I pause to note that when Locke speaks of those who "have a mind to unite for the mutual preservation of their lives, liberties and estates" he announces that he calls these goods "by the general name 'property'." So our lives and liberties are, on the wide definition of "property," as much our property as our estates are. This is a fateful extension of the concept of property. To call my liberty my property leaves it open for me to sell my liberty, sell myself into slavery. Many today, not all I believe, would argue against the right to engage in such a transaction.

Locke's extension of the concept of property is also a basis on which to conceive of my *labor* as my property, hence salable—and far fewer people seem to object to this principle of wage labor. The need and consequence for Locke's conception of labor in these terms is emphasized in a strong and influential criticism, from the left, of Locke's view in Thomas Macpherson's *The Political Theory of Possessive Individualism,* published in the late 1960s, where Locke's view of labor as salable is taken as preparation for labor as alienated, appropriated.

Go back to Locke's description of the state of nature as "full of fears and continual dangers." He will say neither that there is a discrepancy between this and his fantasm of the state of nature as comparable to a state of peace and mutual assistance, nor that this second description is exactly that of Hobbes, since Hobbes insists that when he says a state of nature is a state of war, he doesn't mean actual, continuous fighting; he means insecurity and uncertainty. Can one reconcile, or understand the causes of, Locke's different pictures of the state of nature?

I shall more or less assume the now received view that Locke's state of nature is not, and was not meant to be, accurate history. But I shall assume something further, namely that the idea of a state of nature is also not simply some kind of explanatory myth; or anyway, not a myth of what a state of things was like *before* the establishment of a political order. I take it, that is, that the idea of a state of nature also refers to some selection(s) of reality that Locke saw around him in the social arrangements of his day. Locke gives himself a chance to say that his idea of nature is nothing but a useful fiction. But in a sense he declines the chance.

In section 14 he reports, "t'is often asked as a mighty objection, 'Where are or ever were there any Men in such a state of nature?'" A hundred years later, famously, David Hume, with his superb powers of skepticism, will raise exactly this question, and raise it so comically, and so artfully, that for some it is quite as if we witness the usefulness, the power of conviction, of the concept of the social contract dying on the spot. "In vain are we asked in what records this charter of our liberties is registered," Hume writes. And he continues: "It was not written on parchment, nor yet on leaves or barks of trees." But Locke had already raised the question a century earlier, and given an answer to it. Locke's answer: "The World never was, nor ever will be, without Numbers of Men in that State [of nature]."

To recognize Locke's claim here you do not need to find testimony on parchment or on leaves or barks of trees; you have instead to look at the world in a different way. Locke cites the case of princes and their relation to their subjects as manifesting the logic of the state of nature—namely the fact that there is no political understanding, as described by Locke, between princes, or absolute monarchs, and their subjects, meaning that consent has not established their condition with each "agreeing together mutually to enter into one Community, and make one Body Politick," establishing, for example, an impartial judge, a higher appeal, to settle their mutual grievances. One who has the personal right of life and death over another is in a state of nature with that other. Independent states were, for Locke, on this ground, in a state of nature with respect to one another. Locke is not talking about primitives but about sophisticates.

I find that his description fits a further pervasive circumstance, or raises a further question. Are children who are still subject to their parents' wishes also to count as living in a state of nature with their parents? Parents do not have the immediate power of life and death over their children, but in practice, within wide limits, the parents' treatment of their children is or was unmonitored. (As was that between husbands and wives. If the wife had protectors, would that not increase the idea of a state of nature here too?) Here is a reason Locke might not want to identify a state of nature with a state of war. He doesn't take children—or husbands and wives—to be in a state of war. They *can* be in a sweet state, yet in a state of nature.

The disanalogy with a state of nature is that children and parents, and husbands and wives, do not exist in equal freedom, which they may be imagined to agree to forgo for the securities of society. Prison is not an image of Locke's state of nature. Still, monarchs and subjects were, in imagination, never equally free to consent or refrain from their relation to each other, and Locke perceives them to exist in a state of nature with respect to each other. A reason it would, to my mind, be of interest to pursue such pervasive regions of existing states of nature within and between established societies, is that Locke's influential pictures seem to imply (apart from the denial of international law) that each society continuously and in each generation (and in each individual) has to (re)emerge from a state of nature. In lucky societies this reemergence will take the form of reformation rather than a transfer of allegiance to new oppression, or the convulsion of rebellion.

(I pause, or digress, again—I hope you can accommodate this tendency in me. Perhaps one day I'll find time to justify digressions, anyway of a certain sort, suggesting that they may be understood as something other than digressions, perhaps as rational stages over difficult ground. I pause, I was saying, to note that the third of the most influential contract theorists, Rousseau, did take an image of prison as representing the state from which a self-governing society of laws has to emerge. The great opening line of Rousseau's *The Social Contract* is: "Mankind is born free and is everywhere in chains." Society as it stands, formed by undermining and partial agreements, not the state of nature, is a prison. Rousseau also said that the way a philosopher portrays the state of nature is a projection from his present perception of his society. I shall take this to heart as I work to the conclusion of my account of Locke's *Second Treatise*.)

Going back to Locke's text: Groups of human beings are in a state of nature wherever the particular relation between them called civil government has not been established. And I have said that the question is bound to arise how you can tell when this condition is in fact in effect. Since nothing can establish a legitimate government but the consent of the governed, telling whether it is established is the same as telling whether consent has been established. How can you tell that consent to be governed together has been given? What I took as Locke's answer to Hume's raillery in asking where our consent is recorded only says that we can tell where consent has *not* been given, where pockets or strata of a state of nature inevitably exist. But is there no positive criterion? There may be reasons why the negative here, as elsewhere, is more visible than the positive—as, according to J. L. Austin, there are many ways in which an action may not be free, but no single criterion that shows positively that it is free, no single quality of freedom; as there are many ways in which a statement may be false (an exaggeration, a lie, an understandable mistake, and so on) but no one way in which it is true. But I mean that there may be a reason for the greater visibility of the absence over the presence of consent that is connected with the political function of consent itself. We shall come to this.

I've suggested in effect that you cannot tell whether consent has been given to a society by examining the individual members of that society to determine whether they have—or remember having—given their consent to it. You cannot tell by, as it were, looking. Is consent therefore mystical, or in some other way unreal? Does such a test (as examining the consciousness of individual members) prove that it is? There are other things about a society that you can tell by looking; in particular, Locke's conflicting descriptions of the state of nature may be understood as projections of the conflicts he perceived within the relationships among the members of his contemporary society.

I am thinking of the conflicts described in Macpherson's *Political Theory of Possessive Individualism*, which I mentioned earlier. Here are two features of Locke's experience. He saw men of property, reasonable men, free to enjoy the fruits of their investments, the new men, new powers in society, setting a new social tone, entitled to protection from the powers above and security from the powers below: the new middle class. Again, he saw tremendous inequality in the distribution of these new privileges and wealth. He seemed to regard this as all right, or anyway inevitable, but also as a potentially revolutionary situation, with those living at subsistence waiting to deprive those more fortunate of their fortunes. The founding fathers of the United States saw something not unlike this. They wanted freedom, but also the responsible exercise of freedom. Irresponsibility can come from below or from above. From below, in thoughtless cries for revolution; from above, in blindness to intolerable degrees of inequality and want, depriving citizens of sufficient goods basic to preserving life and pursuing happiness.

The two conceptions of the state of nature fit these two conditions, call them the achievable peaceableness of human nature and the ready bellicosity of human nature. Locke's problem was not alone to justify and encourage rebellion (though it was certainly and famously that), but it was also to justify the extensive possessions of the new middle class, and that means to justify it in terms of the idea (the Christian idea, the Puritan idea) that we are all God's creatures, and therefore equal and free as individuals.

The theory of the social contract fell into disrepute, or disuse, after its formidable philosophical defenses in Hobbes, Locke, Rousseau, and Kant, for reasons some of which are not hard to imagine: first, because of its intractable epistemological problem, the problem of explaining how we know, against appearances, that there is a contract, and what it says, and how it binds later generations, namely those not immediately party to it; second, because of certain apparently heartless moral and social consequences, which in the course of the Industrial Revolution would seem less and less to have produced social distributions of goods that the masses of people who were victims of these arrangements could be imagined to have consented to.

I mention, in anticipation of our turning to John Rawls's *Theory of Justice*, that this text, more than any other of the twentieth century, has served to rehabilitate contractualism in moral and political theory by managing exactly to speak to, to provide reinterpretations of, just those two points. In particular, to present purposes, the epistemological issues of locating consent and positing a state of nature are transfigured, since the object of consent in Rawls's account is no longer to establish and justify a civil government but to accept a pair of principles of justice, ones, moreover, designed to provide, or shape, a *present* judgment of society's worthiness. But since I will, in turn, wish to question whether this shift in the object of consent retains the essentials of what we want of the concept, I will conclude my discussion of Locke with a more textual scrutiny of his discussion of consent than I have found elsewhere.

A form Locke gives to the question of our knowledge of consent is this: How do we know with whom we are in a political relationship? The received view, to which I still know of no exception, is that Locke is weak or confused or dishonest at this crucial point of his theory. It is obvious—is it not?—that not every member of society has given what Locke will call *express consent* to be governed. Every interpretation of Locke I have read takes his notion of *tacit consent* as meant to explain how, in spite of the absence of express consent, political consent has been shown. I suppose Locke needs such a notion. (Call it the problem of interpreting political or moral silence—public or private.) But I do not take Locke as using *tacit consent* for this critical function.

The critical sections in question are 119–122, the concluding sections of chapter 8, "Of the Beginning of Political Societies." I quote the whole of section 119:

> *Every Man* being, as has been shewed, *naturally free,* and nothing being able to put him into subjection to any Earthly Power, but only his own Consent; it is to be considered, what shall be understood to be a *sufficient Declaration of* a Mans *Consent, to make him subject* to the Laws of any Government. There is a common distinction of an express and a tacit consent, which will concern our present Case. No body doubts but an *express Consent* of any Man, entering into any Society, makes him a perfect Member of that Society, a Subject of that Government. The difficulty is, what ought to be look'd upon as a *tacit Consent,* and how far it binds, i.e., how far any one shall be looked on to have consented, and thereby submitted to any Government, where he has made no Expression of it at all. And to this I say, that every Man, that hath any Possession, or Enjoyment, of any part of the Dominions of any Government, doth thereby give his *tacit Consent,* and is so far forth obliged to Obedience to the Laws of that Government, during such Enjoyment, as any one under it; whether this his Possession be of Land, to him and his Heirs for ever, or a Lodging only for a Week; or whether it be barely travelling freely on the Highway; and in Effect, it reaches as far as the very being of any one within the Territories of that Government.

The standard objection against the (supposed) use of the idea of tacit consent here could hardly be more obvious: It is a sheer trick; the central notion securing legitimacy of government is empty. If just *being* in a country, even to the extent of traveling on its roads or taking a lodging for a night, constitutes *consent* (meaning, in this context, tacit consent), then what act of minimum sanity and peaceableness could fail to constitute consent? And then how does this inevitable minimum of acquiescence, say obeying the rules of the road, which may be your unbroken and amiable habit in whatever country you drive, yield the revolutionary result Locke announces? I'm suggesting that it does not, and that Locke quite clearly means that it does not.

In the sections preceding 119, Locke has been asking: What makes a person a member of a political community? And his answer has been: Consent; and moreover, one's own consent. No one else can give it for one, and one cannot, therefore, give it until maturity, when one *speaks for oneself* (the issue I found, in characterizing Liz's perception of Mike in *The Philadelphia Story,* mythologized in Adam's naming of the animals). This is the only way in which an individual, giving consent, comes into the obligations of membership in a society. The opening words of section 119 are, "*Every Man* being, as has been shewed, *naturally free,*" and Locke goes on to announce: "it is to be considered, what shall be understood to be a *sufficient Declaration* of a Mans *Consent, to make him subject* to the Laws of any Government." Whereupon he introduces the distinction between express and tacit consent. It does look, and it has as far as I know uniformly looked, as though the transition to section 119 is to the question: What *constitutes* consent? How do we know when a person has consented?

And in a way this is what is happening. But the topic has shifted. Locke is at the same time moving to a different person *in a different relation* to society. The question of consent is no longer directed to one who is becoming a *member* of society; the question is instead directed to one simply becoming *subject to society's laws* (while not a member). (Try reading the quotation in the preceding paragraph twice, first emphasizing "declaration" and then emphasizing "sufficient" and "subject to the laws.")

These other persons—nonmembers, strangers, aliens, visitors, students, perhaps other long-term residents, perhaps seeking asylum, perhaps seeking mischief, perhaps seeking specialized medical treatment—cannot, for example, vote, but they can, for example, sever all connection with this society merely by leaving it, forgoing its protection and the enjoyment of its comforts. Such a restriction and such an easy freedom do not characterize *members* of a society—and Locke from beginning to end insists that membership requires consent to be declared *expressly*. (It is not immediately clear what could free one from *this* declaration.)

In sum, tacit consent is not a nonvocal, or un-express, form of political consent. It cannot be; and I think Locke consistently means this. How tacit consent is shown is no particular problem, as the instances of uneventful traveling on the highway or lodging for a night, as instances of showing obedience to the reigning laws and customs of the society whose guest you are, are sufficient to show. Locke may be at fault in not sufficiently considering and explaining how *express* consent is manifested. But he is not at fault in giving a wrong, perhaps heartless, certainly undemocratic and illiberal, explanation, one that allows the implication to be drawn that when you express dissent from some action of your government you are withdrawing from membership in society and the protection of its laws. This was something like the interpretation assumed, or advanced, by one of the most famous slogans at the time of the war in Vietnam, seen on many bumper stickers: "Love it [America], or leave it." (The resourceful counter-slogan, also appearing on bumpers, was "Vietnam: Love it or leave it.") Locke's *Second Treatise,* bland and sensible in times of calm, took on a certain fervor in those years, with sudden immediacy in such moments as Locke's saying (in defense against the accusation that his emphasis on consent leaves too much room for rebelliousness among the people) that when a government violates or abdicates its trust *it* is the rebellious party, alluding to the etymology of "rebellion" as returning to a state of war, a war against its own people.

This is what I meant in saying earlier that there may be a reason for the greater visibility of the absence over the presence of consent that is connected with the political function of consent. To consent to be governed is to consent to give up the freedom of nature for the good of society. The function of membership is to give you a voice in what is done in your name, in saying whether what is being done is in fact good. This voice would be worthless unless it was very difficult to lose this membership. Consent is not a matter of joining a consensus on passing issues of the day. Once given, consent cannot be withdrawn as long as the government consented to is recognizable and is effective.

Locke draws the distinction between express and tacit consent as early as the chapter on the beginning of political societies (chapter 8). He does not take up the withdrawal of consent systematically until the nineteenth and final chapter, "Of the Dissolution of Government." The implication thus dramatized is the following general reversal of priorities: while consent begins society, dissent does not end it; rather, society's dissolution ends or cancels consent. (Another asymmetry might prove important. While Locke insists that each individual must give his or her own consent, he does not seem interested in how individuals manifest their individual departures from society, perhaps for the reason that an individual's departure, no matter how existentially backed, does not contribute to the dissolution of society.)

Locke is, however, interested in assessing the causes, in some cases the blame, for society's or government's dissolution. As between blaming "the people's Wantonness" (falsely based attempts at revolution or resistance) and blaming "the Ruler's Insolence" (falsely based exercises of arbitrary power) (section 230), the overwhelming impression of this chapter is that Locke finds blame more likely to fall on the rulers; he describes the people as "more disposed to suffer than right themselves by resistance." Put otherwise, the overwhelming impression is that for my consent to the social contract to be canceled, it has to be taken out of my hands—by public calamity (usurpation of government, defeat in war), which Locke figures in the metaphors of an earthquake or whirlwind. Consent, we could say, has to be withdrawn *for* me, not *by* me.

Does this leave Locke's *Second Treatise* without a conclusion, or a point? His theory of legitimate government, one based upon consent to be governed, was to show that rebellion is justifiable, that is, that there may come a time which produces a rightful cause for resisting and withdrawing consent. But at the end it turns out that by the time you perceive that the time has come, it is too late, dissolution is under way. Well, there is no cure for the misery of a nation in crisis. But there is a difference between hope and despair. And Locke is explicit that "Men can never be secure from Tyranny, if there be no means to escape it, till they are perfectly under it: And therefore it is, that they have not only a Right to get out of it, but to prevent it" (section 220). So perhaps we do not require an answer to the question of what positively shows express consent so long as we have an answer to the question of what negatively shows that this consent is no longer in effect, that it has devolved into our individual hands, that a time has come in which "People . . . may provide for themselves" (ibid.).

Then what is this answer, what shows devolution or dissolution (or the imminent need to prevent them)? Society—as Freud was not the first to notice—inevitably causes discontents. When do discontents become diagnostic of a condition in which (in section 229) "the Rulers . . . employ [their Power] for the destruction, and not the preservation of the Properties of their People?" (Taking "Properties" in the broad definition of "Life, Liberties, and Estates.") Locke's answer, in section 230, may seem too abstract or thin to answer this question of finality (of the perception of a revolutionary moment):

> Nor let any one say, that mischief can arise from hence, as often as it shall please a busie head, or turbulent spirit, to desire the alteration of the Government. 'Tis true, such men may stir, whenever they please, but it will be only in their own just ruine and perdition. For till the mischief be grown general, and the ill designs of the Rulers become visible, or their attempts sensible to the greater part, the People, who are more disposed to suffer, than right themselves by Resistance, are not apt to stir . . . Who can help it, if they [the Governors], who might avoid it, bring themselves into this suspicion? Are the People to be blamed, if they have the sense of rational Creatures, and can think of things no otherwise than as they find and feel them?

But my question persists: How is it known that the "ill designs [or attempts] of the Rulers" have become "visible" or "sensible" to "the greater part"? What has become visible—the rulers' designs and attempts, or the greater part of the people's becoming sensible of their lives' destruction? It is only the people's sense that causes resistance and the desire for change. But this requires a reciprocal perception by the people of themselves. Something in their lives shows a change in the status of their consent. You might say something shows a change in the status of their silence, their not making a "stir." Since being tacit, saying nothing, never expressed their consent to establish and maintain society, there must be a change in their expression that shows their sense of consent to be withdrawing. This may take the form of public demonstrations, or private meetings, but may it also take the form of what Emerson calls "silent melancholy" and what Thoreau more famously called "quiet desperation," which he claims characterizes the lives of the mass of men?

Locke, compared with Emerson and Thoreau, or with Milton's speaking in his tract on divorce of our right to void allegiances and covenants that we "never entered to [our] mischief" (as if we had "conspire[d]" to our "own ruin"), seems uninterested in conveying a sense of, let me say, the quality of expressiveness of lives in the absence of consent. Milton speaks of the effect of tyranny sitting "heavy on the commonwealth" as palpably as "household unhappiness," and he draws the consequences of this heaviness as dispiritedness and disorder in "the life of our grown men" and the neglect of their children, or generally, on the model of an unhappy marriage, a general absence of conversation. As if society at large had become tacit. Locke has, for example, no romance with marriage, but justifies conjugality strictly on the utilitarian ground of providing for the well-known prolonged dependence of human young on human adults. Divorce is in principle irrelevant. While the young are dependent it is unjustified; when no further young are in question it is unnecessary. Nothing in marriage should suggest in the role of husband and father any image of what justifies political authority.

But Locke's point in writing the *Second Treatise* was not alone to justify revolution, and to *describe* a revolutionary situation, but to claim that this situation exists, to *call* for revolution. Peter Laslett's critical edition of Locke's *Treatises* seems to have established that Locke was not simply justifying the "Glorious Revolution" of 1688 after the fact had proven it bloodless, but, having begun the work ten years earlier, was doing the thing he calls stirring himself, and asking his fellows to stir themselves (as in the quotation from section 230). He was running the risk of "ruin and perdition." Was he acting on the perception Emerson would announce a century and a half later, in "The American Scholar," between the two American revolutions, that "the deeper [the scholar] dives into his privatest, secretest presentiment, to his wonder he finds this the most acceptable, most public, and universally true"? He was asking that each of his fellow citizens come individually to a judgment of the state of their lives in common. He was not remaining tacit, and he was asking for the voices of others.

One can perhaps put this another way, marking the various attempts we have seen so far in Emerson, and in Milton, and in *The Philadelphia Story*, and will see in *Adam's Rib*, to relate public and private, society and marriage, social role and individual desire. Go back to the introduction of the distinction between express and tacit consent in section 119. It still seems inescapably obvious to me that when Locke allows that "no body doubts but an *express Consent* . . . makes him a perfect Member" and goes on to note that "the difficulty is, what ought to be look'd upon as a *tacit Consent*," he has skipped a question, namely: What ought to be looked upon as an express consent? Locke speaks of a "difficulty" remaining, but he has turned up no difficulty in identifying the (tacit) consent of foreigners.

And look at the second sentence of chapter 19, "Of the Dissolution of Government": "That which makes the Community, and brings Men out of the loose State of Nature, into one Politick Society, is the Agreement [the express consent] which every one has with the rest to incorporate, and act as one Body, and so be one distinct Commonwealth." This says that apart from our (each of our) consent, a Politick Society does not exist. So that so far as I am in doubt whether I have, or how we have, given consent, I am so far in doubt whether my society exists, whether it speaks for me and I speak for it. And it seems to me that what Locke's wavering indicates is his sense that this doubt is never permanently resolved. (Wavering, I mean, between express and tacit; between the existence of society and the validity of government; between property as things and property as life and liberty.)

That this doubt of the existence of consent, hence of the legitimacy— hence of the existence—of society, is never permanently resolved, strikes me as revelatory of the nature of democracy: of the sense that in a democracy our public and our private lives stand to compromise each other, can as it were be ashamed of each other, that I owe to my society a meet and cheerful exchange to reaffirm my consent, or else a willingness to articulate the public causes of my unhappiness. That there is no measurable limit to my responsibility for the way things are, or to how far the effect of my unhappiness mars the possibility of the general happiness, hence brings into question the fact of our communal existence.

It may be that the idea of myself and my society being in conversation, demanding a voice in each other, is something I was encouraged to by Locke's passage early in the *Second Treatise* (section 9) where he distinguishes between the "Alien" or the "Stranger" on the one hand and "Subjects of the Common-Wealth" on the other, by saying of the alien or the stranger that the laws of the commonwealth "speak not to him, nor if they did, is he bound to hearken to them." By the time of Emerson and Thoreau and Mill, when the issue is no longer to establish the idea of self-government but to assess its costs and its subtler usurpations of voice (to take up the defense of freedom, even eccentricity, in criticism of the demands of democratic conformism), I recall again Emerson's accusation and confession (parodying Descartes) that we no longer speak or think for ourselves, no longer say "I think," "I am," but "quote some saint or sage." As I said in Chapter 1, it follows from this loss of the capacity to outface a doubt of our existence, that we in effect declare that we haunt our existence. The implications for the body politic are immediate, since if I have no voice of my own in which to express my thoughts, I cannot give my consent to be governed, and our condition is that we haunt our society. It cannot hear us.

But here, could we express Emerson's longing for America to discover itself by imagining him to declare, "Man is timid, he is afraid to say 'I think' 'I consent,' but instead quotes, for example, Locke"? Is Emerson's struggle against conformity then a struggle for dissent? But if our language is not our own, why believe that we come closer to speaking for ourselves in our dissent than in our consent? Can't I recognize that the laws of the land "reach" me, "speak" to me, and yet wonder to what extent I am a stranger, an alien, to my society? It is a wondering whether I have consented to *this*, to this way things are. The wondering may be good, if somewhat painful, on both sides. Since it means that each side feels it is to some extent unexpressed, each may undertake to hearken more closely.

Or to turn the question again: What kind of conversation constitutes the bond that democracy, or as Milton puts it, a state in a process of reformation, asks of itself? When Emerson speaks of seeking our unattained but attainable self, I cannot but hear him speaking of America as our unattained but attainable commonwealth. As though a society, like a self, can, in Thoreau's words, be beside itself in a sane sense, its further, or future, version existing within its present.

4

Adam's Rib

1   In a prologue, Doris Attinger (Judy Holliday), discovered in a busy street as a clock advances to 5 p.m., the end of the day's business, proves to have been secretly awaiting the emergence of her husband from a building across the way, in order to follow him to wherever it is he goes after work. (We learn fairly soon that he hasn't been home for several days and nights). When the husband (Tom Ewell) appears, Doris tracks him through the rush hour crowd into a subway, where, bumped by passengers coming through the gate, she drops her handbag, revealing it to contain a pistol. Exiting the subway, a swaggering, unsuspecting, whistling Mr. Attinger leads his wife to an apartment into which he disappears, whereupon she takes out her pistol, consults a pamphlet of instructions in the use of such an implement, shoots the lock off the door, shoves the door open, and fires at her husband and his invitingly clad compan-ion Beryl Caighn (Jean Hagen). The companion screams, the husband falls, Doris collapses, distractedly sobbing, over his body.

2   Newspapers are left at the door of a markedly different class of apartment. A uniformed maid retrieves the papers, takes them, along with a tray of food, to a table outside a closed door, raps on the door, and departs. On the other side of that door, Amanda Bonner (Katharine Hepburn) arises from beside her husband, Adam (whom we may already recognize to be Spencer Tracy), walks to the door, turns the key, opens the door to collect the tray, and carries it to the marriage bed. She opens one of the newspapers as she begins to sip from a glass of juice. Along with these engagements she proceeds to rouse her oblivious hus-band, initially by telling him that he was making noises in the night, but defini-tively by expressing a somewhat boisterous interest in a story on the front page of her paper. It is about the Attinger incident we have witnessed. Amanda says the man had it coming; Adam says, however that may be, the wife has broken the law.

3   They continue the argument in the car as Amanda drives Adam to his office; she then continues on to hers.

4 We find that Adam is an assistant district attorney, who, to his dismay, is assigned the Attinger case.

5 Amanda is also an attorney, in private practice. Adam phones her and breaks the news of his assignment, which he pretends to be proud of, since it implies his special status in the office.

6 Amanda tells her secretary that what she just learned on the phone has broken the back of a female camel, and directs her to make arrangements for Amanda to handle Doris Attinger's defense.

7 Adam takes a statement from Mr. Attinger, who is in his hospital bed recovering comfortably from his wounds, attended by his paramour.

8 Amanda takes a statement from a somewhat distraught but lucid Mrs. Attinger, who is in a detention unit.

9 That night, at a dinner party in their apartment, attended by several judges and also by their neighbor Kip (David Wayne), a songwriter, as cocktails are concluded and dinner announced, Amanda tells one of the judges, in Adam's hearing, that she has taken the Doris Attinger case.

10 After dinner a home movie is shown of Adam and Amanda's country house, for which they have just paid off the mortgage. Adam, seething from Amanda's news, has further to contain himself throughout the enforced silence of the screening, the seething and the silence heightened by Kip's parodic, grating narrative of the film.

11 In their bedroom after the party, Adam tries vainly to get Amanda to change her mind about taking the case. He acts tough but an embrace from Amanda softens him.

12 First day in court. Selection of the jury. Obviously Amanda is going to make a feminist case out of the event.

13 First night after court. In their apartment, after what is evidently a ritual of having drinks together before dinner, and after some mild sexual byplay, they begin, since it is maid's night out, inexpertly preparing a supper of leftovers. Amanda is happy about the heavy coverage of the trial in the evening newspaper; Adam is not happy, and again asks her to give up the case. She says she knows he agrees with what she wants. Kip knocks at their door (Adam reminds Amanda that there's only enough for two at dinner), having the excuse of the newspaper story. He plays a song for them that he's writing about Amanda. Amanda likes the song, Adam does not.

14a Second day in court. The sordid story of the Attingers is brought out in Amanda's and Adam's questioning of the principals of the case.

Adam's Rib

14b Second night after court. The intimacy of their giving each other a massage is interrupted by Amanda's accusing Adam of abusing her: "I can tell a slap from a slug!" She cries, and then kicks him in the shins. "Let's all be manly."

15 Third day in court. The summations. Adam's difficulty speaking when he's overexcited comes into play. He tries to explain to the jury why Amanda's feminist defense of Doris Attinger is laughable, even pointing out that Amanda has dressed Mrs. Attinger in the winning hat that he had brought home as a present to Amanda; but nobody laughs.

16 Third night after court. Amanda arrives late. Adam has finished all the aperitifs himself and is sullen. She follows him from room to room to get him to talk to her. As he begins jamming clothes into a suitcase, he launches into a tirade against her behavior in court and declares that she has fouled up their marriage and its bargains beyond recognition. He allows his anger to say some violent things to her, such that he's no longer sure he wants to be married to the so-called New Woman. He departs noisily.

17 Fourth day in court. After the verdict acquitting Mrs. Attinger, Amanda says she wishes it could have been a tie, and Adam responds by reminding her that they have an appointment with their accountant to go over their taxes.

18 That night, in Kip's apartment, Amanda, listening for a call from Adam, is going over a legal document for Kip. Adam, his hat menacingly low over his brow, enters pointing a gun at them, telling them to get ready to die. Amanda says he has no right to behave so, whereupon, vindicated, Adam rewards himself by eating the licorice gun. There is a general brawl, after which the three go their separate ways.

19 At the accountant's office, the story of what they spend their money on yields further tales of the intimate satisfactions of their life together and, as Adam begins to cry, Amanda suggests they leave for the country house. As they leave the accountant without answers to the rest of his questions, Amanda directs him to finish up with no more exemptions since they like to pay taxes.

20 That night, at their house in Connecticut, various lines of narrative and image and song are tied up, and untied, in their exchanges as they prepare for bed. Amanda, finding in her briefcase the hat Adam gave her as a peace offering after he accepted the assignment of prosecuting Doris Attinger, the hat that Amanda lent to Doris as part of presenting her as an aggrieved wife and mother, now puts on the hat to go with her nightgown. Adam, entering from his dressing room, notices this and puts on his hat to go with his pajamas. Thus equally and ambiguously attired, they discuss the difference between men and women. Adam demonstrates male tears. We leave them, or rather they leave us, continuing their agreeable contesting of each other by other means, as they climb in bed and close a curtain upon the rest of the world.

The even-numbered chapters of this book—which, until the concluding three chapters, are devoted to individual films—are bound to consider, whatever else, two questions: What contribution (meaning roughly, what difference) does the film in question make to the articulation of the genre of which it is (arguably) a member? What are the principal relations the film bears to the text or texts discussed earlier?

About the first of these questions, it is early for you to feel very confident. I have said that there is no a priori, standing, necessary set of features that an instance must exhibit to qualify as a member of (what I mean by a) genre. A set of overlapping, intermediate instances of a narrative preoccupied by a certain range of comic mood, motivating certain heightened inventions of conversation, or expression, the principal characters of which are a pair older than the pair in classical comedy, characters who are already, or have been (at least in fantasy) married and who find themselves on the way to a final state of divorce is roughly where we begin; the narrative accordingly has to track the pair not to their getting together, but to their getting together again, back together. With various exceptions, always to be accounted for, the pair are without children; the woman is never (except in *The Philadelphia Story*) shown to have a mother; if a man is shown with his mother, it is generally the other man, the one who, after the divorce, offers the woman the kind of security her first, excited husband never provided (in short, it is the woman's projected, threatening, mother-in-law); if the woman's father is shown he is, or comes to be, on the side of the daughter's desire, never attempting to call the law down to prevent her marriage.

Take now, for a closer look, my claim that remarriage comedies tend (canonically, generically) to begin in the city and conclude in the country, in Shakespeare's "green world" (often explicitly called in the films, to my undying delight, Connecticut). One could hardly advance such a claim from seeing only *The Philadelphia Story* and *Adam's Rib*, since you wouldn't know from them whether (as I claim), it is *The Philadelphia Story* that must compensate for not beginning in the city or *Adam's Rib* that must compensate for waiting until the end to get to the country (unless it must compensate for anticipating the country by early showing home movies set there).

But *Adam's Rib* has, apart from this, some accounting to prompt of itself, since while it begins unmistakably in the city, it does not begin with either of the principal pair, but presents, in a prologue, a whole opening drama, the stuff of melodrama or soap opera (with the surrealistic comic touch of having the wife consult an instruction manual before she fires the gun). What is the point of the difference in beginning off-center? And what kind of question is that—I mean what might count as an answer?

Suppose I propose the following. The connection is made with the principal pair when, immediately following the prologue, the morning newspaper, containing the lurid story of the outraged, violent wife, makes its way onto a breakfast tray whose presentation, we gather, diurnally (anyway on work days) awakens our privileged hero and heroine. This opening event precipitates the drama into these evidently stable lives, and within the drama's early unfolding the pair find themselves featured in the newspaper. Their neighbor from across the hall, Kip, shows up at their door with his copy of the paper opened to a page featuring the case, saying "Hello, you famous things. Everyone is talking about this," to which the woman of the pair responds, "Yah, that's the idea," meaning that she wants the case to be dramatized, advertised, in order to make visible, sensible, a systematic injustice ("visible" and "sensible," remember, are Locke's words for justifying the people's rebellion).

In *The Philadelphia Story*, too, a family is early subjected to drama in being invaded by the search for news, in the form of two reluctant newshounds, but this time the principal pair, especially the woman, are disgusted by publicity. Only in the very concluding, metamorphosing two shots of the film does the essential newspaper find our pair, who evidently have reconciled themselves to becoming news. And this may be, after all, what the story is of *The Philadelphia Story*, one in which the ordinary behavior of ordinary people is news. Are these ordinary people? What is out of the ordinary? They may have "just more than enough" money than others, but what seems to matter, to them and to us, as we leave them, is that they have been having problems with each other, and that they haven't solved them, and now, having risked marriage again, they are awkwardly kissing.

I have described the penultimate shot of the three principals in *The Philadelphia Story* as a kind of wedding photo, and the ultimate shot of the pair embracing, excluding the third, as ambiguously a news-magazine gossip shot or a wedding photo from an album. But strictly speaking it is at most a rewedding photo, distinguished by the man's not being properly dressed for the occasion. (Mike says, when asked to be best man, "We're going to look like a couple of stowaways.") More important, as we try to assess the sense of its news value, it identifies, in some part, the work of (this) film as the work of a medium of news. For Tracy Lord's former fiancé George, the presence of the publisher of *Spy* magazine makes the imminent wedding "of national importance." It would have been news of a familiar kind ("man bites dog") for a man from the working class to marry into so prominent a family. But if this film is an organ of news for us, it must contain news, or evidence, of a different kind, but still of national importance.

The importance is, according to our concerns with these films, not simply that a happy marriage has been found, but that its happiness, showing marriage to require a double ratification (by itself, by its being chosen out of experience not alone out of innocence; and by its acquiescence in allowing itself to become news, open beyond the privacy of privilege, ratified by society), in effect ratifies its society as a locale in which happiness and liberty can be pursued and, to whatever extent such a thing is possible, preserved. It is thus understandable as a favored expression of consent for this democracy (it may be a reason remarriage comedies are not, so far as I have learned, found in other cultures), showing that, in the present instance, one hundred and sixty four years after the Declaration of Independence, our political society continued to find attestation that it exists.

How seriously may we still be—or were we ever—asked to take this? How seriously do you take the question of being governed by consent? I shall say for myself that I take it all, at a rough guess, about a thousand times more seriously than I do the apparently easily believable theory that Hollywood films were made to satisfy the immigrant fantasies of a small set of Jewish businessmen who became successful as Hollywood producers. Such men, and the money they did and the money they did not control, may have caused untold failures, personal and artistic calamities, spectacles of various kinds, and caused talented and untalented entertainers to be hired, some of whom the camera loved, others not, but they are no more likely to have foreseen any single sequence of such films as we are now considering as they would have been likely to understand, or be interested in, what we are now saying about these films. And these are films quite continuous with what we know as Hollywood films. (That such a group of men occupied the positions of power they occupied at a major stage of Hollywood history is a striking fact, and what difference they can have made in its history is perhaps an interesting and answerable question. The answers one seeks will be a function of what one takes a Hollywood film to be, hence what one takes a film to be, hence what one takes film more generally to be, hence what a film actor, writer, director, cinematographer, set designer, special effects coordinator, editor, producer, censor, audience, studio head, and so on to be, hence what counts as the contribution each can make to conditions of a film's existence, and its consequences.)

Let's notice that *Adam's Rib* also has its ways of identifying itself as something like a newspaper or a document: first, most obviously, in the elaborate correspondences between the film called *Adam's Rib* and the film-within-the-film called *The Mortgage the Merrier* (correspondences somewhat detailed in my chapter on the film in *Pursuits of Happiness*), which, in fictionally showing us the private life of the principal pair out of the realm of their world of work, encourages us to recognize that, as in *The Philadelphia Story*, it is their marriage that is news, as it is the marriage that is taken to court; and second, by using as intertitles between major breaks in the narrative, cartoon drawings that resemble the caricatures accompanying newspaper features. But then let us clearly mark, measured by this similarity, the decisive difference that what happens at the end of *Adam's Rib* is precisely not a willingness for society to be allowed to witness and affirm the state of their marriage (and consequently be affirmed by it). The asserting and contesting of this willingness has been the drive of the narrative throughout the body of the film, taking the marriage into and out of court. But now, at the end, at the entrance to another bed, at the beginning of a further discussion, a further education, the exchanges that constitute the express consent to the marriage are interrupted, postponed, by the urgency of reaffirming the privacy of the marriage, its pursuit of happiness—the struggle of it, the reality of it—unshareable, unratifiable, by society.

It is quite as if what these films will call a good marriage, while having the power to ratify, and receive ratification from, society at large, has at the same time the power to threaten the social order, namely because it reserves a place from which to judge its society, to determine for itself (within the couple itself, but by that fact within that fragment of society itself) whether its desires for a world worthy of consent are sufficiently satisfiable within the world as it is given. (We are, I trust, by now sufficiently alerted to be thoughtful about the role of the newspaper in remarriage comedy. I of course do not predict what we may find—or not find, for example, a sense of why there is no newspaper in *The Lady Eve*.)

I discuss the ending of *Adam's Rib* with some care in *Pursuits of Happiness*, going into what it means by celebrating the difference between men and women. But, as one so characteristically has to learn with a certain pain, one moment of insight may for the moment distract one from a further, even capping, insight. In the present instance, I did discern that when Katharine Hepburn, whose superior education has twice been noted (with appreciation but with some suspicion, both toward Bryn Mawr and toward the Yale Law School) by her husband, asks him what the banal punch line "Vive la différence!" means, he, in the person of Spencer Tracy, knows full well that she is not asking what the French words mean, but what the difference between men and women means. And hence he knows both that he has not answered her by repeating the vulgarity of "Hooray for that little difference!" and also that he can ask her for a reassuring celebration of their difference before discussing the puzzle further. But I had missed something in my discussion then, namely the issue of the relation between the sexes in the suppression of the feminine voice, hence in the development of human expressiveness, hence in human sexuality (according to Lacan, expanding upon Freud).

When in *Pursuits of Happiness* I go into the man's assertion of his equality with women in his ability to produce tears at will, I may seem to be leaving it open whether in this demonstration he is continuing to disparage this ability as beneath a grown-up's dignity, or whether he is demonstrating that if he shows his capacity for being hurt by her, she will be as susceptible to his expression of hurt as he is to hers. I needn't deny either, if both are seen; any more than I need to determine whether what would elicit the woman's sympathy is the humbling expressed by being moved to tears, or the humbling expressed by being reduced to pretending to cry. When the man comments upon his tears by acknowledging, "Oh yes, there ain't any of us hasn't got our little tricks," thus comparing the sameness and difference of men and women, he cannot just be saying that men can fake tears as well as women (both because that would not distinguish between their tricks and because the woman's interest in what he does to produce tears seems to suggest that it is news to her, about either of the sexes).

The official difference between the pertinent tricks of men and women (in our culture) is that women learn to cry in order to manipulate men whereas men, in opposition, learn not to cry in order not to seem manipulable. Since under these systematic pressures the human capacity for expression, for human communication, is incited and distorted (suppressed, repressed, displaced, condensed) on both sides, each side has a chance to find a helpmeet as well as a "competitor" (something Adam, to Amanda's mind unfairly, accuses her of) in the other.

I would like to say: To the extent that Locke's articulation of democratic aspiration still counts in our thoughts, and since the idea of consent is, to my way of thinking, elaborated in our understanding of human expressiveness, the contributions that our films of perfectionist ambition make to the progress of democratic aspiration lies not simply in their attestation of the consent, call it the happiness, all things considered, to be governed as we are, but further in their articulation and display of the dimensions of human expressiveness, of the human registrations and alternations of attraction and aversion, upon which the capacity for judgment, hence for speech, hence for consent or for its withdrawal, depends. (That Hollywood films so often turn away from such powers it is not part of my task here to deplore or to explain. I might say it is rather my task to suggest what it is that is so often turned away from.)

I said in my opening sketches of the perfectionist outlook that in its focus on a way of life rather than on dilemmas concerning individual actions, the particular moral failure perfectionist protagonists risk is that of snobbery. This is hinted at, it seems to me, in the way the victorious counselor, Amanda Bonner, rather avoids contact with the overly reconciled Attinger clan (which now, in a photo opportunity, incorporates the other woman, Beryl Caighn) as she and Adam quit the scene of the trial. As well as in Tracy Lord's contempt for her father's relation with the notorious Tina Mara—but then Tracy is known by all who know her to be what her sister calls "hard," what Mrs. Lord corrects by saying "Tracy just sets exceptionally high standards for herself, and others aren't always able to live up to them, that's all." As though it is unthinkable to the more experienced of the principal women of remarriage comedy that moral squalor could touch their lives (though when Amanda's husband enters her neighbor's apartment with a gun, she might for a moment have a momentary fantasm of herself as providing material for a lurid front page), and impossible for the more innocent of them to have sought consolation outside of an unpassionate marriage (though Tracy's brush with Mike might have left her with some question there: "Why [did you leave me alone in my bedroom], was I so unattractive?"). The women otherwise differ radically in the stage of their perfectionist journeys. Amanda has solved the problems Tracy is still faced with as she begins again; in particular, Amanda is useful in the world, or say she has a voice in her history, and she has found a man who honors and wishes to accompany her on her journey and who does not find her cold. Yet the issue of getting the private and the public sides of her life to affirm each other, neither of them offering false compensation for what the other must be asked to provide, is a problem at the outset, and resolving that one makes room for another.

I have said comparatively little about the men in question. Dexter talks a good game—in some ways the best game in any of the films, and he best fits the portrait of the classical perfectionist sage. How do we account for his transformation into this condition of authority from his tendency to violence (pushing his wife to the ground, socking Mike) and his alcoholism? Does overcoming these failings fit the remarriage genre's demand for an expansive capacity to be humbled? Adam too seems too authoritative to be humbled by words—unless his tendency to stutter under a certain kind of stress counts as being humbled by his own words. And physically he undergoes certain mild indignities, enough perhaps to show him to have merely finite powers—as when he gets into the brawl with Kit, and as when he is caught by the home movie camera with his pants unbuttoned. Let's for the moment leave this question by noting that it is generically odd for the principal man's mother to be present, as Adam's is in the early party for the judges. The compensating feature is that Adam's father is also present, so the possibility of a floating, domineering mother-in-law is explicitly ruled out.

But a long while ago I asked how we are to understand the narrative of *Adam's Rib* to reach the principal pair by means of a newspaper delivered to their door. It would be an answer to say that, unlike the form taken in *Philadelphia Story*, the impinging of the world upon a marriage and its projects does not require anything so complex as the nefarious efforts of a national news magazine and the intervention of a family friend to avoid its powers of spreading scandal, but can appear any day of the week in the daily newspaper of your choice, along with whatever else helps to get your eyes opened to what is happening. Is there not accordingly an implication that one's responses to these deliveries are a measure of one's consent to their tidings, not awaiting a ceremony of acceptance, but achieved in a tacit allowance (not exactly that the facts are as they are recorded, subject to better information, but) that the importance attached to the facts, the relative importance of the maze of events that day, the impression made upon you by their representation, is what it is given out to be—unless you have a way of judging that it is not. Where is trust to be placed? J. L. Austin remarks in "Other Minds" that believing what others tell us is an irreducible part of human experience, meaning that no further evidence is in principle better, more rational to trust, than the human word (presumably both in witnessing something for us and as confessing something to us). Is this a blessing or a curse?

Let me conclude this introduction to further discussion by taking up a trio of events that begin the film proper, I mean that follow upon the delivery of the newspaper into the scene of the pair's intimacy, behind a door shown to us to be kept locked when they are in bed. They are a trio of events that, banal, unremarkable, as they are and are presumably meant to be, are the most direct manifestations, or allusions, to the scene in Genesis in which the prominence of Adam's rib is demonstrated. This film and *The Lady Eve* are the two remarriage comedies in which the originals of the human race are named and their experience in Eden invoked; but since Milton's tract on divorce quotes the line from Genesis (2:18) about the loneliness of the man that has formed the theological basis for marriage for millennia, a line that plays a quite general role in my characterization of the conditions of remarriage comedy, no hint of Eden in the films should, by my lights, go untested. These films feature what in *Pursuits of Happiness* I called the temptation to knowledge, and they are rooted in the idea of the Fall, namely the creation of the human, or more precisely, the creation of the woman, of the difference between the sexes, as the (re)creation of the human. But there is more to be seen in the manifestation, I might even say reenactment, of events in Eden in the Bonners' bedroom.

The trio of events are uncontentiously, if deliberately, describable in the following way: Adam is shown sleeping; a woman arises from his side; she retrieves food which she tastes and which she offers to him (compare Genesis 2:21, 2:22, 3:6). (Perhaps this is four, or five, events.) I claim that further events achieve their resonance from these, in particular the event that begins the drama between our pair, namely the woman's associating the noises Adam made in his sleep with the story her eye falls on of the wife's shooting her faithless spouse, which is the first straw we see laid on the camel's back that, later in her office, she declares to have received the last straw, breaking something in her that leads her to take up the defense of the outraged wife against the outrageous fact that the assistant district attorney assigned to prosecute the case is her husband.

Naturally I am prepared to be told that one doesn't need to go so far afield to understand her wanting to take the case. Who could doubt it? But what I am in these moments seeking to understand is why the woman describes her state as she does (one in which a female back has received a last straw) and why she is part of a story called "Adam's Rib." There may still be resistance to supposing that this film, or any film, can possess answers to such demands for understanding. Would this be a resistance to something about the medium, or the reputation, of film? Or perhaps a resistance against pushing interpretations (too, or very) far? We all, I suppose, know people who would rather say something to the effect: The writers just gave Hepburn that line about the camel's back because they needed a quick way to steer the plot in the direction they had planned, or because of some incident between them we'll never know about. And I suppose we have all heard radiantly irrelevant interpretations that could prompt us to say such reductive things ourselves. Isn't it as a warning against such intellectual stultification that one should bear in mind that criticism, call it the reading of art, is itself an art, and one, it seems, that philosophers have not often practiced. (Kant is more typically philosophical, in this respect, than Aristotle.) Or one might ponder what the motivation, or temptation, to knowledge is. Perhaps it is the temptation to know and say more than we can know and safely say. Perhaps it is the wish to deny that we know all there is to know in order to say what is to be said.

5

JOHN STUART MILL

The issue of knowledge—unsurprisingly, remembering its mythological implications in the puzzle of the creation of men and women—takes indefinitely many forms in remarriage comedies. Given the demand in these films for education, one can formulate the issue as asking: What does the woman want to know? (Of course I enjoy the relation to—or this version of—Freud's question: What does a woman want?) In *The Philadelphia Story* she could be said to want to know how a woman such as she is can be useful in the world. In *Adam's Rib*, the case seems rather to be that the woman wants something to be known, namely wants the world to know that in her private life she and the man she calls husband have made a world of equality (hence that this is possible, and desirable), and she wants the man at home to know that in her public life she is capable of demanding, hence advancing, the cause of women's equality before the law. (In *Gaslight*, to anticipate, and to make it clear that these matters are nothing apart from the experience of the individual films, I will say that the woman wants to know that she is not an object of horror.)

The demand for knowledge (bearing some as yet unspecified relation to what I have called the temptation to knowledge) is a reasonable invitation to read John Stuart Mill, of course including his book *The Subjection of Women* but in its relation to Mill's best-known and more purely philosophical works, *On Liberty* and *Utilitarianism*. Since Mill's study of the subjection of women in marriage is about the legal bondage between the sexes (the last institution in society, Mill says, where slavery is still, in the 1860s, legal), and since the men and women bound in this institution must know that they are, and must know what it is, for whom is Mill's book written? Who fails to know what Mill has to say?

Well, as Freud says, there is knowledge, and there is knowledge. And there is also such a thing as a culture's knowing something *together*, knowing something at the same time the others know, knowing that each knows, knowing as first person plural (something the word "conscience" should suggest), a knowledge that the culture has of itself. I think of it as knowledge that *we* have of, let us say, the path the culture is—we are—making for itself, as it were unconsciously, something that philosophy is in a position to articulate and so bring to consciousness in its way. Philosophers from Plato to Hegel and Emerson and Nietzsche and Heidegger, and in a sense Wittgenstein, have taken this as an essential mission of, or call upon, philosophy. (It requires statistics to know how many of our fellow citizens, those who speak for us and for whom we speak, live in poverty. But it requires something else to articulate what our attitudes to the poor are, and to imagine how this plural attitude can be voiced with confidence.) And then Mill might have something to divulge that only a man, a male, knows about his culture at large.

The issue I want to have awaiting us is not alone the question of who possesses knowledge but who has the right to voice it. With what right does Mill say that marriage puts women in bondage if they themselves do not generally say it, or all perhaps mind it? The right of men to speak for women is, or was as recently as five years ago, when I published my book *Contesting Tears*, sharply disputed, and was brought against me in, for example, a book called *Feminism without Women* by the film theorist Tania Modleski. She was responding in particular to the essays of mine on the melodrama of the unknown woman, a genre which seems to find that freedom from the bondage of marriage requires freedom from the institution of marriage as such. And it is true that my reading of these films sometimes undertakes to speak for women, in place of women, and disagrees with women's accounts of these films, in general and in particular. We shall come to this, beginning in the next chapter.

When Mill wrote *The Subjection of Women* he was one of the most prominent and admired intellectuals in England, the famous son of a famous father, James Mill, the head of an intellectual movement of radical philosophy that had caused historical reforms in English law, subjecting its enshrining of ancient privileges to the glare of the utilitarian principle of, let's say, rational desires, a principle that had been announced and elaborated by the father's friend and idol Jeremy Bentham. The son, John Stuart Mill, among his other works, composed a well-known autobiography that is still fascinating, and moving, in its description of the crisis that entered into this mind unrelentingly trained for a rational existence, one resisting the prejudices of

John Stuart Mill

the age. Educated at home by his father, John Stuart, by his own account, was astoundingly precocious: at three years old he was reading Greek; at six writing essays in Latin; at twenty suffering a nervous breakdown, from which he reports he was helped to recover by reading—material not part of his father's regime of training—English Romantic poetry, for example Coleridge on depression. One image from his year or so of melancholia has often recurred in my thoughts, namely his fantasy that all the combinations and variations of musical tones had been exhausted by Mozart and Cherubini, so that there was no further possibility of original beauty to be discovered. (And that thought forced itself upon a writer's mind a half-century before the intervention of Schoenberg.)

This expression of a sense of the exhaustion of possibility strikes me as the absolute negation of the founding thought of perfectionism, that of an attainable next self in an attainable further society to be found in the reassessment and reconstitution of one's life after a crisis in what appears as its foundation or direction.

To orient ourselves as we turn to Mill's utilitarian outlook, let's remember the distinction I made in the Introduction between the standing classical moral theories. I contrasted the two dominant moral philosophies of Europe and America in terms of whether they base themselves primarily on the concept of the good (on happiness, on the desirable consequences of a course of action) or on the concept of the right (on justice, duty, obligation, on the correctness of the motive as opposed to the consequences of a course of action). Theories based on the good, on the consequences or ends for which actions are taken, are called teleological theories. Theories based on the right, on the obligations or commitments or duties out of which actions are taken, are called deontological theories. The most prominent deontological view (in the English-speaking dispensation of philosophy) is that of Kant. (Hegel is the other great representative here, and within the past decade Hegel has been studied more in American philosophy than, at a guess, at any time since before the First World War. It is well to remember that John Dewey began his philosophical life as a Hegelian and that William James throughout his life found a Hegelian world of totality and closure something to oppose philosophically.) The most prominent teleological view is utilitarianism.

All moral theories have to treat both the good and the right, both consequences and motives. The differences between the theories can be said to be functions of how each conceives the relation between these fundamental notions. Deontological theories give priority to the right, to justice and duty, against the fundamental demands of which individual, or majority, desires have no weight. Teleological theories give priority and independent definition and weight to desires or happiness, and regard a rational society as one which attempts to maximize the amount of good in it. Although the principal writers from a utilitarian point of view have been English philosophers of the eighteenth and nineteenth centuries—Shaftesbury, Hutcheson, Hume, Bentham, the Mills, Sidgwick—Locke's emphasis on consent places him (most clearly since the work of John Rawls articulated the case against utilitarianism, out of a revised contractualist point of view) on the non-utilitarian side of things. If you have seen the rationality in consenting to be governed by an impartial legislature and judiciary and executive, then particular sources of gratification incompatible with that shared system of observances are ruled out as groundless.

A fundamental difference between the deontological and the utilitarian views comes out in their visions of what a reasonable society is, the utilitarian regarding government as a rational administration of resources, the deontological regarding society as always already having agreed upon fundamental principles of justice which neither government nor individuals can infringe as they cooperate or compete in their separate but interconnected rational plans of life.

While Locke, massive as his influence is, certainly for the American political system, is not definitively of either the deontological or the utilitarian outlook, I placed my discussion of him, in conjunction with Milton, after Emerson to open up a philosophical route to understanding the moral claims of the lives depicted in the films whose mysterious powers and fame motivated the line of inquiry of this book.

Given the magnitude of the names and the successes of the utilitarian philosophers in the English-speaking tradition of philosophy, it is not surprising that utilitarianism has been a dominating force in academic moral philosophy. That it is now rather on the defensive (though it has, as we shall see, always had some self-defending to do) is more the result, I think it is generally agreed, of Rawls's *A Theory of Justice*, published in 1971, than of any other single intellectual event. I am not claiming that John Stuart Mill has mounted the most defensible and effective version of the utilitarian view, but as an intellectual figure interesting in himself and pertinent to that

John Stuart Mill

perspective, I am glad to introduce him into our company in working out the relation of perfectionism to its more famous or more respectable neighbors.

I begin with a quotation from chapter 2 of Mill's book *Utilitarianism* (published in 1863):

> The creed which accepts as the foundation of morals utility or the greatest happiness principle holds that actions are right in proportion as they tend to promote happiness and wrong as they tend to produce the reverse of happiness. By happiness is intended pleasure and the absence of pain; by unhappiness, pain and the privation of pleasure. To give a clear view of the moral standard set up by the theory much more requires to be said; in particular, what things it includes in the ideas of pain and pleasure, and to what extent this is left an open question. But, these supplementary explanations do not affect the theory of life on which this theory of morality is grounded; namely, that pleasure and the freedom from pain are the only things desirable as ends, and that all desirable things, which are as numerous in the utilitarian as in any other scheme, are desirable either for the pleasure inherent in themselves, or as means to the promotion of pleasure and the prevention of pain.

Let's first consider Mill's insistence that the principle of utility is both to be the basis of one's personal morality—it is a "theory of life" that assesses my entire mode of existence—and to preside over social criticism, to assess the validity (the justice) of social institutions. Both of these levels have been subjected to objections quite continually and familiarly since Mill's time, but those objections have never succeeded in killing off interest in the theory. It is important to know why. For example, an obvious and early retort against using the principle of utility to guide one's personal morality is that to live for pleasure is not even a candidate for a moral life, it is a debased view of life from the start. In particular, one's most fundamental, or highest, goals are not evaluated (or ought not to be) in terms of whether they yield more pleasure than alternative possibilities. One does not decide whether to invest one's love, one's life, in a friend or in a vocation, on the basis of a greater amount of pleasure or some other advantage that that relationship or commitment will yield over some other.

Mill is wonderfully scornful of this sort of stuffy criticism. To the objection that pleasure is an inferior form of happiness, Mill's answer is that this merely shows an inferior ability to imagine causes and kinds of pleasure. To the objection that pleasure is often unattainable or unsure in society, Mill's answer is that this is a significant criticism not of pleasure but of society's insufficiency in making it achievable. To the objection that pleasure is easy to do without, Mill's answer is that it is indeed commonly, by most people, done without—is this a state we ought to work to make even more common?

Still, Mill knows that there are paradoxes associated with utilitarianism. He distinguishes in *Utilitarianism* between certain kinds or grades of pleasure, which means, in his terms, between the quantity and the quality of pleasure. Jeremy Bentham had famously denied the importance of such a distinction in his motto "Pushpin [a child's game] is as good as poetry," meaning pleasure is pleasure, whoever has it, evidently finding in this reduction the effectiveness and radicality of the utilitarian creed and program of social reform he stood for. Out of Bentham's perception of contemporary English institutions, centrally of the English legal system and prison system at the turn of the eighteenth into the nineteenth century, he was led to say, in effect, "Define pleasure and pain any way you like, society provides too little of the one and too much of the other." For example, notoriously, the death penalty in Bentham's time was prescribed for a great range of offenses—in principle, even for stealing a loaf of bread. If that's the way things are, we are not talking about subtleties of definition. Pushpin is as good as poetry if you are deprived of both. Utilitarianism is devastating in the very superficiality of its critical vision. If a society cannot pass its basic test, it already has reform cut out for it. That it may need reform even if it does pass the utilitarian test is a further matter.

A generation later, Mill was talking about subtleties, and in effect countered Bentham with another equally famous motto, "Better Socrates dissatisfied than a pig satisfied," denying that pleasure is the same everywhere, and denying that it is readily quantifiable. He was voicing a problem that social choice theories always have to deal with: the so-called problem of the interpersonal measurement of utility. *How* much better is a unit of Socrates' pleasure than a unit of a pig's? Ten times? A thousand times? And is it better to be Socrates dissatisfied than St. Augustine or Gandhi dissatisfied? Or better Socrates satisfied than the rulers of Athens dissatisfied? Or better Amanda Bonner satisfied than Adam Bonner dissatisfied? Or better Tracy Lord dissatisfied by the invasion of her privileged privacy than the populous readership of *Spy* magazine satisfied by that invasion?

But things needn't get very complicated to make deep problems for utilitarianism. In my graduate student days, and still when I was writing the earliest chapters that became *The Claim of Reason,* philosophers inclined toward a utilitarian outlook were having to defend it against the charge that even such basic, inescapable social practices as promising and punishing were beyond utilitarianism to justify or to account for. The chapter on Rawls on rules in *The Claim of Reason* argues against certain of these defenses, defenses against certain paradoxical conclusions that seemed derivable from the principle of utility. For example: It seemed that utilitarianism would have to say that if keeping a promise would be somewhat inconvenient for you, give you more pain than you had thought it would, or perhaps give you a little more pain than the pleasure it would yield to the one to whom you made the promise, then you are morally free, or morally right, to break the promise. Such considerations seem to contradict the idea of a promise. Or again: Since the utilitarian point of punishment is to deter others from doing something (as opposed to the deontological view that the point of punishment is retribution for having done something), then, since it would deter effectively (perhaps) to lie about someone's guilt and publicly punish an innocent person, rather than going to the expense and the trouble and the delay and the uncertainty of finding the actual perpetrators and prosecuting them (and maybe they would get off anyway, which would do more harm than good), you should punish the innocent on utilitarian grounds when you can get away with it, balancing the great amount of happiness to many people against the necessary pain to one person (and his or her near and dear).

It is harder to answer these objections than you might think. One familiar line was to say that the principle of utility is not meant to apply to individual actions case by case, but just to general social practices or institutions. That is a line lent plausibility by Bentham's pretty exclusive interest in institutions. But what does it mean to call promising or punishment practices or institutions? Institutions (say, like the court system, or Congress, or banks, or churches, or marriage), have offices, rules, requirements of publicity, of training, or appointment. But any competent member of society can give and receive a promise without benefit of a special appointment or specialized training. If promising is a practice, then so is warning, or urging, or asking questions, or let's just say, talking. (Of course certain particular promises or intentions may require the invocation of a particular institution, and require persons in certain offices to effect or authorize them, say the institution of posting the banns, or taking certain oaths of office. This just seems to show why ordinary promises, everyday ways of clarifying what others can count on, require no special institutional standing. It makes sense to ask for the utility of the institution of posting banns or taking oaths. But does it makes sense to ask for the utility of warning or urging or asking, as such, in short, of possessing language? Having an opposable thumb is of earth-shaking utility. How about the utility of having a body?)

On the other hand, deontologists who insist that promises must always be kept, no matter what the consequences, or perhaps no matter how a situation has changed, become as unintuitive as utilitarians. There are famous tragic tales in which the rigor of keeping an oath turns out to have consequences as horrifying as any to have been averted by making the promise. (A king vows that, if the gods preserve him from drowning, he will kill the first person he meets on land, which turns out to be his son and heir. This is no doubt a fable not merely warning against an inhumanly rigid view of promise-keeping, but against the very making of certain sorts of self-serving or placating vows.)

As for punishment as an institution, utilitarianism cannot (and surely would not wish to) justify it as such; that is, if deterrence from crime could be managed by persuasion or disapproval or by fines rather than by punishment, then, granted that fines and disapproval are less painful than imprisonment and hard labor, for example, there would be no utilitarian justification for punishment. There is a utilitarian justification only for the least amount of punishment necessary to deter, if any, not for punishment as such. In contrast, deontologists do hold that punishment as such is morally necessary, that it is retribution for an evil, for a moral debt to society that must be paid, as it were, visibly and in person.

Utilitarianism continues the Enlightenment's struggle against outworn custom, prejudice, superstition, fanaticism, ignorance, violent injustice, and inequity. It is accordingly comprehensible that the young John Stuart Mill, as he reports in his autobiography, would have marked his discovery of Bentham's principle of utility as providing him with a goal for his existence, a sense for his life, a philosophy, a religion he even says, "in one of the best senses of the word." It made sense of his recognition of the urgency of social change, or, as he puts the matter in *On Liberty,* the need "to make society progressive." That aspiration of Mill's is a reason that the target of his argumentation is so often, and so intimately, what he calls "the moralists," nine-tenths of whom, he says in chapter 4 of *On Liberty,* encourage "moral police" to enforce behavior in regions in which it is none of society's business, regions in which the public, according to Mill, "invests its own *preferences* with the character of moral laws." This is a feature of what I call moralism. What I mean by moralism is something I find to bear a relation to morality that religiosity bears to religion or that aestheticism bears to aesthetics or that scientism bears to science. (I don't ask that such distinctions be taken for granted, or at face value. Some may feel that all religion has become religiosity, that undue attention, say by philosophers, to the arts is aestheticism, that a certain invocation, by nonscientists, of science is scientism.)

It is exactly because Mill wishes laws and institutions to be responsive to human preferences (what we may call desire) that he is so appalled at those who wish to legislate their own desires, not to put first the general happiness of society. These are more intimately his enemies than those who would merely uphold custom, because, as Mill puts it in chapter 3 of *On Liberty*, "there is a philanthropic spirit abroad for the exercise of which there is no more inviting field than the moral and prudential improvement of our fellow creatures." This moral concern directing itself to the moral improvement of the way others live, assuming the security of one's own moral uprightness, is another description, or aspect, of moralism. It is the contrary of perfectionism as well as the contrary of Kantianism. It does not therefore follow that Kant is an Emersonian perfectionist. It does follow that there is a perfectionism (in Kant, wherever else) that is not a teleological view.

Rawls's view of perfectionism served more than any other work to bring this moral outlook back to the attention of moral philosophers, its variance with my own view of the matter is not something I can neglect, nor would want to if I could. The matter is not, as I have stressed from the beginning, a simple one of definition. Nietzsche is cited by Rawls as an extreme case of a perfectionist moralist (Aristotle is taken by Rawls as a moderate case), and as such is ruled out as a serious thinker about morality (at least in that aspect of morality concerned with justice), on the ground that in his supposed teleology, Nietzsche is thought to recognize a basis for allocating the resources or goods of society that is incompatible with the basis given by the principles of justice Rawls advances. Specifically, Nietzsche finds a basis for the unequal distribution of society's goods in differences between persons that, on Rawls's view, do not count morally, or, said otherwise, are morally impertinent. Because the passage from Nietzsche Rawls cites is one that, so I claim, is in effect a rewriting by Nietzsche of passages from Emerson, Rawls is, in his section on perfectionism, simultaneously ruling out Emerson as a viable moralist. This is not an implication I can ignore.

But I can postpone attending to it. We were just looking at one of Mill's outbursts of indignation at the spectacle of the culture that speaks for him, inspired by the philanthropist bent on the improvement of the character always of others. It is specifically against this self-satisfied philanthropy of improvement that Mill becomes most eloquently ironic since improvement is also his goal, but one meant to lead not to further bondage to unjust institutions, but to what he calls liberty. Listen again to Mill's sentence about philanthropy: "There is a philanthropic spirit abroad for the exercise of which there is no more inviting field than the moral and prudential improvement of our fellow creatures." It is a sentence worthy of Charles Dickens at his most gloriously outraged. You can imagine a chapter of a late Dickens novel opening with that sentence and then going on to detail the punishing indignities dished out to those fellow creatures in the name of improving them. (I think here also of Emerson's remarks to the one he addresses in "Self-Reliance" as "Thou foolish philanthropist," touched upon in Chapter 1.)

Now what about Mill's defense of liberty as he presents it in *On Liberty?* Much is said in that book in praise of liberty and in blame of interference with liberty, but is either side (for or against interference) provided with utilitarian arguments to support it? Does Mill say anything that adds up to a claim that liberty makes for the greatest happiness of the greatest number, maximizes the pleasures at the disposal of a social system? On the contrary, it seems, he gives cases in which a person's eccentricity of conduct makes many people around him or her unhappy, causes them pain. Yet this does not, according to Mill, provide moral ground for forcing an eccentric to change his or her ways. Why not? Isn't Mill's utilitarianism faint-hearted here? And isn't it positively absent in his initial summary of his aim, his project in *On Liberty?*

His initial summary goes this way (chapter 1): "The object of this essay is to assert one very simple principle, . . . that the sole end for which mankind are warranted, individually or collectively, in interfering with the liberty of action of any of their number is self-protection. That the only purpose for which power can be rightfully exercised over any member of a civilized community against his will is to prevent harm to others. His own good, either physical or moral, is not a sufficient warrant." Self-protection seems straightforward enough. I can interfere with the liberty of someone who is threatening *my* liberty, or the liberty of others. But "preventing harm to others" has seemed not to be so easy to delimit. Does Mill's utilitarianism generally allow harm to others to be constituted by offending their tastes or thwarting their wishes or refusing to satisfy their preferences? Some critics have felt that Mill's distinction between actions which are self-regarding and those which are other-regarding is undrawable, since any action has consequences and effects beyond the control of its agent, and if we had to consider these as far as our imaginations might run, we would all become Hamlets, paralyzed by the prospect of action as such, as if every act were as risky as shooting an arrow over the house, opening you to hurting your brother. (In fact Nietzsche did perceive us as entering such a stage of paralysis.)

But Mill has a quite clear criterion for specifying what in my conduct "concerns others"—and hence becomes the business of others to control. The criterion is whether what I do violates what Mill calls a distinct and assignable obligation to any other person or persons (chapter 4). Mill earlier describes this as my violating any of another's constituted rights. So what morally concerns others, according to the words of Mill, is not some general way my actions may strike them, or differ from theirs, and even make them sincerely unhappy and accordingly cause them pain. What takes an action out of the self-regarding class, with which others may not interfere, and renders it, in Mill's words, "amenable to moral disapprobation in the proper sense of the term" is specifically, and in each case, my distinct and assignable violation of another's constituted rights. Which seems pretty clearly to say that the openness of my actions to moral judgment is based, is lodged, is vested, in Mill, in Mill's *On Liberty, not* teleologically, on utilitarian grounds, but deontologically, on the obligations to recognize independently specified rights of others. It may be that the rights in question are, or could be, themselves grounded on utilitarian considerations, but Mill doesn't say so in these passages, and the matter seems quite open.

On what, then, is the right to liberty based, according to Mill? Is *On Liberty* a utilitarian text at all?

It is true that Mill says, in the introductory chapter of the book, "It is proper to state that I forego any advantage which could be derived to my argument from the idea of abstract right as a thing independent of utility." But, being Mill, he adds something, out of a sense that the light he wishes to bring to old and dark injustices may at any moment prove dim: "I regard utility as the ultimate appeal on ethical questions; but it must be utility in the largest sense, grounded on the permanent interests of man as a progressive being." The editor of the edition I have most recently read regards this formulation as a reform of utilitarianism. Was Mill's introduction of the quality of pleasure as well as the quantity of pleasure as a criterion of utilitarian judgment such a reform? Or are both an abandoning of the point of the principle of utility? What is "utility in the largest sense"? Can I evaluate whether a certain area of a town is to be opened to commercial use, or whether taxes should be raised, or services lowered, or whether certain actions should be criminalized, or the death penalty be kept on the books, by appealing to utility in the largest sense? Meaning what? That it is better or worse for the human race that a particular section of a town be converted to commercial use?

All Mill seems to mean is that rights and obligations are not to be "abstract" in this sense: that they must be understood ultimately to lead to human good. Well, that is hardly a utilitarian idea. A morality that based human rights on their serving human misery would be insane. Mill may mean, for example, that what is wrong with a tyrant's rule cannot be measured in whether he provides sufficient goods, breads and circuses let us say, to the people, but must be measured in the larger sense of whether tyranny serves the permanent interests of the people. But has he any way to measure what those interests are non-abstractly? Can he claim, from a utilitarian point of view, Milton's perception that tyranny sits heavily on the commonwealth? Mill does claim, two years later, in *The Subjection of Women,* something like this about the rights or powers of husbands.

Take as candidates for the permanent interests of man as a progressive being the trio of the right to life, liberty, and the pursuit of happiness. Can these be defended on utilitarian grounds? Can I say that the possession of life conduces to the greatest happiness of the greatest number, or that the pursuit of happiness conduces to such happiness? But these seem pointless remarks, vaguely humorous, or parodistic of philosophy.

How about saying that liberty is conductive to the greatest happiness? That seems not exactly pointless but mysterious. Does it mean that we should somehow maximize liberty? That might make sense where an institution is seen to have control over a finite supply of liberty—say a school, or a prison, or a navy ship in port. Does it mean that liberty causes greater pleasure than subjection does (since Mill is not talking about metaphysical freedom, freedom as it were from nature, but freedom from subjection)?

John Stuart Mill

93

But if you don't know *that* (that freedom is better than subjection), or don't agree with it (so that freedom is indifferent to you, and perhaps because your pleasure and pain are indifferent to you), then it is hard to see how utilitarianism can get a foothold with you.

And if the pleasure and pain of others are indifferent to you then your obligations can also perhaps get no foothold with you. Human society as such, or its absence, would be indifferent to you. Is Mill attempting to teach us that our pleasures and pains should matter to us? How could we need instruction of that sort? Have we forgotten what pleasure and pain are, or lost the imagination that they may in principle be distributed otherwise than they are in our lives? Have we become unable to recognize that subjection has a new form, that, in Rousseau's words, we are everywhere in chains, and are unable to recognize the fact (fairly obviously taking up Plato's perception of us in his Myth of the Cave)?

I think something of this level of question is part of the feel of Mill's text. He says (in chapter 3) that a person's own character, his or her own individuality, is one of the principal ingredients of human happiness, even the chief ingredient of individual and social progress. This conceives of liberty as the exercise of individuality. So it is not that liberty, conceived as individuality, is justified because it causes (that is, has as a consequence, as part of its teleology, to maximize) happiness; liberty is an element of, a principal ingredient of, happiness. It no more maximizes happiness than flour maximizes bread. What is this to say? Is Mill's fear that we have forgotten the pleasure of acting out of our own desire, as if our only happiness were in being obedient to others?

He does say, as if it is informative (in the sentence preceding that expressing the idea that individuality is an ingredient of happiness), "It is desirable, in short, that in things that do not primarily concern others, individuality should assert itself." Well, "desirable" is a mighty term for a utilitarian. I remind you of its occurrence in Mill's definition of the greatest happiness principle, specifically in his answer in *Utilitarianism* to the question: What ought to be required of the doctrine of utilitarianism to make good its claim to be believed? And here is his reply: "The utilitarian doctrine is that happiness is desirable, and the only thing desirable as an end, all other things being only desirable as means to that end." And now comes one of the most famous, perhaps the most often refuted, argument in modern moral philosophy: "The only proof capable of being given that an object is visible is that people actually see it; the only proof that a sound is audible is that people hear it; and so of the other sources of our experience. In like manner, I apprehend, the sole evidence it is possible to produce that anything is desirable is that people do actually desire it" (chapter 4).

Philosophers have rejected this argument from the start, claiming that it is vitiated by the simple recognition that "desirable" does not mean "can be desired" but "ought to be desired," so the connection with "visible" and "audible" never gets off the ground. I remember one prominent philosopher claiming that Mill must have been sleepy when he fell for this similarity. Such things can of course happen. It may have happened in taking "desirable" to mean "ought to be desired." If I respond to a commission from you by telling you that a site is desirable for a house, I do not imply that you ought to desire to build a house there, but that building a house there is a good idea, that you ought, other things equal, to build there (rather than at any of the other places you asked me to compare this one with). The evidence that you ought to is the same as the evidence that it is desirable to. Similarly, to say that happiness is desirable is not to say that happiness ought to be desired but that it is good to have it, that it is bad if our construction of society is such that we are mostly or unnecessarily deprived of it. And moreover, the connection with visible and audible is not unsound. If something is visible then, given your position and the general configuration of things, you ought to see it, it ought to be in view. And contrariwise, would it not be as paradoxical to say that a thing is desirable if no one has ever desired it or could imagine circumstances under which it might prove to be desirable, as to say that a thing is visible which no one has ever seen or ever could imagine seeing?

But while the argument is not, I find, subject to the kind of philosophical disapproval that has been shown it, there is something strange that it should have been mounted at all. You can say that Mill is to some extent playing with the reader, that when he says "In like manner, . . . the only proof capable of being given that anything is desirable is that people do actually desire it," he is simply indicating that no proof is possible, or necessary, that the most that can be asked is that you test the claim to desirability like any other fundamental empirical claim, where "fundamental" means roughly that the claim requires no particular information or expertise to understand and confirm it. Does the following difference seem to matter?—that while both "visible," and so on and "desirable," as said, have a normative element, in the case of something being "desirable," we are accustomed to the fact that we may find we disagree. ("I can see why you find the site to be a desirable one for building, but I feel sure I can find one still more desirable.") But if one thing is said to be "more visible" than another—say from this location, or painted in these colors—this will be determined by the same, let's say, purely empirical means as were used to determine that it is visible. Judgment, let's say the eliciting and application of criteria, will not play the role it does in determining desirability.

What matters, I find, is not the fact of disagreement, but the emphasis given to the importance that each of us has to speak for himself or for herself. And the relevance to *On Liberty* is then the following: The very point, the peculiar eloquence, of this text of Mill's is precisely a function of the fact that he finds that liberty, conceived as "individual spontaneity," *is not generally desired* in fact. It is said by Mill, in his words, that nowadays it is "hardly recognized by the common modes of thinking as having any intrinsic worth" (*On Liberty*, chapter 3). Then what can it mean—why is it not a contradiction—for Mill, taking as the only proof that something is desirable the fact that people do desire it, to say that liberty is desirable, when he has just asserted that hardly anybody does in fact desire it?

Later in chapter 3 of *On Liberty*, Mill asks a question, pitched in high rhetoric, that I have sometimes taken as the climax of the work as a whole. I shall accordingly quote it in full:

> In our times, from the highest class of society down to the lowest, everyone lives as under the eye of a hostile and dreaded censorship.* Not only in what concerns others, but in what concerns only themselves, the individual or the family do not ask themselves, what do I prefer? Or, what would suit my character and disposition? Or, what would allow the best and highest in me to have fair play and enable it to grow and thrive? They ask themselves, what is suitable to my position? what is usually done by persons of my station and pecuniary circumstances? or (worse still) what is usually done by persons of a station and circumstance superior to mine? I do not mean that they choose what is customary in preference to what suits their own inclination. It does not occur to them to have any inclination except for what is customary. Thus the

* Here let me remind you that this passage is not from Michel Foucault, not even from chapter 4 of Heidegger's *Being and Time*.

mind itself is bowed to the yoke: even in what people do for pleasure, conformity is the first thing thought of; they like in crowds; they exercise choice only among things commonly done; peculiarity of taste, eccentricity of conduct are shunned equally with crime, until by dint of not following their own nature they have no nature to follow: their human capacities are withered and starved; they become incapable of any strong wishes or native pleasures, and are generally without either opinions or feelings of home growth, or properly their own. Now is this, or is it not, the desirable condition of human nature?

Accepting Mill's proposition that the only proof that a thing is desirable is that people desire it, the question he asks, or asks us to ask, is: Do you desire it? It is a question about ourselves; no one is in principle in a better position to answer it than each of us. But Mill has just described the condition of human nature in which precisely this question does not arise. The irony goes beyond any doubts philosophers have felt toward Mill's reasoning. Having established to his satisfaction the principle, based on the distinction between self-regarding and other-regarding acts, and urged that with respect to self-regarding actions we are free to dispose of ourselves, Mill now finds that it is we who are, in the current dispensation of advanced society with progressive aspirations, the threat to our own liberty. As if liberty consists only in the rightful claiming and taking of it, as if it is otherwise an item in pawn awaiting redemption.

The condition of human nature in which we, as we might put the matter, do not ask whether we find our condition desirable is one in which our nature does not exist for us, a perpetuation of the threat I formulated, in reading Locke, as of our haunting society, unable to sense our participation in it. Mill's writing, his philosophical mission as I put it, is to *awaken* us to the question he poses: Is this, is our experience of the currency of our world, desired by me? It is a question meant to show us that we have a right to our own desires, to have them recognized as touchstones for social criticism and reform. A right, one could say, to invoke the principle of utility "in the broadest sense."

It may be felt that my own sense of the world's desirability (so far as it concerns me) is a thin reed on which to base social criticism. But this is a counsel arising from despair. It is the condition of society Emerson described as its "secret melancholy," and Thoreau as the mass of men "leading lives of quiet desperation"—observations I understand as revealing despair to be, in a democracy, a political emotion. That is, "secret" and "quiet" indicate that voices are being withheld from the commonwealth, weakening confidence on both, on all, sides. As if we see no hope of making our lives intelligible. Then there is no hope of achieving a moral, an examined, existence together.

This condition, which we heard Mill articulate, among other ways, by saying that "by dint of not following our nature we have no nature to follow," is one in which, adapting Emerson's phrase, no soul is becoming, none becoming the one it is. If a bible of perfectionism were to be put together, the paragraph of Mill's containing this perception, together with whatever is necessary to understand it, would demand prominence in it.

The perception seems to proceed from a perspective in which a certain distance as well as closeness to his society is maintained, distance enough to see society as a whole, closeness sufficient to hear his own voice in response to his role in it, to express his consent to its existence by chastising it. It is a perspective from which Mill's high rhetoric of, let's say, impersonal invective is called forth. This demand upon eloquence is something that I think we can see throughout Mill's *The Subjection of Women,* where the question "Is this, or is it not, the desirable condition of human nature?" is directed toward the question of marriage—a great question of Mill's day, and, with interruptions, since. And as in the case of his description of the degeneration of humankind in its oblivion of its desires, he demands here a response from the reader which the reader, as she or he stands, in conformity (or conspiracy) with society at large, is incapable of giving—a response that must come from a transformation of perception, of a sense of possibility, created by this writing.

Accordingly, the philosophical mode of Mill's text on the subjection of women, its source of expected conviction, is, as in the case of *On Liberty,* less that of formal argumentation than that of moral challenge: the case of marriage is, in effect, a special case of the want of liberty (Mill, to repeat, calls it "the only actual bondage known to our law"; *Subjection of Women,* chapter 4). As such, arguing against it (on utilitarian grounds, at any rate) is like arguing "against a bad joke" (chapter 3). Can one bring oneself to consider whether slavery causes a greater amount of pleasure in society than its absence would? Abraham Lincoln had to ask a related question: Is the cost of ridding ourselves of slavery—civil war, or the breaking up of the Union—greater than the cost of countenancing it?

But Mill faces no such question. In fact I feel the best help I could be in reading these texts, as it were to locate their rationality, would be to follow out what I mean in characterizing the tenor of his prose here as that of impersonal invective, and specifying the speech act in question as that of chastising, obviously related in some way to that of Emerson's shaming, or humbling. These are instances of what I call passionate speech, which I characterize in relation to Austin's performative speech, extending his analysis of what he calls perlocutionary effect (in contrast to illocutionary force) further than Austin took it.

For the moment let me call attention to two passages from *The Subjection of Women* that bear directly on the essential presence of film in these chapters, the first passage particularly on the genre of remarriage, the second particularly on the genre, indeed on a specific instance, of the melodrama of the unknown woman. The first is from chapter 4:

> What marriage may be in the case of two persons of cultivated faculties, identical in opinions and purposes, between whom there exists that best kind of equality, similarity of powers and capacities with reciprocal superiority in them—so that each can enjoy the luxury of looking up to the other, and can have alternately the pleasure of leading and of being led in the path of development—I will not attempt to describe. To those who can conceive it, there is no need; to those who cannot, it would appear the dream of an enthusiast. But I maintain, with the profoundest conviction, that this, and this only, is the ideal of marriage; and that all opinions, customs, and institutions which favor any other notion of it, or turn the conceptions and aspirations connected with it into an other direction, by whatever pretences they may be colored, are relics of primitive barbarism. The moral regeneration of mankind will only really commence, when the most fundamental of the social relations is placed under the rule of equal justice, and when human beings learn to cultivate their strongest sympathy with an equal in rights and in cultivation.

The Subjection of Women accordingly can be taken to affirm marriage under the sign of "what marriage may be"—but while Mill speaks of its achievable pleasures, as a utilitarian should be expected to do in support of his moral affirmations, he at the same time implies that the principle of utility is unserviceable, either unnecessary or incredible. We are presumably to understand this gesture of declaring words to be superfluous or useless as another indication that we are, in the prospect of the highest manifestation

John Stuart Mill

99

of human happiness, at the limit of proof. But also to take up the idea that the institution of marriage, like that of political society as such, is open to our judgment, requires our affirmation.

That marriage "as it may be" is one precisely that subjects itself to reaffirmation is what I take the genre of remarriage comedy to base itself upon. The derived melodrama of the unknown woman is a narrative in which marriage is rejected as it is given, on the ground that it is the negation of what marriage may be.

Mill's paragraph on marriage as it may be occurs after he has described the family—often, and still, familiarly and sentimentally praised by the moralistic—as a school of despotism. Which raises again the question of the audience Mill takes himself to be addressing. That the audience is sometimes specifically men (of a certain class, of course, namely those with the education to read this tract) is all but explicit in the last sentence of chapter 3: "Women cannot be expected to devote themselves to the emancipation of women, until men in considerable number are prepared to join with them in the undertaking." Probably no sentence in the book more clearly dates it. And while that may have been the empirical truth when Mill wrote (he speaks in the preceding sentence of "a woman who joins in any movement which her husband disapproves" as making "herself a martyr, without even being able to be an apostle, for the husband can legally put a stop to her apostleship"), the idea of a man now, a century and a half after Mill wrote, seeming to assume that feminism, if no longer awaiting, so much as welcomes, his support is something, as mentioned earlier, that particularly invites the scorn of certain women. So I quote, in conclusion, a paragraph from *The Subjection of Women* which only a man is in a position to have written. It is from chapter 3:

It no doubt often happens that a person, who has not widely and accurately studied the thoughts of others on a subject, has by natural sagacity a happy intuition, which he can suggest, but cannot prove, which yet when matured may be an important addition to knowledge; but even then, no justice can be done to it until some other person, who does possess the previous acquirements, takes it in hand, tests it, gives it a scientific or practical form, and fits it into its place among the existing truths of philosophy or science. Is it supposed that such felicitous thoughts do not occur to women? They occur by hundreds to every woman of intellect. But they are mostly lost, for want of a husband or friend who has the other knowledge which can enable him to estimate them properly and bring them before the world: and even when they are brought before it, they generally appear as his ideas, not their real author's. Who can tell how many of the most original thoughts put forth by male writers, belong to a woman by suggestion, to themselves only by verifying and working out? If I may judge by my own case, a very large proportion indeed.

This is a staggering confession, to my mind the most surprising moment in the book. It is one that accuses men, men as prominent as himself, the continuers of European high culture, of systematic plagiarism, of "a very large proportion indeed" of that culture as lifted, unacknowledged, from women. Is it, further, a confession that he only recognizes the woman's voice in himself when he senses it as plagiarized? This is to be put together with his repeated call for the woman's voice. The fascination with the woman's voice and the desire to still and to steal it are direct links to the first of the melodramas of the unknown woman we are to take into account, George Cukor's *Gaslight*, from 1944.

6

Gaslight

1 A prologue gives a glimpse of an event, or an immediate aftermath of an event, whose consequences ten years later will be the subject of the film. The opening shot is of a gas lamp being lit in a London Square, by whose light, in a close-up, a passerby reads in the newspaper that the murder of Alice Alquist, a famous singer, has taken place in this very (Thornton) Square. "Strangler Still At Large." We move to the scene outside the very house of the event, where a young girl is accompanied out of the house and into a carriage by some kind of guardian who is sending her off to Italy to study singing with her famous aunt's old singing teacher and to forget everything that has happened here.

2 That opening had somehow been played by Ingrid Bergman made to look preadolescent. In the following sequence we find a grown Paula (Bergman) in the middle of a voice lesson with Signore Guardi in Italy, practicing an aria from *Lucia di Lammermoor*. The teacher tells her that her heart is not in her singing, that this aria was one of her aunt's great roles, and adds emphatically, "You *look* like her!" "But I don't sing like her. I have no voice, have I?" Not altogether plausibly, he asks if she is in love. The accompanist rises from the piano to say that if the lesson is over he would like to leave. It is Charles Boyer, an actor we know will not remain a mere accompaniment to the narrative to follow.

3 Outside, the accompanist has been waiting for Paula to leave. Evidently this man, whom she embraces and calls Gregory, has won the love of this inexperienced, much younger woman. He importunes her to marry him. She says she wants to go to Lake Como to think about it.

4a In the train she shares a compartment with a visiting Englishwoman, Miss Thwaites (Dame May Whitty), who loves grisly mystery stories and who tells Paula that she lives in Thornton Square in London where a famous singer was murdered ten years ago.

4b As the train pulls into the station at the lake, a gloved hand reaches across the window of the compartment. It proves to belong to Gregory, who pulls Paula toward him in a fervent embrace. Miss Thwaites lets out a small cry of shock.

5 On the terrace of what is evidently their bridal apartment, in a lakeside villa, as they discuss their future together, Gregory tells Paula of his dream one day to live in a house in a London square. Paula is moved and tells him he shall have his house.

6 At the fraught square in London, Miss Thwaites sees that the house of murder is being readied for occupancy after all these years of being closed up. For example, the gas is being turned on. Paula and Gregory emerge from a carriage and are greeted at the door of the house by the guardian who had a decade earlier dispatched her away from it. Gregory pushes open the squeaking door and directs Paula to enter, which she barely manages to do.

7a In the dust and webs and gloom of ten years of oblivion Paula is seized by terror and says that she cannot live surrounded by these memories. Gregory says they'll put all these reminders well away into the attic and buy new, cheerful things.

7b Gregory sits at the piano and plays something accompanying his own memories. Paula opens a letter that has fallen out of a score at the side of the music rack of the piano and reads it aloud. It is a request to her aunt for an interview with her by someone signed Sergius Bauer. At this name, in the first of the uncontrolled outbreaks of rage we will have to endure from this man, Gregory violently snatches the letter from Paula. Realizing that he has shown his hand, he covers himself by saying his outburst was produced by sympathy for Paula's having been reminded of her tragedy.

8a Gregory has engaged a cook, Elizabeth, who is hard of hearing, and a flirtatious housemaid he calls Nancy (wonderfully played by Angela Lansbury, in the first of her film roles).

8b For their three-month anniversary, Gregory gives Paula a brooch that he says was his mother's, and her mother's before her (perhaps he is remembering Othello, a more eloquent psychic torturer), and cautions Paula to be careful not to lose it, reminding her, to her blank surprise, that she has become forgetful in these past few months. He makes her turn around to watch him with elaborate clarity place the brooch in her purse.

8c Nancy says the mistress doesn't seem ill. Elizabeth replies that the master keeps telling her she is.

9a Paula and Gregory are, for their first outing after three months, visiting the Tower of London. As they listen to a guide's tale of the tortures that have taken place on the machines in the Tower, Paula notices that the brooch is not

Gaslight

in her purse. As the recounting of torture continues voice-over, she wanders off to try to recover herself, but Gregory follows, asking what she is doing.

9b Walking across the sunny courtyard of the Tower, the pair pass a young man (Joseph Cotten), accompanied by two children, who out of the blue raises his hat to Paula; startled, she nods almost imperceptibly in return. He says to the children, "I feel as if I had seen a ghost."

9c As we accompany our pair to the Tower's exhibition of the Crown Jewels, we learn that Gregory knows the description of the jewels by heart.

10 Back at the house, Elizabeth, showing Nancy around, answers her question about the top floor by saying that it's boarded up.

11 Gregory and Paula enter. She says she would like to see where he goes out to work on his music every night. He asks to see the brooch he gave her so he can have it repaired. Paula has to confess that it is gone; she empties her purse on the landing of the stair, and gazes at the contents as if amazed afresh. Gregory himself is very perplexed; nay, he is touchingly wounded.

12 In her bedroom that night Paula notices that the gaslight dims. She asks Nancy if anyone else is in the house, and Nancy says no. When Nancy leaves, Paula hears noises, or perhaps only thinks she hears them.

13 Outside the house the young man from the Tower of London encounters Miss Thwaites, who confides in him that something strange is going on in the Gregory Anton house, for example that Paula never goes out. Just then Paula appears at the door, but as she is about to leave, Nancy comes to the door and asks whether Mr. Anton knows she is leaving. She goes back inside.

14a At Scotland Yard, this young man, Detective Brian Cameron, has taken out boxes of evidence from the Alice Alquist case. The head of the Yard, who is his uncle, is angry at this meddling, telling him the case has been closed, and that there is nothing unusual in the niece's coming back to live in the house, which is after all hers. He adds that the jewels were never found. This piques Brian's interest, since there was no mention of jewels in the reports of the case he has read. He declares that he feels something wrong is happening in that house. He confesses that he was introduced to Alice Alquist when he was twelve years old and remembers her as the most beautiful woman he ever saw. The uncle reveals that the jewels had been a present to her from a foreign head of state, so that a potential scandal had to be avoided. (This is the sort of back story one expects from Arthur Conan Doyle.)

14b On his way out of the Yard, Brian encounters a constable of his acquaintance and, learning that he is unmarried, asks him if he would like a more fashionable assignment.

15 Paula is with Gregory in their drawing room. She wakes him by putting a coal on the fire. Now follows a series of events that would drive any sentient creature crazy. Gregory demands that Paula call a servant to put extra coals on the fire, though she thinks that wholly unnecessary. When Nancy arrives Gregory tells Paula to tell Nancy why she rang for her. He also suggests that Nancy might have some hints to help Paula make herself more attractive. When he makes Paula feel that she must be crazy to suggest that he has insulted her before her servant, he begins playing the piano and suddenly reveals that he has theater tickets for tonight. Paula is mad with desire to go out where there are people. She dances to his music in ecstasy. He suddenly stops playing and accuses her of meaninglessly removing a painting from the wall and hiding it. He calls the servants to the room to cross-examine them. Paula has to admit that she does not think either of them has done this meaningless thing. So she can only conclude that it was she. The theater is out. "If I do these meaningless things, then be kind to me. Don't leave me alone in this house. I am frightened of the house. Take me in your arms, please Gregory." He abandons her to her room.

16a Gregory prepares to leave the house, and exchanges flirtatious remarks with Nancy.

16b He leaves the house, walks along the foggy street, and suddenly turns into an alley.

16c In her bedroom, collapsed with fear, Paula experiences the lights dimming and noises emerging as from overhead.

17 Brian, in his apartment, reads an invitation from Lady Dalroy to a recital and reception. He goes early to ask her to seat him next to Paula Anton. Lady Dalroy explains to her husband that she had, at Brian's suggestion, invited the Antons to her party, and then hands Brian Mr. Anton's letter regretting that his wife is too ill for them to accept the invitation. Brian is not surprised.

18a In Thornton Square, Paula is in evening clothes, and when she says, with an unprecedented show of will, that she is prepared to go to Lady Dalroy's party without Gregory, Gregory pretends he was only joking in saying she would have to go alone.

18b As Gregory hurriedly dresses himself to go out, he seems to have a sudden thought.

Gaslight

19 At the party, where Paula is thriving in the presence of the world from which she has been cut off, while they are listening to a performance of Beethoven's "Pathetique" piano sonata, and then the beginning of Chopin's First Ballad, Gregory informs Paula in an undertone that his watch is missing; he opens her purse to show her that the watch is there, just where the brooch wasn't. She cannot suppress her attack of panic, and Gregory has to remove her noisily from the scene, where the piano performance has stopped, apologizing to Lady Dalroy, as they awkwardly walk out, for thinking his wife recovered enough to come to the party. Brian watches them leave with the gravest suspicion.

20 Back in Paula's room, Gregory's accusations become unguardedly wild. He tells her she never had a letter in her hand that first day. He tells her her mother died in an insane asylum when Paula was one year old, and that she has the same mad symptoms as her mother. He then says they will have company, and soon. Paula replies that they will be doctors. Gregory says, "I believe the required number is two."

21 Brian, in the foggy night outside, is waiting, hidden in the shrubs across from the house. As Gregory leaves, Brian and the constable are on the alert. They meet at the entrance to the alley where Gregory had again turned in, and thrown aside a cigarette, and then disappeared. The constable knows Gregory did not exit the alley on the other side. Has he simply taken a back way into his own house? The constable: "It's not against the law." Brian: "It's against common sense."

22 In her bedroom, Paula, lights dimming and noises beginning, runs to the stairwell and screams for Elizabeth. Elizabeth can of course hear no mild noises, and explains the dimming light by saying that perhaps more gas is piped into the house at some times than at other times.

23 In his apartment, Brian is going over a plan of the houses lining the Antons' side of Thornton Square. The constable arrives and reports that Nancy, with whom he, as planned, is keeping company, tells him that her mistress is going away for a long time. Brian is alarmed.

24a Inside the house at Thornton Square, Paula is frantically reading from a book aloud as if to drown out noises in her head.

24b Outside, Brian, when Gregory walks out and away, goes to the door and attempts to convince Elizabeth to let him speak to Mrs. Anton. Paula hears them and says from the top of the stairs that she cannot speak to anyone. Brian approaches her and shows her a glove he says her aunt gave him when he was a child. She recognizes it as matching a glove she had shown Gregory from her aunt's memorabilia. Thus gaining her confidence enough to talk with her, Brian gets her to see the connection of Gregory's nightly comings and goings with the gaslight's goings and comings. Then he notices that the light has dimmed. Paula is mad with relief to have this confirmed. He follows her to where the overhead noise is loudest, namely in her room, and asks what's up there. When she replies that it is all of her aunt's possessions, Brian asks: "You know who's up there, don't you?" A fine question that we are relieved to hear.

25a We see for the first time Gregory in the attic, taking objects apart, tearing stuffing out of chairs, in his hunt for the jewels.

25b Brian asks Paula if Gregory has a weapon. She takes him to Gregory's room where he pries open Gregory's locked desk. "Don't, don't. What am I going to tell him?" "You won't have to tell him anything." A pistol is missing. The letter from Sergius Bauer is present. Brian happens to have Gregory's letter to Lady Dalroy and declares the handwriting of the two to be the same. Paula says she's going out of her mind. Brian says she's being driven out of her mind.

25c In the attic Gregory discovers the jewels, sewn as decorations into the aunt's gown for one of her great roles.

26 Brian and Paula notice that the gaslight has gone back up. Brian rushes out to head off Gregory. But Gregory, this time, reenters the house from above, opening the boarded-up attic from the inside and descending one floor to his room, where he discovers his desk has been broken into. He confronts Paula with this, who says a man was there. Gregory has about convinced her that she dreamed the whole thing (confirmed by Elizabeth, who thinks she is protecting Paula), when Brian suddenly appears, asking, "Am I by any chance part of this dream you're supposed to be having?"

27 The men declare themselves to each other, recognize that both their searches have ended, and when Gregory produces his pistol and fires, Brian knocks the aim off. Gregory flees to the attic, Brian in pursuit. The noise alerts the constable outside, and his pursuit is guided by Nancy, then Elizabeth, then Paula.

28a Paula, alone on her landing, mounts the stairs up to the attic, where Gregory is now bound to a chair, as if rising to where her life had been stored. Brian comes through the door as she reaches it, and she tells him she wants to speak to her husband alone.

28b Gregory asks her to cut him free. She launches into a sort of mad aria in which she says she might have helped him if she had been sane but that in

Gaslight

her madness she is without pity for him. She cries out to Brian, "Take this man away."

28c Gregory says to Paula, mysteriously, "Between us all the time were those jewels." But of course without the jewels there would have been nothing between them to begin with. As Paula says when she learns that Sergius Bauer already has a wife, "Then there was from the beginning nothing." (My reading of the film gives some sense to the idea that this man is motivated by nothing, by emptiness.)

29 On the rooftop, where Gregory had entered and exited the attic, Brian says the long night is ending and asks Paula whether he might come and talk to her sometimes. She touches his arm in gratitude for his kindness. Miss Thwaites appears just in time to respond to the scene with a small cry of shock.

This film is the first instance of the genre of melodrama that I introduce in contrast with—its members exhibiting what I call negations of—the remarriage genre. The constant factor between the genres is that the women of the melodramas are also to be understood in terms of moral perfectionism, and the main contradiction of the comedies by the melodramas is that the woman seeks her unattained but attainable self otherwise than in marriage, the opportunities for which turn out, in her world, to be destructive for her. In two of the four cases I adduce—*Now, Voyager* and *Stella Dallas*—the woman's rejection of marriage has seemed, I believe, to most viewers to be an act of sacrifice by the woman, in Stella's case for the good of her daughter, in Charlotte Vale's case for the sake of her lover. This has set the tone of the reception of the Hollywood melodramas known as (advertised as) "women's films." It is a principal object of my reading of these films to contest this advertisement.

In the other two cases I take in evidence, the man to whom the woman is drawn to share her fantasies of the transcendence of the everyday is precisely one capable only of inspiring the fantasies, not of acting on them. In one of them, *Gaslight*, the man is a true villain who proves to wish the woman, or women, harm, one whose passion for a mysterious, I will say metaphysical, purity (symbolized as jewels) inspires an increasing contempt for his wife, which in turn inspires her, almost fatally, persistently to seek his love. In the other of them, *Letter from an Unknown Woman*, leaving a marriage that was itself a substitute for romance proves to be fatally destructive, as if to under-score the woman's inability to recognize that for her marriage is always fatal, that the man to whom she is drawn to share her fantasies of the transcen-dence of the everyday wishes her, for example, no particular harm, but the magnetism of his need to feed a paralyzed perfectionist aspiration he no longer believes in, or feels capable of, draws her into an affair in which she, as she is, has no existence.

The rejection, or negation, of marriage in the melodramas entails the negation of many further features of remarriage comedy. For example, in the melodramas the woman is always shown in relation to, or in fateful separa-tion from, her mother; she is always shown in relation to a child; if her father, or a figure for her father, is present (sometimes in this genre this figure is her husband), he is never on the side of her desire, but stands upon, and for, the law; the movement of the action is not from the city to a place of reflection and resolution (there is such a place in *Now, Voyager,* one however that is explicitly temporary), but tends to end in the place it began—nowhere more brutally than in *Gaslight.* Given the negation of marriage, the conversation between the principal pair that, according to the theory of remarriage com-edy I am advancing, characterizes those comedies must also be negated in the melodramas, so that the improvisatory and intimate battle of wits becomes an isolating struggle with irony and misunderstanding, not a clear-ing of communication but a darkening of it.

I have described the remarriage pair as preferring to spend or waste time together, as it were doing nothing, rather than to do anything with anyone else. (I first noted this in discussing the Howard Hawks film *Bringing Up Baby,* from 1938, a film I chose, reluctantly, to omit from the course that became this book.) This idea of spending time led to a sense of the different conceptions of time that define the respective genres, the melodramas sketching a past frozen and compulsively active in the present, the comedies proposing an openness to the future, responsive to invention. The sense of a world frozen in meaning, resistant to change, or exchange, is furthered by the heavy symbology of the melodramas, the as it were eternal conflict between light and darkness, good and bad, innocence and guilt, belonging and dis-possession, characteristically associating a heavy mood with heavy weather, and the lifting of the mood with dawn and clearing.

(The idea of the metaphysical as projecting a world of frozen meaning is a suggestion I take from Wittgenstein's *Investigations,* in which he once pictures philosophy's aspirations to purity as stranding human desire in a field of ice, from which the appeal to "return our words from their metaphysical to their everyday use" is to allow us the freedom, the steadiness of ground, upon which to walk again, that is to direct ourselves, to inner and outer goals. Because the detective in *Gaslight* confirms Paula's use of words to refer to phenomena in the world beyond her imagination—to real noises, to light really dimming and brightening—I referred to him, in my book *Contesting Tears,* as her voice teacher. In this application of Wittgenstein's image of the ice field, Gregory is a metaphysician.)

My preoccupation with the film *Gaslight* was originally driven, before I formed the explicit claim that Emersonian perfectionism was the moral outlook of two significant genres of American filmmaking, by the issue of skepticism with respect to the knowledge of others, what Anglo-American philosophy calls the problem of other minds. Continental philosophizing, from Hegel to Heidegger and to Levinas, takes up inescapably our encounter with the other, but as a perpetual struggle, not as posing a further skeptical issue within epistemology that might conceivably find a resolution. In Anglo-American philosophizing, the presence of the other has only since the middle of the twentieth century, in Wittgenstein's *Investigations,* become a featured topic of philosophical investigation. This fact is itself of no little interest to me.

The angle of incidence at which skepticism strikes the film melodramas is different from that at which it manifested itself in Shakespearean tragedy. In the Shakespearean cases I adduce in my book *The Claim of Reason,* the collapse of confidence in our knowledge of others is precipitated by the collapse of confidence in what I call a best case of knowledge, or rather of acknowledgment. Desdemona is the world for Othello, his loss of her is the loss of interest for him in whatever else the world has to offer. But Paula in *Gaslight,* the "niece" of a world-famous singer, seems to be of no interest in herself to Gregory Anton, who merely has a use for her, namely to admit him to the house in which the jewels—which are the world to him—must be hidden, the jewels he had been searching for the night Paula's aunt interrupted his labors and he strangled her.

Unless, perhaps, he has, in the course of realizing his scheme of recovery, become fascinated by this woman's manifestation not of radical Cartesian self-doubt, but of Emerson's perception of mankind as ashamed, too timid, to declare its existence as revealed in its power of thinking, so that it attempts to abandon thinking, to suspend the power of judgment (something Descartes grants us the freedom of will to do), so to haunt itself. As Paula enters her house she becomes its ghost. (In the Shakespearean cases it is the male who doubts, in opposition to the woman who loves. This issue of, let's say, the implication of gender in skepticism will be at the center of attention when at the end of the book we come to consider *The Winter's Tale*.)

Might Gregory have a use also for this condition in her? That he has is suggested by his coming, at the end, to believe, at any rate intermittently, in the fictions he has created for her—he seems really to fly into a rage at her doing crazy things like removing a picture from the wall and hiding it, and stealing his watch (neither of which she has done), and almost to believe she has dreamed that she spoke with a stranger (which she has done in fact), as she dreams everything that happens to her (which he wants to believe, which Descartes in a certain mood seemed able to believe, or anyway not to be able to dismiss).

This, let me say, personal interest of Gregory's in Paula's vulnerability goes rather beyond what in *Contesting Tears* I call Gregory's vampirism, his living off the spirit of women. This perception has been revivified in my recognition, on rereading Mill's *The Subjection of Women* this time, of intellectual men as systematically plagiarizing women's thoughts, perhaps as a spur or supplement to their own originality, perhaps out of a distrust of their own originality. This suggests a route of motivation for men's wanting to know what women know, that it is a projection of their doubts about the worth of their own knowledge, of their intellectualization of their lives.

Another emphasis on the idea of the masculine incorporation, or theft, of the feminine can be seen in a film by Chantal Akerman based on ("inspired by," the credits say) Proust's *La Prisonnière*. Her film is entitled *La Captive*, a literal translation back into French of the English translation of Proust's title. In a round table discussion after a screening of the film, while considering the color or shape given to the concept of love by the, let's call it, absolute compliance of the Albertine character to the wishes of the Marcel character, Akerman spoke of the man of the pair as a vampire, who in effect has already taken the woman's life before her actual accidental or suicidal death. But in the Proustian vampire the man interprets his obsession with the details of the woman's existence as his love of her, whereas in the *Gaslight* complex the man at least begins, we are given to think, in complete indifference to that existence. Well, we are hardly to expect Proustian articulation from a mere

Hollywood film, yet we are not excused from responding to the specific powers of film where they are released.

The thematics of Paula's haunting of her existence shows her eventual, climactic enactment of the cogito, the bare proof of her existence, to be taken in vengeance, as if to declare: Descartes's cogito proof of existence is motivated not simply by the sense that my existence is unproven, but by the sense that it is *denied*. (The archetypal case of the declaration of ignorance as, conceptually and spiritually, an expression of denial, in our culture, is Peter's repeated denial of Jesus.) Among the questions with which I closed *The Claim of Reason* is whether skepticism with respect to others may not be more fundamental than the more familiar case (in analytical philosophy) of skepticism with respect to the material ("external") world of objects. The suggestion is that even with respect to the world, the motivation to doubt is linked with a wish to deny its presence, its incessance. (The denial of denial is explicitly the context of Hamlet's declaration of his existence: "I am Hamlet the Dane." It is declared in refutation of the denial of his right to mourn one with whom his existence is intertwined.) Skepticism with respect to others is not a discovery but a compulsion, a nihilistic despair of the pain of acknowledging separateness.

The conception of (male) knowledge at play in *Gaslight* is represented by Gregory's obsession with jewels. Gregory's last words to Paula are roughly: "Don't try to understand me. Always between us were the jewels. They were a fire in my brain." But at least we can understand that what he requires of intimacy with the world, the condition of his caring about things or persons, is possession. Love as possession, expressed as knowledge, is a way of putting the obsessive force of Marcel's quest in *La Prisonnière*. The fact that both the Proust novel and a significant Hollywood film picture the object of knowledge as one that has to be kept captive, and that the captor accordingly becomes captive to his captive, is a tip to my mind that we have here a contribution to the architecture of skepticism. Gregory is at his virtuosic height of evil when he teases Paula, having suddenly caused elation in her by promising to take her out to the theater, into confessing that she doesn't really "think that Gregory is cruel and keeping you a prisoner." (I merely mention here something that will come up later in the book, when we turn to Shakespeare: that knowledge, shaped by the compulsion to overcome the threat of skepticism, may present itself as an economic matter of private property, as in Othello's and Leontes' jealousy.) The image of the jewels suggests that the relation knowledge seeks is exemplified in the collecting of artifacts, hence in conceiving perception as surveillance of what can be put on display, in principle of the totality of what is real. Gregory's description of the jewels as fire suggests the need to warm his life from outside.

Various paths lead from here. Collecting as a relation to the world recalls the figure of Proust's Swann, against whom Marcel perpetually measures himself, as if his becoming a writer depends upon transcending the point at which Swann's development was fixed. Again, captivation in relation to knowing the world and oneself in it is expressed explicitly in formulations of both Wittgenstein's and Lacan's. In Wittgenstein's *Investigations*: "A *picture* held us captive. And we could not get outside it, for it lay in our language and language seemed to repeat it to us inexorably" (§115). In Lacan's seminar *Freud's Papers on Technique, 1953–1954* (p. 182): "The floating, spoken relation with the analyst tends to produce, in the self-image, sufficiently repeated and wide-ranging variations . . . for the subject to perceive the captating images which lie at the base of the constitution of the ego."

While we have asked how Paula's vulnerability suits Gregory's needs, we have yet to ask how Gregory's obsession suits Paula's needs, if only to notice that her inability to declare or assume or imagine her independent existence in the world subjects her to asking for proof of her existence from this man. She murmurs to the detective's recognition of Gregory as Sergius Bauer, "Then there was from the beginning nothing," but this was true before the revelation that Gregory already had a wife. Paula had called marriage something that secured her against being frightened of existence, a state in which she could achieve the relief of "stopping dreaming." It bespeaks an all but lethal materialization of the idea that the marriage partner constitutes the whole world, as for Othello. (Paula's "aunt" was famously unmarried.)

May we take her helplessness in the face of Gregory's hypnotic suggestions as the extreme instance of what I previously articulated as being humbled by words? This would imply that what Gregory calls Paula's sleepwalking (what I have called her haunting of her existence) is what Emerson calls our remaining to some degree asleep all our waking life (in "Self-Reliance": "There is sleep around our eyes, as night remains all day in the fir trees"). It is the condition that Thoreau perceives as our existing in a trance, from which it is the task of his prose to awaken us. The most famous philosophical portrait of this state, perhaps the original of them all, is Plato's description of human existence, I will say everyday existence, in his Myth of the Cave in *The Republic,* which will come up for us later in this book. The portrait in *Gaslight* adds a terrifying, melodramatic note to this state in showing it in relation to what I might call the paranoia of language, a state in which the simplest of descriptions are taken by the victim, the one who receives words, as accusations. Paula takes the statement "My watch is gone" as the speech act of accusing, which means that every fact accuses her. No wonder she has become terrified of conversation, say become unmarriageable.

There is, however, a word she needs to hear from (as she imagines) Gregory, implied in her begging him not to leave her alone when they return to the house after she loses control at Lady Dalroy's. As they approach her room, she cries out that she is frightened of this room, frightened of this house, frightened of herself. He has accused her of doing crazy, meaningless, twisted things. So the word Gregory withholds, among all those he so willingly suggests to her, is something that will tell her that she is not a figure of repulsion, of horror, unfit for human society. This is the knowledge, the education, she has looked to him for, the want her past has brought her to, as Tracy Lord's has brought her to want to know how to be useful, as Amanda Bonner's has brought her to want something known. Will I be able to formulate such knowledge for the other women of our genres, and if not will I be able to measure how important a lapse this is, either in the films in question or in my ability to interpret them? That such questions are open as we are contracted to go through these works feels like thinking without a net. How different is this from Wittgenstein's insight that thinking, our use of language with each other, occurs with no ground beyond what we can find in ourselves? What alternative do we imagine?

I mention here a still further philosophical location in which to ponder a suggestion that would take us too far afield now but which some of you who share certain of my philosophical tastes might like to pursue. The suggestion of a dimension of paranoia in speech, in what we choose to assert, and to take seriously in what is asserted of us, is given in the way Austin sets up his major work on what he calls excuses, less well known but at least as significant philosophically as his work on the performative utterance. "When," Austin asks in "A Plea for Excuses" (one of the thirteen papers assembled in the third edition of his *Philosophical Papers*), "do we 'excuse' conduct, our own or somebody else's? When are 'excuses' proffered?" His answer is: "In general, the situation is one where someone is *accused* of doing something, or (if that will keep it any cleaner) where someone is *said* to have done something . . . [which is] untoward in [one or another] of the numerous possible ways [of being] untoward." The point of the excuse is "to argue that it is not quite fair or correct to say *baldly* 'X did A'." Not fair just to say X did A (perhaps she was under somebody's influence); not fair to say baldly X *did* A (it may have been an accident); or not fair to say she did simply *A* (perhaps she was doing something else to which A was incidental); or some combination of these. Austin suggests that changing "accused" to "said" may help keep matters cleaner, I suppose in order not to preempt the tone of the speech act in which the description of someone's action is delivered (it may have been closer to a question than to a full accusation).

But what Austin's change more emphatically goes to show, to my mind, is the intimacy between accusing (or questioning) and *saying as such,* which is what I am calling the paranoia of speech. The human being is inherently clumsy, society inherently involves our bumping against each other; civilization depends upon being fair about this, accepting excuses with forbearance and in reasonably good humor, and offering reparations when they are in order, with good grace and in even better humor. Gregory's descriptions of Paula's conduct, or insinuated conduct (not "You stole my watch" but "My watch is gone") leave her defenseless, without excuse, self-accusing, not simply because the descriptions are false but because even if they were true they would be of pointless acts, precisely baffling the issuing of excuses (which go to make clear how and why something untoward has happened), excuses, that is, other than appealing to one's derangement, the precise accusation Gregory wishes to drive Paula to accept.

This is what gives so satisfactory an irony to her concluding cogito aria to her husband, the man in the audience to whom she communicates her unspeakable hatred—as her aunt had communicated her undeclarable love to her lover by displaying on the stage the jewels sewn into her gown, whose significance only the two of them understood—Paula invoking her madness as her excuse not to be able to help Gregory escape. After this tirade, adopting the abuse of language, coating it wholly in irony, she is essentially silent, and the detective's last words to her, asking to come talk to her sometimes, furthers the sense that she is going to have to learn to speak again, where that means learn to trust and entrust words again. She will need a talking companion as before she had a singing teacher, someone with whom the inevitable implications in speech (what Austin calls illocutionary forces and

Gaslight

perlocutionary effects) do not incessantly threaten uncontrollable insinuation. When Paula calls down the stairs to head off the detective, "I can't talk to anyone," we recognize that she is declaring that she has lost the power of speech.

I do not want to claim more insight for this film than it can reasonably be held to hold. It does not give us concrete material for interpreting Gregory's and Paula's deeper uses for each other. But neither do I wish to underestimate the power of the medium of film to present events as credible whose comprehensibility requires and sustains meditation that goes beyond anything the film may know about itself. When—as we shall hear in a later chapter—a woman in *Stella Dallas* says to her conventional husband, "Can't you read between these pathetic lines? Laurel is here. Who has made this happen?" she is in effect giving an instruction in reading a film. To understand the events of a film you have to see what is there, what goes without saying, how each person is where he and she is, why the camera is, and the light is, where they are, questioning what is happening while they create what is happening, between the lines, said as they are forever said, with that tone, look, tempo, pause, evanescence.

I offer some concluding thoughts about why it is *Gaslight* that has prompted these remarks about reading films. Any of the films we consider will have some way of declaring its reflection upon the medium of film. *The Philadelphia Story* raises the question of the relation of moving to still photography, hence to a movie's relation to news in the form of celebrity and gossip; *Adam's Rib* raises the question more specifically of a movie's relation to a daily tabloid, hence to the interest in news in the form of illicit sex and violence. *Gaslight*'s emphasis on the surveillance of a captive object raises the question of the nature of the perception or reception of film, in relation, eventually, to the beholder of paintings and to the presence of a communal audience present with the actors in a theater. It accordingly should question how far the work of the camera is to be understood as that of Foucauldian surveillance, or monitoring, and what our position as viewers, or surveyors, is revealed to be; what it is we wish to know about what Paula knows. I have found it remarkable about Paula's consciousness that she has never inquired further about her mother, or, for that matter, her father, and I have taken the noises in the attic as her knowledge that her life is a ghost story, and was before Gregory's appearance. How do my intentions compare with Gregory's, or the young detective's?

What I have said about skepticism with respect to the other can be related to Levinas's claims for the other. Levinas requires our recognition of the other to be taken in passiveness, a way of saying that we are subject to the other and, contrariwise, that the other is presented to us in an accusatory mode, as if reflecting our inability to recognize him or her. As if the alternative to passiveness—receptiveness—is rejection, which I take as a certain kind of confirmation of the intuition I have expressed in saying that skepticism with respect to the other, the failure of a proof of the existence of the other, is not a discovery but an annihilation. It produces a process of psychic torture. *Gaslight*'s allegorizing of this aspect of the camera's potentiality, presenting the moving image as contributing to a conception of knowledge as capture and vampirism, is an insight that is hard to measure with what I claim are comparable insights arrived at in Mill's and Proust's related articulations.

In a film, unlike a painting or sculpture or piece of theater, we are given (captivated by) a forever fixed, captured, image of a human being in this precise environment, in these precise attitudes and relations, remaining silent or saying precisely these words precisely this way. (In film, contrary to theater, the actor takes precedence over the character.) The events are made to be examined and reexamined, to make one voluble, to be read for their possibilities, like a field of battle or a crime scene. It is a mystery why the convention developed, still in the process of being broken, of viewing a movie only once and, moreover, of accepting as criticism of a film the brief results of impressions upon seeing it once. A way of summarizing the permanence and evanescence of a movie—that it immortalizes the momentary, improvisatory, signature ways in which just this human being sits at a table or lifts a glass or opens a present or pays a taxi driver or crosses a busy street—is to note that films do not have different productions, though they may have different versions (a scene censored here, the ending changed there). They have what are called remakes, but the fascinating, illuminating experiment of Gus Van Sant in attempting to remake Hitchcock's *Psycho* by copying it shot by shot resulted in a so-so film which in effect proved that in an interesting sense there is no such thing as a remake.

Much of what I have been saying in this chapter relates to the conditions of the possibility of films, something that in my first book about film, *The World Viewed*, I call film's material conditions. There I claim that significant films are ones that most creatively explore the implications, one could say the identity, of these conditions. To say that *Gaslight* and *La Captive* both explore the condition of the camera's invasiveness or power of surveillance or vampirism is meant to imply that no way is dictated in which film's conditions are explored by films, and that the discovery of more and less fruitful and original and beautiful ways of exploration, it is the obligation of criticism to respond to and to articulate. If such criticism were to be thought of, with pleasure, as philosophical, this would be a satisfaction to me.

7

KANT

For Mill, in *On Liberty*, the reality of morality is discovered in the overcoming of conformity by inclination or desire. For Kant, the reality of morality is discovered in the overcoming of inclination by duty.

We have heard Mill's eloquence and outrage in the face of, in support of alleviating, human withering and spiritual starvation. For the thinking of a philosopher such as Kant, the eloquence of utilitarianism at its best would not amount to a *moral* judgment. It may be kind, it may be prudent, it requires skills of comprehension applied to real problems, but it does not project a vision in which the rational and moral nature of the human being manifests itself.

But does Mill's outrage sound merely kind or prudent or, for that matter, merely sympathetic? It seems something to call an expression of his moral nature. I do not say Mill has accounted for such an expression, nor that it is clear how utilitarianism is supposed to account for it. The problem is not so much that such a society is judged wrong by Mill for flouting the greatest happiness principle, but rather that the society is unjudgeable by the principle since it (its members generally) does not recognize the right to happiness, does not grasp the liberty to demand it.

For Kant, the very fact that Mill's eloquent appeal is to our *desire*—to what we find *desirable*, to what will make us happy, to what we regard as good rather than what we must know is right—displays the fact that eloquence is unstable, unpredictable. What is right must, as it were, speak for itself. When Mill turns to his reader to ask "Now is this the desirable condition of human nature or is it not?" he bases his appeal, you recall, on an analogy with our senses, not on our reason: As the only proof capable of being given that a thing is visible is that we see it, and so on, so the only proof that something is desirable is that we do in fact desire it.

Let's now, under the pressure of beginning to look at Kant's vision, read

Mill's analogy of the desirable with the visible, or read the difference between the desirable and the visible, by following out my sense of the force (or necessity) of Mill's implied question to his reader—Do you desire this state of human withering?—after Mill has already said that no one desires its opposite (namely, the state of liberty), meaning that no one feels entitled to ask the question of its desirability. This silence is evidently something Mill takes as itself expressive of the undesirable state of society. Mill's question, accordingly, is designed to break the silence, to awaken members of society to their right to ask the question of the incidence, or rather of the absence, of liberty in their lives. How can we understand an analogy here with the question whether something is visible? Surely we do not feel we need an entitlement in order to ask whether a thing is visible or audible? No, but Mill's question about desirability, about whether we desire a given state of soul and society, may be expressed in the form: "Do you see this? Look at what is done. Listen to what we say, and fail to say." The implication, analogously, allegorically, is that if we have permitted a condition of human nature to develop that we do not desire, and have said or done nothing to contest it, we are as if morally blind and deaf.

For Kant this is—reinterpreted—indeed a threat to human nature, but of a kind Mill does not recognize. The deafness is not to the claims of utilitarian routes to happiness but to our deontological route to self-respect, to our sense of right and of obligation. What we are to listen to, Kant calls the moral law. Without obedience to this law (obedience signifies hearing), moral deafness is not overcome, no moral improvement in the human condition is to be expected. If for Kant eloquence is unstable, unreliable, unpredictable, for Mill human misery cannot wait for our more perfect motivation.

Kant is taken by many philosophers to have achieved the most significant and influential recasting of the entire field of philosophy since the classical achievements of Plato and Aristotle and those of the philosopher/theologians of the middle ages. No one thinks this of Mill, so while Kant may well not satisfy his readers in various ways, it is likely to be harder in his case than in that of Mill to say convincingly what is wrong with his thinking—that is, to say something that Kant is credibly imagined not to have thought about and given some answer to.

This is a function of the power of Kant's systematicity—the *structure* of his thinking (what he called proudly his architectonic). This is, in the first instance, a description of the achievement of his *Critique of Pure Reason,* and beyond this of the unfolding of its implications about the validity and the limitation of human knowledge for the field of ethics (in the Second Critique, *The Critique of Practical Reason*) and for the field of, let's call it, aesthetics (in the Third Critique, *The Critique of Judgment*). I guess the interrelations of these three worlds have enlarged libraries around the world over the past two centuries more extensively, and more fruitfully, than any other intellectual project of Western culture.

But the power of Kant's thinking is not simply that he is systematic—that, indeed, he gives a new shape to what philosophical system should be. We might call this a complete unfolding of Reason, on the basis of human reason's systematic investigation of itself. It can be said of this achievement that it showed that philosophy can be a profession. I mean it showed that a professor of philosophy, working in the conditions of a modern university, could produce great philosophical work in meeting, in his way, the obligations of such an institution. The modern philosophers Kant responded to, Hume, Rousseau, Descartes, Spinoza, Leibniz, and so on were not professors of philosophy. And while the classical philosophers might be said to have taught in academies, their lives in their cultures were not ones that we would think of as academic lives. Nor, come to think of it, were those of Mill or Emerson or (except for a brief period in each case) Nietzsche or Wittgenstein.

In Kant's systematization, problems that thoughtful human beings find inescapable seem uncannily to pose themselves *intuitively,* with what I might call a strange familiarity, as the very problems of human life and aspiration, and in the very order of importance, that we had obscurely felt them to have: problems concerning the power and yet the impotence of human reason; concerning the ground of obligation; concerning the communicability of the sense of beauty; concerning the reality of God and of freedom of the will. We need to have some sense of the intuitiveness in this systematic structuring— an overall sketch of the power of these architectural pictures or diagrams and diagnoses of our intellectual life—to prepare for our reading of Kant's relatively short, intensely argued, *Groundwork of the Metaphysics of Morals.* It is this architecture (differences between our knowledge of appearances and our supposing of a realm of unknowable things-in-themselves that generate appearances, of the categories that organize these appearances and the ideas of reason that go beyond them; perhaps most generally of this articulation of the idea of human knowledge as well grounded but limited) that philosophers have been inspired by and struggling with since Kant devised it, philosophers from Hegel and Nietzsche to Heidegger, Derrida, and Wittgenstein.

———————

Before trying to provide this overall sketch I should introduce two pairs of distinctions whose ideas were not original with Kant but which are familiar to philosophers in the form bequeathed to the field by Kant. Kant's project in the First Critique was to show how we are assured that our judgments of the world are objective, not approximations out of our subjective conditions of knowing (putting together sensations to figure what cannot be known to be true of things in themselves), but necessarily applicable to anything we can call a world, a world of objects, how they manifest the conditions of the possibility of our knowing a world at all. The new problem Kant saw in the task of establishing the objectivity or validity of knowledge as such (a problem generally thought to have presented itself to him in response to Hume's skepticism about knowledge) is expressed in a pair of distinctions that, though developed and contested in each generation—in the twentieth century, especially in the analytical tradition of philosophy—remain part of the parlance of professional philosophy; you cannot say what the productive contesting of the distinctions has been without invoking them pretty much in Kant's terms.

One distinction is between two ways in which judgments can claim to be true—either by its predicate "analyzing" its subject, "adding nothing" to its meaning ("Every effect has a cause," "Every widow had a husband"), or else by the predicate "adding something" truly to the subject, synthesizing it with a further concept ("This crack was an event caused by heat," "This woman had a husband"). The former are analytical judgments, the latter are synthetic judgments. The negation of an analytical judgment is a contradiction ("Some widows never had husbands"), or else some kind of riddle; the negation of a synthetic judgment is another synthetic judgment, false if the original was true, true otherwise.

To this distinction in ways of being true Kant adduces a distinction between ways of knowing each kind of judgment is true. Analytical judgments are true by virtue of the meanings of the concepts they contain, known in understanding what is being said, without—or before—consulting one's experience of the world. Kant says they are known *a priori*. Synthetic judgments are known only by—or after—consulting one's experience of the world. Kant says they are known *a posteriori*. The judgments "Every effect has a cause" and "Every widow had a husband" are known to be true, we could say, in the very saying of them. On the contrary, the judgments "Every *event* has a cause" and "Every *woman* has a husband," in the straightforward sense of these words, are not known to be true (or false) just, as it were, by understanding what is said. Summarizing the obvious result of the interaction of these two distinctions: analytical judgments are known a priori, synthetic judgments a posteriori.

Remember that Kant's interest is to determine how judgments can be true *of the world* (of anything we can call a world) *necessarily*, before our experience of the world, necessary to our experience of the world. This can now be put as asking how there can be synthetic judgments that are known a priori. Kant's answer is that they manifest the conditions under which it is possible for a world of objects to be known at all. To know that the law of causation holds of our world is to know that the judgment "Every event [not just, analytically, every effect] has a cause" is true a priori—which is to say, in Kant's terms, true universally and necessarily. To show this Kant has to invent, beyond general logic, what he calls transcendental logic: think of it, in a phrase from Wittgenstein's *Investigations*, as "the basis, or essence, of everything empirical" (§89). *The Critique of Pure Reason* runs in German to something over eight hundred pages.

Something I meant by the architecture of Kant's thought is that he extends his discovery of the significance of synthetic a priori judgments beyond the grounding of our knowledge of the world (and its consequent criticism of metaphysics which thinks to go beyond the a priori conditions that make such judgments possible), and shows them equally grounding in the realms (worlds) of morality (the Second Critique) and of art (the Third Critique). Judgments of what ought to be done are synthetic (for example, that suicide is wrong, that this child is to be cared for, that this worthy man in need is to be helped, that a promise is to be kept). If morality is to be real, say objective, if it is to be shown not merely as a function of my good nature or natural sympathy (shaky reeds for so fateful a task) but as proceeding from and answerable to reason, such judgments must hold a priori. What can be the synthesis between such judgments and a transcendental necessity making possible the existence of, let's call it, a moral universe? Again, an aesthetic judgment is synthetic—"This is beautiful," "This is sublime." Can we determine what makes such judgments necessary, not merely a matter of my preferences, my private, shifting tastes, but grounded a priori in the conditions of possibility of making objective judgments, anyway intersubjective judgments, in this realm at all?

In the case of knowing the objective world, the shared world of objects, the conditions of possibility lie in a complete set of transcendental categories of judgment that can be shown to impose themselves necessarily upon the mode of the deliverances of our senses, our perception of things in space and time. In the case of the world of objects of art, the universality and necessity that define the a priori are imposed by, we might say, the power of our judgments themselves, by their ability to speak rationally in invoking what Kant calls "the universal voice"—which takes the form of our instituting a demand for agreement, a demand imposed upon us by reason (as a consequence of our judgment going beyond our tastes and claiming a basis in the experience of these objects as such) that may nevertheless fail of success. Reason here in effect demands an unavoidable risk.

In the case of the moral world, the a priori grounding of judgment—that without which there would be no such world—is imposed by the moral law, the categorical imperative. So the question becomes: What does a law look like that can command universal and necessary observance?—which is to say, that can show a synthetic judgment to be known a priori, that is, show it to be undeniable even though its negation is not obviously a contradiction, and even though saying of an act that it ought to be done seems to "add" something to it. The answer will have to do with the particular relation of the moral law to the motivation of the judgment upon which my action is based, which is not something added to the action, but something that makes it the action it is.

In the case of the aesthetic and moral judgments it seems to me intuitive to say generally that what carries the force of judgment is the very understanding of what is said, the saying of it as such. In the case of aesthetic judgment my voicing of the universal voice imposes itself on others. In the case of moral judgment, the universal voice of the moral law imposes itself upon me. But the idea of something's carrying the force of truth by virtue of the very saying of it was characteristic of analytical judgments, not synthetic judgments. Does this suggest that what distinguishes the force of aesthetic and moral judgments from judgments of knowledge about the objects of the world is that in the former the distinction in force between analytic and synthetic judgments does not apply, that the role of the imposition of the judgment has to be related in a different way to the authority of the one speaking, or said otherwise, to the origin of the right in confronting another, to an assessment of one's standing with another (and with oneself)?

Even the bare dates of Kant's intervention in Western culture seem significant (as though the lives of private individuals and public events are in some new relation). The two editions of the First Critique, in roughly the first half of the 1780s, were bracketed by the American and the French Revolutions, as though these private and public pairs of events were two faces of the same revolutionary project in human history, namely the realization of a universal realm of reason and freedom in human existence. Hegel most famously undertook the philosophical working out of this vision.

In *Pursuits of Happiness,* where I sketch the results of *The Critique of Pure Reason* as the "foundation" for Kant's moral theory, I present Kant as a philosopher of limitation, hence of aspiration. Philosophy from the beginning conceives humankind in contrast to God—call this conceiving humans as mortals, or as finite (which we might think of as making humans unique not in coming to an end but in knowing that they come to an end). With respect to knowledge, think of it this way: God in his infiniteness knows things as they are in themselves and in their totality— past, present, and future all immediately spread before him. Whereas we finite creatures know things only as they appear to us, in space and in time, as individual substances with properties, subject to causal laws, and so on. Kant transforms our very finitude, our limitedness, into the power that creates the necessary conditions for the possibility of human knowledge of the world.

What we call the objects of the world just *are* what satisfy the human conditions under which we know anything at all. (Hume, the skeptic, had found that we cannot *know* that such a thing as causation operates in nature. We know that certain experiences in fact follow other experiences, but there is no necessity in this connection. Kant answers that the rule of causation— and other rules of the understanding—are necessary in this sense, that if they did not hold of the world there would be nothing we could call a world.) We know Kant calls his insight, and its consequences, a Copernican

Revolution in philosophy. Part of the idea is that, as we have learned to understand the motions of the heavenly bodies as functions of the motion of the earth, the human habitation, so we have to understand the motions (the essential properties) of the objects of knowledge (let's say, the earthly bodies) as functions of the motions (the essential powers) of the human mind and its concepts and perceptions. So part of the idea of a philosophical Copernican Revolution is that it turns our ideas of the relation of earth and heaven upside down again, reconceiving the human habitation at the center of the known universe.

A principal, one might say immediate, consequence of this insight is that we do not know things *except* as they appear to us, or as Kant puts the matter, we do not know things-in-themselves. And the status of the thing-in-itself therewith became, for those caught up in the Kantian revolutionary insight, a great and permanent philosophical question. It is a way of putting Kant's principal legacy, or cause, of German Idealism—the relation of the mind to the world as such, not as its detector but as its creator. We can at once say: Whatever our relation to things-in-themselves will turn out to be, it cannot be one of knowing; on Kant's vision of things, there is strictly no possibility of knowing that the human conditions of knowledge are those which reveal the nature of things apart from those conditions.

In showing that our knowledge of objects, within those conditions, is guaranteed as universal and necessary (which means guaranteed as applicable before we consider any given instance of knowledge), Kant takes himself to have accomplished one of his main objectives in his philosophical project, namely to answer skepticism, to prove the existence of objects "outside of us," in effect to provide a philosophical grounding for the achievements of Newtonian science. At the same time he interprets the price, or limitation, of his answer—namely that we do not know things-in-themselves—as itself a philosophical advance, fulfilling a companion objective of his philosophical project, which in another of his famous phrases, or mottoes, he calls his limiting knowledge in order to make room for faith. This reconciling of the human investments in science and in religion, yielding to each its separate and humanly necessary world, is one of the principal and persisting attractions of the Kantian system.

Kant's solution to what he calls "the scandal of skepticism" is part of what has sustained or nourished my interest in tracing the scandal. Suppose we articulate Kant's solution to the scandal by saying: whatever our relation to the world as such (call this the unconditioned cause of the conditioned world) turns out to be (Kant calls this faith), it cannot be one of knowledge. Then it is a question for me whether this is an answer to skepticism or a further description of its truth.

To have drawn (supposing Kant did accomplish what he set out to accomplish) the precise and final map of human ignorance of what is beyond the conditions in which human knowledge exists (of the existence of God, of the immortality of the soul, and of human freedom)—and to have articulated intellectual capacities within these conditions—represents a traumatic increase of knowledge. The classical empiricists, Locke and Hume, also based their thinking on the human powers of experience, and also wished to follow, or substantiate, the lead of the New Science in pushing forward the world-changing developments in our positive knowledge of the world. And they had also spoken of the limitations of human knowledge—since it is ultimately based upon the deliverances of our senses, which are, in Hume's words, "so limited in extent and duration"—and urged us to confine our intellectual aspirations to accord with our finite powers. But Kant takes two decisive steps beyond this empiricist picture of our indubitable limitations (say in how far our senses reach into the world).

First, in specifying our limits as knowers in terms of conditions of any human knowledge, Kant is able to systematize these conditions in what he regarded as a final knowable form, namely in taking space and time as the forms in which the human senses prepare the world of appearances for our understanding, and in providing the system of Categories of the Understanding (for example, that of causation and that of substances and their properties) in which those appearances are organized into knowledge. He does not deny the empiricist claim that our knowledge of the world begins with experience, but he, as with virtually every other standing philosophical problem or idea, has his own interpretation of the claim: he interprets "beginning with experience" as invoking the *passive* (sensuous) side of human nature, requiring, in order to add up to what we call knowledge, the *active* (intellectual) side, organizing, forming, experience under categories of the understanding, which turn out to be derived from the fundamental forms in which we make coherent judgments of the world, individuated into stable objects with observable, changing properties, related to each other causally, and so on. And again, Kant's settlement has left permanent, contested legacies. For example, whether the intellect is essentially active, required to *impose* itself upon the world, remains a live question for Heidegger, and, on my view, for Wittgenstein.

The second step Kant takes beyond the empiricist's declaration of our limitations as knowers is to recognize the philosophical significance of the fact that the human being will not stay within these limits but will inevitably attempt to transcend them. That they are in a sense to be transcended is recognized in Kant's perception of "making room for faith." But what Kant also recognizes is the human propensity to think of its powers as penetrating beyond the limits of human knowledge, not with faith but with a higher knowledge, rivaling, as I have put the matter, God's knowledge. And, as with everything else Kant touches, he systematizes it; he specifies the ways in which we do (can, must) attempt to transcend our human condition. One of these ways is superstition (claiming to know objects beyond knowledge), another is fanaticism (proclaiming certainties beyond the attestations of knowledge), another is skepticism (criticizing knowledge against an inhuman idea of knowledge). (These distortions of human intellect are studied by Kant in his book *Religion within the Limits of Reason Alone*.)

The intuitive idea captured by this systematization is, I would like to say, the idea of the human creature as essentially *restless*. Kant has a famous motto or formulation for this intuition as well. The opening sentence of the preface to the first edition of the *Critique of Pure Reason* runs as follows: "Human reason has this peculiar fate that in one species of its knowledge it is burdened by questions which, as prescribed by the very nature of reason itself, it is not able to ignore, but which as transcending all its powers, it is also not able to answer." The idea of the human as a burden to itself, tormenting itself, is an idea taken up by the Romantics in the generation succeeding Kant's. What I am calling human restlessness is for me a fundamental, motivating idea of Wittgenstein's *Philosophical Investigations*, a perpetual seeking, perpetually undermined, for what Wittgenstein calls rest, or peace.

The faith for which Kant seeks to make room is faith in the existence of God and in the immortality of the soul, but also in the present reality of human freedom, which is to say, in the reality of morality, which for Kant means in the ability to act in opposition to the laws of our sensuous nature, to those laws which, he has established, govern our knowledge of the world, hence govern us, as members of that world, subject to the laws of causal determination that any material object of that world must obey. ("If you cut us do we not bleed?") How are we coherently to understand our capacity to be guided by reason, how, for example can we know that we will be able to keep a promise if, when the time comes, keeping it goes somewhat sharply against our inclinations? Nietzsche is still marveling at the spectacle: "To breed an animal with the right to make promises . . . is it not man's true problem?" No (other) animal in our world has such an endowment. Kant recognizes this human exception in another memorable formulation, which asks what it means, if I may put it so, to say that the human exists "in" the world—a way of putting matters (I know that for some of you this will be obvious) that I mean to announce the topic of Heidegger's *Being and Time*. Kant's formulation is: Man lives in two worlds, in one of which he is determined [by being fated to the laws of causation], in the other free [to do what reason commands].

In the third section of the *Groundwork of the Metaphysics of Morals*, Kant pictures this doubleness as our having "two standpoints" from which to consider ourselves and our actions (Ak. 453). The sensible, sensuous world is laid out in the system of the First Critique. The other, the intelligible, world is further laid out in the Second Critique and in the rest of Kant's various writings on ethics. Since both of these worlds, or standpoints, are conceived by us as "realms," they are conceived as presided over by laws. And for Kant the giver of law is always and everywhere human Reason.

The field of our sensations—the field opened by our sensorium or manifold of experience—places us in space and time, but it does not reveal a world of objects. We have a sense of before and after and of here and there but not of this and that—in a sense not of ourselves as subjects, what is I and not-I. For this we require Understanding, bringing law to this manifold, articulating it with a further order of universality and necessity, providing us with the assurance that there is a world of objects we share. In Kant's moral philosophy there is, as it were, another, or further, bringer of law, beyond Understanding so conceived, namely Reason, this time bringing law not to a homogeneous but mute order of the senses, but to the chaos of impulses in our sensuous, animal nature. And what it brings is also to be thought of as objectivity.

Think of it this way. Without Reason we would be condemned to the random promptings of impulse, desire, affection, which are by their nature subjective, prompting only to me, and only when they are present. Reason provides us with the idea and the possibility of a shared world, a moral universe by—as in the discourse of the *Critique of Pure Reason*—providing our judgments with universality and necessity. Only here, in the moral realm, reason provides these characteristics not for judgments that yield the possibility of knowledge of objects in the world but for the principle of actions that secures their objectivity in the world.

Is this move from objective knowledge (that is, a knowledge of objects) to objective conduct (or from the necessity of knowledge to necessity of conduct) more than a pun, or a metaphorical shift? Kant seems to trust that the characteristics he has discovered for judgments to be assured a priori of referring to objects, namely that they be universal and necessary, must, applied to moral judgment, that is, to the principle upon which moral conduct is taken, also yield universality and necessity. Of course there are differences: the universality is not assured as the categories of the understanding assure cognitive objectivity, it is a universality in the moral realm that each of us has to bring to our principle of action; and the necessity in the moral realm takes the form of an imperative. But this no longer seems so much like a pun or an allegory as like what you would expect of the difference between knowledge and morality. Kant has shown what this difference is. This profit from philosophical system can seem too good to be true. (Imagine one's surprise when these characteristics of universality and necessity find an intuitive, if transfigured, application to the realm of the aesthetics as well!)

The idea is something like this. Our understanding is objective not because there are objects given to it; rather, our understanding can grasp objects—there can be objects for us—because it organizes experience according to the laws that anything we can accept as a world of objects must obey. Our reason is objective not because we derive the concept of a moral act from experience of the world (where it may be doubted that any act is truly or purely moral); rather, there can be moral acts in our world because reason already possesses a moral law which any act we can accept as moral must obey. In both cases what we, or let's say, what the mind brings to the world is a power that takes it, so to speak, beyond itself, beyond its own subjectivity, in the cognitive realm beyond the present deliverances of the senses, in the moral realm beyond the chaos of its sensuous inclinations. This must be related to Kant's insistence that reason is active, that it imposes its necessities upon existence. Were the senses similarly to be active, rather than passive, their imperative deliverances would be hallucinations.

The distinction between Understanding and Reason is greatly important in the formation of Romanticism, of which Kant is a principal source, where Kant's emphasis on grounding scientific knowledge (as well as grounding the necessity for faith) tended to become a way of confining our loyalty to knowledge and releasing the imagination to explore its own worlds (as in Blake), or to explore the world another way (as in Wordsworth). For Kant there is a further problem. If the understanding is reason applied to the knowledge of objects, and morality is reason applied to the will, is this the same reason at work—is Reason a unity?

We have said that in both its theoretical employment (to achieve knowledge of the world) and in its practical, moral employment (to realize one's duties in the world), reason acts as lawgiver and source of objectivity (that in both employments it is world-creating), but we have also said that these laws apply differently in nature and in morality. Can we specify this difference?

In the case of our knowledge of nature, we have no choice over whether the laws of our reason apply to it or not. What alternative could there be to the knowledge of nature? Ignorance of nature? What would this be? A lack of awareness of any causal regularity, as of the rising and setting of the sun, of the seasons, of the satisfaction of hunger by food, of the relation of planting to harvesting, of violence to death, of the persistence of an object through changes in its condition or its location or its reappearance after sleep? To be ignorant of nature, of the system of enduring objects, as such, would be to be ignorant not of something about the world, or something in the world, but of such a thing as a world at all. What choice do we have over that? To choose such ignorance would be like trying to choose to be an animal or an insect. Or would it require—since animals know something, even a totality of somethings (Heidegger says they are world-poor)—trying to choose to be a stone.

But in the case of our moral conduct, we do have a choice over whether the laws of the moral world apply to us or not. And this is as we should expect: there is an alternative to moral goodness, namely moral evil. This seems implicit in Kant's discussion: to say that the moral law presents itself to us as an imperative or command which we "ought" to obey is exactly to leave it open (to each of us) whether we will, in a given case, in fact obey it. I don't mean merely that we may fall short, despite our efforts, of obeying the law fully, on all occasions. Kant says explicitly that we cannot know about anyone, including ourselves, that our obedience is pure, free of inclination, and that such purity is highly, given our sensuous nature, unlikely. What

I mean, rather, is that it seems we might choose evil, choose to thwart the very possibility of morality, deny its reality.

With the ideas of the possibility, and reality, of morality we are at the door of Kant's *Groundwork of the Metaphysics of Morals*. Let's try to open it.

Put things still another way. In knowledge of the physical world of objects the human mind imposes laws. In its membership in the moral realm (the realm of human subjects) the human mind is *subject* to the law. As Kant also puts the matter (Ak. 412): "Everything in nature works in accordance with laws [including human beings, so far as they are natural things]. Only a rational being has the capacity to act *in accordance with the representation* [or idea] *of laws,* that is, in accordance with principles, or has a *will* [which no merely natural thing has]. Since *reason* is required for the derivation of actions from laws, the will is nothing other than practical reason."

The new science had denied that the upper and the lower worlds obeyed different laws (celestial and terrestrial); Kant asserts that there are different laws, or different ways of obeying laws, for the outer and the inner worlds. That the law of subjection comes from the subject itself, that it is to command what it is also to obey, is the key to what Kant will call moral freedom.

What gives subjectivity this power over itself? I said: In the moral life we have a choice over whether to impose the moral law upon ourselves. But for an action to count as moral we have to choose it—evaluate it—in a particular way, by a particular criterion, as falling under a particular unique law, the moral law, the categorical imperative. This is perhaps Kant's most famous doctrine—that right, moral conduct is guided by a categorical imperative. To understand the doctrine we accordingly need to understand, first, what a categorical imperative is and, second, what it is to be guided by such a thing on particular occasions.

The first issue, identifying a categorical imperative, is comparatively easy to formulate. We know, assuming the idea of reason as imposing a law, that moral judgments take the form of imperatives, that they are "expressed by an *ought*" (Ak. 413). Kant locates the imperative in question through the idea that "all imperatives command either *hypothetically* or *categorically*" (Ak. 414). He continues: "The former represents the practical necessity of a possible action as a means to achieving something else that one wills [or conceivably could]. The categorical imperative would be that which represented an action as objectively necessary of itself, without reference to another end." To offer help at your disposal to a child in distress is an imperative, a duty, that is not dependent or contingent on the hypothesis that you will receive money or a medal, or even some secret personal satisfaction, for your trouble, but is unconditional, or, Kant will sometimes add here, objective. If we were, in an image of Kant's, beasts or angels, we would respond to such a situation as our nature dictates. In the case of animals, an instinct will lead a mother to protect her young; in the case of angels, good is as it were the natural law of their being. The idea of an *ought* is in both cases out of order, indeed is in order only for the mixed or dual or divided creatures we humans are, who sometimes call their kind the rational animal.

So Kant's problem is something like this: How can such an imperative, an ought, a duty, be derived by reason from a law, thus showing that duty acts unconditionally, or as Kant puts it, that "duty is not as such an empty concept" (Ak. 421)? (Christine Korsgaard, in her introduction to the translation published by Cambridge University Press, puts this as showing that "morality is real.")

This perception of duty, or obligation to show duty's purity, is one within which Emersonian perfectionism will not seem a moral outlook at all, not now because it is taken as providing an essentially unjust teleological distribution of resources, but because its concerns for others are characteristically for friends, hence based on attraction not obligation. But the conversations characteristic of moral perfectionism, as exemplified in our genres of film, concern issues that seem to me morally real, indeed ones which make up the fabric of serious relationships—issues such as whether judging the lives of others according to elevated standards might not indicate a frigidity of character; or whether it is justified to risk a client's case in court in order to dramatize a social wrong; or on what basis slaps and even slugs are forgivable; or what conditions there are under which equal moral conversation is undermined. To exclude such matters from the realm of morality would seem to me to confine morality either to claustrophobic scruples or to parliamentary debates on legislation.

(I anticipate here my sense that the featured four examples Kant presents after introducing the first formulation of the categorical imperative seem to me fantasies of essentially isolated, friendless people. From this sense, the claim that in Kant duty is shown not to be empty seems prejudicial. Conversations in which friends explore whether an act is indeed your duty, meaning any of your business, as well as meaning your inescapable business, and whether if it is, it is to be denied the name of doing your duty if you do it, for example, out of guilt, or remorse, or joy, seem to me to be of the essence of a moral life and to leave open what makes duty real.)

The second issue before us, understanding what it is to "derive" a duty from a law, is harder to formulate, the topic of endless debate. What is this law, and what is this derivation?

The law appears with quite melodramatic suddenness, or rather out of the identification of the reality of duty expressed as an unconditioned imperative imposed by a law of reason. Here is the moment (Ak. 420–421):

> When I think of a *hypothetical* imperative in general I do not know before-hand what it will contain; I do not know this until I am given the condition [the incentive under which I will do what is asked]. But when I think of a *categorical* imperative I know at once what it contains. For, since the imperative contains, beyond the law, only the necessity that the maxim be in conformity with this law, while the law contains no condition to which it would be limited, nothing is left with which the maxim of action is to conform but the universality of a law as such; and this conformity alone is what the imperative properly represents as necessary . . . There is, therefore, only a single categorical imperative and it is this: *act only in accordance with that maxim through which you can at the same time will that it become a universal law . . .* The universal imperative of duty can also go as follows: *act as if the maxim of your action were to become by your will a universal law of nature.*

Something tremendous is to have happened here. Whether or not it is to have the force of an argument, Kant calls it the explication of a concept, of "what the concept [of duty] wants to say" (Ak. 421). Kant immediately goes into his four examples of duty to clarify the force of his discovery, namely to show that the attempt to escape a duty leads to a contradiction of the moral law conceived as a universalizing of the message of your act.

The first example is of a man considering suicide, evidently an escape from the duty of self-preservation. Kant declares that the maxim of his action is: "From self-love I make it my principle to shorten my life when its longer duration threatens more troubles than it promises agreeableness" (Ak. 422). "It is seen at once," Kant declares further, that universalizing this maxim into a law of nature would contradict itself since it uses self-love, which is to further life, to destroy life. Since it could not, therefore, be a law of nature, it opposes the supreme principle of all duty, namely the Categorical Imperative."

I don't know how many among the army of Kant's admirers who have interpreted this text, and in particular these examples, which are hard to ignore, actually believe in this idea of contradiction, either as a description of a person's motivation or as part of a conversation persons might have with themselves (or others) to dissuade them from suicide. Counting myself among Kant's admirers, while no doubt not a Kantian (unless Wittgenstein and Heidegger are to be counted as Kantians; they surely are made possible by Kant), I do not find Kant's descriptions here compelling. How important this is is a matter of how important you find examples to be, and philosophers differ dramatically on this issue.

Yet there is surely something deeply intuitive in the thought experiment of universalization that Kant asks us to perform. His claim that "it is seen at once" is essential to his thought that duty has no conditions: to recognize its categorical nature is "to know at once what it contains." It is the very form, the pure form, of what is imperative. Is there a way to capture its importance without having to believe that universalizing it contradicts, or makes impossible, a fantasied law of nature and hence opposes the moral law? I know of no commentator (which perhaps says little, although I have done my share of reading and listening to lectures on Kant) who asks what the intuitive force of the idea of a "maxim" of an action is. Kant more or less assumes the obviousness of the idea and uses it to explain how an action in accordance with duty is "derived" from reason, namely because the objective principle of morality, the moral law, applies not to the action directly (as, for example, motives do in the form of passions or inclinations) but to its subjective principle, which Kant calls its maxim, which it generalizes.

Given the trouble readers have had identifying "the" maxim of an action, together with its essential importance to Kant's argument, it seems extraordinary that Kant assumed it as obvious. Indeed, among the most remarkable features of the idea, to my mind, is Kant's insight that actions indeed *have* maxims. (We are more or less familiar with the idea that speaking is a mode of acting; we are perhaps less familiar with the idea that acting is a mode of speaking—an idea however that seems pervasive in Freud and in Shakespeare.)

It occurs to me that Kant may simply have been extending the ordinary idea of a maxim as a piece of encapsulated practical advice—"Early to bed and early to rise makes a man healthy wealthy and wise"; "Neither a borrower nor a lender be"—which in effect guides and generalizes action. But is

Kant assuming that every action is guided in this way? What is *the* maxim of your action now, that is, what are you doing and why are you doing it? Are you sitting quietly in a classroom or studying philosophy or satisfying a requirement or testing whether your interest in literature or theology can be taken where it wants to go without a detour into philosophy, and are you doing any of these things, or countless others, out of self-love, or self-punishment, or to please your parents, or out of defiance of your parents, or to delay a career in the law, or to win a bet, or out of sheer joy? This indefiniteness in the description of an action alerts us to the task of locating Kant's apparent ease in selecting a maxim. The circumstances he describes in each of his four examples are ones in which a person is pictured as *being stopped from acting* by asking himself a question (in the fourth Kant asks the question on the person's behalf), namely whether the maxim can be universalized, willed as a universal law.

The prohibition, or sense of transgression, thus occurs *before* the universalization takes place. Before acting the man knew to question his proposed conduct. How did he know this? With respect to the suicidal man, Kant says he was "still so far in possession of his reason that he could question whether [his act] would be contrary to his duty to himself"; with respect to the second man, who is about to make a false promise, Kant says "he still has enough conscience to ask himself: is it not forbidden and contrary to duty to help oneself out of need in this way?" The state of such a man seems to be one that presents the thought of an act as a temptation; and it is this temptation which identifies the act whose maxim must be subject to the test of the law. And shall we say that the temptation is caused by an obscure awareness of the law, or that the sense of temptation, of a tainted, self-serving motive, produces the idea of the law? And do we say to a despairing person contemplating suicide, or imagine him saying to himself, that he is acting self-destructively out of self-love hence contradictorily or incoherently? We might, and it may be just the thing to say. But it might equally mean that we had not taken his despair seriously. Have you already talked with him about the sources of the despair?

In identifying moral worth with acting out of duty, out of respect for the moral law, Kant from time to time shows his scorn, or directs his irony, toward the idea that benevolence can substitute for duty. For example, at Ak. 398: "To be beneficent where one can is a duty, and besides there are many souls so sympathetically attuned that . . . they find an inner satisfaction in spreading joy around them and can take delight in the satisfaction of others so far as it is their own work. But I assert that in such a case an action of this kind, however it may conform with duty and however amiable it may be [and deserving of praise, since "it fortunately lights upon what is in fact in the common interest"], has nevertheless no true moral worth [and does not deserve esteem]."

Note that phrase "take delight in the satisfaction of others so far as it is their own work." It has—does it not?—that ring of Dickensian irony I noted in Mill's praise of a contemporary "philanthropic spirit" that is concerned with the moral conduct of others. And sure enough, in the following sentence Kant names the "philanthropist" about whom he expresses the following fantasm, that "the mind of this philanthropist was clouded over by his own grief, which extinguished all sympathy with the fate of others" and that "he nevertheless tears himself out of this deadly insensibility and [benefits others in distress] without any inclination, simply from duty; then the action first has its genuine moral worth"; it "give[s] himself a far higher worth than what a mere good-natured temperament might have." That Mill expresses as great a scorn for "mere benevolence" as Kant does at least shows that this perception does not require a new explication of the concept of duty and morality.

And mightn't one feel, despite Kant's assurance, that a philanthropist's being able to tear himself out of a deadly insensibility is as thin a reed on which to base the alleviation of distress as the unpredictable occurrences of what Kant once scornfully describes as "melting sympathy" (Ak. 399)? It may be said that Kant leaves plenty of room for less melodramatic, more everyday, observances of the duty of beneficence (for example, Ak. 398), and that Kant's case (what I have somewhat meanly characterized as a fantasm) of the difficulty in alleviating distress out of duty serves only to make vivid what duty demands, not to portray the context in which it always operates.

But is it the case that fulfilling everyday duties (helping someone rather frail onto a trolley, laying in groceries for a friend with the flu, not yielding to favoritism in giving a grade or voting an award, hearing out a friend in grief, not cheating on taxes) gives one a higher moral worth if one fulfills them grimly or affectlessly rather than with occasional feelings of mild satisfaction, mild exasperation, or relief, and with no thought in the world whether everyone else does such things or not? (Here I think I may be risking that moral snobbery which I identified as the characteristic vice of perfectionist aspirations.) What is certainly true is that what ought to happen, anyway what is necessary, in furtherance of the cooperativeness of our lives should not depend upon the beneficence or benevolence of individual others. If it does, that is not a sign of a lack of individual, ordinary moral worth, but of a poorly formed society, a society with too great an incidence, or opportunity, for unsociability, or for corruption, or for tyranny. (I assume something of this sort is a guiding insight of Rawls's *A Theory of Justice*.)

Some Kantians, for perhaps reasons or sentiments of these kinds, have found Kant's further formulations of the categorical imperative (Kant says his three formulations say the same thing) better to capture the sublimity Kant finds in the moral law. The first formulation (which we were just considering) is called the Formula of Universal Law. The second is the Formula of Humanity: "*So act that you use humanity, whether in your own person or in the person of any other, always at the same time as an end, never merely as a means*" (Ak. 429). The third formulation of the moral law is Autonomy or the Kingdom of Ends: "the *principle* of every human will as *a will giving universal law through all its maxims*" (Ak. 432). This third formulation makes explicit that others legislate for me as well as I for them, that I am at once the law's subject and its sovereign, that in obeying it I am obeying myself, which is to say, in obeying the law I act autonomously. This formulation joins us, so far as we join ourselves to it, in what Kant calls a kingdom (or realm) of ends.

The idea that those who aspire to a moral life (I might say a philosophical life, more anciently called an examined life), already live, as it were, in an association (real or imaginary) other than the one manifested in our everyday world of imperfect laws and enforcements and unstable or unworthy incentives is a deeply attractive one. I have described something I take as its analogue, from a perfectionist outlook, as the idea of an unattained but attainable further state of society present within this one. (That there is equally a worse state within this one is stressed, as we shall see, in the picture of communal degeneration in Plato's *Republic*.)

I have stressed that construing the Kantian corpus of texts continues to provide instruction and enjoyment for many philosophers. It is not practical for us to go further with it. I have wanted to make intuitive just enough of it to suggest its decisive importance for Emersonian perfectionism, for what Emerson found undeniable yet unsatisfactory in the Kantian settlement.

I noted earlier the transcription of the vision of Kant's *Groundwork* in the opening sentence of the last paragraph of Emerson's "Experience": "I know that the world I converse with in the city and in the farms, is not the world I *think*." And the paragraph goes on to give Emerson's solution to his version of the problem that Kant says, in concluding the *Groundwork*, "we cannot solve." "It is impossible for us to explain, in other words, *how pure reason can be practical* [which would be exactly the same task as to explain *how freedom is possible*], and all the pains and labor of seeking an explanation of it are lost" (Ak. 461, 459). What I am calling Emerson's version of this unanswerable question is his picturing himself as being asked: "Why not realize your world?" He has just said that he has "not found that much was gained by manipular attempts to realize the world of thought," meaning by efforts to make reason practical, by individual acts of will (what Emerson calls "solitary examples of success")—hence presumably much would be gained only by a change in our ways of life. But then these will have to change precisely not through willing but by "patience and patience," through which "we shall win at the last." Which is to say, not by action but by suffering, of which Emerson's continuous example is his writing, which continuously and patiently gives expression to his aversion to the ways things are, that is, to the ways he and his countrymen keep things.

I am not here, plainly, going to attempt to convince you of the plausibility of Emerson's proposal; it would be satisfaction enough to convince you that he composed "Self-Reliance" with the *Groundwork* as if open at his elbow. Since I can hardly now undertake to verify this, I can at least indicate something of the way the Kantian concepts of autonomy, conformity, and constraint play decisive roles in "Self-Reliance."

For Emerson, the foundation of morality, of the expression of my freedom, can also be said to be based on a law I give to myself (as the title "Self-Reliance" at once suggests). Of course Emerson is going to be devious or duplicitous in his formulation, out of his sense of truly satisfying words as ones that have been reclaimed from their counterfeit currency. When he says, for example, "No law can be sacred to me but that of my own nature," and continues by saying "Good and bad are but names readily transferable to that or this; the only right is what is after my constitution; the only wrong what is against it," he means by "constitution," as he always does, his private makeup as well as the Constitution of the United States, call this the expression of a universalization of that private makeup. So to consult his constitution, sacred laws to which he is subject which at the same time bind (in principle all) others in a realm of ends, is already to invoke a conversation that has to consider not only what is necessary but what is possible, given what is actual, a conversation that is simultaneously a criticism (Kant says "assessment") of my private projects and of my society's.

Emerson also declares himself subject to what he recognizes as constraint, as when, having invoked the figure of "the true man," he declares, "You are constrained to accept his standard." But this Emersonian constraint is precisely not expressed as an "ought." Rather, it is as like a desire as like a law; Emerson figures it as a form of attraction, as if to my further self. For the true man is what we each may stand for: "I will stand here for humanity, and though I would make it kind, I would make it true." (I merely note the occurrence of that Shakespearean "kind," indicating both generality and partiality.) "Stand here for" describes us as able to bear up as representative men, reciprocally drawing each other on to "the possible of man."

The need for a transformation in the idea of constraint, of a distrust of the moralistic "oughts" current in society, arises, I believe, from Emerson's speaking of "conformity" as being the virtue most in demand, and announcing "self-reliance" as its aversion. I hear it in relation to such a characteristic passage from Kant's *Groundwork* as this: "The often anxious care that most people take of [their life] . . . has no inner worth . . . They look after their lives *in conformity with duty* but not *from duty*" (Ak. 398). Kant is careful not to despise conformity with duty, but merely places its value lower than that of the reality of duty.

Emerson's—and Mill's—scorn of conformity indicates a sense that something in human life has changed, that most people who have some choice in their lives are as afraid to insist on their own desires as they are unable to determine their duties by discounting those desires. Instead they quote, they imitate, *they go along.* Hence in addition to the true man, Emerson invokes (something I called attention to in Chapter 1) a second figure to remind us that, as it were, our lives are ours—the figure of young boy who "gives an independent, genuine verdict" "on such people and facts as pass by" by "never cumber[ing] himself" about consequences, about interests, which is what Kant requires of independent, categorical imperatives. The boy arrives at his independence by an "unaffected, unbiased, unbribable, unaffrighted innocence," an independence Emerson calls neutrality (free of interests and of inclinations), achieved in an innocence that in each life will soon be lost, never to be returned to. Kant's moral law in effect promotes an analogue in adult terms of this judgmental neutrality or innocence. The issue, as I indicated at the opening of this chapter, that Mill (and Emerson) see in this proposal is that our problem is not (or is no longer) one of a threat to the moral life by the power of inclination or desire but a threat to desire by the power of conformity. Conformity now sits upon the commonwealth, in Milton's image, like a tyranny. Mill speaks explicitly of the tyranny of the majority; I am taking his metaphor with some seriousness.

I have sketched Kant's vision with the aim of being able to suggest usefully that Emerson's "Self-Reliance" and "Experience" are a kind of rewriting of the *Groundwork of the Metaphysics of Morals,* the concluding paragraph of "Experience" offering a solution to (or a transfiguring of) the problem of making the will practical, that is, according to Kant, to the problem of freedom, which Kant says he cannot solve. Emerson's solution, or direction of solution, is, in an image of Wittgenstein's, not to keep pushing at the door, but to open it toward you. Instead of making the will free by making it effective (using "manipular efforts"), Emerson recommends learning patience, suffering, standing for mankind (bearing up under the pain of my humanity, under, say, the discrepancy between the world I know and the world I see).

This may sound (it may be taken to be) perfectly empty, as if it says: the way to make the will effective, at least not to be baffled by its relation to the world, is just not to do anything—at least the will will no longer be baffled! What I take Emerson, rather, to be saying is that we have to reverse our lives, reconsider the magnitude of our claims upon the world, and its (consequent) claims upon us. In Emerson's words mankind is still pictured as living in two worlds, but the worlds now are not those of nature and of understanding, perennially, ineluctably in metaphysical combat, but those of society as it stands and as it may become—hidden in, in struggle with, the present.

The principal pairs in remarriage comedy form, as I propose them, a third image of moral exchange (after Emerson's images of the boy passing judgments from his innocence, and of the man becoming the true man) designed to make us worthy of membership in a realm of ends. The proposal can be framed as a reconsideration or reformulation of what a maxim is and what making it a universal law comes to.

First, take the idea of a maxim—as a subjective principle of a human action—as recognizing that human actions speak, that they have (interpretable) significance, something not governable by the laws of nature. The

Kant

141

conditions of conduct—for example, that they are motivated and have consequences (emphasized in every moral theory) and take place in specific contexts, more or less opaque, and can go wrong in a hundred specific ways—can no more determine what I do than the laws of grammar determine what I say. That my actions are part of the life form of talkers (as Wittgenstein characterizes the human, at *Investigations* §174) makes them *open to criticism*. That I am open to, perhaps responsive to, the criticism of being insensitive, cruel, petty, clumsy, narrow-minded, self-absorbed, cold, hard, heedless, reckless (careless is the marvelous charge made of Daisy and her crowd in *The Great Gatsby*) is as much a mystery as my being open to the charge of being imprudent or undutiful or unfair. That we are not transparent to ourselves means that such criticism demands confrontation and conversation. The mystery is not that we are impure but that we can be moved to change by speech, and (hence) by silence.

Second, the idea of willing the maxim of the action (at the same time) as a universal law of nature creates the world in which I act, and makes me responsible for the world. It is now mine. (This is a feature of moral judgment not, I believe, transferred by Kant from the idea of a judgment of knowledge, from the implicit inclusion in judgment of an "I think.") Contemplating the consequence of universalizing my example of conduct, I stop to ask myself a question, namely whether I *want* a world in which my example is universalized. (A version of Mill's question about a world without liberty.) A world in which I authorize breaking promises when it is convenient or useful for me is one in which *giving my word*, which is to say, speaking, is no longer possible. This is not a contradiction. It happens to some extent in each life each day, where I do not recognize what I am saying.) I am responsible for the world of my action, for example, for preserving in it the possibility of exchange. Does wanting a world in which my legislation is reciprocal with another's make me worthy of participation in a realm of ends? The conversation of the pair in remarriage comedy is an image of such a realm, an attestation of its reality. You cannot enter the realm of ends alone. And if two achieve reciprocity, the realm exists, or let me say, it is attested, in a world in which it is doubtful for whom I speak and who speaks for me.

Can we choose between these images of a realm of ends? Kant's insistence that we never know absolutely whether we are acting merely in conformity with the moral law or purely for the sake of it makes us mysterious to ourselves, but to my mind, as I have been implying, rather in the wrong way. It

should not create either cynicism or complacency or despair about ourselves. These consequences of Kant's vision of the moral law seem as likely as
its creating a humbleness or wariness in ourselves. These are what moral
conversation is about, and about what we should do given our impurity, our
finitude, imperfection. That our purity of motivation in obeying the moral
law is impenetrable to us is no more mysterious or revelatory about us than
that our motives and desires generally are not transparent to us and yet that
we can, in caring about ourselves, make them less dark, articulate why one
person or object or state of the world appeals to us and another repels us;
nor more mysterious than how caring about another can produce the extent
of devotedness it does.

Kant's repeated expressions of scorn about sympathy, and his distrust of
passion, and his constant recourse to the grimness of spirit in which obedience to the moral law most clearly stands forth, has throughout the history
of Kant's reception caused suspicion. Austin may well have been thinking of
Kant when, in defending his conception of the performative utterance
against the charge that it presents promising (and wedding and betting and
bequeathing and christening) as just saying some words (in *How to Do
Things with Words*), he mocks the alternative to his presentation as one that
requires "an inward and spiritual act," the sort of metaphysical mystification
that he believes causes moral chiseling.

To the charge that his account takes promising, betting, bequeathing, and
so on to be just the saying of some words, Austin's answer is evidently unsat-
isfying, indeed it is no answer at all. Yet it suggests that Kant's interest in the
(always imperfect) purity of our motives in, for example, keeping promises
is less interesting, philosophically and morally, than the fact that so
impressed Nietzsche, namely that we can make them rightfully, meaning that
we on the whole keep them, having bound ourselves to them, that the slum
of ourselves need not be put in order before we, most of us, much of the
time, act with reasonable faithfulness. (This merely human faithfulness is an
expression of our misfortune—Emerson's boy, in the irrecoverable power of
his neutrality, is innocent of what Emerson calls "pledges," a notion I can't
help thinking is at play in Nietzsche's remark about promises.) To say that we
manage such faithfulness as we do because we have the power of reason (or
"still" have some conscience left) just repeats the puzzle. It is worth asking
how Nietzsche's perception of the animal capable of promising differs from
Kant's expression of awe at the presence of the moral law within.

Must we choose between the idea of the realm of ends as a world we can want and for which we are responsible, and a realm of ends as one in which (as Korsgaard sees the matter) we "reason" about our plans? The conversations of the pairs in our films achieve, I have noted, the humbling, the chastening Emerson describes and the films exemplify. The cause in Emerson's case is sublimity and majesty in receiving words I know to be mine, coming from afar. I compare this with Kant's reception of the law. May we say the moral law is humbling, chastening? That it is ennobling is not incompatible with that claim.

Suppose the pervasiveness of Kant's *Groundwork* in Emerson's "Self-Reliance" is as great as I claim. We might ask what this closeness of texts means, why it exists if philosophy is always in revolt against its past, or rather its present (the fact that the past is not over). For that reason.

8

It Happened One Night

A familiar form of narrative opens by laying out a time and place in which a character or characters in whom we are to take an interest are described as carrying on a way of life, and then the plot proper, as it were, begins with an element of change or interruption breaking into this world. An obvious instance is Jane Austen's *Pride and Prejudice,* where the interruption of the ordinary days of this little world is the unheralded appearance in it of a pair of rich and handsome bachelors. Sometimes the narrative opens precisely with the element of change, noted as such, hence implying the ordinary state of affairs that has been interrupted. Austen's *Emma* is an example (Emma's lifelong companion and mother figure has married and left Emma and her father to shift, with their servants, for themselves). *Hamlet, King Lear,* and *Macbeth* begin with interruption; *Othello*'s element of change is delayed slightly, with Iago's information that Othello and Desdemona have eloped.

In just one of the classical remarriage films considered here the interruption is simultaneous with the opening of the narrative, when in *His Girl Friday* the camera follows the woman of the principal pair (played by Rosalind Russell) as she, as we will shortly learn, returns with an announcement to the newspaper world she left in order to get a divorce from the ruler of that world. All our other remarriage comedies open differently, namely with a brief prologue in which an event is depicted (a man leaves a house in silent anger, angered further upon witnessing his putter broken in half; a woman follows her husband to an assignation and shoots him) that is discontinuous with the plot proper but which poses as it were the problem, or the terms of the problem, that the plot is to solve, namely to get a certain kind of pair back together from their self-imposed interruption. The point of the lack of prologue in *His Girl Friday* seems to be that the pair have never had an ordinary life, but only interruptions, the life of newspaper people. (We will at some point recognize that none of our pairs have had an ordinary life, if that means a way of life they do not question. It is a way of understanding the interruption between them that the world calls a divorce, that their life has, perhaps momentarily, cracked under the strain of their criticism, call it their perfectionism.) A point of *It Happened One Night* is the rapidity with which the pair establish something that feels to them, and us, for all their bickering, or because of it, like an ordinary marriage.

---

1 A prologue shows Ellie Andrews (Claudette Colbert) escaping her father's control (by diving off his anchored yacht), having refused to take food from him and declared her refusal to accept his annulment of her wedding ceremony, contesting his vow that she and the man she has chosen "will never live under the same roof."

2a The escape of Ellie Andrews proves to be headline news. At a bus station, presumably in Miami, Ellie, to avoid recognition, has asked a woman to go to the sales window to purchase a bus ticket for her.

2b A star reporter, Peter Warne (Clark Gable), in a drunken oration delivered in a phone booth to his editor in New York, with whom he is evidently familiarly at odds, quits his job before the editor can fire him again.

3 When Peter boards the waiting bus, he discovers that the only free seat, in the very back, is filled with stacks of newspapers, to be sold to the passengers. He makes room for himself by throwing the stacks out the window onto the loading platform of the station. As Peter comes forward to collect his suitcase, the bus driver objects to his treatment of the remunerative papers. As Peter is facing him down, successfully, Ellie eases past the two men, and when Peter returns to the seat he has prepared for himself, he finds Ellie comfortably ensconced there. He determines, whatever her judgment, that the back seat, which is his by discovery and argument, has room for two.

4 It is evening when the bus leaves. The next morning we discover the pair still together in the small space of the back seat, but now Ellie is trustingly asleep with her head on Peter's shoulder and his sweater wrapped around her shoulders. She awakens slowly and then suddenly realizes that something has changed during the night. A little later she will say to him, "I hope you don't misunderstand what happened last night." It is quite unclear what she thinks, or thinks he thinks, has happened.

5 As Ellie is leaving the bus at a rest station, she tells the driver that she may be somewhat late returning, so he will have to wait for her. Peter's reporter's suspicions are aroused by this ignorance of the everyday world and assumption of superiority to it, and he is waiting for her when she returns late to discover that the bus has departed on time.

6 He confronts her with her picture on the front page of a newspaper. She offers him money to help her continue her escape to her, as it were, husband. He is contemptuous of her presumption. They take the next bus, leaving that night, and do not sit in adjacent seats. On the bus a loudmouth makes a pass at her and is called off by Peter claiming her as his wife. As the man scrambles away and Peter takes his place beside her, he begins taking charge of her life, budgeting what they can spend, beginning with getting the money back for the expensive chocolates she has just bought from the vendor on the bus. A Frank Capra community of the ordinary forms on the bus, expressed by a group song; Ellie is pleased that Peter joins in. It is raining heavily and the bus is disabled by a mud slide. The passengers will have to spend the night in an auto park (predecessor of the motel).

7 Peter rents a room for them as Mr. and Mrs., assuring her that his only interest in her is in getting her story, exclusive, which will be his means back to the newspaper job he has just lost. As an earnest of his good faith he strings up a blanket between the twin beds, saying something like, "Not as thick as the Walls of Jericho but a lot safer." The effect of the invisible woman inadvertently stirring the blanket as she is undressing in the darkened cabin introduces the register of the erotic into the proceedings. In the darkened cabin, in beds separated by the blanket, they have their first serious exchange of thoughts.

8 Ellie is awakened in the morning by the sound of an airplane passing overhead—her father's private plane, guiding the search for her. After a refreshing shower in what for her are exotically primitive and communal conditions she returns to the cabin to discover Peter preparing a delicious meal for them, including a doughnut, which she has evidently never had before; and he has pressed her rain-soaked clothes.

9 Private detectives sent by her father are checking the guests in the motel. Peter and Ellie put on a show for them, convincing the detectives that they are a solidly unexceptional married pair by the way they shout threateningly at one another over obscure differences. They are extravagantly pleased with their performance.

It Happened One Night

10 At a rest stop that night, the loudmouth, who has also recognized Ellie's picture in the newspaper, indicates to Peter that he wants to make some money out of keeping quiet about Ellie's whereabouts. Peter frightens the man into running away and keeping his mouth shut by telling him that her disappearance is the work of a vicious gang of criminals. Peter takes Ellie away from the bus trip, since he isn't sure of the permanent effectiveness of his ruse.

11 He carries her (over his shoulder, suitcases in his hands) across a star-filled stream into a pastoral landscape where, as he is making up beds of straw, their attraction to each other is made explicit to us and very nearly becomes explicit between them. Again he provides food for her, foraging for, it turns out, a bunch of carrots.

12 The next morning we encounter them walking down an empty country road. She is limping, and goes over to sit on a fence. Peter claims to be an expert in hitchhiking, a boast that proves to be empty. Now follows one of the most famous moments in the history of American film, as Claudette Colbert walks to the side of the road and, by showing a shapely leg, brings the next car to a violent halt.

13a Peter is sullen as they drive off, and when the driver stops for food, Peter says they aren't hungry, not allowing their pennilessness to be the excuse for Ellie to "gold dig" the stranger for a meal. As they are sitting at an outside table, the driver runs from the restaurant out to his car and takes off with Peter's and Ellie's belongings. Peter runs after the car.

13b As Ellie is waiting by the road, Peter astonishingly turns up alone in the car, and the two continue on their journey. Having the night before refused to eat the carrots, she now finds the bunch in Peter's coat and tentatively munches this food of humility.

14 The third night of their adventure on the road they stop at another auto park three hours from New York, a stop Peter says he finds unnecessary and foolish. Again he strings up the blanket, this time as though it is an old, familiar, but obscure custom of theirs. In their separate beds, she asks him, across the blanket, if he's ever been in love, or wanted to be, and he tells her about an island in the South Pacific, a transcendental scene of innocent sky and water as he describes it, where he has longed to take a woman who would love it as he does, "but they don't make them [women] like that any more." This declaration inspires a climactic declaration from Ellie, who appears on his side of the blanket confessing her love for him and her readiness to join in his vision. He is taken by surprise and rebuffs her.

15 She has cried herself to sleep, but Peter has been thinking, and across the blanket/screen asks for confirmation of her declaration. In response to silence from her side, he looks over the blanket and then, as if in response to seeing her asleep, dashes out of the cabin.

16 In New York he convinces his editor that he has the story he went after, that it has become his story as well as Ellie's, and receives in return the thousand dollars he evidently feels he needs to make his dream come true.

17 At the auto park, the suspicious, disapproving owners have found that the man has made off with the car; they awaken Ellie to the fact of his disappearance, whereupon she calls her father to come to her aid.

18 Driving back from New York, Peter is elated by his success, and expansively sings and waves to strangers as he anticipates telling Ellie of his private resolution of the situation. Almost back, he encounters a police-escorted limousine coming the other way, and sees Ellie inside, between her father and her annulled partner. The air goes out of one of Peter's tires.

19a Peter takes the thousand dollars back to his editor, tells him he was just joking about the story, but the editor has been convinced of its truth by the power of its writing. He puts some money in Peter's coat pocket and says, "When you sober up, come see me."

19b His face away from our view, empty liquor bottles in the foreground, Peter is going through the headlines of successive newspapers, each epitomizing Ellie's progress, the last one, agreeably for our purposes, reading "Ellie Andrews Remarries Today." Peter phones Ellie's father, who, he says, owes him money. The father asks him to come out to his place and Peter, after an initial refusal, says he would like to see for himself what kind of circus they are running.

20a Ellie's father extracts from Ellie a confession that she loves Peter Warne, that he is "marvelous," and that she has no feeling for the inept prig she engaged herself to to get away from home, but that it doesn't matter anymore, since Peter holds her and her father in complete contempt.

20b When Peter shows up, the father, prepared to pay him the thousands in reward he had announced, discovers that what Peter wants is reimbursement for twenty- or thirty-odd dollars and cents he spent on Ellie during their trip. The father writes the check and asks Peter if he loves Ellie. After avoiding the question Peter furiously acknowledges that he does, but also that he is screwy.

20c Peter emerges from the father's study into the central hall of the family mansion to see Ellie in the midst of a gay episode of drinking with her fashionable friends. Peter hurls a contemptuous "That's perfect" at her and leaves.

It Happened One Night

21 The wedding has begun. As the father accompanies his dazed daughter down the long aisle he tells her that Peter loves her, that her phony husband can be bought off with a pot of gold, and that her car is waiting at the side entrance. In response to the minister's asking if she will have this man to be her husband, Ellie dashes off, her long veil flying, across the grass. Newsreel cameras (ours presumably among them, knowing news when it finds it) turn to follow her, see her jump into her car, and watch the car speed off out of the reach of whoever might wish to stop her. Her father lights a celebratory cigar.

22a The owners, this time benign, of yet another auto park, this fourth night, discuss their peculiar new guests. The husband reassures his wife that the pair are married all right, but expresses his puzzlement that the man asked him to find him a toy trumpet.

22b In a darkened room a trumpet sounds and a blanket comes tumbling down. (From which side of the blanket the sound had come we do not know.)

––––––––––––

We are already alerted by the idea of what I am calling a genre that the members of it will emphasize, or discover, different or further features of the genre. I say the members are in argument with the genre, by which I mean that some feature or features of one member will quite inevitably seem at first not to fit with the features of others, hence that each is in argument over what defines the genre. (This is not true of all useful ideas of what constitutes a genre. Argument marks what I call genre-as-medium, which I contrast with the idea I call genre-as-cycle, which used to characterize Hollywood films under the titles of westerns, gangster films, musicals, women's films, screwball comedies, and which still characterize the episodic and serial continuities of character and situation essential to television sitcoms, detective and hospital soap operas, and so on.) In the case of *It Happened One Night,* the earliest member of the genre of remarriage comedy I propose (1934), at least two features are clearly at variance with what we have derived or predicted from the members of the genre we have considered so far, *The Philadelphia Story* and *Adam's Rib.* First, and most obviously, the pair in *It Happened One Night* are not officially married until the final sequence, so this sequence cannot strictly speaking be understood as their remarriage, nor, it should follow, can the film as a whole be called a comedy of remarriage; second, remarriage comedies end in a place Shakespeare calls the green world, a place of spiritual perspective, a mythical Connecticut, hardly represented by an undistinguished motel.

Such "variances" require, according to the laws of genre-as-medium, compensations, or what amount to additional revelations of the genre. Accordingly, while Peter and Ellie are not married, strictly speaking, until the very end of the film, the film makes clear from the beginning that there is a question about what marriage "strictly speaking" is. The film calls it, as noted, "living under the same roof," and that, strictly speaking, is something Ellie and Peter have repeatedly been shown to be doing. What is more, under their various roofs what we have seen them doing is behaving as if they are married—Peter declares as much to the loudmouth, and the pair enact marriage in sufficient, tawdry detail to convince hardboiled private detectives that they should not be disturbed in their bickering and undoubted state of matrimonial bliss. We might come to consider such things, in a new age, as revised marriage ceremonies, publicly forming the ties that bind.

Again, while minimal motel rooms lack the accoutrements of Adam and Amanda Bonner's paid-off house in Connecticut, let alone those of national importance that provide the setting for the Lords of the Main Line outside Philadelphia, those minimal dwellings have that without which no setting would serve the function required by the remarriage process, call it a place to call home, a locale permitting the pair's recovering of their intimacy, the privacy (of consent, call it) without which there is, in their more perfect union, no marriage. That this happens at night is something that *It Happened One Night* particularly emphasizes.

As I note in *Pursuits of Happiness,* whereas Shakespearean comedy and romance, as characterized by Northrop Frye, emphasize the succession of the seasons of the year, remarriage comedy characteristically organizes itself around the succession of day and night. An exception in Shakespeare is *A Midsummer Night's Dream,* where the unresolved tensions of the day (not only between generations and between young lovers, but notably between the royal pair of the play's world, Theseus and Hippolyta, Queen of the Amazons) are shown to be expressions of strife among the invisible forces inhabiting night. This feature was notable, even perhaps first brought to the fore, in Peter Brook's great production of the play in the early 1970s; the idea is still active in the expert, gorgeous, and intelligent, yet, I found, somewhat cold, recent film of the play starring Kevin Kline as Bottom, Michelle Pfeiffer as Titania, and Stanley Tucci as Puck. It is curiously registered or prefigured in *The Philadelphia Story,* where, among other references to the Shakespeare play, I suggest as an instance the suggestion by the Cary Grant character (the character itself being a combination of Oberon and Theseus, making happen everything that happens) that what Dinah saw out her window the previous night (among other things, her sister Tracy in Mike's arms) was a dream.

Not to lose the line of thought thereby suggested, and yet not to pursue it now, I just call to your attention Nietzsche's proposal, in *The Birth of Tragedy,* that the aesthetic access to theater is to treat what is happening in front of your eyes as the staging of a dream. With the birth of cinema in the years after Nietzsche's death, the dream force of drama became as it were automatically available in the powers of film, not always to its benefit. This, further, seems a difference of the medium of film from that of television: if film is a dream machine, television is an information machine.

As in *Adam's Rib,* in *It Happened One Night,* after a prologue, day and night are in careful alternation, in which the events of the day (the time of judgment and criticism and explanation, of taking matters to court, of budgeting money, of giving lectures on such fateful matters as doughnut dunking and piggyback carrying) are exchanged at night for fantasies of union, of a world of perfect justice and of freedom. Marriage seems presented as a state in which a pair can make intact the forever (until death parts them) repeated oscillation from one of these worlds to the other. As in *The Philadelphia Story,* in *His Girl Friday,* as we shall see in due course, the match between night and day is secured in the action's spanning part or all of one night and parts of one or two of the night's adjacent days (perhaps a span of some twelve hours in *His Girl Friday,* and of something over twenty-four hours in *The Philadelphia Story*).

Against these calculations, we shall be alerted to the different dispositions of day and night, light and dark, in the remaining comedies, *The Lady Eve* and *The Awful Truth,* where we should be able to note considerations that compensate for their differences—to show why it is that the latter ends precisely at midnight, and why in the former the crisis of estrangement occurs at night and the reestablishment of intimacy occurs in daylight. There is already the suggestion here that the peculiarity of the hurried reshuffling leading to the remarriage at the conclusion of *The Philadelphia Story,* with its surrealistic, or say dreamlike quality (Dexter and Mike and Liz are all dressed in inappropriate clothes), is associated with its happening at midday, as though its promised intimacy remains, as it were, to be seen.

I have often been asked why it is, or whether it is true, that remarriage comedies are no longer made, given my insistence on their preeminence among comedies in the opening two decades of the Hollywood talkie. I think it is true to say that there are many good films made that have remarriage elements in them (I'm grateful that people, strangers as well as friends, continue to let me know about certain of these films), but the genre can no longer be said to inspire a continuous series of such films, and in any case as a genre does not have the importance it once did in forming the concept of what a Hollywood film is—nothing like a genre-as-medium now plays such a role, but only something like a genre-as-cycle, such as the *Star Wars* series, or other sci-fi technological explorations such as *The Matrix* or *Men in Black*, which have much to recommend them, including philosophical interest, but nothing quite like the development of one soul's examination of another and a consequent contesting of social institutions, matters such as are featured in classical remarriage comedy. Such matters must seem like luxuries in the face of the question whether the human soul and society as such are to survive. (I do not take the case of *The Matrix* to show moral encounters between master and disciple since the master is not changed by the encounter and the disciple is not enabled to live a better life in the world he had known. An understanding of its combination of religiosity with advanced technology requires a separate development of the ideas of perfectionism and of associated green and black worlds.)

By films with remarriage elements in them I have in mind such films as *Moonstruck* (with Nicholas Cage and Cher), which emphasizes the incestuous intimacy underlying marital intimacy and relies on a talent for dialogue that is at once morally severe and intellectually inventive; and *Groundhog Day* (with Bill Murray and Andie MacDowell), which emphasizes the necessity of improvisation and repetition in achieving the mutuality or reality of marriage; and *Four Weddings and a Funeral* (with Andie MacDowell and Hugh Grant), which underscores the contempt for conventional marriage that nevertheless fails to still the desire for and the quest for marriage of another kind; and *Say Anything* (with John Cusack and Ione Skye), which elaborates the inevitable feature of classical remarriage comedy in which the pair become incomprehensible to (most of) the rest of the world, which may be taken as the essential moral risk perfectionism runs, since at the same time it fully recognizes the moral demand for making itself intelligible—but first, in the case of our couples, to each other.

It Happened One Night provides an apt occasion for raising this issue since the relatively recent *Sure Thing* (again with John Cusack), while it cannot quite count as a remake of *It Happened One Night*, contains a number of reasonably explicit references to that earlier exemplar: for example, a young man, who is a writer, accompanies a young woman on a cross-country trek to meet up with her fiancé, who proves not to be worthy of her, a trek which involves an incident of hitchhiking that includes an unscrupulous driver, and in the course of which the man of the central pair lectures the woman on how to drink beer, and in which the woman's father, at a distance, supplies them with money to keep them independent and together (in the form of the woman's discovery that her father has outfitted her with a credit card).

It would be a contribution to understanding why the remarriage genre is no longer what it was, to understand the difference of texture in a comedy that features as its leading man Clark Gable in comparison with one that features John Cusack. (An initial surprise is that one would—I at first was one who did—imagine that the difference between classical and later remarriage comedies must have to do essentially with the fact that there are no longer women capable of or interested in the central roles in classical remarriage comedy. But it turns out that the absence of appropriate men is the more telling fact. Such is my intuition, at any rate.) Cusack's charm and wit are formidable, but they depend upon his conveying an air of actual youth, of innocence untried, to make him a candidate for the young woman's attention. The difference from classical remarriage comedy, with such men as Gable, Cary Grant, James Stewart, and Spencer Tracy, may be put starting with the fact that these men are given authority by their experience, by their having staked their innocence against the need of "taking their place in society," so that their capacity for inventiveness, improvisation, allowing themselves to behave with their marriage partner in ways incomprehensible to the rest of society, are entered upon knowing that they are risking a certain standing in the world that it has been important, costly for them, to establish.

The absence of full-blown remarriage comedies accordingly suggests that men have become unable, or less able, with good spirits, to let their social station, so far as it is established, become jeopardized by acting on unexpected, awkward desires, as if the awkward were as such illicit—less able, we might say, to maintain their sense of identity without its ratification by social role. It thus quite accurately denies the general condition that perfectionism depends upon, the knowledge of oneself as, let's say, transcendental with respect to one's given subject position as defined by society. (The actor who comes to mind as emerging with the temperament and talent to project a mature risk of adventure is George Clooney, as in *Oh Brother Where Art Thou* and *Ocean's Eleven,* both of which are remarriage adventures, but in which the remarkable adventures are not shared with, but are something like the cost of, the woman. (The former film makes various references to *The Odyssey,* the mother of all remarriage adventures, in which marriage is pictured as its own adventure, containing what the principal pair call its "secret signs.")

My sense—but this would have to be worked out in detailed study—is that a vital difference between classical and recent remarriage comedy has to do with the role, or idea of, or faith in, education, so massive an issue for both the comedies and the melodramas we consider in this book. In the comedies, while the woman is subject to an education from the man (her choice of a man is a function of her choice of one from whom she can receive and respect an education), the man, in recompense, wants to know what this woman knows (a version of knowing what she wants), so that he is chosen as one for whom she is an education. In *It Happened One Night,* as said, this takes the form of the man wanting what he calls "the woman's story." When it becomes *his* story, he finds that there is something essentially more that he wants, something he does not know how to acquire. In the more recent versions, or fragments, of the genre, the young woman may be presented as explicitly better educated in society's eyes than the man (in *Say Anything,* she has won a prize scholarship to Oxford; the young man enables her to accept it by accompanying her on the transatlantic flight, which she mortally fears), but her attraction to him is a function of his knowledge of himself, somehow affording him knowledge of the value of life, that gives him an independence of society as it stands (as in *The Untamed Heart,* with Marisa Tomei and Christian Slater), which has evidently taught her some complexity in her unforced consent to existence within it. Such motifs emphasize the feature of the classical versions that shows the pair to be mysterious to the rest of the world.

I am aware that while I may have, in my little elaboration here of the concepts of night and day, broken some new ground in my discussion of *It Happened One Night,* and indeed of remarriage comedy more generally, I have not rehearsed, or given an indication of, the details of the reading of the film taken up in my chapter on the film in *Pursuits of Happiness,* which ranges over matters from taking the memorable blanket in the film as an image of a film screen, which reveals what it hides (for example, the erotic reality of the live woman photographed for the film and shielded, as we are shielded from her, by the screen), suggesting that the camera, or rather the entire apparatus of film from the necessities of the camera to the requirements of the projector, is to be understood as a set of Kantian conditions making possible the work of cinema as such; to enumerating foods offered, refused, and accepted, in the film, in which, as I propose, hunger is identified with desire and imagination, or say with fantasy—running the risk of seeming to deny or slight the fact that at the time the film was made, in 1934, still within the time of the Great Depression, people by the millions were going hungry.

As an emblem of so much I cannot go into here, and of matters that I hope you will be moved at some point to pursue further, I shall discuss one image from *It Happened One Night* that I knew I had not accounted for in *Pursuits of Happiness*. It was some years after the publication of that book that I seemed to find the point of the image in question, one whose very unobtrusiveness, or what I called its nothingness, my experience kept insisting was pregnant but whose significance I had been unable to find words for. It's the sort of thing that I should think anyone who thinks about the arts (or anything else) is more or less familiar with; it is an instance of the half exasperating, half glorious, fact that in works one cares about, new aspects continue to dawn, sometimes ones whose significance is so plain that it is hard, after it has dawned, to imagine having missed it.

The image in question follows the couple's second night together, in which they slept in an open field, on separate, chaste mats fashioned by Peter from a stack of hay, after departing from the company on the bus. We encounter them now at the fateful hour of dawn, as they are walking on the empty road on which they will soon famously stop a car to hitch a ride.

I take the mood of the pair, and the few words they exchange that break a silence otherwise broken only by faint sounds of birds, to be suffused by the strength of the mood of the night from which they have awakened. In my chapter on the film I characterize that mood by invoking what I call "the American transcendentalism of Capra's exteriors." In thus aligning Capra's work with the thought of Emerson and of Thoreau, I was trying to locate one of Capra's signature emotions—the experience of an ecstatic possibility as of a better world just adjacent to this one, a possibility this actuality expresses in an all but unnoticeably ordinary setting, hardly marking itself as symbolic in force; a possibility we could (in romance, in an access of the promise of justice) as it were reach out and touch.

My sense of this experience was formed, in retrospect (hence improbably to be reached after just one viewing of the film), in part from the memory of the series of shots of Claudette Colbert—I mean Ellie Andrews—in the pair's ensuing night in a cabin (their third together), responding to the man's meditative invocation, in response to her asking whether he has ever been in love, of "those nights when you and the moon and the water all become one and you feel you're part of something big and marvelous." The description seemed to me (and I imagined, to Ellie) to be the expression of an old fantasy of the man's but at the same time of his fresh memory of the previous night the two of them had spent together in the open field. The description, taken in itself, is not much more than newspaper filler. But set to the man's entranced recitation, and authorized both by the woman's entranced responsiveness to it and our own memory of their night in the moon-bright field and of their arrival there by fording a stream filled with reflected stars, the words can take on the weight of a passage from *Walden*. The stream is shattered by stars; it is an image of something Thoreau calls "sky water."

Capra's transcendental moments derive in part from German Expressionist cinema (as Emerson's transcendental thought derives in part from classical German philosophy); they display the mood of a character stretched across that character's setting. But the German settings tend toward the closed and their mood toward the haunted; Capra's tend toward the expanded and their mood toward a tortured yearning. If one does not find, or will not permit, the mood, the Capra moment is apt, in its intensity and obviousness of sentiment, to produce titters, as from emotion with no visible means of support. (I have noticed this more than once in college audiences, where the film may be screened not in a theater but in a made-over classroom, and in the presence not of strangers, where your response remains your own, but of your classmates, sitting as it were in judgment of the sophistication of your responses.)

Here is the moment I concentrate on: the pair are on the road walking together away from us. The shot lasts about thirty seconds, during which the pair have the following exchange (the woman speaking first):

"What did you say we're supposed to be doing?"
"Hitchhiking."
"Oh. Well, you've given me a very good example of the hiking. Where does the hitching come in?"

"Uh, a little early yet. No cars out."

"If it's just the same to you I'm going to sit right here and wait 'til they come."

I have reported my initial, persistent sense of the "nothingness" of this shot (remarking the spareness of its imagery, the conventionality of its words, the apparent offhandedness of the characters' manners), and confessed at the same time my sense of the transcendental mood of the night before continued in this early gray morning. But my next response was to feel: Certainly the mood continues. This just means that the powerful, expressionistically enforced mood of the night before persists, for us and for them. How could it not, given that the sequence of the night before had climaxed with an extreme close-up of the pair resisting an embrace; they are, on the road, unreleased. But then again I felt: No. I mean the mood persists not just as in memory but as present, continued by, expressed in, the new setting at dawn. The spareness, the conventionality, the offhandedness are somehow to be understood with the same expressionist fervor of the moonlit night scene. Of course in the new setting the cosmos will not be concurrent with the words that are said, but rather the words will have to be heard as covering, almost, the attraction of the mood. Even the variance of the pair's individual manners suggests the covering—the man somewhat depressed, the woman somewhat manic. So I imagine them as moving together but each keeping to himself and herself, filled with thoughts of each other, trying to accommodate to what has passed between them and to their knowledge that they each know what the other is going through, including an unreadiness to become, or a perplexity in discovering the right to become, explicit.

My critical claim is that this understanding is not a guess on my part as to how a couple of other people must be, or ought to be, feeling, based on what I know of their time together; but that it is a reading, a perception, of what I am calling the transcendental mood of this utterly specific shot now before us, a reading of its very nothingness. To substantiate this claim I must provide this reading.

I begin by repeating the title description I suggested in introducing the shot, and dividing it into four segments:

The pair is on the road / walking / together / away from us.

I take up the segments in reverse order.

Away from us. It is my general impression that the motion picture camera held on a human figure squarely from behind has tended to inflect some significance of human privacy and vulnerability, or self-reflection, of the capacity or necessity to keep one's counsel. I hope everyone can recall analogous shots of Charlie Chaplin's Little Tramp in a walk away down a road. Beyond noting the Chaplin gesture as providing sublime instances on film to capture human isolation, exposure, and hopefulness, I note that such a shot naturally constitutes the sense of an ending of a film. What is such a shot doing, then, in *It Happened One Night,* at something like the center of the film? This is in effect to begin asking: How does this specific shot inflect the range of associated shots that invoke the sense of privacy, thoughtfulness, vulnerability, and so on?

Together. The pivot of inflection is that while the pair still keep their individual counsels there is union in their moving in concert exactly away from *us.* It is, as I have emphasized, an essential feature of the genre of remarriage comedy that the films defining it close with some indication that the principal pair, in reentering the state of matrimony, are crossing some border that leaves us out, behind, and with no visible secure embrace of their own, nothing to insure the risk that they will find, or rather refind, their happiness. In *The Philadelphia Story* the pair freeze into still photos: in *The Awful Truth* the pair at the close are metamorphosed into figurines on a Swiss clock; in *His Girl Friday* they run away from us down a flight of stairs, the man first; in *The Lady Eve* a door closes in our face; in *Adam's Rib* curtains close; in *It Happened One Night* a blanket falls in a darkened room. Yet the centered walk away down the road we are considering here does also feel as if something is ending, hence as if something is beginning, some psychic border being crossed. It is this undefined openness, as if leaving the past behind them, that constitutes this particular inflection of vulnerability, of thoughtful anticipation.

Here is a place to pause for an instant to see whether the words of this sequence are as unremarkable as we have assumed. What becomes of words on film can prove to be as significant a matter as what becomes of people and things on film. Take the line, "Oh, well you've given me a good example of the hiking. Where does the hitching come in?" I hope you can come to the place—it again may not happen on a given viewing (who says all films are meant for one viewing?)—of wondering whether "hitching" here pertains to getting hitched, and even to what Katharine Hepburn refers to in

The Philadelphia Story (having to explain to her assembled wedding guests about the successful failure of her wedding plans) in saying "There's been a hitch in the proceedings." Not only was this man on this road with the woman supposed to be helping her return to her so-called husband, but generally hitches in hitching are the study both of classical comedy and (reshaped in significance) of remarriage comedy. I find the thought reinforced by the surprisingly touching fact that the woman on the road is limping; she walks with a hitch. So Capra's shot immediately, ironically, informs us that hitching has already come in, more or less before our eyes, that the tying of the (hitch) knot, the entanglement of lives, is on the way and will not, for some happy reason, come undone. (This sketches the moral of the remarriage structure.)

Walking. What they are doing is walking together on a road, hiking until hitching. This fact began to take on thematic importance for me some time after a colleague inquired whether I had thought about the range of vehicles in the film, suggesting that they form a little system of significance as striking as the system I had found in the various foods consumed in it. Thinking this over (there is a yacht, a bus, a roadster, one or two limousines, a flight of motorcycles, a freight train, a private passenger plane, a helicopter), it seemed to me that the vehicles mostly emblematize or differentiate matters whose disposition in this film we know independently—power, isolation, vacuity, the capacity for community. Whereas the system of foods and their modes of preparation or gathering provides the basis of relationship that serves to establish and measure acceptance and rejection.

Even so, the intuition of significance in the system of vehicles seemed to me right. I have come to understand it in its contrast as a whole with—hence its emphasis upon—the human fact of walking; as I had taken the system of foods as a whole to emphasize the human fact of hunger and of imagination. Being on the road and being hungry are familiar images of the Depression of the early 1930s. Hollywood comedies of the period are often chastised as fairytale distractions from the terrible realities of those years. I do not deny that some were, maybe most. But the best among them were tales that continue the extreme outbursts of hope in human possibility that were also part of the realities of those times; otherwise the persistent popularity and instructiveness of a number of such films would seem to me inexplicable. I have said that hunger in *It Happened One Night* stands for the reality of imagination, the imagination of a better world than we have made. Now

I wish to make explicit a companion representativeness in its idea of walking together. Accordingly let us consider where it is the pair are walking.

On the road. In four of the seven definitive remarriage comedies the denouement of mutual acknowledgment is achieved, as said, by a removal of the pair to a place of perspective that, following Shakespeare's psychic or allegorical geography, I call "the green world." I find that *It Happened One Night* compensates for its lack of this more or less explicitly mythical location by its presentation of perspective acquired on the road, which is the classical and no less mythical location of picaresque quest and adventure. In its interpretation or displacement of the green world as the location of adventurousness, improvisationally achieved romantic remarriage becomes an interpretation of marriage as itself the process of quest and adventure. The virtue in demand becomes less the capacity to manage the repetitions of marriage than to keep up with its varying desires.

There is another declaration of this road as a mythical or psychical locale. After Gable's lecture to the woman about the three modes of thumbing a ride and then his proving to be impotent to stop the first three cars that pass by, the road suddenly produces, as from nowhere, an unending stream of cars rushing past his abashed thumb and disappearing around the bend into nowhere, as if the proper rebuke to this male expansiveness is to publish the man's failure to stop each and every car on earth. This cosmic rebuke, as by the medium of film itself, sets up the succeeding rebuke by the woman, who stops a car by showing some leg, thus proving once for all, as she says happily to the gloomy man, "that the limb is mightier than the thumb," call it the ascendancy of nature over convention.

It was in connecting, more or less consciously, the idea of the road as the equivalent of a spiritual realm of perspective and adventure with the persistence of a transcendental sense of dawning landscape as calling out a moment of openness and beginning, and with the specific cosmic rebuke of male assertiveness, that I turned, for the first time in years, to Walt Whitman's "Song of the Open Road." I remind you of what is to be found there. The thirteenth section opens as follows:

Allons! to that which is endless as it was beginningless,
To undergo much, tramps of days, rests of nights,
To merge all in the travel they tend to, and the days and nights they tend to,
Again to merge them in the start of superior journeys . . .

The fifteenth and final section concludes:

> Camerado, I give you my hand!
> I give you my love more precious than money,
> I give you myself before preaching or law;
> Will you give me yourself: will you come travel with me?
> Shall we stick by each other as long as we live?

The mood is of course different from that of the shot of our pair on the empty dawning road. But if you will take Whitman's closing questions as lines for the invention of a new wedding ceremony, they match as perfectly as any I know the questions and the tasks proposed by the (perfectionist) comedy of remarriage. (By the invention of a wedding ceremony I mean a task of these comedies that they share with Shakespearean theater, as in *Antony and Cleopatra* and *The Winter's Tale,* where I have taken the closing scene of each, one apparently of a suicide, the other apparently of a statue magically coming to life, in effect to constitute an unheard-of wedding.) It follows that I am proposing the shot of this pair on the road walking together away from us as a wedding photo.

Even if you will take it so for this moment, you may not for the next. Not every moment will yield to, or require, the mood of Whitman's ecstasies and exhortations, any more than every moment can tolerate, or use, the sentiments and elations of Frank Capra. But I imagine that these artists themselves composed knowing this, even that they meant to declare it, respectively, of the nature of poetry and of film, to acknowledge their intermittence of effect, our evanescent readiness for them. Or in Emerson's words from "Experience": "Since our office is with moments, let us husband them." Or as Wittgenstein will put a similar thought: "What dawns here lasts only as long as I am occupied with the object in a particular way." We have perhaps most poignantly in film, something we have in any art, the opportunity to find, but always the freedom to miss, the significance of the nothing and the nowhere.

Am I claiming that Capra is as good as Whitman and Emerson? Am I saying that he intended the matters I have invoked to account for my mood with a moment he has provided? These are reasonable questions, deserving reasoned answers. Until then I may put my approach to them this way. Capra shares certain of the ambitions and the specific visions of Whitman and of Emerson, and he knows about working with film roughly what they know about working with words. If your fixed view is, however, that no film (anyway none produced in the Hollywood sound era) could in principle bear up under any serious comparison with major writing, then our conversation may, if it has begun, be at an end; for I would take the fixed view, or attitude, as representative of a philistine intellectuality fully worthy of the philistine anti-intellectuality from which we more famously suffer.

Well, that discussion of walking was written, for a general audience, in 1985. You can see, from the hauteur of its last sentence, evidence of my sense of embattlement in thinking to bring film into a philosophical classroom, which is what I did two years later when I taught the first version of the course in which this book originated. The particular edge of embattlement was, I should acknowledge, my sense of feeling unappreciated—here was I, bringing what should have been pleasure and instruction to my fellow citizens about objects of common interest, but instead of receiving the news as a gift they seemed to take it as depriving them of something. I had forgotten, it seems, that this is a characteristic fate of philosophy, at least in any somewhat novel form. But here and now, in this book that was born in a classroom, we have the time to explore further this feature of philosophy's reception. The anger it causes is an essential subject foregrounded, early and late, in Plato's *Republic*, a text we come to in not so many chapters. (By the way, to return to the last sentence of my earlier article on the image from *It Happened One Night*, the idea of philistinism is something we will, in Chapter 11, see Nietzsche embattled against; it is an idea he develops in part out of his reading of Emerson on conformity.)

9

RAWLS

I ended my discussion of Kant by reinvoking his achievement as the philosophy of limitation (I might say finitude), in which human reason is perceived as the bringer of law, hence the creator of realms or worlds, indeed of both of the worlds in which the human finds habitation, namely, the world open to the senses, hence science, and the world open to intellect alone, the latter being the realm of freedom, of immorality, and of deity. There are various names for these worlds, since there are various aspects to them. The former is called the phenomenal or sensual world (the world of things as they appear to us), the latter is called the noumenal or intelligible world (the world of things-in-themselves). There is in each world a barrier, or something that can present itself as a barrier, against what I am calling the human's inhabitation of it. The barrier in the realm of the phenomenal or sensuous world in which objects are known, that is, subjected to the conditions of knowledge, is those conditions themselves, conceived as limitations of our capacity to know things as they are in themselves. (But "limitations" is a prejudicial picture of what are articulated as conditions of the possibility of knowing anything as such. I am limited to walking because I have a bruised ankle and cannot run, or because I haven't a horse or a carriage or roller skates, but not because I lack wings.)

The barrier in the realm of the intelligible world is to my inhabitation, whatever that will mean, of the realm of ends. The barrier to the knowledge of things-in-themselves is that I cannot experience them (as they are). The barrier to the knowledge of, or entry into, the realm of ends is not a necessary incapacity of experience; it is in principle realizable. I have specified the barrier as my not being able to enter that realm alone; it is a realm of reciprocity, demanding my treating others as ends, never merely as means, and of my being responsive to others' treatment of me in that light. Here again, a condition presents itself as a limitation. In the sensuous world of knowledge I know I cannot but obey these conditions; in the intelligible world of freedom and command, I cannot know that I am purely obeying them.

Kant's vision yields the suggestion that I can act now in such a way as to represent my participation in the knowledge of such a compound place or state. I do so, for Kant, when I act not only in accordance with the moral law, but for the sake of the moral law. I claim an analogue of this inhabitation for the exchanges of the principal pair of remarriage comedy, their representation of a world that can be unequivocally desired. Their marrying means that their intelligibility to one another is not shared in their wider society as it stands; this is emphasized in their requiring a degree of unintelligibility to that society. At the same time the fact of their representing something to this society (running up against the limits of their intelligibility to it) counts as their consent to it; consent ensures that we are compromised by our society's inevitably at best partial compliance with the principles of justice; but the compromise is worth suffering to the extent that the society is committed to the reform of itself. This assumes that our society embodies justice good enough to warrant defense, say loyal opposition. Our pleasure in the behavior of the remarriage pair accordingly becomes a measure of our distance from the kingdom of ends, the reign of the principles of justice. Rawls needs such a measure.

Taking Kant's realm of ends as an eventual just state of society and a perspective or standpoint from which this state can be glimpsed now is an idea that finds a new representation or picture in Rawls's *Theory of Justice* (1971). Let's begin with an early description Rawls gives of his purpose in this work (p. 22): "My aim is to work out a theory of justice that represents an alternative to utilitarian thought generally . . . to all . . . versions of it." This resembles but is not exactly Kant's project. For Rawls, "an alternative to utilitarian thought" means an alternative to what utilitarianism as a theory and practice wishes to accomplish, namely to provide a basis not alone for motivating individual actions morally (or put otherwise, for providing a philosophy by which to conduct one's private life); but as well a basis for mitigating social misery by social means, beginning now, to the extent possible within the terms of justice (that is, not by revolutionary dispossession of one class or status in favor of another).

Utilitarianism, as said, had been the most familiar moral doctrine of

English-speaking universities (together with a form of what seemed to many the moral skepticism of the reigning philosophy of logical positivism, according to which value judgments, moral judgments chief among them, were not strictly speaking meaningful judgments at all) in the somewhat disorganized period of moral philosophizing in the decades before Rawls's book appeared. The criterion of utility, or the greatest happiness principle, was a rational weapon to use against claims of privilege and claims of the intrinsic or historical value of the arrangements of certain institutions. Rawls also requires a weapon against these abuses, but he begins by being impressed—as a growing number of others were—by intolerable consequences of paradoxes of utilitarianism of the sort I sketched in discussing Mill's views, paradoxical consequences concerning the concepts and institutions of promising and punishing, as well as general dissatisfactions with its proposals concerning pleasure as the sole basis of the moral life.

Rawls summarizes these consequences once as follows (p. 26): "There is no reason in principle [according to utilitarianism] why the greater gains of some should not compensate for the lesser losses of others; or more importantly, why the violation of the liberty of a few might not be made right by the greater good shared by many." What, on this view, would rule out the argument that if a small religious sect or deviant sexual group greatly offends the sensibilities of a large number of townspeople, then even though they do not threaten the fundamental liberties and rights of others, they—forcibly if necessary—may be restrained? Though others before Rawls found such consequences unjust, no one in the century just past has been as systematic and successful at articulating the basis of an alternative conception of the relations between justice and rationality as Rawls has been.

How might we think about the extraordinary success of *A Theory of Justice* in the world? There are various—non-exclusive—possibilities. One is: Academic, or professional, moral philosophy (in the English-speaking tradition) was in the 1960s, with some exceptions, largely moribund, importantly because it was rendered abstract and defensive by logical positivism, or say by the hegemony, across the borders of academic disciplines, of scientifically inclined philosophizing, which attacked the rationality of moral, religious, and aesthetic judgments as such—something that has chronically been the case in Western philosophizing since the time of Plato. A second possibility is that Rawls's adaptation of social contract theory, linking it to the theory of rational choice, brought it into connection with economic theory and with legislative possibilities and judicial necessities. A third reason for the particular success of *A Theory of Justice* is the timing of its appearance, namely at the beginning of the 1970s, in the wake of years of student-led uprisings over the war in Vietnam. That war was something almost everyone was by then looking for a way out of; it was a period, moreover, that incorporated the intellectual and moral climate of the years of the civil rights movement of the 1960s. *A Theory of Justice* provided a systematic account of democracy's procedural powers for criticizing and reforming itself (against, as it were, the various more radical calls, ecstatic or frightening or repellant, depending on your point of view, for revolution). For example, it had room in its system for a reconsideration of the basis of civil disobedience, something increasing thousands of students had been invoking in scores of venues over the better part of a decade.

A fourth reason I might suggest is that this remarkable systematization serves a humbler, daily purpose for our moral lives, as a kind of moral encouragement, giving earnest that our good wills are parts of one another's, a kind of palpable sense that our individual efforts are not lost, or invisible, in that way pointless—a counteracting of one direction of moral despair, a nemesis of Emerson's Essays, call this nemesis demoralization. Rawls follows Kant's lead in seeking a system that interprets intuitively one's sense of questions of morality and of rationality, as if only the systematic can provide the clarification to oneself of one's fugitive, transient intuitions—intuitions on which one nevertheless bases one's most fateful decisions. This use of the systematic seems precisely the intellectual virtue that failed utilitarianism—its tremendous power of the intuitive against a social and legal system grown irrational, arbitrary, and unfair dissipates in the face of the consequences of its own justifications. We can say that Rawls demonstrates the power of the systematic within morality as such—as if the very texture of justice, thought of in a certain (intuitively satisfying) way (Rawls calls his theory justice as fairness) is itself grounded in the idea of the systematic.

One might think of the intuitive clarification of systematicity as capturing several ancient features in the visual representation or iconography of justice: as holding in one hand a balance, and in the other a sword, and as blindfolded. Justice balances differences in order and in weight of conflicting claims; it yields decisions or choices that are final, fatal; it is blind to certain differences between conflicting parties, for example to differences of social station and of talent and taste, as well as to the consequences of letting justice be done. (The fact that justice is personified as a woman may capture the sense of a perspective taken from outside the established hierarchies of a given social dispensation, hence the sense of treating each person as an individual, respecting their differences so far as they do not infringe the freedoms of others.)

The purpose of Rawls's systematicity is to identify principles for setting up the basic structures of social institutions that have exactly these features of just adjudication (achieving a weighting of claims, blind to irrelevant differences, that is, treating each person subject to the institutions with equal respect, and issuing in stable decisions) which all who are affected by the outcome will recognize as just, including (in principle) those who are on the losing side. What Rawls calls his two fundamental principles of justice speak to, reinterpret systematically, the issue of balancing or weighting (or put otherwise, argue for detailed articulations of the metaphors or images of balancing and blindness; the fatality of the sword seems comparatively easy to gloss).

The principles of justice are refined gradually, beginning with the formulations on pages 60–61. The final versions are given on pages 302–303.

> *First Principle:* Each person is to have an equal right to the most extensive total system of equal basic liberties compatible with a similar system of liberty for all.
>
> *Second Principle:* Social and economic inequalities are to be arranged so that they are both (a) to the greatest benefit of the least advantaged, consistent with the just savings principle, and (b) attached to offices and positions open to all under conditions of fair equality of opportunity.
>
> *General Conception:* All social primary goods—liberty and opportunity, income and wealth, and the bases of self-respect—are to be distributed equally unless an unequal distribution of any or all of these goods is to the advantage of the least favored.

There are two Priority Rules:

> *First Priority Rule* (The Priority of Liberty): The principles of justice are to be ranked in lexical order and therefore liberty can be restricted only for the sake of liberty. [Lexical ordering: certain principles are to be satisfied before others come into effect.]

Second Priority Rule (The Priority of Justice over Efficiency and Welfare):
The second principle of justice is lexically prior to the principle of
efficiency and to that of maximizing the sum of advantages.

One sees immediately how these principles and priorities modify utilitarianism's greatest happiness principle. From "What Utilitarianism Is," chapter 2
of Mill's *Utilitarianism:* "The creed which accepts as the foundation of
morals Utility, or the Greatest-happiness Principle, holds that actions are
right in proportion as they tend to promote happiness, wrong as they tend to
produce the reverse of happiness. By happiness is intended pleasure and the
absence of pain, by unhappiness, pain and the privation of pleasure." In
Rawls's *A Theory of Justice* such a principle is not (though incomplete) irrelevant; but it is held to apply only subsequent to the assessment of liberty. And
when issues of pleasure and pain do become relevant, the question of their
distribution is to be assessed before considering whether, as it were, their
"increase" is warranted. (These principles themselves come into effect only
on condition that there is a bearable minimum of goods available for all.)

Now what is our stake in these principles? What does it mean to say that
each person "is to have" a certain level of liberty, or to say of primary social
goods that they "are to be distributed equally unless . . ."? This makes it
sound as if we are setting up a just society, not already living in one in which
all these distributions and priorities have already found a most particular
and defended materialization, with whatever outcome justice and power and
fortune or misfortune have reached in struggling among themselves. I shall
emphasize that strain in Rawls's view that takes the idea of a democratic
society (one in which each member possesses the means and rights for a life
of "self-respect") to be one in which its citizens sense that they are somehow
in the process of creating it. You can say that the principles of justice are simply principles of evaluation or criticism, not ones we are in a position to put
into practice. But Rawls's claim is that they can be seen to be *our* principles,
so that the extent to which our society does not meet their demands is an
indictment of ourselves by ourselves. How is this shown?

Rawls offers us a thought experiment (something like what lawyers call a
hypothetical) to show that these principles of justice are "ours" in this sense,
that they are the principles we would choose to govern us if we had convened
to order ourselves into a society, under the specific condition that we were
choosing without knowing our position or state in that society, what our

social or natural fortunes (wealth, offices, talents, energies, and so on) would be. Rawls calls this thought experiment one in which we choose these basic principles behind a veil of ignorance, out of the stance (characterized by arriving at the veil of ignorance) he calls "the original position." The idea of an original position is obviously enough an interpretation or articulation of what a social contract theorist such as Locke has in mind when he invokes the picture (what more can it be?) of "giving up" our liberties in the state of nature in order to gain the advantages of being governed together by common institutions of legislation and adjudication. And like the classical contract theories, Rawls's idea of the veil of ignorance carries the air of a quasi-historical or mythical claim, and its hypothetical character has created analogous doubts. Rawls's distinct advance over the classical theorists (notably avoiding room for the kind of objection we found Hume voicing against Locke's idea of the original contract) is his explicitness that this hypothetical stance is one we can, and do, adopt now, in the present, whenever we attempt to assess and defend or criticize our society's standing with respect to the demands of justice.

This proposal joins the discussion of fundamental moral assessment at the point I was stressing in contrasting Kant and Mill, at which Kant asks whether I can universalize the subjective (individual, private) maxim of my action, and Mill asks whether I can want my society as it stands, manifesting not only the lack but the fear of liberty. Locke's answer, we found, taking the form of asking whether his consent was intact, was ambiguous as between the question—should his consent be withdrawn, in response to repeated and intolerable abuses of government, forcing an interpretation of the government's actions as breaking its side of the bargain of consent—whether it is simply the government that is overthrown, or the fabric of society as such. (And since his tract on government was to justify revolution, this ambiguity was, I suggested, perhaps necessary.) Rawls's comparable question ought, as it were, to be: Is my society one I can imagine having chosen, or rather one I can accept as the consequence of my choice?

But in fact such a question for Rawls does not declare itself uncontroversially to my mind, since he takes his adaptations of the various clauses of contract theory (of the state of nature as becoming the original position, of the common institutions of government and law that remove us from this state as requiring the veil of ignorance), to mean, in the case of consent, that what the members of a society consent to is not society at large but specifically the two principles of justice (see, for example, pp. 11, 180). It would then seem to follow that we consent to the present dispensation of a society that bears up under the critical eye of those principles, given the knowledge that no actual society will satisfy them perfectly. Presumably an acceptable society is then one that satisfies them, while partially, with a system of justice good enough as it stands to warrant defending. But how is "partial compliance that is good enough to defend as it stands" to be determined?

At a juncture important to my reading of his view, Rawls in effect claims that my sense of living in a society which in my judgment exhibits a favorable degree of partial compliance is one in which, in response to an expression of resentment leveled by an aggrieved member (permanent or impermanent, I believe) of that society, I can say that my conduct is above reproach (p. 422). (What "in effect" means here is critical. Rawls does not explicitly claim what I find him implicitly to claim here.) I could not justly say so if the aggrieved member can show that a specific institution is unjust, or more unjust than any realistic alternative, or that someone has injured him; but if he cannot show any of this then his claim to suffering amounts morally to an expression of envy (p. 533).

But what is my relation to one whom I accuse of envy or else accept as the victim of justified resentment? And what is the force of my being "prepared to say" anything at all to such a cry of injustice? Is what I called the point of fundamental assessment in my relation to my society addressed by the task of defense that Rawls assigns one committed to his or her society, or is that task designed, rather, to show that there is no such question to be addressed to it, but only a preparedness to answer questions of specific abuse? We have to go further in describing Rawls's theory in order to be able to treat such matters.

Like Mill's, Rawls's theory is ameliorative. It wishes to mitigate the brute facts of natural inequality and social inequity in human society. Unlike Mill, Rawls is anti-meritocratic: while each of us is, within the law, entitled to enjoy the fruits of our talents, fortunes of birth, and hard work, no one is *entitled* to a more advantaged position *because* of these accidents or accomplishments. Indeed justice will require protecting others against *too* disparate a share of goods as a result of these fortunes, and against any transgression of, or exception to, the right of liberty thought to be warranted by them. Rawls presents, or refines, a new contribution to a series of pictures of distributive justice proposed over the course of our civilization. Aristotle saw justice as giving to each his due. Marx saw it as giving to each according to his need. Rawls sees it as giving to each according to principles ensuring universal self-respect and fair procedures.

It is possible to find Rawls too, well, procedural, too rule-bound, too indifferent to unexplained suffering, too rigorous. Something comparable to what I said in this connection about Kant seems to me pertinent in the case of Rawls: it is morality itself, specifically justice itself, that is rigorous. Treating oneself as just one voice in a system of equal voices—no more and no less than this—is rigorous. Rawls's view might be said to mitigate as much as to, and because it undertakes to, systematize rigor.

Now moral perfectionism, as I conceive it, raises a different concern at a different point in the system—without questioning anything said so far in describing Rawls's view. Intuitively, the issue may be expressed as a question about the image of justice's sword, namely whether it is drawn in offense or in defense. Is it raised against an individual within its dispensation? Or against a competing social order? If against an individual, it implies that one has offended justice by placing weights in the scales that violate the priority of liberty or the judgment of the least advantaged. If against a competing system, then there again seem two possibilities: (1) it is defending its own dispensation of justice as such, as a system (its honor, as it were, is the necessity, and sufficiency, of its blindness and balance, in comparison with any other ordering or weighting of primary goods); or (2) it is defending justice against injustice as such, call it tyranny.

I would like to ask: What, more concretely, is what I just called the honor of justice, the good of it, I mean of the dispensation of justice pictured in *A Theory of Justice,* presumably that from which our society is more or less to be derived? The region in Rawls's theory that I wish this question to throw light on is epitomized for me in the following early passage (p. 13): "Whenever social institutions satisfy these principles [of justice] those engaged in [those institutions] can say to one another that they are cooperating on terms to which they would agree if they were free and equal persons whose relations with respect to one another were fair."

I focus in my book *Conditions Handsome and Unhandsome* on that idea of what, under a just structure, we "can say to one another." I call this idea of the communication made possible by the sharing of just institutions *the conversation of justice.* This phrase, fairly plainly—in view of the genre of comedies that I take as exemplifying one happy, or happy enough, realization of lives in a just (enough) structure—is meant to emphasize that my invocation of conversation, while it means talk, means at the same time a way of life together.

"Conversation" is taken by me to represent perhaps a different goal or ideal, or a different inflection of the goal from that of "cooperation," as Rawls puts the context of justice. My reservation, or question, is not so much directed to Rawls's particular systematization as to his evaluation of the consequences of his system. "Cooperation," as a general state of social interaction, suggests the idea of society as a whole either as having a project or, at the other extreme, as being a neutral field in which each can pursue his or her own projects. Intuitively, these extremes are analogous to aspects of the interesting institution of competitive games. "A game of baseball" may be taken as the project of playing a particular game; at the other extreme, "the game of baseball" may be taken as the general conditions under which the game being played counts as baseball, conditions specified by a weave of descriptions and various kinds of rules and principles.

The virtues in most request in this analogy, those going into what we might call the temperament of cooperativeness, are a certain kind and degree of participation and forbearance, in which the limitation of mutual involvement is paramount and well defined. In the moral life, the game is never over—until it is over—but your responsibilities for the game are confined to the position that, let us say, natural selection and social fortune have placed you in. (The comparison of moral institutions with games, in particular baseball, is broached in Rawls's early paper "Two Concepts of Rules." Rawls does not, I believe, refer to this influential paper in *A Theory of Justice.* But Christine Korsgaard, one of Rawls's most influential successors, does refer to it in her Introduction to the Cambridge edition of Kant's *Groundwork,* and I believe an essential idea in that paper is retained in Rawls's later working out of his theory. There is a chapter on "Two Concepts of Rules" in my *Claim of Reason.* I find what is said there still to be pertinent; it will come up presently.)

The idea of "conversation," in contrast, emphasizes neither a given social project nor a field of fairness for individual projects. (Nor, as I have insisted, does it deny the importance of these ideas.) What it emphasizes is, I might say, the opacity, or non-transparence, of the present state of our interactions, cooperative or antagonistic—the present seen as the outcome of our history as the realization of attempts to reform ourselves in the direction of compliance with the principles of justice. The virtues most in request here are those of listening, the responsiveness to difference, the willingness for change. The issue is not whether there is a choice between the virtues of cooperation and of conversation. God forbid. The issue is what their relation is, whether one of them discourages the other.

The imperative to conversation is meant to capture the sense that, even when the veil of ignorance is lifted, we still do not know what "position" we occupy in society, who we have turned out to be, what our stance is toward whatever degree of compliance with justice we have reached. To know such things is to have a perspective on our lives, on the way we live, and this is precisely the province of what I call, of what interests me in, moral perfectionism. The idea of conversation expresses my sense that one cannot achieve this perspective alone, but only in the mirroring or confrontation of what Aristotle calls the friend (what Nietzsche calls my enemy, namely one who is, on my behalf, opposed to my present, unnecessary stance), what Emerson calls the true man, the neutral youth, my further, rejected self. My sense of this outlook can be put this way: Without the register of moral perfectionism Rawls's theory cannot reach its goal of being able to say (to oneself, if no further) that one is above reproach, or rather, to do what that claim, were it sayable, is meant to do.

It is my sense that good readers of Rawls do not attach the intensity of importance to his idea of conducting oneself beyond reproach that I attach to it. But my view is that some such claim expresses something of the very object of his labors. His theory, humanely, is designed, in achieving justice, to reveal the limits in degree and range of responsibility I have to accept for the unexplained or irreducible misery of the world. I take it, in that regard, to be meant as in the line of work, as I recall Georges Bernanos to put the matter in *Diary of a Country Priest*, that seeks to preserve us from dying of pity for the world (without becoming pitiless). I do not, however, believe that Rawls's theory has shown that we can in good faith say (to others, therefore in good conscience to ourselves) that we have constructed a life that is above reproach. But it may suggest another avenue of response, or expression, to a similar, but decisively different, effect.

To say how I see this it will help to go back to the comparison of moral imperatives with the defining rules of games as broached in Rawls's "Two Concepts of Rules." This paper, published in 1955, was written during the period in which paradoxes of utilitarianism—particularly those I mentioned in connection with discussing Mill, concerning utilitarianism's apparent inability to justify such morally essential acts as promising and punishing—were receiving as it were a last, for some quite convincing, register of justification. (The paradoxes of utilitarianism in view, I remind you, were that it allows you to break a promise if keeping it would cause you a little more pain—perhaps summed together with that of a companion—than breaking it would cause to the one you would disappoint; and that it allows you to punish an innocent person if the unhappiness caused to that one and a small number of others is less than the happiness of a large number of people in imagining justice done.)

The thought of the new defense of utilitarianism was that the principle of utility was best, and was meant to be, applied not to the assessment of individual acts but to the practices or institutions within which those acts mean what they do, are what they are. There is no paradox in giving a utilitarian justification for the *institutions* of promising and of punishing, that is, no paradox in saying, for example, that it is better on the whole for a society to have among its institutions or practices one (call it the practice of promising) which disallows asking whether it is better on the whole to do something (namely, to do something you have promised to do). The utilitarian justification for the institution of promising is, roughly, that it ties down expectations and hence furthers cooperation. The utilitarian justification for the institution of punishment is that it deters further harmful acts of the kind punished. Rawls's paper was effective in making this distinction clear, which he accomplished by distinguishing, as his title announces, two concepts of rules, call them defining rules and guiding rules, the former of which define practices, the latter of which guide individual acts.

Allow me to summarize, or epitomize, the conclusions I draw about this in *The Claim of Reason.* I focus on the following two excerpts from Rawls's paper:

> The practice view leads to an entirely different conception of the authority which each person has to decide on the propriety of following a rule in particular cases . . . It doesn't make sense for a person to raise the question whether or not a rule of a practice correctly applies to his case where the action he contemplates is a form of action defined by a practice. If someone were to raise such a question, he would simply show that he didn't understand the institution in which he was acting. If one wants to perform an

action specified by a practice, the only legitimate question concerns the nature of the practice itself ("How do I go about making a will?").

This point is illustrated by the behavior expected of a player in games. If one wants to play a game, one doesn't treat the rules of the game as guides as to what is best in particular cases. In a game of baseball if a batter were to ask "Can I have four strikes?" it would be assumed that he was asking what the rule was; and if, when told what the rule was, he were to say that he meant that on this occasion he thought it would be best on the whole for him to have four strikes rather than three, this would be most kindly taken as a joke. One might contend that baseball would be a better game if four strikes were allowed instead of three; but one cannot picture the rules as guides to what is best on the whole in particular cases, and question their applicability to particular cases as particular cases.

As an admiring and grateful student of J. L. Austin's, I note that it takes more than two concepts of rules to "define a game," if that means to specify what counts as playing it (let alone playing it well—and a certain grasp of what goes into playing it well is essential to the idea of knowing the game). But my quarrel with Rawls was over the sense in which games "illustrate" the moral life. Rawls's example of baseball imagines a player "challenging" its rules in a way that shows the "player" either not to know the game or else (to put it, as Rawls says, kindly) to be making a joke (or, to put it unkindly, to show that the player has suffered a moment of lunacy, perhaps even shows not only that he doesn't know what baseball is but that he doesn't know what playing a game is). And this seems not to show how challenging a rule in games illustrates something about moral practices but on the contrary to suggest that there is in the moral life nothing that plays the role of a defining rule in games.

The presence of defining rules might be taken as defining what a game is, why games are fun, I mean why they can be *played:* you know in advance of any given game essentially what all your responsibilities are; this goes with being able to *practice* them. In the moral life a competent challenge is one that is inherently open to discussion. If I deny that I was wrong not to fulfill a promise and all I mean is that I found that it was better on the whole, say it increased the amount of pleasure in the world, if I went to the movies instead, then I have suffered a moment of lunacy, or perhaps rage. It is no cause for intellectual or moral alarm if someone doesn't know the rules of baseball, doesn't know the game of baseball. It might be fun to undertake to teach (certain of) the principal rules and conditions to him or her, in contrast, say, to those of cricket. But it is reason for intellectual and moral alarm if I am to conclude that a mature person doesn't know what a promise (or pact) is. (The sacredness of promising is a familiar enough fact of human life to participate in the action of tragedy, for example in Euripides' *Hippolytus*.) So what am I asked to imagine if I am asked to imagine having to say to a mature person something like: "You evidently do not know what a promise is. It might be fun to teach you"? Yet something analogous to this is evidently what I have to say if I am asked to back up my declaration of being above reproach.

When Rawls introduces the idea of one's conduct as above reproach (p. 422), the context is that he is considering a person's rational plan of life, a plan in which, if things work out badly, one need not blame oneself for having made an earlier decision (I suppose for such decisions as having made what turns out to be a bad investment, or having refused a particular offer of marriage, or not having had children, or having taken a job that seemed lucrative instead of staying in school, and so on). But he also compares caring about one's future self (making a life plan) with caring about others, and he does say that a rational plan is a plan about which one "can say that at each moment of his life he has done what the balance of reasons required, or at least permitted" (ibid). I relate this "can say" to what I called the conversation of justice, as in "those engaged in [just social institutions] can say to one another that they are cooperating on terms to which they would agree" (p. 13), or as in the suggestion that to one who for the moment doubts the validity of his moral promptings as a whole "in a well-ordered society there are many things to say" (p. 514).

So I am taking it that "above reproach" is something that is imagined as serviceable to say (since to oneself) to another who questions your life plan, since that plan affects everyone whom you affect. In particular I imagine that the claim, leveled against those who express resentment, is to be taken as formulating something that you can say to one (perhaps one whom you have known all your life) who expresses resentment at your good fortune (pp. 532–533), perhaps at your freedom of choice, seen as the result of your large inheritance and your powerful connections. The sense I get is that the claim is meant to work the way invoking defining rules works: your resentment shows you don't know the rules of the game. This is what I hear "I am above reproach" to say. In imagining it as said to oneself Rawls takes it as a counter to misfortune. In imagining it said to others, I take it as a defense of fortunateness. (I'll come back to this in a moment.)

I have implied that it is not a morally acceptable (or perhaps only that it is always a morally questionable) thing to say, on the ground that, modeled on the analogy with games, it suggests that the other is morally incompetent. It also implies that the state of our society is more transparent than it is. (Rawls invokes the recognition that "envy is not a moral feeling"; p. 533. I am saying, comparably, that "above reproach" is not a moral claim. Another may award you the description.)

A competent moral agent might, uncontroversially, have sufficient reason not to fulfill some promise (the implicit conditions are not realized, or there is an illness in the family and I have made arrangements for a colleague to appear in my place). There can be arguments over the weight to give various considerations, but that is the nature of the moral game, a reason conversation is essential to it. That there is at a particular juncture nothing to discuss is the result not of applying a rule but of staking a particular claim or defining the choice of a particular position. Of my conduct in games it is true that if I play hard within the rules and conditions, it makes sense to say that my conduct has been above reproach. I may have failed to make a play and let in a run, or in the boxing ring even caused a death, but (granted that my effort was scrupulously hard and unquestionably within the rules) however I may suffer from this, I deserve not reproach but sympathy (partly because I cannot escape my own self-reproach).

It is, so I claim, understanding institutions to function like promises and both to be defined by rules that enables Rawls to appeal to the idea of conducting himself so as to be above reproach. He says in *A Theory of Justice* (p. 344): "Promising is an action defined by a public system of rules. These rules are, as in the case of institutions generally, a set of constitutive conventions. Just as the rules of games do, they specify certain activities and define certain actions . . . If one says the words 'I promise to do X' in the appropriate circumstances, one is to do X, unless certain excusing conditions obtain." But this, in the light of the insistence on constitutive conventions and defining rules, makes it seem that we can agree whether a promise has been made, or excusably left unfulfilled, the way we can agree that a batter is out or that a will is valid. Whereas we rarely solemnly say the words "I promise to do X" (except to a child), yet I may justly be taken to have promised to do something by a simple gesture, verbal or not, of accord. And if I have not done what I said (or signaled) that I would do, there may be understandable disagreements about whether I did all I could under the circumstances, or at least all I could to mitigate the harm my inability caused. No rule tells me when I may end the conversation unilaterally; it is my judgment, not a rule, that lets me conclude that I did what I could. Then why cannot I express the judgment "I did what I could" by saying "I am above reproach"?

My qualm about Rawls's "above reproach" may be expressed this way: It makes me the judge of my obligations, but in a way that removes me from the consequences my verdicts have upon others, as if I were acting from the recognized office or station of a judge. Here is an indication of the importance I attach to questioning the idea that promising is a practice defined by rules. No office is required, or comprehensible, for my entitlement to make or to accept a promise, any more than to speak responsibly, and none I occupy in general dictates for me the limits of a promise, nor shields me from the consequences of precipitousness in making a promise (or, for that matter, in expressing an intention) or of laxness in breaking or interpreting it.

The issue of resentment comes up for Rawls in the section on the problem of envy, where in distinction from envy (which Rawls, following Kant, conceives as one of the vices of hating mankind, p. 532), Rawls conceives that resentment can be justified where an institution can be shown to be unjust or where injury has been done by others. But again my sense is that a necessary shield of protection against false cries for justice has been made too thick. Rawls distinguishes, again following Kant, cases of what he calls benign envy, as follows: "We may remark upon the enviable harmony and happiness of a marriage or a family, . . . or say to another that one envies his greater opportunities or attainments . . . [without] ill will intended or expressed" (p. 532). But in the former case, this may be remarked of a family enjoying distinctly lower means than your own. (It may or may not be a condescending remark.) Now take it that you have seen a family profit over the years from a compounding set of interwoven advantages, of inheritance and education and employment and promotion, so that mediocre talent and intelligence and effort on the one side have amassed position and security out of all proportion to the talent and intelligence and effort and good will on the other.

One may hope you would sufficiently recognize the rewards of virtue in itself to keep the self-destructiveness of envy at bay; but suppose, thinking of your children's lessened chances for success if not for happiness, you exclaim to this family of long acquaintance (if you do not swallow the exclamation, to the detriment of your relation with them) that you resent their complaisance in their achievements and distrust their love of a country which has bought their affection and dulled their sense of inequity. You may not know to which institutions you can point as unjust, nor to any other persons who have done you specific injury, but your resentment does not seem to you irrational. There is nothing you contemplate asking anyone to do about the discrepancy of advantage—but then there is nothing you may be asking or expecting any-one to do if you indeed could, as Rawls says, show why an institution is unjust or how another has injured you. There is nothing a single other of your acquaintance may be able to do to correct the role of influence in gaining admission to a desired institution, nor to monitor the carefully shaded reservation you have been told that a given person has included in a letter of recommendation for you which in effect kills your chances of admission. What fardels are simply to be borne in the inevitable, at some point irreducible, frictions of society is not a question that can sanely come up at every moment.

But how I respond, as a member of the favored family, to your outburst of resentment and indignation is fateful to what I want of my society, to its democratic aspirations. To say something to the effect of "I am above reproach" is to end my relation with this other, and to that extent to injure the texture of my society. To say something to the effect of "These are frictions and fardels you just have to bear" is to claim a standing with this other sufficient to correct with finality her or his judgment of another's situation, appropriate (non-pompous, non-presumptuous, non-dismissive, non-frigid) hence only in very particular circumstances.

Here I recall that I am distinguishing between cases in which what I have to respond to is not my misfortune but my fortunateness. It is the case pertinent to the examples of moral perfectionism as exemplified in remarriage comedy, where the happiness of the pair often seems tied to unequally distributed gifts of some kind—if not of money then a gift of or a talent for life, perhaps one can say. The immediate context of Rawls's appeal to being above reproach is one in which I am defending myself against the self-reproach of not having done enough to prevent or hedge against my own misfortune. That is one cause of depression.

In the opposite case—self-reproach for not having done enough to prevent or hedge against or alleviate the misfortune of others, intimates or strangers—claims upon one's beneficence (especially upon one most apt to have his or her goodness taken advantage of) can produce debilitating demands against which one's very sense of fairness or of equity may leave one defenseless. I say, in particular, that there is no definitive rule of institutions that can be cited for this purpose. What is at stake in denying this aspect of the analogy of morality with games (the lack of defining rules in morality) is this. There is no definitive defense, nor should there be in a democracy, against the sense of being compromised by the partiality, the imperfectness, of one's society's compliance with the principles of justice, when, that is, that partiality is one from which you gain relative advantage.

I may make it a rule to give to charity five percent of my disposable income. That cannot be said to be definitive of the institution of charity. Others at such a point may invoke the idea of duties to oneself to combat excessive duties to others. (Here I am indebted to a conversation with Barbara Herman, author of *The Practice of Moral Judgment*.) But I am not sure that I find that to be an either intellectually or morally clear or satisfying idea. How, for example, can I go about combating a promise I made to others or an expectation others are justified in having of me, with something I am forced to call a promise I made to, or an expectation I have of, myself? I know how to accept a good excuse for another's breaking a promise to me. If the other was in all honesty too sick to give a guest lecture for me, or too strapped to lend me (more) money, that is that. But for me not to give a promised lecture I would have to be in traction, or otherwise visibly incapacitated or endangered or exhausted, to feel fully justified. What promise could I conceivably have made to myself to combat this promise to appear? I may have taken stock of my life and found that my sense of obligation to a segment of family or friends or profession has grown out of control. I have no time for myself; my life is on hold. I may express this by saying that I have promised myself to make time to read more, write more, walk more, spend more time with my children, or their children, follow the doctor's advice to cut back on activities that I know cause me stress, and so on.

This suggests that I want to (or should) modify my life. But the change of existence I contemplate, and may even be said to owe myself, has no bearing on my commitment to appear tomorrow as promised. It takes as much preparation with others who will be affected by this as it takes in reeducating myself. Which suggests that "promise to myself" is a figure of speech— not, of course, an arbitrary one, since what it suggests is that the change

I contemplate is rightly up to me alone, and that it is within my power, and that if I fail to put the change into effect I will have cause to question my knowledge of myself, my care of myself, even my trust of others to respect my decisions for myself. I may feel something like disappointment in myself, perhaps over my cowardice in the face of disappointing others. But it is not the same as the guilt, the destructiveness, I would feel in breaking a promise or ignoring a just expectation.

What is coming into play here is the difficult notion of, if one can express it so, the rights of desire itself. In the background here is Kant's fateful picture of a realm of inclination that as a whole is to be contrasted with, and discounted in the face of, a realm of duty. Also in the background is Mill's picture of a realm of conformity in which the discounting of the realm of inclination, or let's say idiosyncrasy, has been internalized, or let's say universalized. In the chapter on Mill I contrasted Kant's idea of the conflict between freedom and inclination with Mill's conflict between freedom and conformity. In Kant freedom depends upon freedom from desire, in Mill upon the freedom for desire. (Does this signal a change in Western culture from a tradition continuous from the time of Greek philosophy through Kant, that reason, and a rational, moral life, is threatened by unrestrained passion, to a view that passion, and a happy life, is threatened by unrestrained reason—a change brought about by whatever has brought about rationalized, commodified, mass societies?) While Mill is hardly to be understood in *On Liberty* as recommending the rights of one's own desires over the just claims of others, he does evidently want the expression of desire to be included within what is justly mine, as part of what makes society worth consenting to and defending. But then he owes more development to the idea implicit in his text that it is the stifling of the necessary expression of desire that causes the crippling or stunting of the conforming selves he perceives as making up his society.

But if "above reproach" is morally treacherous, and "duty to myself" is obscure, then what is my defense against claims against my advantages, how do I live with what I just called my defenselessness against my compromise by society's imperfection, from which I happen to profit? Here is where the moral ambience, or ambivalence, of perfectionism in remarriage comedies presses in.

There is in each of these films a moment at which the world of the fortunate, of which the principal pair are evidently a part, is impinged upon by the world of the unfortunate, and we are invited to ask how the fortunate (whom we are asked to, and on the whole allow ourselves to, identify with) may be imagined to justify their position in a democracy. The answers given fairly explicitly in the films are hardly intellectually satisfying. In *The Philadelphia Story* one explicit answer is Tracy Lord's saying to Mike, in getting acquainted, that what Mike calls "lack of wherewithal" doesn't "always matter" and citing her fiancé as an example of one who began with nothing; and later Mike concedes that although Dexter Haven is "born to the purple," Mike has discovered that "he's a very nice guy." So we are told that there are exceptions and escapes from the misery of lack; not much political insight there. But at the end, when George, "the people's choice" (generically, or allegorically, George is the temperament of melancholy which classical comedy must expel), flings at the assembled friends his curse—"You and your kind are on your way out, the lot of you!"—we know, or used to know, that that is true enough. The daughters who will inherit from this father will want to be, as Tracy says, "useful in the world," and childless Uncle Willie's estate will perhaps begin some Foundation for something publicly worthwhile.

So one question of morality the films pose for themselves is whether, or to what extent, our attractive pairs find for their protected regions of privacy a sufficient justification in their alliances with the eventual and inevitably rougher world outside and beyond. In *Adam's Rib,* Adam and Amanda are brought to see, for a moment at least, that their marriage is subject, if not so unprotectedly exposed, to the same vulgarities and brutalities as a marriage less cushioned with "wherewithal." In *It Happened One Night,* the upper-class woman is shown to have a good, if uneducated, heart and mind when she gives all the money she has at hand to a woman who has fainted from hunger; and we are supposed to know that the man with whom she now reciprocates love is blessed with a conviviality that will not allow him to live on ill-gotten or ill-inherited gains. These couples are all in motion, all assessing their position in the world.

If it is at them that the question of resentment and outrage is leveled, "above reproach" and "duty to self" are not only out of order but out of character. Their responsiveness to others, on which the films insist, means to me that their response to a charge of unbearable discrepancy between their positions and those of the mass of society would, in effect, be to take it seriously, which means to consider that the charge comes from a competent agent, one who knows the rules of their shared institutions as well as they do. It means, consequently, to let the questioning of their fortune cause them to ask whether they wish to confirm their consent to a society in which their favored position has depended, however much they feel they have earned or deserved it, too much on their social connections, on their genetic and developed powers of quickness and charm, and on luck. So they are forced to become conscious, as it were to taste the fact, that their society is in some measure at best in partial compliance with the principles of justice. My impression of their lives is that they will all, out of different perspectives in the different cases, affirm their consent to their society as embodying good enough justice to warrant whole-hearted defense. But now they consent in the consciousness that their society's partiality compromises them in relation to justice, implicates them in some measure of injustice.

Shall we say they are consenting to being compromised? Then the question becomes: Where does the joyousness, the happiness, they manifest and elicit come from? Shall we say that the happiness is compromised, that the pursuit of happiness is from the beginning compromised?

The questioner of one's position (I assume this is, in a society affording widespread civility, most often oneself) asks, in effect: How do you live with yourself, knowing and seeing what you know and see? To my mind, as I have been saying, there is no justification, that is, no assertible reply, of the form: Because this, the way things are, is an exemplification of the game or realm of justice, or of justice good enough to defend. This would carry the implication I have already deplored—that of treating my questioner as morally incompetent. (Moreover it seems liable to Kant's criticism of moral examples: We cannot know that any given empirical action or institution actually fulfills the condition of dutifulness we claim for it.) Nor is it even accessible or assertible justification to say: Because my society is in good enough compliance with the principles of justice. Or: It is as good or better than any other with comparable resources. Or: The human cost of changing it more rapidly than it is changing already would be too high.

I have faith that these things are true; I judge that they are. To have that faith is the wager of democracy, the faith a democracy stakes in itself. But I do not now, in general, have any better knowledge of these things than you. I cannot *inform* you of these things. I am not morally more competent than you. But if not then your rebuke of me stands to show that I am morally compromised. How I live with this determines my contribution to the moral life of my society.

If your charge does not shake my faith, then to answer your charge my recourse, after reflection, is to be inclined to say: "This is simply what I do, where I am, and reasonably happily. I find that I do consent to this society as one in which to pursue happiness." And since I do, I show this consent in whatever happiness my personal fortunes, social and natural, allow. Of a certain temperament, my consent is based on my sense of my society's openness to reform. Of a different temperament, my consent implies an alienation from the discontent of others. In a democracy, happiness is a political emotion, as depression is; each is a contribution, oppositely, to the general mood in which our joint faith in our enterprise is maintained, the one to its possibilities, the other, perhaps, to its present obstacles to its possibilities. (This is why Emerson and Thoreau recorded the secret despair and the quiet desperation of their fellow citizens, and recorded at the same time their own surprises by joy. I have said that this extremity of mood was, in effect, their prediction of the Civil War.)

I pause to remark on an allusion that some of you may recognize in the preceding paragraph. When I fashioned my—undefensive—reply to your charge of my unwarranted or inscrutable advantage by saying, or being inclined to say (I'll alter it to catch the light another way), "This life is mine, it is simply how I live, what I do, where I am, what has become of me, and not unhappily," I was alluding to, imitating, a passage from Wittgenstein's *Investigations* (the one I call its scene of instruction). The passage, at §217, runs in part as follows: "If I have exhausted the justifications I have reached bedrock, and my spade is turned. Then I am inclined to say: This is simply what I do." Wittgenstein's discovery is of a critical impasse in the mutuality of our concepts. In my view of philosophy one should not seek sides (rely on "isms," perhaps one can still say) in settling its puzzles and perplexities. At *Philosophical Investigations* §133: "For the clarity that we are aiming at is indeed *complete* clarity. But this simply means that the philosophical problems should *completely* disappear." There is no question of a totality of philosophical problems that are to be systematically solved. One can also say: Philosophical problems are not solved *polemically*, which etymologically says, not by taking sides. "Complete clarity," glossed as problems "completely disappearing," implies that there are no sides left. I would say: Nothing (nothing to doubt) is left unexpressed.

This absence of polemic, which marks what Wittgenstein understands as the solution of a philosophical problem, is by no means my view of political perplexities and disputes. I have invoked it to differentiate the political from the philosophical at this level of (dis)agreement, or absence of justifications; hence implicitly to criticize a political interpretation of the scene of instruction. I have put the difference by saying, schematically: philosophical arguments must not be won (philosophy does not conquer by victimization); political arguments must not be lost (the conversation of justice must not be lost, or else the political becomes a realm of victimization). (For those interested in pursuing this interpretation of the political implications in Wittgenstein's scene of instruction, I have taken it further, as part of my criticism of Saul Kripke's reading of this scene, in my book *Conditions Handsome and Unhandsome.*)

The point of relating a political "This is simply what I do, what my life is" to Wittgenstein's philosophical twin of the remark is to extend my essential claim about Wittgenstein's scene of instruction, namely that its response to hitting bedrock is meant as *weak,* temporary, open to continuation. What is raised here is a corner of the issue of the relation of general philosophy to the political and the moral. Rawls wishes to keep individual eccentricities in choosing the economy of a life's goods free of any constraints other than the lexical priorities required by the principles of justice, in particular (in the second principle) those suggested by the intervention of philosophical theories of higher and lower values. Your eccentricities of taste should neither bear upon nor be borne upon by your neighbor's. This is the brunt of Rawls's distrust of what he calls moral perfectionism.

It is true that Emerson's perfectionism, as I see and offer to defend it, suggests a life into which philosophical perplexity has inserted itself. Into the swirl of issues involved here I merely cast the following thought: Perfectionism, as I find it defensible, is concerned not to dictate a specialized economy of pursuits, any more than to urge a maximization of certain pursuits throughout society. Its intervention in human life is justified only by the perplexities of human life itself—I have epitomized philosophy's mode of intervention by saying that it does not speak first. Philosophy exists only where it is called upon. Emerson's "boy," speaking still from his neutrality, is too young for philosophical inhibition. And, as Emerson emphasizes, once the crises of experience overtake him, in the form of philosophical catastrophes—irrationalities, disproportions, incommensurabilities, irreversible choices, unsurveyable consequences—there is no return to innocence. If one says this means that perfectionism holds philosophy to be an inescapable register of human life, hence of moral encounter, so be it.

Rawls, as said, does not seek to justify consent to society; or rather, he interprets the clause of contract theory concerning the consent of the governed as, in his refiguration, finding an analogue in consent to the principles of justice. According to my understanding of his idea that "each aspect of the contractual situation can be given supporting grounds" (*Theory of Justice*, p. 21), this means in practice that each aspect finds its analogue in what he calls his "expository device" (ibid.) which collects such ideas as that of the original position and the veil of ignorance and justice as fairness. I am in effect suggesting that something is left out of the idea of consent when it is refigured or transposed as consent to the principles of justice; and perhaps suggesting that the clause in classical contract theory requiring consent to society finds a different natural extrapolation from Rawls's expository device. It is for this purpose that I have singled out my qualms about his ideas of being "above reproach," of promises as institutions, and of institutions as defined by rules.

And I have arrived at an odd fact. Contract theory is developed to show why one consents to give up certain advantages for certain others, principally giving up unrestrained freedom for fairness and security in being governed. Rawls's theory of justice emphasizes, beyond this, why one should not only consent to be governed together, but consent to a present arrangement in which one is relatively disadvantaged. The reason is, remember: "Whenever social institutions satisfy these principles those engaged in them can say to one another that they are cooperating on terms to which they would agree if they were free and equal persons whose relations with respect to one another were fair." But, since "each person finds himself placed at birth in some particular position in some particular society, and the nature of this position materially affects his life prospects"—since, in other words, our positions are likely to be materially different from one another's, some more advantaged than others—it is those in relatively advantaged positions who are going have to remind those relatively disadvantaged that the terms under which they are operating or cooperating come "as close as a society can to being a voluntary scheme," namely one to which consent is owed. (Those in relatively disadvantaged positions will have to say this to themselves.) Grant that Rawls has accomplished this feat of justification for specific principles of justice.

In going on to ask what the consequences might be imagined to be of the idea of consenting to society as it stands—which is not hypothetical, however critical, but actual—I come upon what I called the odd fact, or let me say the apparently odd question: Why are those relatively *advantaged* prepared to consent? Who is to remind them of society's worthiness for consent? Themselves? Those still more advantaged? But why would they need reminding? Doesn't it seem that the cause of their consent is obvious? If the other is assigned to cut the cake and you to choose the first piece, then if you see and choose an advantageous cut, why would you object to the consequences of the procedure? (This is why what I call "consent from above" may not seem a genuine issue.) Yet in a democracy I have to worry that if the cuts increasingly come out in my favor, I must be profiting from some hidden hand, even if I cannot say where a particular injustice or injury lies, or lay. The closer society comes to presenting itself as a "voluntary scheme," which is to say, the more it seems to me that I am responsible for the way it is, the more I am exposed to asking myself whether I can want a society with the present degree of inequality in it, even when the inequality is in my favor. (This is why consent from above remains a problem.) As if with the advent of democracy a new sense of political guilt, arising from a new civil intimacy, becomes possible, from which, as it were, hierarchy had protected us.

Perhaps this may be pictured as the sense that while, if asked now to step behind the veil of ignorance, I would agree to those principles, but with the awareness that others—that I myself from time to time—do not act with the conviction or imagination that we have participated in choosing these basic principles together. The sense is one not simply of assessing relative disadvantages, but of feeling left out of the basic decisions of the society—of, as I put it in *The Claim of Reason,* lacking a voice in my history. The sense is that society is not mine. This implies that the sense of a society as a voluntary scheme, in which "its members are autonomous and the obligations they recognize self-imposed" does not do something the classical theorists wanted from the sense of a social contract, namely to *remove* me from a state of nature, make a political being of me, create a polis to which I *belong.*

The worry about consent from above is a worry that the alienation of the relatively advantaged is as great a threat to the life of a democracy as is the alienation of the relatively disadvantaged (especially where, as in the United States, so many are greatly advantaged). (One can say that consent out of advantage is less costly psychically than consent despite disadvantage, since you can out of your own will divest yourself of any excess that feeds your guilt. But if morality is not in place in a society of angels or saints, the inability to achieve personal equality with the disadvantaged can be thought to be more costly.) The threat is not of resentment and envy but of a guilty disdain and snobbery—a tendency to distance oneself from the cultural costs of democracy, from the leveling down of taste, the mendacity of public discourse, the intolerance of difference. The disdain may be understood as a reaction to blunt the guilt of advantage, a coarsening of political imagination that makes one indifferent to inequity and acquiescent in the state of nature that exists (as Locke noted) wherever shared consent is not in effect.

The Emersonian perfectionists observe these lives of their society and recognize that these lives are not ones they can with a good heart unequivocally desire, however much they will, with a certain unlightness of heart, obey the society's laws. Rawls identifies perfectionist dissatisfaction with the observation of a lack of cultivation, epitomized by some taste for the arts. But the lack, in Emersonian terms, is of a liberality of thought, of an imagination of adventure, and of a degree of joyousness and wonder in the differences of others, to all of which each has a right to aspire. The arts matter, accordingly, to the extent that they are the indispensable touchstones of such ideals.

The justice in the title "screwball comedies," used to name a Hollywood genre that indiscriminately includes comedies of remarriage, is the suggestion of these comedies as a whole that America's high promise to itself to be something new to the world leaves it without protection against the (self-)reproach of failing to live up to that promise. This lends to its citizens, at their best, their tendency to be—in Clark Gable's self-description in *It Happened One Night*—screwy.

10

Mr. Deeds Goes to Town

1 The film opens with a prologue, here simply of a car plunging off a road, killing its driver, its sole occupant.

2 The ensuing sequence opens into the confusion of a newsroom, where reporters are intent on learning and breaking the news concerning the mystery of who is heir to the careless and perhaps heirless millionaire who died in the crash. We get the idea that the sense of life as ruled by accident and the unsurveyable consequences of actions will be the subject of the narrative to follow.

3 The millionaire's lawyers (Cedar, Cedar, Cedar, and Budington) locate the heir, his nephew, a country bumpkin, Longfellow Deeds, who lives in Mandrake Falls, upon whom the lawyers and their press agent, named Cobb, decide to call personally. They have difficulty communicating with the first citizen of Mandrake Falls they encounter: "Do you know Longfellow Deeds?" "Yes indeedy," is the man's reply, and he continues on his way into a barn. When he reemerges they ask where he resides. The man asks "Who?" When they convey the idea that they want to know where Deeds lives, the man offers to drive them in his car.

4 The housekeeper says Deeds is not home, and rebukes the driver for not taking them to where he knows Deeds is. He replies that they told him they wanted to know where Deeds lives.

5 The housekeeper explains that Deeds is famous in town as a poet who writes sentiments on postcards, and she reads the visitors one of them. Asked whether Deeds is married, she replies that he is looking for a lady in distress. When Deeds (Gary Cooper) walks in, and is introduced, he sits down, picks up his tuba to insert in it the object he holds up proudly and calls a "new mouth-piece," saying he's always losing them to kids who use them for pea shooters. (Nothing further is ever explicitly made of the allegorical possibilities in the fact that a lawyer in American slang may be called, irreverently, a "mouth-

piece.") Told that he has just inherited twenty million dollars, Deed tests the new mouthpiece, and the housekeeper asks whether they would like lunch. Deeds, assuring the puzzled lawyers that he has heard their news, asks why his uncle has left him the money since he doesn't need it. The whole town shows up at the train station to give him a sendoff; he plays the tuba in the band that anchors the celebration.

6 In the lawyers' office in New York, we learn that the corporation's books must be protected from examination, and the chief Mr. Cedar assures the others that he will succeed in getting power of attorney from the childish Mr. Deeds.

7 A furious woman rails at a passive man that *they* should share the inheritance. The man says he can't help it that his uncle didn't like him.

8 In a newspaper's crowded office, its editor is chastising a group of reporters for not being able to get an inside story on Deeds, who is news. They clear out, except for Babe Bennett (Jean Arthur), who is preoccupied in practicing casting a knot in a small piece of rope with one hand. The editor says she's the one who can get the story and he'll give her a paid month's vacation if she'll do it. She accepts.

9 Deeds is being measured in his newly inherited mansion for a tailored suit. Mr. Cedar is present and informs Deeds that acting for Deeds, if Deeds will give him power of attorney, is done for no extra money. Deeds says that isn't natural and asks to go over their books. (Later, the idea of nature plays an explicit, if comic, offstage role.)

10 The Friends of the Opera attend upon Deeds, elect him chairman, and indicate that they expect him to make up the year's deficit, $180,000. When Deeds asks whether they sell tickets, they reply that ticket sales, though the performances are sold out, are naturally insufficient. Deeds denies that this is natural and suggests that they must be putting on the wrong kind of shows. (This is a tip that the kind of show Deeds thinks may be right is instanced in the one we are viewing, a Capra movie. Hence the issue is raised concerning the relation of film to opera. If we haven't time to go into this relation in this chapter, it will surely come up later in connection with *The Lady Eve*.)

11 Back to the suit fitting, Cobb offers to get women for Deeds. Declining, Deeds remarks to his valet that Cobb speaks of women as if they were cattle. The valet, who is evidently as uninterested in women as he is in cattle, replies "Everyone has their own tastes."

12 Deeds slides down a long, curving banister to the entrance hall of the mansion, and escapes his bodyguards by locking them in a closet.

Mr. Deeds Goes to Town

13   Outside, at night in the rain, Babe is waiting across the street in a car with two photographers. As Deeds leaves the house, she alerts the photographers to follow, gets out of the car and reaches the other side of the street in time to let Deeds see her walking slowly, unsteadily. He follows her, she faints, he lifts her up, she says she just walked too far looking for a job.

14a   Deeds and Babe are discovered in Tullio's, a bustling restaurant whose sign promises that here you "Eat with the Literati." Deeds is enjoying watching Babe's pleasure in eating, and says, "You were a woman in distress, weren't you?" The waiter informs Deeds that some writers have come in, and points them out at their "large round table."

14b   The writers have invited Deeds and Mary (as she has introduced herself to him) to their table. They ask him questions about his methods of writing; he responds modestly, saying he's not a great writer like them; then when they ask him to recite some of his poetry he realizes they are treating him condescendingly. As he rises to leave, he says "I guess all famous people aren't big people." The two writers flanking him rise with him to protest his leaving and with two punches he knocks them down. A third writer catches up with him as he and Mary are leaving, and drunkenly but sincerely praises him (it is a brilliant aria by a clearly recognizable character actor of the period): "A writer with a straight left and a right hook! Brother, you have added a week to my life. Let me show you New York."

15   A montage of newspaper headlines indicates that Babe Bennett has named Deeds "The Cinderella Man." She has covered the night on the town in which, among other things, Deeds fed doughnuts to a horse.

16   The next morning, Walter, his valet, awakens Deeds at midday and they discover that he doesn't remember much of the night before, for example that he was brought home by two policemen who had discovered him and the writer in their shorts yelling "Back to Nature."

17   Cobb, the press agent for the lawyers, enters (played by Lionel Stander), furious at the uncontrolled newspaper headlines. He tells Deeds that punching people in the nose is no solution. Deeds replies that sometimes it is the only solution.

18   After a nighttime tour on the upper deck of a bus, Deeds and Mary are in front of Grant's Tomb. Mary says most people find it a letdown. Deeds says it depends on what they see—and he gives a sentimental account of Grant's dreams, Lee's heartbreak, and Lincoln's vision of a great new nation.

19 The lawyer Cedar, unable to extract the power of attorney, thinks the other relatives of Deeds' uncle may be useful for their nuisance value.

20 Sitting on a park bench with Babe/Mary, Deeds says people have the Saint Vitus' Dance; they work so hard living that they forget how to live. After this unattributed citation from Thoreau, he then explicitly quotes Thoreau (inexactly): "They built grand palaces but they forgot to build the noble men to live in them." Babe says Deeds reminds her of her father. They discover a shared love of music and sing a duet as she shows how she learned from her father to use drumsticks. A fire engine passes, sirens on, and Deeds, as an auxiliary fireman, runs to join the fighters.

21 Babe in her friend Mabel's apartment finds she can no longer go on with her subterfuge. Deeds phones her. He's in bed, lying on his back. He says he couldn't sleep and that he's working on a poem. "It's hard for me sometimes to say things, so I write them." Babe tells Mabel that she is crucifying him. Mary replies that it's been done before. "He's got goodness in him, Mabel."

22 While Deeds is lying on the bed, now playing the tuba, his valet comes in. Deeds chases him out, yelling at him, onto the landing, and on to the stairs. On the stairs he hears his yells echoing. This interests him. He stops chasing and involves his valet and two butlers into trying their echoes; then gets them into hooting all together. "Let that be a lesson to you," he says as he departs, satisfied.

23 After a further montage of Babe's stories, ending with "Brilliant Reception Set for Tonight," we witness the gala, with the opera people much in evidence.

24 Deeds shows up at Mabel's apartment and tells Babe/Mary he threw the people at the party out of the house and that he wants to talk to her. They go for a walk. He tells her when he was young he used to talk to an imaginary girl friend. "I hoped she would turn out to be real." Returning to the apartment, he asks Babe to read the poem he's been working on. She reads it to both of them, a declaration of love that contains the line, "I'm . . . speechless in your presence." When, moved to tears, she finishes, he says, "You don't have to say anything now," and runs away down the night street tripping over a sequence of trash cans.

25 Babe tells her editor she's quitting, that Deeds has proposed, that she's going to lunch at his house and will take the risk of telling him the truth.

26 Deeds is overseeing preparations for the luncheon table. Cobb enters with proof that Mary is Babe Bennett. Cobb phones her newspaper and puts

Deeds on the phone. He asks her if she wrote the stories. Cobb is stunned and moved to see that Deeds is brokenhearted.

27 Deeds says that he's going back home, that they can have the estate. As he is dressed for departure and headed down the sweeping stairs, there is a disturbance at the door and a crazed man forces his way in and confronts Deeds with his frivolous escapades open only to the super-rich, feeding doughnuts to horses when thousands of men are out of work and their families are starving. When Deeds accuses him of being a "moocher" like all the rest, the man takes out a pistol, then comes to his senses, and collapses in grief. Deeds sits silently and encouragingly with the famished man at the table he had helped prepare for lunch with Mary, watching him, over the careful flowers, eating mechanically, still dazed, drinking out of a gold-rimmed glass.

28 This time a montage of headlines declares "Deeds To Give Fortune Away; Stuns Financial World; Unemployed Storm Deeds' House." In that house, Deeds is interviewing men who have applied to him to receive acres of land, a cow, and seeds. Police come in with a warrant for Deeds's arrest on grounds of insanity. Cobb says he'll phone Deeds's lawyer, Cedar, only to be told that it is Cedar who has filed the complaint against Deeds.

29 At the County Hospital, Babe is not allowed to see Deeds, and Cobb pleads with him to defend himself when his sanity trial convenes. But Deeds has fallen mute. Cobb encounters Babe in the corridor of the hospital and accuses her of crucifying Deeds.

30 The last montage of newspaper headlines, announcing the trial, declares: "Deeds Refuses Counsel."

31 Roughly the final twenty or twenty-five minutes of the film depict the astonishing trial. Deeds sits silently in the dock while witness after witness describes each of his charming foibles, as well as his plan to give away his money to the needy, as proofs of insanity. When at last, after Babe Bennett is accused of loving Deeds, and confesses it, and the courtroom crowded with the jobless men Deeds had planned to help fills with shouts to him not to abandon them, Deeds speaks up.

32 His defense is mostly to show that his eccentricities, like playing the tuba at all hours, are no stranger than any of the inexplicable things people do to help them think; and as for his plan's being crazy, he reports that Mr. Cedar offered to withdraw his complaint against Deeds for a share of the fortune. The implication that if he's crazy everybody is crazy, is essentially the testimony that the two unworldly sisters from his home town give in observing that everyone is "pixilated," except the two of them. Deeds' summation, after he says to the judge, "There's just one more thing," is to knock down Mr. Cedar. The chief judge declares Deeds the sanest man that ever walked into his courtroom, and the crowd erupts in joy, carrying Deeds out of the court in triumph.

33 The room is empty except for the two sisters at the side and, alone in the center of the room, Babe. Deeds, disheveled, his jacket ripped from the exuberance of good fellowship, escapes back into the courtroom, closing the heavy doors behind him, picks up Mary as if she were a child, or a woman in distress, and stands in place while she covers his shining, bewildered countenance with kisses.

This film's explicit invoking of Thoreau, motivated by Longfellow Deeds's experience of Grant's Tomb and of Times Square as emblems of what Deeds calls America and its threatened loss of its ideals, is as extreme an expression of Emersonian perfectionism as I have found on film. But this film's particular role in this book is to force the consideration of how this representative of the "screwball comedy" differs from (other) members of the genre of remarriage comedy.

We can never go far wrong in picking up the remarriage genre by the handle of its conversation. Deeds and Mary's exchanges have nothing of the witty confrontation of their remarriage cousins. They are full of Deeds's painful sincerity and Mary/Babe's irony, at first indifferent and eventually tortured. (Jean Arthur, for those who love the era of films represented by the classical remarriage comedies, is one of the most admired of the stars of the period, her career ending early, with her untypical role as the good wife in *Shane*. Her range of passion, from ironic backtalk to pure pathos, is unsurpassed among the great stars, the equal of that of Barbara Stanwyck and Irene Dunne and Carole Lombard.) Babe and Deeds are not exactly instructed by each other in their imagined ideals (as the couple in remarriage comedy characteristically are); they merely have to believe that in each other, in Deeds's words, what they imagine has turned out to be real, and to hope that bad timing is overcome in time for them to believe it together.

The emphasis on conversation is, nevertheless, as essential to *Mr. Deeds* as it is to the comedies of remarriage, but it occurs at a different level, perhaps one could say a more metaphysical level. Deeds's problem is not to keep his end up in establishing an equal and reciprocal battle of self-examination, but to keep heart in the point of talking at all. At the trial, Babe accounts for his silence by asking why he should talk when his words have been invariably twisted against him ever since he came to New York. But she is expressing only her own guilt. His problem with speech had begun long before New York, as he reveals in saying, "It's hard for me to say things sometimes, so I write them" and again in telling her later, leading up to his poem of proposal to her, that when he was young he invented an imaginary friend to talk to, that is, to enable him to talk. But talking is established as a revelation of human existence from virtually the beginning of the film's narrative when the lawyers from New York visit Mandrake Falls and have that species of Zen exchange with a local beginning "Do you know Longfellow Deeds?" to which the man answers "Yes" and is evidently satisfied that he has fully answered the question; and when this same man understands that they are interested in who Deeds is he replies, "Longfellow Deeds, he's very democratic, he'll talk to anybody," thus setting up the issue of the popular in culture as signaled by the name Longfellow and by this Longfellow's composing verses on postcards.

I mention mostly in passing the great subject raised in the film of the relation between the serious and the popular in modern culture, broached early when Deeds suggests that the opera association is putting on the wrong kind of shows, and emphasized when Deeds explicitly declares to the writers he meets at the eatery of the literati that he knows his writing is not great, as theirs is, but indicates that his work has its place in human encounters. The place of the great writers in this restaurant, and in the world (call it New York), is named when the waiter points them out, at the "round table over there." This would in its time unmistakably have referred to the Algonquin Round Table, so called because a group of writers associated mainly through their relation to the *New Yorker* magazine met for lunch at the Algonquin Hotel.

The *New Yorker* at that period (say from the late 1920s through the 1940s) represented a remarkably high level of, let us say, public American intellectual sophistication. The best of its writers, such as James Thurber and E. B. White, produced work of lasting note (in these two cases especially, significantly, their superb books for children); George Kaufmann and Moss Hart wrote for Capra and for Broadway; the likes of Preston Sturges (writer, director, and producer of *The Lady Eve*) might sometimes join them. But none exists, or aspired to exist, in the realms occupied by Hemingway, Faulkner, Scott Fitzgerald, Eudora Welty, Katherine Anne Porter, Marianne Moore, Wallace Stevens, William Carlos Williams. Yet the *New Yorker*'s stratum of, as it were, stylish intelligence, associated with the then thriving culture of Broadway theater and hence overlapping with a significant segment of Hollywood writers and directors, is one that supports a justified nostalgia when New York inspires nostalgia—for more people than those who have lived there.

For a critical view of this stratum of culture, I recommend the chapter on the *New Yorker* in Robert Warshow's recently reissued *The Immediate Experience*. In his short life, Warshow wrote for, among other publications, the *Partisan Review*, the literary-political quarterly associated with the so-called New York Jewish intellectuals flourishing from the late thirties to around the late fifties. Warshow was untypical of that group in taking film with great seriousness.

Another feature of that entire, heterogeneous but interconnected intellectual ambience is that no one in it spoke for philosophy. The only contemporary American philosopher with the charisma to compete with these cultural icons was John Dewey, and it is no easier to imagine a conversation around that Algonquin round table with him in it than one including Wittgenstein, or Heidegger. And by the time, in the late thirties, the refugees from Hitler came to America to establish logical positivism as the avant-garde of philosophy, the field had become academically professionalized beyond the reach of sophisticated general intellectual exchange. So, apart from my personal grief that a generally educated American culture has failed to find in itself room for a general knowledge of a few high points of the history of philosophy to hold in common (as would be expected in Europe among those claiming a university education), I confess that I do not know, and it may be significant of more than my personal limitations that I do not know, whether in *Mr. Deeds Goes to Town* Capra and his writers are mocking the writers of the round table for being overly cultivated or for failing to be cultivated enough.

Then there is the connection of speech and silence associated with violence as epitomized in the awe with which the prominent writer in the restaurant hailed Deeds as "a writer with a straight left and a right hook." It raises the question whether writing is to carry the weight of a punch or whether punching results from an insufficiency in speech, as in Melville's *Billy Budd*. Speech as essential to the human polity has been part of our concern from the beginning, when I have invoked Aristotle's perception of speech as the condition of political life, and political life as essential, or natural, to human existence. (Inevitably this will be further stressed when we turn to Aristotle's treatise on ethics in Chapter 19.) And expression as essential to individual human existence has been part of our consideration since I emphasized Emerson's "Self-Reliance" as, in effect, an enactment of Descartes's cogito argument: it understands human existence as taking one's existence into one's speech—Aristotle will call something like this taking one's life upon oneself. We might think of it as accepting responsibility for being the one you are, hence, as perfectionists may put the matter, for becoming it—and demanding this fundamental gesture from others. Without this acceptance of radical responsibility, as for each jot and tittle of one's deeds and words, politics tends toward the exchanges of ghosts. One could think of Deeds's scheme for giving new land and a cow and seeds to farmers who have lost their farms, as his providing them not alone with their means of livelihood but at the same time with their means of expression. It is not aimlessly that he quotes Thoreau's transcendentalist vision.

Of course this is not much in the way of a political program. But neither is Mill's *On Liberty* or Locke's *Second Treatise of Government* or Rawls's *A Theory of Justice*. They envision tests for the governance of a society that those governed can want and can find worthy of consenting to. Deeds's idea is that a society in which people cannot express themselves (call this a society that cannot hear itself) has debarred itself from receiving consent, which is to say, from legitimacy. (The secret melancholy and quiet desperation Emerson and Thoreau perceived in their fellow citizens meant politically to them a state in which consent can be neither given nor withdrawn. Deeds's visibly falling silent, accordingly, is his identification with this state of mind, figuratively his condemnation of a society that has destroyed the point of speaking. (This is a fair description of how Austin and Wittgenstein perceive the consequence of language becoming metaphysicalized. The question for them is to locate the human responsibility for this. Here is where they fundamentally differ, namely in the terms in which they criticize philosophical failure.) The credibility of Deeds's condemnation is what accounts for the sense of hysteria in the efforts of the good people in Capra's world to get him to speak. Then the task of the film's narrative is to reveal the conditions under which the resumption of speech becomes possible for him.

―――――――――

Here I shall adapt, or incorporate, some paragraphs from an earlier essay of mine on *Mr. Deeds Goes to Town*. I called the essay "What Photography Calls

Thinking," taking my cue from Deeds's defense of human thinking as an expression of something about the human body. In taking the human body in motion as an inescapable subject of movies, I in effect adduce the motion picture camera as a further defense, or ratification, of Deeds's vision of the human body as essentially nervous, restless. While this may seem to be about the most trivial feature of human beings, the fact that they are fidgety, it is also the feature of human mortality that the *motion* of motion picture photography cannot fail to capture. When Deeds, speaking in his defense, cites doodling, nose-twitching, knuckle-cracking, ear-pulling, and nail-biting—these are not examples of the "failed actions" Freud includes in his portrait of the psychopathology of everyday life, but they are a further field revealing the nontraumatic region of the (interpretable) limitations of our control over our bodies—his speech becomes a kind of voice-over narrative as the camera illustrates each of these involuntary movements in close-up, assembling his evidence. This underscores Deeds's alliance with the camera. It is his acknowledgment that to provide such illustration or evidence is a power and a possible glory natural to the moving picture camera, that the most apparently insignificant repetitions, turnings, pauses, and yieldings of human beings are as interesting to it as is the beauty or the science of movement.

The camera's knowledge of the metaphysical restlessness of the live body at rest is internal to what Walter Benjamin calls cinema's optics of the unconscious. Under examination by the camera, a human body becomes for its inhabitant a field of betrayal more than a ground of communication, and the camera's further power is manifested as it documents the individual's self-conscious efforts to control the body each time it is conscious of the camera's attention to it. I might call these recordings *somatograms* (cf. cardiograms, electroencephalograms), to register the essential linking of the pattern of a body's motions with the movements of the machine that records them. We seem to have no standing word for what somatograms record. "Mannerisms" is partial in its noting of characteristically recurrent behavior; "manners" is partial in its attention to social modification. The plain word "behavior" has the right generality, but in a time still unpredictably marked by the psychological and philosophical sensibility of behaviorism—in which behavior is reduced to something outer, from which something inner (call it mind) has been scooped out—the expressiveness of the range of the restless is more or less incomprehensible.

Mr. Deeds Goes to Town

Emerson's essay "Behavior," from *The Conduct of Life,* is an effort to reha-bilitate the concept of behavior, along with that of manners, to return the mind to the living body. Here is a sample: "Nature tells every secret once. Yes, but in man she tells it all the time, by form, attitude, gesture, mien, face and parts of the face, and by the whole action of the machine. The visible carriage or action of the individual, as resulting from his organization and his will combined, we call manners. What are they but thought entering the hands and feet, controlling the movements of the body, the speech and behavior? . . . The power of manners is incessant,—an element as uncon-cealable as fire." Emerson's effort of conceptual rehabilitation constitutes this marvelous essay as a major contribution to the aesthetics of cinema (as well as to the aesthetics of acting, a coincidence hardly merely coincidental). (That he implicitly links the mind, or call it spirit, with fire, invokes an ancient intuition of philosophical thought.)

Deeds's name for the condition that causes universal fidgetiness is *think-ing.* "Everyone does silly things when they think," he declares. He uses the word "think" or "thinking" repeatedly, each time emphasizing an idiosyn-crasy. Why playing the tuba is part of his particular somatogram is of course a further question. (Is it that the tuba is only very accidentally a medium of outstanding virtuosity but is almost inherently sociable and encouraging, keeping the rhythm going in early jazz bands, always forming the basis for celebratory marching bands?) The more pressing question for us is why or how Deeds has been brought to break his silence in order to speak of the connection between thinking and silliness—or why speaking of this connec-tion is what allows him to speak. Why is it now that he is willing to claim his identity and his contribution to the polity and his personal happiness against the villainous incomprehension of the world?

I take his appeal to the concept of thinking with greater philosophical seriousness than others may be prepared, right off, to grant it. Deeds's per-ception of fidgetiness discloses an essential feature of the human, not simply of the animal, body; it marks a creature in which the body and its soul do not everywhere fit. (This does not deny, on the contrary it ratifies, I trust, the insight Wittgenstein articulates in the *Investigations* in saying, "The human body is the best picture of the human soul.") I wish to leave open the ques-tion whether this is true of the human creature as such, or whether it may be true only of the human creatures in our epoch, and especially true of those creatures in the period of late capitalism that Deeds's social program of redistribution defines, one in which a large number of evidently hardworking, un-envious, independent people are needlessly being deprived of what they need in order to make a living. "Need" is another recurrent term of Deeds's discourse. I have reported his being puzzled by his uncle's bequest since he (Deeds) doesn't need it. His word for those who do not wish to do their fair share of work is "moochers"; he is shown to be indiscriminate in his application of this term.

That fidgetiness means, or proves, thinking will be as striking in our opening glimpse of Cary Grant's nervous hands in *His Girl Friday,* in Chapter 18, as it is in Deeds's naming it in Gary Cooper's tuba playing now before us. At the same time, I have taken it to prove that the *desire* to think, as Heidegger emphasizes in the opening paragraph of his fascinating lectures from 1951, *What Is Called Thinking?* (an awkward translation, as perhaps any would be, of *Was Heisst Denken?*), is essential to the possibility of thinking. It is the connection of thinking with the human desire of the possible, of realization, that prompts me to see in Deeds's words, and the way he uses them, a recapturing in the everyday of Descartes's perception of what thinking itself proves, namely the existence of the human. Here is the cause of my finding that when Deeds begins to speak, defending his sanity, he is performing, as the climax to be expected in a melodramatic structure, a version of Descartes's cogito, taking on the proof of his own existence, against its denial by the world.

Some will be unwilling to grant this degree of seriousness to Deeds's courtroom lecture on silliness and thinking. They may wish to protect their sense of the serious by suggesting that Deeds's words are at best a parody of philosophy, not the thing of philosophy itself. I am sympathetic to this. At about the time I was first immersed in finding my way through the events of Capra's *Mr. Deeds Goes To Town* I was finding cause to suppose that at some stage serious philosophy may come to manifest itself as—one could say, to exist most immediately as—a parody of philosophy. This is after all a reasonable way to try grasping the mood of Emerson's use of Descartes's saying "I think," "I am"—namely quoting it and in the same breath implicitly criticizing his own quoting of it, as if performing a little demonstration that every word we say risks parody. All have been said before. Well, of course, otherwise they wouldn't be *words,* parts of a (shared) language.

But how can words carry the expressive weight each of us gives them—or counts on—on the thousands of varying occasions each of us thousands, millions, of speakers pronounce them? The exchange of words has been compared with, allegorized by, the exchange of money. Wittgenstein alludes to this in the *Investigations*, §120: "Here the word, there the meaning. The money, and the cow that you can buy with it. (But contrast: money, and its use.)" But a soiled, dim, yet legible twenty dollar bill is worth no more nor less than that crisp one, fresh as mint. Supposing, of course, that neither is counterfeit. But here the disanalogy between words and money asserts itself. It is as if I am responsible for ensuring that my words, as legible as anyone else's, are not counterfeits of themselves, that they are backed by my meaning, here and now.

(I think here, by the way, of the once-famous occurrence in the film *Mr. Deeds* of the word "pixilated"—probably not in the treasure chest of most speakers' vocabulary before the film was released. It is, in an aside, explicitly defined by an otherwise unremarked character in the film as connected with "pixies"; but it could have done its work, been successfully introduced into the community of the courtroom, without explicit definition. That this calls attention, as it were, to our confidence in playing free and easy with the general run of words—or to what may seem the groundlessness of this confidence—is perhaps a reason James Joyce introduces the word into *Finnegans Wake*.)

I was pushed to the idea of Emerson's parodying Descartes in the course of reading and writing about a couple of stories by Edgar Allan Poe, in which I seemed to discover apparently parodistic adoptions, or adaptations, of the cogito argument. (This essay, "Being Odd, Getting Even," appears in my book *In Quest of the Ordinary*.) Which in turn prompts me to add here that the perception of our inability to pronounce, as it were, on our own, or for ourselves, our cogito, taking upon ourselves our existence, is part of a perception that we, so far as we have a say in the matter, persist in a state of preexistence, as if metaphysically missing persons, ghosts. Emerson's word for this state of lacking words of our own is "conformity." It obviously has precursors in Romantic perceptions of the human as dead, or deadened, and it is a specific conceptual precursor of Nietzsche's "last man" (in *Thus Spoke Zarathustra*), hence of Heidegger's *Das Man* (in chapter 4 of *Being and Time*).

But does the perpetual risk of parody ensure the perpetual lack of (intellectual, philosophical) authority, a matter essential to Descartes's broaching of the issue of the cogito? One could say: The point of the proof in saying "I think" is not alone that it must be said, or thought, in taking it upon myself, but also that no one else can, that is, no one can say it for me. This is the issue, as expressed in this film, of what allows Deeds to break his silence, to take upon himself authority in his speech. Recall his quoting Thoreau's observation that people have the Saint Vitus' Dance. This is the more familiar name for the disorder called chorea, found mostly in children and associated with temporary brain dysfunction. In Deeds's fantasm (and for that matter in Thoreau's) there is no distinction to be made between Saint Vitus' Dance and human behavior as such, as it has become, as if human behavior is now in general the result of brain damage. When the two comically dotty old sisters testify—under friendly cross-examination by Deeds in the courtroom—that not only Deeds but everyone except themselves is pixilated, they discredit their earlier testimony (or disrupt the conventional, or say conforming, implication of that testimony) that Deeds is, in the judge's term, "peculiar." Everyone thereupon apparently agrees that this shows the sisters to be mentally incompetent, anyway incompetent witnesses. But the only difference between their view of the world and Deeds's view is that Deeds does not exempt himself, any more than Thoreau exempts himself, from the madness of the world. Perhaps this is what philosophical authority sounds like.

To dismiss Deeds as too silly for philosophical thought is to deny him a voice in defining what silliness is, a concept essential to his explicit view of the human. And if we deny him this voice, how are we different from the corrupt prosecution, who would exercise an analogous denial by having him declared insane? And how do we understand the muteness that prepared the condition, you may say the seriousness, of his cogito? The woman who loves him screams out that he is being crucified. (Frank Capra, not unlike other artists, finds the figure of Christ near at hand for identifying the posture of his heroes in their moments of rejection. Some will find this an unredeemably coarse habit, perhaps in the way Nietzsche found Luther's intellectual habits sometimes to be coarse.) Without going that far, the question remains how far we credit the grief, the sense of rejection, that this hero's extended muteness bespeaks. Our answer to that question determines how seriously we take this man's (intellectual) seriousness, or for that matter, Frank Capra's and his writers'.

I am expressing here an anxiety you have heard from me before, a function of my knowing quite well that lovers of classical American movies not uncharacteristically take such philosophical remarks as occur to me in thinking about such films to be needless and pretentious, and that professional students of film are in particular often not prepared to credit such company for American movies. My knowledge is further colored by the comparatively benign attitude of colleagues in professional philosophy for whom such speculation may be fit for an intellectually frivolous hour.

It has been urged upon me that such dismissals should not matter to me so much. And in fact it may be that things have changed more than I know in the years since *Pursuits of Happiness,* and half a decade later my reflections on *Mr. Deeds Goes To Town,* were first published. Yet I think one sees in the work of Emerson and of Thoreau that analogous dismissals have mattered as much to them. I would not wish to hide from myself the possibility that some such dismissal is irreducible in these regions, that it goes with the territory. What territory? So far, wherever philosophy is haunted by being irreducibly in struggle, or in league, with its parody (as from its beginning it knows itself in struggle with sophistry, its envious twin); and wherever film (like any art?) knows itself subversive of what it serves, putting everything it touches on trial.

To provide a fair test of the question of Deeds's intellectual seriousness, we would need to *place* Deeds in that courtroom, arrive at him, derive him, from the paths of his narrative and cinematic development, something we can only suggest here. I'll draw to some conclusion by asking about the role the camera plays in Deeds's willingness to speak and to claim his happiness with the woman, taking on two ideas that are already well in play here—one is Deeds's linking with the camera as he in effect provides a voice-over lecture on its revelation of thinking (in nervousness); the other is Emerson's perception that we are mostly incapable any longer of taking on our existence by ourselves, by acknowledging our fatedness to thinking. My thought here is that while my thinking, call it the mind's declaration of presence to itself, no longer secures my conviction in my human existence, the camera proves that existence, in a compensatory action, by the mode in which it accepts the presence to it of the live human body, in particular by its registration of the body's apparently least intelligent property, its fidgetiness, its metaphysical restlessness. In Descartes the proof of my existence was that my thinking cannot doubt itself; after Emerson the proof of my embodied thinking is that it cannot be concealed.

Am I saying that the camera is necessary to this knowledge? Descartes says that my existence is proved "each time I say 'I think,' or conceive it in my mind." Must I commit myself to saying that my existence is proven (only) each time the camera rolls my way? I ask a little license here. My idea is that the invention of the motion picture camera reveals something that has already happened to us, hence something, when we fail to acknowledge it, that is knowledge of something fundamental about our existence which we resist. And the camera also reveals and records that resistance—recall that, in the course of Deeds's lecture to the court, each time the camera follows his attention to a person's body's motion, that person's reflex is shown to be to attempt to hide the motion. We can think of what the camera reveals as a new strain either in our obliviousness to our existence, or in a new mode of certainty of it.

If the price of Descartes's proof of his existence was a perpetual recession of the body (a kind of philosophical counter-Renaissance, now in the name of strict science instead of stern religion), the price of an Emersonian proof of my existence is a perpetual visibility of the self, a theatricality in my presence to others, hence to myself. The camera is an emblem of perpetual visibility. Descartes's self-consciousness thus takes the form of embarrassment. (Recall once more Emerson on introducing Descartes: "Man is timid, he is afraid to say . . .")

Deeds is accordingly the name of one who sees the stakes in this altered condition and who submits himself to the camera's judgment, permits its interrogation, its victimization, of him. It is an unlooked-for species of bravery. Psychologically, submission to a somatogram—to the synchronization between body and camera—demands passiveness, you may say demands the visibility of the feminine side of character, male or female. Capra's mastery of the medium of film, or his obedience to it, guides him to make certain that we are aware of the beauty of Gary Cooper's face, and in two instances he photographs him posed as in a glamour shot of a female star, lying on his back across a bed, capturing his full length from a vantage just above his head. (He is, in one instance, playing the tuba, perhaps to distract us from what is happening, perhaps to give us a hint that more is happening than we might think.) Cinematically, submission to the camera declares what I have called the natural ascendancy on film of the actor over the character, so that the rightness of its being specifically Gary Cooper who plays Deeds comes here to the fore. Capra is interpreting the embarrassment (say the self-consciousness) of the Emersonian proof—that thinking cannot be concealed—in terms of Cooper's world-historical capacity for depicting shyness; and vice versa, giving a metaphysical interpretation of this American mode of shyness.

Narratively, the condition of Deeds's happy ending is that his victimization be interpreted, or redeemed, as his particular willingness to reverse roles with the woman. We have repeatedly been told of his boyish wish for romance, his wish "to rescue a woman in distress." Jean Arthur asserts once for all her superiority over Deeds in the realm of deeds, call it the masculine realm, by pretending to him to be such a woman. She has ridiculed exactly that wish of his by naming him The Cinderella Man—ambiguously suggesting that he is as much in need of being rescued as he is in a position to provide rescue. But this, in turn, is the expression of her own condition of romance, her wish to discover a man for whom she could make it all right that he has been badly frightened by desire and perhaps left a slipper in making his escape.

He has twice run from her, each time at a moment when his desire was importunate. Early, as noted, when he runs to the fire engine from the park; then later, elaborately, when, as she completes reading aloud the poem he has composed for her, he races down the night streets, in a solo of awkwardness that cinematically registers the falling of an American male in love. In the courtroom his starting to speak is the sign that he has stopped running. He claims the woman's love by acknowledging that the shoe fits, that he was, so to speak, at the ball, that he has desires and can ask her to rescue him from his fear of expression.

The man's willingness to speak, to express desire, comes in response to the woman's courtroom declaration, under cross-examination, that she loves him (a familiar Hollywood topos). I think we are entitled here, further, to understand the man's reading of this woman's declaration of love as a signal of her own distress. Thus, after all, she grants him his wish to rescue, to be active, to take deeds upon himself, as he grants her wish to her. So this film participates, with comedies of remarriage, but in a distant register of human mood, in the comedy of equality and reciprocity.

The words with which the man breaks his silence are "I'd like to put in my two cents"—which is still useable American slang for expressing an opinion. Why would this man, whose adventure recounts the inheriting and attempted bequeathing of one of the richest fortunes in the country, initiate his willingness to quit his silence and to claim the inheritance of his existence, his right to desire, by speaking of speaking as an issue of giving a modest sum of money, or an issue of modestly adding to a communal giving of money? Of course one can bring any number of ideological suspicions to bear here. I think the film deserves also the following line of consideration.

Exercising the right to speak not only takes precedence over social power, it takes precedence over any particular form of accomplishment; no amount of contribution is more valuable to the formation and preservation of community than the willingness to contribute and the occasion to be heard. Further, unlike twenty million dollars—or the $180,000 the Friends of the Opera ask from Deeds—the contribution of two cents is one that can likely be responded to equally by others; it leaves your voice your own and allows your opinion to matter to others only because it matters to you. It is not a voice that will be heard by villains. This means that to discover our community a few will have to be punched out, made speechless in their effort to usurp or devalue the speech of others—one interpretation of Deeds's repeated violence, punching men on the jaw. It is a fantasy of a reasonably well ordered participatory democracy. It has its dangers; democracy has; speech has. If the motion picture camera contributes its uniqueness to help keep the perfectionist, utopian register of democracy alive, that is power and glory enough to justify its existence, a contribution somewhere between two cents and the largest fortune in the world.

11

NIETZSCHE

We may open a path into Nietzsche's *Schopenhauer as Educator* by looping back to a guiding idea in my response to the film *Gaslight,* namely to what I called vampirism, an attempt to capture the way the apparently independent male in that world lives off the light—the spirit—of an evidently dependent female. Not only is he casually stealing her light each night, but this stealing is in service of another attempted theft, of another woman's secret possession (which also, we learn in the film's last lines, presents itself to him as a wish or need to receive light: the jewels "were a fire in my brain"). So this portrait of the negation of marriage is one in which a woman's casting her lot with the world of men leads to a house, with a respectable address, that is a prison, a house of terror or horror; and to an intimacy that serves to drive the woman mad. This becomes at the same time a portrait of a man who has no inner life of his own, one who can live only with infusions from others, a man of conformity and good manners and cultivation (he is a musician) who lives a second, secret, nocturnal life of theft, not a body-snatcher but a soul-snatcher. He and others call what he does alone at night his "work." It suggests the question: How are men of cultivation "supported"? (The linking of conformity with secrecy is something Emerson records in speaking of humankind—too timid, or ashamed, to announce the cogito—as "skulking" and "peeping," in contrast with his own claim to "stand here for humanity.")

The man of *Gaslight* is one grisly realization of what, adapting Kant's term, we can call the completely heteronomous human, whose every action, absolutely without autonomy, is motivated from outside. He is not so much immoral—putting his satisfactions before the rights of others, failing to meet certain specific obligations—as unfit for the moral life altogether, immune to moral criticism, incapable of moral conversation. He hypnotizes, but he is hypnotized. He cannot exactly be said to be conventionally envious or covetous; before that he is motivated by emptiness.

The woman's recovery from her subjection, namely her announcement of her existence, her demanding the burden of thinking for herself, expresses itself in the form of what I called a mad aria, specifically one that recalls her aunt's famous role as Lucia di Lammermoor, a dagger in her hand. So the fate or history of the *cogito ergo sum* argument, said to begin modern philosophy, here manifests two ironic registers: first, instead of solving the problem of madness, the woman in saying "I think" accepts a position that in that moment is indistinguishable from madness, call it a state of incomprehensibility to others (almost to all others); second, what seems to give her the power or spirit or life to take this announcement upon herself is that she at the same time takes upon herself the identity, that is to say, the voice, of her aunt. So *whose* existence has she proved? (One might say, anticipating a turn the characterization of the genre of the unknown woman will invite when we get to *Stella Dallas*, that she is on the way to proving that motherhood, this power of originality or creativity, exists in her life. But at the moment we are asking whose existence, or identity, she has proved, if the basis for the proof comes from accepting her identification with the woman she has grown up calling her "aunt.")

I might say: An argument is set up—in the task of claiming your own existence, the thing Emerson and Nietzsche follow the Romantics (harking back to the Greeks, to Pindar) in describing as "becoming who you are"— between two forms or ideas of theater, one represented by a kind of hypnosis, associated with eyes and looking, which deprives one of one's identity; and a competing theater associated with ears and listening, which grants identity. The cogito is an advance over hypnosis, but what verifies the identity it grants? (In Descartes's Second Meditation: "I have proven that I am a thing that thinks. But what thing am I?") Perfectionism, as in Nietzsche's *Schopenhauer as Educator,* requires the guidance or inspiration of an other, a figure both Nietzsche and Emerson call the true man. Nietzsche speaks of this figure as a teacher and as an exemplar. What ensures that we are not merely imitating, mimicking, this example?

The problem of imitation haunts philosophy's establishment in Plato, and in a further form it is in full flower in the work of Emerson and the work he inspired in Nietzsche. In both forms it is at stake in the two places I have found it dramatized in *Gaslight.* It arises in the question whether I have found the identity of my voice, whether I am saying what I think or only quoting some saint or sage. And it arises in the question whether the human world exists. It presents in effect a new relation between appearance and reality. When philosophers traditionally invoke this contrast, there is no sense that what is real does not exist—in Plato it is a realm of being whose perfection our realm of the senses only imitates ("participates in" Plato says, as if it draws what reality it has from being in touch with the higher realm and its unity); in Kant it is a humanly unknowable realm posited by us as the cause of the matter of our experience. Even if you take a philosopher such as Hume to say that there is, for example, no table beyond the order of our ideas, there is not, for him, as it were, some gap in reality, some imaginably better or realer place where the model or cause of what we call a table might exist: the one our senses confirm *is* the table.

But in Emerson and Nietzsche, the human beings we know, hence the human institutions we participate in, are, with certain exceptions, as such infected with unreality. And there are no instances of the human, in some realer or higher state, in some other realm. We are what, here and now, is what there is of the human, and we are, or it is, lacking; we are not what we are meant to be, not what the human expects of itself. (No doubt this is a certain characterization of the human being's uniqueness in creation.) When Emerson says, in "Self-Reliance," "I stand here for humanity," he means simultaneously that he bears up under the painful realization that he is representative of the poor creatures that exist today in human form, and also that he stands as a sign of the human state we (including, of course, him) aspire to. Both he and Nietzsche speak of these creatures, of us, as phantoms and ghosts.

Schopenhauer as Educator is an early work, published in 1874, when Nietzsche was thirty years old. A dozen years later, in *Beyond Good and Evil,* he no longer calls for the realization of the human, but for the overcoming of the human in the over-man: the present men and women we encounter are, after all, *human, all too human,* the title of the book he published in 1879. *Beyond Good and Evil* carries the subtitle "Prelude to a Philosophy of the Future." The philosophy of the future awaits the philosopher of the future. *Beyond Good and Evil* characterizes the philosopher as the man of tomorrow and the day after tomorrow. A new preface to *Human, All Too Human,* printed the same year as *Beyond Good and Evil,* uses the same formula. As does, the following year, the preface to *The Gay Science.* What so excited Nietzsche about this formulation? In German, the unremarkable English phrase "tomorrow and the day after tomorrow" translates the German *Morgen und Übermorgen.* Take the prefix Über- as Nietzsche uses it, among other places, in *Übermensch* (Superman, Overman, Beyond-Man), and *Übermorgen* means something like super-morning, over- or beyond-morning, a new day, the future. Then the idea is that the future, the new day, will be brought about only by, or confirmed only with the appearance of, the new man, the beyond-man. The future is not simply later than the present but requires "a great separation" (as in the new preface to *Human, All Too Human*), namely a splitting from (or within) the self that sustains the present, an overcoming of this present, living "in contradiction to the present" (Emerson had said: in aversion to the present state of conformity to the present). And this, as the words say, is something happening in (and to) the present.

I cannot forbear taking this apparent digression a step further. (I trust you by now are aware of my tendency not to suppress such impulses, and I hope somewhat sympathetic to them, seeing the value in them of suggestions for further work.) In the same decade as Nietzsche's *Beyond Good and Evil*, the 1870s, George Eliot published her two great novels, *Middlemarch* and *Daniel Deronda*, full of the learning and speculation of a masterly mind. The idea of a new day creating and created by a new human being—call this the taking of a step into a further, attainable, self—is something perceived by Eliot as itself going forward in as it were a new ordinary, or dailiness of existence. The thought is epitomized in Daniel Deronda's being moved to speak of "what is happening every day" as "the transmutation of self" toward a world closer to the heart's desire. This may be understood as a perception within a religious register of experience, but it is tied to a vision of what marriage, with its ordinary and unremarkable reciprocity, may be. As such, these novels are precursors of, preparations for, the aspiration of the vision in remarriage comedy, along with the novels of Jane Austen.

In *Schopenhauer as Educator*, whatever the human creates partakes of human unreality, its fraudulent or pseudo or apparent or false or artificial existence. Two issues will concern us most directly, that of apparent or fraudulent philosophy and that of apparent or pseudo culture. I anticipate the importance of this emphasis in approaching Nietzsche's text for the following reason. Rawls speaks of Nietzsche as an instance of those he names moral perfectionists, who call for an unjust amount of goods to be allocated to cultural institutions. But this is the reverse of what Nietzsche calls for, which is for genuine philosophy to become the judge of current cultural institutions, which are themselves the enemy of genuine culture, philosophy itself to have no subsidy from the state. And Rawls regards Nietzsche as worse than he has said, since these expanded institutions are themselves to be in service mainly of that tiny number of individuals who are recognized to be geniuses. Even if, as I trust, it becomes plain that, in Nietzsche's meditation on Schopenhauer, Nietzsche shows himself diametrically opposed to this charge, there might be others whom the portrait fits. But who would take them seriously? Those who argue for more subsidy for the arts than seems just, and who are to be taken seriously, need not do so on any grounds short of arguing that it is good for society at large.

I find Nietzsche's Untimely Meditation on Schopenhauer to be a particularly fateful crossroads in the reading and viewing I have chosen to discuss in these chapters, for two immediate reasons. One: This text of Nietzsche's is drenched with thoughts of Emerson, thoughts, that is to say, inspired in one of Emerson's best readers. Two: It is the text of Nietzsche's from which Rawls quotes in the passage on extreme perfectionism in section 50 of *A Theory of Justice*. We shall be moving in this chapter from the first of these facts to the second.

Often a sentence in Nietzsche's text is a recasting, through Nietzsche's temperament, of a sentence of Emerson's. The opening paragraph of "Self-Reliance" ends, as we have noted: "Work[s] of genius . . . teach us to abide by our spontaneous impression . . . Else tomorrow a stranger will say with masterly good sense precisely what we have thought and felt all the time, and we shall be forced to take with shame our own opinion from another." The opening paragraph of *Schopenhauer as Educator* ends: "The man who does not wish to belong to the mass needs only . . . to follow his conscience, which calls to him: 'Be your self! All you are now doing, thinking, desiring, is not you yourself.'" The earlier part of Nietzsche's paragraph attributes the common quality of men that prevents heeding this call to "laziness," adding that "men are even lazier than they are timid," as if he is warming up to a conversation with Emerson, querying whether it is quite right to say that "Man is timid . . . He dares not say 'I think,' 'I am'"—though the first sentence of Nietzsche's second paragraph continues: "Every youthful soul hears this call and trembles when he hears it; for the idea of its liberation gives it a presentiment of . . . a happiness to which it can by no means attain so long as it lies fettered by the chains of fear and convention." "Youth" "chains" "fear" "convention" (that is, conformity) are explicit in "Self-Reliance," which, if it does not picture the soul as "trembling" with presentiment, notes its "vibrating."

Nietzsche introduces the idea of being ashamed of oneself (in the face of genius) somewhat later (I think not until section 6), and then in the same paragraph he rewrites a passage of Emerson's from "The American Scholar," namely "This revolution [in human aspiration] is to be wrought by the gradual domestication of the idea of Culture. The main enterprise of the world for splendor, for extent, is the upbuilding of a man. Here are materials strewn along the ground." "Upbuilding" virtually pronounces the German *Bildung,* that signature word simultaneously for education and for culture, which peppers Nietzsche's text on Schopenhauer. When the accent is on what we mean by (an individual's) "education" Nietzsche specifies it as *Erziehung*—hence the title *Schopenhauer als Erzieher;* when it is what we mean by (a society's) culture, Nietzsche specifies it as *Kultur.* It is what he calls one's "consecration to culture," the sign of which is that feeling of shame without distress, that "[hatred] of one's own narrowness and shrivelled nature" that is the condition, further, for one's feeling of sympathy with the genius incessantly overcoming "our dryness and apathy" and "in anticipation for all those who are still struggling and evolving [*werdenden,* developing], with the profoundest conviction that almost everywhere we encounter nature pressing towards man and . . . failing to achieve him, yet . . . producing the most marvelous beginnings . . . so that the men we live among resemble a field over which are scattered the most precious fragments [*bildnerischen Entwürfe:* artistic projects]."

I repeat Emerson's words: "Revolution . . . of the idea of Culture. The main enterprise of the world for splendor . . . is the upbuilding of a man. Here are materials strewn along the ground." The differences are as notable as the coincidences. Both passages convey the idea of the current ground of what is called human existence as the floor of an artist's studio, littered with sketches and experiments. But where Emerson speaks of the upbuilding of a man as "the main enterprise of the *world,*" Nietzsche speaks of "*nature* pressing toward man." Accordingly, where Emerson speaks of *revolution,* Nietzsche speaks of *evolution.* We must recognize in this difference a radical difference in their cultural contexts (granted the decisive similarity that neither of them remained within any social institution of education): Nietzsche repeatedly asserts the exhaustion of the age and its culture, whereas Emerson as insistently calls for the discovery of America, whose culture has barely begun.

Nietzsche's Darwinism is a controversial topic, and his personification or animation of nature is obvious ("nature presses toward man"; and he also calls nature an artist). But there is an intellectual tendency that more decisively confirms his difference from Emerson, the tendency Wittgenstein would perceive as the metaphysicalizing or absolutizing of the difference between nature and culture, the call for culture to transfigure [*verklären*] or to redeem nature, what Nietzsche calls physis. Whereas for Emerson, the process of what he calls transfiguration (one of the two characteristics he assigns to thinking in "The American Scholar"—the other is conversion) goes on in each word, each day, combating the condition in which "every word they say chagrins us." In my book *This New Yet Unapproachable America*, I say that for Wittgenstein the redemption of culture from decline goes on, for philosophy, diurnally. I am alluding to that claim for Wittgenstein in contrasting Nietzsche's metaphysics with Emerson's everyday. This is not the way Nietzsche actually uses the term "metaphysics" in *Schopenhauer as Educator,* where he attractively uses the idea of man's "metaphysical disposition" as his demand to answer the question "What is existence worth as such?" "Do you affirm this existence in the depths of your heart?" That is a question Emerson was equally determined to raise.

I don't mean to give the impression that one could sensibly list the Emersonian echoes in Nietzsche's text: while some are I think beyond argument, others are in various degrees speculative. Are Nietzsche's "moments and as it were bright sparks of fire" in whose light "we cease to understand the word 'I,' there lies something beyond our being which moves across into it" echoes of Emerson's "gleam of light which flashes across [our] mind" and returns to us something we have rejected from our "I" and that was hence beyond us? This connection with what is beyond us as we stand is something Emerson finds taught to us "in every work of genius"; it is our rejection of our own genius that makes us "skulk" and "peep." Nietzsche puts the matter this way, not in his first but in his second paragraph: "There exists no more repulsive and desolate creature in the world than the man who has evaded his genius and who now looks furtively to left and right . . ." When Nietzsche says "being truthful means: to believe in an existence that cannot be denied," I hear Emerson in "Self-Reliance" calling upon us to speak with necessity. And I notice that in speaking of "the three constitutional dangers that threatened Schopenhauer [and that] threaten us all," I note that Nietzsche's German, spelling "Constitution" with a "C," is using the English word, in homage, so I imagine, to Emerson, whose signature use of the word always means both the state of his disposition (in German, *Geschaffenheit*) and the Constitution of the United States (in German, *Verfassung*).

But if these links are real in connection with such guiding concepts as culture (together with its debasement), and genius (together with its evasion), and transfiguration, and conversion, and conformity (Nietzsche sometimes says sociability), then we may expect to find links anywhere between them. This is something whose importance and detail has finally to be left to each reader, depending on how illuminating or essential he or she finds the issue to be, given specific understandings of and ways of reading each of these figures.

Before discussing an uncontroversial relation between them—namely that Nietzsche explicitly cites, or alludes to, Emerson twice in his Schopenhauer text, early and late, both times to Emerson's "Circles"—I add a note on what I earlier called Nietzsche's querying Emerson's appeal to timidity, rather than laziness, as the common failing of mankind. The significance of the idea of laziness for Nietzsche is its existence in the mode of "killing time," a matter pertinent to the name Nietzsche gives to his text as one of his Untimely Meditations. Whatever else *Unzeitgemässe* may be understood to mean, it certainly refers to the relation a philosopher bears, or undertakes, to his own time. I imagine that Nietzsche may be thought to be in disagreement with Emerson's saying, in "Self-Reliance," "Accept the place the divine Providence has found for you; the society of your contemporaries" when Nietzsche refers to himself as a "stepchild" of his times. But what Emerson's phrase here contrasts with is the idea of accepting the place *society* has found for you, which might be, for example, as your stepmother's and stepsisters' servant, hence not conceivably a future princess. And the concept of time makes more explicit than Emerson does the difference he, and Nietzsche, insist upon between philosophy and history, and the vision they share—none more telling—about the need for philosophy to discover the future, the genuinely new.

That the originality, or genuineness, or true humanity, these perfectionists demand of human existence requires a reconception and achievement of a genuine future, one not merely a continuation of the outworn past, is not, as suggested, explicit in the earlier texts of theirs I mainly quote here, *Schopenhauer as Educator* and "Self-Reliance." A while ago I mentioned the change in Nietzsche's later invocation of the philosophy and philosopher of the future. In Emerson, a concentration on the theme of Old and New is guiding for the great essay "Experience," written several years after "Self-Reliance."

Returning to the uncontroversial relation between these figures, namely that the younger explicitly cites the older (though Emerson was still alive, just seventy, when *Schopenhauer as Educator* was published, he was moving past his writing years), I remind you that in Nietzsche's earlier citation, or allusion, to Emerson there is some explicit clowning in introducing the words. Nietzsche writes: "Who was it who said: 'a man never rises higher than when he does not know whither his path can still lead him'?" Emerson, who quotes the saying and attributes it to Cromwell at the end of "Circles," does not mention its quotation in Cardinal de Retz's *Memoirs,* from which he presumably learned of it and quoted it. Then to whom should Nietzsche attribute the citation? Perhaps to both Cromwell and Emerson, if he learned of it from Emerson; perhaps to Cromwell and Cardinal de Retz, if he knew of it from the cardinal, but then he should nevertheless mention his knowledge of Emerson's having already quoted it. (Cardinal de Retz, Emerson, and Nietzsche all quote what Cromwell said, but only Cromwell *said* it. Meaning just what, that only he meant it? Surely not; Emerson and Nietzsche, at least, say it because they mean it. Then because Cromwell was the first to say it? But first, who knows whether that is true? And second, what would that prove?—that it was new, original? But none of the words are new. Then because the thought is new. That seems unlikely. Is it not like, "Do not let the left hand know what the right hand is doing"?) I like to think of Nietzsche's clowning here as a recognition of Emerson's problematizing of the relation between quotation and saying, specifically to the sense of the quoting of Descartes's *cogito (ergo) sum,* and the implication that, let us say for an American, everything has been said and nothing has been said, everything read and nothing read. But a European of the highest cultivation— Nietzsche, for example—has his own way of saying that.

Perhaps the significance of this problematic of quotation can be seen as shifting Kant's doctrine of freedom from the register of action to that of speech. Kant had found that morality and freedom (the origination and autonomy of our actions, free of determination, free of heteronomy, of which imitation, say conformity, is a rampant expression) depend upon acting not only in conformity with the law but for the sake of the law. I am asking whether it makes sense to say that for Emerson and Nietzsche freedom, originality, in our thinking depends upon our speaking not merely in conformity with words but for the sake, as if to achieve the meaning, of our words. As if these writers are claiming that we do not—to some unmeasured extent—know the meaning of what we say. This is something Emerson states many ways, and something his and Nietzsche's continuous practice of punning and metaphorizing may be understood to dramatize.

Take an apparently banal observation from "Self-Reliance" such as "[man] is no longer upright." We know that narratively, or thematically, or allegorically, this means that we are no longer forthright, honest, upstanding, trustworthy, let's say reliable; it evokes the most familiar image of moral respectability and honorableness. But coming in the immediate context of the claim of man's being timid and not daring to say, and being ashamed, and the broader, mediate context of posture, centered on standing, and following a standard, and eventuating in understanding, and collapsing in leaning, skulking, stealing, peeping—we know uprightness names the posture of the human being standing on hind legs, eyes toward heaven (as in a famous outburst of Kant's praise of our moral capacity), namely as having just evolved out of the trees and come to earth. So the resultant force of "man is no longer upright" becomes: man has as it were suffered a setback (another fall, one could say), which has left him everywhere less than human (Mill will say: distorted, crippled; Nietzsche will say: degenerated), and in such a way that he is incapable of the necessary condition of morality (according to Kant, the capacity to stand on his own, that he be autonomous). (If moral perfectionism can be understood as meant to repair this setback, to establish the condition of moral agency, and if one understands perfectionism as the moral impetus of Plato and Aristotle, then it is as if at the establishment of Western philosophy there was already the recognition of the possibility of human setback, that the soul, like the state, was capable of a lapse back into animality, unfit for the conversation of justice.)

This Emersonian judgment of universal imitativeness is a vision of the world of humankind—shared around the middle third of the nineteenth century (beginning, say, two generations after the French Revolution, anticipating the American Civil War, America's completion of its Revolution)—as a scene of incessant heteronomy, looking solely to borrow or steal thoughts for private interest and the approval of others; in a word, a world of conformity, depersonalization, philistinism, simulation, exteriority. It is a vision in which it is questionable whether morality can any longer judge the world, one in which we have lost faith that, become skeptical whether, in what Kant pictures as the inscrutable workings of our motivation, we are capable of acting for the sake of the law.

In Nietzsche's terms, we are in danger of losing the sense that, before the demands placed upon us by culture, there is, or is access to, that region in each of us of the uneducable, the nonliterate—think of it as the implacable desire for satisfaction, for expression, something Schopenhauer calls the Will, something Freud followed Schopenhauer in speaking of as the instinct of Eros, a matter I know I mean to capture in speaking, in my reading of Wittgenstein's *Investigations,* of human restlessness. In *Human, All Too Human,* Nietzsche calls this the place of *Ursinn* [literally meaning something like the origin of meaning], which may be taken as a primordial demand for sense, a demand as original and clear as a baby's cry. I think of it as an attestation that there is perpetually a further possibility of ourselves, which it is the task of the genuine educator to encourage us to find. It is at the same time a demand for the further possibility of culture, call it the provision of the means of expression.

The vision of the demand for a transfigured future, expressed as a sense of the exhaustion of present culture, perhaps accompanied by a demand for the renewal of culture, call it a vision of modernity, seems shared by many of the major writers (let alone painters and composers) of the nineteenth and twentieth centuries. Apart from our Emerson (hence Whitman, Emily Dickinson, through at least to W. C. Williams) and Nietzsche and Ibsen and Mill, and so forth, there are Blake and Baudelaire and Melville and Kleist and Schopenhauer and Kierkegaard and George Eliot and Flaubert and Proust and Joyce and Thomas Mann and Kafka and Rilke and Beckett and Heidegger and Wittgenstein. (I mention only a few peaks of achievement that should exist beyond murmur. "Major" as an attribute of a writer and thinker does not always coincide with "favorite," or with the diurnally most valuable.) The vision is not to be refuted, but confronted (as these writers in their various ways confront it). Which is to say, if it is real for you, the world of this vision is to be redescribed, reobserved, readdressed; I like to say, recounted. This is not accomplished alone.

I said a while ago that there were two immediate reasons for calling Nietzsche's *Schopenhauer as Educator* a particularly fateful crossroads in the texts discussed in this book. The first was its drenching itself with Emerson's thinking. The second, to which we now turn, is its existence as the text of

Nietzsche's that Rawls cites in depicting the extreme form of what he calls moral perfectionism.

Let's begin by looking at the passage Rawls quotes—or rather, fascinatingly, as he says, quotes as cited in a selection of sentences from the translator Hollingdale's book on Nietzsche: "Mankind must work continually to produce individual great human beings—this and nothing else is the task . . . for the question is this: how can your life, the individual life, retain the highest value, the deepest significance? . . . Only by your living for the good of the rarest and most valuable specimens."

This can sound bad. Such a passage puts Rawls in mind (as it has many others) of possible justifications of slavery, spiritual and otherwise. Rawls continues:

> If it is maintained that in themselves the achievements of the Greeks in philosophy, science, and art justified the ancient practice of slavery (assuming that this practice was necessary for these achievements), surely the conception is highly perfectionist. The requirements of perfection override the strong claims of liberty. On the other hand [i.e., moving from the strict to the more moderate and reasonable doctrine of perfectionism] one may use the criterion simply to limit the distribution of wealth and income under a constitutional regime. In this case it serves as a counterpoise to egalitarian ideas.

But having come from a bout of comparing Nietzsche with Emerson, I ask myself whether the intimacy I find between them suggests that what they advocate is something like slavery, and that they want more money, or more of some material thing, or more freedom for themselves and people they regard as like themselves, than for others? I find not. Like philosophers from Plato to Rousseau and Thoreau, they perceive around them their countrymen as it were in chains, but they do not *recommend* this condition to them. Then what do they want? Why does Nietzsche give, perhaps deliberately or purposefully, so lurid an impression?

Take the sentence from Nietzsche that Rawls quotes as ending: "Only by your living for the good of the rarest and most valuable specimens." That is actually not the end of Nietzsche's sentence, which continues: "and not for the good of the majority, that is to say those who, taken individually, are the least valuable exemplars." This can still sound bad.

I note two or three causes for suspicion in understanding this to mean that you are to serve, act on behalf of, the gains of a great one against the aggregate gains of a great many. Though the term "specimens" translates the same German word as "exemplars" does (*Exemplare*, which occurs in both places in Nietzsche's text), a specimen is a sample of something, a representative or typical instance of a group or mass, of a plant, an animal, a mineral, whereas an exemplar is a supreme or perfect instance, worthy, if there is a choice, of emulation. Taking certain persons as exemplars to be emulated means that acting for their good or gain is acting on the basis of *what you take as their idea or conception* of good or gain; you let that guide your life. You are often wrong, almost fated to be wrong, in realizing your idea of their conception of good; that is why exemplars such as Emerson and Nietzsche say they do not want followers. The background thought, contrasting living "for" the rare one with living for the many, is that you are already imitating one or the other of these individuals; so your initiating task is to find one to follow from whom you can learn what it is to follow an idea on your own behalf, to find the one you are. If anyone correctly lives "for," on behalf of, another, it is the exemplar, not the follower.

As the text continues, there is the most blatant evidence, the plainest statement, that "the rare and most valuable exemplar" is not *another* person. The one who "at last . . . may appear who feels himself perfect and boundless in knowledge and love, perception and power, and who in his completeness is at one with nature, the judge and evaluator of things" (compare this with Emerson's boy in his neutrality) is your own "higher self." "Anyone who believes in culture is thereby saying: 'I see above me something higher and more human than I am; let everyone help me to attain it, as I will help everyone who knows and suffers as I do.'" I am confined; the path cannot be taken alone; but it is to be my attainment. When Nietzsche goes on to say that "only he who has attached his heart to some great man is by that act *consecrated to culture*" and that "the sign of that consecration is that one is ashamed of oneself without any accompanying feeling of distress," he is not saying that one is to consecrate oneself to that great man; that figure only produces in you the "sign" of, the pointer to, the consecration. You leave him behind, along with your shame.

The obvious manifestation Nietzsche gives us of this response to greatness is his relation in this meditation to the figure of Schopenhauer. It is young Nietzsche's consecration (or memory of it), his pledge to attain *his* future. Schopenhauer has been left behind as the writer of texts that require specific interpretation, which receive none explicitly in this text of Nietzsche's.

But if Nietzsche means what seems plain to me, oughtn't he have been clearer? Could he have been clearer? Two considerations suggest that he is as clear as possible.

First, this future—further—self (predicted by his consecration to culture, which "is the child of each individual's self-knowledge and dissatisfaction with himself") is not describable in advance. "Culture demands of him, not only inward experience, . . . but finally and above all an act, that is to say a struggle on behalf of culture and hostility towards those influences, habits, laws, institutions in which he fails to recognize his goal." This is a "further stage" in "the production of true *human being*."

Second, the difficult path toward culture is one on which the individual is subject to confusion as between finding himself and finding or founding another. Which is to say: the determination of the true "goal of culture" must face and as it were compete with the "misemployed and appropriated culture," that pomp and promotion of culture which is all "around you" and which is driven by powerful forces, various forms of what Nietzsche calls "greed." There could be no position free from subjection to confusion and disorientation about one's goal short of the task of replacing what is at first an "obscure impulse" to culture with a conscious willing.

I said that Rawls distinguishes between strict and moderate perfectionism. Nietzsche was his example of strict perfectionism. For Rawls, the "strict principle of perfectionism" is as follows: "it is the sole principle of a teleological theory directing society to arrange institutions and to define the duties and obligations of individuals so as to maximize the achievement of human excellence in art, science, and culture." In such a formulation the ideas of "excellence" and "culture" are taken as known quantities rather than as fields of struggle between greed and salvation, so the criterion begs the question of culture Nietzsche wished to raise. I specify two further points that make this principle irrelevant to Nietzsche's proposals.

First: That the principle is, as a principle of justice must be in Rawls's theory, one that social institutions are to obey, assures not only its irrelevance to Nietzsche's argument, since society as it stands can precisely do nothing to help further the goal of culture, which Nietzsche (with, I assume, deliberate provocativeness) characterizes as the transformation or redemption of nature. Exactly on the contrary, the present culture of society is the enemy of culture as it is called for. These ideas can be given a Kantian articulation. The moral law can be said to "redeem nature," nature taken as the world of inclination. And acting in conformity with the law can be said to be the enemy of acting for the sake of the law, which alone is morally redemptive. Then Nietzsche, as a transfiguration beyond Kant, can be said to focus on Kant's assertion that we cannot ever be certain that we are indeed acting for the sake of the law, and to go on to articulate his (Nietzsche's) consequent impression of human life as using conformity to the law as a cover for a despair of ever acting—or trusting others to act—for the sake of the law. This amounts to an impression of a perfect state of moralism, a stultification of individual and social freedom and originality.

Second: In Nietzsche's (and Emerson's) perfectionism there is nothing to maximize and no distribution to be equalized (other things, specifically liberty and opportunity, being as equally balanced as possible). The only thing there could be to maximize would be what Nietzsche and Emerson call genius, and that is perfectly distributed already, each individual having his own. So Nietzsche's proposals do not count as a teleological moral theory at all. Perhaps it is not exactly what we would call a moral theory at all. (I have been suggesting that perfectionism is directed at the precondition for moral thinking. Though it is hard not to understand Nietzsche's demand for making oneself intelligible—beginning with oneself—as the beginning of moral thinking.) But that is something different from finding in it a recipe for enforcing a wildly unjust, anyway unequal, distribution of the goods at society's disposal. Nietzsche goes out of his way to say that the philosopher, in his role as judge of his culture, cannot afford to be in the service of any state institution, hence cannot, in his culture, serve in the office of professor. He praises Schopenhauer's father for making his son financially independent; otherwise Nietzsche may be implying the necessity of the poverty of the sage.

Rawls's principle of perfection in its moderate version, making it not the sole but a supplementary principle modifying the strict principle of distribution and its orderings, brings out further the mismatch between Rawls's and Nietzsche's concerns. According to this moderating principle, one should get more wealth and income than others because of one's "talent" or one's "higher" "style and aesthetic grace." But not only is such a criterion antithetical to Nietzsche's contempt for current measures of aesthetic value; his fundamental idea of culture, what he calls "the secret of culture," is not that it provides something but that it removes something, namely obstacles to genuine, transforming culture. So the idea of the "moderate principle of perfectionism" as wishing to justify "public funds for the arts and sciences" as they stand is, for Nietzsche, not a contribution to solving the problem of culture but, if anything, to intensifying the problem.

But if the question whether it is in general good public policy, justified morally, for a society to use public funds, or provide incentives to the use of private funds, to endow art museums and subsidize symphony orchestras and opera and theater companies, and so forth, is at best irrelevant to Nietzsche's concerns in *Schopenhauer as Educator*, or would even be treated with the contempt Nietzsche shows toward official current culture, many others do have an interest in the question. I am one who does, and yet the manner and extent to which I am a perfectionist would not mitigate the outrage I would feel toward a proposal to accept such support at the price of depriving others of their just claims to liberty and equality. My argument for the support would accordingly not appeal to any deserts that may accrue to consumers of culture with special talents and refined tastes. (This needs no argument, and suggests no surprise, given some moderate attention to the principles of justice. The presence of universities does not ensure that all will thrive in discovering themselves there, nor prevent some from using its credential merely for private social advantage.) My argument would seek to identify the good that may be understood to accrue to the life of society at large from the opening of artistic treasures and potentialities to broader access, competing with other modes of contributing to the good of that life, raising questions, as philosophers from Plato to Rousseau to Thoreau to Wittgenstein to Freud have done, of what the necessities of life truly are, and of what the complex and shifting identity of a culture, what it thinks and how it thinks of itself, asks that each of us should at a minimum command. Why would Nietzsche's name come up at all in this connection?

The broad answer I have would be articulated in drawing out the implications and conditions of what I have been saying about his, let's call it, criticism of culture, manifested in its beginning stages in his early Untimely Meditation on Schopenhauer. One way to think of this is as the attempt, or need, to inherit, as part of the criticism of religion, the task of religion as a criticism of life, after the authority of religion has become questionable. "How does the philosopher [whom Nietzsche contrasts here with what he calls contented professors of philosophy; he has in the preceding paragraph unmistakably described Hegel] view the culture of our time? . . . He almost thinks that what he is seeing are the symptoms of a total extermination and uprooting of culture. The waters of religion are ebbing away and leaving behind swamps or stagnant pools"; Nietzsche speaks of this as a "turmoil of secularization." This turmoil involves Nietzsche simultaneously in the criticism of the current standing and purpose of philosophy and politics and theater and music and education. The extravagance of ambition and claim here may strike one as immodest to the point of insanity. But then one should consider how often rather more modestly cultivated and talented writers write daily or yearly texts as from an assured, or say contented, perspective on all such matters. (The fact that Thoreau and Marx and Kierkegaard and Nietzsche all warn against reading the newspaper every day I understand as a warning that the consequent sense of needing to defeat bad—simulated—philosophy would be further incited to take over the task of philosophy.)

Now that philosophy is the possession of everyone, its ancient tendency to arrogance is joined, or replaced, by immodesty, to the point of shamelessness. The hunger of our culture for some reasoned, philosophical criticism of our lives is, I judge, essential to the success of Rawls's *A Theory of Justice*. That I find the book more stinting than perhaps it had to be in its treatment, or its reasoned rejection of attempting to treat, its sense of the nature of philosophy and of the arts in its criticism of society from the perspective of justice, does not, I trust, detract from my gratitude for the gift of it.

There is, however, a more specific matter concerning Nietzsche's pertinence to the moral criticism of our lives, and raising a different moral charge that can justly be brought against his perfectionism—one that Nietzsche brings forth in *Schopenhauer as Educator,* at the beginning of its section 8. He is speaking of the "conditions under which the philosophical genius can at any rate come into existence in our time ["at any rate" meaning, I suppose, at any rate emerge if not flower] despite the forces working against it." And again I urge the counter-reading of Nietzsche against the impulse to take him as an elitist indifferent to justice. "The philosophical genius" is not a person with a particular talent or virtuosity but names a spirit in which life may be lived, dangerously, perhaps self-destructively, a life whose conditions Nietzsche describes as "free manliness of character, early knowledge of mankind, no scholarly education, no narrow patriotism, no necessity for bread-winning, no ties with the state—in short, freedom and again freedom" (ibid.).

Now comes the moral charge Nietzsche himself imagines and accepts against his perfectionism: "Whoever wants to reproach him [the one living philosophically], as Niebuhr reproached Plato, with being a bad citizen, let him do so and be a good citizen himself: thus he will be in the right and so will Plato." (Niebuhr was an early nineteenth-century German historian of Rome.) Those claiming the life of philosophical genius or inspiration can be said to be bad citizens—according to the attributes Nietzsche has just claimed for the life of philosophical genius—not because they are necessarily lawbreakers or violators of the principles of justice, but because they necessarily criticize the life of these laws, and so seem malcontent, ne'er-do-well, footloose, irresponsible (or, in an idea featured in Emerson's "Self-Reliance," whimsical), without proper credentials, presumptuous in what they think they know from their observations of mankind, and without shows of patriotism (an absence perfectly compatible with love of country, a fact the enemies of philosophy like to deny). In a word they seem to live *against* the spirit, or rather against the actual life, of the laws—at any time short of the eventual good city, the achieved realm of ends.

It is the city as it stands that makes it and genuine philosophy dangers to each other. It is out of such a perception that Plato invokes the idea of philosophy's imagined city, the city in which philosophy is openly and freely called for and practiced, the city of words. ("Our manners have been corrupted by communication with the saints" is the way Thoreau casts the thought of, let's say, philosophy's irritability.) So the one claiming the life of philosophy, always groundlessly, is rightly reproachable for disturbing the peace. But he is right too (if, or to the extent that, he is a Plato), because the laws and the life of the laws, in any era, demand criticism, because our society and its culture—if it has justly won our consent to be governed by it—is not what it calls upon itself to be. So the very existence of philosophy, in an imperfect world, calling upon the world beyond the compromised materializations of our time, is inherently "untimely"—meaning both that it is disruptive and that it ignores history, apparently indifferent to the inevitable causes and excuses for compromise with justice, and interested only in justice's presence or absence.

But now: a conflict of rights has been a way of characterizing tragedy. (Not all tragedy. Not that of Lear, who has no right to what he unleashes; surely not that of the Macbeths, and certainly not that of Othello, who do not know what is wronging them; and Hamlet's knowledge that he has no right, yet no choice, is part of his tragedy.) Antigone, since the featuring of her play in Hegel's aesthetic theory, is perhaps the central case here. Then the question is, if this play is a conflict of two rights, why it is we side with her, against the state. If one is right, that is, a good citizen, in reproaching Plato for being a bad citizen; and Plato is right, that is, a good philosopher, in reproaching his city for being false to philosophy, hence to itself so far as it wishes to claim philosophy; then shall we say that the willingness for tragedy appears as a condition of morality, exacting a trail of martyrs to the truth—perhaps enacting just small, undramatic martyrdoms, enduring various forms of disapproval, unacknowledgment, isolation? How could such a conflict have a resolution *within* morality?

Or is the martyrdom rather more dramatic than this says? I mean, can we see that the modern writers I listed as examples showing a tendency toward perfectionist aspiration are in opposition with the main tendency of academic moral philosophy from Kant and Hume to Rawls? Plato exiled much of poetry from his ideal city on the ground that the poets tell lies about the gods and wrongly portray the character of heroes. Are moral philosophers prepared to say that some principal segment of major writers over the past two centuries have told lies about the character of human beings? If not, and if accordingly these writers have been right about their fellow creatures (at least as right as any group is recognized to be), then their being so characteristically exiled from moral philosophy suggests that the disciplinary strife between the study of philosophy and of literature is touched with tragedy.

I break off here with a transitional change of register. Nietzsche's text is painfully pertinent to assessing what we might call the cultural standing of movies. Are they inherently part of low or popular culture, where this might mean that they are comprehensible only as some mode of entertainment? Or are they as various in quality and design as the things called books are, namely some of them belonging to low, others to high, culture? Or is that distinction of service only outside the range of Hollywood films, which are as such low? Or is the distinction between high and low now out of service altogether, since the advent of what is called post-modernism? *Now, Voyager,* to which we turn next, should be a particularly fruitful example for us, since its reception has been explicitly split, between those for whom it remains one of their favorite films and those who see it as essentially sharing the values, and having the value, of the advertising campaigns mounted by its Hollywood studio upon its original release, tying it in with advertisements for a line of cosmetics and other beauty and hygienic (viz. dietetic) tips designed to make women loveable (to men and to mothers).

12

Now, Voyager

1   A block of stone with chiseled letters spelling VALE occupies the opening shot; since the block is isolated, and seems to be in front of a mansion, it is probably not a grave marker (exactly).

2   Inside the house, we recognize, after a scurrying of servants, the matriarch of the premises (Gladys Cooper), giving orders. She hears an unfamiliar noise coming from the entrance hall, which proves to be a man of self-confident respectability and unconventionality, Dr. Jaquith (Claude Rains) knocking the ash out of his pipe into an ornamental vase the size of an average human being.

3   He has entered with two women, of different generations (they turn out to be mother and daughter), Lisa (Ilka Chase) and June (Bonita Granville). Lisa asks the matriarch not to call the doctor she has brought to interview Charlotte (Bette Davis), the daughter of the premises, by the title of Doctor.

4   Charlotte, coming down the stairs, overhears her mother speak of her to Dr. Jaquith as a late child, "my ugly duckling"; Charlotte's consequent attempt to retreat back up the stairs is thwarted by being noticed. Her mother defiantly addresses the doctor by his professional title. He explains, in an attempt to get past the daughter's fears and her mother's suspicions and disapproval, that what he does is not frightening, or even unusual; he says people come to him, and his place in the country, Cascade, when they have lost their way. His business is from time to time to say to them, "Not this way; that way."

5   Charlotte abruptly leaves the room, but Dr. Jaquith follows, asking her to show him around this impressive pile. As she turns away and continues her retreat up the stairs, he persists in following her and commenting on the house. He gains her confidence sufficiently that she accedes to his request to see her own room.

6   Her room reveals that Charlotte carves ivory boxes artistically, stocks cigarettes, hides forbidden books, and keeps a diary, which she insists that Jaquith read and which comes to life for us in flashback, telling centrally of a sea

voyage young Charlotte took with her mother, who kept her away from other passengers and interrupted her tryst with a young ship's officer whose offer of marriage the mother vetoed. The memories of these events and the sense of their having made her into an unattractive spinster companion and servant of her powerful mother produces an episode of hysterical sobbing in Charlotte and a cry for Dr. Jaquith's help.

7 The return downstairs is again broken up when Charlotte, mercilessly teased by her niece June (who protests it is nothing new), rushes out in tears.

8 Charlotte's mother protests that "no member of the Vale family has ever had a nervous breakdown." Dr. Jaquith retorts, memorably, "Well there's one having one now. I suggest a few weeks at Cascade."

9 At Cascade, Charlotte has notably, if not radically, improved. She is relieved to learn that, with Jaquith's encouragement, Lisa has arranged a cruise for her which will delay her having to face the return home for some months. To mark the termination of her treatment, Jaquith hands her a slip of paper containing a quotation, remarking, "If old Walt [Whitman] didn't have you in mind, he had plenty of others just like you," and departs with a thrillingly casual " 'Bye." Charlotte reads aloud from the slip: ". . . Now voyager sail thou forth to seek and find." Call this the end of Act I.

10 Charlotte makes a second entrance down an inclined plane; this time instead of a mansion's stairway it is a gangway from a cruise ship into its tender; and this time instead of as a reclusive spinster it is as a tentative figure of mystery and glamour. The theme of metamorphosis is heralded. Charlotte is introduced to the awaiting group as Renee Beauchamps.

11 She is paired for the shore trip with Jerry (Paul Henreid). They have lunch on a sun-drenched terrace; he is, in the face of her reserve, preternaturally charming and attentive, a quality that, for good or ill, will never fail him; she tells him her real name is Charlotte Vale, a name he recognizes as associated with Boston. He asks if she would mind helping him shop for presents for his daughters; she replies that a spinster aunt is the perfect person to help select suitable presents for young ladies. Returned to the ship, Jerry gives Charlotte a small present of perfume he has bought for her as thanks for her help and shows her a photograph of what he calls his "harem," containing a wife whose depressed expression he says doesn't do her justice and two daughters, the younger of whom, Tina, sitting apart, evidently his favorite, is a cause of his concern. Charlotte surprises Jerry and herself by asking whether Tina knows she wasn't wanted. They agree to meet for dinner.

12a We see Charlotte rushing around her stateroom to find appropriate evening clothes among the wardrobe Lisa and their common friend Renee Beauchamps have supplied her with for the voyage.

12b As Jerry and Charlotte are having drinks before dinner, as he compliments her on the elegance of the butterfly ornament on her shawl, he notices a tag pinned to it out of her sight. "Someone has been playing a joke on you." "The joke is far funnier than you think." She asks him to unpin it and read it; it reveals that the clothes were left for her, with instructions pinned to them instructing her in when and how to wear them. Her attempt to escape further exchange is momentarily blocked by the sudden appearance of a pair of old friends of Jerry's. After arranging to meet them later, Jerry finds Charlotte out on deck; it is her turn to show a photograph of her massive family. Jerry asks where Charlotte is in the picture, and who the fat lady is with the heavy eyebrows and all the hair. Bette Davis is entrusted to deliver one of the great, and greatly strange, lines in the history of American film: "I am the fat lady with the heavy eyebrows and all the hair." She adds that she has been sick and is still not well. Jerry's genius for taking things in stride is in full evidence here.

12c Jerry and Charlotte have made a friendly foursome with his friends, and the wife of the pair describes to Charlotte how Jerry has, out of his gallantry, been trapped by his wife into remaining in a loveless marriage. Charlotte's heart is touched, and she agrees to spend time together with him in, as they enter the harbor of, Rio.

13a Driving in the hills above Rio, an incompetent chauffeur disables their car. They are forced to spend the night alone together in a vacant cabin, doing what they recall that New Englanders refer to as "bundling." A signature moment from Act 2 of *Tristan and Isolde* is unmistakable on the sound track. (No one I have asked has noticed, or anyway remembered, this. Perhaps they had viewed the film only once; and perhaps this is a tip that some films are not made to yield up their significance on one viewing; or perhaps, for those who eventually remember it, it is an instance marking the register of an irreducible privacy played upon in viewing a film.)

13b The next morning over coffee, Jerry confesses to Charlotte his love for her and asks her to stay with him in Rio, suggesting that she rejoin the cruise by flying to Buenos Aires three days later.

13c That night, on a hotel terrace overlooking the city, Jerry performs the trick of lighting simultaneously a pair of cigarettes and then handing one to Charlotte. He asks her if she believes in immortality and whether she is afraid of getting burned if she gets too close to happiness, to which she replies that she is immune to happiness. They embrace with the fervor of hopelessness.

13d At the dock in New York, Lisa and June do not at first recognize the dashing woman in the black hat descending the gangplank, surrounded by equally dashing, admiring, voluble friends. Call this the end of Act II.

14a Back in Back Bay, Mrs. Vale disapproves of Charlotte's metamorphosis and says that she expects her to resume her old duties as a daughter as well as to wear her old clothes, which she has had taken in to fit her new condition. Charlotte deftly dodges these demands without precipitating an open break. The mother, sensing rational defeat, causes herself to trip and fall down the stairs. She is put to bed watched over by the nurse who was supposed to be kept on only while Charlotte was away, and dispatches Charlotte downstairs to receive the rest of the family at a dinner arranged to welcome Charlotte home.

14b Charlotte astonishes the family with her good looks and assured command of the situation. A youngish widower, Elliot Livingston, has been invited along, whom she knew as a child; he asks whether he might call her sometime.

14c Mrs. Vale is surprised and pleased by Elliot's attentions to Charlotte. When Charlotte goes down to receive Elliot in the entrance hall he asks why, mysteriously, she always wears white camellias and never lets him buy them for her. She answers: "Just a personal idiosyncrasy. We're all entitled to them."

14d At a party at Elliot's sister's house before a symphony concert, Charlotte reencounters Jerry; they pretend to be strangers. Left alone to get acquainted, he tells her, in a voice underneath their public exchange about the architectural job he is doing for the host of the party, that he is still horribly in love; in a corresponding tone she answers that she is proud and agrees to his request to stop by her house, briefly, after the concert.

15a Instead of stopping by, he phones her to say that he has learned she is engaged to be married to Elliot Livingston and that he's taking the next train out of Back Bay Station.

15b She finds him on the train platform and says she wanted to tell him about Elliot, that Elliot is a fine man, whose virtues and sensibility and intellect, however, of course do not compete with Jerry's. Jerry says he has been a cad. She replies that she knew what she was doing as well as he did, and asks him what the feminine for "cad" is.

16a Charlotte breaks the engagement with Elliot, which seems as much as anything to relieve him.

16b When she informs her mother of the break, the mother becomes enraged, and among other insults, hurls at her the observation that "I would have thought you would be ashamed to spend your whole life as *Miss Charlotte Vale!*" Charlotte responds roughly that tyranny takes many forms and that if her mother is an instance of maternal tyranny, she wants nothing to do with it. Whether because of Charlotte's news or because of her rebuff, her mother slumps, shocked into a loss of consciousness, which proves to be fatal.

17 Charlotte blames herself for everything, and on a train which we know to be headed for Cascade, tells herself that now she will never have "a home of your own, or a man of your own, or a child of your own." Call this the end of Act III.

18 As she enters Cascade, Charlotte reencounters the head nurse, whom she knows well, says she's tired and wants to go right to her room, but then notices a young girl whom the nurse is cajoling to eat something and then to join the other young people in a game of Ping-Pong. Charlotte recognizes the girl as Jerry's daughter Tina; she persuades the exasperated nurse to let her take Tina with her to get her car attended to, suggesting that she might be able to get her to eat something.

19 In an ice cream parlor, Tina tells Charlotte she is worried about her father. Charlotte, to Tina's jubilant surprise, suggests she telephone him right now, and gives her coins for the telephone. Tina tells her father that her new friend who arranged for the call is named Vale, and then says, "No, not the kind you put over your face." After the call, Tina's confidence in Charlotte is secured and her appetite revives.

20 Charlotte becomes Tina's friend, nurse, and companion, holding her in her bed at night when she has fits of crying, taking her camping, and ultimately gaining Dr. Jaquith's acquiescence to take Tina to live with her in Boston. Call this the end of Act IV.

21a Jaquith and Jerry pull up in a car at the Vale mansion, about which Jaquith remarks its look of a relic, only to enter into an interior that has metamorphosed into a noisy, convivial scene of a crowd of young people roasting wieners in the once-dead fireplace. Jerry sees Tina and Charlotte at the top of the stairs, Tina radiant in a party frock; as she runs down and into his awaiting arms, he says, as he embraces her but looks over her shoulder up at Charlotte, "I love you"—a difficult moment to witness.

21b In the drawing room, stretched out together on the floor, Charlotte and Jaquith are going over architectural plans for a wing Charlotte is adding to

Cascade. Jaquith asks whether she is the same woman who a few months ago had not an interest in the world, and upon her agreeing that she is not, he tells her he's putting her on his board of directors. They have a life together.

22 Learning that Jerry is in the adjacent room and wants to speak to her, she goes to him to learn that he is planning to take Tina away. He explains to the bewildered Charlotte that Tina is happier than he has ever known her to be but that he cannot go on causing such sacrifices from Charlotte, taking from her and giving nothing in return. Then follows one of the most remarkable exchanges I know of Hollywood dialogue in its confident, uncontestedly dominant years, in which Charlotte angrily accuses Jerry of being piously conventional and Jerry responds to her anger by saying that its genuineness proves to him that their love is intact, bigger than both of them, and so on. The concluding line of the film is endlessly famous, perhaps over the decades as much mocked as admired, admired all the more because so easily and unstably mocked: "Oh, Jerry, let's not ask for the moon; we have the stars." The camera moves outside and rises to reveal a star-filled, moonless sky.

I have been surprised by the number of people, old and comparatively young, who have told me that *Now, Voyager* is their favorite movie. I am unsure of the source of my surprise. I am moved each time I view the film, and I have a healthy, even growing, respect for the intelligence and the stylishness, almost to the point of abstractness, of its writing, and for its superb performances; but I suppose I imagine that others who share something of my unshakable commitments to philosophy and literature will be less forgiving of the invitations to campiness in receiving the film. I have tried to include, in my summary, a few of the most memorable lines from its script. Oscar Wilde no less, I seem to recall, composed among his aphorisms one that mocks the idea that writing a libretto is an inferior form of writing, Wilde implying that this genre has its own, demanding, forms of difficulty. Surely this is an equally valuable observation about film scripts. How the lines of *Now, Voyager* can so much as be said in all seriousness, without camp or any other grain of distance that would deprive them of the weight they depend upon, it would take a considerable feat of literary criticism to explain. Which is only to say that it bears explanation.

In my chapter on the film in *Contesting Tears,* I go at some length into, for example, the script's concentration on names and changes of names, and its register of animals, in which the butterfly and the implied swan (in the phrase "ugly duckling") bear the brunt among them of suggesting metamorphosis. (An allusion I do not mention there—should it be mentioned?—is Charlotte's adding a "wing" to Jaquith's construction.) And I detail the heavy symbology of hats and shoes and glasses and ivory boxes and smoking and flowers, as befits classical melodrama. Above all, I suppose, I contest the idea of Charlotte as "sacrificing herself" for Jerry and his child, which I have found to be the common reading of the film. Whatever sacrifices Charlotte has made were accomplished long before there was a Jerry in her life. I also discuss Bette Davis's powers as a screen presence, having to do with her virtuosic ability to project moods edged with hysteria, a power that enables her notable capacity for enacting extremes of self-revelation and self-concealment.

My indicating large breaks that divide the narrative into five "Acts" is meant to register a signal difference between the melodramas and the comedies engaged in this book, namely the difference in the scale of time each spans. (A further, or prior, difference in the conceptions of time projected by each genre will be emphasized when we come to the discussion of *The Awful Truth*, in which time as frozen in the past, in the melodramas, is explicitly noted as contrasting with an openness to inventiveness and a revised future in the comedies. *Now, Voyager* is the only one of our melodramas that closes by actually depicting a step into a certain revised future.) The melodramas depict the principal woman in two states of her life, call them a state of innocence and a state of experience, years apart. The comedies depict time spans ranging from less than twenty-four hours (excluding the brief, epitomizing prologue of *The Philadelphia Story* and what can be understood as an extended prologue preceding the pair's separation in *The Awful Truth*) to as much as four days or, in *The Awful Truth*, a few weeks. (*The Lady Eve* is exceptional in requiring two indefinite lapses of time, neither of which imagines a change in the physical or psychic state of the woman, except for her voice. The exception stands to be explained, perhaps precisely by its noting of the importance of the woman's voice, perhaps because there is a melodramatic cause, moments of passionate vengeance between the man and the woman, that needs resolution.)

Now, Voyager is a perspicuous case in which to note further generic differences between the melodramas and the comedies, certain "negations," as I call them, of the remarriage structure by the unknown-woman melodramas. The fundamental difference, I suppose, is that in the melodramas marriage is explicitly rejected as part of the woman's perfectionist ambitions. A related difference is that in the melodramas the principal woman's mother is always present (or memories of her are a presence) and the principal woman is herself presented as a mother. Again, in the comedies the perfectionist step into the future is taken by the pair together, reinventing what is to be called marriage, whereas in the melodramas the man is psychically fixated and it is the woman alone who seeks change, permits herself metamorphosis, sometimes to her mortal danger (as in *Gaslight*), sometimes to the destruction, as well, of others (as in *Letter from an Unknown Woman*). (Two of our four melodramas are, it may be worth noting here, based on bestsellers from the period, rather better novels than their consignment to present oblivion would suggest, written by Olive Higgins Prouty, *Now, Voyager* and *Stella Dallas*.)

A final difference I emphasize here is the fate of conversation, which in remarriage comedy presents itself as mutual education and constitutes what is revealed as the validity, not to say legitimacy, of marriage; whereas in the related melodramas conversation, the opening of mutual understanding, is defeated, negated, by irony. The closing exchange between Charlotte and Jerry is explicitly about the moral issues, and implicitly about denying the moral issues, in a father's conveying his child away from its mother into the hands of another woman. We have to believe that the mother does not want or love the child, and the film's effect depends upon our believing that Charlotte does both want and love her, and will do well by her. Whether the natural mother has given her permission for this arrangement, and is competent to do so, is nevertheless a further matter. Were this to be considered, the film would have to face the possibility of further tragedy, which its melodrama displaces. It is, however, I find, morally admirable of the film that it does not displace the permanent tragic effects of Charlotte's having grown up under the care of an unpermitting mother. Charlotte, as testimony to her immunity to happiness, hardly smiles (except once, around strangers, and mildly during the episode with Jerry in Buenos Aires), a characteristic marked particularly for me by just the hint of a smile that shows when she answers Jaquith's question whether she is the same woman, a moment suggesting her harboring a secret.

The moral pertinence of the dialogue of the concluding sequence of the film is emphasized by the man's failure to grasp what is going on. What

Charlotte says to him is true about the child being theirs and about the house in which she is to be reared, differently from Charlotte's rearing in that house, being a place to which he will return, knowing that he is loved there. But she does not correct his insistence that she is proving their love for one another to be what it was, or might have been. She allows him to think he knows her; hence the irony of this climactic moment. The importance of this matter is its contribution to the question of what perfectionism shows moral reasoning to be, most particularly the question of what constitutes one's standing in confronting another person with moral questioning.

It is my impression that in established academic moral philosophy the question of moral standing, if it comes up at all, is grounded in one's conviction that one knows what is good or right for the other to do, so that the philosophical issue is essentially how to provide convincing, rational reasons for one's conviction; put otherwise, the point of the conversation is getting the other to agree to, or to do, something. This is one feature of what I sometimes refer to as the risk of moralizing morality. The point accordingly assigned to moral conversation is that of rationally persuading the other to agree to, or to do, something that you are, independently of the conversation, persuaded that she ought to do. (Sometimes this is quite appropriate, as with a child, where the sides are in a sense not equal. This raises the issue of the relation of authority to morality. Kant cautions against confronting the other on the ground that one cannot know the consequences of the intervention. A reasonable worry. My concern is rather that one may not recognize one's own agenda.)

Kant, as we saw, is exempt from this charge of moralism since the moral law applies in the first instance to oneself. But Kant's caution in confronting others makes it something of a mystery what the basis of rational moral conversation can be. In the case of what I call Rawls's conversation of justice, one is given ground too easily, as I see it, for dismissing the confrontation by another. My counterproposal is that in confronting another with whom your fate is, by your lights, bound up (either generally, as another human being, or more specifically by your cares for and commitments to the other, casual, institutional, or permanent), you risk your understanding of the other as of yourself—it is part of the argument you have initiated, or accepted the invitation to enter, to determine whether you have sufficiently appreciated the situation from the other's point of view, and whether you have articulated the ground of your own conviction.

Now, Voyager

Charlotte's choice at the end to treat Jerry as morally and intellectually unequal to her—doing privately what she decides, not without reason, is best for him and the child, and, perhaps, for her as well—means that she is limiting the moral ground she shares with this man, in favor of what she calls "preserving that little strip of territory" which is their secret and which limits the moral ground between them and the public world. Various paths lead from these thoughts. One path concerns the sense that the worth of a society is tested by the cost of the secrets that have to be kept from it. Another concerns the dangerous necessity, sometimes, of refusing moral ground with another altogether, in effect denying them the human fellowship moral encounter presupposes. An extreme case here is represented in Claude Lanzmann's film *Shoah*, in which, in interviewing an unapologetic concentration camp guard, Lanzmann lies to him about keeping something in confidence. I know some who feel that this must count as a moral failing on Lanzmann's part. In my gladness to be implicated in this failing, or refusing, of moral relationship, I do not count myself as immoral; perhaps as unsaintly.

Now, Voyager is a central document to consider in an examination of the recurrent figure of the psychoanalyst in the history of cinema. For all the fascinating intimacies between psychoanalysis and film—both of them originating in the last decade of the nineteenth century; both bound up, explicitly or implicitly, with the vulnerability and expressiveness of women; each arguably responsible for a greater effect on the human being's perception of itself than any other science or art of the intervening century; neither able to gain the respectability of a stable position within the academic world, in some part because, I dare say, of the unexhausted subversive reserves of each—I know of no systematic effort to articulate the conditions of these intimacies, however many psychoanalytic interpretations of individual films have been offered and however frequent have been the cinematic presentations of psychoanalysis and psychoanalysts (running into the hundreds in Hollywood alone, especially if one is not asking for a clear differentiation there between psychoanalysis and psychiatry). For someone of my intellectual tastes and debts, a convincing articulation of these intimacies will have to account for the fact that neither psychoanalysis nor cinema has received the measure of attention from philosophy that each calls out for (of course there are exceptions), each calling into question whatever philosophy had hitherto known as representation and reality, pleasure and pain, understanding and ignorance, remembering and imagination, intention and desire.

I note specifically that I speak, or wish to speak, under the sign of what I have elsewhere called Freud's ambivalence toward philosophy. I do not mean simply the evidence indicated by Freud's taking the trouble to deny that psychoanalysis is philosophy—a trouble expressed in his denying the identity no fewer than twelve times—but I mean as well an all but explicit ambivalence in his speaking, as in chapter 4 of *The Interpretation of Dreams,* of being led to feel "that the interpretation of dreams may enable us to draw conclusions as to the structure of our mental apparatus which we have hoped for in vain from philosophy." The ambivalence may be read in this assertion's meaning equally that our vain waiting for *philosophy* is now to be *replaced* by the positive work of something else, call it psychoanalysis; and/or that our *waiting* for philosophy is at last no longer vain, that philosophy has now been *fulfilled* in the form of psychoanalysis.

Either way, psychoanalysis is seen as some sort of successor of philosophy, but I am rather attracted to the latter, stronger side of the ambivalence, which takes psychoanalysis as some sort of transformation of philosophy— as if, after a millennium or so in which philosophy, as established in Greece, carried on the idea of philosophy as a way of life, constituted in view of the (perfectionist) task of caring for the self, call this philosophy's therapeutic mission, and after another millennium or so in which philosophy has seemed prepared to discard this piece of its mission, psychoanalysis has discovered methods which can make good on philosophy's originating goal of liberation (as in Plato's image of our lives as those of chained prisoners in a cave), methods still using dialogue of a kind, but now inflected with injunctions about saying whatever comes to mind, and about free association, and about interventions guided by the progress of transference, which may appear to be anti-philosophical methods, teasing, not training, reason with its dialectics. Then it must be the task of psychoanalysis to show, as Freud says with respect to knowledge, that there is reason and then there is reason.

This shadowing of philosophy within psychoanalysis is pertinent to the image of psychoanalysis, or anyway psychotherapy, sketched in *Now, Voyager,* directed by Irving Rapper, not one of Hollywood's most noted directors, but one who had the talent and the luck to preside over a remark-able, one might even say transcendent combination of script and actors and technicians and convention provided by the studio system of classical Hollywood filmmaking. But to say how I locate the philosophical pertinence, I have first to place this film, as it comes to me, within two conflicting, or incommensurable, frames of reference.

A received view takes the film as one of what Hollywood named "women's films," rediscovered in the 1980s as part of the emergence of the new femi-nism which became, among other of its intellectual accomplishments, the major unified force within film studies (in the United States at least). This phase of feminism tended fairly uniformly to distrust such films, and the Hollywood that stood behind them, seeing them (even when recognizing their considerable art) as luring their primarily female audiences to excessive investments of feeling and identification with their narratives, placing them-selves in service of a conventional patriarchal hierarchy between men and women, confining women to their roles as mothers and wives when not arraying them as commodities.

Here one may be treated to depressing descriptions of the institutions of Hollywood advertising and publicity, which included the phenomenon of the "campaign book" or "press book" that studios distributed along with their films, instructing individual theater owners in ways of marketing the pictures. The principal commodity connections established in the press book for *Now, Voyager* are beauty products and fashion tips to make the woman viewer as glamorous as, for example, Bette Davis and therefore lov-able to whomever she wishes to be lovable to. But of course it is the point of a kitsch perspective that it can reduce any object or event to kitsch. It should, to my mind, be of interest to ask how it is that movies as such are particu-larly vulnerable to such a perspective. It is not enough to say that many movies are in fact works of kitsch. So are many paintings and poems and novels. This does not on the whole tempt us to take up this perspective on paintings or poems or novels as such.

Film's critical vulnerability is a question raised by a second frame of ref-erence, one at odds with the received view of the "woman's film." It is a requirement I impose on the choices of the films I take, from which to develop the laws of the two genres chiefly adduced in this book, that they be films of cinematic, or say aesthetic, value, by which I mean two things pri-marily: (1) that I judge them to be of value (in Kant's sense of aesthetic value, the test of which is my declaration that they provide me with a pleasure I am compelled to share with others), a judgment I demand that others agree with (knowing that my subjectivity may be rebuked); and (2) that I am prepared to account for my insistent pleasure by a work of criticism (brief or extended) which grounds my experience in the details of the object, and in which I show that the object is, in roughly the sense Walter Benjamin develops in "The Concept of Criticism in German Romanticism," criticizable, we might say interpretable. What is not criticizable in this sense is not a work of art.

I therefore owe you some examples of gestures of criticism to establish the proposal that, to take our present case, *Now, Voyager* has in it that which resists, or rebukes, reductive description, indeed resists all criticism, in the sense that it invites and contests response, seeking as it were a voice in its judgment. Before discharging that obligation, I add one more comment about the genres of comedy and of melodrama (and certain related films) in relation to the figure of the therapist.

Two of the seven core comedies of remarriage and two of the four derived melodramas contain therapist figures. It is true to say of this small sample of films that in the comedies the therapist is a comic, marginal figure, evidently more distorted in character than those he treats (as in *Bringing Up Baby*, with Katharine Hepburn and Cary Grant, and *His Girl Friday*, with Cary Grant and Rosalind Russell, both directed by Howard Hawks). In the melodramas, the therapist is a serious character, even a leading one (as in *Now, Voyager* and in *Gaslight*). (The figure of the therapist I identify in *Gaslight* takes the form in this narrative, for interesting reasons, of a young detective, who has an exchange with the maddened central woman in which he confirms the accuracy of her sense-perceptions and insists, effectively, that she knows who is causing the ghostly noises overhead in her bedroom. Freud himself, as least as early as 1915, early in the *Introductory Lectures*, compared the scrutiny of an analyst with that of a detective.)

In fact I know of no exception to this postulate of the difference in the therapist figure in comedy and in melodrama (except that in film noir, the figure may even be the villain). It is borne out in related melodramas (for example, in *Random Harvest*, with Ronald Coleman and Greer Garson, and emphatically in Hitchcock's *Spellbound*) as well as in related comedies, such as the comic Viennese courtroom doctor in *Mr. Deeds Goes to Town*. In *Mr. Deeds* the hero, in a sense respecting the subjectivity opened up in psychoanalysis, adduces evidence that all human beings, including the psychiatrist, "do silly things when they think," which amounts to the assertion that the creature who thinks, that is to say, the human being, is inherently and inveterately "nervous." As Freud phrases the matter, "self-betrayal oozes out of every pore," a condition known to every novelist and detective and fed upon by the motion picture camera. If it were not widely shared but unarticulated knowledge, Freud's relating of these betrayals to those of dreams and jokes and neurotic symptoms would not have been the world-historical discovery it proved to be.

The artistry or "criticizability" of such films suggests determining some explanation for this difference between comic and melodramatic environments. We might say, for example, that in a comic world, where desire is present, joyous, but disruptive, to mistake it for madness is itself comic; it will find its own way out. In a melodramatic world, where desire is denied, or fixated, perhaps a source of horror, liberation must come from outside, from the capacity to attract and tolerate help. In *Now, Voyager*, at the close of the initial interview of Dr. Jaquith and his patient Bette Davis, this guarded, melodramatically suspicious woman is reduced to tears and cries out to the doctor, "Can you help me?"—to which he responds mysteriously by saying, "You don't need my help." I say mysteriously because he is not refusing her plea; but if he is granting it, why isn't his answer a flat lie? She patently does need (his) help. I take his line as a peculiar compression, meaning something like, "I'll help you come to see that you are not helpless." No doubt we are to understand this man as maintaining a certain mystery about himself, but the writing requires a characteristic Hollywood abbreviation or allegorizing in narration that I find extraordinarily hard to characterize.

Let's get further into the film *Now, Voyager* by following out its depiction of the initial interview between therapist and patient. It is not literally depicted as such an interview. For one thing it takes place not in the doctor's office but in a Back Bay mansion in Boston. When Charlotte's evidently distinguished mother, or matriarch, disrupts Charlotte's encounter with Dr. Jaquith, Charlotte takes her cue to leave and Dr. Jaquith follows her out of the room. What happens next is what I am calling "the initial interview" to underscore the remarkable fact that what ensues between this pair obeys essentially all the recommendations in Freud's classic statement "On Beginning the Treatment" (1913)—but obeys it backward, in two respects.

The first half of Freud's paper concerns issues around the scheduling of appointments and money, and it is of the nature of the particular case in question in *Now, Voyager* that the woman in question is not in a position to make such arrangements for herself, but only through the mother. A climax in the relation between this daughter and her mother will turn in part explicitly on the mother's threat to cut off financial support unless the daughter returns to her former state of obedience to the mother's wishes, to which the daughter replies, indicating that she has thought of taking an ordinary job, "You see, I'm not afraid, mother," and then is astounded by the simple truth, as it were the originality, of her own words.

The second half of Freud's paper concerns the importance of letting the patient do the talking, very much including finding a starting point, throughout the session, except for the analyst's announcing the analytical rule of suppressing nothing that comes to mind. (I have variously noted it as a point of affinity between them that neither philosophy, as I care about it most, nor psychoanalysis speaks first, that their essential virtue is responsiveness, or the shunning of conventional response, which sometimes expresses itself in silence.) But it appears that Dr. Jaquith does almost all of the talking when the two leave the room, as they walk up flights of marble stairs and enter Charlotte's own room where, after further conversation, Charlotte reveals, with mounting agitation, a story from her adolescence of a traumatic sea voyage with her mother, a revelation that produces the tearful, frantic plea for help.

My claim, however, is that one is invited—that Jaquith invites Charlotte—to understand the entire encounter as one Charlotte initiates and perpetuates, beginning with understanding Jaquith's following Charlotte out of the drawing room as if she has invited him to. (This is no more surprising than the fact that she turns out to permit it.) Then when he says he'd like to be shown around such a house, Charlotte continues walking up the stairs, which might be taken as a refusal of his request but which he takes as an initial response to it: he follows her up the stairs, saying, "That's right, I have already seen the ground floor." And when, after she identifies an upstairs room as her mother's, he says, as if it had been offered, that he would like to see *her* room, she mounts another flight and pauses before a door with a key in her hand saying, "She locks her door, doctor. Significant, isn't it?" (This comment indicates that she's been doing some exploratory reading on her own, another matter her mother will later explicitly deplore.) Again he refuses a conventional response—in this case, conventionally Freudian—saying: "Well, it signifies that it's your door. I've never heard it said that a woman's room is not her castle," which may be taken as a false or conspiratorial gesture of intimacy, but may also be granted as testing the possibility of rapport with this prospective patient, one of the principal tasks of the beginning interviews as articulated in Freud's paper.

Of course I would not claim, even if I were certified to do so, that these exchanges are literal or mimetic representations of authorized technique; but I emphasize their, so to speak, allegorical aptness, for a pair of reasons. Among the suspicious theorists of Hollywood film alluded to earlier, one notes that *Now, Voyager* does not show us any instance of the implied analytical treatment. But the allegorical abbreviations of analytical purpose I cited, in their accuracy to that purpose, seem to me to respect Freud's familiar insistence that one cannot understand psychoanalytical procedures by being shown them, that what one learns, from outside as it were, is hearsay. But there is a further reason for my emphasis on analytical purpose.

The picture of the analyst given in *Now, Voyager* is that of a sage, or say a philosopher; and while that picture is something that suits one dimension of the figure of Freud—one internal to the process of analysis—it is one Freud accepted no more than he fought against it (it is surely one of his reasons for wishing to dissociate his work from that of philosophy). Putting aside for the moment Freud's major cultural works, who but one prepared to withstand the title of sage, who is at the same time a therapist, would write papers such as "Transience" (1915) and "'Civilized' Sexual Morality and Modern Nervous Illness" (1908) and the pair entitled "Thoughts for the Times on War and Death" (1915)? The first paper is a contribution to what I would like epistemology to include (a study of our apprehension of the world as nature) as much as it is a perception of the incidence of mourning. The second paper prepares us to recognize that a firmer perception of a balancing must be arrived at between the requirements of instinct and those of civilization, for the sake of both, than either can achieve within its own frame. The third and fourth (the pair) end with the line: "If you want to endure life, prepare yourself for death." And who but a therapist who is at the same time a sage would portray a patient as "marooned within her illness" (*Introductory Lectures*, 18th lecture)—thus casting himself as one who assigns himself the task of discovering her for herself. One of the characteristics of being marooned that Freud specifies is the inability to give gifts; so it is nice to find in *Now, Voyager* that markers on Charlotte's therapeutic path are once the giving and once the receiving of a gift (her gift to Dr. Jaquith of one of the ivory boxes she carves is heavily remarked upon when the two return to the drawing room; her acceptance of a gift from Jerry is the beginning of their affair).

Beginning, as an analyst must, from the fact of transference, Lacan has most famously accounted for the element of the sage as "the one supposed to know"; but Lacan seems, to some disgracefully, to have enacted that role as much as he analyzed it. And naturally the extent to which sagacity is required in a course of psychotherapy is a function of what one expects of a course of therapy. It is not the least of the affinities of psychoanalysis with philosophy (with, that is, some strain of philosophy, to my mind most helpfully represented, perhaps I should say, in the later philosophy of Wittgenstein) that philosophy too, in its way, has to deal with the renunciation of knowledge, with the question whether knowing how to undo false knowledge is itself an extension of what is known.

The overarching image of therapeutic change in *Now, Voyager* is that of metamorphosis: one should not underestimate a narrative that can sustain a pivotal moment in which a stylish, mysterious woman can show an attentive man on the moonlit deck of a ship a photograph of her family and declare, truly, "I am the fat lady with the heavy eyebrows and all the hair." This is not simply a smart, literary-philosophical moment declaring human identity to be inherently ambiguous, or ironic. She still is, as she says, whatever the world sees, the fat lady with the heavy eyebrows . . . and she is at the same time not, and never was, however she imagined and defined herself, (identical with) the fat lady. But there is also evidence that fatness means, and meant, something to her, say that it is symptomatic, and that we are to speculate about its meaning. At the end Jerry identifies Tina, his child, whom Charlotte has befriended and helped when she returned to Jaquith's clinic, as their child; and we have seen Charlotte comforting Tina in bed, their bodies spooned together, saying to herself, "This is Jerry's child," as though she has been delivered of it. But it is Charlotte's mother whom she says has caused the fatness, and her mother seems to have been both father and mother to her. We are not in a position to draw hard conclusions about how she may imagine that a child had been put inside her.

But neither I think need we accept the inviting idea that the film wishes us to understand that Charlotte is sexually repressed because of her mother and cured of this by a love affair. That things must be more complicated is suggested in the early exchange between Charlotte and Jerry, alone on a midnight hotel terrace some days after their car accident isolated them for a night together before a fire. Jerry is already beginning his song of love and extrication. He asks, "Are you afraid of getting burnt if you get too close to happiness?" to which Charlotte replies, "Mercy, no. I am immune to happiness." He again: "You weren't immune that night on the mountain." And now her reply raises an essential question of the film: "Do you call that happiness?" Then his refrain: "A small part. There are other kinds . . . If I were free, there would be only one thing I want to do—prove you're not immune to happiness."

Evidently Charlotte had found genuine sexual satisfaction with Jerry, and she will be grateful for that to the end. But why is it important to her to deny that it could bring happiness? I think we know enough about her not to attribute this to Jerry's conventional imagination of providing her with what she calls "a home of her own [and] a man of her own." When her mother calls her "my ugly duckling," I suppose the most prominent of the figures the film provides of transformation, the mother is conventionally misinterpreting the figure, taking it that Charlotte is in fact ugly and is fated to be a misfit. But the fantasy of the ugly duckling (fundamental to the film) is not just that the creature is not ugly; she is not a duck at all, but an unrecognized swan, latently beautiful. Charlotte is shown to be capable of physical transformation into a glamorous presence (is Bette Davis really beautiful? and does it matter?); but her insistence on immunity to happiness suggests that what she is remains unrecognized, perhaps unrecognizable. (It seems reasonable to suppose that she will never come to the end of mourning for her life.)

When a proper suitor later is courting her he asks why she never lets him send her the white camellias she habitually wears when they go out in the evening. She replies, "It's just a personal eccentricity. We're all entitled to them." There is, I think, strong reason to take her to be alluding, among other things, to something like a homosexual side to her makeup. An essential part of the reason for me to take her meaning so is my sense that Jerry is attracted precisely to this side of her, to what they both understand as her morbidity. "I've been sick," she says when she shows him the picture of the fat lady, "and I still am." And in their amorous exchange on the terrace he confesses, "Ever since the night you told me of your illness, I haven't been able to get you out of my mind, or out of my heart."

The matter of her identity is taken to a new level when, in the penultimate sequence of the film, Charlotte and Dr. Jaquith are stretched out on the floor of that drawing room in her mansion—itself transformed, after the death of her mother, from a mausoleum into to a festival hall full of young people—looking over plans for the new building Charlotte is funding for Jaquith's Cascade, and he stares at her to remark: "Are you the same woman who some months ago hadn't an interest in the world?" She replies, simply but with Bette Davis mystery, "No." What these two discover together, looking like a couple well along in marriage, is that she is unknown—that the various names and labels that have been applied to her (another pervasive theme of the film) are none of them who she is. That this is a desirable therapeutic result I would like to maintain from a philosophical point of view of what the self is, something which no set of predicates can in principle exhaust, indeed something to which, as Heidegger takes *Being and Time* to demonstrate, no predicate applies, in the way predicates apply to objects. This idea of the self—always and never my possession, always to be discovered—is fundamental to the idea of perfectionism explored in these chapters.

From the encounter with Jaquith on her drawing room floor, Charlotte moves to her final, famous exchange with Jerry, about which it is generally understood that Charlotte sacrifices any new life of her own in favor of a sterile pact with Jerry to remain faithful to the memory of their hopeless love, a view with which I thoroughly disagree. It seems to me instead that we are shown that Charlotte perceives Jerry's destructive guilt to be about to cause further destruction, in the form of removing his daughter from Charlotte's protection and love, and shown further that he is incapable of responding to Charlotte in her assumption of her freedom and power. Accepting the fact that he has reached the limits of his powers of comprehension, she allows him to delude himself in peace.

There is no time now to articulate what elsewhere has taken me considerable care to make this claim plausible—including an understanding of the unforgettable closing line of the film: "Oh, Jerry, let's not ask for the moon; we have the stars." So I conclude with the acknowledgment that I am not unaware that interpretations I find convincing of lines and moments of films that I admire often do not at first find conviction in others. I attribute this—I mean in cases where I know some have by some eventually been accepted—to a further fact or condition shared by psychoanalysis and by philosophy as I care about philosophy most (the one seeking to do for individual inhabitants of a culture what the other seeks to do for the culture as a whole—and what is this difference?), as manifested in a mode of thinking that wishes to make itself responsible to each of these institutions. What I have in mind here is the sense of impertinence or strain in philosophical or in psychoanalytical interpretation when one is at the moment outside the experience which gives these interventions their life. (This is a reason interpretations are difficult to arrive at and to accept. They are not to be believed as statements of fact are, or not believed. Accepting or rejecting them requires work, a shift, of the self. Sometimes the shift is small, sometimes it is transformative.) To me this means that it is the never-ending task of the therapeutic mission, whether in the clarifying and liberating practices of philosophy or of psychoanalysis, to rediscover the reality of such work in one's experience, a reality in each case, therefore, whose access essentially runs the risk of becoming lost to a culture.

13

IBSEN

Why Ibsen? Which means, in our context, why feature him in a consideration of what I am calling moral or Emersonian perfectionism? I listed in my chapter on Nietzsche a dozen writers of the past two centuries, more literary than professionally philosophical writers, from Blake and Wordsworth to Goethe and Kleist to Whitman and Thoreau to Flaubert and Proust, who might serve as well as Ibsen to rebuke philosophy, in its dominant professional dispensation, for its comparative shunning of the perfectionist strain in moral thinking. I might answer by saying that it matters particularly to me that Ibsen became the most significant playwright in the lapse of time from Shakespeare and Racine to the middle of the nineteenth century, by taking as his subject for observation what can be seen precisely as a sequence of debasements of the search for a perfectionist existence.

To say why this matters it will help to do a little recapitulating. One way I earlier located perfectionism as a strain of moral thinking, I cannot say how fancifully, was to invoke Socrates' explanation to Euthyphro that the questions that cause hatred and anger—specifically unlike questions of measurement or science—are disagreements over the just and the unjust (we might say right and wrong), and the good and the bad, and the honorable and the dishonorable. The emphasis in Socrates' third pair, the honorable and the dishonorable, suggests to my mind more strongly (of course the other pairs will also consider it) the evaluation of a way of life, rather than of a choice of a particular course of action, for which particular reasons are owed. This emphasis is essential to what I am calling perfectionism, epitomized in the modern period in Emerson's formulation of our perpetual moral aspiration to an "unattained but attainable self."

Other formulations of perfectionism are the Romantics' more famous "become the one you are," taken up as a banality, but one to be given new life, in Heidegger's *Being and Time* (perhaps the banality is related to

Shakespeare's having given the line about being true to yourself to Polonius), adapted in Emerson's "have the courage to be the one you are" (in his essay "Considerations by the Way") and in young Nietzsche's transcription of conscience as saying "Be your self! All you are now doing, thinking, desiring, is not you yourself." To remember something of this kind echoed not long ago in the U.S. Army's recruitment advertisement, "Be all that you can be," is to bear in mind that perfectionism has debased forms, something that is apparently as essential to it as that philosophy itself has its debased forms, its intellectual competitors, insisted upon since its inception in Plato. My reservation about Rawls's portrait of perfectionism is not simply that it develops from what I understand to be a misreading of Nietzsche, but that the misreading is one that takes Nietzsche to be praising the very state of culture that he finds debased (fraudulent, false, fake, and so on) and, what is more painful to me, that it is based on sentences that show Nietzsche's indebtedness to Emerson at its most intense and intimate.

As manifested and attested in the films I adduce for their Emersonian outlook, perfectionism's attention is generally not focused on headline moral issues such as abortion, capital punishment, or euthanasia (plenty of other films are), and hence may not seem to some to be a moral theory at all. Indeed, as I have noted, it is the apparent unconcern of the couples of remarriage comedy with such matters, as if they are above ordinary moral confusion, that suggests their signature moral failing to be that of snobbery. But how else is one to think of the conversations of Katharine Hepburn with Cary Grant, of Hepburn with Spencer Tracy or Jimmy Stewart, of Barbara Stanwyck with Henry Fonda, of Clark Gable with Claudette Colbert, touching upon inattentiveness, contemptuousness, brutality, coldness, cowardice, vanity, thoughtlessness, unimaginativeness, heartlessness, deviousness, vengefulness, other than as one soul's examination of another, and of itself—which I suppose to represent moral encounter?

Ibsen's *A Doll's House,* the primary focus of this chapter, is less an exposure of the harm caused by debased or failed perfectionist ambitions—as are *Peer Gynt,* and *Hedda Gabler,* and *The Wild Duck,* and *Brand,* and *Rosmersholm,* and the massive double play Ibsen regarded as his masterpiece, the rarely attempted *Emperor and Galilean*—than (as the other plays also are) an exposure of the harm caused in failing to honor or recognize perfectionist longings. Elsewhere I have discussed *A Doll's House* in connection with a picture Rawls presents of resentment, or a sense of injury, in *A Theory of Justice.* The suggestion is that the climactic exchange between Nora and her husband in this play forms a test of that strain in Rawls's theory of what I call the conversation of justice.

Ibsen is another of the monumental names we take up in this book and perhaps the one, compared with those previously on our minds—Emerson, Locke, Kant, Mill, Nietzsche—that is most apt to be vague, or dead, to contemporary students. If so, that has happened in the past couple of decades, although Ibsen's plays continue to be retranslated and produced. And you never know what may happen to the reputation of true artists or thinkers. However far any of them may seem to recede from public attention, someone somewhere is rediscovering them, reading them as if they are the first to read them. I think this is what I mean in calling a work great, not having to do with the size of its fame but with something like the permanence or inexhaustibility of its interest, that just when you had as if thought you were beyond it, you find it ahead of you. Perhaps advancing age puts one more on the lookout for such surprises; but inexhaustibility is surely a function at the same time of a sense of the new, since the sense of permanence is of survival into, and even because of, a new time.

The young James Joyce in 1901 wrote a letter on the occasion of Ibsen's birthday (he would have been in his early seventies), celebrating his life of achievement and saying, "I hail you as one of the young generation of artists for whom you have spoken." (A happy moment, doubtless, for each of them.) James Joyce is electing himself, as you would expect, to the position of spokesperson of the young generation; but what is interesting at the moment is his accomplishing this by speaking publicly to Ibsen.

We might as well open our discussion with the unavoidable question about *A Doll's House:* Is Nora right or wrong to leave the house? Is it good or bad of her? Her husband thinks she is horribly wrong, thinks it is obvious that she is being undutiful, to him, to her children, to her religion. Does she perhaps have utilitarian grounds on which to combat this? She is a mother who loves her three children, married to a man of some position who dotes on her; his sensibility is no doubt restricted, so his appreciation of her is restricted; but they are, as is clearly signaled, sexually attracted to each other (when he pleads that if she will just stay they can live as brother and sister, she replies that he knows they couldn't hold to such a bargain). What does she want?

Shall we calculate for her? Let's see: she will cause intense pain to at least four people we know about (one husband and three children), perhaps for the rest of their lives. And what does she cause for herself to counterbalance this destructiveness? She doesn't seem to anticipate pleasure. On the contrary, she anticipates something like isolation and desolation. So she is creating displeasure all the way around. If she is right, or justified, in closing the door behind her then the play seems to constitute some kind of repudiation of utilitarianism as a personal morality (if not yet its repudiation as a theory of social choice—Mill, you remember, hailed it as both). (Other plays of Ibsen raise the question of social choice, notably *An Enemy of the People* and *Emperor and Galilean.*)

Then let us try Nora's perplexity further from a deontological, or Kantian, point of view, and attempt to apply to her case Kant's moral law, the categorical imperative. In Kant's *Groundwork of the Metaphysics of Morals,* one of the most persistently controversial short texts in the history of philosophy (in this it resembles Descartes's *Meditations*), Kant insists that what he says, in particular his formulation of the moral law which is the foundation of morality, is obvious or intuitive, in this sense, that as soon as I recognize that morality, "the reality of duty," requires the idea of an unconditional or categorical imperative imposed by a law of reason, "I know at once what it contains" (Ak. 420). (Something like obviousness is also an essential claim of Descartes for his cogito argument and for his original proof of God's existence from the presence of the idea of God in him; he characterizes obviousness as clarity and distinctness. By the time of Wittgenstein's *Philosophical Investigations,* obviousness, and the defeat of false or sham obviousness, can be said to be a dominant objective, in content and in form, of his whole project. (The obviousness he seeks is translated by perspicuousness. Specifically: *übersichtliche Darstellung* is translated as "perspicuous representation." It is a matter of continuing controversy.) What articulates or expresses the reality of duty, the categorical imperative, I remind you, in its most famous form, is as follows: "Act only in accordance with that maxim through which you can at the same time will that it become a universal law. . . . The universal imperative of duty can also go as follows: act as if the maxim of your action were to become by your will a universal law of nature" (Ak. 421).

What seems obvious here is that this is some unobvious way of saying that we are to ask ourselves what would happen if everyone acted as we propose to do. We might accordingly suppose that this consideration is on a par with one or another floating fragment of ignorable or cautionary wisdom, such as "Do unto others as you would have them do unto you," or "To thine own self be true," or "God helps those who help themselves." But this would leave unaccounted for two clearly essential but unobvious elements in Kant's formulation, namely those of a universal law and of a maxim.

Some light is shed on the idea of universal law if we examine Kant's two further formulations of the categorical imperative (he insists that all three say the same, but some Kant scholars find the further formulations more intuitive). The first, which I just gave, is called the Formula of Universal Law. The second is the Formula of Humanity, which goes this way: "So act that you use humanity, whether in your own person or in the person of any other, always at the same time as an end, never merely as a means." The third is Autonomy or the Kingdom of Ends, which stresses "the principle of every human will as a will giving universal law through all its maxims" (Ak 432).

I noted in my chapter on Kant that the last formulation joins us, so far as we join ourselves to it (recognizing others as legislating for us as well as we for them), in what Kant calls a kingdom (or realm) of ends—a deeply attractive idea to me, suggesting that those who aspire to a moral life (I have sometimes said, a philosophical life), already live, as it were, in an association other than the one manifested in our imperfect everyday world—the world of Emerson's conformity, of Nietzsche's philistinism, of Pascal's distractions, of Hume's sociability, of Rousseau's sense of imprisonment, of Kierkegaard's or Marx's alienation, of Heidegger's sense of chatter, of Wittgenstein's sense of exile. These are perfectionist perceptions of the way we live—the sense of personal crisis given a social projection. I have formulated this projection, extending an Emersonian thought, as the idea of an unattained but attainable further state of society, a state somehow present within this one. (The place Kant assigns to a perfectionist impulse seems less to be here than in the sense of our approaching purity in being able to act not merely in accordance with the moral law but for the sake of the law.)

That the categorical imperative, which Kant calls an objective principle, applies not directly to my action, or to what may be taken to be its motives or its consequences, but to the maxim on which I act (which Kant calls the subjective principle of the act), was for a long time a stumbling block for me, since it is not obvious how to decide what *the* principle is on which I am acting at a given time. For me a permanent contribution in Kant's theory is the very idea that my actions bespeak themselves, that they are interpretable, as my words are, that they are expressive. (As Freud describes the condition, something we had occasion to note regarding Mr. Deeds's theory of human thinking and restlessness, "self-betrayal oozes out of every pore.") That speaking is a mode of acting—which even those who will not cite J. L. Austin's name seem to accept—is no more or less true than that human acting is a mode of speaking (intentional, purposive, deliberate; confirmed in the ways it can be blind, aimless, heedless, thoughtless). (The idea of an act as based on a maxim suggests that "maxim" in Kant bears some relation to its ordinary use as indicating a familiar guide to conduct, related to an adage, such as "An eye for an eye" or "All's fair in love and war." Such thoughts are, we might say, not so much to be derived by universalization from my action as culturally stored universalizations awaiting adoption by my need to justify my conduct.)

We were going to test Nora's act of closing the door behind her in Kantian terms. How then shall we articulate the maxim of her action? Is it something like "If your husband disappoints you, leave him"? But that seems tantamount to saying that we have no concept of marriage; and Nora doesn't seem to be thinking this. Does expanding it help: "If your husband disappoints you and accuses you of talking like a child, leave him"? But she is also leaving the children. So then is she, as it were, saying, "When your husband shows his unheroic nature and accuses you in effect of being incompetent to raise the children you have had together, leave both him and them"? But how about the fact that he may have been speaking, as married people do, out of fear and anger and confusion, shown by his beginning to show remorse as he becomes convinced that his wife has changed? Could we imagine: "When you feel that the world you have shared has been shattered, that your judgment and confidence have been so undermined that you are no longer capable of understanding whether you belong there or nowhere, that the idea of sharing intimacies with this man suggests violation, and the idea of rearing children a mystery, but that there is one ray of possibility that somewhere you could learn to think and to speak again, then leave that world to find that place"?

What would it be to imagine this as a law of nature, governing the behavior of people universally? I do not imagine the streets suddenly full of people, women mostly, leaving pleading families and sympathetic friends for parts unknown. Is that because I cannot think that many people are in the condition described by this law, or because I cannot imagine that even many who are in that condition are made so as to be obedient to such a law? But then in the latter case, am I not conceiving that an untold number of households harbor fugitives from that law? Or has all this become moot since divorce has become an increasingly easy social option? In any case, or because of these various cases, there does not appear to be an obviously satisfying Kantian solution to Nora's dilemma. That there should not be such a solution is, to my mind, already suggested by her husband's very insistence that there obviously is one, implied in his direct appeal to her duties toward her family and her religion—and on what stronger ground than that it is unthinkable (to him) to imagine a world in which everyone did what she proposes? But of course my sense here is a function of my taking her husband to be in the wrong when he advances the idea that what she proposes is unthinkable (an idea that he in effect retreats from). Which does not prove that she is right.

I said divorce has become increasingly easy. How easy is easy? Nora's case is in various ways extreme, but while divorce has since her era become familiar to us, it is still serious moral business. There must for serious people be serious grounds for, as in Nora's case, leaving a person bereft with whom you have lived in the way of marriage. And the grounds are apt to be, if less absolute than Nora's, still a matter of what is intolerable and what seems possible. And a moral response to Nora (one, let's say, that treats her not merely as a means but at the same time as an end) seems to require not the construction of a law she is prepared to see become universally controlling, but an offer of conversation, or of imagination, to help determine whether what may appear as conditions of such a law are in fact determinative and fixed conditions of her life, or whether there are possibilities of change other than the ultimate change she has arrived at. (Put otherwise, we are to see that her decision is not based solely on inclination or disaffection, but rather on the contrary, to recognize that there are powerful inclinations and affections in play that she is precisely resisting, and to consider both that she may or may not be transparent to herself in weighing her desires and that she is going to have to act one way or another in partial darkness to herself.)

Emerson might well describe Nora as acting on what he calls Whim, taking a short way to the recognition that she is unjustified by utilitarian or by Kantian reasoning. Here it would be clear that the Emersonian Whim is anything but equivalent to the Kantian inclination or incentive. It makes no sense to say of Kant's incentive what Emerson says of Whim, that he hopes it may be better than Whim at last (that it is neither whimsical nor whimpering). But his reasons and explanations have run aground, come to an end.

And just here, at the pertinence of conversation, we are given the climactic irony of the drama. The person with whom Nora could imagine having such a conversation is precisely the one with whom such a conversation is not possible. Should that fact have gone into my articulation of the grounds of her maxim? For example, "And if the only person you can talk to will not talk, then . . . "? In fact Nora does include something of the sort when she invites Helmer to talk by saying that this is the first time they have sat and had a serious conversation in their eight years of marriage. But this invitation is avoided when Helmer indicates that he doesn't understand what she means. What I called an irony is what Nora describes as requiring the greatest miracle ("the miracle of miracles") to achieve, namely a genuine marriage between them. Or in my lingo: For them to have the conversation that would save their marriage they would already have to be (in effect) married. And they, she announces, have never been in that state.

But if we are to confront Nora as an end, not merely as a means to illustrate our own theories or inclinations, namely if we are to offer her our imagination and conversation, we have be to assured that we know all we can about how she herself perceives her condition. She says, very late, that she has to consider her duty to herself. Does she mean, or is she trying as it were to mean, that the categorical imperative does not apply to her, in this case? Or is she treating Helmer merely as a means, using his obtuseness as an excuse to get out from under commitments that have become onerous to her? Remember that the second formulation of the categorical imperative, about never treating humanity merely as a means but also always as an end, directs us to treat as an end "humanity in others *and in ourselves.*" So when she says "duty to myself" is she invoking the categorical imperative on her own behalf? How would that go?

The idea of duties to oneself is a treacherous one, as I emphasized in my chapter on Rawls. It seems meant to adjudicate (in my favor) between duties directed to others and duties directed to myself. What kind of conflict does such an idea wish to express? Do I weigh whether to keep a promise I made to you or to keep one I made to myself? (Suppose you are my younger brother. For some reason I am thinking of the situation depicted in the Frank Capra film *It's A Wonderful Life,* which had a great effect on me when I saw it in my early college years.) But we seem to be in the wrong register. If I make a promise that conflicts with another commitment, I am in trouble. If I take on a commitment that proves to exact more than I imagined, or am capable of, I am also in trouble. In both cases there is hell to pay—someone is going to have to sacrifice something. Isn't the claim of duty to myself merely a way of saying that the sacrifice is not going to be mine? Look at it differently. If you want something for yourself, say an education (as in the cases, however differently, both of Nora and of the James Stewart character in the Capra film), it may well be important for you to have it. But why call it your duty to provide it for yourself, rather than, for example, the good you have desired for yourself almost above all others?

I feel like saying that "duty to oneself" is only in play if the context is taken to be more basic than adjudication of competing demands (following my feeling that we were in the wrong register in seeking to weigh duties to self against duties to others). What Nora wants a way of saying is that there *is* no rightful duty she has as a wife and mother that costs what is asked of her— her existence as a human being.

Here the third formulation of the categorical imperative, that of the Kingdom of Ends, seems most pertinent: "the principle of every human will as a will giving universal law through all its maxims." The virtue Kant sees in this formulation of the systematicity or reciprocation in every human being's legislating for humanity (for the humanity in others and in oneself, apart from the private interests of any) is that it shows that in being subject to these laws each is subject to laws that each has, as it were, pro-mulgated; each is both the sovereign and a subject of the kingdom of ends. Now it is as if, in the face of Helmer's reminding her of her duties, Nora perceives the opposite face of the systematicity of human wills, namely that everyone else legislates for her, but in such a way as to deny reciprocity with her own powers of legislation. She finds herself, one could say, in a state of nature with respect to the world she knows. Her decision is to exile herself from that world, to find whether, in acquiring the education she senses her-self to crave, she, as she will be then, or the world, as she will then know it, is right.

Is this rational? Is she justified in sacrificing others and herself as she stands, for herself as she may be? (And is the concept of sacrifice called for here? Does it falsify her own sense of the degrees of pain at stake?) My answer must be, it seems, that we have no grounds for an answer. No utili-tarian or Kantian grounds. The former is repudiated; the latter begs the question of what is dutiful. A perfectionist answer remains possible: that Nora feels the force of an unattained but attainable self. It is not incompatible with the principles of justice as formulated by Rawls: she wants no greater goods for herself than for others, on the contrary she is headed for drastically less; and as for depriving others of their liberties, her claim is precisely that she has been living without liberty. But does the question of her rationality, or justification, depend on imagining future outcomes of her decision that will seal whether it is right or wrong, rational or irrational? In that case, is she making a wager on her life where the stakes are the happiness of four other human beings? Is there a right to make such a bet?

Lacking grounds here is I suppose a cause of a memorable formula of George Bernard Shaw's book *The Quintessence of Ibsenism,* in which Shaw, perhaps the most famous playwright then at work in Europe or America, undertakes to explain—by devoting a few pages in plain words to each of Ibsen's plays, and then drawing what he calls their "lesson" and revealing what he calls their "technical novelty"—why Ibsen was in his time the greatest writer in the world. The formula, given in answer to the imagined objection that Shaw has forgotten to reduce Ibsenism to a formula, is that "its quintessence is that there is no formula."

I suppose Shaw likes teasing us with the sense that he is avoiding trying to characterize Ibsen's achievement when what he has formulated is precisely what he takes each of Ibsen's plays to undertake to prove. Shaw spells out his idea by saying, "What Ibsen insists on is that there is no golden rule," and he glosses this immediately by continuing, "conduct must justify itself by its effect upon life and not by its conformity to any rule or ideal." Shaw boasted, when accused by a German scholar on his Ibsen book's publication in 1891, of having read Nietzsche's *Beyond Good and Evil,* that hearing that question was the first time he heard the name Nietzsche. This is quite believable for 1891, but Shaw later flaunted his reading of Nietzsche, as in his play *Man and Superman.* Indeed, in the 1912 edition of the Ibsen book, Shaw identifies Nietzsche's call for the Superman with what can be taken as the defining idea of the Ibsen's play *Emperor and Galilean,* namely its call for a man of the future who will "swallow up" both the emperor of the world (Caesar) and the emperor of the spirit (Christ), now tragically at odds. Though Shaw's sophisticated superficiality may sometimes grate on the nerves, he is reading or anticipating his encounter with Nietzsche with reasonable accuracy in declaring that "conduct must justify itself by its effect upon life." This recalls the theme of *Schopenhauer as Educator,* that the metaphysical meaning of the truthful man's activity is to pose and to answer the question, "What is life worth as such? . . . Do you affirm this existence in the depths of your heart? Is it sufficient for you?"

A typical instance of Shaw's application of his discovery of the nonexistence of a formula is his sort of reading of readings of *A Doll's House*, as for example when he announces: "When you have called . . . Nora a fearless and noble-hearted women or a shocking little liar and an unnatural mother, [and called] Helmer a selfish hound or a model husband and father, according to your bias, you have said something which is at once true and false, and in both cases perfectly idle." Elsewhere he says of such readings, for or against, that nothing in Ibsen can prove them false, that it is Ibsen's point to provide evidence for both sides.

I mentioned a technical novelty Shaw defines by means of which "*A Doll's House* conquered Europe and founded a new school of dramatic art." The novelty is the promotion of what Shaw calls "discussion" rather than action as carrying the drama of the work. It is therefore the more surprising, perhaps, that Shaw's endless epitomizings of the plays' alternative possibilities of interpretation seem to leave out precisely any room for our participating in these discussions, which amounts to leaving out—I would say, blocking out from the audience's attention—the characters' subjectivity.

When I found that Nora's perplexity demands not the application of a law but the offer of conversation, I wanted to imply that my relation to her and her play takes place in the mode of conversation. I cannot, or should not, judge her action apart from assessing my willingness or my refusal, for example, to take her wager in company with her, or perhaps take her plunge, with no thought that anything other than the present can justify the risk. She may be wrong in supposing that she will be able to bear up under her deed. She may return to her house defeated after two months. If I feel this, it may be my duty to raise the question. But given the velocity of her revelations about the world, it is hard to imagine that she can stop to calculate her resources. Something strikes her as so appalling in her life that she would rather not go on living than live like this (she has told Helmer of her contemplating suicide). Who but she can judge that? Can we say anything more about what is under her judgment? We know she judges her marriage to be a sham. But many others have doubtless come to some similar conclusion. (Hamlet's relatives try a comparable argument on him: Many others have lost their fathers, they remind him. "Why seems it so particular with thee?")

Ibsen

When I phrased Nora's wager, or risk, as taken in the face of not knowing whether she would be able to bear up under her deed, I was alluding to an idea of Nietzsche's which some of you might want to follow up. In *Thus Spoke Zarathustra*, Nietzsche sketches a portrait of a figure he calls The Pale Criminal, representing the fate of human action as marking the actor with the unbearable consequences of his own striking out at, or into, the world. As though doing anything remarkable enough to be noticed as *your* action, one that is to be laid at your door, is risking becoming identified as nothing more than the doer of just that deed—not merely *what* you are but *who* you are is an adulteress, an informer, a draft dodger, a shoplifter, an unfit mother, a God-denier, a terrorist—put otherwise, the deed absorbs the power of your subjectivity. It used to be said, in my graduate school days, perhaps it still is, in introductory logic classes, that we must not confuse two meanings of the word "is," the is of predication and the is of identity. I could not imagine how anyone could *confuse* saying, for example, "The shoe is brown"—a straightforward case of predicating a property of an object—with some idea that the object (a shoe) is identical with (or equals) its property of being brown. It was not until I read Heidegger's *Being and Time* that I recognized the systematic possibility, in the case of human existence, that I might "confuse" someone's being characterized by the predicate of professor or wife or acrobat or Jew or prisoner or short or beautiful or intelligent or maimed with someone's being identified or equated with or absorbed by one or other of these characteristics. Heidegger builds his theory of human existence on the idea that the fundamental characters of human subjects do not apply to them as predicates apply to objects, that they are not in the world as one object is in another, nor near nor distant from each other as objects are near or distant from each other.

Torvald Helmer's actions bespeak anything but a realm of ends, and his is the world Nora has adopted. Put otherwise, Helmer treats others, and himself, always as a means, demanding, where he is not putting himself in the position of, subservience. In Nora's case he uses her "kindly"; he loves her, to whatever extent he can love. (The final scene is only harrowing if his live love for her is not denied. I have never seen it played so.) But for all his claims to duty, no one, including himself, is treated by him as a lawgiver in the realm of the spirit. He does nothing without an incentive, acting always out of passion, dominated by a craving for respectability. This associates Torvald with the lawyer and blackmailer Krogstad, whom Torvald cannot tolerate, as if he recognizes him as his own double—as if what Torvald once calls the "atmosphere of lies" in his house is one of emotional blackmail, of which he, in his accusation to Nora of her undutifulness, is precisely guilty. The question of his imagination of Nora's humanity is at stake in his conventional pet names for her ("songbird," "skylark," "squirrel"). Nothing wrong with pet names surely, but for him they echo like threats: be these things, only these, or be unloved.

Helmer's sense of his own humanity is expressed in his saying, "No man would sacrifice his honor for the one he loves." Nora's reply is to say, "Thousands of women have." So *this* prospect, of sacrifice, is not what she regards as stifling her existence. Would Kant think such women have been morally wrong in sacrificing their honor? Does it not follow from the unconditional imperative to treat oneself as an end that one not dishonor oneself? Then is there not such a thing as a moral tragedy, in this case a forced choice between dishonoring oneself and causing another to be dishonored? What Nora knows, indeed declares, is that she would have acted on the maxim "Do not let the one you love be dishonored by you." But her imagined way to avoid that is to commit suicide, and that for Kant contradicts the moral law, its maxim cannot be universalized. Nora in fact rules out universalizing whatever her maxim will prove to be when she says, "All I know is that this is necessary *for me*." And she draws, I think, the right conclusion from this, I mean the sense of the weakness of her position, which proves to be the strength of it.

When Torvald reminds her of her religious duty to her family she replies that she doesn't know what religion is any longer; and when he goes on to try to "rouse [her] conscience," saying "You must have *some* moral sense," she replies, "Well, Torvald, it's hard to say; I don't really know." Her moral existence is at stake, some would say her soul, and she has only her newly achieved ignorance to stand upon. "I must find out which is right, the world or I." (This bears comparison with the moment in Kant's *Groundwork* where he says that one about to do something morally unjustifiable has "some" or "enough" conscience left to apply the moral law to himself. I asked how we are to understand that this remainder or fragment is enough to check desire, as opposed, say, to the fear of discovery and disapproval, presumably morally unworthy incentives.)

At an analogous moment Mrs. Linde, Nora's friend, describes herself as having sold herself in rejecting Krogstad years ago and marrying a richer man whom she did not love. Krogstad now rebukes her, saying she had no right to throw him over. She replies, anticipating Nora's response: "I've often asked myself if I had the right . . . I really don't know." I understand her to be asking equally whether she had the right *not* to marry more profitably, which is to say, whether she had rights at all. Did she have the right to act on her desires? Do desires confer rights? She would presumably have been willing to universalize the maxim that one act so as not to feel, and be, "sold" by one's decisions; but that itself would seem to assume a trust in, or place a value on, one's desire that may already be ungrounded, to put one's own ahead of the desires of many others, for example, those of parents. This is the sort of question utilitarianism cannot, even forbids itself to, help with: for it, desires count the same no matter whose they are.

That Nora does not wish to repudiate moral reasoning is shown by her appeal to her duty to herself, something she calls "another duty," one opposed to her duty to her husband and children, one that she claims is "more sacred." Where do these distinctions come from in her? These are the opening moments of this woman's claiming her right to exist, her standing in a moral world, which seems to take the form of having at the same time to repudiate that world. No wonder she would be both bewildered and lucid. I feel the moment as one of witnessing someone trying to invent or discover language for herself.

This is confirmed in her response to Helmer's attempt at rousing her conscience by saying, "Before everything else, you're a wife and mother." In a way he does rouse her conscience, namely to a fuller declaration of itself, and in opposition to his claim. She replies, "I don't believe that any longer. I believe that before everything else I'm a human being—just as much as you are . . . Or at any rate I shall try to become one." So that is the translation, or expression, of what she means by "duty to herself." And now comes the confirmation of the sense of her discovering language, giving herself words: "I can't be satisfied any longer with what most people *say*." This is not quite Emerson's "Every word they say chagrins us," but it partakes of the sense of needing to rethink all one's words. Recall the moment Nietzsche describes as religion having lost its authority as a criticism of life, leaving us in a "turmoil of secularization"; in Ibsen as in Nietzsche, this opens the question of the authority of morality as a criticism of life, as opposed to life as a criticism or test of the value of morality.

The idea of becoming a human being seems counter to Kant's assurance that humanity is in your own person or in that of another and is to be used always at the same time as an end, never merely as a means. How can you "*try* to become" one who is to be used at the same time as an end? You are or you are not an end in yourself. Any more than you can *try* to use others as ends. You do or you do not. Nor is the idea of becoming human exactly to be articulated as a matter of being true to oneself, because what Nora has discovered is not her true self. Her discovery is rather that she has allowed herself not to have a self, or to claim a self, at all. If we think of this as not allowing oneself to claim the power to say what does and does not belong to oneself, then it is a description of a state in which one is powerless to judge the world. (I am thinking here of Freud's idea of the origin of judgment in the power to accept or reject the incorporation of the world, in his paper "Negation.") When Nora says she really doesn't know, that it's hard to say (a wonderful expression), whether she has some moral sense, she is not expressing an uncertainty about some fact about herself but an ignorance of her relation to her experience. The inability to judge amounts to the lack of that possession of speech which Aristotle declares fits one for membership in a polis, makes one able to participate in a Rawlsian conversation of justice.

Let's move to a conclusion by noting that the play closes, after all, in a religious register, upon the image or invocation of a miracle, indeed of a greatest miracle, one produced by this woman's sense of having lived a life of violation, of having accepted the denial of her existence as a human being, the realization of which makes her want, as she cries out near the end of the play, "to tear herself to little pieces" (perhaps as if to show the world, which she cannot tear to pieces, what she thinks of its worth). She describes the miracle as creating between her and Torvald a genuine marriage, namely a change which would be redemption.

There is a change associated with salvation in the Christian Bible, First Corinthians 15 (a portion of which Emerson quotes in "Self-Reliance"): "Behold! I show you a mystery. We shall not all sleep, but we shall all be changed, in a moment, in a twinkling of an eye, at the last trumpet. For the trumpet shall sound, and the dead shall be raised incorruptible, and we shall be changed. For the corruptible must put on incorruption and the mortal must put on immortality." Linking this to the change called marriage puts marriage (whatever that will be recognized to be) under mortal, or say religious, pressure in the modern world, namely to achieve incorruptible union in a world none of whose corruptible institutions can validate the fact of genuine marriage, not church or state or family or gender or allowed sexuality. The uncanniness of the fit between Paul's Letter to the Corinthians and the end of Ibsen's *A Doll's House* is unlaughably comic, or dreamlike, when you consider that the twinkling of an eye in which Nora's change comes about occurs at bedtime, when, as Torvald abruptly discovers, she is not, and he is, preparing to go to bed ("We shall not all sleep"). But perhaps it is no more comic or dreamlike than Ibsen's use of the image of changing clothes as a modern parable for being changed.

Some extreme statement is being suggested here about the secularization of modern life, about the relocating or transforming of what is important or interesting to human life, as if turning our attention from celestial to terrestrial things, or rather suggesting that their laws are not different. (This relocating of importance and interest is what in *The Claim of Reason,* following my reading of Wittgenstein's *Philosophical Investigations,* I call the recounting of importance, and assign as a guiding task of philosophy.) The specific turning of our concern with heaven back toward our lives on earth is something that preoccupied Marx, who wrote in his "Introduction to a Critique of Hegel's *Philosophy of Right*":

> It is therefore the task of history, now that the truth is no longer in the beyond, to establish the truth of the here and now. The first task of philosophy, which is in the service of history, once the holy form of human self-alienation has been discovered [presumably in man's sinfulness in disobeying God], is to discover self-alienation in its unholy forms [evidently in man's appropriation of another man's labor]. The criticism of heaven is thus transformed into the criticism of earth, the criticism of religion into the criticism of law, and the criticism of theology into the criticism of politics . . . So where is the real possibility of a German emancipation? We answer, in the formation . . . of a sphere that has a universal character because of its universal sufferings and lays claim to no particular right, because it is the object of no particular injustice but of injustice in general. This class [the proletariat] can no longer lay claim to a historical status, but only to a human one . . . The complete loss of humanity . . . can only recover itself by a complete redemption of humanity.

That "redemption" here was interpreted as "revolution," and revolution as a particular form of violence, is one of the dominating facts of the bloody twentieth century. Another less noticeable fact is Marx's little clause that declares philosophy to be in the service of history. It is Heidegger's curse, and to that extent philosophy's, that, at least for a while, Heidegger wished this role for philosophy. It is against this idea that I insisted on Nietzsche's insistence, following Emerson's, that the philosopher will live in aversion, in contradiction, in criticism, of whatever, necessarily imperfect, dispensation prevails.

I cite Marx's text here, as one culmination of Hegelian thought, because it seems to capture the right level at which Nora finds herself helpless to claim that her case represents a brief against the world; she cannot claim her suffering to be representative. I might put the point of invoking the passage from Corinthians by claiming that Ibsen, in secularizing it, indeed domesticating it, is announcing that the task before humanity is no longer for the mortal to put on immortality, but rather for the pre-mortal (the songbird and the doll, for example, but Helmer's behavior is equally, let's say, mechanical, or in Emerson's term, conforming) to put on mortality, to become responsible for their lives of finitude, to become intelligible to themselves and to each other. So I see Ibsen as taking his literary task to be one of making a new form of revolution or transformation intelligible (as the perfectionists Emerson and Nietzsche explicitly do).

This is the way I understand Ibsen's saying, in a speech given in 1898, "I have been more the poet and less the social philosopher than people generally seem inclined to believe." He thus accepts that he is both poet and social philosopher, but puts poetry in the foreground. I take this to mean that he proposes no social solutions to the social distress he describes, but that he divines and presents this distress in ways philosophy may not. And it seems to mean more particularly that even though his great breakthrough as a dramatist came when he gave up writing his plays in poetry, his dramatic prose is meant to continue by other means the density of poetry.

Here I might just refer to the continuous sense, in an Ibsen text, of what is sometimes called dramatic irony, a character's saying something whose meaning is fundamental to the issues of the drama but is unglimpsed by the character who says it. (As when Helmer wants to make a bargain with Nora by agreeing not to discuss a matter further, not seeing that his life with her depends upon their not discussing matters at all; or as when Dr. Rank says he is auditing his inner economy and means his state of physical health, not his moral position as a friend of this family; or as when Nora notes that Helmer can't bear seeing dresses made, not yet recognizing the implications of her husband's inability to bear seeing the conditions of the pretty things he likes, call it their seamy side.) (One might say of Wittgenstein's and of Heidegger's descriptions of our unexamined ordinary lives that they are marked, in their obliviousness of their significance, by dramatic irony.) This continuous air of something unsaid, unheard, unseen, in Ibsen's medium of exchange is the glaring fact of it that Bernard Shaw's idea of "discussion," at least as exemplified in *A Doll's House,* leaves out of account. And this is the play, after all, that Shaw cites as the definitive moment in which Ibsen became an international figure.

I should add that sentence by sentence Ibsen's work in English translation doesn't by itself announce the kind of interest I claim for it. James Joyce learned Norwegian in order to read Ibsen. I haven't done that, so my claims for the plays come from having read and seen a reasonable proportion of them enough times that the recognition of, let's say, the suffocation of significance (meaning its pervasiveness and its unspeakableness) has come through for me (when it has) as it were despite the flatness of the translations I know. This is a conviction whose basis I wish I understood better than I do.

My emphasis on irony in Ibsen's language is one source of my emphasizing this feature of the language of the melodramas of the unknown woman. And Nora's climactic declaration of Helmer's inability to provide an education for her as her proof that they are not in a state of marriage is an idea I am not sure I would have come to in defining the comedies of remarriage without Ibsen's example.

14

Stella Dallas

1 Opening shots establish the workday's end in a factory in a New England mill town in the years after the first world war. A young woman (Barbara Stanwyck) appears at the picket fence of a house watching the mass of mill hands leaving the factory; she is evidently awaiting the appearance of a particular worker. A close view isolating a man among the exiting crowds—evidently some type of manager, at home in his well-kept suit of clothes—appoints him as the object of the woman's interest. On spotting him, she ostentatiously opens a small book as if to appear oblivious of anything but her regard for literature. The object of this theater, who had stopped to light a cigarette, resumes walking vigorously along the sidewalk, directly past the woman reading at the gate, his attention uncaptured. A young worker comes into view and raucously teases the woman ("Stella's got a fella; only he don't know it"), enters into a masquerade of her perhaps awaiting her dear brother and attempts to embrace her, to which she responds sharply, "Get your filthy hands off me." He opens the gate of the fence and walks to the house.

2 In her room, we find her reading, evidently not for the first time, a saved feature page of a newspaper, from which we learn that the man we have just seen walk past is Stephen Dallas (played by John Boles with an expertness easy to underestimate), from a prominent midwestern family, who has broken off his engagement to a society woman and left his home town as a result of the scandal of his father's bankruptcy and suicide.

3 The next morning, as Stella and her inexpressive mother grimly prepare breakfast for her grim father and her jocular brother, and sandwiches for their lunch at the factory, the brother refuses the food as intolerably cheap and boring and storms out. In a close-up, Stella, reflectively studying herself in a cheap mirror, is hatching a plan.

4 She appears in Stephen's office at the factory, apparently helpless in her search for her brother, who, she reports, has forgotten his lunch. It is too late to

deliver it to him, but Stephen and the factory's fortunate owner, who is in a high mood from a successful business trip and who recognizes Stella as part of a family whose members have long worked for him, accept the offer of sharing the lunch she has prepared (that is, purchased, extravagantly, on her way to Stephen's office), and they compliment her roundly on her sisterly concern and her talent as a homemaker.

5 Stella and Stephen Dallas are at the movies, where we view with them a silent romance ending with a sudden embrace at a formal ball. Walking away from the movie house, Stella confides in her new friend that she has enjoyed keeping company with him and that she wants him to educate her, so she can talk like him and his friends and like the people in the movie she is remembering with absorbed admiration. He replies that he has enjoyed her company as well, and is grateful for it, urging that she should not wish to be anything but herself, advice that makes her cringe. They embrace.

6 Stella has not slept in her room at home. The mother and brother attempt to disguise this fact from the father, whose primitive suspicions are melodramatically aroused and who orders that Stella and her things be removed from the house. The brother is drawn outside when a car pulls up to the house, and rushes back inside shouting the news: "It's all right! They're married!" This concludes a kind of Prologue, expert in maintaining interest in its extreme condensation of expository material.

7 Stella, transformed, in assertively expensive afternoon wear, is returning to her apartment with her husband and her maid and her new baby. After three weeks in the hospital she is eager to go out, especially to accept an invitation to the River Club, much to Stephen's displeasure and disapproval.

8a At the River Club Stella, having somewhat scandalously agreed to dance with glad-handing Ed Munn (superbly played by Alan Hale), contrives to leave the table where she is seated with Stephen's boring friends and get herself introduced to Mr. Munn's lively circle of companions.

8b Back in their apartment, Stella greets Stephen's evident disapproval of her behavior by saying, roughly, "Okay, let's have the lecture about how I act and talk. Only don't tell me how to dress." Stephen tries to reason with her, asks her to distinguish between what is important and what doesn't matter, and tells her he has been promoted to a job that requires moving to New York. She at once refuses to accompany him and her attention is fully captured by her baby daughter Laurel, who is waiting patiently to be nursed.

9 In an indifferent housedress, in her apartment feeding her daughter, now in a highchair, and visited by her friend Ed Munn along with her brother and his girlfriend, Stella remarks, "Laurel's been a real pal now that Stephen is in New York. I hardly know I have a husband." As Stella is trying to calm an air of unwelcome gaiety created by the drinking and smoking and general high spirits of her visitors, Stephen Dallas appears at her door and feeds his disapproval with his misinterpretation of Stella as encouraging these proceedings. When he threatens to take their daughter away from such an environment, Stella grabs the child to her and fiercely orders him away.

10 In New York, Stephen encounters his former fiancée, now Mrs. Morrison, and her three young sons. He learns that she has recently been widowed.

11 Stella is sewing Laurel a dress; from the size of the dressmaker's model Stella is using, we realize that Laurel (Anne Shirley) is now an adolescent. Laurel's high-toned high school teacher (evidently Stephen is supporting a privileged, private education for his daughter) calls upon Stella at home to ask her permission to take Laurel into town to visit museums and go to the theater. Stella agrees, saying Laurel takes after her father in her taste for such things.

12a To keep Stella company, Ed travels with her on a train ride to town to buy favors for Laurel's birthday party. They are old friends by now and he, obviously not for the first time, suggests that they add something more to their friendship, to which Stella replies that Laurel absorbs her reserves of serious feeling for others. ("I don't believe there is a man in the world who could get me going again.")

12b Ed is inspired to play a practical joke on their solemn fellow passengers, introducing some itching powder into the assembly. Ed and Stella are so overcome with laughter at the ensuing spectacle of surprised and intensifying itching that they are forced to quit the scene.

12c Their noisy entry into the adjacent train car is particularly noted by a pair of richly black-clad matrons, one of whom remarks chillingly, "Women like that shouldn't be allowed to have children." The colleague to whom she offers this observation is Laurel's teacher, she into whose cultivated hands Stella had recently delivered Laurel.

13 On the memorable day of Laurel's birthday party, we witness each excruciating stage in the disintegration of mood as Stella, Laurel, and the maid open messages informing them that, one after another until the guest list is exhausted, no one is able to attend.

14a Laurel, on her regular visit to New York to be with her father, is this time surprised by being taken with him to stay at Mrs. Morrison's marvelous house. She is dazzled as if by the realization that such perfect places can exist. Mrs. Morrison helps her unpack and is impressed by her wardrobe, even more impressed when Laurel says that her mother made all the clothes.

14b At the end of her stay, during which she has become at home, Laurel tells her father that Mrs. Morrison is the loveliest lady she ever knew, "except, I mean, for my mother."

15 On returning home to Stella, Laurel describes this new experience and this new vision of being a lady in poetic terms. When she realizes that Stella's feelings have been hurt, she comforts her, we can say mothers her, by helping her peroxide her hair. Stella has invited Ed Munn to have Christmas dinner with them, as if she has become afraid to be with Laurel on intimate terms.

16a Ed turns up drunk with a raw, plucked turkey under his arm, which he insists on taking into the kitchen and trying, against Stella's efforts to dissuade him, to shove into a cold oven.

16b Laurel answers the front door to discover, to her delight, a radiantly smiling Stephen, who has arrived a little early to collect her for their Christmas in New York. Stella manages to guide Ed and the turkey unseen out of the apartment by the kitchen door.

16c Stella avoids greeting Stephen until she has hastily transformed a somewhat overly fussy dress into the kind of plain but elegant black gown Stephen appreciates. He asks whether he can take Laurel away a bit early to attend Mrs. Morrison's Christmas party, but he is so taken with Stella's reserve and elegance that he soon offers to have dinner with her and Laurel and take a later train. Stella has trouble restraining her tears of gratitude. As Stephen goes to the phone in the entrance hall to change his train reservation, Ed Munn reappears with his turkey, and, eventually recognizing Stephen, retreats with desperate embarrassment and remorse. Stephen hangs up the phone in resumed disapproval, saying there really isn't, on maturer thought, time enough for them to stay. As he and Laurel disappear together and the door closes on them, and on her, Stella stands with her back to us, facing that door.

17 In a lawyer's office, Stella is informed that her husband wants to set her free in order to clarify her position. She says her position is that she has a marriage license and she intends to clarify the way things have been going by receiving a divorce settlement sufficient to show Laurel the kind of good times Stephen has harbored for himself all these years.

18a A montage of shots shows Stella shopping for a makeover wardrobe, with notably many pairs of shoes, and getting the full treatment at a beauty salon.

18b At a fancy resort hotel for the right people, Stella has stayed in her room, away from the myriad forms of elevated entertainment and socializing the resort offers; but when Laurel says that she has met a boy, a friend of the Morrisons', Stella makes her appearance. It produces one of the great melodramatic fiascos in the history of classical film narrative, when everyone but Stella recognizes that she is dressed with grotesquely flamboyant inappropriateness, perfectly outfitted for ostracizing.

18c Laurel, at an ice cream parlor after having gone bicycle riding with the boy and his friends, hears jocular remarks that other young people are making about someone looking like a Christmas tree, and notices, in the same wall-length mirror in which they see the object of their amusement, that the object of their humor is her mother, wandering rather aimlessly outside. Managing to slip away without being seen by Stella, Laurel rushes in near hysteria back to their hotel room to get the two of them packed and gone. When Stella returns to the room, Laurel says she wants to leave because of a quarrel with the boy. Stella wants to fix the situation, but Laurel is adamant.

19 In the sleeping car of the train, Laurel overhears a conversation in which one fashionable young woman tells another that the Christmas tree spectacle was Laurel Dallas's mother; Laurel looks down from her upper berth toward her mother, and Stella pretends to be asleep and not to have heard; Laurel climbs down to cuddle with her, clearly an old, reassuring gesture of theirs.

20 Stella appears at Mrs. Morrison's wonderful house, drawn with the effort of controlling her tortured feelings, to ask whether, now that Stephen is going to marry Mrs. Morrison and live in this house, it would be convenient to have Laurel live with them. Stella says she wants to get on with her life, and besides, Laurel likes the sorts of things they can give her that Stella doesn't enjoy. Mrs. Morrison is stirred to the depths by this display of magnificent motherly sacrifice. The women's connection is so strong as to suggest that each has found a mother.

21a When Laurel is told by her father and Mrs. Morrison that she is to live with them, and that this is her mother's idea, she recognizes instantly, in agony and ecstasy, that her mother did indeed overhear the conversation on the train. She departs at once, saying that her home will always be with her mother.

21b Mrs. Morrison informs Stella by telegram of these events, and Stella proceeds to stage a verification of her supposed desire. She goes to look up Ed Munn, whom it turns out she has not seen in months, in his rooming house, where, unable to rouse him from a drunken stupor, she picks up from his bureau a humorous photo of him which, arriving back in her apartment, she places on her mantel; and then, putting a lowdown jazz record on her phonograph and lighting a cigarette, she sits cross-legged on her sofa pretending to be reading a Love Story magazine, altogether presenting a picture of wantonness to her again gullible daughter, who walks in with her reparative fantasy of living with her mother forever. Stella feigns surprise at seeing her and impatience to get on with her life beyond being a mother.

21c Laurel returns to Mrs. Morrison's house in a state of bewildered rejection, to find that her father and Mrs. Morrison have received a note from Stella saying that by the time they receive it she will be Mrs. Ed Munn. Mrs. Morrison recognizes the truth of the matter, saying to the benumbed Stephen, "Can't you read between these pitiful lines? Laurel is here. Who has caused this?"

22 Mrs. Morrison's house is in a state of wedding preparation. Laurel, in a wedding gown, is reassured by Mrs. Morrison that if her mother knew she was getting married nothing in the world would prevent her from being present.

23 It is a rainy night. We find Stella milling with a crowd of onlookers outside a brilliantly lit window of the house which reveals the formal wedding ceremony in progress inside. At its completion, with the bride and groom embracing, Stella turns away and walks almost toward us, with a reviving, swaying walk and an enigmatic expression of smiling through tears whose interpretation might have invited, given the persisting interest in this film, more speculation than it seems to have received.

———————

This is the third of the melodramas of the unknown woman that we have considered, and the earliest produced (1936; *Now, Voyager* is from 1942; *Gaslight* from 1944; *Letter from an Unknown Woman* from 1946). As with *Now, Voyager,* its script was adapted from a book by Olive Higgins Prouty. Its generic obligations are fulfilled fairly straightforwardly—the principal woman is presented as being a mother and as having a mother; it is essential to her language and conduct that they are systematically and ironically misunderstood; education and its transformative power are thematized; the narrative spans, or recapitulates, a substantial period of years; the power of setting and costume is heavily emphasized, absorbing the brunt of the tendency of melodrama to heavy symbology; while the film does not open and close in the same house, there is a house that is climactically returned to; the woman rejects marriage as the arena in which she is to discover a life for herself.

My accounts of these melodramas in *Contesting Tears* all tend to take the form of contesting a received reading of the films as fairly unquestioned tales of a woman's self-sacrifice. There is a reasonably straightforward (I do not say complete) explanation for this. The melodramas of the unknown woman were from the beginning taken as belonging to the genre of "women's pictures," more recently called "weepies." This amalgam characteristically contained films in which a woman, prevented (perhaps accidentally) from marrying the man she loves, remains faithful to him in the shadows of what furtive moments they can steal together, a figure of rumor and unfulfillment (an example is *Back Street,* from a novel by Fanny Hurst, with Irene Dunne). This narrative is at odds with the narrative of the melodramas of the unknown woman, which however may be taken as comments upon melodramas of illegitimacy, as we might call them.

Other women's films range from *Camille,* which, like Verdi's *La Traviata,* is made from Alexander Dumas's *La Dame aux Camélias,* and which provided Garbo with one of her greatest roles; to *Imitation of Life,* with Lana Turner; to *Mildred Pierce,* with Joan Crawford playing a mother whose dedication to her ungrateful daughter is unrequited to the point of the daughter's stealing her lover; to *An Affair to Remember,* with Cary Grant and Deborah Kerr, in which the accident that keeps the pair apart is literalized as being struck by a car, which somehow means that the pair can get back together. What is surprising is that in the renewed interest in these films inspired by the dominant strain of feminism in modern film studies, this general view of the melodramas we consider in this book, as narratives of a woman's sacrifice (in particular *Stella Dallas* and *Now, Voyager*), remains, so far as I know, uncontested. And in this renewed interest, the specific genre of women's films defined here is rather disapproved of than celebrated.

It is not surprising that my readings of the remarriage comedies do not take a contestatory form (except in the implied sense that the films are worthy of more serious critical attention than they have mostly been shown) since there are no received readings of that genre to contest (beyond an understanding that lumps its films with what were and are called "screwball comedies," a title so far as I know that has still received no definite characterization).

My efforts in doing what I call reading a film often have to do with showing that the film resists casual efforts to dismiss it as, let's say, a popular effort to entertain for a couple of hours, with tears or laughter, and to convey a transparent, congenial message—with showing, on the contrary, that it may be understood as touched with an interest and an ambition usually reserved for an accepted work of some kind of art. I do not deny that movies, of the kind represented by the comedies and melodramas we are considering, are made to be interesting and satisfying on one viewing (drawing tears, laughter, thrills) and without serious thought (like pieces on conventional music programs). (This raises the, for me, fascinating question of why a piece of music is appreciated so essentially in its endless repetition and familiarity, whereas with films, even in the era of videos, DVDs, and classical movie television channels, it is still common to hear that a reason not to see a film is that one has already seen it.) So what motive can be found, for anyone not professionally or pedagogically required to view a movie *again,* and when so much movie criticism is guided by swiftly arrived-at judgments of thumbs up or thumbs down, of life or death, to *think* about one's experience of a film? We might start an answer by taking in the fact that such thinking normally occurs in discussion, and about films seen recently, which suggests that it is difficult to think about a film alone, difficult, to begin with, simply to recall the events of a film thoroughly enough to provide evidence for a thought.

In the discussion after the class at the University of Chicago viewed *Stella Dallas,* I proposed we test our powers of recall—let's call it our group memory—by attempting to reconstruct the film together. We were able to do what no one present could do alone, namely to give a satisfyingly complete sketch of the sequence of events. What one, or most, could not remember, another remembered, often prompted by a classmate's hazy suggestion. I don't claim that any group of comparable size (roughly twenty-five people) could do this; our group contained dedicated, avid students of the subject, and before viewing the film they had read my chapter on it in *Contesting Tears.* If I were a betting man, however, I would bet that any group, even one as small as three or four, with a moderate, temporary interest in a film could go far enough in this effort as to surprise themselves with their capacity for collective memory.

In a famous sequence—one of the most unforgettable in classical American cinema—Stella Dallas's appearance dressed in an outlandish outfit makes her an object of ridicule to the refined society gathered at an exclusive resort hotel. The received, indeed ingrained, understanding of this sequence, unchallenged so far as I know, takes its shock to precipitate Stella's plan to separate from her daughter, an act, on this understanding, of pure self-sacrifice. In *Contesting Tears,* I challenge this understanding as expressed in an impressive paper by Linda Williams, "'Something Else Besides a Mother': *Stella Dallas* and the Maternal Melodrama," the most careful and elaborated exposition of this understanding I am aware of. Because my reinterpretation is so strictly at odds with that view, and because what I shall say at first increases the pain in following the narrative (while, I trust, in the long run serving somewhat to counteract it), and because the evidence for my reinterpretation is hard to keep in mind, and because I have found no better way to articulate my alternative proposal, I am going to incorporate large stretches of that articulation in what follows here.

The received interpretation of Stella's self-sacrifice is based on the assumption, as expressed in Williams's essay, that Stella at the resort hotel is "as oblivious as ever to the shocking effect of her appearance" when she makes "a 'Christmas tree' spectacle of herself." My thought is that the pressure of this interpretation is excessive, too insistent, that there is massive evidence in the film that Stella must know exactly what her effect is there, that her spectacle is therefore part of a strategy for traumatically separating Laurel from her, not a catastrophe of misunderstanding that causes her afterward to form her strategy.

The evidence that Stella knows her effect at the resort hotel turns on her conclusively authenticated knowledge of clothes, that she is an expert at their construction and, if you like, deconstruction. The principal authentication is given in the sequence in which Mrs. Morrison, the highest and most humane judge of propriety in this depicted world, helping Laurel unpack her suitcases on her first visit, is impressed, even moved, to learn that Laurel's mother has herself made all of Laurel's beautiful, and exactly appropriate, clothes. Moreover, Stella's knowledge of her own effect is separately authenticated in the sequence in which we are shown her hurriedly and surely alter a black dress in which to receive Stephen, who has turned up early to take Laurel away for Christmas. The resulting, not quite basic black dress is not exactly expressive of Stella's taste (though her alteration has demonstrated that it is just a rip and a stitch away from her taste), but it certainly satisfies Stephen's. He even goes so far as to suggest, in response, that he and Laurel might take a later train in order to stay and have dinner with Stella, who is thrilled by the suggestion. But when Ed Munn barges in drunk, in a virtuosically destructive sequence, brilliantly played on all sides, Stephen reverts to the appetite of his disappointment and takes Laurel away at once, and Stella learns the futility of appealing to the taste of those who have no taste for her. This represents an unforeseen answer to the education she had asked Stephen for at the beginning of their association. Here he shows how effective a teacher he is.

It is this learning, on my way of looking at things, that precipitates the scandal in the resort hotel. Stella appeals there, as it were, to the distaste of those for whom she knows she is distasteful. Why take it as certain that her overstatement in clothes in this sequence exactly expresses her own taste, any more than her understatement in the black dress exactly expresses her own taste? On my theory of the film, Stella's plan for Laurel's separation from her begins much earlier than when she raises it on her visit to Mrs. Morrison at home, after the sequences at the hotel and in the Pullman car with Laurel afterward. I take the mark of its beginning to be precisely the close of the sequence of her final lesson from Stephen, as she stands in that black dress, her back to the camera which dwells on her as she faces, in what reads as self-absorption, the closed door behind which Stephen and Laurel have disappeared.

Why *must* the Christmas tree spectacle be conceived as expressing Stella's unexamined taste? It can be seen (something I claim the melodrama of the unknown woman contests) as something enforced by a supposedly transparent, homogeneous ideology of a Hollywood intent on punishing raucous, unsociable, single mothers. It surely fits the pattern of so many North-American families of the period—notably exemplified in the second generation of immigrant families, such as mine, whose parents craved a life of acceptance for their children in the greater American culture from which they were themselves debarred. Neither idea accounts, for example, for my sense that Stella in her strategy at the hotel seeks disapproval. What is the benefit of public disapproval?

I note briefly the cinematic elaboration of ideas in the sequence in which Laurel's young companions, seated along the stools of the resort's ice cream parlor, watch Laurel's mother in the wall-length mirror before them and banter gleefully about what they name this "Christmas tree" spectacle. This vision of Stella is one in which she is seen only indirectly, as she stands in a space behind the space of those viewing her in the mirror; one senses that they are not in a position to see who she is as a person. The unreality of these viewers' view is confirmed by their arriving at it in view of each other, encouraging each other in their exhilarating power to ostracize. The immediate effect upon Laurel, when her attention is drawn away from the boy with whom she has just exchanged certain tender vows and she notices what these companions are laughing over, is that she sees her mother for the first time through the massed, hard eyes of others. Stella has picked a harsh mode for Laurel's education in objectivity. Since I have elsewhere spoken of the medium of film as one in which reality is behind us, as if at any time ready to pounce, like a revelation, I take this moment in *Stella Dallas* to set up a moment in which this tendency in film questions itself, and the place of reality may equally be read as a place of illusion.

Linda Williams speaks of Stella in the course of the film as "increasingly flaunting an exaggeratedly feminine presence that the offended community prefers not to see . . . But the more ruffles, feathers, furs, and clanking jewelry that Stella dons, the more she emphasizes her pathetic inadequacy." I see no such linear buildup. Stella's taste in her self-presentation is generally more flamboyant than it is refined; but only once, at the resort hotel, is it egregious to the point of scandal. (And as for "pathetic," so good a witness as Mrs. Morrison, in describing Stella's late letter claiming she intends to marry Ed Munn, says to Stephen, "Can't you read between these pitiful lines? Laurel is here. Who has caused this?" That is, the lines pitifully fail to conceal the power of Stella's decisiveness.)

I count six events in which representatives of respectable society take offense at Stella's presence (apart from, or later than, the prologue where Stella's father gives orders for her to leave the house when he discovers she hasn't slept in her room): (1) Stephen's reaction to Stella's fun and earrings at the River Club; (2) Stephen's shock coming in upon a scene of liquor and song in which Ed Munn and Stella seem to be sharing the care, or ignoring the care, of infant Laurel; (3) the schoolteachers' contempt for Stella's boisterousness as she and Ed Munn, having left the train car in which Ed has done his bit with the itching powder, lurch into the parlor car; (4) Stephen's revulsion as Ed Munn returns to Stella's apartment while Stephen is expansively phoning for a later train; (5) the chorus of reactions of the older generation, but most vocally and individually of the younger, at the resort hotel; and (6) Laurel's horror at her mother's cliché masquerade of desire by listening to jazz, smoking a cigarette, and reading a cheap woman's magazine—it is a scene from such a magazine, or from a movie.

Stephen retains enough human intelligence early in his and Stella's history to recognize that "the earrings don't matter." And his later two revulsions, at Ed Munn, are caused by episodes not merely not of Stella's flaunting but of displays which she is trying to stop. The aftermath of the itching-powder episode is the single instance I recognize in which Stella is oblivious to her giving offense, and there nothing is flaunted; unless one feels, I think rightly, that she is being excessive in her loud appreciation of Ed's practical joke, a display I readily forgive as being the only reciprocation she is prepared to offer in return for Ed's devotion. And this causes no general disapprobation, nothing beyond the violent contempt and meanness of the two high-minded schoolteachers who in response prevent Laurel's schoolmates from attending her birthday party. As for Stella's painful flaunting of her sexuality before Laurel, this involves no general increase of feathers, furs, etc.; it is an enactment of a specific setting staged as for an assignation. This leaves the Christmas tree spectacle at the resort hotel as the only event, among the six events of Stella's giving offense, in which she scandalously, publicly flaunts the excessive piling on of ornamentation.

If there is no "pathetic inadequacy" here, but a conscious decision to face not only the necessary, in principle shared, pain of separation, but the unshared pain of enforced separation, then how are we to think about what Stella accomplishes in sending Laurel away? And since I am in effect questioning Williams's perception that "the final moment of the film 'resolves' the contradiction of Stella's attempt to be a woman *and* a mother by eradicating both," how are we to take Stella's ecstatic walk toward us at the film's close? I have said that Stella's plan is not pathetic but effective. What has it effected? Uncontroversially, it has placed Laurel with her father, in the house of Mrs. Morrison Dallas (I assume this marriage is by now to be assumed, without having been said or shown) and without being, in the short run at any rate, laden with guilt. But who is Mrs. Morrison (Dallas)? What is her house?

It seems generally recognized that her place may be located by the brilliantly lit, horizontally rectangular window, hardly avoidable any longer as a figure for a film screen, through which, in the film's final sequence, Stella views Laurel's wedding. (Hardly avoidable now, yet on the whole avoided for some decades of the seven since the film was made. Has our repression of film's power of significance all at once been overcome?) The general idea seems to be that Stella has placed Laurel into the fantasied film world that we had seen Stella absorbed in when we were early shown her and Stephen out together, at the movies, and she was asking Stephen to educate her to be unlike herself. Hence it may be easy to think that at the end Stella gets her wish, if somewhat more ironically than in a classical ending, and, eradicating herself and seeing her daughter as a publicly unapproachable star, identifies herself as the star's creator, to her own infinite but necessarily private satisfaction.

One of the most influential ideas in film studies during the 1980s and beyond (associated particularly with the work of Laura Mulvey) was that (especially Hollywood) films have been made under the sign of satisfying and ratifying the patriarchal, male gaze. Apart from contesting the evidence for this claim, I have proposed that film assaults the human sensorium at a more primitive level than the (anyway the nontotalitarian) enforcement of an ideology can maintain. Film's enforcement of passiveness, or say victimization, together with its animation of the world, entertains a region not of invitation or fascination primarily to the masculine nor even, yet perhaps closer, to the feminine, but primarily to the infantile, before the establishment of human gender, that is, before the choices of identification and objectification of masculine and feminine have settled themselves, to the extent that they will be settled.

I assume that films such as *Stella Dallas* and *Gaslight* and *Letter from an Unknown Woman* and *Now, Voyager* could not attain their power—which I am not interested now to distinguish from the power of works in the other great arts in Western culture—apart from their discovery of one or more of the great subjects, or possibilities, of the medium of film. I claim of remarriage comedy that its subject, or a way of putting one of its principal subjects, is the creation of the woman with and by means of a man, something I describe further as a search for the new creation of the human, say of human relationship, which implies that friendship and mutual education between the sexes are still a happy possibility, that our experience, and voices, are still to be owned by each of us and shared between us, say by dispossessing those who would dispossess us of them. I have formulated the subject of the melodrama of the unknown woman as the irony of human identity. And I have formulated the narrative drive of the genre as a woman's search for the mother.

And now, having introduced the dimension of infantilization in the viewing of film (cutting across cultures, races, genders, generations), I will articulate this subject further as the search for the mother's gaze—the responsiveness of her face—in view of its loss, or of threatened separation from it. (The psychoanalytic work of Melanie Klein is critical here.)

That film gazes at us (or glares or glances) aligns it with the great arts, though its specific way of animating the world—unlike poetry's or painting's or theater's—is unprecedented, still being absorbed, worked through. We will doubtless think of animation as something that must be brought to works of art, say in terms of the powers of each of the arts to produce psychological transference, or as Emerson puts it, to return our thoughts to us with a certain alienated majesty. The formulation in terms of the search for the mother's gaze should take us at once to Stella at the end of what we are shown of her existence, placed before, barred at a distance from, the shining rectangle of her daughter's departure into marriage, replying to a policeman's demand for her to disperse with the rest of the viewers by saying: "I want to see her face." What do we imagine her to (want to) see?

I have already implied that some will take her to satisfy herself of Laurel's satisfaction, since this proves to her her own power to have provided it. But now we have to consider her walking away from the world of the transparent and reflective screen. I imagine the walking away to express the completion of her education: she learns that the world of the screen, whose education in the world of refinement had at the beginning made her cry with longing, is not for her. But "not for her" is perfectly ambiguous. The accepted view, of Stella at the end sacrificed as a mother and as a woman, takes Stella at the end still convinced of that world's incalculable desirability, to taste her belonging to it through her gift of it to and from her daughter.

My opposed view takes Stella to learn that the world Laurel apparently desires—of law, church, exclusiveness, institutional belonging—is not to her own taste. (I say apparently; Laurel seems in a trance. Where is her mother?) She walks away from that world, and from the only person she has loved, continues to love. What is that window/screen? What, walking away, does she walk toward? Why almost straight toward us? May we imagine that we have here some Emersonian/Thoreauvian perfectionist image of what Nietzsche will call the pain of individuation, of the passion Thoreau builds *Walden* to find, expressed as his scandalous pun on mo(u)rning, the transfiguration of mourning as grief into morning as dawning and ecstasy? And if just possibly so, wouldn't this be just one more proof that metaphysical speculation about freedom or self-creation is a cover for social injustice? Needless to say, such a speculation may be appropriated in this retrogressive way—as may the world of Emerson and Thoreau in general. They seem indeed, as steadily as these films, readily to permit, if not quite to invite, such a way of appropriation. My heart is set in the one case as in the other on making out another way.

How did Stella get to her position in front of the rectangle of the wedding ceremony? The explanation for the window being open to view is given a little sequence of its own as Mrs. (Morrison) Dallas says to her butler, "I told you those curtains weren't to be drawn. Open them please." After they are opened and the butler withdraws, she walks to the window, gazes out, and says to herself, "Yes." In this woman's expectation that Stella will appear at that window, the film screen is being identified as a field of communication between women. Putting this together with my suggestion of the search for the mother's gaze, may we understand Stella to be drawn to the window as her search for the mother's gaze?

Isn't this backwards? Isn't Stella the mother, the source of the desired gaze, not its desirous object? But how is this distinction to be understood?

Does the fact or position of motherhood negate the fact or position of daughterhood? I do not mean merely that every mother is a daughter. I mean that we have repeatedly seen Laurel mothering Stella, typically in scenes of her sensing Stella's sense of rejection—at the unattended birthday party, and peroxiding Stella's hair after returning from her initial visit to Mrs. Morrison's house, and preparing to leave the resort hotel while Stella cries like a child being treated unfairly, and on the train after Laurel hears other passengers recount Stella's spectacle earlier that day at the hotel and identify her as Laurel Dallas's mother. So it does not follow from Stella's wanting to see Laurel's face through the window that what she wants is to gaze motheringly upon it more than to be gazed upon by it.

And remember the extended sequence between Stella and Mrs. Morrison, the feeling of which is present in Mrs. Morrison's responsibility for communication through the medium of the shining window. I remarked that Stella is convincingly childish at the end of the resort hotel sequence; then on the train back home she is essentially silent, only recovering her voice in the subsequent sequence, at Mrs. Morrison's house. I find that Stella presents herself there, and is received, no more as a mother than as a child, with her hesitant questions about whether this fine lady and Stella's husband, as it were, are going to, or would plan to, get married, and with her motives disguised in a way that mothers are bound to see through. Mrs. Morrison, as the interview is closing and the two women rise from a sofa, cannot keep her hands off Stella. I do not say that this clinging is as to a daughter more than as to a mother; it seems rather that the blurring between these positions continues. So it is also Mrs. Morrison's gaze, real or imagined, coming to Stella from the screen she gazes at.

In the infantine basis of our position as viewers, Stella's gaze before the window, as the camera gives it to us, is the mother's, backed by mothers; and as Stella turns to walk toward us, her gaze, transforming itself, looms toward us, as if the screen is looming, its gaze *just* turned away, always to be searched for. (For what it grants; for what it wants.)

When Stella, as she and Stephen return from the River Club, tells him not to try to educate her (in matters of clothes, which implies not in how to be a woman), what this betokens, in both of our genres of film, is that the woman does not recognize a marriage between them. What Stella learns from the late gaze of the screen, from Laurel's and Mrs. (Morrison) Dallas's acceptance of each other, is that Stella has the right not to share their tastes, that she is free to leave not just this marriage but any marriage, which she had allowed herself to believe would transform her. Her education of Laurel has included the refutation of Laurel's outburst to the initial attempt to transpose her to the house with her father and Mrs. (Morrison) Dallas: "My home will be with my mother for as long as I live." Stella's instruction is to teach Laurel otherwise, to cause her to cry over separation, as for a solace preceding one's own happiness, not replacing it.

The striking source we have come upon earlier for the connection between a woman's leaving her husband and their children on the ground that there is no marriage between them because he is not the man to educate her, and setting out on her own to find that education, is Nora's exit from the doll's house, a house of what she feels as illusion, moralism, and anxious pleasures. (From Stella's rejecting what Stephen has to teach it does not follow that she has put aside her craving for knowing where she is to be at home in the world.) In fancying Stella walking away as one continuation of Nora walking out, there is the additional moment to consider of her walking toward us. The mother's gaze she has received from the window/film screen replaces the education she wished for from the early screen she had identified with the world of the man she married. The ratifying of her insistence on her own taste, call this her taking on the thinking of her own existence, the announcing of her *cogito ergo sum*, happened without—as in Descartes's presenting of it, it happens without—yet knowing who she is who is proving her existence. Her walk toward us, as if the screen becomes her gaze, is allegorized as the presenting or creating of a star, or as the interpretation of stardom. This star, call her Barbara Stanwyck, is without obvious beauty or glamour, first parodying them by excessive ornamentation, then taking over the screen stripped of ornament, in a nondescript hat and cloth overcoat. But we know she has a future, a knowledge that extends to a conviction about Stella Dallas, both about her artistic expertise in creating clothes and her capacity to make things happen according to her desire. The knowledge of Barbara Stanwyck's creation of this character is ratified not just because now we know—we soon knew—that this woman is the star of *The Lady Eve* and *Double Indemnity* and *Ball of Fire*, all women, it happens, on the wrong side of the law; but because she is presented *here* as a star (the camera showing that particular insatiable interest in her every action and reaction), which entails the promise of return, of unpredictable reincarnation, or say metempsychosis.

15

FREUD

The first thing I did after graduating from the University of California at Berkeley with a major in music and enrolling as a composition student—having had a portfolio of my material accepted at the extension division of the Juilliard Conservatory—was to recognize that music was no longer my life and thereupon to avoid my composition lessons. The next thing I did was to realize that I was in a state of spiritual crisis. My solution to that realization, not to say my expression of it, was to decide that I had learned nothing in college and to resolve to know and to see everything worth knowing and seeing. This led me, or released me—with several months to myself in New York before having to confess to my parents that I was now there under false pretenses—to attend the theater or the opera almost every night and to see at least two films a day and to begin reading whatever it was that people called philosophy.

Along with books with philosophy in the title I found my way, because of correspondence with a friend from university days, to Freud's *Introductory Lectures on Psychoanalysis.* That proved to be the first book of ideas I read with the hypnotic attention and identification that reading novels had from an early age produced in me. While I had studied essentially no philosophy in college (except for a semester course in aesthetics, which as I recall it, required no reading), I had heard that philosophy had something to do with examining one's life. So I was surprised to find Freud repeatedly denying that what he did was to be called philosophy, since it was nothing if not an examination of one's life. At some stage I came to feel that if he had to deny it so firmly, there must be strong reason to affirm it. It took rather a longer time for me to become Freudian enough to recognize that if he denied so many times that he was philosophizing, then it must on Freudian grounds be concluded that he knew, and for some reason feared, that the denial was not exactly true.

I mention this, I suppose, because the text of Freud's I adduce now—"Delusions and Dreams in Jensen's *Gradiva*"—in the course of filling out further the picture of moral perfectionism, is, while unmistakably marked with Freud's touches of irony, humor, pride, seductiveness, and iron-like modesty, remarkable in his corpus of work in two obvious respects: first, it is the most extended, consecutive psychoanalytic interpretation of a literary text by this author whose writing includes countless literary allusions and interpretations; second, it contains, I believe, the most persistent emphasis on Freud's idea or sense at once of his break with advanced Western thought, as represented in philosophy and established science, and at the same time, with greater insistence, of his continuity with the high literary tradition of Western culture, or what he calls "imaginative writers" (whom "we are accustomed to honor as the deepest observers of the human mind") and with those he names "the ancients" and "the superstitious public."

The text Freud examines is Wilhelm Jensen's novel *Gradiva: A Pompeiian Fantasy* (1903), in which an archaeologist, Norbert Hanold, becomes obsessed with a woman portrayed in a relief from the ruined Roman city of Pompeii, goes to Pompeii in search of her, and finds instead a real woman, Zoe Bertgang, a friend from his childhood. The form the continuity with literary tradition takes in Freud's essay goes so far as not only to find insights in his allies, rediscovered and given theoretical illumination by the new science of psychoanalysis, but to assert that the method of analysis, which Freud was so proud to have discovered, and which he links with the world-historical discoveries of Copernicus and of Darwin, was also already possessed and presented, if one knew where to look, throughout civilized life:

> The procedure which the author [Jensen] makes his Zoe adopt for curing her childhood friend's delusion shows a far-reaching similarity—no, a complete agreement in its essence—with a therapeutic method which was introduced into medical practice in 1895 by Dr. Josef Breuer and myself, and to the perfecting of which I have since then devoted myself. This method of treatment . . . consists, as applied to patients suffering from disorders analogous to Hanold's delusion, in bringing to their consciousness, to some extent forcibly, the unconscious whose repression led to their falling ill—exactly as Gradiva did with the repressed memories of their childhood relations.

It is because of Freud's insistence on a continuity (granted decisive discontinuities) between psychoanalytic thinking and practice and perceptions

Freud

and practices notable in everyday life, that I take up this text now in relation to both my understanding of philosophy and my interest in the genres of film I say represent moral perfectionism, primarily the remarriage comedies. Both philosophy and comedy (and of course tragedy, recognized as therapeutic as early as Aristotle's lectures called *The Poetics*), have therapeutic dimensions of which the Jensen fable, in Freud's interpretation, can be seen as an allegory, as Freud takes the fable as an allegory of psychoanalysis. Most generally these allegorical connections turn on the presence of delusions from which the sufferer has to be, as Freud characteristically puts the matter, awakened; and on the further characterization of the one suffering the delusion as feeling himself a prisoner of his circumstances. This sense of imprisonment, of the need for liberation, is critical both for Wittgensteinian philosophizing and for Emersonian perfectionist aspiration. I have sometimes called it the crisis from which the wish for philosophy and for a morally comprehensible life begins.

We might start as Freud does, after introducing his interest in the fable, with an attempt to summarize its contents—for the benefit of those, he is careful to say, who have already read it. Even before this, he summarizes "the story [as] set in the frame of Pompeii and [dealing] with a young archaeologist who had surrendered his interest in life in exchange for an interest in the remains of classical antiquity and who [is] now brought back to real life by a roundabout path which was strange but perfectly logical." This may be taken as a fair epitomizing of the story of *The Lady Eve,* the film with which I have paired Freud's text—with the classical archaeologist replaced by a zoologist, a scientist interested in the study of an even deeper past (of evolution and of religion), that of the snake, an interest explicitly cultivated in antithesis to, as a substitute or sublimation for, an interest in women, call it love. Perhaps the uncanniest of the relations between Freud's text on Jensen's text and Preston Sturges's *The Lady Eve* is that in both the therapeutic leading of the man back to life is accomplished not only by a woman but by a woman who appears to the man, delusively, as two different women.

Here I ask you, even more fervently than I did (or meant to be doing) in the case of *Stella Dallas,* to see how you would summarize what happens in Jensen's *Gradiva.* Does it open in a university town in Germany where our hero Norbert Hanold is fascinated by a relief of a girl walking in a particular way, an object he has had a plaster cast made from and hung on his wall; or does it open in Rome, where he first encountered the relief; or in Pompeii, where he found himself after an obscure impulse prompted him to make a springtime trip to Italy? And what is the relation between his dream of this girl dying in the ancient city of Pompeii on the day of the city's destruction by the eruption of Vesuvius and his finding himself chasing through the crowded streets of his town (which one?) in his pajamas, after a figure whose walk he glimpsed from his window and felt was similar to that of his Gradiva, a signature gait he had tried unsuccessfully to imitate? And what convinced him that the girl portrayed in the plaster cast was real and (or because) living in the same city with him? And what allowed him the step of recognizing that the place they were contemporaries in was not, by accident, ancient Pompeii, but familiar, daily, contemporary Germany, where they had grown up across the street from each other? And then how, after this accept-ance of reality, does Freud account for Jensen's going further and adding an erotic ending to this happy discovery of reality?

I don't ask for an account of the buildup of evident symbols in the story—flowers, the sun, the canary, the lizard, the shift of names. There are so many symbols that Jensen's text may read more like one of our melodra-mas than our comedies, though its air and its aim are comic. What Freud registers as "the frequency with which the author puts ambiguous remarks into the mouths of his two principal characters" is related to what I note as the irony of the conversation in the melodrama of the unknown woman. In those melodramas, in contrast to the exchanges in the comedies, communi-cation is blocked between the pair, as when Gregory in *Gaslight* tells Paula at one time that she must forget all these things, and at another time that she is forgetful, or when Paula, in her revenge, mocks Gregory by pretending to have misplaced the dagger she has just found and melodramatically dropped. But in *Gradiva*, the principal woman uses irony on the principal man's behalf, in response to, as a kind of match for, what Freud calls the compromises of the man's delusion, which expresses the conflict between his conscious and his unconscious desires, so that she both speaks to what in him is concealed from his light, and at the same time shows him the direc-tion in which to bring it to light. As when she asks him: "I feel as though we had shared a meal like this once before, two thousand years ago; can't you remember?" When he can allow himself—supported by the reassurance of her sharing something, accompanying him, in his torn consciousness—to remember what she suggests that he must remember, he will be cured, or let us say, released. This understanding is specifically what never happens in our melodramas, or rather never happens in congenial time.

But are we to take with full seriousness Freud's assertion that "The procedure . . . Zoe adopt[s] for curing her childhood friend's delusion shows a . . . complete agreement in its essence . . . with a therapeutic method which was introduced into medical practice in 1895 by Dr. Josef Breuer and myself"?

Since the relation between this pair I take as a kind of model, or allegory, of what goes on in a perfectionist conversation, as illustrated in our comedies; and since the appearance of Freud in our list of philosophical perfectionist texts requires specific justification; I am going to spend much of this chapter giving some instances of ways I relate psychoanalysis with philosophy, as I care about philosophy most. Most philosophers in my tradition, I believe, relate to psychoanalysis, if at all, with suspicion, habitually asking whether psychoanalysis deserves the title of a science. I am not here interested in that question. I am for myself convinced that the corpus of Freud's writing, and a considerable amount of writing that depends upon it, has achieved an unsurpassed horizon of knowledge about the human mind. Accordingly I would not be satisfied with an answer that declares psychoanalysis not to be a science, if that answer denies that horizon of knowledge. But if psychoanalysis is declared to be a science, the house of science will be changed. (I am mimicking, with appreciation, a perception expressed— independently, I assume—by both Walter Benjamin and Robert Warshow, namely that if film is understood to be an art, the house of art will be changed.) Given my conviction in the discoveries of psychoanalytic thinking, I am interested that it has accomplished them with methods that intersect with those of philosophy, as I care about it most. In emphasizing this intersection, I will not have space in which to discuss most of the details of Freud's reading of Jensen's text, though I mean the elements I touch on to help in prompting a detailed reading.

In a paper published a year or two before the *Gradiva* study, entitled "On Psychotherapy" (1905)—still early in the establishment of psychoanalysis, but after *The Interpretation of Dreams*, and *The Three Essays on Sexuality*, and *The Psychopathology of Everyday Life* had all been published—Freud says this:

> It seems to me that there is a widespread and erroneous impression among my colleagues that this [psychoanalytic] technique of searching for the

origins of an illness and removing its manifestations by that means is an easy one which can be practiced off-hand, as it were. I conclude this from the fact that not one of all the people who have shown an interest in my therapy and passed definite judgments upon it has ever asked me how I actually go about it . . . I am now and then astonished to hear that in this or that department of a hospital a young assistant has received an order from his chief to undertake a "psychoanalysis" of a hysterical patient. I am sure he would not be allowed to examine an extirpated tumor unless he had convinced his chiefs that he was conversant with histological technique.

Freud is here talking about, and to, doctors of medicine. Is he making an exception in the case of Zoe's technique, which is surely not that of a quali-fied expert? How is her case different?

Well, negatively, neither Zoe nor her creator Jensen *calls* what she is doing psychoanalysis; so that particular element of pretension is absent. And pos-itively, and more significantly, Freud, as said, likes to insist that his insights into the human mind have been anticipated by the creative writers of our civilization. His claim for himself can be said to be that he has systematized the culture's powers of insight into a new science. And then again, what he says in unstinting praise of Zoe is that her procedure is in complete agree-ment with the therapeutic method of psychoanalysis "in its essence." How do we understand this? In a sense she does not use the psychoanalytic "method" at all, if this means such things as demanding free association from her charge, her as it were patient; enforcing upon him the fundamental rule of psychoanalysis, namely that of saying what comes to mind regardless of its apparent insignificance; and holding to the routine of appearing and depart-ing at agreed-upon times.

"In essence" seems to come to two things, or one compound thing: that Zoe speaks to Norbert from within his private world of significance, call it his delusion, and speaks so as to use her ancient love for this man to show him a way back from his "surrender of his interest in life" (words from Freud's summary of the fable)—from, as Freud phrases it in "On Psychotherapy," his "aversion from sexuality, his incapacity for loving." One can even say that Zoe is not infringing the psychoanalytic principle that "the method is [not] applicable to people who are not driven to seek treatment by their own sufferings, but who submit to it only because they are forced to by the authority of relatives." I think we may imagine Norbert exactly to be presenting himself to Zoe as if seeking relief from his own sufferings. Anyway presenting himself as incapable of concealing that he is in a tortured state with respect to her (how can she, having grown up with or near him, not take his misrecognition as directed, in inescapable knowledge, to her?), a state of some kind of helpless lunacy. I suppose this is not the least appealing form an expression of love might take.

In a remarriage comedy not included in this book—Howard Hawks's *Bringing Up Baby,* from 1936, another film with Katharine Hepburn and Cary Grant—a comic psychiatrist portentously announces to Hepburn, who memorizes the announcement and carefully repeats it upon reencountering Grant, whom she met earlier that day and has just caused to take a pratfall: "The love impulse in man often presents itself in terms of conflict." That film, in certain respects, fits Freud's discussion of the *Gradiva* story more closely, in mood and in theme, than any of the other comedies: in mood because of Grant's seeming to be in some unnamed state of stupefaction or suspended presence throughout; in theme because of the question repeatedly raised between the pair of who is following whom (invoking explicitly Freud's noting that our attempts to flee from our desire only direct us toward it) and because the woman proves at the end to have been right (the man confesses it) in her perception that all the time he was saying he wanted to get away from her he was having the best time he ever had.

Recall my generalization that in Hollywood films of the classical period the psychiatrist is a serious figure in melodramas (beyond *Now, Voyager,* think of Hitchcock's *Spellbound,* Mervyn LeRoy's *Random Harvest,* Max Ophuls's *Caught*) but a comic figure in comedies (beyond *Bringing Up Baby,* there is *Mr. Deeds Goes to Town*). I have read that the figure of the psychiatrist occurs in films from the classical period, extended perhaps by a decade, several hundred times. I haven't checked my claim about the contrast between melodramas and comedies systematically, but the generalization does prompt one to think about why psychoanalysis should have both a comic and a tragic (or earnest) face.

It is not sufficient simply to attribute a more realistic ambition to the earnest face and take the comic as a way of resisting psychoanalytic insight. This leaves out various considerations: the fantastic popular success, and consequent debasement, of psychoanalysis in the United States over the decades in question—think of the currency of the idea of a Freudian slip, to go no further—may act as a kind of massive resistance to it, or inoculation against its serious form. Psychoanalysis seen in the double aspect of the comic and the tragic suggests a view of being human in which comedy and tragedy are as closely linked, and as far apart, as the pair of simple masks, of laughter and of tears, that emblematize all the works of theater, all the ways our civilization has devised for making comprehensible, or as Aristotle says, imitating, what humans are capable of. This closeness and distance are forever recorded in, and for, psychoanalysis as early as 1905, when to the understanding of the symptoms of hysteria and obsession, and the meaning of dreams, and the traumatic and trivial misadventures of everyday life, Freud adds an understanding that jokes too are motivated by unconscious conflicts and compromises. (Wittgenstein observes, in *Philosophical Investigations*, that a certain class of jokes sound the depth of philosophy.)

Still something seems strange, or unannounced, in Freud's insistence on the essential agreement of Zoe's methods with those of psychoanalysis. Her story is too happy, too sunny I might say, for the essence of the travails of psychoanalysis, and the difficult and measured return to life it promises at best, to be essentially captured in it—as if Freud in his taking up of the fable is romanticizing his own achievements. (I am indebted to Steven Affeldt for this perception and for other influences on this chapter.) Zoe's moments of exasperation in her "treatment" of Norbert do not, for example, really show that she is prepared for what Freud calls (in "On Psychotherapy") "unpleasantness of various kinds" in real psychoanalytic treatment. Something else is going on in Freud's insistence on this therapy of love.

One source of his, to my mind, quite justified pride, I can't help thinking, is his sense of having freed the study of the mind from the hold of philosophy. (Just what he includes under this title it would be valuable to have specified. To what extent is it confined to naming the reigning academic philosophy of his era in Austria and Germany? He surely does not mean to free the study of the mind from its connection with the thinking of Schopenhauer and Nietzsche, for example.) The Editor's Note preceding the translation of Freud's treatment of Jensen's *Gradiva* in the Standard Edition of Freud's works speaks of Freud's discussion as "perhaps the first of his semi-popular accounts of his theory of the neuroses and of the therapeutic action of psychoanalysis." But the interspersed semi-popular accounts of his theories do not account for the tone of his long retellings of the Gradiva narrative in his extended reading of this text. It seems to me that Freud is basking in the idea that he has discovered and explained a talent distributed throughout our culture—possessed by anyone who can be compared with "an unusually clever girl" like Zoe, by those who carry in themselves, let us say intuitively, a therapeutic touch powerful enough to divert potential tragedy into romance. As though the unhappiness that civilization visits upon its respectable members is compensated for, to the extent possible, by a portion of these individuals' possessing an amateur capacity for undoing that unhappiness. In "On Psychotherapy" Freud says of psychoanalytic treatment, that is, psychotherapy, that it "may in general be conceived of as . . . a *re-education in overcoming internal resistances.*" Philosophy and its sages were those who had claimed this psychic therapeutic role of re-education heretofore, most famously in Plato's portraits of Socrates teaching.

This competition with philosophy is what, in Chapter 12, I mentioned as an ambiguity in a claim of Freud's in *The Interpretation of Dreams*: "These considerations [on the operation of two psychical forces or systems, namely the conscious and the unconscious systems] lead us to feel that the interpretation of dreams may enable us to draw conclusions as to the structure of our mental apparatus which we have hoped for in vain from philosophy." The ambiguity, or ambivalence, I bring out by recognizing two natural readings of the implied relation of psychoanalysis to philosophy. What I suppose is the common reading takes the remark to say that our vain waiting for *philosophy* is now to be replaced by something else, the thing Freud named psychoanalysis; but the remark can equally be taken to say that our *waiting* for philosophy is at last no longer vain, that philosophy has been fulfilled in the form of psychoanalysis. That this form may destroy earlier forms of philosophizing is no bar to conceiving psychoanalysis as philosophy.

I cannot now say that this effort to escape or replace philosophy is more frequent in this early period (still only ten years away from his and Breuer's opening investigations establishing psychoanalysis) than it is later. In "On Psychotherapy" Freud notes as if in passing: "Our unconscious is not quite the same thing as that of philosophers and, moreover, the majority of philosophers will hear nothing of 'unconscious mental processes.'" In what is in effect a companion essay, "Psychical Treatment," he goes a little out of his way, in placing mental treatment as part of the history of medicine, to emphasize that from ancient times mental treatment had been part of medical treatment known to physicians, but that it had been left behind when, in the nineteenth century, medicine shook off its dependence on "what was known as 'Natural Philosophy' and . . . came under the happy influence of the natural sciences." And Freud goes on to say: "It followed, as a result of an incorrect though easily understandable trend of thought, that physicians came to restrict their interest to the physical side of things and were glad to leave the mental field to be dealt with by the philosophers whom they despised."

But perhaps in this essay (for which the editor's note was never reprinted in Freud's lifetime) Freud has to be particularly careful of his scientific credentials since the title of the essay is "Psychische Behandlung (Seelenbehandlung)," thus in effect calling attention to the fact that the German word *Seele* is closer to the English word soul than to the word mind, and then the second paragraph says something scientifically shocking:

> Foremost among such measures [treatments which operate in the first instance and immediately upon the human mind—*auf das Seelische des Menschen*] is the use of words; and words are the essential tool of mental treatment. A layman will no doubt find it hard to understand how pathological disorders of the body and mind can be eliminated by "mere" words. He will feel that he is being asked to believe in magic. And he will not be so very wrong, for the words which we use in our everyday speech are nothing other than watered-down magic. But we shall have to follow a roundabout path in order to explain how science sets about restoring to words a part at least of their former magical power.

In *Gradiva,* the dissociation from philosophy is not so different. Freud has just described "in correct psychological technical terms" Norbert Hanold's psychic state when his childhood experiences were aroused, namely that he remained unconscious of them: "When [he] saw the relief, he did not remember that he had already seen a similar posture of the foot in his childhood friend . . . but all the effects brought about by the relief originated from this link that was made with the impression of his childhood." And Freud continues: "We are anxious that this unconscious shall not be involved in any of the disputes of philosophers and natural philosophers . . . When some thinkers try to dispute the existence of an unconscious of this kind [one that is active], on the ground that it is nonsensical, we can only suppose that they have never had to do with the corresponding mental phenomena, that they are under the spell of the regular experience that everything mental that becomes active and intense becomes at the same time conscious as well."

Freud

291

Here Freud appeals to his reader's experience for conviction in what he says, and, equally important for us, characterizes the failure to be responsive to that appeal, to be as it were unconscious of the experience in question, as a condition of standing under a spell (*stünden im Bann:* spell, charm, ban, interdiction, excommunication); and moreover the spell is precisely that of what we may call everyday life, "the regular experience that everything mental that becomes active and intense becomes at the same time conscious as well." To become conscious of this spell upon us, namely conscious of the action of the unconscious in our everyday experience, requires us to grasp the magic of words, that is, the extent to which we believe in their magical powers. (What Freud calls the "watered-down magic" of everyday words is related to what Emerson, in "The Poet," calls their "fossil poetry.")

The idea I am prepared to derive from Freud's characterization here is that the figure of the patient in the Jensen fable—as Freud says of the figure of the analyst, or her procedure—is in complete agreement "in essence" with the discovery of psychoanalysis. This is the emphasis I have had in mind in agreeing that the fable is an accurate allegory of psychoanalysis. What the figure of Norbert (the "patient") allegorizes, in his delusion, is the state of every human being before discovering the truth or reality of his own experience, namely that it is a life-and-death struggle with unconsciousness, that its unawareness of what it is expressing at every moment, despite itself, is a kind of delusion. But as a delusion is "essentially" how Plato in the *Republic* pictures everyday (or "ordinary") experience in the Allegory of the Cave. This is an essential condition for recognizing the therapeutic motive in Plato's, or Socrates', philosophizing, namely the motive to turn us from, free us from, this imprisoned experience of the everyday.

What this comes to in Freud's description is that the discovery of the reality—one might say the contemporaneity—of one's experience is one and the same fact as the discovery of the reality of psychoanalysis. (By discovering the contemporaneity of one's experience I do not mean alone discovering that it is present, but discovering what it is present with— unconsciously.) One might even say that the psychoanalytic therapeutic process is one in which the reality of psychoanalysis is always being rediscovered. I would like to say something comparable about philosophy as I care about it most. It is perhaps for this reason that psychoanalysis and philosophy are subject to distrust—the reason, I mean, for being aware that each is subject to debasement and charlatanry. (This is a sound enough reason for wanting to find a method of philosophy that secures it against imitation—say the method of logical analysis. But this is where I came in all those years ago in finding my way to philosophy. I kept finding that its methods, attractive and indispensable as they may be, were characteristically used to proscribe my interest in topics close to my heart.)

The famous philosopher of roughly the middle of the twentieth century who has meant most to me, most helped me find my way to what I wanted in philosophy, is Wittgenstein. (Austin is another, but he is not on the same scale famous; Heidegger is even more famous, but of more limited help.) And Wittgenstein's *Investigations,* alone among these influences, describes its methods as "like" therapies.

Some philosophers I have great respect for have taken offense at this claim (at least as made for Wittgenstein by philosophers of less originality than he), supposing it to mean that what is in mind is therapy from the desire for philosophy altogether. Why take it this way, rather than taking it to join philosophy's own ancient commitment to therapy—namely to free the human being from the chains of delusion? Wittgenstein calls the chains those of bewitchment and of being held captive by images (compare Plato's appearances); and the methods he speaks of are such as constructing language-games, eliciting criteria for the application of concepts, finding intermediate cases, investigating grammatically related ideas (for example between what the meaning of a word is and what explaining the meaning of a word is). Why such methods—like, and decisively unlike psychoanalytic methods, such as following the psychoanalytic rule and producing free associations—may be said to free us of delusion is surely something that should be open to discussion. That Wittgensteinian philosophizing and psychoanalysis both essentially hark back to childhood (a rare gesture in philosophy), and that both are processes of reeducation, are related points of similarity, hence of difference, between them.

I call attention, beyond these ponderable affinities, to a description, or allegory, Freud proposes of analytic technique in "On Psychotherapy" which is curious in itself and which oddly matches a fundamental claim Wittgenstein makes for his philosophizing. It occurs as Freud is explaining his grounds for having given up eight years earlier the use of the technique of hypnosis. "There is, actually, the greatest possible antithesis between suggestive [viz., hypnotic] and analytic technique—the same antithesis which, in regard to the fine arts, the great Leonardo da Vinci summed up in the formulas *per via di porre* and *per via di levare*. Painting, says Leonardo, works [by] apply[ing] a substance . . . where there was nothing; sculpture, however, proceeds . . . [by] tak[ing] away from the block of stone all that hides the surface of the statue contained in it." This analogy has the severe drawback, in comparing the technique of suggestion unfavorably with that of analysis, of counting painting inferior to sculpture, a drawback one might have thought would have made Freud think better of using it. But it brings to light a feature of analysis whose importance evidently seemed to Freud to outweigh the discrepancy. "The technique of suggestion . . . superimposes something, a suggestion, in the expectation that it will be strong enough to restrain the pathogenic idea from coming to expression. Analytic therapy, on the other hand ["concerned with the origin, strength and meaning of the morbid symptoms"], does not seek to add or to introduce anything new, but to take away something, to bring out something."

I think of Wittgenstein's description of his work in the *Investigations* that insists "It is . . . of the essence of our investigation that we do not seek to learn anything *new* by it. We want to *understand* something that is already in plain view." It does not seem quite right to characterize Freud's material as already in plain view, but this is perhaps less important a difference than the further similarity that, as Wittgenstein's practice shows, he seeks to remove something (a temptation, a picture, an illusion of making sense) that meets with resistance. As Freud goes on to say after the Leonardo passage: "I have another reproach to make against this method [of suggestion], namely, that . . . it does not permit us . . . to recognize the *resistance* with which the patient clings to his disease and thus even fights against his own recovery [a point Plato emphasizes in telling the allegory of the Cave] which alone makes it possible to understand his behavior in daily life." I should add, in recounting the crossing of paths in Freud and Wittgenstein, that I am less satisfied with Wittgenstein's well-known mottoes for understanding the resistances of philosophers to his methods, as when he speaks, for example, of their being misled by grammar. This to my mind obscures what it is that philosophers *want* from their ratiocination, a matter Wittgenstein also wishes, of course, to bring to light.

Before concluding this excursion on Freud's invocation of and competition with philosophy, motivated by the sense of a pride or pleasure he takes in his discussion of Jensen's fable, I come back to Freud's speaking of what one of his patients called "the talking cure," what he calls the cure by words, by remarking: "We shall have to follow a roundabout path in order to explain how science sets about restoring to words a part at least of their former magical power." I wish I understood this remark better than I do. I am not satisfied to leave it with the earlier discussion I devoted to it. Let us approach it differently.

Freud's emphasis on the magical powers of words cannot just mean what Bertrand Russell meant in saying, roughly, against Wittgenstein's emphasis on ordinary language, that ordinary language embodies the metaphysics of the Stone Age, meaning, I guess, that consulting ordinary language will tell you, for example, that physical things "obey" laws, and that a storm can be "threatening," and that objects "have" properties, perhaps that the sun rises and sets, perhaps that there are ghosts since we are afraid of them, and that fictional beings exist because we can name them, and that we can have things (literally) in or on our minds. Why would Freud with his new science wish to "restore" to words the power (supposing they have it, or retain it) to instill such notions?

Let us take it that what Freud has in mind here is less the meaning of our words than the saying of them, the effect of our speech on others, which can range from the devastating to the thrilling, from the obscuring to the illuminating, and from the confining and proscriptive to the liberating. But for words to have the power to liberate, to reeducate, something has to happen to both analyst and patient in the therapeutic relationship that can seem to require the restoration of the magic of words, namely that the analyst's words be lent the investment that the phenomenon of transference makes possible, and that the patient find words that genuinely match, say express, childhood impressions that were absorbed with an understanding that never reached words contemporary with them, or were covered with words, perhaps enforced by one's elders, that falsified their significance.

Something like the reverse is the effect of Wittgensteinian methods, which undertake something like an effort to free ourselves from philosophy's chronic wish to instill our words with, or require of them, magic ("Surely no one else can have THIS pain!"—striking oneself on the breast), by reminding us of the ordinary cases in which words have their genuine effect, a process that invites disappointment, since on its first approach it seems to deprive us of, rather than to give us, something precious, call this the possession of ourselves. In Plato's *Republic*, the approach of redemptive philosophy is greeted by the inhabitants of the Cave with murderous hostility.

Freud

By the philosophically diminished time and place of *Stella Dallas*, the wish for education presents itself initially to the woman as precisely a means of escape from herself, signaled in her absorption by the images of the magic figures of the silent film we watch her watch. The man accompanying her, whom she associates with those figures and whom she has chosen to educate her, tries to teach her a better way, but he is himself caught and sees Stella as a means of escaping from himself.

We should not neglect an obvious oddity, so far not emphasized, in Freud's insistence on Jensen's fable of psychotherapy as giving to the figure of the analyst a technique in essence in complete agreement with Freud's own. I mean the plain fact that the role of the analyst, of Freud before all, in the Jensen text is taken by "an unusually clever girl." Might not this have something to do with Freud's pleasure in discussing the text? He says that Zoe "could carry out this task [of bringing to the man's consciousness the unconscious whose repression led to his illness] more easily" than an analyst, that she is in "what may be described as an ideal position for it." What makes it ideal? Freud contrasts her position with an analyst's having no memory he shares with the patient and having to call a "complicated technique to his help in order to make up for this disadvantage." This sounds humorous, like saying that the analytic technique has to make up for the disadvantage of not possessing the power of telepathy. Zoe is as mystified at first by Norbert Hanold as an analyst might be; more mystified in obvious ways. Her advantage lies, one could say, in being her, that she brings his thoughts to consciousness simply by presenting herself to him, which hardly counts as carrying out a task. I think Freud's humor here expresses his sense that her advantage is simply and precisely that she is a woman, I might say, speaks with a woman's voice.

I have two reasons for this suggestion. One reason is elaborated in the "Postscript" in *Contesting Tears*, in which I speak of canonical philosophy as requiring the suppression of the feminine voice (whether that possessed by a male or a female, working with the idea that both sexes have both voices). The other reason is that so many of the films and texts discussed in this book, in pursuing their task of reeducation, place women primarily and explicitly in the role of educator. This is patently true of *The Lady Eve*, and of *Letter from an Unknown Woman* (though the education in both cases in a sense fails catastrophically); and true of Henry James's "The Beast in the Jungle," in which the educative role of the woman is essentially the subject of the piece, and transcendentally true of Shakespeare's and of Eric Rohmer's

The Winter's Tale; it is even true in the perhaps over-obvious irony of George Bernard Shaw's *Pygmalion,* where the obsessively didactic master-teacher Henry Higgins learns of the existence of other human beings through the woman he thinks he knows he has created.

I want to mention another sly, or say suggestive, moment in Freud's text that contributes to its sunny, even elated tone. The concluding line of his text (apart from the Postscript he added to the second edition in 1912) reads this way: "The wish to be taken captive by the girl he loved, to fall in with her wishes and to be subjected to her—for so we may construe the wish behind the situation of the lizard-catching—was in fact of a passive, masochistic character. Next day the dreamer hit the girl, as though he was dominated by the contrary erotic current . . . But we must stop here, or we may really forget that Hanold and Gradiva are only creatures of their author's mind." (The marks of elision in this quotation are not mine, but Freud's.) Remember that Freud had announced, near the opening of his discussion, a fundamental teaching of psychoanalysis, namely "It is our belief that no one forgets anything without some secret reason or hidden motive." What would be Freud's hidden motive for "really" (not just for the sake of the fiction?) forgetting that the fictional characters he is imagining are fictional? How do we fill in the elision?

Is he saying that he is about to push his analysis further than a fictional text can sustain? But he's been pushing it no less hard, it would seem, throughout his discussion. Is he expressing a danger that he will as it were become infected by Norbert Hanold's capacity for delusion, since we can describe Norbert's condition as one in which he has identified a real person with a fictional person? Has Norbert "forgotten" something? What *is* it to forget such a thing? Advanced literary theory in recent decades has accused traditional narrative techniques—epitomized in the classical Hollywood expertise in so-called direct or invisible editing—of being designed to make us forget the unreality of a fiction, as if this expertise had been designed to steep us in delusion. But this says nothing about our supposed state of delusion. We seem to know what it is to believe a lie—anyway we know it as well as we know what it is to believe what someone says, true or false. We know, for example, the role of confirming the truth by further testimony, or by checking for ourselves. But what is it to believe in a fiction? Do we look for confirmation from others, or check for ourselves, to learn whether Hamlet exists, or Charlotte Vale, or Camille Beauchamp? Freud says that what we (he and his reader complicitly?) forget is that Gradiva and Norbert Hanold are only creatures of their author's mind. This seems to distinguish our threat of forgetting from Norbert's case, since we can hardly accuse him of forgetting that Gradiva is only a creature of her author's mind (if we think of the author as Jensen)—but perhaps we can say that Zoe's task is to plant the seed of realization in Norbert's mind that he (Norbert) is Gradiva's author.

It strikes me that Freud is suggesting that Norbert's delusion is an allegory not alone of an exceptional outbreak of delusion, but at the same time of the inevitable process in which the human psyche finds its objects of love, through a negotiation of conscious and unconscious attractions. It would be the sense in which we are the unsought authors of our lives. (We were invisibly editing our minds millennia before film was made to discover the knack.)

When Emerson, in "Self-Reliance," is feeling most estranged from his fellow citizens, or most averse to them, and cries out "Every word they say chagrins us," it is in immediate response to his having observed: "[Their] conformity makes them not false in a few particulars, authors of a few lies, but false in all particulars. Their every truth is not quite true." He is using "author" here, it seems to me, in something like the way Freud is using it in speaking of the danger of forgetting about the author (though Freud is writing in a darker place and time, anyway older, than Emerson's). An "author of lies" is not merely the utterer of them but the creator of the characters who utter them, and of their scenes, and of the forms they take. This is presumably why Emerson says "To talk of reliance is a poor external way of talking," and why he asks "Who is the Trustee?" namely of self-trust. It makes no less sense to speak of characters in a fable trusting the author who created them than it makes to speak of our character as trusting the author in us of our wishes and deeds and utterances.

But if this isn't how to think of the self-relying that Emerson has in mind—as of one aspect of the self-reflecting, dual self, as standing on the other half, as on a rock—what is? What is wrong with the picture is that it seems, in combating conformity, to detach one's self from the rock of others only to attach itself to another fixity, this time within; whereas the liberation of the self is precisely to let it become unsettled, to let what is thought to be great and important "dance before your eyes." The forces playing for our lives, outer and inner, are unsparing if not always unkind. The call to self-reliance is in effect a caution neither to hope nor to despair.

The technical form of the issue of attachment in Freud called "object-choice"—how it is one finds oneself attracted to one person rather than another—is one of the most elaborated in psychoanalysis, as suggested by Freud's *Three Essays on the Theory of Sexuality,* published two years earlier than the essay on *Gradiva.* This issue is fundamental to the narrative of remarriage, as one of Freud's most remarkable formulations makes clear: "The finding of an object [of love] is in fact a refinding of it." Freud's way of putting this in his Gradiva text is to say: "It was as though they [the principal pair] were struggling towards each other and each were trying to assume the other's character." I think of the happy mood in Freud's discussion as a response to a tale in which a happy ending is well deserved, the "debt to life" easy to pay, an earnest of the validity of his discoveries which show that the path through the perils of childhood and the fortunes of encounter, recorded in the delusions of every human mind, constructing fictional objects for itself, can achieve an acceptable measure of happiness in an acceptable number of instances (though this latter especially may come to seem itself a delusion).

The perfectionist vision is that the journey toward each other, finding the next self in finding the next phase of the object, will become for each a journey together of continuous interest. To outsiders, as remarriage comedy repeatedly demonstrates, such a couple will seem incomprehensible. (Wittgenstein asks himself: "Where does our investigation get its importance from, since it seems to destroy everything interesting; that is, all that is great and important?" His answer, as I read *Philosophical Investigations,* is that the task of philosophy is to ask whether we know what is important and interesting to us.)

Among the many things left unclearer than I would like in what I have been saying, one thing is quite clear to me, namely that I have been steered through this material by the consciousness that we were to discuss *The Lady Eve* in connection with it. I mentioned early the coincidence of the Preston Sturges film with the Gradiva material, of there being two versions of the same woman providing an education for a young scientist who has used his intellectual calling to turn away from the society of women. And the father of the woman in the film (not Eve's fictionally imaginary father, but Jean's fictionally real one) tells his companion con artist that Jean says she is going to teach her brand-new husband a lesson. We'll have a chance to see what the lesson is and whether it was successful (that is, therapeutic) and to what degree it mocked itself and to what degree it then discarded its mockery.

I will not, in this book, get to trace the implications of Freud's text for remarriage comedy in its other instances. For example, is Norbert's attacking the fly that has settled on Zoe's body—an attack that offends her—a slap or a slug (recalling a central exchange between Amanda and Adam Bonner)? And how do members of the genre other than *The Lady Eve* compensate for the lack of a past childhood of the pair together, perfectly essential to the Gradiva fable? And is the requirement Freud notes of "the aggressiveness which is a man's inevitable duty in love-making" simply dated, and was it already dated by the time of the classical remarriage comedies, or do these films maintain some comparable asymmetry between the sexes in some other form?

16

The Lady Eve

1 In a prologue, Charles (Henry Fonda, later Hopsy) and his companion Muggsy (William Demarest) are accompanied to a paradisiacal water's edge, where they are taking their leave from a research team of naturalists after a year up the Amazon. Charles, an amateur ophiologist ("Snakes are my life"), makes a brief farewell speech praising the team's dedication to science, saying he wants nothing more from his life than to spend it with men of knowledge, such as those present. A river steamboat takes him and Muggsy far enough out to sea to intercept an ocean liner, which he is to board.

2 At the railing of an upper deck of the liner, Jean (Barbara Stanwyck) says to her father, Harry (Charles Coburn), as they watch Charles begin to climb a ladder onto the ship, "I hope he's terribly rich." Harry replies, "He'd almost have to be to stop a ship." Jean observes that she is always the one having to con suckers into a card game with them, her father never stooping to steer a woman. She drops an edenic apple onto Charles's pith helmet as he mounts the ladder.

3 In the ship's dining room, abuzz with excitement about the new passenger, having already informed itself that he is the scion of Pike's Ale, Jean is looking through her viewfinder, or crystal ball—in other words, into her hand mirror—to see and interpret what is going on behind her as Charles enters the room and all eyes (especially women's eyes) are trying to attract the glance of the unwitting celebrity. "They're none of them good enough for him," Jean decides, as she puts her foot backward into the aisle Charles is marching along and trips him into a sprawl on the ground. She announces that this contretemps is Charles's fault and that since he's broken the heel off her shoe he'll simply have to take her to her stateroom to get another pair. They leave the dining room arm in arm to the consternation of all who failed to manage exactly that.

4 There follows a notable scene of shoe-selection and perfume-inhalation in her cabin, the upshot of which is that the man, who, because of his father's ale business, is nicknamed Hopsy, has fallen completely under her spell.

5 Jean and Harry invite Hopsy to play a three-handed game of cards, in which they bait the hook by letting him win a few hundred trivial dollars. They compliment him on his card playing, and to thank them, and explain his powers, he does a card trick for them. They are simply amazed by it.

6 The next morning, Muggsy does some checking and demands that the purser look into the background of Harry, Jean, and their partner Gerald (Melville Cooper). Charles tells Muggsy to stop worrying, that he himself does card tricks. Muggsy observes, sensibly, that they may know some tricks he hasn't seen.

7 Jean reports to Harry and Gerald that the young man is in love with her. Harry is not surprised, and is altogether delighted. "We're going to play some cards tonight, and I don't mean Old Maid." Jean says that this time it's different, that he's touched something in her, that maybe she's in love too, that she's going to go straight. Harry protests that Charles has some of their money. She concedes that they can get that much back. Harry adds, "And with a little interest." Jean tells Harry he doesn't get it, that she won't allow it ("I'm not your daughter for free you know"), and she snatches a fixed deck out of Gerald's hands as she turns on her heel.

8 Charles is not so lucky that night, but he is much luckier than he knows, since most of the time when Harry is about to make a killing, Jean, when she deals, thwarts his cheating. The game winds up with Charles owing them a thousand dollars, and when Jean leaves to get a wrap, she returns to discover that Harry has won $32,000 from Charles playing double-or-nothing "to wipe out the foolish debt" that Charles, by now an intimate, has incurred. Jean pointedly asks Harry what he's going to do with Charles's check, and Harry, feigning that he always intended to do so, dramatically tears it up. Walking out, Charles says to Jean, "That was some lesson your father taught me." Jean and Hopsy go out on deck, where he makes an elaborate, sentimental speech to her about his feeling that he has known her since she was a little girl. She confesses a reciprocal feeling but says they must be sensible about the future ("They say a moonlit deck is a woman's business office").

9a The pair are strolling through the ship when Hopsy is surprised to discover that they have arrived at his cabin door. Jean mocks, but goes along with, his "surprise."

9b Upon entering the cabin Hopsy discovers another surprise, that the snake he is taking back with him from his year up the Amazon has got out of her cage. This time Jean lets out unfeigned screams of terror and runs out into the corridor, continuing down several flights of stairs, Hopsy in hot pursuit, and when she arrives at her cabin demands that Hopsy look under her bed to see whether the snake is there.

10a The next morning, Jean wakes from a dream with another scream. Her father rushes in from his adjoining cabin, and they have an intimate moment in which she confesses her love for Charles. As her father, sitting on her bed, rather absent-mindedly practices a trick shuffle and deal, she says, "Harry, tell my fortune."

10b As Hopsy awaits Jean for breakfast, the purser appears and hands him an envelope that turns out to contain a photograph of Jean, Harry, and Gerald, with a caption identifying them as professional gamblers and con artists.

11 Jean appears in person, glowing with anticipation. When Charles hands her the photograph, crushing her spirits but causing her to say that she was only waiting to tell him until he knew her a little better, he tells her that he received the photograph his first day on the ship, that he has been, in effect, the one doing the conning.

12 As the passengers are assembled to disembark, Jean stares with hatred at Charles and wishes he hadn't got off scot-free. Her father shows her that in fact he had never torn up Charles's check, but palmed it.

13 At the races, Harry, Jean, and Gerald run into Curly (bald Eric Blore), an old member of their world of artistic cheating, who tells them of his life as a titled Englishman ("Sir Alfred McGlennon Keith at the moment") retired to a country house in rural Connecticut making a sweet living playing bridge for money with the rich and unsuspecting locals. Jean, recognizing the name of the town, asks if he knows the Pike family, of Pike's Ale. Curly replies that Horace, the father, is a regular at cards with him (and raises some question about the competence of his backward son). She arranges to visit Sir Alfred as his niece.

14 The Pikes throw a party for her at their mansion, where, surrounded by men, she is the life of the party, telling tales, in an elaborate British accent, about how hard it was for her to get to "Conneckticut." Charles makes several kinds of fool of himself, first by insisting that he knows the woman they are calling Lady Eve, then by believing implicitly Sir Alfred's deeply private revelation of his family's secret that Eve has a half sister who looks exactly like her, whose father was a groom on their estate, a handsome brute called Harry, and with each thunderbolt of news Charles contrives to trip over something or bump into something that each time forces him to go to his room and change his soiled clothes. Muggsy is beside himself with suspicion; Charles tells him that he (Muggsy) doesn't understand psychology.

15 Eve, at Sir Alfred's house, tells him that Charles doesn't recognize her because on the boat they had this awful yen for each other which colored their perceptions. She also reveals her plan to extract a marriage proposal within weeks.

16 She and Charles, exploring his estate on horseback, are drawn to dismount by the beauty of the sunset. Charles launches into the same speech he made to Jean on the prow of the ship, about feeling he has known her for a lifetime. It is difficult to see how she could, even if she wanted to, ever take him seriously again.

17 We are given a montage of various segments of the kitchen staff of the Pike establishment engaged in wedding preparations, ending with a glance at the wedding itself.

18 Harry is complaining to Gerald about having had to keep away from his own daughter's wedding. The two of them discuss what Jean might mean by saying she's going to teach Charles a lesson.

19 In their honeymoon train compartment, as they prepare for bed, Jean decides to spin a yarn concerning some earlier marriage of hers, or rather near-marriage. Warming to her task, she goes into a list of former lovers that threatens to last as long as Scheherazade's stories, until Charles stops the train and jumps off in a driving rain, slipping down a muddy bank.

20 In Horace Pike's office at his brewery, his lawyers are gathered to arrange a divorce settlement. Reached by telephone, Eve/Jean tells Horace that she doesn't want money (to the uncomprehending chagrin of Harry and Gerald) but asks instead only that Charles come to her and ask her for his freedom. Charles refuses (to the uncomprehending chagrin of Horace's lawyers). Jean/Eve, learning from Horace that Charles is leaving in a few hours to take the same ship back to the Amazon, consults her wristwatch.

21 Charles, strolling through the ship's dining room, trips over some obstacle. Hearing Jean's voice and seeing her standing over him, he discovers that the old obstacle has miraculously asserted itself again. This time he is instantly thrilled, no sooner arises than embraces Jean, orders unending bottles of champagne for the Colonel (Harry), and decisively takes Jean out of the room.

22 In her cabin, he starts to explain to her that he is married, but that it wouldn't have happened if she hadn't looked so exactly like her; and as Jean replies, "You still don't understand," and he replies in turn that he doesn't want to, she confesses that she is married too, and gently closes the door in our face.

23 The camera, still steady on the closed door, watches it slowly open wide enough for Muggsy furtively to slip out and close it behind him. He observes, quite undeniably, "Positively the same dame."

A summary of a film comedy written and directed by Preston Sturges suffers most in missing the continuous, virtuosic precision and intelligence of his dialogue, in no case more than in that of *The Lady Eve*. Sturges is one of the most remarkable minds to have found expression in Hollywood. Not until after the end of the Second World War, with the reception in America of the outburst of filmmaking in Europe—including films of Truffaut, Godard, Fellini, Antonioni, Ingmar Bergman—did an American audience become accustomed to finding a film written and directed by the same person. And Sturges's tight corpus of comparatively small-scale films occupies a treasured place in the hearts of those who care about the world and art of film; for example, beyond *The Lady Eve*, there are *Sullivan's Travels* and *The Palm Beach Story* and *Hail the Conquering Hero*. An instance of this particular esteem is recorded in the title of the Coen brothers' recent film *Oh Brother, Where Art Thou?* (with George Clooney and John Turturro), one of the most notable films of the past few years. It is worth taking a minute to say how that title inscribes a Sturges film.

The hero of *Sullivan's Travels* (played by Joel McRea, who is also the male lead in the remarriage comedy *The Palm Beach Story*, an interesting actor of considerable range, but less well known than the male stars, his natural competitors, of the remarriage comedies of the period discussed in this book) is a filmmaker whose great success is based on making thrillers with little intellectual or political content, and who wishes to make a film about something true and important, about suffering. The travels of the film's title are those taken by this director, who escapes the world of Hollywood escape in order to experience the suffering of, after all, most people in the world, in preparation for making his important film of witness. The narrative takes him to the bottom of the world, in the form of being falsely convicted of murder and sentenced to a southern chain gang, where he discovers that the laughter provided by a Hollywood cartoon may provide the only rare moments of respite in a stretch of fully desperate existence. He contrives to be recognized in this place of anonymity, and returns to Hollywood to apply his hard-won insight, which means leaving unrealized his film of suffering.

The title of his projected work was to be *Oh Brother, Where Art Thou?* The Coen film, which opens in a southern chain gang, realizes this unrealized work by, as it announces, adapting (or more accurately, silently remembering names, and imagining sequences to realize them, from) episodes of the *Odyssey* (the Sirens, the Cyclops), taking as the overall adventure the return of an extraordinarily resourceful, or resilient, man to his native town to reclaim his sought-after wife (and children). The challenge the Coens take up, or depart from, in Sturges's fantasy of witnessing suffering, and which they seem to declare as part of their film (indeed of their corpus of fascinating films), is neither to record nor to distract from suffering. It is rather to witness, on the part of people who recognize, despite all, that life may still hold adventure, say hold out a perfectionist aspiration, but that to sustain a desire to meet the fantastic, unpredictable episodes of everyday modern existence, one must, and one can, rationally and practically, imagine that one will, at need, discover in oneself, in the register of passion, the resourceful persistence of Odysseus, and the mixed, but preponderant, favor of the Gods, call it fortune.

To give a taste of Sturges's writing, I am going to quote at some length from the extended exchange between Jean and Charles the second time they discover themselves quite alone in her cabin. Their exchange is a satire of ideals, proposing the film more largely as such a satire (as Ibsen composes melodramas of ideals), perhaps attempting to move beyond this vision by satirizing its own suspicions. The exchange begins after the woman has recovered herself from having run screaming from his cabin down to her own (suddenly hearing of an escaped snake), pursued by the man, whom she orders to search for the snake in and under her bed. She manages things so that they somehow trip each other, with the result that she is lying back comfortably on her chaise lounge and he is sitting on the floor awkwardly alongside her, whereupon they begin talking earnestly together as she plays absentmindedly with his hair. She asks whether he has ever thought of getting married, and he replies, dreamily, that snakes are his life ("What a life" she remarks to no one in particular), and that he has told his father that he isn't interested in the ale business. When she wonders whether there is any difference between ale and beer, Hopsy replies energetically that his father would have a fit if he heard that, explaining that one of them is brewed from the top and the other from the bottom, or the other way around, and concluding, "Why, there's no similarity at all between them."

Differences between similar things will considerably ramify as a theme of the film: differences, of course, between men and women; but also differences among women (Jean tells Hopsy, "the good ones aren't as good as you think, and the bad ones aren't as bad"); differences between sincerity and theater; and differences, as we might put it, of each human being from itself, torn from itself, repaired by itself, comically or tragically, as perfectionism persists in reminding us. Here is the part of the exchange I have in mind:

She: "So you say that's *why* you never married?" [namely because of the absolute difference between beer and ale].

He: "Oh, no, it's just that I never met her. I suppose she's around somewhere in the world."

She: "It would be too bad if you never bumped into each other."

He: "Well . . ."

She: "I suppose you know what she looks like, and everything?"

He: "I think so."

She: "I'll bet she looks like Marguerite in *Faust.*"

He: "No. She isn't as . . . bulky as an opera singer."

She: "Oh. How are her teeth?"

He: "Huh?"

She: "Oh, you should always go out with good teeth; it saves expense later."

He: "Now you're kidding me."

She: "Not badly. You have a right to have an ideal. I guess we all have one."

He: "What does yours look like?"

She: "He's a little short guy with lots of money."

He: "Why short?"

She: "What does it matter if he's rich? It's so he'll look up to me, so that I'll be *his* ideal."

He: "That's a funny kind of reason."

She: "Look who's reasoning. And when he takes me out to dinner he'll never add up the check or smoke greasy cigars or use grease on his hair. Oh yes, and he won't do card tricks."

He: "Oh."

The Lady Eve

She: "Oh, it's not that I mind *your* doing card tricks, Hopsy. But naturally
you wouldn't want your ideal to do card tricks."

He: "I shouldn't think that kind of ideal would be so difficult to find."

She: "Oh he isn't. That's why he's my ideal. What's the sense of having one if
you can't ever find him? Mine is a practical ideal, one you can find two or
three of in every barber shop, getting the works."

He: "Why don't you marry one of them?"

She: "Why should I marry anyone that looked like that? When I marry, it's
going to be somebody I've never seen before. I won't know what he looks
like or where he comes from or what he'll be. I want him to sort of—take
me by surprise."

He: (dreamily) "Like a burglar."

Jean has become increasingly relaxed as her combination of needling and
contradiction and seductiveness has played itself out, while Charles, with
increasing pain and absorption in the woman's words, after his year up
the Amazon, by that last line has become so wrapped up in the woman's
aroma and in the sound of her voice and her spell of images that he virtually
finishes her thought for her.

Let's note two or three turns in the exchange that bear on our particular
preoccupations. It is most obviously, as noted, an exchange about what Jean
calls ideals, especially about the fact that we all have them and that we are all
confused about them. This is most strongly and fundamentally theorized, or
based on fundamental theory, among our texts, in Freud's commentary on
Gradiva. The persistence, and persistent confusion, in what Freud calls ego-
ideals prompts, to my mind, some of the most memorable and useful commentary I know in Lacan's developments out of Freud. (Those of you who
have time and inclination may be surprised by the lucidity and usefulness of
Lacan's early Seminar entitled *Freud's Papers on Technique, 1953–1954.*) More
specifically, utilitarianism as a way of life seems pretty clearly mocked in
Jean's advice to marry someone with good teeth because it saves money later.
While Jean concedes she's kidding, she qualifies this by saying "not badly,"
meaning I suppose that she is merely exaggerating—after all we've been
shown a world, recognizable as our world, in which the attention of large
numbers of people is attracted by a man solely on the ground that he is rich
(and perhaps single). And then Kantianism may be being mocked in the idea
that you wouldn't want your ideal to do card tricks, with its suggestion that

fundamental choices about one's life with others are inevitably and validly made with some irreducible element of what we may call moral taste, going beyond the judgment accomplished through universalizable principles.

But beyond and before any such specifics, there is the intimacy gained in the sheer fact of a conversation in which the mind is moved, challenged, educated, elated. Hopsy declares explicitly enough that the encounter, fully including the exchange of words, has aroused him. Jean teases him about this ("Why, Hopsy!"). It may be that this is the point to which she has generally led and teased men before conning them in offering nothing more, or rather before leaving them with less than they had. But this time something has happened to her that wasn't in the cards.

A way of putting what has happened is to consider that she sees a step more deeply than the film's audience on an early viewing, into Sturges's demonically clever device of having Charles repeat to Eve the identical prelude to a declaration of love that he produced (I suppose invented) for Jean. I have called it the most difficult moment of the film to watch, since it seems to undermine Charles's seriousness so decisively as to threaten to make his fate uninteresting to us. But Eve/Jean recognizes the fact that trumps the insincerity of this fact, namely that it is, despite all, to *her* that he repeats the words, that he has never loved anyone *else*. Granted he "thinks" he knows she is not the same woman. But he has had to get himself into mental contortions and to swallow an incredibly tall stack of tales in order to convince himself of this—that is to say, in order to make love to the one woman he loves. So I am taking it that when Eve turns solemn on the train, after Charles jumps off and slips on a bank of mud, she is not simply feeling guilty for her treatment of this mug, and not even simply realizing that she has deprived herself of someone she has had genuine feeling for, but recognizing before all that his protestations to her of love have been, however deviously arrived at, helplessly sincere. This is confirmed for her when he tells her at the end, "It wouldn't have happened except that she looked so exactly like you"; so *exactly* (a critical point of Lacan's analysis of the ego-ideal); it is you; positively the same dame. (The same aroma; the same body; the same face and hair; the same yen. Just not the same voice. How important this is is perhaps measured in his being unable to assess the lying narrative of uninteresting promiscuousness she feeds him on the train.)

What is more, Charles/Hopsy's repetition of his fantasy of seeing Eve/Jean as a little girl is a comically blatant version of a fundamental feature of the genre of remarriage comedy, namely that the principal pair feel they have known each other forever, that they in effect began life as brother and sister. Then romance takes the form of divorcing from that incestuous intimacy into the discovered intimacy of strangers. Another pure version of a feature of our comic genre is the notation, in Eve's conversation with Horace about the divorce, concerning her rejection of a settlement by money, that what is between the pair is incomprehensible to the rest of the world.

There is a variation in *The Lady Eve* from the genre's tendency to end with enlightenment in the green world of Connecticut—as we saw in *Adam's Rib* and will see in *The Awful Truth*, and saw compensated for in *It Happened One Night* (where enlightenment is compensated for by continued adventure) and in *The Philadelphia Story* (where the green world is the world of national adventure) and will see compensated for in *His Girl Friday* (where the green world is replaced by a black world, known to the pair to be in need of their efforts of repair). The variation in *The Lady Eve* is that the film ends where it begins (as is required by the companion melodrama of the unknown woman), and that Connecticut is displaced to occupy most of the second half of the film. One might conjecture that the explanation, or compensation, is produced by the melodramatic elements of the comic narrative which require their own resolving. But I am inclined to put more weight on the fact that in this film Connecticut is taken over by an impostor who, for ample reason, uses it to achieve darkness rather than light (or causes only her own, isolating enlightenment).

Another variation of this film from what I take to be the canonical form of the genre is that the principal man's mother and father are present, a variation the film shares with *Adam's Rib*. But in *Adam's Rib* this variation accents the quality of fatherly authority in the temperament of Spencer Tracy, whereas in *The Lady Eve* it emphasizes the quality of Henry Fonda as innocent, vulnerable (his dominant temperament famously in the earlier *The Grapes of Wrath*), specifically as needing to assert his independence of his father, not from his tyranny, which Horace seems to lack, but from something like his disdainful indulgence of his son. Fonda's authoritative side (evident in *My Darling Clementine*) leaps into the film with his reappearance at the conclusion in the ship's dining room and his ecstatic refinding of Jean, or refalling for her.

As literally as in Freud's study of *Gradiva*, *The Lady Eve* materializes Freud's tracing of human sexuality as epitomized in *Three Essays on the Theory of Sexuality* in the formulation: "The finding of an object [of love] is in fact a refinding of it." Then what shall we say has become of Eve? The man evidently neither seeks nor refinds her; so shall we say he never found her? (Found what?—Eve's apparent refinement without what Jean's father calls Jean's ribaldry?) Freud's epitomizing formulation serves to turn the investigation around, so that we ask who the ones are who do the finding and refinding, here most obviously asking after the relation between Charles and Hopsy. This suggests asking what the relation is in human character between innocence and experience, or vulnerability and authority, or acceptance and rejection, learning to say yes and to say no, ideally a never-ending learning. May we conclude that the finding of the self is a refinding of it, the re-creation of it? Something of the sort is what perfectionism proposes, that no state of the self achieves its full expression, that the fate of finitude is to want, that human desire projects an idea of an unending beyond.

I close this reintroduction of Sturges's film by adducing a wonderfully illuminating text through which to view the issues of Jean/Eve's and Hopsy/Charles's parallel splitting, namely Wagner's *Tannhäuser*. Sturges's sound track uses the opening strain of the Overture to *Tannhäuser*, revealed in the ensuing opera as The Pilgrim's Chorus. (This is one of the tags from classical music so absolutely famous as to serve as comic commentary in a thousand animated cartoons. The various and profound relation of the medium of film to that of opera is a great subject in itself.)

Tannhäuser is about two women who are opposite aspects of a woman's powers of love, call them the profane and the sacred, where each is lethal and each promises redemption. *The Lady Eve* is about one woman who plays two opposite women, each of whom pretends, and cons the man into believing, that she is someone she is not. Tannhäuser sings a song to the "wrong" woman, that is, he repeats the very song he associates with Venus, the Goddess of Love, to the virginal Elizabeth. It is a transgression that precipitates his banishment from respectable society to seek redemption in Rome, on the intercession of Elizabeth. In *The Lady Eve,* the man's faux pas, so to speak, in repeating his aria-like declaration of sentimental love, with equal sincerity, to a "second" woman also precipitates the man's banishment. And he is again redeemed, let's say brought to his senses (if not yet to his intelligence), by the intercession of the very woman to whom he had been apparently unfaithful in sentiment.

If, as in a convincing Bayreuth production of *Tannhäuser* in the late 1970s (a video of which is commercially available), the roles of Venus and Elizabeth are sung by the same woman (Gwyneth Jones), the relation between the Wagner and the Sturges is underscored, each further illuminated. You recognize in the Wagner an explicit bar against taking Tannhäuser simply to have singled out the wrong woman for his song of love; and you are helped to consider with respect to *The Lady Eve* that, while it is next to impossible to imagine that the man does not recognize the second woman as the first, since she has not materially changed her looks, it is equally impossible to suppose that the man does not perceive that she has, however, distinctly changed her tune. So we are forced to ask how big a change that is. And ask further whether the gaze or the voice is the more essential in marking the object of desire.

I have elsewhere described film as our opera, taking the violent depths of its concerns into the heart of the culture's views of itself after opera, while masterpieces continued to be composed through the twentieth century, had lost the magnificence of the position it held among the arts when Wagner and Verdi were alive. It seems to me reasonable to consider that film's relation to opera is a key to film's achieving artistic and popular heights so soon after its (silent) technology was perfected.

17

PLATO

What makes anything the thing it is? What is in question can be anything from being a scarf to being a tyrant to being red to being bigger than something else to being good to being in love to being you. And who is best placed to know what the thing is? Plato is the one generally praised or blamed for starting philosophy down the road to look for answers to such questions. If you have the thought that to know this thing is a red scarf you have first to know that this thing is a scarf and that it is red, and then the thought that *this* thing cannot tell you that all the things you call scarves, so different from each other, are scarves; and the thought that *this* color cannot tell you what all the red things in the world have in common; and if you have the further thought that what a scarf is and what red is cannot be something arbitrary and changing and destructible (since if all scarves and all red things were destroyed, what it is to be a scarf and to be red would not have been touched); and if you conclude that every way every thing might be is something determined from the beginning of the world, and that what determines this cannot be *in* the world (in as it were what meets the eye), but must exist in an eternal, unchanging world, a world of perfection therefore to which our world and everything in it aspire, or you might say imitate, then you are following Plato, who called this perfect model of all that does or could exist the realm of Ideas or Forms.

If you follow Aristotle you will think that what makes a thing the thing it is, still calling this thing its Form, must reside within the matter of the thing itself, holding it within the realm of imperfection, as if each thing that exists is striving to become what it is, to realize itself. (Those of you who have come across the long poem *Paterson,* by the marvelous, enduring William Carlos Williams, will remember the refrain "No ideas but in things." It is for an American to wonder whether this physician from New Jersey can have, or can have not, been aware that he was epitomizing Aristotle at the same time that he was charting a direction to poetry.) If you think the knowledge of what the thing itself is is a matter beyond human powers, and that our human limitation imposes upon anything we can relate to as an objective world, a world apart from us, what it is we will consider the things of that world to be, you are following Kant. Such matters, invoking what is still called the problem of universals or the problem of predication, are today, for some philosophers, at stake in technical theories of truth.

Heidegger, in his *Being and Time,* regards the things in the world called human beings to be such that what characterize them (as human, not merely as things) are not universals or predicates, but something we might call (harking back to Aristotle, as Heidegger says we should do) possibilities or potentialities (Heidegger calls them *existentiale*). A philosopher such as Wittgenstein, in his *Philosophical Investigations,* has been thought by some to have dispersed the problem of universals by a simple piece of advice: "Don't say: 'There must be something common, or they would not be called "games"'—but *look and see* whether there is anything common to all" (section 66). (Attend to what meets the eye.) This is thought by others, to put it mildly, to beg the question. (But it is hardly more dismissive than Aristotle's dismissal of the importance of the separate eternality of Plato's Forms, as we shall see in a passage from *The Nichomachean Ethics.*) But for me the advice is a sort of comic preparation for Wittgenstein's persistent claim, in dead earnest, that "it is grammar that tells what kind of object anything is" (section 373)—a claim that seems to amount to the vision that our everyday language penetrates the world, or I would rather say that the world penetrates our everyday language, to an extent that other philosophers find, if not mystical, simply incredible. Conviction in it evidently asks a turn of the imagination as decisive as Plato's condescension toward variable, perishable, everyday objects. It is hard to know philosophically what has sent one down a particular road of thought (a progress sometimes thought of as eliciting our assumptions). It is equally hard to know what the human restlessness is that creates our dissatisfaction with our present stance, or what the resistance is that refuses to admit either satisfaction or dissatisfaction.

Remembering our restlessness should remind us that we have not touched on the companion question I raised in raising just now the question of metaphysics in the prejudicial form "What makes things the things they are?" (prejudicial as opposed simply to asking what things there are)— namely "Who is best placed to know what things are?" In *The Republic,* in which the question of justice is raised, Plato says that it will be easier to recognize the thing (the presence) of justice first in characterizing a city than in characterizing a person, but it turns out that the just city is one in which persons (some among us) can undergo the rigorous (difficult, systematic, and long) education necessary to a life of justice, so the justice of a city is a function of the justice, and the knowledge of justice, of its inhabitants. Education is pictured in *The Republic* (in a profoundly influential image) as a path upward, from darkness to light, concluding in a perfect state of perception and comprehension of the Forms. Emerson's related counter-image, at the opening of "Experience," is of our finding ourselves someplace on a series of stairs, perceiving those stairs below us that we have ascended and those above us that we have not reached (without a first or last).

We shall in our time with Plato concentrate largely on how he describes the beginnings of the path, namely on the darkness within which the desire for a step toward another, liberating perspective asserts itself. The practical reason for this, as in a thousand other cases, is the choice not to seem to try to do everything. But there is a philosophical justification as well. Since the perfectionism I am interested in drawing out, that I see in Emerson first among others, does not envisage, even deplores, the prospect of arriving at a final state of perfection, I am more interested in paying attention to the ways in which the initiating impulse to the further self may present itself in different temperaments of thought—the beginnings of philosophical stirring which no perfectionist can ignore—rather than in arguing with the various ways in which such a quest may or may not be seen as coming to rest. In Wittgenstein's *Investigations,* the impulse to question ourselves comes to rest on, as it were, each stair; at each, it remains open whether the impulse to a further questioning will present itself.

(Not every world, or circumstance, is one in which such a quest can be continued. Tragic and comic worlds are typically inhabited by those embattled against a world that would change them against their wills. One can think of such figures as using the energy of perfectionist ambition in service of their constancy, their resistance to change that is *not their own*. Who imagines Falstaff, or Othello, or Cleopatra, or Don Giovanni, in quest of a further self? We might conceive such figures as beyond the reach of philosophy. Philosophy might accordingly either regard them with pity, or terror, or envy. We must bear this in mind when we eventually come to consider Plato's distrust of theater.)

This chapter begins the last third of the book. We can look downward at a considerable number of stairs we have mounted—Emerson, Locke, J. S. Mill, Kant, Rawls, Nietzsche, Ibsen, Freud, and a film comedy or melodrama to be paired with each. I hope the sense is growing that neither the beginning nor the order of these works was inevitable. Any of those that have succeeded Emerson, and any yet to come, might have preceded him—indeed when you are moved to pick up an Emerson text in the future, they will all have preceded him. And so forth. The stairs Emerson pictures at the beginning of his great essay "Experience" are such that each is one on which we have *found* ourselves, and in some measure, therefore, one on which we have attained some further reach of an attainable self. The idea, or dream, of this book is that each of us will be enabled to take these steps in conversation with the successive pairs of works we have committed ourselves to spend a fraction of our lives with.

There are various reasons why a conversation may, in a given instance, fail—not every moment, certainly not every assigned moment, is apt to create a good encounter with a stranger, not even with a friend. The conversations of moral perfectionism, asking where you find yourself, are not incompatible with those, more familiar in moral pedagogy, that require reasons for performing or not performing a particular action. I have said that a reason for my emphasis on the moment of perfectionism is my sense that without it moral reasoning runs the danger of moralism, of, we might say, encouraging acting for the sake of conformity (as in Helmer's confrontation with Nora at the end of *A Doll's House*, or George's with Tracy Lord near the end of *The Philadelphia Story*, or Jerry's with Charlotte at the close of *Now, Voyager*, or Stephen's with Stella in the early scenes of *Stella Dallas*).

What is at stake bears equally on film (and its audience, hence variously on the other great arts) and on moral thinking. It bears on film and its audience, because I take the instances of film in evidence here as among the masterpieces produced in the Hollywood of their era, and, being among the most admired and memorable, as revealing and instructing American culture in ways that are still not fathomed philosophically. And the idea bears on moral thinking because while, as I've emphasized, Emersonian perfectionism does not on the whole take up front-page moral problems such as abortion or capital punishment, it informs, or is implied by, the larger portion of ways in which ordinary human beings confront and question each other's conduct and character every day, distinguishing a slap from a slug, smarting from a slight, meeting a reasonable request ungraciously, inflicting irritation on an innocent object instead of upon the more frightening one who has caused it, withholding deserved praise or gratitude, withholding deserved rebuke, instances of an untold number of the little deaths we deliver or suffer day and night.

Plato's *Republic* might be included with those works I have noted as amalgamating philosophy and literature (primarily Emerson and Nietzsche), since his writing is an enduring object of praise for its artistry, hence as an object of curiosity, standing in a paradoxical relation to its all but obsessive desire to rid the good city of most art, great or small. We shall have to ask whether this paradox is a trivial or a decisive fact about *The Republic*. This work might also be linked with Freud's, since Plato's too can be said to have established a new kind of psychological theory, one moreover, in its picture of the mind as divided in three unequal parts, posing perhaps the fundamental issue of ethics and of knowledge, namely how to bring one's life under the tutelage of reason. For us the text of *The Republic* represents primarily a familiar place from which to locate the full beginning of what we understand philosophy to aspire to be, the establishing of a prose, call it a set of conditions, under which we can arrive, let us say, at an understanding of our responsibilities for our words and deeds as under the assessment of reason, requiring an understanding both of the authority of reason and of the kind of creature humans are that we recognize the worth of our obedience to authority.

With respect to the characterization of perfectionism, *The Republic* is not only the most extended and systematic treatment, or portrait, among the great philosophers of the perfectionist perception of the moral life—a perception of it as moving from a sense and state of imprisonment to the liberation of oneself by the transforming effect of what can be called philosophy—it also consistently portrays philosophy's address to that process as directed not to the assessment of individual acts as right or wrong, good or bad, but to the evaluation of the worthiness of ways of life, an earmark of perfectionist ambition. In a fine and useful recent commentary on *The Republic*, Nickolas Pappas puts a similar point by saying: "The conversations of Book I constitute a progression away from conceptions of justice that look for that trait in some feature of the *actions* one performs, toward a view of justice as a characteristic of the *person* performing them. Hence ethics will concern itself not with commandments but with accounts of the virtues."

I suppose for this reason, a study that puts emphasis on the assessment of a person and on a way of life, as opposed to features of actions and reasons for actions, is sometimes called virtue ethics. I do not myself think of perfectionist moral theory quite that way, perhaps because of the suggestion that there is a known list of virtues (Plato's favorites in *The Republic* are justice, wisdom, courage, and moderation) that analysis should seek to discover, and also because my emphasis on perfectionism is associated with a philosophical outlook—marked by intellectual temperaments as different as Emerson and the later Wittgenstein—that does not, so far as I know, characterize what may be called virtue ethics.

With respect to the format of invoking films in connection with each discursive text, this might accurately be taken as an homage on my part to Plato's vision in *The Republic* that the power of art is so massive and, let's say, insatiable, in its competition with philosophy's plans for human happiness that it must be banned almost entirely from the good, or the philosophical, city. Painting and poetry (meaning primarily tragedy) are the arts that bear the brunt of Plato's antagonism, painting primarily for a metaphysical reason (namely that it is not of reality) and tragedy in addition because of its role, in Homer and in the Greek tragic writers, Aeschylus, Sophocles, and Euripides, as the most favored and powerful source of moral instruction in Athenian culture. To attack them, knowing their power, is at once to place Socrates in confrontation with Athenian moral consciousness as such, the place from which he evidently wishes to announce philosophy's contradiction of his culture's way of life, let's call it their values. (Of all the ways one may and must question the accuracy of Plato's portrait of Socrates to the historical Socrates, hence of the changing allegiance of Plato's thought to that of Socrates, one fact seems constant throughout the dialogues' attack on customary life as Plato casts it, namely that it is the life of a city that puts Socrates to death, an act whose intertwining of inevitability with a lack of necessity seems to encode the fate of philosophy as such in the public world, the fact, hence, from which that fate is to be interpreted.)

I do not claim so tremendous a role for the films I discuss here in relation to philosophy as Plato claims for tragedy, yet they have, in the vastness of their audience and in their power to affect it, claims over any of the other arts, high or low, to have provided moral education for the culture contemporary with them. This was registered, at relatively low levels of intellectual effort, in the mid-1930s, early in the rise of talking film's popularity, in the justification for instituting a moral code of censorship for movies. Four and five decades later, in the 1970s and 1980s, when public censorship was more nuanced, academic criticism of film achieved a certain height of intellectuality when much of advanced film studies was undertaking to attack what it understood as the effect of film on its audience, especially Hollywood film. This took two major forms, a Marxian-derived attack on the ideology of Hollywood as the perfect, that is transparent and homogeneous and unresistant, instrument of the commodification of culture achieved in late capitalism; and an attack on Hollywood's construction of women, a deployment of film's undeniable pleasures in service of underwriting women's subjection to the satisfaction of men.

Film studies has recently declared itself in need of reconception, and I hope part of this reconception will take the form of a wish to understand how it got to its present form. Part of seeking that understanding, were I to attempt to trace it, would be to follow out my impression that the wholesale attack of film studies upon a large portion of its subject was driven by a moralism as intense as Plato's obsession with poetry. I cannot avoid the feeling that a fear of the power of film remains insufficiently analyzed.

But film studies is not my profession, and any judgments of mine about it are essentially anecdotal. What I wish to emphasize is that my periodic turn to writing about film, theoretically at first (in *The World Viewed*) and later critically, has been meant precisely to articulate philosophically what I can divine of its power as a medium, and to demonstrate critically that in genres and oeuvres of its major achievements, including ones among its most popular, it undertakes to criticize itself, and its cultural origins, in ways that we have come to expect of the high modernist arts. We shall see a small but notable instance of this in *His Girl Friday*, when the light turned on a prisoner under interrogation is identified as the light by which the motion picture camera does its work.

That other Hollywood productions, even the bulk of them, provide evidence for one's worst fears of cultural repression, may be true. But that is not news. It is part of the debasement of culture, its splitting into high and low, that comes with democratization, something culture's democratic critics should not, therefore, be so quick to despise. All this was under way before the rise of the new Hollywood special effects spectacles, which has revealed to those in charge of the breakdown of the old studio/star system new magnitudes of profit and risk in the making of movies, a new system so genuinely driven by the autonomous life of capital that it directly threatens the making of reflective films. But criticism of this development has been blunted in advance by the casual, often condescending, criticism of an era that deserved better.

Film's particular pertinence to Plato's distrust of the effects of the arts is something that will emerge in full flower when we take up the great Myth of the Cave in Book VII of *The Republic,* which virtually predicts the existence of film a couple of millennia before its materialization. The presence of various myths or allegories is a well-recognized feature of the composition of Plato's *Republic,* and a reasonable, even practical, explanation of their presence is to say that, while as Plato insists, argumentation is the primary business of the philosopher, he wants his work to be understood also by those not (yet) trained in philosophy, so he illustrates the results of his argumentation with what he calls "images," which he will identify as producing a lower form of knowledge than philosophy aspires to. One problem with this explanation is that it is not clear who Plato intends to read his writing, other than philosophers, as perhaps a teaching manual. But since the text portrays, in addition to Socrates, younger figures we might call friends of philosophy (and an enemy of it, Thrasymachus, who might be won over to it), we should include them among its intended audience, and then ask when friends of philosophy are to read it.

My own interest in Plato's text as pertains to this book is a function neither quite of its argumentation nor of its images and myths as illustrations of its argumentation, though both play an essential role in what I shall say about it. Rather I take its uniqueness (by virtue of its historical position as well as by the extensiveness of intellectual range in metaphysics, epistemology, aesthetics, politics, ethics, and religion it brings to bear on issues of perfectionism, of, let me say, the constitution of the better self in the imagination of the better city), to warrant using it—experimentally as it were—as a source of what I call a thematics of perfectionism. The idea is to consider that every feature of the text is, or may be, an essential feature of what perfectionism demands, or aspires to.

But what counts as a feature? In *Conditions Handsome and Unhandsome,* I put together a list of 28 topics of Plato's *Republic* that I propose as its thematics of perfectionism, beginning with "a mode of conversation." Because of its general, ample applicability (in similarity or in difference) to themes derivable from our other texts—while no other text could contain all or only the themes of *The Republic,* in the way it contains them—I have placed the list of its features that I have distinguished at the end of this book for easy, anyway for equal, reference. A topic much on my mind as I look at that list is whether or how Plato's idea of continuous matching of a type of soul with a type of city as a city declines (or improves) applies to the aspiration of democracy I see in remarriage comedy. If I say that the aim of Emersonianism, I might say the aim of these chapters, is to suggest the richest conception of perfectionism compatible with, and indeed essential to, a democratic disposition, then the question arises as to whether, or in what sense, the democratic city is an image of its citizens, or whether it is precisely of that city that it can be said the face of its citizens remains open to their imaginations.

After demonstrating the significance of a certain form of conversation in turning the self around and guiding it to a path of enlightenment—speaking of education, of distinguishing true from false necessities, of the debasement of philosophy and culture and justice, and the soul—Socrates' dramatization of his argument ends (from the beginning threatening the violation of his injunction against the public dramatization of human lives) by declaring that their city, their theoretical city, made of words, their words in the foregoing conversation, is the only one a philosopher will participate in, and in effect invites the reader to become a citizen of that city, joining in the competition between the work of philosophy's prose and of tragedy's poetry for the privilege of making things happen to the soul. This ends Book IX, leaving the concluding Book X for further reflections on art—so essential a power in imagining the just city, so treacherous a power within the city—and departing with a great myth of death and rebirth.

In what I have said so far I have stressed perfectionism's conception of morality as evaluating ways of life rather than assessing individual actions, and at the same time indicated that moral philosophy occurs in Plato's *Republic* not as a field of philosophy isolated from an isolated metaphysics and epistemology and aesthetics, and so on. Also, in mentioning the attention to the virtuousness of the one acting rather than to the virtue of an act of that one, I do not pursue the analogy Plato pursues—in seeking to determine the particular virtues of justice, moderation, courage, and wisdom—between various more or less virtuous souls and the counterpart societies that have produced them and that they sustain, and undermine. Nor have I explicitly stated what appears to be the guiding question of Plato's *Republic,* namely "Can an unjust person be happy?" which has produced Socrates' questioning as to the nature of justice, of happiness, and of a person (or soul).

But the present chapter has as part of its past my discussion of Rawls's *A Theory of Justice,* and Plato's question should be made explicit in view of, or against the background of, its contrasting with my implied formulation of a guiding, but unannounced, question of Rawls's text, namely "Can a just person be happy in an unjust world?" where this question turned out to require considering the extent to which even one relatively advantaged feels compromised by the degree of injustice he judges to be present in his society, to which he consents, as I put the matter, from above.

But if my summary of Plato's *Republic* does not contain the fact that, as anyone would say, it is a search for the definition of justice, in the soul and in the state, and for the relation between justice and happiness, then in what way is it a summary? In my defense I can say, negatively, that I was trying to avoid the usual effort of summary as taking one through the text Book by Book, which is without question one way it is productive to do things, respecting the order of the text, but which, I find, can also violate my experience of the text, or muffle my interest in it and memory of it. I am now interested to note that many of the first dozen features of *The Republic* I have listed are ways of recounting the events of the opening of the Myth (or Allegory) of the Cave, which occurs only in Book VII, after preparation by more than half of Plato's text.

Let us have Socrates' description before us:

> Next, I said, compare the effect of education and the lack of it upon our human nature to a situation like this: imagine men to be living in an underground cave-like dwelling place, which has a way up to the light along its whole width, but the entrance is a long way up. The men have been there from childhood, with their neck and legs in fetters, so that they remain in the same place and can only see ahead of them, as their bonds prevent them turning their heads. Light is provided by a fire burning some way behind and above them. Between the fire and the prisoners . . . there is a path across the cave and along this a low wall has been built, like the screen at a puppet show in front of the performers who show their puppets above it.—I see it.

See then also men carrying along that wall . . . all kinds of artifacts, statues of men, reproductions of other animals in stone or wood fashioned in all sorts of ways, and . . . some of the carriers are talking while others are silent.—This is a strange picture, and strange prisoners.

They are like us, I said. Do you think. . . . that such men could see anything of themselves and each other except the shadows which the fire casts upon the wall of the cave in front of them?—How could they, if they have to keep their heads still throughout life? . . .

Altogether then, I said, such men would believe the truth to be nothing else than the shadows of the artifacts . . .

Whenever one of them was freed, had to stand up suddenly, turn his head, walk, and look up toward the light, doing all that would give him pain, the flash of the fire would make it impossible for him to see the objects of which he had earlier seen the shadows . . . If one then compelled him to look at the fire itself, his eyes would hurt, he would turn round and flee toward those things which he could see . . . And if one were to drag him thence by force up the rough and steep path, and did not let him go before he was dragged into the sunlight, would he not be in physical pain and angry as he was dragged along? . . .—I think he would need time to get adjusted before he could see things in the world above.

What has justified my starting my list of features of *The Republic* by noting the fact of conversation, and what can justify the immediate leap to, or association with, the Cave? That there are questions here is hardly surprising, given a pair of prior, standing interests of mine in conversation. The more obvious interest is in the nature of the exchanges featured in, to begin with, the film comedies and melodramas adduced in this book. The less obvious interest is something that has been on my mind explicitly at least since I wrote the opening sentence of *The Claim of Reason* (arrived at late in revising that manuscript, and providing perhaps the most prominent touchstone for whether a reader finds that my manner of doing things is sensible or insupportable), a sentence meant to be striking if only because of its length (those who deplore it have taken the trouble actually to count the number of words in it, somewhere just over two hundred), made so by me in order to raise as memorably as I could the question of how and where and for whom philosophy is called upon, that is, begins. And this is tied for me to some level of the question of why we speak, as if to make us wonder at the fact of language, which by now we will take as creating wonder at the possibility and the necessity of the political. It may seem to amount to wondering what our stake is in others, why we care about them. Not everyone will agree offhand that that is a genuine, or sensible, question.

Plato goes to some trouble to stage the onset of conversation, not as it were taking for granted his philosophical medium of dialogue but suggesting both a craving for it and a reluctance toward it. Both craving and reluctance are epitomized in the gesture, near the beginning of *The Republic,* in which someone (a slave it happens) stops Socrates from leaving to walk back to Athens from the port of Piraeus by catching hold of his cloak and expressing the wish of an acquaintance for him to stay. I note immediately, something I first emphasized in speaking of the beginning of Wittgenstein's *Philosophical Investigations,* that philosophy does not speak first; a fact I sometimes express by saying that philosophy's first virtue, as it matters most to me, is responsiveness. Wittgenstein's book opens with a quotation from St. Augustine, to which Wittgenstein's opening remark is a response. The trick of *The Republic* is that Plato casts the entire dialogue as narrated by Socrates, so that with its opening word Socrates is already speaking. (To whom? To us? But still on the first page it is noted that speech is ineffective, is pointless, if someone refuses to listen. It doesn't say there—does it anywhere?—what counts as listening. Responsiveness, perhaps. But that is the question, not an answer.) There is already the suggestion that philosophy's silence is the most, or first, seductive feature of it; or put otherwise, that there is something in philosophy that makes one crave its response. That there is something in it that, in certain moods, perhaps in most, is repellent, or boring, is perhaps obvious enough. Both effects are registered in the reasons given Socrates to persuade him to stay, namely that there will be a torch race on horseback for the goddess tonight (a new goddess of Piraeus whose celebration was the cause Socrates had noted for his appearing there), and that after dinner they will be joined by many young men and they will talk.

I note that these beginnings emerge from ordinary encounters in the public street, among acquaintances, and that I take the opening of the allegory of Cave, which is the opening of the journey to philosophy, to be Plato's portrait of the everyday, the customary public space in which philosophy is first encountered. So there was no "leap" to the allegory when I in effect began my list of features by recording its opening events; they are a certain "allegorical" recapitulation of the opening events of *The Republic.* But in that case, we are alerted in turn to go back to the (literal) opening, an apparently benign public encounter of acquaintances, prepared to find in it unnoticed delusion and aggressiveness.

What constitutes delusion will take time to emerge. We get a show of aggressiveness soon enough in the figure of Thrasymachus and his contempt for Socrates' praise of justice. And there is that initial aggressive joking expressed by Polemarchus to Socrates in noting that he and his friends out-number Socrates and his companion Glaucon and could force them to stay, to which Socrates proposes persuasion as an alternative—as if preserving the question of the relation of speech and violence, in particular the question whether speech disperses violence or whether it is a form of violence. (Later Socrates will distinguish modes of speech, not merely at large between the poetry of tragedy and the prose of philosophy, but between discussion and dispute.)

But there is a still more specific link between the opening of the reported discussion of *The Republic* and the Allegory of the Cave, one forged if we go back not alone to the beginning of the action, and the anticipation of philosophy in antagonistic exchange, but to the beginning of Plato's text. Its opening words are "I went down" (namely, to the Piraeus); and I am prepared to take this, in retrospect, to be illuminated by the going down into the cave of the everyday. (Retrospective illumination is an important mode of understanding in Freud's thought. And I am glad to invoke the expertise and experience of Nickolas Pappas, in his commentary on *The Republic,* as confirmation of my surmise about the link of the opening going down with that figured in the cave allegory. I am indebted to Pappas's text in other respects, and recommend it strongly to your attention.)

I do not expect, perhaps I do not simply want, your immediate agreement as to the importance of this connection of two descents. Does this mean that I do not want to disguise the violent element in lecturing, keeping potential interlocutors silent, demanding interest in what interests me? I leave the issue by noting two other occurrences of the notation of descent. (I may have passed others by; if you come across any of interest I'd like to hear about them.)

Near the beginning of Book IX (576d,e; 577a), Socrates, coming to the conclusion of his argument about whether the unjust can be happy, and reaching agreement with Glaucon that the tyrant, the unjust ruler of an unjust city, is the most wretched man, asks Glaucon whether his "judgment

[is] the same with regard to [the] happiness and wretchedness" of their respective cities. Socrates adds: "And let's not be dazzled by looking at one man—a tyrant—... but since it is essential to go into the city and study the whole of it, let's not give our opinion, till we've gone down and looked into every corner." And Socrates goes on to caution the same about judging the happiness or wretchedness of the individual citizens of the city: "The person who is fit to judge them is someone who *in thought can go down* into a person's character and examine it thoroughly, someone who doesn't judge from outside, the way a child does, who is dazzled by the façade that tyrants adopt for the outside world to see, but is able to see right through that sort of thing," someone who sees the tyrant "stripped of his theatrical façade." These occurrences—of the gesture of descending—mark the violence of mature judgment in assessing the lives of others, examining what others would keep out of sight in the corners of the city, or the soul, stripping them of their pretenses. These are evidently further effects of what Socrates means by discussion, which is, as refined by him, his only instrument for arriving at a mature judgment of cities and souls.

Dwelling here on allegory and imagery, I should amplify further what I meant by saying that I am as attached, in reading Plato, to myth as to argument. About Plato's or Socrates' arguments I might say that I am no more generally convinced by them than their interlocutors often seem to be. What to my mind is permanent in them, fresh every day, is the perception that the assertions of our fellow citizens, including ours to them, or to ourselves, need to be confronted, questioned, stopped, in ways that are apt to strike their proponents as violent. We are, after all, telling them that they do not know what they are saying.

Argument by counterexample is one way of showing them this, as when Thrasymachus asserts that justice is matter of getting an advantage for oneself and Socrates counters by considering that doing justice is a virtue like practicing a craft and notes that people do not practice a craft—medicine, say—for their own advantage but for the advantage of their patients. What Thrasymachus asserted is accordingly proven false; and since he could have recognized its falseness by bethinking himself further, the encounter shows that he did not realize what he was saying. Argument by what Wittgenstein calls language games is another mode of confrontation to similar effect. (If the confrontation is of the self with itself, the violence may be expressed by tapping the butt of one's palm to one's forehead—even if unobserved.)

About Plato's myths, my attachment to them is not simply that they are images, easier to appreciate than arguments, and not that they illustrate, and make more convincing, the conclusions or premises of Plato's arguments—such testimony is familiarly given. My attachment to Plato's myths is more likely to be rather that they illustrate, hence potentially extend, or expose, turns of philosophical thinking that I have found myself convinced by. This suggests that my idea of the history of philosophy is that it can be approached only out of philosophizing in the present. No present will illuminate all of it, or be illuminated by all of it (unless Hegel, and perhaps Heidegger, are to be believed); and some dispensations of present philosophy will leave next to no room for mutual illumination with the past (if Descartes or Hume or Quine is to be believed).

I note an instance whose specific relation to work of my own I had not noticed until this time through *The Republic*. It concerns Socrates' image of the human being within the human being in Book IX—where he asks for the imagination of a monster in man-like form molded seamlessly from a large lion and a small man together with a "multi-colored beast with a ring of many heads that it can grow and change at will" (588c,d,e). The point of the image is to demonstrate "what someone who praises injustice [and justice] is saying" (589a,b), that is, to show them that they have not known what they are saying, about justice or about the human. I found myself thinking of a somewhat bizarre passage in part 4 of *The Claim of Reason* in which I had come to a sense that the skeptic with respect to others is imagining that the other might be simulating human responses (not feigning this or that sensation, but sensuousness as such, so to speak), and I in effect try to grant what it is to imagine this by asking whether what we take to be human beings can be imagined as beings in human guise. The point of the image is to suggest that those who ask for assurance that a human body goes with, or is evidence for, a mind inside it do not know what they are asking. (That this passage from *The Claim of Reason* also mentions the imagination of metempsychosis, the transmigration of souls, will turn out to be pertinent.)

Speaking more generally, Wittgenstein's *Philosophical Investigations*, as I have taken a number of occasions to indicate, has been for me one of the two or three most convincing philosophical texts of the century in which I spent my first seventy-four years. So naturally I have been interested to discover what the grounds of that conviction have been, to learn from it what I take conviction to be. I might say that it was an important step in this discovery to articulate the *Investigations'* idea of philosophical progress not as from false to true assertions, or from opinions to proven conclusions (say theses), or from doubt to certainty, but rather from the darkness of confusion to enlightened understanding, or say from illusion to clarity, or from being at an intellectual loss to finding my feet with myself, from insistent speech to productive silence (perhaps in the form of thinking through an image).

The relation to Plato is therewith made, I trust, palpable enough. But it may be no more accurate to say that Plato's Myth of the Cave illustrates Wittgenstein's progress than that I came to characterize Wittgenstein's progress in such ways because of my having first read Plato.

Now take a further step in *The Republic*'s description of the Cave, to the early moment in which the prisoners, having as it were been confronted with their chains, turn themselves around and face the fact of their bewilderment, manifested as their not knowing how to tell shadows from the objects which cast them. I have wished to align this turning around with two formulations about turning in *Philosophical Investigations*: "Our examination must be rotated around . . . the fixed point of our real need" (sec. 108); "What we do is return words from their metaphysical to their everyday use" (sec. 116). The former captures the sense that philosophy's task requires a reorientation of thought, and one which amounts to a reorientation, if momentary, of one's life, invoking implicitly the idea, important early in *The Republic*, of our entrapment in false necessities. The latter formulation, speaking of returning rather than turning, challenges the claim of Plato's myth to describe the trajectory of a total, unified human life.

The idea of returning language to itself, as it were, is something that has to happen every day, in response to each incursion of the metaphysical, of the insistence to know what cannot be known, or say what cannot be said, or mean what cannot be meant. The everyday to which we may be said to turn ourselves back is not a place (except in myth), and our repetitive call to release ourselves from fixated images does not describe a continuous direction (as demanded by Plato's myth of the Divided Line, the companion image to the Allegory of the Cave). *The Republic* and *Philosophical Investigations* share the perfectionist sense of one's intellect, or life, as enclosed, entrapped; and share the sense of liberation as requiring the intervention of a new or counter voice—in Plato figured as an older friend already in love with, let's call it, truth; in Wittgenstein internalized as the voice of correctness or say of reason, perhaps speaking as from a promised or revised community. (The two voices, one of sensuousness or temptation, and one of intelligence or correctness, are a way, as said, that I sometimes cast Kant's idea of the human as living in two worlds. But in the *Investigations,* there is a field beyond the two voices. You can think of it as acknowledging the literary conditions of philosophy, which must share the language of everyday life, or think of it as the silence surrounding the possibility of talk.)

The *Investigations* does not share, indeed it stands against, the *Republic*'s idea of a goal of perfectibility, a foreseeable path to a concluding state of the human. The idea of life's journey, say the quest to take one's life upon oneself, to become the one you are, is no longer expressed in the image of a path, but rather, I would say, in the very idea of walking as such, in contrast to a chaos of slipping and sliding or to the nightmare of paralysis. The measure of direction, or progress, is not assured by a beacon from afar, or what seems to be meant by what today is sometimes spoken of as a moral compass, but rather pointed to by what Emerson figures as a gleam of light over an inner landscape, and which concretely is guided, and tested, by whether the next step of the self is one that takes its cue from the torment, the sickness, the strangeness, the exile, the disappointment, the boredom, the restlessness, that I have claimed are the terms in which *Philosophical Investigations* portrays the modern subject.

By a step that "takes it cue" from these conditions I do not mean one that attempts to escape them, but one that judges the degree to which these conditions must be borne and may be turned (some might say sublimated) constructively, productively, sociably. This puts tremendous weight on one's judgment, critically including one's judgment of whose judgment is to be listened to most attentively.

Evidently I do not find that listening to reason is exhaustively expressed by the ability to produce and to be moved by argument. Sometimes it requires refusing to listen to arguments. Sometimes it requires demanding that one's own voice be listened to, taken into account. I am impressed by Freud's discussion of judgment (in "Negation") that relates the act of judgment to the most basic of instincts, the oral instincts, in which saying no is related to a primitive reaction of disgust, to a wish to spit something away from one's insides, and saying yes is related to a wish to incorporate something (remember Lady Eve: "You mean he actually swallowed that [the story about the identical half-sisters]?"; "Like a wolf."). But disgust is open to education, and the education provided by a culture is open to the political of the culture; hence one's power of judgment is going to be forced to conform with a current political dispensation or forced to oppose it. But this is essentially the vision of Plato's *Republic*. Neither the moral law, nor God, nor calculation can get beneath the necessity of judgment. Independence of judgment, call it autonomy, depends upon neither losing your capacity for recognizing your disgust nor taking it as beyond criticism.

Plato's Cave uncannily anticipates a movie theater—from behind you, a source of light casts shadows of moving objects upon a wall in front of you which you take for real things and real people. In *The World Viewed* I express this by saying that, on film, reality is behind you, wishing by saying so to capture the idea that you have to turn yourself around in order to see how things are and that the seeing will take you by surprise, as by a further familiarity, as a touch on the shoulder.

But before saying what I can about how I come to a different evaluation of an art of drama and of the visual than Plato has done, I should clarify a claim I made earlier in passing, namely that the representation of the everyday in the Allegory of the Cave casts the everyday as a scene of something like illusion or delusion. I don't mean exactly what Plato seems to mean, namely that you think you see things that are not there; I mean rather, or as well, that you do not, even cannot, see fundamental things that are there, the conditions, let us say, of what is there, of our ability to speak of what we know.

Let us put aside what it is that Socrates is supposed to see, the one supposed to see everything. I recall first that the portents in his opening words, "I went down to the Piraeus," are not discovered until the Myth of the Cave in Book VII and, in Book IX, the recognition that judgments of happiness and wretchedness essentially require going down into the city, looking in every corner (576d,e). This may remind us that we never know why Socrates went down to Piraeus, I mean what importance he attaches to saying a prayer to a goddess whose cult is new to that place, since he also says he was "curious to see" the festival planned for this first occasion, and since we learn in a few minutes that what keeps him from leaving Piraeus seems to be the promise of another festival which Polemarchus says will be "well worth seeing," featuring a torch race on horseback and providing the opportunity for talk with some young men. Since, moreover, the significance of "talk," or say of the justice of speech, and the worth of seeing, may be said to be principal subjects of *The Republic,* Polemarchus may be said not to know what he is talking about, and we, who are told what he has unremarkably said, may be said not to know what we have heard.

And then consider the fact that Socrates' first direct report of his own words, in answer to Polemarchus's observing "It looks to me, Socrates, as if you two are starting off for Athens," is his reply, "It looks the way it is, then," thus announcing at least half the epistemological quest of philosophical talking, as it is portrayed in *The Republic*—to get things to look the way they are, shadows as shadows, and things that cast shadows as things that, in the presence of light, cast shadows. (The other half of the quest will be to get the Forms of things, call them the ideas of whatever is, to be free of looking, that is, to be invisible—the thing itself, free of its presentations to us, open to the intellect alone.)

So what happens to my claim that philosophy does not speak first, in view of the fact that the opening words of this text, indeed all the words, are those of Socrates? But does it really seem that Socrates has indeed spoken first? Do not the opening words "I went down to the Piraeus yesterday" rather unmistakably imply that a question has been asked, or that a word, perhaps a letter, is known to be awaited? Who, then, is Socrates counting on being interested in where he was yesterday, that is, in what is (still) on his mind today? (He is not just describing how it is he is tugged at by someone who wants to stop him and hear what he has to say. He is enacting it.) Who other than we, present at his text, are now his audience? Then who are we to be interested in what he says? And to get us to ask this question, namely to participate in the work of the text, seems sufficient philosophical reason for the text to begin as it does.

I once claimed that the only audience of philosophy is one performing it. But how are we inspired to such performance by a sentence that locates its utterer? (It is not uncommon. Compare the opening of *Walden:* "When I wrote the following pages . . . I lived . . . a mile from any neighbor . . . Now I am a sojourner in civilized life again." Or the opening of Emerson's "Self-Reliance": "I read the other day . . ." Or the quotation opening Wittgenstein's *Investigations,* which haunts what follows: "When my elders . . .") Evidently the idea is to suggest a standing question about our own whereabouts, in particular now, stopped in front of this text. Where are we? Which requires asking: Where were we (namely when we were rudely interrupted, turned aside from our false needs, a turning that is initially disorienting)? Emerson's opening of "Experience" simply states, rather than implies, the issue of philosophy: "Where do we find ourselves?" For Wittgenstein, in his *Investigations*, philosophy begins in loss, in finding oneself at a loss: "A philosophical problem has the form; 'I do not know my way about.'" The question we have been brought to ask, that we did not know we were asking, produces the sense of illusion, of reality passing us by, that demands philosophizing.

I have spoken sometimes of the ordinary as the missable, the unobserved, what we could call the uncounted, taken not as given but for granted. The sense is that every word we say shares, and may reveal, the fate, or destinies, we have found, for example, in the opening words of *The Republic*—missing or underestimating the significance in its self-location, its invitations to stay and witness, and to talk, and its noting of being stopped by being tugged by the cloak, and the project of finding things to look the way they are. In now emphasizing that the philosopher has to lead or get us to see this perpetual, unlimited, vulnerability of our, and of others', words and deeds, I recognize that "to lead or get us" suggests that we actively shield ourselves from this open, unsurveyable field of ungroundedness, ground giving way from us on all sides, in principle with each word. This is what Freud implies early in picturing the psyche as surrounding itself with protection, or say resistance, to the incessance of stimuli from outside and inside.

If each word had to be sounded for its powers before we entrusted ourselves to it, we would be able to say nothing, never come to the beginning, let alone to the end, of a sentence. Some philosophers spook us, or themselves (not alone Derrida), with this thought; they speak, for example, of meaning as always deferred. Who would deny that our words mean more, and other, than we ask them on a given occasion to say? That is reason enough to be interested, as I am, in the fact that meaning is—also—*not* deferred, that I can mean, now, here, exactly, precisely, accurately, fully, assuredly, what I mean, for instance that here are five red apples. (Absolutely exactly? Metaphysically fully? I would guess not. How does that come up? Perhaps in my leaving it obscure why I have said this to you.)

And yet, of course, I may at any time in fact be wrong, my assertions raked by unassessed dangers, unmonitored trusts, lacks of insurance. I say I am certain that the cat is on the mat and it proves to be the case that she is not. A reason I might persist in saying that nevertheless I was certain—if I was, but, as it were, the fact I asserted is dead—instead of repeating, as it used to be put, that no empirical statement is certain, is that that repetition would not relieve me from the responsibility of having asserted my certainty initially, since certain is what I *was*. My judgments are ineluctable grounds for judgments against me.

The issue of the essential vulnerability of human action and speech to "slips" is central to the work of thinkers as different as J. L. Austin and Freud. In Austin's "A Plea for Excuses" what emerges is that, in contrast to Freud's vision of the human being as a field of significance whose actions and words express wider meaning than we might care to be questioned about, Austin's vision is of the human being as a field of vulnerability whose actions and words imply wider consequences and effects and results—if narrower meaning—than we should have to be answerable for. I have described Austin's work, epitomized in the paper on excuses, as criticizing the injustice of our speech (especially as it is prompted by metaphysical stirrings)—as when he speaks of our "unfairly" describing (accusing) someone of having done something without recognizing the mitigating factors in play. For Freud our speech is inexorably just, though it may take considerable pains to discover wherein the justice of our expressions lies.

I might address the issue I see here in the following question: To what extent is the intuition of the everyday as a scene of illusion—whether pictured as in Plato's Cave, or taken up in Schopenhauer's invocation of Maya, or in what Western religion can call putting off the old man for the new—articulated in philosophy's study of, let's say, the logic or grammar (comparable to what Lacan calls the symbolic) of language? What is left out (meant in philosophy to be left out, or overcome) is what we might call the essential symptomaticity of language (comparable to what Lacan calls the imaginary). We might think of it as whatever it is reason has to strive with. In *The Claim of Reason* (pp. 94–96), I distinguish between the economy and the aesthetics of speech, the former referring to the control of concepts by criteria, the latter to the revelations of myself by what I find worth saying, or not saying, as and when I speak, or hold my tongue. My efforts in philosophy generally, I think, can be said to aspire to bear in mind that the achievements of reason are to be measured by the justice they do to what reason has to overcome. And by the question of who, and by means of what agency, is to do this measuring, which may require a relocation or reconfiguration of reason.

Which perhaps brings us to the question of the relation of philosophy and the arts, with which Book X, the final book of *The Republic*, principally concerns itself. Since with the end of Book IX the argument over the nature of justice in the city and in the soul, and over whether justice is profitable, or phrased otherwise, whether the unjust can be happy, is concluded, it is unclear what work a Book X has left to do. The Platonic theses concerning the hierarchy of grades of reality and the hierarchy of the powers or parts of the soul that correspond to each grade are in the main repeated—that knowledge proper is only of an intelligible, eternal world while opinion is of an imperfect, impermanent visible world (more specifically, imagination corresponds to shadows and reflections or appearances; trust or opinion applies to things, namely artifacts, plants, animals; thought is of mathematical objects; intellection, the highest grade of knowledge, is of Forms, the highest grade of being). (I take the translation of the grades of knowledge and reality from Pappas, who mostly takes them from Alan Bloom's translation of *The Republic*.)

And the idea that the visible participates in, or imitates, the intelligible world again finds itself illustrated most vividly in the arts, in painting most plainly, where the arts are declared to be as it were doubly or hyper-imitative—the painting of a bed imitates a thing in the world which imitates, in order to be the imperfect thing it is, the Form or Idea of a bed. From which the argument against most poetry and painting follows. Put without elegance, but so as to remind you of the main premises: Art imitates appearance, not reality. Since reality is alone the object of knowledge, alone addresses itself to the rational, namely the highest part of the soul, art appeals to nonrational regions of the soul. The moral life, the just life, is the life presided over by reason, is the life of reason. In appealing to the irrational, art corrupts the soul, discourages its aspiration toward the summit of the soul and of being. Therefore art, or most of it, can have no role in a city in which the life of reason can be aspired to and achieved. Art, or most of it, is to be denied existence in the just city.

Plato's assumption of the just city's power to control the degree and character of the art that may flourish in it, as part of controlling the degree and content of the education to be provided to each of the three classes of its members that the highest and smallest class proves to itself to be appropriate for each, has caused some to regard *The Republic* as a precursor of modern totalitarianism. I don't myself find the comparison to be a particularly enlightening one, though it was something of a burning issue in the years after World War II, crystallizing in arguments around Karl Popper's portraits of Plato and Marx in *The Open Society and Its Enemies*. (It was an unforgettable part of my initiation into philosophy, in the late 1940s at UCLA, to hear Paul Friedlander, an admired commentator on Plato and a refugee from Hitler's Germany, end a class on the first book of *The Republic* by giving his testimony, I might say bearing witness, to his reading of Plato by saying—I seem to remember his very words—"I have the experience of teaching in a classroom beginning to be filled with youths in black shirts and boots, and I said to myself, 'I know this is not what Plato meant.'")

One reason I do not find it enlightening to examine whether Plato has designed a totalitarian society is that the examination too readily leads to an anachronistic discussion of censorship. The control of thought in a mass, technological society, like the tests for allegiance to it—let's say the possibilities and depths of privacy that have to be plumbed, and created—go beyond anything Plato's text can be thought to contemplate. What impresses me more forcibly, every time Book X of *The Republic* comes into discussion, is that we still do not have convincing accounts of the difference between education and indoctrination, and do not know on what basis we wish, for example, to shield children from movies, and, more intensely, television, more carefully than from, say, *Richard III* or *Macbeth;* and, perhaps most puzzlingly to me, why so many adults are incurious about what their own relations to movies and to television are, which can take up so many precious fragments of a life.

The most striking innovation in Book X is the introduction of the image of the immortality of the soul. It is an old Socratic topic, especially in those dialogues depicting Socrates' life and death. But the concluding Myth of Er, which presents an image of the rewards and punishments of life after death, seems to go against the drive of *The Republic,* which concerns the rewards and punishments of a just and unjust life within this one life. There might be various explanations of its presence at the end, ranging from the wish for a parting literary flourish to a desire to declare that nothing has been said in this text that is incompatible with belief in the immortality of the soul, thus adding a further, more popularly graspable, motivation for "holding to the upward path," as the concluding paragraph of the text summarizes the life of the just. But this is not the role assigned to other myths and images in *The Republic*—most notably the Myth of the Cave and the image of the Divided Line—which are rather taken as illustrating theses that are also the subject of philosophical argumentation within the text. This seems to me possible in the case of the Myth of Er.

I take my cue here from another observation of Pappas's, in which he is comparing *The Republic* to Aristophanic comedy: "The comedy's progress takes its protagonist from [an] enclosure in the earth to a new life outside it. Since . . . no narrative structure occurs as frequently in *The Republic* as does that of rebirth out of a cave, we have at least one literary reason to read Plato as an Aristophanic author." The Myth of Er, presenting a vision of metempsychosis, of the transmigration of souls, locates the place at which souls emerge up out of the earth, as well as down out of heaven, where they have spent a thousand years living, in tenfold measure, the consequences of an earlier stay on earth, now to choose again their next lives, or their chances in it, in the form of a choice among bodies strewn along the ground. I assume this is how we are to imagine "choosing a life" in the myth.

The choices detailed are, for example, of Orpheus—which is to say, "the soul that had once belonged to Orpheus"—"choosing a swan's life" and of a swan's choosing "to change over to a human life," of "Epeius, the son of Panopeus, taking on the nature of a craftswoman," of Atalanta choosing the life of a male athlete. (She is said to have been swayed by "[seeing] the great honors being given" to him. Perhaps we are vaguely to imagine that the lives are somehow played out before the released souls in quest of a new life, in some lapse of time; but in my sometime craving for the concrete, I cannot resist the sense of the life being as it were marked on the body, variously readable by souls in want of a body to belong to.) I do not see how the justice or injustice of our present lives makes us keener or poorer judges of our chances in reading and choosing life in a future body whose necessities and possibilities are unexperienced by us. But as an explanatory myth of our moral risks in our present body, that is in our present life (to leave this body is to leave this life), it seems a reasonably unvarnished cautionary tale.

It describes our relation to our body as one in which we have chosen it, meaning mythically that we are choosing our lives, chancing our souls, taking upon ourselves an unforeseeable field of responsibility, of responsibility for making ourselves intelligible, in each choice we make, or leave unmade. The readiness for one's life implied in such a vision does not strike me as exhaustible in ideas of calculating consequences (utilitarianism) or of universalizing a given principle of action (Kant) or in specifications of assignable consents (Rawls).

It is, in its present application, the idea of choice, or of an alteration of life, expressed as metempsychosis, that interests me more. Taking this feature of the Myth of Er as about our present life and as illustrating the totality and trauma of real change in the progress of the soul, each movement out of the Cave (turning, confusion, walking up, being dazzled, returning changed, that is, without returning to the same), or upward on the Divided Line, is to be thought of as coming to life, a further life, being reborn, a moment of metempsychosis, in which a soul, altered by life (618b: "The soul is inevitably altered by the different lives it chooses"), chooses its own (altered) body again, that is, assesses again its rewards and punishments.

I spoke a moment ago of the earlier books of *The Republic* as assessing rewards and punishments not in a future life but "in this one life." But seen as a series of unpredictable incarnations (where a mistaken choice may be repeated for an unlimited number of lifetimes), it is no longer clear that what we live is "one life" rather than a sequence of lives, as discontinuous as they are continuous. Like Er, we awake (each day) without knowing how we got here; unlike Er, we have (as Emerson reminds us) drunk somewhat too heavily from the water of Lethe, yet remembering enough to consider that we are already living a future life, reincarnating one past but open to one present, already possessed of the fact, if not the shape, of our immortality, such as it is. That we are the successors of ourselves (in our "journey from here to there and back again," 619e), and not necessarily succeeding in a given order or direction (but capable of choosing upward or downward or neither), is a reasonable figure of the perfectionist life, seizing crises of revelation, good or bad, clear or confused, as chances of transformation. A drawback of the figure is that it leaves us perhaps completely changed but with nothing visible or reportable that seems significant enough to have made the difference. Unless, remembering Plato's image of the human being within the human being—part of the construction of a man-like form molded seamlessly from a large lion and a small man together with a "multicolored beast with a ring of many heads that it can grow and change at will" (588c,d,e)—we can report that we have altered the number and gaze of one or other of the heads in that inner ring of heads, say moods.

Since metempsychosis, or transmigration of souls, or reincarnation, may seem something of a reach in this day and age, even as allegory, I might add that such ideas should be no harder to swallow imaginatively than Freud's ideas of psychic incorporation (as furthered in the work of Nicolas Abraham and Maria Torok, *The Wolf Man's Magic Word*), supplemented by recollecting the countless passages of our consciousness in which we recognize ourselves to be, for example, feeling a shame or grief not of our own as it were, but perhaps of our mother's or father's, or recognize ourselves as pronouncing a word in the voice or with the inflection, or take upon us for a moment the posture, of a friend or of an admired or a feared stranger. The necessity as well as the possibility of metempsychosis would then be prepared by the fact that we are already the subjects of souls to whose migration into us we have accommodated ourselves. So a critical moment of the myth of transmigration is the leaving of our body, ridding ourselves of an identity, a moment mentioned but not dramatized in Plato's myth, which simply assumes that after a thousand years the time comes for sloughing off existence, whatever form it may have taken, not considering whether we have left it with reluctance or relief. How souls come to inhabit us may be taken to be the subject of what is called our identification with others, actual or narrated or dramatized. Then it has been the focus of discussion in *The Republic,* and contested, recurrently since early in Book III, under the title of what Plato calls imitation.

It pleases me to add that the idea of metempsychosis within this life (as opposed to which one?) is taken with full gravity by the novelist thought by many to be the greatest of the twentieth century, Marcel Proust (though perhaps it could be shown to be a topic shared with James Joyce and with Thomas Mann), exemplified in such a passage as the following, from the last pages of volume 2 of *In Search of Lost Time:*

> But our knowledge of faces is not mathematical. It does not begin by measuring the parts, it takes as its starting point an expression, a sum total . . . Although expression may suffice to make us believe in enormous differences between things that are separated by infinitely little—although that infinitely little may by itself create an expression that is absolutely unique, an individuality—it was not only the infinitely little differences of its lines and the originality of its expression that made these faces appear irreducible to one another. Between my friends' faces their coloring established a separation wider still . . .
>
> On certain days, thin, with a gray complexion, a sullen air, a violet transparency slanting across her eyes such as we notice sometimes on the sea, [Albertine] seemed to be feeling the sorrows of exile . . . At other times, happiness bathed those cheeks with a radiance so mobile that the skin, grown fluid and vague, gave passage to a sort of subcutaneous glaze which made it

appear to be of another color but not of another substance than the eyes; sometimes, when one looked without thinking at her face punctuated with tiny brown marks among which floated what were simply two larger, bluer stains, it was as though one were looking at a goldfinch's egg, or perhaps at an opalescent agate cut and polished in two places only, where, at the heart of the brown stone, there shone, like the transparent wings of a sky-blue butterfly, the eyes, those features in which the flesh becomes a mirror and gives us the illusion of enabling us, more than through the other parts of the body, to approach the soul . . . Each of these Albertines was different . . . It was perhaps because they were so diverse, the persons whom I used to contemplate in her at this period, that later I developed the habit of becoming myself a different person, according to the particular Albertine to whom my thoughts had turned; a jealous, an indifferent, a voluptuous, a melancholy, a frenzied person, created anew not merely by the accident of the particular memory that had risen to the surface, but in proportion also to the strength of the belief that was lent to the support of one and the same memory by the varying manner in which I appreciated it. For this was the point to which I invariably had to return, to those beliefs which for most of the time occupy our souls unbeknown to us, but which for all that are of more importance to our happiness than is the person whom we see, for it is through them that we see him.

If it is the ability to take expression as a starting point in order "to approach the soul," meaning to become impressed by the infinitely little differences that separate this soul from all others, make it unique, that requires us to interest ourselves in such a thing as the transmigration of souls (that is, in bringing such a concept into the court of reason), then it should come as no surprise that many of us, lacking Proust's abilities for registering impressions, see no need, or have no interest, in such a project. But perhaps also as something of a surprise that this may imply a limitation in our interest in proving to ourselves the existence of others.

Plato

18

His Girl Friday

1 A camera moving leftward through the newsroom of a big city newspaper pauses at the opening doors of an elevator to discover a man and woman it then begins to accompany back in the direction from which it came. The woman, soon to be identified as Hildy (Rosalind Russell), in a defiantly smart hat, who seems to know where she is going, pauses to say hello at the switchboard, whose operators return her warm yet mildly sardonic greeting in kind, suggesting a shared past of civilized suffering, and revealing that she has been away for a while. She turns to the man accompanying her, Bruce (Ralph Bellamy), to ask him to wait while she briefly interviews her now former husband and boss Walter (Cary Grant), who is the paper's managing editor.

2 The camera continues to follow, or rather slightly lead her, down an aisle of "Hello, Hildy's" and bantering returns, into Walter's office, where the man himself (Hildy had asked the operators whether "the lord of the universe" is in) is primping in a mirror. In the fast and erotically tinged talk and backtalk between them, peppered with glancing reminiscences and recriminations, she eventually decides that the reason she stopped by to talk to him, on her way from divorcing him in Reno to setting off with her fiancé for home in Albany, is to tell him to stop sending her incessant telegrams attempting to change her mind. (If that's really what she wanted from him, she could have sent him a telegram.) When she, perhaps accidentally on purpose, lets it slip out that this new beau is waiting outside, Walter insists on meeting him.

3 Walter theatrically confuses Bruce with an old man also in the waiting area, then calls concerned and admiring attention to Bruce's thorough preparations against the possibility of inclement weather, and finishes by insisting on taking the pair to lunch. He affably motions them into a waiting elevator, and Hildy as she passes him says out of the corner of her mouth, "Won't do you a bit of good, Walter," to which Walter replies publicly, in his grandest good humor, "No, no, glad to do it."

4   At lunch Walter tries to trick Hildy into interviewing a prisoner, Earl Williams, falsely accused, for political reasons associated with an impending election, of deliberately murdering a policeman. He argues that Hildy could save the poor fellow's life by turning public opinion in his favor. Hildy starts getting interested in the journalistic possibilities, but then recognizes it as a trick of Walter's, who has someone else who could do the interview. Walter, conceding her point, levels with her, suggests a straight business proposition, and appeals to Bruce to take his side, emphasizing Hildy's special talent for this kind of writing. Hildy then makes a successful counter-proposition: Bruce sells insurance, and Hildy will do as Walter asks if Walter buys a very large life insurance policy from Bruce.

5   Hildy shows up in the pressroom of the Criminal Courts Building, explaining that she is taking a last assignment before quitting the miserable life of a newspaperman. She learns from her fellow reporters that Earl Williams is insane, but that the mayor and his creature the warden insist that he is fit for execution (the reporters point out that it was a black cop Earl chanced to shoot and that the black vote is large).

6   After an insurance company doctor has given Walter a physical in his office, Walter reminds Bruce to phone Hildy and tell her the certified check she has demanded for Bruce's commission is signed; Hildy, in response, antici-pating Walter's capacities, insists that Bruce, while Walter is out of the room, put the check in the lining of his hat. As Bruce leaves the office, Walter points him out to Louis, a shady combination of Ariel and Caliban, who fol-lows him.

7   In the Criminal Courts Building, Hildy bribes her way into the holding cell where Earl Williams awaits his fate. His first words to her are "I'm inno-cent." The interview consists in Hildy's leading him to the idea that the reason he fired the gun (which he had no sound reason to have or to shoot) was that, as he was passing his days sitting in the public park since losing his job of four-teen years, he had overheard one of the soapbox orators there speak of "pro-duction for use," and after all, the use of a gun is to shoot. Earl accepts the explanation with a show of genuine illumination. Hildy, depressed from her benevolent further confusing of a bewildered victim, leaves the death cell, wishing Earl good luck.

8   Molly Malloy, a distressed woman whose sympathy for Earl when she saw him wandering alone at night in the rain led her to take him back to her room, walks into the pressroom to accuse the newspapermen of heartlessness and distortion in reporting her and Earl as having a love nest. Hildy walks in

His Girl Friday

341

unobtrusively, sits down at her desk, and begins to type as she listens to Molly. The men further ridicule the woman (out of habit, but one understands as well, out of guilt), and Hildy comes over to protect her and leads her out of the pressroom, closing the door behind them.

9 The reporters walk aimlessly about the room, uncomfortable and silent. After a long moment, Hildy returns, pauses in the doorway to observe the scene, and comments, calmly and brutally, "Gentlemen of the press."

10a The phone rings for Hildy. It is Bruce, who tells her that he has been arrested for stealing a watch. Hildy rushes out to rescue him. His first words are "I'm innocent," which is no news to Hildy. She threatens the cop in the precinct with a story in the *Morning Post* if he doesn't release Bruce, who he knows didn't steal the watch they found planted on him. In the cab Hildy, making sure the check is still in Bruce's hat, asks him for his wallet, which he discovers, not to Hildy's surprise, is missing; Hildy had taken the precaution of demanding as they separated at the restaurant that he turn over all his cash to her, namely $500, which Bruce informed her is their entire savings. Arriving back at the Criminal Courts Building, Hildy tells Bruce to wait in the cab.

10b In the pressroom the reporters are listening with impressed concentration as one of their number reads from the interview left in Hildy's typewriter. The one reading observes, "Anyone who can write like that won't last three months in retirement. I'll give three-to-one odds on it." Hildy enters, taking him up on the bet. She phones Walter and tells him she wouldn't cover the burning of Rome for him if they were just lighting it up. She wants him to listen to the sound of her tearing up her interview with Earl Williams. ("I bargained to write it, I didn't bargain not to tear it up.") As she begins collecting her belongings, she launches into a farewell to the newspaper game.

11 In the warden's office, a psychiatrist is about to give Earl a final sanity test. The psychiatrist and the sheriff exchange pleasantries about the fearful annoyance of having to appear in the newspapers, and agree to share the lime-lit burden of the inevitable interview and photograph of themselves. The doctor darkens the room and directs the light of an enormous lamp into Earl's face, and Earl says, "I'm innocent."

12 As Hildy stands at the threshold of the pressroom, finishing her valedictory address to her comrades, machine-gun shots ring out and sirens go off everywhere. Someone shouts "Earl Williams escaped"; the other reporters rush out, leaving Hildy standing alone. She is dazed, then coming alive she rushes to the phone: "Get me Walter Burns, quick. Walter, Earl Williams has escaped. Don't worry, I'm on the job."

13 In the pandemonium outside the jail, Hildy tackles the jail guard she earlier bribed.

14 Reporter after reporter enters the pressroom, phoning to bring their papers up to the minute. By the time Hildy enters, it is empty again. She closes the door and phones Walter to tell him she's got the story of the escape exclusive. "The jailbreak of your dreams." The gun Williams used was the warden's, who gave it to him to reenact the killing. Hildy says it cost her $450 to get it, and it was Bruce's money, and he's waiting in a taxi for her. Walter puts his hand over the phone, asks Louis to take 450 counterfeit dollars to Hildy at the Criminal Court Building. At the same time, he dispatches Louis's brassy blonde girlfriend to encounter Bruce in a taxi parked outside that building. Walter assures Hildy that the money will be there in fifteen minutes.

15 As she waits, more reporters enter the pressroom with bits of news. The warden makes an appearance and is pressed by the reporters to confirm whether there really is, as he claims, a red menace. Bruce phones to tell Hildy that he is in jail again, this time for "mashing." As he begins describing the woman who entered the complaint, Hildy at once understands. She tells Bruce she can't leave right away. The mayor enters and the reporters ask whether the jailbreak will affect the election, a possibility that the mayor elaborately finds incredible. The warden announces excitedly that his rifle squad has located Earl; the reporters rush out to the scene.

16 The mayor and the warden go up to the warden's office, and as the former tells the latter that he's taking him off the election ticket, the door opens to reveal Mr. Pettibone, a large man in a bowler hat with an open umbrella—evidently a mythic messenger of some kind. He tells them he comes from the governor with a reprieve for Earl Williams. The mayor, aghast, looks at the document and reads aloud "on grounds of insanity." The phone rings, the warden picks it up and reveals that Earl Williams is surrounded. He asks the mayor what to do. The mayor hands the reprieve back to Mr. Pettibone and tells that perplexed personage that he never delivered it, promising him, as he nudges him out of the office, to give him a good-paying job and to fix his wife and to take care of his child's school problems. Then as he lights a cigar he says to the awaiting warden, "Shoot to kill"; the warden relays the message.

17 Louis shows up at the pressroom to give Hildy the 450 apparent dollars. She also demands Bruce's wallet, which Louis reluctantly produces. When instead of accepting his offer to take her to the train station Hildy further demands that he go down to the precinct and free Bruce, Louis, who wants nothing to do with police, runs away. Hildy picks up the phone and before she can finish a sentence, in a startled isolating shot, she slowly hangs up the receiver and stares at Earl Williams walking toward her, having just entered by a window. She tells him he doesn't want to kill anyone, and as he agrees a window shade suddenly snaps up behind him, which he wheels around and shoots at. He vacantly hands the gun to Hildy, who runs to lock the door and turn out the lights, since the shot will have given him away. He says he doesn't care any more. Hildy phones to tell Walter she needs him. Bruce calls on another phone and hears her tell Walter that she has Earl Williams. There is a knock on the door. Hildy cracks open the door. It is Molly, who is frantic that they are about to shoot Earl down. Hildy tries to send her away but Earl calls out to her not to leave. As soon as Molly is in the room, reporters knock and clamor at the door; the women hide Earl in the only large receptacle in the room, a rolltop desk. Hildy goes to the door and turns the lights back on before she unlocks and opens it.

18 Two reporters enter with questions, first of all one about what Molly is doing here. They, joined by the rest of the gang, phone their papers with the news that Earl was not found. They get to speculating about where Earl might be, for example, still right here in this building, and they become suspicious at Hildy's apparent encouragement for them to leave and search for him. Bruce's mother comes in looking for her son, saying she knows they have captured a criminal. The reporters turn on Hildy, who protests that the mother has misheard what was said. Molly, standing across the room near the windows, attracts their attention by crying out that she is the only one who knows where Earl is and now they'll never find out. Walter and Louis are shown to enter the room precisely as Molly leaps out of the window Earl had entered by, or one next to it. The reporters abandon Hildy to rush to the window, look down into the courtyard and learn that Molly is alive. The room clears except for Walter, Hildy, Louis, Bruce's mother, and Earl invisible inside the desk. Hildy wants to talk about Molly, but Walter insists on learning where she has Earl, which is why she sent for him. Walter directs Louis to take Bruce's mother and hide her somewhere. Louis introduces himself to the mother and in one gesture lifts her up and flings her over his shoulder, then disappears with her.

19 Hildy is beside herself. Walter talks sense into her by saying that this is a revolution, that her story will throw out a corrupt regime, that they will name streets after her and put statues of her in the parks, that she's stepped up into a new class (which really startles her). They start writing the story. Walter phones Duffy, his assistant editor, to tear out the front page, and to get hold of a group of wrestlers to carry a desk out of the pressroom.

20 Bruce shows up, having wired Albany for a hundred dollars to bail himself out. He asks where his mother is, and asks for his money. Hildy, to his surprise, hands him his wallet. Bruce pleads with Hildy to come with him for the life she's always wanted, while simultaneously Walter tries to get words in edgewise and otherwise to Duffy, intermittently telling him to stick Hitler in the funny papers, and later to leave the rooster story alone, "That's human interest." Bruce finally says he's leaving on the nine o'clock train and Hildy asks, gesturing to the story in her typewriter, "Can't you see this is the most important thing in my life?" Walter has also intermittently been on the phone with the wrestlers, who are delayed by difficult women in coming to get the desk.

21 Hildy remembers, painfully, that Bruce said he wasn't coming back. Louis enters completely disheveled, managing to relate that his car ran into a squad car of police racing down the wrong side of the street. He doesn't know what became of Bruce's mother; perhaps she's dead. They start calling hospitals; Hildy tries to leave but is pushed back by reporters entering along with the warden and assorted policemen. Walter orders the warden out of the pressroom; as Hildy tries to get away, the gun Earl handed to her falls out of her purse. The warden identifies it as his gun, hence the one Earl used to escape, to the delight of the reporters. The warden puts Walter under arrest.

22 Bruce's mother enters with more police and accuses Walter of kidnapping her. Walter denies that he has ever seen her, emphasizing his sincerity by rapping three times on Earl's hiding place and receiving three raps back from Earl. The warden is prepared to shoot through the desk, but Hildy prevails upon him to give Earl a chance to come out peacefully, which he does.

23 The room empties again, except for Walter, Hildy, a policeman who puts handcuffs on them and guards them, and the exultant warden, whom the mayor enters to congratulate. As the mayor and the warden gloat over their triumph, Mr. Pettibone, umbrella and all, appears again with the reprieve, saying that these two refused to take it earlier and tried to bribe him; he also makes obscure and dire references to his wife's attitude. The mayor and the warden express their unbounded, transparently profound, pleasure and relief in the reprieve of an innocent man, and Walter and Hildy in turn promise them ten years in jail when the *Morning Post* appears in a special edition.

His Girl Friday

24 In the opening sequence of the film, Hildy had accused Walter of reminiscing irrelevantly; now she reminisces about an earlier brush they had with the law, before they were married, the time they stole a courtroom exhibit of a stomach to prove foul play, and hid out in a hotel room where they—Hildy pauses, looking for the right words to suggest that that was when they entered on their adventures together. Walter reminds her that they could have gone to jail for that, too.

25 Walter suddenly becomes earnest, and says goodbye to Hildy, assuring her that a wire from her will bring Bruce happily to meet her at the station in Albany. She protests that she has to finish the story, and Walter tells her he'll write it himself, though it won't be half as good. He explains that he had been jealous and sore that Bruce could offer her the kind of life he could never give her. One last time the phone rings and again it proves to be Bruce under arrest, this time accused of passing counterfeit money. Bruce tells Hildy that it was she who gave it to him. She hangs up and begins sobbing. (We hear music arising for the first time.) Walter seems genuinely alarmed, calling her Honey and saying she's never cried before. She blubbers out that she thought Walter was sincere this time, that he was going to let her go without doing anything to stop her, that she didn't know he had Bruce in jail again, that she thought he didn't love her any more. "What were you thinking with?" is Walter's answer to this amazing outburst. So she, recovering, tells him to send down some honest money to the jail to bail out Bruce, and Walter, merry again, phones back Duffy to tell him not to do anything, that Hildy is staying to write the story, that she never meant to leave. And when he says they're getting married and, consulting Hildy, says it's to be in Niagara Falls, he is asked by Duffy to cover a strike in Albany, which is after all on the way to Niagara Falls, and, again consulting Hildy, Walter agrees. The two exit walking fast, him first, her holding the bags.

I might note at the outset that Walter's order to Duffy to tear out the front page, that Hildy is staying, is an allusion to the play *The Front Page,* from which Howard Hawks and his writer Charles Lederer have torn the original role that became our Hildy, making what was originally a man's into a woman's part. I confess that I found the remake of the film, called *The Front Page,* which keeps the male Hildy role intact, steeped as I was in the Hawks transfiguration, to be largely flat, however expertly acted by Jack Lemmon and Walter Matthau. Of course it could be of great interest to track the endless consequences of such a difference (no doubt as part of tracking the relation of each of our films to their sources, in plays or novels or stories); but I do not foresee an interest in me to do this with the systematicity that would make it worthwhile. I merely caution you that what I take up here about these matters is a response solely to the Howard Hawks film with Rosalind Russell and Cary Grant.

I have gone on with my summary of the film at greater length than in other cases, finding as I proceeded that it was particularly hard to recall in enough detail to justify anything I would be likely to want to emphasize. I have viewed the films discussed in this book enough times to trust myself to give a reasonable summary of each of them from memory, occasionally prompted by my notes. But in the case of *His Girl Friday* I found I could not manage the account after a certain point unaided by another viewing. This became interesting to me. The opening two sequences, after the prologue, namely Hildy's return to Walter in his office and the subsequent lunch at Walter and Hildy's familiar restaurant, their home away from home (Walter's office being another such home), were no problem. Each was a substantial conversation about a particular issue, Hildy's engagement to Bruce be married in the former, Walter's proposal of the interview in the latter; the issue in each case is broached, discussed, and a conclusion arrived at. This roughly continues to be the pattern through Walter's insurance physical examination and Hildy's interview with Earl Williams. But about now, with Hildy's return to the pressroom and Molly's rebuking of the male reporters, things change, the world seems to change. This perhaps comes to a climax after the sirens go off and Hildy is drawn to forget about her farewell to Walter and to their escapades in facing down the mischief of the world. From now on no single issue is in focus, no conversation develops and achieves a decision, anything can happen, nothing can be made to happen.

I began to find that I could not remember exactly the times Bruce phoned to say he was in jail, nor precisely when and how his mother happened to be in the pressroom just when she was needed, nor, for example, how Hildy happened to have both Bruce's wallet and the 450 counterfeit dollars in it ready just in time to hand to Bruce when he appeared (who had bailed him out of jail?). And just when do we cut away to the warden's office for the sanity test, and again later when Mr. Pettibone enters? Any misplacement of one of these pieces blocks out the fit of another. This surely is essential in accounting for the fundamental fact of generic difference of *His Girl Friday* from its fellow members in the genre of remarriage comedy.

We can characterize the difference in the new setting by noting that the image of a Shakespearean green world (the Connecticut of most of the other members of the genre) is here replaced by a black world, identified with the chaotic, dangerous state of nature as described by Locke in his *Second Treatise of Government* and by Hobbes in *The Leviathan,* two of the three classical, most famous, sources (along with Rousseau's *The Social Contract*) of the social contract theory of the legitimacy of government. Walter says to Hildy that they are in a revolution. Revolution is an essential topic of classical contract theory, as is the question of how the state of revolution is recognized and who is entitled to declare that such a state obtains. That Walter says this to Hildy in private, and in a fantastic set of declarations about her once-in-a-lifetime chance to wipe out corruption, is a parody marking the grave fact that a genuine, deep problem for the contract theorists is posed by this matter of recognizing when a government is no longer intact or has broken faith with its charter. This is part of a larger register of conceptual farce running through the language of the film.

As is not unique to this film within the works of Howard Hawks, one finds various broad allusions to a fascination with the human behind. (I think immediately of the sequence of double entendres in *Bringing Up Baby,* Hawks's film of some four years earlier.) In *His Girl Friday* I recall four verbal allusions to this region of human anatomy: (1) "Stick it in the classified ads"; (2) "Earl Williams is hiding under her piazza" "Tell her to stand up"; (3) "What was the name of the mayor's sister?" "You mean the one with the wart on her—?" "Yes," "—Fanny"; (4) "Hildy, you're stepping up into a new class!" "Huh?" Without being overly pedantic about this, one is entitled to some curiosity over its insistence. I confess that it took a while for me to register the significance of Hildy's abrupt "Huh?," although Walter's reference to class contains the allusion literally. The first three allusions are blatant vaudeville. The last is just between Hildy and Walter—perhaps a reference to whatever went on in their early cohabitation in a hotel room that they could have gone to jail for.

The point I would like to formulate here is not of some hidden meaning but rather of a general implication of unsurveyable interaction between the political and the erotic (or, if you prefer, the psychological), or the chaotic public and the illegitimate private. That finding the political fugitive Earl

Williams should be a matter of (or analogous to) finding something lost in our confusion over what our anatomy hides, and reveals, and of whether that confusion is in particular something natural or social, suggests that the state of nature is one not only essentially pre-political but pre-human, something occurring before the flowering of human sexuality. Here the ancient insight of Aristotle of language as the condition of the political joins the insight of Freud (elaborated by Lacan) of human desire as a (an unfinished) social (or say joint) construction, or reconstitution, of human desire out of biological need, of language as reaching in its expressiveness to the depths of individual construction and reconstitution. And that Hildy should become convinced of her vocation ("Hildy, this isn't a story, it's a career!"), a step into her further self, by understanding Walter's saying "You're moving up to a new class!" as a step into (erotic) freedom, suggests that she perceives in that "Huh?"—as if she has been punched into insight—that her desire for ridding the world of political corruption is at the same time her desire for sexual liberation. But what then are the terms of that liberation?

Let us take the moment in which Hildy is transfixed by the gunshots and sirens expressing Earl Williams's escape, as she is abandoned in the pressroom, as her recognition that she too is a victim of circumstances, in need of escape, and that Walter is key to that condition, to why she is in that place, at that moment—perhaps not to discover that she can choose to leave but perhaps that she is free to choose to stay. To do what?

Here I am remembering the film from its ending, taking what is discovered there as epitomizing the pair's perfectionist quest. Weighing the ending of each of the films of both of our genres is something one learns to be as important as pondering the conclusion of a poem. How can this possibly be? Can there be something to call a popular genre of film having such power that those creating within it, who learn to give all they can to the genre, can be taken beyond their expected strengths? For example, notice that, for all the supposed knowledge of the "happy end" of Hollywood comedies, none of the comedies of remarriage ends with an unequivocal kiss. Either the embrace is invisible (a door closed in our faces) or else the embrace is compromised (by visible awkwardness, physical or psychological), or, as in the present case, postponed, out of a certainty that there will soon enough be time and place for it.

What Hildy achieves at the end is Walter's affirmation of his love for her (as direct as such a thing can be from Walter: "What were you thinking with?"); what Walter achieves is her recognition (a recognition as willing as she can make it, given its cost) that he cannot give her the life she wanted from Bruce (admitted by Walter without denying that the want was, is, genuine). What I called, in my summary, Hildy's amazing outburst, through her sobbing, namely her declaration that she thought he was going to let her go without doing anything to stop her, seems to make explicit her nearly insatiable need, no doubt required by the very way Walter satisfies it, for proof that he will continue to go to any lengths to keep her with him, and keep her interested. The entire narrative of the events of this film can be taken as a wedding ceremony, Walter's answer to Hildy's opening announcement to him—invitation, one might rather say—implied in her informing him that she is divorced and is getting remarried and that Walter must stop trying to stop her. How can she doubt that he has been doing nothing but accepting the implied invitation to stop her? Her tears show her relief in knowing that he knows it. Divorce may be, as Walter tells her from the beginning, "just some words mumbled over you by a judge." Marriage is not.

Why pair *His Girl Friday* with Plato's *Republic*? We should hardly expect any film, or set of films, or set of any imaginative works, to exhaust a text which, as much as any, founds the aspirations of philosophy. And, as I had occasion to suggest in taking up Plato's text, its Myth of the Cave, so uncannily prophetic of the technology of motion picture projection, is alone enough to justify pairing it with any film. But we can be a little more specific.

The black world of this film not merely takes the place of the green world as the source of what insight is available to the human mind in certain of its straits, but occupies the bulk of the film after its not insubstantial beginning in the worldly bustle of a big city. And while we see the pair making a certain exit from that world, we see no more of a different world; we have moved deeper into the same world, or say into the conditions of that world. There is no obvious way to get to the green world; there is no obvious way to leave the black world.

In Plato's description of the stages of devolution of the human city (from aristocracy to timocracy, to democracy, to tyranny), each creates the souls to match it. In the good city, Plato's city of words, fit for philosophy, there are, over the mass of members any city is made of, a smaller class of educated guardians, and, out of them, a small class of philosopher-rulers. Each class has its virtues and its capacities for knowledge. The knowledge contained in newspapers, the highest knowledge attainable in the black world, far from philosophical knowledge, is yet better than the illusions of the everyday that chain one into fixations of irreality in Plato's cave. Newspapers recognize the irreality of our condition, if not an alternative reality, and that itself unfixes the chains, the first "step into a new class" as Walter puts it, the first impulse of perfection.

A democracy must not contain a separate, privileged class to guard the city; for each member of the democratic city, it is his or hers to guard. Those who consider themselves a class of guardians, privileged to take the lead, will not recognize the good which should reign over the common life, but will, pursuing the only good they know, and in ignorance of the very concept of the common good, put their own stamp of private power on the city. In the black world the fantasy of being jointly guided by justice as fairness cannot be assumed; it is to be awakened.

Those inclined to a step of freedom in their lives enter the cave not to save its (other) victims, but to root out the false benefactors the mass of victims attracts. A moment of reprieve is the best you can hope to offer others. Whether they will accept it as the chance for self-liberation is not up to you. A black world, like any world according to Plato, creates its own virtues. The virtues required for the limited good you can do in a black world (all the world we know there is) are, as divined by this film, for example, deviousness, charm, wit in the face of danger, a knowledge of what is of human interest, the appeal to others through sentiments you may not be in a position to authenticate, hardness in the face of desperation you cannot alleviate, a dangerous addiction to freedom, and an immunity to flattery and other bribes. (Are these virtues? Vices?)

Call this a picture of comic stoicism. It is a life that can call upon the mysterious unseen powers beyond oneself, presenting itself to a benevolent judgment that takes pity upon, even sees the justice in, at least the necessity of, our transient insanities. While it is not a life (or a world) that has much interested moral philosophers, it seems to form the stock-in-trade of such observers of the human spectacle as Montaigne, Pascal, and Nietzsche in his aphorisms.

19

ARISTOTLE

With Aristotle, Plato's pupil, we have the only other philosopher to rank in the founding of Western thought, and in influence upon it to this day, with Plato himself. The editor of the *Cambridge Companion to Aristotle*, Jonathan Barnes, in his Introduction to the volume, puts Plato's influence second to Aristotle's, and adds: "Plato's philosophical views are mostly false, and for the most part they are evidently false; his arguments are mostly bad, and for the most part they are evidently bad." I don't suppose these are meant as reasons for putting him second in world influence. Sufficient and evident reasons for putting Aristotle first are, I suppose, his influence on Catholic philosophy and theology and the fact that his arguments in science were so far from being evidently bad that they were still what had to be contended with two thousand years after they were advanced, in establishing the Copernican-Galilean-Newtonian New Science at the turn of the sixteenth into the seventeenth century. And yet I have found pleasure in going back to a text of Plato's that I have often missed in Aristotle, whom I am used to reading, to the extent that I have read him, out of dutifulness.

Of course one must read Aristotle's *Nichomachean Ethics* in a course on moral perfectionism. Who could put the general issue of perfectionism more strongly, or with deeper reference to what is central in philosophizing at large, than Aristotle's saying: "We are in so far as we are actualized, since we are in so far as we live and act"? Actuality is contrasted in Aristotle with potentiality, and the power to be attracted to a further self, or state of the self, is what perfectionism's idea of the journey motivated by dissatisfaction with one's present condition of unchosen or unnecessary restriction depends upon. Heidegger's working out of human existence, in *Being and Time*, as essentially characterized by possibilities (not by properties, as objects are) whose actualization as *my* possibilities is manifested in my claiming my authenticity from what he calls the everyday (a derivative of Emerson's conformity), seems an inheritance from Aristotle. It might itself be a point in understanding Heidegger's advice to study Aristotle for sixteen years before beginning to philosophize on one's own.

But this time, returning to the *Nichomachean Ethics* has been different for me, leading to a less forced absorption in its progress than I have hitherto experienced. Such a good encounter may happen at any time, and one is always glad for it; but there is, I realize, a particular reason behind this new appreciation. I attribute it to my having in recent years been variously led to reengage the writing of my teacher J. L. Austin, on several issues. One of the most significant issues for me was one I mentioned in the chapter on Plato, when I invoked Austin in connection with taking the Myth of the Cave as opening with a scene of the ordinary, in which we find that we do not know what we are saying. And I went on to speak of our unsurveyable exposure to the world and to language, to the necessary vulnerability of our language, as revealed in what both Freud and Austin call "slips." The consequences Freud and Austin find in this human vulnerability are different (in some ways opposite, since for Austin the significance of a slip is to reduce an act's intentionality, for Freud to expand it); but for each thinker the result is peculiarly revelatory of their respective procedures.

Austin's study of slips is recorded, or summarized, in his paper "A Plea for Excuses," where he attributes his interest (and inspiration) in pursuing the topic, call it the topic of responsibility, to Aristotle, or rather to his sensing that Aristotle's critics were wrong in thinking that, in speaking of the various ways in which we cannot be held responsible for an action, Aristotle was avoiding the issue of saying what responsibility *is*. A certain relation of Austin's "Excuses" to the *Nichomachean Ethics* is obvious enough when we compare certain passages. Consider these two from *Nichomachean Ethics:*

> Virtue, then, is about feelings and actions. These receive praise or blame when they are voluntary, but pardon, sometimes, even pity, when they are involuntary. . . . What comes about by force or because of ignorance seems to be involuntary. What is forced has an external origin, the sort of origin in which the agent or victim contributes nothing—if, e.g., a wind or human beings who control him were to carry him off. (1110a)

> For the cause of involuntary action is not ignorance in the decision, which causes vice; it is not [in other words] ignorance of the universal, since that is a cause for blame. Rather, the cause is ignorance of the particulars which the

action consists in and is concerned with; for these allow both pity and pardon [excuse], since an agent acts involuntarily if he is ignorant of one of these particulars. [To adapt an example from Austin: it is blameworthy not to know the universal that it is wrong to shoot your neighbor's harmless donkey; but it is pardonable, or pitiable, at least to some degree, to have shot the donkey by accident or by mistake.] Presumably, then, it is not a bad idea to define these particulars, and say what they are, and how many. They are: (1) who is doing it; (2) what he is doing; (3) about what or to what he is doing it; (4) sometimes also what he is doing it with, e.g., the instrument; (5) for what result, e.g., safety; (6) in what way, i.e., gently or hard. Now certainly someone could not be ignorant of all of these unless he were mad. (1111a)

And compare them with this passage from Austin's "Excuses":

When are "excuses" proffered? In general the situation is one where someone is *accused* of having done something . . . which is bad, wrong, inept, unwelcome, or in some other of the numerous possible ways untoward. [The topic concerns blame, not praise.] Thereupon he, or someone . . . will try to defend his conduct or to get him out of it. [In the latter case, you] admit that it wasn't a good thing to have done, but . . . argue that it is not quite fair or correct to say *baldly* "X did A." We may say it isn't fair just to say X did it; perhaps he was under somebody's influence, or was nudged ["e.g., a wind or human beings who control him carried him off"]. Or, it isn't fair to say baldly he *did* A; it may have been partly accidental, or an unintentional slip. Or, it isn't fair to say he did simply A—he was really doing something quite different . . . Naturally these arguments can be combined or overlap or run into each other.

Aristotle's discussion of the involuntary, and of incontinence, constitutes his answer to a central doctrine of Socrates', that virtue is knowledge, that you cannot knowingly do wrong; whereas it is Aristotle's view that virtue is doing what is right in the right way and at the right time and place and to the right person and in the right way, "and so on." The moral of which is, as Aristotle summarizes it (1144b), "In that [Socrates] thought all the virtues are [instances of] intelligence, he was in error; but in that he thought they all require intelligence, he was right." (Or, put otherwise, we in a way know and in a way do not know what is right when, to our dismay, we do what is wrong.) Austin's very silence on this point indicates to me that he finds Aristotle's reply to Socrates to be definitive.

But Austin's relation to Aristotle is more extensive. I hear it in the justification Austin offers for pursuing the topic of excuses. "In ethics we study, I suppose, the good and the bad, the right and the wrong, and this must be for the most part in some connection with conduct or the doing of actions. Yet before we consider what actions are good or bad, right or wrong, it is proper to consider first what is meant by, and what not, and what is included under, and what not, the expression 'doing an action' or 'doing something.'" I relate this emphasis on the priority of acting, acting as such, to the claim of Aristotle's I cited as an epitome of perfectionism: "We are in so far as we are actualized, since we are in so far as we live and act" (1168a). The relation I see is not, clearly, that Austin shares Aristotle's metaphysics of potentiality and actuality, but simply that he is responding to, and agreeing with, something in Aristotle's emphasis on acting and is seeking to find his own sense of what makes it important in what Aristotle, at the close of *Nichomachean Ethics*, speaks of as "the philosophy of human affairs."

This is, what is more, roughly how I think one should understand Aristotle's reply to Socrates on knowledge and virtue. Nowadays it is almost inevitable to think of it as the refutation of an argument. But if philosophy may be thought of as, let me say, the critique of importance—a contesting of what the world, or any of its inhabitants, takes to be, as Wittgenstein phrases the matter, "great and important" (call this the world's values)— then I would rather say that Aristotle's reply is meant to preserve what he finds important in Socrates' claim, namely something about the internality of the relation of intelligence and acting well, call this doing what is called for. I do not have to claim that preserving what matters, what is of genuine interest, is more important than refuting what is false, or overstated, or misdirected. But to leave what is to be preserved unstressed leaves out something essential in what I crave from philosophical exchange, including the exchange of philosophy with its history.

The connection of Austin with Aristotle is more extensive than this suggests. Methodologically Aristotle is forever noting what is and is not said. Sometimes this refers to his collecting common, often conflicting, opinions about ethical matters. Sometimes it retells an adage or proverb ("Call no man happy until he is dead.") Sometimes it tells what something is. ("If someone returned a deposit unwillingly and because of fear [or under compulsion], we should say that he neither does anything just nor does justice, except coincidentally" (1135b). I suppose that Aristotle, instead of appealing to what we should say, could have said the same in the form: To return a deposit unwillingly, out of fear or compulsion, is not to act justly; it is a coincidence that it is just. Austin works in a register that permits him to shift from language to reality at any time. I do not say that Aristotle is therefore an ordinary language philosopher. I say that Austin has preserved, by purifying and systematizing, something whose importance he can be imagined to have learned from his study of Aristotle. To get this relation right would be, to my mind, a contribution to (not, maybe, what we might call the history of philosophy, but to) the history of how a philosopher responds to, even creates, his or her history. That this is not always the way philosophy continues is irrelevant. That it happens at all is cause enough for wonder. And it has a further effect. Not only does it illuminate a present philosopher's work. It may heighten something that makes us look harder at the past, as though it unpredictably awaits actualization. We'll come back to this.

Before leaving Austin I cannot forbear remarking on something more precisely in his relation to Aristotle. I reported that Austin's interest in the topic of excuses began with his sense that Aristotle's critics were wrong about the significance of Aristotle's work on responsibility. What Austin actually says is that he came to his interest when he began "to see the injustice of this charge." The idea of an injustice of speech repeats something Austin says in his opening paragraph, in recommending the subject of excuses to philosophy, namely that he "owes it to the subject to say" that it has provided him with "the fun of discovery, the pleasures of co-operation, and the satisfaction of reaching agreement," which philosophy had so often been made barren of for him.

Can we imagine that Austin fails to recognize that the idea of the injustice of speech, or of the *owing of words*, is precisely the topic of the way he conceives the subject of excuses, namely as matter of what it is "fair to say" and "not fair just to say"? I would say, moreover, that the justice of speech is the preoccupation of Austin's philosophizing throughout, in general and in particular. (I wish the title of what came to be called "ordinary language philosophy" had been one that recognized that the justice of speech was its subject.)

I have suggested that the justice of speech can be taken as the method and goal of Aristotle's philosophizing as well, at least in the *Nichomachean Ethics*. This would be important enough, since that text ends by indicating that it is to be continued in Aristotle's *Politics*, with its early emphasis on the possession of language as the condition of the association of human beings in a polis. The implication of what I have been saying here is that the discovery of standing possibilities of injustice in our descriptions of our lives together threatens the conditions of that association. Errors in our view of the relation of knowledge to virtue can have drastic consequences in our view of what laws should be adopted, for example in what provisions there will be for mitigation by excuses.

Let's move toward the text of the *Nichomachean Ethics* a little more systematically. As general orientation I point to the obvious ways in which its perspective differs from both utilitarianism and Kantianism. In comparison with utilitarianism, Aristotle emphasizes myself, this individual, the development of my character, as the touchstone of goodness and rightness—so forcefully and continuously that some have found his theory to be an ethics of selfishness, not a *morality* at all, a theory in which the welfare of *others* counts only derivatively. (This is surely a reason Rawls classifies Aristotle as a moral perfectionist, though of course in a form as reasonable as possible, in contrast with Nietzsche's cultivation of heavy paradox.) But then Kant, in comparison with utilitarianism, focuses on my individual motive for conduct, in determining the application to it of an a priori, universal principle. Here the contrast is with Aristotle's focus on the individual circumstances—discriminating the correct time and place of the action, its proper object (that is, the person to whom it is directed), and manner, and so on. Here it is the exercise of my perception of a situation—not an intellectual grasp of necessity, but an empirical judgment, an a posteriori cognition, of practical intelligence, of course one that has been educated in a certain way—that determines the course I shall take.

For our purposes here, two of Aristotle's characteristic concepts, or doctrines, are paramount—that of happiness and that of friendship.

The title of my book *Pursuits of Happiness* comes, of course, from America's Declaration of Independence. But it is meant as well to allude to happiness as presented in moral philosophy, and perhaps first of all in the *Nichomachean Ethics*—not exactly because of Aristotle's particular doctrines (though his discussions of the role of pleasure in happiness go beyond the treatment of the subject, in their subtlety and patience, in any other of the incontestably philosophical texts discussed in this book), but because the idea of happiness is more famously examined in his text than of the others in view here—and these are a fair sample of the landmark texts of the field.

I recall for you the opening of *Nichomachean Ethics*—or rather, the recapitulation and extension of the opening on its third page (in the scholarly numbering, 1095a):

> Since every sort of knowledge and decision pursues some good, what is that good which we say is the aim of political science [of which ethics is the first half; Aristotle's *Politics* represents the second half]? What [in other words] is the highest of all the goods pursued in action? As far as its name goes, most people virtually agree [about what the good is], since both the many and the cultivated call it happiness, and suppose that living well and doing well are the same as being happy. But they disagree about what happiness is, and the many do not give the same answer as the wise.
>
> For the many think it is something obvious and evident, e.g., pleasure, wealth or honor . . . in sickness he thinks it is health, in poverty wealth. And when they are conscious of their own ignorance, they admire anyone who speaks of something grand and beyond them.
>
> [And here Aristotle takes a crack at Plato's Idea of the Good as the highest point on the journey out of the Cave:][Among the wise,] some used to think that besides these many goods there is some other good that is something in itself, and also causes all these goods to be goods.

This sets the stage for the rest of Book I, and in fact for what happens through Book VII of the ten books of the *Nichomachean Ethics*. Since for us it is the concluding three books of Aristotle's text that are most pertinent, I shall trust that I have said enough generally in locating a certain texture in Aristotle's procedures to encourage you through its earlier books if I now simply in effect remind you of their progress and then spend the bulk of this chapter considering the last three books. Let me alert you to how this goes.

At 1095b: "But let us begin again from [the common beliefs] . . . For, it would seem, people quite reasonably reach their conception of the good, i.e., of happiness, from the lives [they lead]; for there are roughly three most favored lives—the lives of gratification, or political activity, and third, of study." At 1096a: "We had better examine the universal good, and puzzle out what is meant in speaking of it. This sort of inquiry is, to be sure, unwelcome to us, when those who introduced the Forms were friends of ours; still, it presumably seems better, indeed only right, to destroy even what is close to us if that is the way to preserve the truth. And we must especially do this when we are philosophers; for though we love both the truth and our friends, piety requires us to honor the truth first . . . There is no common Idea over [all the ways good is spoken of]." At 1096b: "Moreover, Good Itself will be no more of a good by being eternal; for a white thing is no whiter if it lasts a long time than if it lasts a day." This seems simply to be a one-line rejection of the heart of Plato's vision of the transcendental realm of Ideas or Forms, hence of the imperfection and imitation of perfection in our actual realm of existence.

But let's continue. Still at 1096b: "Even if the good predicated in common is some single thing, or something separated, itself in itself, clearly it is not the sort of good a human being can pursue in action or possess; but that is just the sort we are looking for in our present inquiry." This concessive remark, "*even* if the good [is] predicated in common" refers back to Aristotle's argument at 1096a: "Good is spoken of in as many ways as being is spoken of. For it is spoken of in the category of what-it-is, as god and mind; in quality, as the virtues, in quantity, as the measured amount; in place, as the [right] situation; and so on. Hence it is clear that the good cannot be some common [nature of good things] that is universal and single." This sentence expresses a sensibility cut from the same cloth that composed the one following of Austin's, from his *Sense and Sensibilia:* "Many philosophers, failing to detect any ordinary quality common to real ducks, real cream, and real progress, have decided that Reality must be an *a priori* concept apprehended by reason alone." I may not have liked, or like, the implication Austin draws that philosophers are merely wily or drunken, or something, in their quests, but I knew, reading that sentence of his, that so far he had me there.

Back to Aristotle's Book I. At 1097b: "Well, perhaps we shall find the best good if we first find the function of a human being. For just as the good, i.e., [doing] well, for a flautist, a sculptor, and every craftsman, and, in general, for whatever has a function, seems to depend on its function, the same seems to be true for a human being, if a human being has some function . . . What, then, could this be?" Ruling out mere life, shared with plants and animals, and the life of sense-perception, Aristotle goes on at 1098a: "The remaining possibility, then, is [that the human function] is some sort of life of action of the [part of the soul] that has reason." Then follows a proof ending this way: "Each function is completed well when its completion expresses the proper virtue. Therefore the human good turns out to be the soul's activity that expresses virtue."

Aristotle

359

We are almost at the goal of locating happiness. At 1100b: "It is the activities expressing virtue that control happiness, and the contrary activities that control its contrary [neither of which are accordingly controlled by fortune]." "This conclusion agrees with our opening remarks. For we took the goal of political science to be the best good; and most of its attention is devoted to the character of the citizens, to make them good people who do fine actions [which is reasonable if happiness depends on virtue, not on fortune]." And finally, at 1102a: "Since happiness is an activity of the soul expressing complete virtue, we must examine virtue; for that will perhaps also be a way to study happiness better." We have reached the concluding paragraphs of Book I, which launch us into the subject of virtue, the subject of the bulk of *Nichomachean Ethics*.

Book II takes up one of the two main branches of virtue, the virtues of character (for example, of temperance and bravery), introducing them with the famous definition of virtue as the mean between extremes; Book III deals with the preconditions of virtue (such as that virtuous action be voluntary); Book IV takes up other individual virtues (generosity, magnanimity, mildness, truthfulness, wit, shame); Book V is devoted to justice as a virtue; then in Book VI comes the other main branch of virtue, virtues of thought (expressed in scientific knowledge, craft knowledge, intelligence, understanding, wisdom, deliberation, consideration); Book VII deals with two main issues, the problem of continence (hence further into Socrates' proposal that to know the good is to do the good) and the role of pleasure in the good. Then Books VIII and IX move, with questionable preparation, to the topic of friendship. The concluding Book X recapitulates earlier material but then veers off, so many readers have felt, in ways incompatible with what has gone before (in that respect not unlike Book X of *The Republic*).

The material on virtue could easily fill a book. Let me, bearing in mind the goal of relating our texts in moral thinking to our genres of film, add a few further thoughts on happiness and then turn to the all-important topic (for the remarriage comedies) of friendship.

In the Declaration of Independence human happiness is announced, along with life and liberty, as a revolutionary goal, a revolutionary emotion one could say, the drastic loss of which potentially (on Locke's grounds) is justification for the overthrow of a government—it is a state of the loss of political life and liberty within which happiness could be pursued. I do not, that is, take "life, liberty, and the pursuit of happiness" to be mentioning two public goods (life and liberty) and one private good (happiness), but three public goods, three dimensions of our communal lives, the (threatened) loss of any one of which is a state of things amounting to political despair. (What constitutes the difference between political and private relationships is not an issue for Aristotle as it is for us. For Aristotle, every thing, and every one, has its and his or her natural place, and seeks that place.) In Aristotle happiness is not a revolutionary goal; different grades of it are fit for different grades of human beings; so far as we are alive and active, we pursue happiness, an inevitable and respectable condition.

Far from implying that I wholly agree with Aristotle's view of things, my title's allusion to his work is as much a rebuke as it is an homage. Remember his saying: "They [we human beings] disagree about what happiness is, and the many do not give the same answer as the wise." Thinking of the pairs in remarriage comedy, I ask: Are they among the wise or among the many? The fact that they are happy, or happy enough, and acceptably so, by the many *and* the wise, is something essential in my admiration of them; something that seemed to me at first, and now, to warrant study. Well, what *is* the basis of the pair's happiness in remarriage comedy? Is it, to take Aristotle's alternatives, "something obvious and evident, e.g., pleasure, wealth, or honor" or "something in itself [that] causes all these goods to be goods"?

My suggestion in *Pursuits of Happiness* is that they are committed to finding "happiness without a concept." This idea is an adaptation of a rhetorical discovery of Kant's in his *Critique of* (aesthetic) *Judgment,* in which he calls the particular pleasure yielded by the experience of art "pleasure without a concept." What this means, intuitively, is that pleasure in an object is not a determinate property of a work of art, like its size or color, but is something *to be* determined by the kind of analysis of an object we expect of criticism; determining it is a task, of description, of connection.

"Happiness without a concept" means to me, beyond this, that the pair who find themselves happy in one another are engaged in a conceptual as well as, let me say, an experimental journey. What is to be called marriage is, in irreducible part, an intellectual undertaking—a certain demand for understanding, a certain willingness to press for an understanding of the conditions of that understanding. In this process, the thing happens that Mill describes as "looking up to each other" and that Aristotle, and Emerson

Aristotle
361

in his way, describe as taking the good person as the measure of goodness, one in whom what the good is, in practice, is recognized.

Here is the cause of the emphasis on conversation in these films. Aristotle's topic of defining the good does not loom large in Emersonian perfectionism as manifested in remarriage comedy. The conversation decides. The conversation is it. What is it?

The emphasis on the pair's learning what living together can be challenges what seems to be a necessary assumption of the moral life made by Kantians and by utilitarians, that in a case in which a decision is to be made, or you are stopped to question yourself, there is one right thing, the best thing, to do, and that this is discoverable (by calculation or by formulation of a maxim that is universalizable—our dominant forms of moral reasoning). I suppose this is pertinent where the relationship is adversarial. But it seems not to be where the state of the relationship is itself the measure of the good.

Aristotle speaks of friendship in its highest form as the desire to live together, by which, as commentators suggest, he means not necessarily living under the same roof but something like spending time together. My formulation for this has been to say that for the pairs of our comedies what they do together is less important to them than the fact that it is together that they do it. (This can be abused. One isn't thinking of the Macbeths as models here, or Bonnie and Clyde. The latter have made up their minds what it is worth doing together, what keeps them together; it is what they call robbing banks. The Macbeths have never asked themselves what it is worth doing together, only what the other expects them to do together; and they know soon enough that they have killed sleep. I do not expect moral reasoning of any kind to be of interest to those who have killed sleep.)

Then let us turn our attention to Aristotle's treatment of friendship, a topic that plays a larger role in his thinking about human affairs than, apparently, in that of any of the other moral thinkers we have taken up. Indeed, in utilitarianism and Kantianism, how could it be anything but corrupt, unethical, to allow the relationship to a friend to influence one's calculation of the greatest good of the greatest number or the application to oneself of the moral law? Aristotle's effort to understand the role of friendship in the moral life is a reason I was glad to have the title of my remarriage book allude to his outlook. At the same time, there is another obvious rebuke to Aristotle's vision leveled by remarriage comedy, namely that friendship in them is primarily manifested through the relation of a woman and a man, whereas Aristotle says no such friendship can exist, on the ground that the relation is not one of equality.

Is this rebuke worth saying? Isn't Aristotle's archaic notion just to be dismissed and his views declared irrelevant at best to the concerns of modern perfectionism manifested in our films? But even discarding his declaration of essential inequality as something our culture has moved past intellectually, an issue of friendship between men and women remains controversial, namely in posing publicly the role of the erotic in friendship. All my friends are evidently committed to the idea of friendship between men and women, I mean as compatible with an exclusive marriage, but I know comparatively few such friendships of any serious elaboration which are not those of women with women or men with men. The last of the films discussed in this book takes up this question in a remarkable way, and in the context of meditating on one of the greatest of dramatic works underlying the remarriage narrative, I mean Eric Rohmer's *A Tale of Winter*, a meditation on Shakespeare's *The Winter's Tale* so constant, on my view, that it in effect raises the question of the competition of film with theater as such.

It is against the philosophical importance Aristotle attaches to friendship that the radicality of the idea in remarriage comedy may perhaps most readily be seen—the idea that not state, not church, not children, and not sex, or gender, validates marriage, in the absence of something that looks like what Aristotle means by the equal friendship of character. This relation is what Aristotle calls friendship for virtue, the highest form of friendship among the three types he distinguishes, reaching beyond friendships for utility and friendships for pleasure. These are intuitively as distinct as relationships in which each looks up to, and cares for, the other; and those joined for mutual advantage or convenience, as in business; and those consisting of shared amusements, say hanging out together. It is an attraction of Aristotle's weddedness to the world of affairs that almost any relation of cooperation or mutuality—any we might say that furthers sociability—may be seen to manifest some register of friendship, as between host and guest, or seller and buyer, or a ruler and his swineherd. But while Aristotle can say that character friendship includes the two lesser grades of friendship he distinguishes, the relationships drawn in remarriage comedy seem to demonstrate the possibility.

That there are problems to be contended with in Aristotle's view of friendship is indicated in the very way he turns to the topic. The closing two sentences of Book VII (the last focused on questions about virtue) and the opening two sentences of Book VIII (the first of the two chapters on friendship) read this way: "So much, then, for continence and incontinence and for pleasure and pain, what each of them is, and in what ways some [aspects] of them are good and others bad. It remains for us to discuss friendship as well. After that the next topic to discuss is friendship; for it is a virtue, or involves virtue, and besides is most necessary for our life. For no one would choose to live without friends even if he had all the other goods." Aristotle does not speak this way about the individual virtues of generosity, wit, truthfulness, mildness, shame, intelligence, or about any given virtue of the intellect— namely, that we would not choose to live without them. It seems as though he is assigning to friendship the importance of happiness itself, as in Book I: "We regard something as self-sufficient when all by itself it makes a life choiceworthy and lacking nothing; and that is what we think happiness does." We must come back to this.

Two problems with Aristotle's view have attracted recent scholarship. First: Can only those advanced human beings capable of the friendship of character be said to have genuine friendships, or do ordinary people, stuck in friendships of advantage or of use or of the enforced provision of pleasure, have friendships worth the name? (Underlying this is surely the question why Aristotle calls certain relations those of friendship at all, for example that of host and guest. I think of the distinct shock, not without its pleasures, when Charlotte Vale's mother tells her, on her return from her therapeutic months away from home, to remember that she is a guest in her mother's house, and Charlotte courteously replies, "Well then mother, your guest prefers to sleep in *this* room.") Second: If the best life is one of self-sufficiency (basing itself on virtue, as a shield against the turns of fortune) why does it *require* friends?

The second issue seems to me the more important. The first seems to be answerable by considering, as my example from *Now, Voyager* suggests, the *range* of relationships Aristotle calls friendship and the special importance he gives to character. Friendship is an epitome of everything he says about *any* of the "degrees" he distinguishes among "affiliations"; there are degrees of friendship as there are degrees of character. Whereas the question about the necessity of friendship to the *best* life is why the *even the highest* friendship is necessary to it. I want to try an answer to this question in conjunction with the puzzle about Aristotle's new evaluation of happiness at the end of the *Nichomachean Ethics*—namely his apparently sudden claim of "theoretical study" as the supreme element of happiness.

I have encountered two main views of this new evaluation, both of which take it as obvious that the overwhelming drift of Aristotle is toward a life that is balanced among the claims of the various parts or functions of the soul, hence that the intrusive exclusiveness of the contemplative life, or life of study, as providing the happiness of the highest function of the human, is something that has to be explained or corrected for.

One view is that Aristotle is simply emphasizing, as presumably most moral philosophers will, reason or rationality as essential to the good life. The human makeup—unlike animal instinct and grouping—in order to live with others, or reasonably with oneself, seems to require a faculty of, let's say, economy among limited resources and between conflicting desires within and between persons. But if this is the issue, Aristotle needn't have taken "theoretical study" as the image of reason that is required. Philosophical wisdom (*sophia*) is divided into two: one of them is theoretical study (*theorien*), the other is practical wisdom (*phronesis*). Now with practical wisdom we have both the idea of the highest life and the life of balance among competing needs. But it is hard to understand why, if Aristotle meant this, he didn't say so. Why indeed he seems to insist on something else (on theory, not practice).

The other view is that the intrusion of *theorien* as the highest life is a straight reversion to Plato's view, a view explicitly mentioned (without endorsement), as we saw, at the opening of the *Nichomachean Ethics*. So at the end of his treatise, Aristotle's attempt to overcome Platonism fails him, or else leaves him in struggle with it. Two features make it Platonism that is to be explained or corrected for: First, it takes the best life to be the life of philosophy; second, it relates the life of contemplation or theoretical study to the divine: "We ought to make ourselves pro-immortal" (another recent translator says "immortalize ourselves"). So uncharacteristic does a transcendentalist Aristotle seem to one scholar that he takes more seriously than others have the view that the passages on theoretical study in Book X were not by Aristotle himself but by an editor of his notes.

But these scholarly proposals—that Aristotle is merely emphasizing the importance of reason to the good life; that he is still struggling with Plato; that the text is corrupt—seem to me either too casual or too desperate. I propose trying out the idea that the final three books go together, that the last is not a reversion or corruption of Aristotle's view to an incompatible Platonism, but is a response to the preceding two books on friendship.

It is a disputed question what weight Aristotle puts on the idea that in the genuine friend "one can observe one's own actions." Some kind of otherwise unavailable pleasure, and otherwise unavailable knowledge is in view. Remember Aristotle's various formulations: "The blessed person decides to observe virtuous actions that are his own; and the actions of a virtuous friend are of this sort. Hence he will need virtuous friends" (1170a). "The excellent person is related to his friend in the same way he is related to himself, since a friend is another himself" (1170b). "Someone's own being is choiceworthy because he perceives that he is good, and this sort of perception is pleasant in itself. He must, then [in order to perceive his own being], perceive his friend's being, together [with his own], and he will do this when they live together and share conversations and thoughts" (ibid.).

Grant, then, that there is no doubt about the desirability, or rather the necessity of the friend in Aristotle's conception of the best life. My suggestion is this. It is taken for granted by the scholars I have read that the "study" (*theorien*) Aristotle takes to represent the occupation of the highest friendship is the same—that is, it is a study of the same things—as defined in other works of Aristotle, for example, the study of mathematics or physics. But suppose the "study" in question is a study of what this book—the *Nichomachean Ethics*—is about, namely, friendship and its role in the best life in human affairs. Could there be such a study? I mean, Aristotle famously warns, early in the *Nichomachean Ethics,* against searching in philosophizing about human affairs for the same degree of exactness that, so to say, nature and numbers yield (1094b). Now suppose what is different about Book X of this text is that it somewhat contests or modifies this methodological claim, so as to emphasize the relation of the idea of *theorien* (or theory) with ideas of perceiving and gazing. (The English word "speculation" gives both registers, intellectual and sensuous.) It is a register of the concept always commented upon, if in footnotes. This would still not mean that we can reason more exactly about human affairs than ordinary practical wisdom allows. But the reasoning might have its own conditions of origin and goal, its own completeness or accuracy or depth.

My suggestion is that, in particular, the origin and goal of the study that constitutes the highest activity of friendship is precisely the study that takes friendship, this friendship in particular, as its object. It is to achieve a new perception of your life, new speculation about it, but one whose condition is the friendship itself. Only in the state of friendship is it possible to "study" it, to perceive it—there is nothing of the kind otherwise to perceive. Of course there is something of a paradox here: the condition of friendship, the study that makes it possible, is not possible until the friendship has already been achieved. But is this a greater, or lesser, paradox than Aristotle's formulations which recognize the friend as another myself, and announce that in order to perceive myself I must perceive my friend's being together with mine? Then Aristotle's observation that we achieve such perceptions in living together and in sharing conversations and thoughts should constitute the solution of the paradox. Following Aristotle's mode in suggesting that, since he finds that happiness expresses virtue, examining virtue will be a way of studying happiness further, I am suggesting that examining what constitutes conversation, or sharing thoughts, will be a way of studying friendship further.

This may seem a little too good to be true, I mean too convenient from my point of view about what our film comedies can do, to be credible. But I have claimed that these films have made a discovery about the medium of film that allows it a certain competition with the mighty work of Shakespearean romance. And suppose we take it that, although Aristotle does not give examples of what these conversations will sound like, they will not be so different from the weight and the topics of the *Nichomachean Ethics*. That text, even given its form as notes, is pervaded by "what is said," by the wise and the many, so that it gives the impression of a writer in conversation with countless representatives of a culture. And I have already said that Socrates' depiction of conversations in *The Republic* opens with the sense of his answering a question. The dramatic difference in our films is that the equality demanded by Aristotle, between the participants in the highest form of friendship, is not established before their conversation; it rather seems the goal of their conversation. In arriving at it they, as Mill puts the matter, "look up to each other," as it were granting and overcoming inequalities as they study themselves in each other. The transcendence in such relationship, its "immortalization" of myself, is not one that comes from a metaphysical height, but merely from beyond myself as I stand, still within the human, contesting Plato, not succumbing to him. The friend becomes, as it were, my next self. (A book may call on this unattained self, Emerson attests—depending, of course, on our reading's being willing to take it to heart. A book, Aristotle says, may be a further actualization of its maker, who then loves it as a child. Then as such it is better, more advanced, than its maker.)

There is perhaps a further hint about how Aristotle thinks of conversation in his adding to his description of the way friends are together—almost at the end of Book IX, that is, at the end of the discussion of friendship, as he anticipates turning again to the topic of pleasure in Book X, as if reminded of the particular pleasures of friendship: "For in the case of human beings what seems to count as living together is this sharing of conversation and thought, not sharing the same pasture, as in the case of grazing animals" (1170b). Of course the idea of humanity as approached through its difference from animality is a familiar gesture throughout the history of philosophy. But the specification of the fantasm of sharing the same pasture catches my attention here—as though Aristotle is saying friends do share a pasture, only not one that grazing animals have a use or need for. Here I think again of the relation of the instinct of hunger to the human power of judgment—of incorporation and rejection to saying yes and saying no—which Aristotle regards as natural to the human (precisely as natural as language and politics). Nietzsche speaks of the link of philosophers with grazing animals as their both having the capacity to ruminate. Aristotle's image of conversation suggests that friends are each other's pasture, providing indispensable food for thought.

It may be that conversation between friends will in fact turn mostly to what Aristotle elsewhere calls theoretical study. But if the highest friendship has the transformative, definitive effect on the best life that Aristotle suggests, then any study entering the friends' conversation will be affected by the friendship, lent interest by the fact of the friend's interest. Take so low an interest as that of film comedy. It can be considered as a realm of amusement, or as one of a business or "industry," or as an art with its own call upon plot and poetry and character and the passions, one that provides its own promptings to speculation, raising issues of the place of entertainment, and of comedy or tragedy—and of this instance of entertainment or art—in the quest for taking one's life upon oneself in the light of (the highest) friendship. If these reflections are taken less as interpretations of Aristotle's text than as some improvisatory responses to it, I will be unable to object. I might, though, add that they seem to me to do no more violence to the text than the competing proposals seeking to save its appearances, and that they serve rather better to keep in conversation with it.

Having come this far I take one further step that I wouldn't dream of trying to prove, but merely to report, as an undertone of Aristotle's progress of thought that, having repeatedly perceived it, I cannot get clear of. The undertone comes out perhaps most clearly in a conjunction of remarks in Book IX (1168a): "Being is choiceworthy and lovable for all. We are in so far as we are actualized, since we are in so far as we live and act." (Compare, from Book X, 1175a: "Everyone aims at being alive . . . And life is choiceworthy.") The undercurrent I sense is in the idea that human existence, my life, is my choice; that I have, before I know the difference between good and bad lives, to say yes to being alive and to the world in which I am to live.

I have to—on pain of what? The undercurrent is an anxiety that some do not affirm this, do not take their lives upon themselves, so to speak. That one chooses life, or not, was the moral I drew from Plato's Myth of Er. It seems to me a way of taking a suggestion of the opening words of *Nichomachean Ethics:* "Every craft and every investigation, and likewise every action and decision, seems to aim at some good." Aimlessness is evidently open only to the human being. (Who therefore is the only creature capable of nihilism, as at the close of Nietzsche's *Genealogy of Morals:* "Man would rather take the void for his purpose [or aim] than be void of purpose.") (I might locate my response to Aristotle on friendship by saying that it places friendship in the role not alone of making my life visible but of showing it to be affirmable. Is this vulnerability incompatible with self-sufficiency?)

A few paragraphs into *Nichomachean Ethics,* Aristotle quotes Hesiod as follows: "He who understands everything himself is best of all; he is noble also who listens to one who has spoken well; but he who neither understands it himself nor takes to heart what he hears from another is a useless man." That paragraph has opened by declaring, or warning: "We need to have been brought up in fine habits if we are to be adequate students of what is fine and just, and of political questions generally." But if part of being "brought up" is being initiated into language and its restrictions and amplifications, that which makes the life and the study of political questions possible, then "taking to heart what he hears from another" precedes "understanding everything himself" as its condition. Listening to each other, speaking one's judgment with a point that matters to others who matter to you, is the condition of the formation of a polis, the reason Aristotle makes language the condition of the highest of human formations. His declaring, in the early paragraphs of his *Politics,* that one unfit for political association, one for whom political association is not natural (the association within which—or of which—all other alliances are established), must be a god or a beast, is unforgettable.

Thinking of it, I identify what Aristotle sees in Hesiod's useless man as the naturally unpolitical man, one who is inherently unsociable, a beast—but a beast the way a man can become a beast. (That natural beasts do not have language and therefore do not form the association of a polis is essentially a rephrasing of the point that language is the condition of such an association, not an additional, remarkable declaration.) That this is not an imagination of a natural beast is shown in Aristotle's going on to describe such a creature as "the worst of all animals" (fallen from the best, the human gone wrong) and as a "savage being." I recall with something of the same alarm Plato's myth of the man within the man, the human form as containing a small man, a large lion, and a gigantic, many-headed beast, and recall further that Plato compares this beast with legendary monsters such as the Chimera and Cerberus. Since both Aristotle's "savage being" and Plato's fictional monster are created specifically within a discussion requiring the imagination of a figure incapable of a life of justice, I assume Aristotle's image to invoke Plato's.

In Plato's argument the figure, entering late, is to show that one who asserts that injustice is to the benefit of the unjust man does not know what he is saying. But what is the significance—it seems more a reminder than an argument—of the fantasm of a monster at the opening of Aristotle's *Politics,* the work on human association that continues the *Nichomachean Ethics?* Is it to caution that a few souls are going to have to be ruled out of the polis, left at best to wander the fringes of civilized life? Or does it mark a continuing philosophical anxiety, namely that we do not know why (hence not to what extent) some humans are unnatural, insufficiently realized as human? (In another repeated image of Aristotle's, this would amount to someone's "being asleep or inactive throughout his life" [1095b], which he later describes as "living the life of a plant" [1176b].)

Then to some extent we fail to know something, we remain unassured, about our existence, about the degree of our actualization, which is never perfect. It is familiar for thinkers, Emerson among them, to claim, or seek, the God within. (Levinas attributes the idea, surprisingly but fascinatingly, to Descartes.) Plato has given sense, in his way, to the idea of the monster within, as if he marks a sense that there is an irreducible part of us which craves the unsocial, not so much the unjust as the absence of the concepts of the just and the unjust altogether, a craving, let's say, for the natural, which presents itself to Aristotle as the unnatural. (Is it our irreducible potentiality for monstrousness, some lure of the unsocial, that is the object, according to Aristotle's *Poetics,* of the pity and terror that tragedy is to purge us of?)

I suppose I would not be prompted to this line of thought apart from my taking something like the anxiety over listening to each other—over the necessity to count on (given our separateness, call it our existence in nature) our mattering to each other—as fundamental to the work of Wittgenstein's *Philosophical Investigations.* It is commonly taken as obvious, it is surely obvious, that for Wittgenstein language is as it were a public, shared fact. It is to my mind exactly as true, and as important to Wittgenstein's thought, that language is subject to our unsurveyable powers of repudiating it, finding it metaphysically disappointing, its sharing coming to seem a superficial feature of it, or a feature of its superficiality, call it its relative or conventional objectivity, leaving my world inherently private.

The principal image of this fragility in my hold on my language—the image that causes me, I think, to speak of the issue as expressing anxiety—is the repeated realization that the teacher's power of instruction comes to an end before the separateness of the other, who has to go on with a concept on his or her own (to "understand everything oneself"). It is as the teacher exhausts what can be said, and teacher and pupil fall silent with each other (then and there, subject to limitations of time, imagination, patience, good will, and to what we might call a tolerance for anxiety), that one feels it becomes the responsibility of teaching to provide a reason for, a point, an aim, in speaking at all; a responsibility of philosophy, so far as philosophy, as in the *Investigations,* conceives of itself as instruction, instruction however in what no one could manage just not to know. (A reason for speaking, having something to say, is the sense that you will be listened to.) As if the world might, apart from the heart for philosophy, lose its interest, which accordingly must be, we can say, awakened. Of course some will say philosophy may contribute to this loss of interest. I do not deny it. But this only says that the impulse to philosophy is, or has become, natural to the human, not to a particular class of humans, and that it often, perhaps most often, appears as unwelcome, and is brought to an end before it comes to, brings itself, on each occasion of its arising, to an end.

If taking an interest in the world is the sign of choosing your life, I should perhaps add that happiness cannot be the reason life is chosen, because you cannot know whether your life will be happy. (When Aristotle quotes the proverbial "Call no man happy until he is dead," he considers that even that date may still be too soon.) Any more than you choose to obey a government because it is advantageous to do so. It is yours before you know its particular economy of injustice. In a crisis you may choose to reject the government. It may not take what we recognize as a crisis to choose not to live, let's say to sleep life out. It is this possibility as arising specifically in adolescence, in facing the choice of adulthood, but speaking to anyone open to doubt about what makes life choiceworthy, that causes Emerson and Thoreau sometimes to specify their commitment to address themselves to those they call the student, or to recall a youth, with what words of encouragement they have. It is a distinct part of my gratitude to them.

20

The Awful Truth

1   In a prologue, at the Gotham Athletic Club, Jerry Warriner (Cary Grant) is about to get a sunlamp treatment sufficient to make it appear that he has spent the last two weeks in Florida "even if it takes all afternoon." He tells a passing acquaintance who is brandishing a squash racket, "What wives don't know won't hurt them." And he adds, "And what you don't know won't hurt you." He invites the acquaintance to come home with him that afternoon for protection, I mean for drinks.

2   Entering the house with several acquaintances, Jerry discovers that his wife Lucy is not at home. He invents the explanation that she is at her Aunt Patsy's place in the country, an explanation which collapses when Aunt Patsy walks in looking for Lucy.

3   Lucy Warriner (Irene Dunne) enters, in evening dress, followed by Armand Duvalle, her singing teacher, with a story about chaperoning a dance and then on the road back having the car break down miles from nowhere, and spending the night at a most inconvenient inn. Jerry mockingly pretends to believe the story and is complimented by Armand for having "a continental mind." The guests take the cue to leave; so, in a way, does Jerry, who says his faith is destroyed; Lucy says she knows what he means and tosses him an orange with "California" stamped on it that Jerry had sent to her as from Florida. She says he has returned to catch her in a truth, to which he responds by calling her a philosopher. He in turn philosophizes, in a speech which includes the lines "Marriage is based on faith. When that's gone everything's gone." She asks if he really means that and upon his affirming it she telephones for a divorce.

4   Her lawyer, on the phone, repeatedly tells Lucy not to be hasty, that marriage is a beautiful thing. He is repeatedly interrupted by his wife, asking him why they have to be interrupted, whom he repeatedly invites, each time covering the phone, to shut her mouth.

5 In court to begin divorce proceedings, Mr. Smith (the couple's fox terrier) is tricked by Lucy into choosing to live with her. Jerry asks for visiting rights.

6 Aunt Patsy wants to get out of the apartment she and Lucy share and have some fun for a change. (Since they are dressed in evening gowns, we rather get the idea that this is not the first time they have found themselves all dressed up with no place to go.) Lucy objects that they haven't an escort. Aunt Patsy stalks out and comes back with their neighbor from across the hall, Dan Leeson (Ralph Bellamy), whom she has in effect rescued from going out alone. Dan declares that he's from Oklahoma, in oil; when Aunt Patsy draws the implication that he's marinated, he, somewhat to our surprise, gets the joke, even boisterously. Jerry takes this moment to appear for his visiting time with Mr. Smith, whom he accompanies at the piano. The others leave.

6a The next morning Dan's mother warns him in general about women and in particular about that kind of women.

6b Aunt Patsy warns Lucy against acting on the rebound, pointing out to her that her toast is burning.

6c 6a continued.

6d 6b continued.

7 In a nightclub Jerry's friend Dixie Belle sings and enacts "My Dreams Are Gone with the Wind." On each recurrence of the title line, air jets from the floor blow Dixie Belle's flowing skirt up higher and higher—she finally gives up trying to hold it down, or in other words, throws up her hands.

8 Just before that, Lucy and Dan had entered the club and taken a table. Jerry takes Dixie Belle over to introduce her; when she leaves for her act, Jerry invites himself to join Dan and Lucy. On meeting Dixie Belle, Lucy had sincerely complimented Jerry on finding himself a nice companion, evincing considerable surprise at his good taste. Now, after witnessing her act, Lucy seems uncertain about it.

9 When Jerry corrects Dan's impression that Lucy dislikes dancing, Dan, from whom we learn that he is a champion dancer, alertly draws her onto the floor. The music changes and Dan is moved to take over the floor with a display of his champion jitterbugging. Jerry so thoroughly enjoys Lucy's taste of country life that he tips the orchestra to repeat the same number. He pulls up a chair to the edge of the dance floor, sits legs crossed, arms draped before him carelessly, perfectly, fronting the dancers and the camera, looking directly at the world with as handsome a smile as Cary Grant has it in him to give, in as full an emblem of the viewer viewed—the film turned explicitly to its audience, to ask who is scrutinizing whom—as I know in film. I think of it as a hieratic image of the human, the human transfigured on film. This man, in words of Emerson's, carries the holiday in his eye; he is fit to stand the gaze of millions. (What fits Cary Grant, or anyone, to stand this normal condition of a film star? It cannot be some independently definable property that differentiates them from each of those millions.) Call this the end of Act One.

10a Lucy and Dan at the piano in his apartment make a duet of "Home on the Range."

10b Jerry enters to discuss their business deal about a mine.

10c Dan's mother comes in with a piece of gossip about Lucy; Jerry sort of clears her name with a speech of mock gallantry that includes the line "Our marriage was one of those tragedies you read about in the newspapers." The mother shows she is still not satisfied, whereupon Lucy retreats to let her and her son sort the matter out between them.

11 Lucy returns to her apartment to find Jerry there, rewarding himself with a drink for having, he says, given her that swell reference; she haughtily refuses his offer of financial help, and laughs heartily as the piano top falls on his hand. As they walk toward the door for Jerry to leave, Dan knocks. Lucy opens the door, which serves to conceal Jerry from Dan, who apologizes for his mother's suspicions and insists on reading Lucy a poem of love he has written for her. As he embarks on it, Jerry, from behind the door, prods Lucy to laughter with surreptitious pencil jabs in her ribs. The phone rings, on the other side of Jerry. Lucy answers; we are shown by an insert that it is Armand; Lucy asks whoever it is to wait and puts down the phone; as she crosses back past Jerry to complete her exchange with Dan, behind her back Jerry picks up the phone and learns who it is that Lucy has concealed on the other end. Lucy gets rid of Dan by giving him a kiss; he departs noisily. Lucy makes an appointment into the waiting phone, handed to her by Jerry, for three o'clock the next afternoon, explaining to Jerry after she hangs up that it was her masseuse. Jerry finally leaves, saying he's just seen a three-ring circus.

12 At three o'clock, evidently the next afternoon, Jerry forces his way into Armand's apartment only to embarrass himself on discovering Lucy in the middle of a salon song performed for a small attentive audience, Armand accompanying her at the piano.

13 The next day in her apartment, Lucy, having faced her unfaded love for crazy Jerry, has written a letter calling it off with Dan. She places the letter on her mantel and asks Aunt Patsy to deliver it for her.

14 The farce now blossoms. Each party shows up to apologize to Lucy. Mr. Smith precipitates the tangling as he fetches Armand's hat for Jerry, whom it doesn't fit, similar as it is, and try as he will. The two men find themselves alone together in Lucy's bedroom, Armand to have avoided Jerry, Jerry to have avoided Dan and his mother, who have appeared from across the hall. From the bedroom the two men dash across the living room past the assembled others and out the door. Dan says, a moroser if wiser man, "I've learned a lot about women from you, Lucy: I've learned that a man's best friend is his mother." As he and his best friend begin their exit, Aunt Patsy takes Lucy's letter from the mantel and hands it to him: "Here's your diploma." Call this the end of Act Two.

15a Mr. Smith barks at the society page of the newspaper Lucy is reading; it says that Jerry and Barbara Vance are to be married as soon as his divorce is final, which incidentally is today.

15b The newspaper comes alive in a montage of Jerry and Barbara's whirl-wind romance, which mostly consists of their attending or participating in society sports events; the sequence reads like the society segment of, say, a *Movietone News*.

16 Lucy appears at Jerry's apartment to say goodbye on the eve of their final divorce decree. She recites a poem Jerry wrote for her early in their relationship. She introduces it by saying, "This will hand you a laugh," but neither of them is tickled in the ribs. They sample some champagne that Jerry has ready in an ice bucket, as if he was expecting this visit. It turns out that the life has gone out of the champagne; evidently they are unable to cel-ebrate either divorce or marriage. To account for Lucy's presence when she answers a phone call from Barbara Vance, Jerry invents the fable that his sister is visiting from Europe, then after a pause explains that she can't accom-pany him to the Vance household that evening because she's busy and any-way she is returning to Europe almost immediately. Lucy remarks that he's slipping.

17 That night, at the Vance establishment, Lucy, in a racy costume, interrupts a flagging family occasion with an indecorous display as Jerry's low-down sister. She claims to be a nightclub performer and gives them a modified version of Dixie Belle's "Gone with the Wind" rou-tine. ("There's a wind effect right here but you will just have to use your imagination.") Jerry joins her on her exit from the song and dance.

18   They drive to their conclusion in Connecticut.

The path to the green world is portrayed here in more detail than in any member of the genre (except *Bringing Up Baby*), and the effect is to suggest, something said but not shown in *The Lady Eve*, that there is no clear way to get there, no obvious predictable path and no obvious vehicle; it is, in short, a mythical locale. On leaving the Vance mansion, the pair enter an open car whose radio squawks intolerably. Lucy, pretending to be drunk (she is obviously in a heightened state of mind), causes the radio's behavior, as if it speaks her mind. Then on a darkened, unmarked road, two motorcycle policemen stop the fleeing pair for speeding. As Jerry is talking with the officers, Lucy releases the hand brake of the car, sending it down a small embankment to slam against a tree. She asks the officers to give them rides on their motorcycles to her aunt's place, only fifteen miles from where they are stopped, where they can properly be identified. They behave like children, riding on the handlebars of the motorcycles, making rude noises, she fairly manic, he fully solemn. On arriving at the country house and being identified, Lucy treats the policemen as if they were valued servants. Lucy evinces blank surprise when the husband of the couple who take care of the house says Aunt Patsy is not there, and then, claiming to be exhausted, bounds up a flight of stairs—all of which Jerry recognizes as some kind of continuation of the charade she has been putting on as his sister and as Dixie Belle.

They occupy adjoining bedrooms, as it were playing dress-up in clothes borrowed from the elderly housekeepers, he in a nightshirt, she in a nightgown patently too large for her. How they overcome the difficulties of getting the closed door between them to open, and to stay closed at the right time, is a saga in itself. Lucy says they have a problem. We could call it a problem in finding an escape from their having backed their way toward an edge of divorce which neither wants—an escape, or escapade, having to do with wind effects, with a cat that as it were protects Lucy from Jerry, to Lucy's chagrin, and with a cascade of philosophy falling from each of them. Along the way she says: "Things are just the same as they always were, only you're just the same, too, so I guess things will never be the same again." And he: "Things are different, except in a different way. You're still the same, only I've been a fool. Well, I'm not now. So, as long as I'm different, don't you think things could be the same again? Only a little different."

A passage from Plato's late dialogue *Parmenides* bears a clear and comic resemblance to this exchange:

> *Parmenides:* Then, that which becomes older than itself, also becomes at the same time younger than itself, if it is to have something to become older than.
>
> *Aristotles:* What do you mean?
>
> *Parmenides:* I mean this.—A thing does not need to become different from another thing which is already different; it *is* different, and if its different has become, it has become different; if its different will be, it will be different; but of that which is becoming different, there cannot have been, or be about to be, or yet be, a different—the only different possible is one which is becoming.
>
> *Aristotles:* That is inevitable.

The conjunction reveals, or affirms, a double revelation: first, that the thoughts of one of the most complex pieces of philosophy ever composed are recognizably recapturable in contemporary conversation, or in the representation of such conversation by a clever writer who may or may not have studied Plato in college; second, that there is something in the sublimest philosophy that can strike one as comic.

The pair's exchanges lead, through further intricacies, to their representation by apparently miniature Swiss figurines coming separately out of a Swiss cuckoo clock at the stroke of midnight and disappearing together back into the clock. An obvious implication is that, while at midnight their divorce decree becomes final, they are allegorized as doing then the precise thing that automatically voids the decree, namely "cohabiting." So are they (re)married or not? Since the clock takes the form of a chalet, a dwelling of the sort they are literally inhabiting, their reentry into it suggests that they are reconceiving their sense of past, present, and future, or say their relation to time, to what it means to inhabit its repetitions together.

Perhaps the deepest contribution of this film to the psychological exploration of the genre of remarriage comedy is its emphasis on the requirement of the genre that the pair have known each other forever, hence that they are, or have been, something like brother and sister—the original intimacy which must be broken if a different intimacy, that of strangers, or of the exogamous (ultimately, the difficult recognition of the separation, the otherness, of others), is to be achieved. That this should be combined with registering Lucy's difference from herself, or her double nature as socially refined and as erotically risky, each epitomized in the delivery of a different song, and each complexly, expertly executed by Irene Dunne, amounts to several strokes of cinematic and narrative brilliance. And these are joined in by the strong, but apparently backward, or say original, ways Cary Grant reacts to each version of Irene Dunne—when she is refined, by falling all over himself; when she is raucous, by managing to show his appreciation of her spiritual daring by visibly controlling his admiration of her and by displaying his connection with her to the assembled company in forming a walk-off with her to end her Dixie Belle impersonation.

I mention here the fatal contrast to Jerry's appreciation of Lucy's voice when Dan asks her, after their duet on "Home on the Range," whether she, who accompanies them on the piano, has ever had any lessons. The question of voice and its non-negotiable demand for recognition is here made explicit, yet all but disguised by the drift of the narrative. In the sequence preceding the climactic sister act at the Vance household, Lucy appears at Jerry's bachelor apartment to mark the day that is to achieve their divorce. As a toast of farewell, after Jerry pours the champagne, she says, "I remember the first drink we ever had. In your best manner you offered a toast. You said—this will hand you a laugh: 'Lend an ear, I implore you. This comes from the heart; I'll always adore you. Until death do us part.'" (Another fatal comparison with Dan's poetic effort to her a few sequences earlier.) Before they can consult the implications of their both being moved, and as if to distract them from consulting themselves, Barbara Vance phones, discovering that Jerry has questionable company. We accordingly never have time to consider the peculiarity of the phrase "Lend an ear." It asks, of course, for another's attention to your voice. But it could also be taken to ask for help with your own ear, to confess a sense of inadequacy in your isolated capacity to respond, a desire and willingness for reciprocation. (Precisely a recognition of limitation, call it finitude, that Dan Leeson, in his duet with Lucy, had shown himself incapable of.) The ensuing routine in the bosom of the Vance family can then be understood as Lucy's responding to Jerry's old desire for her attention and for her provision of instruction in his capacity for hearing.

Go back for a moment to the mysterious road leading to their concluding night in the country, and their mishap with the means of transportation. There is a realization here of the earlier instance of a story of late-night mishap on an isolated country road, as Lucy and Armand enter the house to encounter the just-returned Jerry and his acquaintances. There Jerry had scorned the story, and Lucy had countered with scorn, precipitating an impasse of mutual credibility that precipitated the drastic measure of, let's call it, the standing threat or option of divorce. On his own adventure with Lucy on a country road, Jerry has the chance to recognize the intuitive impossibility that the fun Lucy is having with him could resemble any fun she might have found during her night with Armand.

But then why doesn't he see this in his initial encounter with this foolishly simple European and his continental mind? We have to count it to Jerry's credit that he trusts Lucy's seriousness sufficiently to wonder what this apparently uncompetitive manikin can provide for her that is beyond his American capacities. And indeed his incapacity again proves to concern his failure (even his) to have recognized the range of Lucy's voice, the single attribute Armand is hired by her to concern himself with. Jerry is, as the genre of remarriage characteristically shows the spiritually ambitious man to be, fated to make a further, explicit, expiatory, fool of himself.

Lucy's voice teacher's name is, as revealed by a close-up of the card on his apartment door the afternoon Jerry invades what proves to be a musicale, "Armand Duvalle." This is, deliberately or not, a misspelling of the Armand Duval who is the love interest in Dumas's *La Dame aux Camélias* and of the George Cukor film of that play entitled *Camille,* arguably Garbo's greatest role, with Robert Taylor as Armand. (Here are tragedies of the sort one might read of in the newspapers.) Since *Camille* was made several years after *The Awful Truth,* and since, in Verdi and Piave's *La Traviata,* another adaptation of the Dumas play, the names of the characters are changed to characteristically Italian names, our Lucy's Armand must come directly from Dumas. What might the point be? I have to think that the director of *The Awful Truth,* Leo McCarey (and his scriptwriter, Vina Delmar), are less making a little easy fun of European pretension (just a little fun, since Lucy's salon song carries weight in the narrative and is sung by her in French), than balancing a perception of an American overvaluation of European cultivation with an American undervaluation of cultivation (as represented in Dan's bragging about having had no voice lessons): Dan and Armand seem mild caricatures of each of their nationalities as seen by the other's. The sophistication of Lucy's and Jerry's sensibilities is accordingly confirmed in this regard by their being free of such prejudices.

Perhaps more directly, the name emphasizes that this Armand cannot possibly be taken as the erotic threat to an established relationship that Dumas's Armand patently and fatally is, hence that the obstacle to the continuation of Lucy's and Jerry's marriage is not external, but lies within each of them.

This is another description of what I called a moment ago their crisis, or impasse, of mutual credibility. It would indicate why the moral perplexities in wanting a mysterious, perhaps uneventful, two weeks of unmonitored freedom; or of arranging a recital as an assignation; or of feeling unlistened to, or of being unspoken to, or unspoken for—why these perplexities are not assessable by utilitarian calculation or by Kantian law. There is not some action for either of them to take whose pros and cons or whose universalizability requires addressing, like offering better gifts of fruit or flowers, or vowing never to spend another night out of the house, come what may.

There is an unspoken attunement of moral perception that conditions, and calls upon, our ability to make ourselves intelligible to each other. The sense of attunement lost, in an encounter in which only through the other do you reach to your attunement with yourself, is a way of framing the perfectionist moment. I find myself thinking, perhaps extravagantly, of Cathy's saying, in *Wuthering Heights*, "Heathcliff is more myself than I am"; or, in *Great Expectations*, of Pip's saying to Stella, "You have become part of my character." Perhaps extravagantly, but I cannot think irrelevantly. While these may not express common intensities of moral dilemmas, both are expressions of a recognition of moral intimacy, of a sense of doing mortal harm and being threatened with irreparable harm, unsensed in its stakes by the rest of the world. Can I trust the perception of one who does not respect the anguish in these outcries? But how is respect shown here? By moral confrontation? Who has the standing for this? Then by recognizing that whatever course is to be taken, suffering is to be clarified and acknowledged? It is an awful, an awesome truth that the acknowledgment of the otherness of others, of ineluctable separation, is the condition of human happiness. Indifference is the denial of this condition.

What I called the inner obstacles sheltered by Lucy and by Jerry are in a sense revealed by what overcomes the obstacles—in Jerry's case, as said, by his demonstration of being knocked out, or brought to his senses, by each of

Lucy's opposite songs, in Lucy's case by her demonstration of her Dixie Belle earthiness as bound up with the even more dangerous closeness between her and Jerry in her sisterly intimacy with him, no less a puzzle to her, surely, than to him.

Shall we make a stab, in this context of Armand's ambiguous presence, at interpreting what Lucy means by saying that Jerry, in arriving home before her entrance with Armand, has caught her in a truth, which leads Jerry to accuse her of being a philosopher and to agree to a divorce? Evidently being caught marks the awfulness of this truth. Well, what is true about being discovered in company with Armand, which seems to be Lucy's meaning in saying she was caught? Given what we have been saying, we could answer that it is her realization that love catches you, that no matter what accidents befall you or who you happen to bring home with you, you love where you love. Another awful truth of finitude is that, unlike gods, we mortals are not generally reliable mind readers, so that love between mortals, to be known, must be spoken. This requirement is emphasized in the genre of remarriage comedy by the man's having to claim his right to speak of love to the woman, to ask for reciprocation; as it were, to go first. Perhaps it was to remind Jerry of this requirement that Lucy brought Armand home with her. (And perhaps this is how Hildy and Walter understand his apparent inconsiderateness in going through doors and gates and down stairs—barriers of any kind— ahead of her.)

Another drawback of mortality, of human speech and thought, is that going through doors, or getting them open, is not as straightforward as one would like to imagine. It can demand, and inspire, poetry; and require the disguise, or revelation, of exotic songs and dances; and the taste of flat champagne; and singing a duet with a terrier; and wearing an ill-fitting flannel nightshirt; and inviting the aid of a high wind. (Is improvisation a virtue?) And after that it still can await a flurry of philosophy to try to get one's own mind and its body together and in the same direction, let alone in concord with another's mind and body. The wonder is that the craving for clarity is available to two in conversation when it is denied to either alone.

A concluding thought. Remarriage comedies are a specific, limited genre, habitually included in hasty journalistic reports of films within the massive (differently conceived) genre familiarly known as "screwball comedy." Sometimes I try to reconcile myself to this confusing inclusion. But sometimes I have objected to the indiscriminateness of this idea, which is no more illuminating than the title "women's film." I agree that it is no less illuminating. But there is a moment in *The Awful Truth* which I take to be a declaration that this film is not to be classed with screwball comedies. It occurs in the sequence following the two-men-in-a-bedroom farce, when Lucy reads in the newspaper about Jerry's engagement to Barbara Vance, whom Aunt Patsy describes as a "madcap heiress," namely the character supposed to be the distinguishing feature of screwball comedy. (This fits very well an interesting film such as *My Man Godfrey* with William Powell and the great Carole Lombard, which no one would suppose to be a remarriage comedy.) I take Aunt Patsy's identification as suggesting that a film featuring Jerry's romance with Barbara Vance might constitute a screwball comedy (except that Barbara is not witty), thus implying that the film before us not one.

21

HENRY JAMES AND MAX OPHULS

In this chapter I am going to focus on both a literary text and a film melodrama—Henry James's "The Beast in the Jungle" and Max Ophuls's *Letter from an Unknown Woman*. James's story—many people find it the best of his shorter fictions—is quite concentratedly concerned with what, so to speak, makes a woman unknown (a certain kind of woman unknown to a certain kind of man—but how they are special, and whether they are special, is part of the subject of the story).

In James's story, when a man and a woman, John Marcher and May Bartram, neither of them still young but neither of them attached, attract each other's attention among a group of visitors to a great English country house, the symmetry of being strangers vanishes when the woman tells the man that they met on an earlier occasion and that he confided to her the secret sense on which he founds his life, namely, that he is marked out to have something altogether singular happen to him. He has not confided this to anyone else, and May Bartram now agrees to base a friendship with him on waiting with him to find out how this singular event will manifest itself. The story follows their conversations over the remaining years of their lives, which consist of their assessing the nature of the beast which is to appear and of the bargain they have entered into to consign themselves to awaiting its appearance together. For him, it will pounce.

For Ophuls's film, too, let me begin with a summary.

---

1 *Letter from an Unknown Woman* opens with a title establishing our location as "Vienna 1900." Through a rainy night, a horse-drawn carriage draws up to a darkened building where the young man we will know as Stefan Brant (Louis Jourdan) is being dropped off at his apartment by two friends who, it emerges, are to serve as his seconds in a duel at dawn. The friends indicate that

in his life of amorous escapades he has this time gone too far. He brushes off their seriousness by replying that he doesn't mind dying, but that he hates getting up early.

2   Inside his apartment he tells the servant waiting up for him, "This is one appointment I won't keep," and directs him to pack a bag for an extended stay out of town. The servant hands him a letter delivered earlier that evening.

3   Stefan glances at the letter as he begins to change his clothes for the journey. A woman's voice recites the letter's opening: "By the time you read this I may be dead." His attention is captured, and the bulk of the film takes place as a manifestation of the letter, with intermittent voice-over narration by the woman.

4   The film takes us back to the woman's (Lisa's, played by Joan Fontaine) first encounter with Stefan, on the day he moved into her apartment building and caused a stir, generally by the process of his grand piano being hoisted up to his apartment, specifically in Lisa's breast by her imagination of the life of art and its demands and celebrity and misunderstanding implied by the empirical fact of this difficult and delicate mechanical project of the piano movers.

5   Soon after, Lisa maneuvers her way into Stefan's apartment by helping his servant carry a rug up the back stairs. The recited letter tells him—and us—that as she listened to the sounds of his practicing the piano, she began preparing herself to be worthy of him and his world, by paying attention to her appearance and by reading biographies of "the great musicians."

6   Lisa learns that her widowed mother, with whom she shares an apartment, has accepted an offer of marriage and that the man—whose utter lack of distinction we are shown through Lisa's offended eyes—will remove Lisa and her mother from Vienna to set up house in Linz.

7   Frantic at the thought of giving up her fantasied life in Stefan's world, Lisa steals away from the station where her mother and new stepfather count their luggage and blessings as they await the train for Linz, and returns to the apartment building to throw herself on Stefan's mercy and—who knows?—love. No one answers the door at his apartment; she sits for hours on the stairs leading up away from it; and when, that night, Stefan eventually reappears, it is in the company of another woman. Lisa gazes at them as they, oblivious of her, enter his apartment. She departs for her fate in Linz.

8   Linz is a garrison town in which Lisa's mother, the mother's husband, and the colonel of the troops stationed there, with whom the husband has some kind of business connection, are preparing with great excitement for

Lisa's expected acceptance, this very Sunday afternoon, at the weekly summer band concert, of an offer of marriage from the colonel's nephew, a rising young officer in the detachment.

9 As he and Lisa stroll together across the town square, the young officer cites the Sunday military band concert as proof that Linz, as well as Vienna, can boast of providing music for its residents. In a complexly photographed interview, Lisa interrupts the introductory gestures of what is obviously an approach to a proposal, blurting out that she is not free, that she is promised to another. The colonel and young officer depart, not disguising their sense of injury; the mother and her aspiring husband are dumbfounded.

10 In Vienna, Lisa is employed as a model in a fashionable dress shop. (The brilliant sunshine in Linz may alert us to the fact that the scenes in Vienna to which, from now on, we are party are set at night, or at dusk or dawn.) A male client asks the manager of the shop for an introduction to the new girl, but the manager tells him "She's not like the others; she goes home after work."

11 We follow Lisa after work to a place where, as she has in effect stationed herself across the street from her old apartment, Stefan, alighting from a carriage, notices her and crosses to her. As he says something like "I know this will sound banal but I feel we've met," and as he attempts to introduce himself she interrupts him by saying, "I know who you are."

12 They walk together—perhaps one notices that they pass a small saint's shrine built into a wall along the street—and find themselves in a restaurant where Stefan is well known. He obliges a stranger by autographing a program of one of his concerts; the program compares him to the young Mozart.

13 The pair take an open carriage through the winter night to visit the Prater amusement park, where they eat candied apples, ride on an imaginary train, and dance until they are the last couple in the pavilion. He plays for her after the orchestra has departed; she is entranced beyond recall.

14 He shows up at the dress shop to tell her that he has to leave town for a series of concerts and asks her to meet him to say goodbye at the train station.

15 He is glad to see her arrive at the station, and as soon as they have greeted, he is called to board. He calls back to her that he will return in two weeks.

16 Lisa's voice-over notes that they will never again see each other alive. As the camera observes Lisa walk away down the platform, and continues to watch while she becomes smaller to the point almost of invisibility, certainly of indistinguishability, the dark spot marking her disappearance begins growing again and moving toward us, but now, we make out, in the form of a nun, walking in a hospital corridor, who enters a cubicle to the bedridden Lisa and asks her to reveal the name of the father of her child. Lisa refuses.

17 An older, richly dressed Lisa is ready to leave for an evening at the opera with her husband, a high-ranking officer; her son Stefan, some ten or eleven years old, asks if he can sleep in her bed until she gets back. She agrees and suggests it might be a nice gesture if he would begin calling the man she has married by the honorary title of father, since he has cared for them both so well.

18 On the staircase of the elaborate foyer of the opera house, with Max Ophuls's signature camera exploring the elegantly crowded space from a path passing among the chandeliers, accompanied by Lisa's voice-over speculating on metaphysical chance and fate, Lisa notices Stefan, as have others in the crowd, whose remarks about him Lisa overhears, to the effect that he has found amusements and talents other than music to occupy him, at the cost of his promise as an artist.

19a Seated in the box beside her husband, she is haunted by the idea of Stefan's presence; she complains of feeling ill and tells her husband that she will recover herself by leaving, alone, to lie down for a while. In the hallway she orders her carriage.

19b As she reaches the bottom of the staircase she is accosted by Stefan, who insists, however strange and banal it may seem, that they have met and that he must see her again. She manages, in her evident agitation, to leave without agreeing.

20a As she makes her way through the doors and out of the opera house, she discovers that her husband is already awaiting her in their carriage.

20b On the ride home he asks her what she intends to do. She says she has no will of her own, only Stefan's. Her husband, remarkably sympathetic, tells her she is gravely mistaken.

20c At home, in some kind of shadowy trophy room, with guns and swords mounted on the walls, her husband's sympathy has lessened and he tells her that if she leaves there will be no turning back. Upstairs, as Lisa wakes young Stefan to take him to his own bed, he calls out, "Goodnight, Father," one of many such ironies in the melodrama.

21 Again at the train station, Lisa is saying goodbye to this younger Stefan, whom she is sending back to boarding school early; this time it is her turn to say that she will see him in two weeks. She repeats it as she watches the train begin to pull out, "Two weeks." A conductor appears suddenly in the hallway outside the boy's compartment, anxiously telling an assistant that that cabin was to have been quarantined. We see a covered body being wheeled down the train platform on a stretcher; someone in the attending crowd mutters, "Typhus fever."

22 From a distance along the street past Lisa's and Stefan's old apartment building, we see Lisa disappear into its entrance. The distance turns out to be that of the carriage in which her husband has evidently been waiting, to see what his wife's decision will be. Seeing it, he tells the coachman to drive on.

23 We watch Lisa mount the stairs to Stefan's apartment, from the exact perspective from which Lisa waited all day for him the day her mother and stepfather left for Linz. This time Stefan is at home, and by chance unoccupied. We watch Lisa enter his apartment as she had silently watched Stefan enter it with a woman all those years ago. She is now that woman, as the camera insists by repeating its striking gesture of accompaniment and surveillance from Lisa's earlier vigil.

24 Stefan compliments Lisa for managing to get away so soon after their meeting at the opera, and sends his servant out, recognizing that it is somewhat late, for some supper ("the usual" he adds). Lisa climactically recognizes that, for all Stefan's convincing recent display of tortured, unsatisfied memory (for all anyone knows, including himself, he had been in that moment sincere), he has by now fully recovered the talent for amusement for which he has, perhaps, sacrificed his talent for art (a sacrifice the invocation of which in any case is part of his routine of amusement), and he is charmingly treating her as the usual end for him of an evening's adventure. The recognition sends Lisa reeling out into the night, along whose deserted streets she shrinks from a drunken man's attempts to invite her company, and vanishes across an empty square.

25 In what seems to be the hospital in which we found her after her initial separation from Stefan, we witness Lisa writing the last words of her letter to him, the last of her life, "If only . . ."

26 In Stefan's hands, back in the present, the letter shows that it has been sent on to him by the superior of an order of nuns. The effect of reading the letter upon Stefan is to visit upon him a crush of exactly remembered images of the distant episode with Lisa—banal images of their visit to the Prater amusement park, ending with that of his lifting the veil of her hat in his apartment just the other night. His stopping to read the letter that evolves into our film has used up the time in which he had intended to escape from the appointment of the duel. (What time has it used of ours, what time does art take?)

27 He says to his mute servant, "You recognized her," which the man confirms by writing her name on the letter, in effect counter-signing it, as if standing in for the (mute) director of the film, who is sending simulacra to us of figures who will be dead.

28 Outside the building, as Stefan goes to keep his appointment to face his death, he turns back to see a present, hallucinated image of Lisa standing beside the entrance door as she had the first time they encountered each other, the day he moved into his apartment there.

29 He looks down with rueful resignation, then turns and enters a waiting carriage, which, as it departs, is followed by another.

I should mention something on my mind, in relation to the perfectionist motivations of both the film and the story. Both concern a man who feels stopped or lost in his life, as if unfinished or paralyzed, who is awaiting some form of omen or signal or experience that will free him or show him a fate beyond the stance he has achieved in the world. This is figured in Emerson's "Self-Reliance" by that humbling gleam of light which reveals to you your refusal to break free of expectation and conformity and discover your own judgment of the world, which amounts to declaring your own existence. I broach the idea in *Contesting Tears* by proposing that James is in this text rewriting, or, less melodramatically, systematically commenting upon, Emerson's great essay "Experience." That essay of Emerson's can be taken as investigating the causes of the difficulty in the way of acquiring one's own experience, or say the freedom of one's experience, which requires a willingness to imagine that the thwarting of one's desire for the world can be overcome. Emerson's essay is not exactly about the debasement of perfectionism but about the difficulties, or painfulness, or suffering, hence inevitable setbacks, in the way of meeting its demands for transformation, for changing one's life and (hence, however invisibly in the moment) the life of the world.

A way of summarizing what I take to be Emerson's criticism of previous philosophy's idea of experience—say in Locke and Hume and in Kant—is to reinterpret what it means to take experience as based upon impressions. These former philosophers classically take impressions to be the result of a causal relation borne to me by the world. In Emerson, my impressions are my interpretations of the world, the way I experience the world, the basis of my judgments of its worth, how it matters to me, impresses me, or not.

What I am caused to do and what I am free to do are then subject to my investigation.

Let's start with three elements shared by the James story and the Ophuls film that seem uncontroversial enough. First, in both of them the man fails, in the beginning, to recognize who a woman is when we are shown their reencounter. Second, in neither case does the woman tell the man who she is, or understands herself to be; in both she takes herself to know who the man is, what he wants of himself. Third, when he recognizes who she is, or what she has meant, a high moment of melodrama is precipitated: in the film the moment is the man's covering his face with his hands; in the story it is the concluding moment at which the man throws himself on the woman's grave.

We will recognize the connection of these melodramatic instances with the light-hearted, not to say comic, versions of the failure of a man to recognize a woman in *The Lady Eve* and in Freud's "Delusions and Dreams in Jensen's *Gradiva*." It suggests itself that in genres so much about education, the identification of a woman is the form the man's education takes. What might this mean? If we arrive at a discussion of this point, it is bound to be tied to the question why, in the melodramas, unlike the comic versions, the woman is not therapeutic for the man, though in some sense he asks her to be, anyway asks her to rescue him, or "watch with him." (There is a certain distinct strain of imagery in the James story concerning ships, as if it is from shipwreck that the rescue is to take place.)

An obvious difference between the film and James's story is that in the film the woman never tells him (in person) that they have met, and had a child. Whereas in the story the woman does tell him about their meeting and has to remind him, to his astonishment, that he had divulged to her a secret that amounts to the secret of his life.

The woman in *Letter* informs the man, when the child is dead and she is dying, in her letter, which will have the consequence of killing its addressee, why she did not tell him earlier who she was. She says she wanted to be the one woman who did not ask him for anything. (So she wanted him to die instead?) And don't we want to ask what, in "The Beast in the Jungle," May Bartram gets out of not speaking, that is, out of not telling John Marcher what he eventually insists that she knows? Which would be to ask what it is she gets out of accepting the role of waiting or watching with Marcher, namely to see whether the "it" that is to happen to him, that he is being "saved" for, happens, or whether it is a fatal, if laughable, illusion? Marcher asks himself what she gets—mostly by way of asking whether he isn't being selfish or egotistical in asking for her companionship in what he calls this "vigil." Do we ask whether she isn't getting just what she wants—the lifelong companionship of what she considers "her man" without sexual obligations? Or is it easier for us to accept the man's point of view, because everyone knows that Henry James could not conceivably have married, and many suspect they know the reason for this?

James's tale can indeed seem laughable, which is the response John Marcher repeatedly fears may be directed at him, the thing he particularly notes, with gratitude, that May Bartram does not conceive. Yet I join those who place it among James's greatest short fictions, adding along with it two other of his late, long stories, "The Birthplace" and "The Jolly Corner." All three stories are about what we can think of as being haunted.

Evidently the fantasy of a life lived waiting for life to happen finds an anxious, or perhaps eager, response that is more widespread than one might have imagined. Is the reading (influentially broached by Eve Kosofsky Sedgwick) according to which Marcher is taken to be closeted by either a well-grounded or an ill-grounded panic over his homosexuality widespread enough, I mean specific and general enough, to account for this response? I find the reading important and plausible, and I am duly suspicious about my being somewhat resistant to it. Not exactly about its being only partially true. "The Beast in the Jungle" is a story about a friendship (between a man and a woman) providing a "cover" for each of the friends. But the more plainly the homosexual pertinence asserts itself, the more that itself can seem a candidate for a cover story.

Let us start with a small moral, or a small conception of the moral issue involved, pertinent to our concern with perfectionism as an alternative register of the moral life.

I have noted that John Marcher's moral imagination, skirting the laughable, early turns on the question whether he is being selfish or egotistical in pulling May Bartram into his idiosyncratic orbit of self-fascination. He considers, and asks her, what her "compensation" (an important Emersonian concept) can or should be for her attention to him. He first imagines her presence at the great house, to which, as the story opens, he is among the party invited, to be paid for by her through her "services" to the place, and he initially (that is for most of a lifetime) sees her in terms of her usefulness, which he repays with thoughtful and expensive birthday presents and by taking her systematically to the opera season and participating in late suppers afterward prepared by her. His mind in this register forms a kind of parody of utilitarianism. (Perhaps the pair are understandable as a parody of Aristotle's second grade of friendship, friendship for utility.)

That Marcher, for that very reason, fails the test of the Kantian moral law is clear enough: he does seem to be contradicting the categorical imperative to treat others never merely as a means but also as an end. But James, I think, gives us enough ground to withhold this judgment, if in no other way than by taking Marcher's consciousness of May Bartram as false from the beginning. He may imagine that the subjective principle of his action is: If one holds the key to your fate, use that one to find it out. But suppose the maxim is closer to something like: If the only one to whom you have been able to speak from the heart reveals that she has taken what you said to heart, and will cleave to you, cleave to her. The categorical imperative doesn't seem to decide for you whether a course of conduct is morally necessary, or possible, unless you are altogether clearer what it is you propose to do than John Marcher is. Or put otherwise: Marcher doesn't propose to do anything, other than "wait." He doesn't know why he has chosen May Bartram for his ultimate confidence, and she is his only route to finding out why.

I find myself coming back to the opening question of Emerson's "Experience"—"Where do we find ourselves?"—which I take as emblematic of a perfectionist quest for orientation, responded to as such by Nietzsche, explicitly in the second sentence of *The Genealogy of Morals*: "How should we find ourselves since we have never sought ourselves?" Ideas of finding, hence of losing, hence of succeeding and failing, come up early and late in James's "Beast in the Jungle." In "Experience," the idea of finding, or as Emerson also puts it, discovering, is associated with America, which Emerson there calls "new yet unapproachable." The words "new" and "old" are recurrent in both this Emerson essay and James's story; in both, I imagine, to sound the American world. This will have to come back when I take a moment to specify more fully evidence of the connection between these texts. For the moment I specify two contexts of the occurrence of the idea of loss, or being lost, that show the range of its effects.

A late paragraph in James's story begins "He [Marcher] found himself wondering," which I read as suggesting that he came to know himself in the philosophical mood of wonder. And the cause of the wonder was a change he reports as absolute between his old sense and his new, namely between his old expectation of something revelatory to come and his new sense of nothing left to come. In the next paragraph he expresses this new vision as of "the lost stuff of consciousness," and identifies his quest of it—or his wager, either to "win it back or have done with consciousness for ever"—as becoming for him "as a strayed or stolen child to an unappeasable father." This to my mind takes him to Emerson's identification of himself in "Experience" as the father of a child lost, who finds that grief teaches only that he cannot grieve, meaning perhaps that grief is not what he had expected, it is not close enough to the fact, suggesting an insufficiency in human consciousness as such. (I compress these ideas in order not to lose them and their connections; they will come back.)

The other context I take initially to measure the range in the concept of loss appears in the second paragraph of the story, where John Marcher is affected doubly by May Bartram's face, namely both "as the sequel of something of which he had lost the beginning," and as conveying "that the young woman herself hadn't lost the thread." So are we to take it that May Bartram presents herself to him as a descendant of Ariadne, who holds the thread for Theseus of his return from the maze; that accordingly the Beast in the Jungle is an interpretation of the Minotaur in the maze; that in the modern world, call it America, we know that obstacles to our desires are no longer at the center of a construction (say stories we tell ourselves), but that we are the Daedaluses of our own haunted, empty mazes, constructed in memory of, say in the loss of, romantic, monstrous quests; that we wander into the unsurveyable alleys of doubt and disorientation in order not to see what stares us in the face; that the monster to find whom we are willing to risk losing ourselves in the maze is the one we flee, namely the young woman holding the thread?

Or is the absconded monster, therefore, ourselves? (Such matters are virtually announced as threads, as continuations—or rewritings—of the story in James's later "The Jolly Corner," written in the aftermath of the experience of writing about his long return to America, in *The American Experience,* in the years immediately after "The Beast in the Jungle.") But if so then why does May Bartram not inform John Marcher of his mistake, since she seems always to have known the truth?

Is what she knows unsayable, let's say unnameable? (This is an important concept in Emerson's "Experience.") At the end (in the penultimate paragraph of the story) Marcher will evidently name the "it" that was to happen to him: "The name on the table [the gravestone] smote him . . . and what it said to him, full in the face, was that *she* was what he had missed . . . He had been the man of his time, *the* man, to whom nothing on earth was to have happened." So the stone says something to him, something that the woman could not say. But in what sense "could not"? For her to say "I am what you have missed" would not have been true, so long as she had the strength to say it. So did it become, as it were, true—only when she was dead? And then who was there to inform him of the truth? Who can inform you of what you either already know or can never really know?

Some of you will recognize this last formulation as a problem addressed in Wittgenstein's *Investigations*. I give it expression here because the disarmingly casual opening sentence of the James story flags an interest in the conditions of speech, of what can be said, of what is worth saying, by both declaring and denying the interest: "What determined the speech that startled him in the course of their encounter scarcely matters, being probably but some words spoken by himself quite without intention—spoken as they lingered and slowly moved together after their renewal of acquaintance." And everything that follows seems to turn on why something was said or on forgetting something that was said or on beseeching someone to say something or on characterizing the topic of speech.

Now what am I doing in speculating about such possibilities? Am I suggesting that James's prose is a maze, that to follow its thread is an act of seduction designed to have us "watch" with its characters (as May Bartram contracts to do with John Marcher early in the story), in which case we are warned that our (reading) lives depend upon our not missing something, and in all fairness allowing ourselves to ask and to say what it is we get out of it, what compensates us for attending to this complex, famous, late, difficult, writing, a writing that divides audiences, who may find it inviting and opulent, or uninviting and evasive? To respond to the tale seems to require matching, or competing with, its prose. And I have barely begun.

Before continuing with that, let's ask whether there is a comparable competitive response to such a work as the film *Letter From an Unknown Woman*. What are its ways of defining the level of response that it asks from its viewers? The question, and a direction of answer, is posed in the idea of a letter from an unknown woman. The letter is, in the first instance, the name of something that the film is about, whose writing and whose reception the film depicts. But the letter also *is* the film; its title identifies itself as a letter, which more or less materializes the letter that it depicts, hence radically changes the audience for which it is composed. Does the fact that there is accordingly some identity between the letters suggest that the composer of the film is declaring himself as an unknown woman? Or that he undertakes to speak for this woman, to incorporate her voice (-over) in his letter? It is not exactly the *same* letter, since it knows something the depicted letter does not know, principally what the effect of the letter will be. (Which?)

I have said that the depicted letter participates in causing its recipient's death. How? By making him lose track of time, holding his attention through its narrative until it is too late for him to escape from the duel? But what it more directly causes—so the maker of the film asserts—are the images it awakens, or returns, that is, supplies, for the man. What relation is being proposed between the woman's words and the (man's) film's images? Does the film wish to be taken as an illustration of the images the woman intends and the man receives? Or does it confess that it usurps the man's imagination, dictates to him what he is to realize? And was the woman's letter somehow meant to have its death-dealing effect? The writer of it had led her honor-bound duel-inclined husband to her former lover's door.

An importance of the question how the woman's letter was meant is that *we* are the recipient of the film that calls itself *Letter from an Unknown Woman*. We can say that it means to awaken images in us, and to make us lose track of time. But is it thereby supposed to do us harm? Is it supposed to deal us some kind of death? Or to produce the death of something whose expiration does us good?

Well, how does the film conceive of itself? Let us take it in its general and obvious presentation of the genre whose title I have adapted from the film, the melodrama of an unknown woman, a genre derivable from remarriage comedy, which is to say, one which negates principal features of that genre of comedy. Let's briefly rehearse them. (1) The woman is presented as a mother, and (2) her mother is present. (3) Her desire comes in conflict with the law, represented in the formidable form of her father-like, military husband. (4) The film ends where it begins, not in an elsewhere of possibility, a green world. (5) It depicts what I have sometimes hastily called a world of women; or perhaps it is two worlds, at least—one of high fashion, with an air of prostitution, and one of religion. (6) The past is not an imagined, shared place of happiness, as in the comedies, but it holds an unredeemable curse in store. (7) Time is not recurrent, as in the comedies, but frozen; it will pounce, as in the last sentences of "The Beast in the Jungle." When things in these environments occur at the wrong time, there is no matter for laughter. And (8), pervasively, communication or conversation is everywhere undercut by irony. There are ironies at various levels—at the level of dialogue, at the level of images, at the level of camera motion.

Melodrama thrives on the blatant, so let's begin with so blatant a thing as the repetition of the phrase "two weeks." Stefan says it first when Lisa arrives at the train station to see him off for his concert tour, from which he will not return; and later Lisa says it when she sees, or sends, their son Stefan off on essentially the same train, to his death. Separation from this man, and what comes from him, represents death for this woman. To take her seriously is to take this seriously. When, near the end, she confesses to her husband in their carriage after the opera that she never had any will but Stefan's, hence that she is helpless to break off from him, as her husband reasonably asks her to do, she is in effect declaring that she has never been in conversation with either man, but has kept herself hidden from both. (Unless, as in *A Doll's House*, her leaving precipitates what Nora calls her and her husband's first serious conversation—but Lisa, unwedded to life, is far from a Nora.) Lisa has never been in conversation with Stefan, except in her imagination, if conversation requires two wills in play. Only so would they humanly share pastures.

No less blatant is the irony, at Lisa and Stefan's final encounter, when she at last is admitted to his apartment and Stefan welcomes her by, as he would with any such visitor, ordering a late supper and leaving her for a moment to open a bottle of champagne. He calls out to her, fooling with the bottle, "Are you lonely out there?" and she replies, realizing that she after all is unrecognized, "Yes. Very lonely." She replies—to whom? To him and to us, simultaneously meaning opposite things, hence in irony: lonely consolably, and lonely inconsolably. She takes his flirtatious question as a death sentence.

Then there is the irony in the repeated notion of "having many talents." Lisa first says this, of her son, as she and her husband prepare to leave for the opera; and then, at the opera, the phrase "talents, and perhaps too many talents" is overheard, used of the son's father as a kind of dirty side-swipe at what the father can do with women apart from play the piano for them. Again, there is the irony of the coachman saying at the end of the alienating conversation in the coach, the serious conversation of divorce, "We're home, Sir." And back at home the boy, whom the mother awakens to guide him back from her bed to his own, manifests his compliance with his mother's request to him, before she and his stepfather left for the opera, to call this man "Father," now exactly after the woman has made that irrelevant in deciding to send him away from this father too.

In all of this, symbology continues to be laid on with the usual trowel: there are endlessly repeated heavy iron fences and grates and windows and doors that separate people from their desires, and trains transporting ones you care about to separation and death in clouds of smoke, all serving to emphasize the contrast of black and white, as do shots taken outside at night on largely empty, snow-covered streets.

Let's see more specifically how this film conceives of its own working, how it defines the nature of film and the responses that film asks for. It contains, more or less obviously, certain emblems that may be taken to represent the nature or fact of film. And Max Ophuls's camera, famous for its intricate and elaborate movement, has its particular ways of declaring itself.

I begin with what I am calling emblems of the fact or the nature of filmed figures and of their audience. One of these emblems is a wax museum. The pair come upon it the winter night they drive out in an open carriage to the Prater amusement park in Vienna. A wax museum is a place in which famous or infamous human beings have been duplicated in a malleable, impressionable substance—a reasonable simile for being duplicated on film. The dialogue here is critical. The woman asks, "Will they make a wax figure of you?"—already confessing her interest in his promise and notoriety. This immediate declaration of duplicated, or duplicitous, figures is virtually daring us to see that the film is, let us say, alienating itself, questioning the basis of its existence, questioning our presence there, our fascination. What are we looking at? They have (Max Ophuls and his crew have) already made a wax figure of the man—and of her, which she does not notice, hence does not notice that she has made an inner wax figure of the man, as the materialization of her desire, as one does. He answers the question she asks by a question of his own: "Will you pay a penny to see me?" Her reply recognizes the stakes in her question: "If you'll come to life." He will come to life, apparently, but too late, and it costs him his life. (We haven't discussed whether John Marcher has come to life as he casts himself face down on May Bartram's tomb. What did May Bartram mean by saying "It is never too late"? Does this mean, never too late to contest melodrama?)

Lisa had, when her family was, on her mother's remarrying, taking her away from Vienna, walked alone through her family's empty apartment, and mused to herself (that is, she is speaking the voice-over throughout this film; the letter is hers, whoever else's), "Will these rooms ever come back to life? Will I?" So she is looking for resurrection, for transformation, for escape. The film will, in its figures for itself, such as the wax museum, taunt her with its own powers, or images, of resurrection. This is the beginning manifestation on her part of perfectionism, since she is asking herself in what world she belongs.

What is wrong with her idea? We already know, however things will work out, that her consecration to culture, as Nietzsche had put the matter in his Untimely Meditation on Schopenhauer, was not in favor of her further self, but has been in favor of another, this cultivated man. That it is to or for him and his piano-playing that she is consecrating her life she makes explicit in her lethal letter to him ("Quite consciously I prepared myself for you"). Why does this sound so joyless, especially recalling Nietzsche's expressions of the ecstatic in his discovery of freedom? What is morally suspicious about her decision? Is it that she is sacrificing herself for the man, or let us say with Kant, treating herself as a means? Or is it that she is assigning a debt to the man that is unknown to him? I do not doubt the sincerity of her telling him in the letter that she wanted to be the one woman who asked him for nothing. Then either she was not up to the wish or else it was from the beginning a terrible bargain.

A second emblem of film announced in this film is provided by the statue, the image of the goddess that never arrives. It is a figure Stefan describes in his final sequence with Lisa in his apartment, one for which he says he is waiting, as for a tomorrow that never dawns. Something that would compensate Lisa for the bargain of waiting with him is that, alone among the parade of women through that apartment, with as it were their compensation of false promises, she would discover herself to him as the goddess who would release him into his life. But the idea of waiting for such an event had long ago been abandoned by him, replaced by the wax pleasures of using the idea of the event as part of his seduction ritual. When she runs out of the apartment, in distracted horror, may we attribute to her some sense not simply of his failure to recognize her, either as a woman or as a goddess, but of her neglect in not having told him of his son?

Such absorbing bargains as Lisa and Stefan have made, or John Marcher and May Bartram, do not seem well recognized, not pertinently criticized, by our philosophy—neither by utilitarian calculation, nor, very clearly, by Kantian maxims. I have indicated a pertinence to the idea of treating humanity in oneself or in another never merely as a means, but this does not seem demonstrable in the present cases through universalizing maxims. If you say to Lisa that she cannot will that everyone consecrate themselves to another human greater than themselves, she can reply that she is fulfilled in this other, or, as she puts it, that she has no will but his. Then you have to say something like: Do not abandon the basis of your human dignity by abandoning the moral life altogether, which demands essentially that you exercise your own will. But now this sounds argumentative, prejudicial. Kant wished to prove that duty is real, not an empty concept. But duty that stands in the way of providing this man with the will to live, to become what he is, seems an empty concept to this woman.

Can we tell whether her fatal acceptance of her failure is an acceptance that his nihilism is greater than her faith, or a recognition that her fantasy of rescue and responsibility was never more than one more adventure in his temporizing with life, waiting for his life to happen to him? Can we tell this in the case of John Marcher? If not, are we to take this as more evidence that, since Kant wrote, a degree of privacy has entered into the modern subject that craves an intimacy of understanding not expressed in classical moral relationship?

Kant was aware, indeed insisted, that we can never know the degree to which, in the recesses of our natures, we act purely for the sake of the moral law. But it is as if this knowledge—bound up with an ungovernable sense of the masquerade and pious violence of the world—of our inadequacies and our desires for transcendence and purity, can come to dominate our view of morality, which no longer assures us of our humanity. Or else we come, as I have suggested happens in perfectionism, to regard the discussion of morality, of what proves the reality of moral relationship, to be part of moral conversation. It is that juncture of human existence, expressed as consent to the world of others, which, in my chapter on Aristotle, I called the necessity of choosing our life, and assumed from this the obligation of a philosophical education to provide the knowledge of what makes a life worthy of choice.

The emblems of wax figures and of statues of goddesses eternally absent, as images of what it is to view a film, seem to be taken up and elaborated in the most extended allegory of film delivered in this film, namely, the sequence in which the pair go to the sideshow inside the Prater park that consists of the make-believe travel around the world in the fake train compartment. That sort of setup, with the garish landscape scenes mechanically rolled past a window that opens as from a train, was a popular amusement for a few years during the first decade of the twentieth century, before actual movies caught on as the dominant form of popular artistic entertainment. It was called, after its inventor, a Hale Tour. I mention a few salient features of that allegorization of this film by that setup.

It shows the audience of the film (represented by the pair in the compartment) to endow the passing scenes presented to them (some rather obvious travel poster paintings) with incomparably more emotion than those painted panoramas can be expected to call for in themselves—as if this allegorized response to film reveals the response to film as inherently excessive, say inherently melodramatic. But then, where, in response to the arts, can one's response not be said to be excessive? Works of art are only dumb objects, are they not? Where is all this emotion coming from? Let's go further. The allegory shows that a projected film is, after all, just a nineteenth-century setup, a mechanical contraption. It runs on tracks and rollers, fed and tended by essentially bored functionaries, for whom the idea of magic in this contraption is either funny or sad, if they have the energy to be either. This suggests that a certain overly magical response may be taken as the other side of the sense that the actual world—the one represented, and eclipsed by the representation—is in itself quite tawdry and boring; these attitudes seem called for by each other.

I think of a description from section 6 of "The Beast in the Jungle": "[Marcher] visited the depths of Asia [in response to May Bartram's death], spending himself on scenes of romantic interest, of superlative sanctity; but what was present to him everywhere was that for a man who had known what *he* had known the world was vulgar and vain." A moment, perhaps, of perfectionist disillusionment (or fake disillusionment—nothing can be taken at face value in these matters).

Another pivot of allegory from the Hale Tour contraption to the response to actual films—beyond excessiveness and disillusionment—is that the response of the pair isolated in their false compartment to the passing rolled landscape is essentially one of nostalgia. The man gets out after they have seen the thing once and says to the operator, "We will revisit the scenes of our childhood" (perhaps as if they have just constructed a child-hood together). Viewing a film as a return to childhood has come up more than once in our discussions, for example in reference to *Stella Dallas,* where I identify the screen as the source of the mother's gaze. More specif-ically, the scene of this depicted audience of a moving image shows it to be finding escape (that is, in imaginary travel), and to provide a context, in the man and the woman's physical and psychological isolation together, for mutual seduction.

(The intimacy of this small "audience" raises again the question, broached in my *World Viewed,* whether there is such a thing as a "total audience" for a film—as for theater, spoken or sung—or whether an audience for a film essentially consists in pools of companions; in which case it would be neces-sary to break into the isolated pools in order to involve a total audience in the experience of these works. I take from this necessity the suggestion that there is something essentially transgressive in watching films, something illicit. Perhaps the special-effects spectaculars that have inundated Hollywood in recent decades are indeed media for a total audience, in which the power to fantasize and identify is overwhelmed, regimented rather than provoked.)

What purpose is served by these emblems or allegories? If Ophuls is declaring his film to deal, inevitably, in excess emotion, nostalgia, and seductiveness, then presumably he is providing perspective on these forces, alerting his audience to his art, which is to trace them to their human sources, to provide for them what understanding, sympathy, say catharsis, is available to him.

Let's stay close to the film by taking up the second major way in which film defines the response it seeks: not now by finding emblems of itself but by the ways the camera finds in which to declare its work. Max Ophuls, as said, is famous as a filmmaker for the exceptional fluidity of his camera, allowing it to roam and rise over a room as if sweeping across a universe. I take further two moments of virtuoso camera movement in *Letter from an Unknown Woman.*

The first is the opening of the sequence at the opera in which the camera describes its most extravagantly luxurious motion of the film, moving from left to right, then up, following a stairway, past the chandeliers that Ophuls loves to take in his foregrounds, as if to measure his progress, as perhaps to say that no matter how attentive and privileged a vision the camera may offer, its view is partial, drawn one way rather than another, from here rather than there. Here it searches a field or world of unmitigated glamour, of codes of uniformed power and honor, a world of irreversible, unredeemable consequences, as in war. That depiction of, and in some measure participation in, a world of surface and danger is described in the monologue of the voice-over, in which Lisa's reading/thinking her letter seems here not to dictate but to interpret what the camera, in its apparent freedom, is doing. It proposes a long speculation about "Passing faces, so many, and every step counted; and yet none is lost that is to be found. I know now that nothing happens by chance." Is this what we understand ourselves to see here? That everything passes and that nothing is lost that is to be found is a reasonable characterization of the work of the motion picture camera, which makes the evanescent permanent. Nothing follows about what its freedom is and how it wagers with chance.

This is under investigation in the art of cinema. Ophuls's camera is to be taken as providing meditations on chance, on counting steps, on always and never losing what it finds given to it, as if film instills images that we never assuredly escape, subjecting us to its subjects, speculating on its victimization of us, as, according to Emerson, language condemns us to meaning.

Philosophers will wonder whether what we know of the world is dependent or independent of our contribution to this knowledge, the answer to which seems to determine whether we can have objective knowledge of the world or at most intersubjective agreements about it. Photography's intervention into our culture strikes a new note in this problematic. Put it this way: Reality plays a causal role in the creation of a photograph unlike its role in any other medium of art—in painting, in theater, in writing (fictional or otherwise). The absolute dependence of photography on the world at the same time declares its separateness from the world. The world can no more dictate what of itself is given to the camera to reveal of it than it can dictate what of itself is given to language to be said of it. Our revelations reveal our freedom, what of our freedom we can claim.

The second way Ophuls's camera declares its work is in its power of absolute repetition, a power that neither painting nor theater enjoys, or suffers. (In an age of reproduction, it is striking that the replication of a photograph is not a reproduction of it but another print of it. The subsequent object is not less original; it may be more or less preferable to the antecedent, a valuation that then becomes a matter of judgment.) I speak in my essay on

Letter From an Unknown Woman in *Contesting Tears* of two sets of repeated images, ones I call death-dealing and death-enhancing. (The exactitude of the recurrence is an image of Lacan's discussion of the ego-ideal's demanding, demanded, search for its object. Perhaps the greatest, most concentrated, treatment of the implacable violence in this search is Hitchcock's *Vertigo*.) Now I call attention to the repetitive power of the camera's motion and its positions. I have in mind the narrative moment in which Lisa, in a final, futile effort to escape from moving with her parents from Vienna to Linz, appears at the door of Stefan's apartment, and we have the celebrated complex motion in which the camera slides up from the unanswered door to show Lisa from the back, where she has been sitting all day long, and where upon on a sound of voices from below the camera turns to let us see what she sees at the bottom of the stairs, a scene of Stefan's entering the apartment building with another woman, walking up the stairs with her, to the landing just below where Lisa is seated motionlessly, unnoticed, and then, as the camera slowly swings to watch them with more exquisite pain, their passing into his apartment. We will climactically be given this identical, complex camera progression a second time (counting its steps, losing nothing), with Lisa cast as the woman entering Stefan's apartment.

How we read this repetition will epitomize how we read the film. Has Lisa got her wish to be the woman, one of them, that Stefan ends his evening adventures with? But a wish, of course, always with the proviso that she be seen by him in her difference, as, so to speak, redemptive of empty repetition, redemptive of time. Is she giving him a chance, just after having denied that anything happens by chance? Then is it fated that she not tell him of the difference that she has had his child? Her declaration that she wanted to be the one who asked him for nothing has to be set against her evidently expecting him to recognize her as the meaning of his life, that is, to recognize himself as the meaning of hers.

I said the repetition of the camera motion is exact. But what it depicts is not quite exact. The difference the second time is that Lisa's earlier position seated on the stairs, as spectator of her future, is unoccupied. Our old position, however, is reoccupied by us, and now from there we absorb Lisa's position as spectator and desirer. And what do we desire for this man and this woman? Punishing things or redemptive things? And on what moral grounds? It is we who are being tested, being given a chance.

Henry James and Max Ophuls

403

I have noted that in both James's story and in Ophuls's film there is a moment in which the man's depicted horror (so James calls it) at realizing (what James also calls) the "void of his life" seems to dictate, anyway suggest, a response to the events of the tale we are now in possession of, not perhaps to imitate this response, but to respond to it. In the story the response is the recognition that causes the man to throw himself on the grave; in the film it is the recognition that causes the man to cover his face with his hands.

But to respond to these responses of the men is to recognize how we understand them, stand under their effect, bear up under their knowledge. Most particularly, to recognize whether we imagine in each case the man's response to include a perception of the woman that we share, or else contest, or whether we imagine his response as a continuation of his "selfishness," a matter of his regret at his own missing of his chance, with some elegiac tinge of guilt at his treatment of the woman; whether, that is, we imagine the man to have achieved some perception of, some perspective on, what the woman has suffered and what her suffering has caused them both. That some ambiguity may be irreducible here is shown in my reading of Stefan's gesture of response as he finishes Lisa's letter and is assaulted by earlier images of their time together—covering his face with his hands—as ambiguous as between not wanting to recognize something and not wanting to be recognized.

James's words depicting this moment of insight (or insight still missed) are more elaborated. I quoted earlier the sentence in which May Bartram's tomb is described as saying something to John Marcher that May Bartram could not say, namely that she, or rather that missing her, was his beast. The conjunction of saying and missing is rubbed in in the preceding sentence: "He gazed, he drew breath, in pain; he turned in his dismay, and, turning, he had before him in sharper incision than ever the open page of his story." James is famous for his indirection. But he is, because of it, also violently direct. He had said a few paragraphs before this one: "The open page was the tomb of his friend." The open page before us of James's story, which John Marcher recognizes as his story, declares itself to be a tomb, in which something which is the object of desire—of our desire, if we read the story with desire—is buried, something we have missed. (This is I suppose the deepest connection of James's story and Emerson's "Experience.")

This makes the story ours. But is James counting merely on the idea that what makes it ours is some universalization of the experience of missing out on one's life, his text the tomb of our desires? (It is a characteristic enough American experience, from Jay Gatsby to Citizen Kane to Blanche DuBois to the James Stewart character in *It's a Wonderful Life*.) Or is James at the same time specifying something about the story before us, open as a tomb, namely that in however much time, in whatever interval of our life, we have spent with it, we have missed something? This seems to imply that James has undertaken to compose in a finite space a work of infinite implication. Something of the sort may be taken as defining the ambition of serious writing. This would measure the density of writing with that of certain dreams, whose interpretation, as Freud notes, may reach so deep into the endless complexity of the real as to baffle further interpretation. I'll sketch the sort of thing I mean by going back to the connection I proposed at the outset between James's story and Emerson's essay "Experience."

I suppose I should confess that when John Marcher appeals to May Bartram to tell him what she evidently knows and what he has become afraid not to know, and he adds, "You've had your experience. You leave me to my fate," I understand him to be mentioning two of Emerson's greatest essays, "Experience" and "Fate." I say I confess it, uncertain whether I am asking you to believe it. But belief is here not necessary, since the link I find unassailable between the James story and Emerson's "Experience" lies in the congruence of sense and rhetorical flair between James's "He had been . . . *the* man to whom nothing on earth was to have happened" and Emerson's "I grieve that grief can teach me nothing, nor carry me one step into real nature."

No doubt I am encouraged in my view by James's characterizing Marcher's interest, and loss of interest, in what he calls "the stuff of his consciousness," as something that became for Marcher "as a strayed or stolen child to an unappeasable father"—it is an accurate account of Emerson's portrait of himself in "Experience," in which he reports the death of his child two years earlier as the most significant instance of his experience, the one from which he derives his account of experience's incapacity to get the world, or the loss of the world, closer. And I am prepared to verify that what Emerson specifies, in his poem that prefaces the essay, as "The lords of life," something like moods in which the world as a whole presents itself to the mind—"Use and Surprise / Surface and Dream / Succession swift and spectral Wrong / Temperament without a tongue / And the inventor of the game / Omnipresent without a name"—are all present in James's story. In such a frame of mind I take the repeated notation of "impatience" in Marcher's self-rebuke, after saying to the ill May Bartram "I know nothing"—"He was afterwards to say to himself that he must have spoken with odious impatience, such an impatience as to show that, supremely disconcerted, he washed his hands of the whole question"—to remember Emerson's critical repetition "Patience, patience" at the end of "Experience." Whether James thereby implicitly accuses Emerson of having washed his hands of the question of action in the world, accuses him of resembling John Marcher more than Henry James, or whether James associates himself with an Emersonian accusation of Marcher, may be left open.

Some interesting recent writing on James, collected in the *Cambridge Companion to Henry James*, continues the line of identifying James with his apparent alter egos who devalue the life of action in favor of a life of consciousness, most notably with Lambert Strether in *The Ambassadors*. One critic, Eric Haralson, takes James to be contesting the idea of male forcefulness by proposing an exploratory life of experience or consciousness as an alternative to an active sexual life; another, Martha Banta, takes James more specifically to be combating Theodore Roosevelt's preaching of maleness as doing things, making things happen, critical among them fathering a family. The evidence for these contexts is impressive on both accounts. But I am taking James, in this encounter with Emerson, to be meeting the issue on the ground Emerson stakes out, the ground of philosophy, challenging with Emerson the American trust in conquering the world by iron and annexation; it would not be a new world so conquered.

So when James presents his formula for John Marcher as "the man to whom nothing on earth was to have happened," it is possible to read this as taking "on earth" in contrast with Marcher's fate to have things happen only transcendentally, implicitly leveling at Emerson, projecting upon him, criticism of James's (and his apparent alter egos') adoption of inaction and consciousness. James and Emerson both seek an alternative to the compulsion to action seemingly demanded by the still-awaiting promise of America. As if for them the frontier (said by Frederick Jackson Turner to be closed in 1903, the year of James's story) was closed long ago, with the demand for self-reflection, the country thrown back upon itself, in actualizing and preserving itself, as with the Declaration of Independence and the arguments leading to the Civil War. For Emerson, the poverty of "these bleak rocks" of

America was perhaps sufficient, even ideal, for philosophy; for late James they were perhaps not enough for high art.

I earlier emphasized an air of a perpetual danger of the comic surrounding John Marcher's expectation—and his own sense of his expectation—of redemption in one unnameable experience. Six years after "The Beast in the Jungle," in the ghostly love story "The Jolly Corner," Henry James provided a no longer young man with a redemptive experience and with a woman waiting to interpret it with him, and this time earned for them an active, erotically charged ending ("he drew her to his breast"). But this was still one man conquering, that is, facing, the ghost of his missed life, with the help of a philosophical woman to teach him that what is missed is always the present. James had, in the years between these stories, written large this theme of taking one's existence upon oneself, when, in *The American Scene*, he moved from seeing in himself a returning ghost, to entrusting his hopes for a live future to the chance of America.

With the proposal of the need to rethink the relation of philosophy and literature, and their tasks in America, to question philosophy's ideas of the active and the passive, to reconsider the relation of men and women, to plot the transition from a ghostly to a shared existence, I mean to suggest routes of the dispersal of these texts of James and Emerson into the endless complexity of the real.

Has John Marcher, when we see him last, understood May Bartram's saying to him, "It's never too late"? That is, does his plunge onto her entombed body express his knowledge that he loves her, or that he does not? In neither case is it clear that she is what he missed. If he did not love her, then he missed more than her. If he does love her, what is too late? (I don't say nothing is.) This question can be taken as explored in Eric Rohmer's meditation on Shakespeare's *Winter's Tale*, as we shall be seeing.

Both what is missed and whether one loves are questions to which one in a perfectionist mode must demand responses of himself or herself. Lisa's perfectionism, like that of her model Stefan, is morally debased; each awaits another to justify, to take responsibility for, their coming into existence. Marcher's perfectionism, though he fears it may be debased, or as he puts it, selfish, is rather based on what we might call a metaphysical mistake. He wants another to say to him what only he can say—in effect wants another to *be* him, which is the perfect negation of the perfectionist quest to become oneself. He has avoided the question that would have forced him to recognize in what sense his beast is May Bartram, namely why it is she whom he singled out to tell of his sense of his singularity. She could have asked this question of him—for it is she who voices the question both of them take as obvious, namely whether his sense of awaiting something isn't simply, as it were, awaiting the beast of falling in love (which she identifies for him as being overwhelmed). He asks her whether she asked him this question when they first met and he told her his secret sense. Her reply is evasive: "I wasn't so free-and-easy then." What she evidently recognized even then is that talking love is love talk, initial gestures of lovemaking. So why didn't she tell him? Did she show him?

22

G. B. SHAW
Pygmalion and *Pygmalion*

The film *Pygmalion* is so faithful to Shaw's play that a summary of the film is pointless for those who know the play. They differ in certain important details, and these will be noted when their significance can be assessed.

In some ways George Bernard Shaw is the slightest—the most dated—of the writers discussed in this book; yet Shaw is widely considered the best dramatist between the age of Ibsen, Strindberg, and Chekhov and that of Brecht and Beckett, indeed by some to have been the most influential writer alive during the period, let's say, between the two world wars. *Pygmalion* was written in 1912 and published (in English) in 1916. It's hard to think of a play purely cleverer, but it is not as ambitious as Shaw's *Saint Joan,* or as what many consider his finest play, *Heartbreak House,* both written after the experience of the First World War. I would love to be able to articulate what the palpable but elusive sense of his limitedness is. It does not, I think, lie in what he calls his "didacticism," and prides himself on. Who is more didactic than Brecht, or for that matter, Ibsen? And it does not lie in the slightness of his ideas; he has many and they are important. Is it a matter of his coldness? But Professor Higgins will give Eliza Doolittle a little discourse defending the coldness of a way of life identifiable as one Shaw ratifies.

But I find *Pygmalion* greatly useful to these chapters on moral perfectionism, for various reasons. Shaw's reading of the myth of Pygmalion and Galatea, as told in Ovid—where Pygmalion falls in love with his statue Galatea and asks the gods to bring her to life—in terms of a man's training a woman in the further possession of language, brings the myth within range of the guiding demand for education in remarriage comedy; and at the same time Shaw's reading readily lends the creation myth to the interpretative reversal of it in the remarriage genre, in which it is the woman who seeks creation and in which the man is shown to suffer education (hence further creation) by the woman. I add that it is easier to imagine the various writers, adaptors, directors, actors, involved in the creation of the films I adduce here, not to have read any of the previous texts discussed in this book—with the exception of *A Doll's House*—than it is to imagine them not to have read, or seen, *Pygmalion*. Its very fame makes it the more fascinating for me that the aspect of Shaw represented in Professor Higgins fits Rawls's picture of perfectionism (as I presented it in Chapter 9) more closely than does the work of Nietzsche (as presented in Chapter 11).

Is *Pygmalion*, then, a remarriage comedy? It breaks the genre to the point of defiance, and yet this doesn't seem to neutralize its remarriage feel. (It is quite as defiant of classical comic demands, in insisting on the difference in age of the principal pair, and in the mysteriousness of its conclusion.) But perhaps I feel this just because of the way I envision the ending of the play. Or more precisely, because of the way I envision its sequel.

I am going to take with complete, some will think morbid, seriousness Shaw's preface to the play. This writer, whose individual prefaces to his plays are in their way as notable and interesting as the plays themselves that they preface, declares, in the opening sentence of his preface to *Pygmalion*, "As will be seen later on, *Pygmalion* needs, not a preface, but a sequel, which I have supplied in its due place." But the sequel Shaw provides, which declares itself to demonstrate that Eliza marries the adoring but helpless Freddie, seems evasive and arbitrary. The predominant idea of the sequel is that Higgins's mother has spoilt him for other women: "Eliza . . . was instinctively aware that she could never . . . come between him and his mother (the first necessity of the married woman)." Hence: "Unless Freddy is biologically repulsive to her, and Higgins biologically attractive to a degree that overwhelms all her other instincts, she will, if she marries either of them, marry Freddy. And that is just what Eliza did." What happened to the "if"? And what are we to make of the fact that Higgins ends the play not simply announcing that Eliza is going to marry Freddy, but announcing it with "roars [of] laughter"? Is he laughing because he is relieved of the responsibility of taking a hand in, as the other characters keep pestering him to think about, "What's to become of her?" Or is it because Freddy is the perfect choice for her to "marry" since he is too slight to come between Higgins and his Eliza? And is that because, according to remarriage ideas, the quality of conversation between Higgins and Eliza means that they are already married? But also according to those ideas, while there may well be sexual problems, there is not an acceptance of sexual absence.

Shaw's "sequel" interests itself more in Freddy's sister Clara's transformation, and in the nature of the shop or shops that Eliza and Freddy make a living from, than it does in how Eliza expresses the fact that Higgins remains, in Shaw's words, "one of the strongest personal interests in her life . . . [given the assured absence of] another woman likely to supplant her with him." This further manifests evasiveness. Why does Eliza not feel supplanted, as it were in advance, by his mother? What is the source and distribution of gratifications in these households? Is it that Higgins is supposed to retain Eliza's mind, what he calls her soul, and gladly cedes the rest to Freddy? But her body and voice, physical voice as well as spiritual, have also from the beginning of their connection attracted Higgins's undivided attention and molding. In my chapter on Ibsen, in which I tipped my hat to Shaw, I also criticized Shaw for his inability or unwillingness to convey his characters' subjectivity. But in *Pygmalion* he seems positively to attempt to conceal the subjectivity he has conveyed, as if he has given up on describing the nature and distribution of the satisfactions he proposes, meant to conquer our demand for a romantic ending.

I should specify what I had most emphatically on my mind in saying that this play of Shaw's defiantly breaks generic laws of remarriage comedy. Most obviously, the mother of the principal man is essentially present, and the father of the principal woman is not on the side of his daughter's desire, if he is at the same time obviously not on the side of the law. I would initially also have had in mind Shaw's effort to play down the importance of marriage as the conclusion of romance, except for a suspicion that his blatant fooling around with marriage in his sequel, and his mystifying of it in Higgins's concluding roars of laughter, instead serve to keep the importance of marriage on our minds. But if we persist in some thought that the pair have divorced and that, in an, as it were, legitimately expected sequel, the woman returns to the man, namely that this narrative is to be understood in terms of remarriage expectations, then where are the compensating features in this welter of conversation, education, and laughter?

Let's try to assess the radicalized importance of the idea of speech or conversation as the medium of the play. There is a satisfying brilliance in using the idea of teaching phonetics as a figure for, let's say, the acquisition of speech as such, hence the idea of "making a lady" as a figure for "creating a woman." It seems to raise any and every issue about the conditions of speech, from Aristotle's taking speech as the condition of the polis, to the imagination of a better world in which the conservation of justice can be held without compromise, to Prospero's giving Caliban language and profiting from it by being cursed, and in between to invoke images, in an American second-generation immigrant, such as the present writer, of the pain of first-generation immigrants to America whose accented language belongs neither to the old nor—without comedy or tragedy—to the new world. When Higgins describes to his mother the thrilling interest of "taking a human being and changing her into a quite different human being by creating a new speech for her," and adds, "It's filling up the deepest gulf that separates class from class and soul from soul," I am reminded of learning that in the immediate aftermath of the American Revolution (which I had rather tended to devalue in importance in comparison with the Civil War), there was a revolutionary change in the way ordinary people spoke to each other.

But of course Shaw's play leaves the fact that the new Eliza has no place in society—no place to find out "what's to become of her" in a way that adventurously discovers what she may become—to be merely a personal not a social question. Which perhaps only shows that Higgins is no socialist, whatever Shaw's convictions may have been. But the fact that Shaw goes to some length, in his imaginary sequel, to imagine Clara's transformation into a socially conscious follower of the writing of H. G. Wells, but never imagines that Eliza, who can read, and who is attested by Higgins and by Colonel Pickering to have an ear of genius, is fit for, or has a taste for, some such education into the world she now inhabits, suggests something blocked for Shaw—as if Higgins had written the sequel.

There is that marvelous stroke of having, in the opening of the play, Higgins's taking down what people are saying interpreted by bystanders as a sign that he is a police informer, which we might understand as raising the idea that police powers are required to enforce proper speech as well as to keep those without it in their proper places. But nothing comes of that perception, no recognition of the psychic costs of correctness to match the social costs of incorrectness. Of course one might take the criticisms of Higgins's character as evidence that this blindness is a sign of his personal limitation. But criticisms of him in the play (anyway in the film) do not go beyond accusations of his childishness and rudeness. Moreover, the opening moment of Higgins's notetaking as something more than scientific recording, might be considered as a figure for his (or for Shaw's) dictating what should be said, hence for Shaw's own "didacticism," something he assigns to all genuine art.

This will all come back. As will, perhaps more insistently, the interpretation of impropriety as the suggestion of prostitution ("I'm a good girl I am"), which carries the further implication of society's essential prostitution of its institutions, enshrined in the institution of marriage (an old theme of Shaw's, as of socialists more generally), called by Eliza "selling oneself" (upon which, at one stage, she observes that "We were above that sort of thing in Lisson Green," where she grew up).

I do not want my solemnity to mask the fact that Shaw is both using and satirizing the idea of proper speech as a determinant of social position and value. The figure of Eliza's father is, in some ways less ambiguously than Eliza, a mark of the satire. But Shaw's play strains under the satiric weight, since all the play can claim is that Eliza has, and will be, "passed off" as a lady, not that she has become one. True, she says that what makes a lady is being treated as a lady, but that is an expression of her still limited point of view. And what is that point of view? Everyone asks what's to become of Eliza. But what has already become of Eliza? In the Anthony Asquith film, Wendy Hiller plays the scene at the ambassador's ball as if she is in a trance, which suggests that her relation to Higgins is as Trilby to Svengali. Yet it is later that night that she finds it in herself to oppose and leave him. (If only, as it turns out, to go to his mother.) The figure of Svengali, by the way, indicates that there may be an idea suggested that Higgins's choosing Eliza for his experiment was not the mere chance it is offered as being—but that he was already, as Svengali was, attracted by the woman's voice.

So perhaps we should concede that this play of Shaw's is not meant to talk political sense, and concentrate on his, or rather Higgins's, claim that creating language fills the gulf between souls.

Before concluding that, I should locate Shaw's particular stripe of social idealism, taking a leaf from Eric Bentley's valuable book *Bernard Shaw*. Bentley includes Shaw's idealism in the line of aristocratic Victorian socialism, as distinguished from the French utopian line (associated with such names as Saint-Simon and Fourier), and from the German scientific line (culminating in Marx), and from the Russian anarchist line (for example, Bakunin). Behind Shaw stand the names of Carlyle (so important to Emerson, and to Thoreau), and Ruskin, and William Morris (Shaw's stage directions identify Higgins's mother as surrounded by Morris designs). Here again are names out of fashion. But Morris is still a saint of any program, theoretical or practical, of any institutional scope, serious about the artistic crafts; and John Ruskin's immense achievements in the criticism of painting and of architecture, for all the mannerism and hectoring he assaults the reader with, are still discovered for the force of his intellectual passion and the originality of his perception, by serious readers of every generation, as he was, for example, by no less than the young Marcel Proust, who translated him into French.

So it is worth saying that the idea of an aristocratic Victorian socialism is not merely paradoxical. Aristocratic perfectionism and socialism have a common enemy—the bourgeoisie empowered by capitalism—what Shaw calls the middle class and its morality, what Nietzsche called philistinism, borrowing from what Emerson called conformity. Both Victorian or Emersonian perfectionism and socialism assume that the privileges of traditional aristocracy are, by right, over with. One could say that the aristocrats among the English socialists wish to see socialism acquire certain of the educated tastes, if essentially none of the possessions, of the older aristocracy; as certain American socialists wish to see socialism embody certain of the political ideas of liberalism, such as individual freedom. We have had occasion to mention that attacks on the middle from either side can be taken in bad faith: from the side of the disadvantaged, out of envy; from the side of the advantaged, out of snobbery. It seems clear that Eliza's father is portrayed as free of bad faith and Higgins as simultaneously proud and oblivious of his.

Higgins's imagination of the good city, the city of words, is expressed when he and Eliza are at the end discussing whether she will come back to live in Wimpole Street. She accuses him of treating her badly, of wanting her back only to be of service to him. He replies that he treats everyone the same. Colonel Pickering treats a flower girl like a duchess; he, Higgins, treats a duchess like a flower girl—in short, as Eliza puts it, the same to everybody, and Higgins agrees. He goes on to justify his manners: "The great secret . . . is not having bad manners or good manners; but . . . behaving as if you were in Heaven, where there are no third-class carriages, and one soul is as good as another." This is just the sort of leap over the present, to a combination of the essential and the ethereal, that drives to distraction those who seek genuine social reform.

But sometimes the glibness of Shaw's arguments seems to express a recognition that there are no stable answers to the issues he raises. Shaw, in his sequel, describes Mrs. Higgins's effect on her son as twofold, first setting "a standard for him against which very few women can struggle," and second "effecting for him a disengagement of his affections, his sense of beauty, and his idealism from his specifically sexual impulses." This seems to leave Higgins with over-refined personal and political and artistic impulses and under-refined sexual ones, if any at all.

We have, by the way, heard in the play very little about these impulses. He mentions Milton as representing the language to which Eliza should aspire, and compares her unfavorably with the architecture of Covent Garden, but says nothing about how we might measure ourselves favorably with them. And then there is his tirade to Eliza running, "Oh. It's a fine life, the life of the gutter. It's real: it's warm: it's violent: you can feel it through the thickest skin: you can taste it and smell it without any training or any work. Not like Science and Literature and Classical Music and Philosophy and Art. You find me cold . . . Very well: be off with you to the sort of people you like. Marry some sentimental hog or other with lots of money, and a thick pair of lips to kiss you with and a thick pair of boots to kick you with."

The idea of an erotically uncharged sense of beauty seems a strange one for the man who quotes Nietzsche twice in his sequel, the Nietzsche who in *The Birth of Tragedy*, sec. 21, invokes the Dionysian and who declares that he can speak about music only to those "who, immediately related to music, have it in, as it were, their motherly womb." Yet Shaw quotes Nietzsche's famously garish remark "When you go to women take your whip with you" and, without interpreting it, seems to pick it up roughly by the right end, as warning that what you will have to overcome is not exactly your subjection to unruly women, but rather their willingness for unlimited subjection to you, call this your craving for idolization and pity. (Think of Stefan in *Letter from an Unknown Woman;* and of Jerry in *Now, Voyager.*)

So when he (Professor Higgins) speaks of "creating a new speech for her [Eliza]," it is possible that he means it is for her to use for purposes unpredictable by him. He in effect says so often enough. Yet at the end, when she defies him, he exults: "By George, Eliza. I said I'd make a woman of you; and I have." As a self-identification of himself, in his difference from the mythical Pygmalion (who had to pray to the gods to "make a woman"), it all seems too pat. It confirms a suspicion that Shaw says only what he knows he means, that he never writes beyond himself, that his fine inventiveness is a substitute for a certain level of surprising discovery as he goes, leaving signals of further work to be done, that writers closer to the heart never fail to provide. But this thought reminds me that Pygmalion lends his name as the title of the play, not Galatea, and not the two together; yet I feel that I have been, since I tend to take Eliza's side of things, thinking more about what would satisfy her than what would satisfy Higgins, and leaving the issue of his relationship to his mother, and in a different register his relation to the author of the play that creates him, in too superficial a state.

I mentioned that Higgins's taking dictation of what people say can be understood as a figure for dictating what they are to say; that is, as a figure for writing a play, this play. This seems to be emphasized in the authorial intervention early in the speech of the figure (it turns out to be Eliza) called The Flower Girl: "Here, with apologies, this desperate attempt to represent her dialect without a phonetic alphabet must be abandoned as unintelligible outside London." The effect is, from then on, to make the status of her dialogue indistinguishable from that of the characters whose speech it is unambiguous that he is creating as the writer of the play. But as a playwright it is his apparently quite understandable, non-miraculous job to create women, and men; and we could also say it is his job "to take a human being and make her into a quite different human being by creating a new speech for her"— for example, to make a flower girl out of a duchess, or to make a flower girl into a "consort for a king."

In *Pygmalion* the implied issue in how duchesses and flower girls are made out of each other is how duchesses are made out of, as it were, born duchesses, how they get treated as duchesses are expected to be treated. Eliza speaks of not wishing to deny the difference between Higgins and her, but Shaw does not explain these differences, for example, does not undertake to show us the Eliza who knows more than Higgins about "girls who bring men like him down to their level."

The deliberateness of the confusion, or allegorical relation, between the metaphysical difference between things (like statues, or photographs) and people on the one side, and the theatrical difference between character and actor on the other, is blatant in a climactic exchange such as the following:

Higgins: "I shall miss you, Eliza . . . I have grown accustomed to your voice and appearance . . ."

Eliza: "Well, you have both of them on your gramophone and in your book of photographs. When you feel lonely without me, you can turn the machine on . . ."

Higgins: "I can't turn your soul on. Leave me those feelings: and you can take away the voice and the face. They are not you."

Eliza: "Oh, you are a devil."

This is fairly obviously as serious as Shaw gets explicitly in this play, and it is at the same time a gag about the job of the playwright to create characters who convey feelings. There are greatly important and interesting philosophical issues that seem to me to be set in motion by the confusions of these sets of differences. One issue is not simply the sorting out of the difference between character and actor, involving the difference between the fictional and the actual, but concerns, I would like to say, the irreducible involvement of the theatrical in everyday life, doubtless a function of the nature of human consciousness, whose consciousness is self-conscious, or say whose consciousness is irreducibly a consciousness of the consciousness of others of itself.

Is Shaw's inventiveness meant to make us notice and ponder such questions, or is it meant to distract us from them, or from noticing that he has not taken the responsibility for working them out, dramatizing them?

Now about that mother. Her presence is so important that the compensation for her defiance of the requirements of the remarriage genre must be compensated by herself, by the way she defies them. Hers is too important a presence to be described generally as her spoiling her son for other women by her power to provide beauty and intelligent companionship in his life, while leaving him free to live as he chooses. These would not preempt the felt need for another object of love unless it was also the provision of intimacy. And then how would one distinguish the fact that the mother is taboo as a sexual object from the apparent fact that the association of beauty and intelligent understanding and freedom with this woman has made all women taboo as sexual objects for him? (And evidently all men.)

To answer, I have to sketch my own sequel to the play. I ask why Eliza, having said to Freddy, whom she encounters in the street after her quarrel and break with Higgins, that she is going to put a hole in the river, turns up the next day under Mrs. Higgins's protection? Mrs. Higgins's apartment plays the role of a green world. But my question is why Eliza assumed she would be welcome there. Eliza has been said by Higgins and Pickering, as we have seen, to have an ear of genius, and I am taking it that she heard something in Mrs. Higgins, a promise call it, that she realized she wished to accept, something that indicated she would be as at home with Mrs. Higgins as with her son on Wimpole Street. What she heard comes out in the intimacy of Mrs. Higgins's understanding of Eliza the next day—not merely as expressed in her sharing of Eliza's rage against the two men ("I'd have thrown the fire irons at you"), but in her understanding that she was to accompany Eliza to Eliza's father's wedding ceremony, as if to legitimize and protect Eliza's presence there, as a mother might. (Mrs. Higgins had earlier remarked not only on Eliza's father's tracking her to Higgins's house, but on the fact that no mother had done so.) My proposed sequel finds that Mrs. Higgins, recognizing that Eliza and Henry are necessary to each other, in effect adopts Eliza. This makes it possible for Eliza to live in both houses, or live in one and find periodic refuge in the other, and also to make her, being in the relation of sister to Higgins, a taboo sexual object for him, in which the aim-inhibited erotic impulse requires no further explanation.

While I have characterized my fantasied sequel as a proposal and a sketch (as Shaw's proposed sequel is), I would not want to leave the impression that I feel it to be more weakly grounded than I do. It has what I might call a general or literary and a specific or theatrical origin; I mean merely that there are two points at which Shaw demands an interpretative sequel from the reader and audience.

The general point is that Shaw insists on the necessity of a sequel but provides one himself that feels merely possible, a cover for being unconvinced by the play's ending. (I would rather try out, at the level of the merely possible, the idea that Higgins acts on his early idea of taking his talent into the Music Hall, where Eliza either joins him or gets him to withdraw from this indignity by agreeing to return to live in his house.) The specific point is the mystery of what Mrs. Higgins is unable to write at the close of Act III, expressly in response to her exasperation with "you two infinitely stupid male creatures," her one loss of control, to our knowledge. Since what she is exasperated by is the men's obliviousness to their responsibility for Eliza's future, which they have irreversibly affected, it seems hard not to imagine that what she "tries resolutely to write" is something that will secure that future, hence ensure Eliza's and Henry's closeness but sexual independence—Mrs. Higgins expresses a slight alarm about that at the end

("I'm afraid you've spoilt that girl, Henry. I should be uneasy about you and her if she were less fond of Colonel Pickering")—and allow Eliza to keep Freddie as an erotic plaything if she requires one.

I have argued that remarriage comedy invokes two necessary divorces for discovering happiness in what one might call a marriage—a divorce from the immediate attachment to one's parent(s) and a divorce from the intimacy in the pair's "having grown up together," that is, from their as it were secondary incestuousness. Higgins has no motive for either of these divorces, so to preserve what I persist in taking at the decisive remarriage elements of conversation as intimacy and education, and the presence of the green world, and the absence of (other) children, I require of a credible sequel that it make envisionable the narrative resolution as forming a sort of compromised comic remarriage ending—a compromise in which a perhaps puzzled acceptance of chastity is being weighed in the balance against every other human satisfaction. In this sense, the sequel is not romantic. But there is a childishness and productiveness in the relation which is eccentric enough in its claims upon happiness to place serious claims upon our attention.

A parting thought. Higgins, we recalled, speaks to his mother about language as "filling up the deepest gulf that separates class from class and soul from soul." Having concentrated on the relation of souls, I ask where Higgins's idea of a "gulf" between souls comes from, I mean as something that is to be overcome, or "filled up." It seems, on the contrary, only when a gulf is opened between them, and Eliza, along with Mrs. Higgins, can say goodbye to him, that he no longer regards her as "a millstone round [his] neck." Since it is part of my idea of remarriage comedy that it deals with what philosophy names the problem of other minds, I am glad to find Shaw opening his play to this issue, the issue, let's say, of becoming human to each other. But while it seems obvious that part of granting humanity to another is recognizing the other as possessing (human) language, this leaves unanswered how that possession enters into my recognition of *this* other, my recognition of him or her as, so to speak, mine, mine to respond to. Higgins recognizes Eliza's reality when she opposes him. That is understandable; as is his missing her. He says that what he misses when she is gone is her soul, which he wants to turn on. The obvious difference between your turning on the recording of a voice and your turning on that voice is that the recording does not respond to you, not, at any rate, now. But what is it to want to be responded to now? Why, in the version of the play I use, is Higgins left laughing?

And what, in the film (whose script was adapted by Shaw himself), is its particular proposed sequel to the play, ending with Eliza returning with the line from offscreen, "I washed my hands and face before I come, I did," and Higgins, having been shown longing for her return, turning mysteriously away from her, suppressing a smile, and saying, "Eliza, where the devil are my slippers?" Are they proposing to start again and try for a different ending? Or are they taking up Henry's suggestion of the three of them living like old bachelors? How do bachelors live? It may be part of the nature of film that it wants to leave open, more clearly than theater, the fantasy of romance between Higgins and Eliza. In that case we should note that this possibility is managed by, in the film, somewhat flattening the character of Higgins's mother, removing her two passionate outbursts, which played heavily in my proposed sequel emphasizing her relation to, I called it her adoption of, Eliza. In the film she calls her son and his friend Colonel Pickering "child-ish," but not, as in the play, "infinitely stupid males"; and her attempt to write something, in a state of exasperation at men (expressed in the line "men!, men!!, men!!!")—a departure from the evidently more usual letters of concern or courtesy or of business that occupy her time at her desk—is gone. These excisions make it harder to envision my sequel to the play, which imagines making Eliza the mother's protégée. But not, I think, impossible. What, for example, do we now make of her interest in attending Mr. Doolittle's wedding, and her telling Eliza that the two of them will go in her carriage, which in the film seems quite unmotivated? This might be tip enough to stage a performance along the lines of their unspoken understanding.

23

SHAKESPEARE AND ROHMER
Two Tales of Winter

Like the previous chapter, this one concerns both a literary text and a film—
in this case, not a film that is a close adaptation of a text, with tantalizing differences, but a film that is something like a commentary on a text. Eric
Rohmer's film bears, in French, the title *Conte D'Hiver,* which is almost the
canonical French title of Shakespeare's *The Winter's Tale.* I shall, to distinguish it from the play, translate it as it is advertised in English, namely as
A Tale of Winter.

The play and the film are relatives of the genre of narrative I have named
the comedy of remarriage. That this narrative ends, not as in classical comedy, with a marriage, but with a remarriage, means, as I have emphasized,
that the narrative begins, or climaxes, with a divorce, or some equivalent separation, not at any rate with some simple misunderstanding, or defiance, or
confusion (as in *A Midsummer Night's Dream*); so the adventure of getting
the pair not simply together (which had already happened), but together
again, back together, is not one of overcoming external obstacles to their
union, but one of overcoming internal obstacles. What this overcoming
requires is not a moral reevaluation of particular actions or decisions that
have come between them, but the revision and transfiguration of their way
of life. In a phrase, the dimension of morality raised in these narratives is
that of Emersonian perfectionism.

Overcoming an inner obstacle is manifested in *A Tale of Winter* as what
Rohmer's character Loic calls a resurrection, and characterizes as fantastic.
I note his claim in a gesture of gratitude to Northrop Frye, whose *Anatomy
of Criticism* made so strong an impression on me when it appeared in the
years I was beginning to teach. In Frye's description of Old Comedy the
woman of the principal pair undergoes something like death and resurrection. Frye explicitly contrasts this with the example of (unspecified)
Hollywood comedy. But some equivalent of resurrection or rebirth is blatant

in *The Philadelphia Story* (as Mike carries Tracy like a child in his arms from a body of water and Tracy raises her head to say that she is not wounded but dead), and in *The Awful Truth* (as Lucy, by let's say metempsychosis, becomes Jerry's sister). And since marriage, as I have argued, is an image of the ordinary in human existence (the ordinary as what is under attack in philosophy's tendency to skepticism), the pair's problem, the response to their crisis, is to transfigure, or resurrect, their vision of their everyday lives, something that requires, in words I recall George Eliot gives to Daniel Deronda, "the transmutation of self" which "is happening every day." The form the revision takes I have articulated as recognizing the extraordinary in what we find ordinary, and the ordinary in what we find extraordinary. The particular slant given to this perception in Rohmer's meditation on Shakespeare's *Winter's Tale* can be said to be an interpretation, or transfiguration, of the woman's fatal patience, and impatience, in "The Beast in the Jungle" and in *Letter from an Unknown Woman*.

In Rohmer's film, a pair of young lovers, Felicie and Charles, as they part, having spent an indefinite portion of the summer together at the seashore (perhaps it is an island), arrange to meet again. Charles is temporarily traveling outside France and can provide no useable address, and the address Felicie gives him proves to be incorrect.

We cut to five years later, some days before Christmas, and find Felicie to be the mother of a daughter, Elise, whose father is the unlocatable man of that summer adventure. With each of the two men now in her life (Loic, a philosopher, and Maxence, the owner of a beauty salon in which she is employed), each of whom wishes to marry her, Felicie discusses her inexplicable dumbness in having given the wrong address to the love of her life. She also discusses with them, and with her splendid mother, with whom she and her daughter live when she is not staying at Loic's house, her ideas about love. She makes clear to each of the men that she does not love him as she loved Charles. She tells Loic that she loves him and is grateful to him for his friendship but is not intensely attracted to him; she is attracted to Maxence physically and, when he tells her he has left the woman he was living with, she decides that she loves him enough to live with him.

She and Elise move to the city of Nevers with Maxence, who has bought a salon there, but the following day she recognizes that, as she tells him, she is not madly in love with him and therefore was mistaken in believing she could live with him. This revelation has something to do with a revelation she had earlier that day while she was visiting a cathedral with Elise, who insisted they go inside (something Felicie herself had no interest in doing) to see the Nativity scene.

Back in Paris, Felicie tells Loic she has not returned to begin again with him. She wants to have his company however, and they go together to a performance of Shakespeare's *The Winter's Tale,* of which Rohmer's film shows most of the final scene of resurrection. The play affects Felicie profoundly. Afterward she and Loic discuss the play and Felicie relates her experience of it to her revelation in the cathedral, where, she announces, she felt alive to her existence in a way she had experienced only once before, five years earlier with Charles. She describes her senses of true and false faith in a way that impresses Loic, not least because he hears in her words an unlettered discovery of insights brought to philosophy by Plato and by Pascal and Descartes, and she concludes that, whether Charles returns or not, she will not live in a way that is incompatible with their finding each other again.

It is by now the day of New Year's Eve. As she and her daughter are returning in a bus—one of the many vehicles, private and public, we have seen them in around Paris—to her mother's house for a family gathering, they encounter Charles. He is with another woman and Felicie, after saying to Charles that she was dumb to make the mistake with the address, grabs Elise's hand and dashes off the bus. The woman Charles is with is a friend who knows about the contretemps with the address and is not surprised when Charles rushes after the pair. What Felicie and Charles find to say to each other in the public street, and how their ecstatic yet ordinary re-encounter is related to the ecstatic and metaphysically extraordinary re-encounter staged at the close of Shakespeare's play, it is a proof of Rohmer's genius to discover.

I have been finding Rohmer's film to contain—more with each viewing—surprising and beautiful confirmations of the sort of claim I made for *The Winter's Tale* in an essay I published in 1986. At the opening of that essay I note that at the end of Shakespeare's play a dead five- or six-year-old child is left unaccounted for. And I sense that Rohmer's camera's repeated cuts, in *A Tale of Winter,* to five-year-old Elise alone, is as if to assure itself of her existence. Yet confirmation in Rohmer's film of my earlier thoughts on the Shakespeare play was initially hard for me to believe.

Shakespeare's *The Winter's Tale* is split into two parts. The first part comprises Acts I through III, in effect a compressed tragedy revisiting the insane intensities of jealousy interrogated in *Othello* (the madness made starker by the absence of a separate Iago, but lodged in a more emotionally plausible rival). The second part, somewhat longer, comprises Acts IV and V, working through its great pastoral celebration of nature in Act IV to a transcendental, nearly religious, return in Act V of reality which tragedy, or something like it, had denied. (How near the religious the return is, and in what sense near, is an explicit question, both of the play and of the film.) The emphasis of my essay on *The Winter's Tale*, extending the preoccupation of my companion essays on Shakespearean tragedy, is on the world-destroying skepticism formed in Leontes' mad state of mind in the first part of the play. Rohmer's film, on the contrary, seems as it were to skip that first half and to begin with an epitomizing of the late-summer festival engaging a country town, which makes up the bulk of the second part of Shakespeare's play. Rohmer transfers the jollity of this pastoral setting to a montage of a pair frolicking on a beach and taking photographs of each other and biking through the woods and fishing and cooking and making love, which seems precisely to avoid the part in which Leontes' madness drives the plot.

So before getting into Rohmer's film's response to, or perhaps its competition with, Shakespeare's play—one may even find in it more generally a declaration of film's competition with theater—let me just indicate what I have argued about Shakespearean tragedy in relation to philosophy's concern, through so much of its modern period, with the crises of knowledge associated with the religious and scientific revolutions of the sixteenth and early seventeenth centuries, linked with the names of Luther and Galileo and Newton. Modern philosophy is familiarly taken to begin with Descartes's subjectifying of existence (as Heidegger envisions the matter), showing the power of doubt to put into radical question the existence of the world and of myself and others in it, retrievable only in my recognition that I cannot doubt that I think, backed by the consequent discovery that my thinking ineluctably recognizes, as it were bears the imprint, of the existence of God. Much of subsequent philosophy—professional, academic philosophy at any rate—has retained the skepticism but lost the route to God, making the existence of the world a persistent, epistemological problem of knowledge perpetually unjustified. My claim for Shakespearean tragedy has been that, in the generation preceding Descartes's beginning of modern philosophy, Shakespeare was already, in the main characters of his tragedies, exploring characters whose destructiveness can be seen to arise out of this epistemological lack of assurance, but in each case directed to a different topic, a different way in which the foundation of a life seems to give way before a moment of doubt, casting the world into a hostile, worthless chaos. In Othello's case it is a doubt, expressed as jealousy, about Desdemona's faithfulness; in the case of King Lear it is about whether he is loved; in Hamlet's case about the worth of human existence, about the curse of being born, of being mortal; in Macbeth's case about the identity or nature of his wife.

In *The Winter's Tale*, Leontes' wish to kill the world, what of it is his, arises from something that, while resembling Othello's consuming jealousy, is more directly related, as I there emphasize, to a response to his wife Hermione's pregnancy, expressed as a doubt that his children are his. My essay on *The Winter's Tale* elaborates an argument for this emphasis; in what follows here I shall simply assume and assert it. Leontes' madness is magnified as it is shown to spread to his doubt that his five- or six-year-old son is his, from its concentration on the unborn child almost come to term in Hermione's body. For this present pregnancy he has at least the grace, or curse, to construct evidence identifying an alternative father, his returned childhood friend Polixenes. That *The Winter's Tale* differs from the plays in which skepticism produces only tragedy—so that it is traditionally classified as one of Shakespeare's late romances (together with *Pericles, Cymbeline,* and *The Tempest*)—I find marked specifically by a peculiarity of Leontes' basis for doubt (whether his children are his), which is (unlike the doubts in the major tragedies, which are about faithfulness more generally, or about the worthiness to be loved, or about the worth of human existence, or about the nature of one's spouse) not a doubt that a woman is apt to be vulnerable to. What would it look like for Hermione to doubt whether her children are hers? I am careful to say that it does not follow that women are in general not vulnerable to what philosophy calls skeptical doubt, only that where they are, their doubt of existence is apt to be expressed otherwise than toward their progeny, and in some emotion other than doubt. (They may have some anxiety about the father of their child.)

I am going to argue that Rohmer does in fact reveal in the figure of Felicie a kind of skepticism (one centered on questions about herself but somehow bound up with her sense of disappointment in others), and that it too is overcome by something that resembles faith but that is also to be distinguished from what we may expect of faith. This suggests that the first, tragic half of Shakespeare's *The Winter's Tale,* as well as its reparative second half, is after all under discussion in Rohmer's *A Tale of Winter.* But if so, then something in Felicie's strangeness to the world, let's call it her stubbornness or perverseness, which everyone around her feels in her—it seems part of her attraction to them as well as of her annoyance or puzzlement to them, say her mystery, her unknownness, something she feels in response to herself—this perverseness must function in her world in something like the way Leontes' extravagant and lethal strangeness functions in his world.

Here, if it can be made out, is a remarkable result, since it means that the consequences of melodramatically tragic action, to which human folly subjects us, is active pervasively, below the level of notice, in the world of everyday existence, the insistent habitat of Felicie. In my various discussions of skepticism, in relation to Descartes, Hume, Kant, Wittgenstein, and so forth, principally worked out in my book *The Claim of Reason,* skepticism *contrasts* with what, in reaction to the skeptical threat, we can see as ordinary or everyday life. Skepticism breaks into that life, with a surmise that I cannot live with, that the world and I and others are radically unknown to me. I *must* find a way to put this doubt aside—perhaps through what Pascal calls the taste for distraction, or what Hume depicts as the desire for sociability, or what Kant calls recognizing the necessary limits of human understanding, or what Wittgenstein calls the limits of my language. But if Rohmer's suggestion is valid, our temptations to skepticism, or say to a knowledge beyond human powers, are unannounced and may be at work anywhere, woven into the restlessness of vacations at the beach as well as into the business of getting along every day with others back in town, walking along the streets with them, and through tunnels and down and up stairs in their company, riding with them in trains, and subways, and buses, and automobiles.

In order to pursue this counter-vision of Rohmer's, I am going to take Rohmer seriously as a thinker, one whose organ of thought is the motion picture camera. "Take him seriously" means grant him the power to be engaging intellectually claims made by writers such as the five he cites specifically. In addition to Shakespeare, there are E. M. Forster, Victor Hugo, Pascal, and Plato. Forster's novel *The Longest Journey* is under discussion early, as Felicie returns to Loic's apartment to tell him she is leaving him for

Maxence. The passage in question is one, at the opening of the novel, in which a character imagines a cow standing in a field and—in an epistemological mode made famous by Moore and Russell at Cambridge in the years between the world wars—is moved to speculate (in contrast, as I recall it, with the cow's contentment) on the doubtfulness of our knowledge of the existence of the external world. (There is a comparable cow at the opening of Nietzsche's first Untimely Meditation, on history.) Toward the end of that same evening, Loic recites a poem of Victor Hugo's with immense flair, at the same time both movingly and quizzically, dramatizing an intellectual cast of mind that both attracts Felicie and puts her off. He is identified as a trained philosopher and a believing Catholic, neither of which Felicie trusts. (It may be pertinent that E. M. Forster's *A Passage to India* and Victor Hugo's *Les Misérables* and *The Hunchback of Notre Dame* are significant novels that have also provided the bases of notable films.)

As Loic, later, drives Felicie to his apartment after they have gone together to the performance of *The Winter's Tale* (their going together happens more or less by chance when Felicie visits Loic to tell him that she has suddenly left Maxence, but not in order to return to Loic), their discussion of the play focuses on signature passages in the writing of Pascal and of Plato, neither of whom Felicie has read but whose intuitions—what Loic calls her "instinctive science"—capture something essential in what these monsters of intellect have brought to the cultural table. Loic says, impressed by the accuracy of Felicie's formulations, "You're killing me." It would be a possible measure of Rohmer's seriousness to suppose that he has meant his camera to validate, or discover, the fact that instinctive science, anyway, instinctive philosophy, should be expected to begin in the articulation of an individual's intuition, before or beyond education. (This would form a comment on the debasement philosophy suffers when it arises from articulation without intuition, giving the impression of thoughts as mere, or empty, words. This is a way of putting what distresses both Loic and Felicie, in different, conflicting, ways, in that earlier discussion in his apartment, which touched upon skepticism and metempsychosis, the transmigration of souls, the topics of Pascal and of Plato that come up in the long car ride.)

But what does it mean to say that Rohmer's camera can "validate," or "discover," intellectual origins? What is revealed to it? What attracts its attention? What authorizes its witnessing? A Rohmer film characteristically includes a passage in which a woman is taken out of the ordinary by a transcendental moment, a declaration that the world we are given to see, like the words we are given to mean, is not all the world there is, and not all we mean. A favorite instance of mine is in Rohmer's film *Summer* (also called *The Green Ray,* perhaps to distinguish it from his film *A Tale of Summer*), in which a woman, wandering away from a boring dinner party, becomes lost in an indefinite stretch of trees, and as a wind animates the trees into a state of shivering, the woman begins to sob, one would not say from a fear of being actually lost, and if from a sense of aloneness, then no more from loneliness than from a perspective of a place in nature in which she feels unencumbered, we might say feels no longer out of place, shaken by an ecstatic sense of possibility. (I note that in Rohmer's *A Tale of Winter* there is a shivering tree in the poem of Hugo's that Loic recites.) The ecstatic insight Felicie will attain during the car ride is achieved by evidently opposite conditions. There she and Loic, whose love for her she accepts but cannot return, are not open to stirring wind and sky but enclosed together in a small, cave-like space, cut off from the world, human and natural, wrapped together in the woman's mood.

In that mood, stirred by Shakespeare's play, Loic raises the most obvious question about the play, namely whether the woman at the end is brought magically back to life or whether she is to be understood as not having died. Felicie explains to Loic that, although unlike her he is a believer, he does not recognize faith; as if whether Hermione had died or not died is inessential to the play's issue. Felicie goes on to inform Loic of a fact that he will be surprised by, that on the day she left Maxence in Nevers, she found herself praying, and what is more, praying in a church. So we have accordingly in *A Tale of Winter* to consider two kinds of time—a time of the experience of transcendence (in the church, and at the play) and a time of articulation or understanding of that experience (in the car ride). Freud's name for this temporal relation is *nachträglich* (meaning supplementary or extra), but his use of it (notably in the case of interpreting the primal scene) is not simply that something supplements or augments what has been experienced, but that in returning to what has happened, that is to say, in retrospect, the return reveals it for the first time, as if the first time it happened was in a dream. (I take Emerson's linking of Intuition with Tuition, a link he calls thinking, to be such a relation.) Dreams enter remarkably into Shakespeare's text of *The Winter's Tale,* as when Hermione says to Leontes, "You speak a language that I understand not: / My life stands at the level of your dreams," and Leontes replies, "Your actions are my dreams." These are explicit announcements that what happens requires a time for understanding or recognition. And I note in addition that the idea of what happens leaves its mark on Rohmer's text. Various people say: "It just happened"; "The things that happen"; "It could have happened to anyone." In a Freudian world of human interaction almost nothing *just* happens, so to justify the qualification "just" requires the most careful attention. We shall therefore have to come back to this.

We know as soon as we know that Rohmer is producing a meditation on Shakespeare's play, not merely including comments here and there about certain of its themes, that he cannot avoid the maximum theatrical stake of Shakespeare's structure, namely to consider whether the statue's being replaced by life *holds,* or "works," theatrically, whether the audience is given enough motive to stay with the moment. I know prominent and gifted Shakespeareans who cannot find, or have not found, that that concluding scene does hold them, the scene of awakening or resurrection. This constitutes a drastic criticism of a work that for gifted others achieves the highest level of theater. By "not avoiding the maximum theatrical stake" I mean that Rohmer creates an analogous moment in his film, namely in the return of a long-absent parent.

Whether this moment holds us in Rohmer's film does not so much depend on overcoming scientific incredibility—chance encounters in a bustling city are familiar enough events—as on whether we are held moment to moment, from the recognitions of and by the lover/father Charles to the concluding ecstasy of the line "These are tears of joy" and its repetition by the child, who thereby receives a concept she cannot then and there encompass. Its time of understanding, or revised understanding, if it comes, is years away. The film's attention to the child's absorptions suggests to me that the line joining tears and joy, taken from her mother, begins in her some measure against which to criticize the lesson so much of the world likes to teach, namely that existence is inevitably as melancholy as most grownups assume is natural to the human condition.

But when do we know that Rohmer's film is serious about—is measuring itself against—Shakespeare's play? I suppose an early incontestable moment—a fixed, topological point of identity between these works—is Felicie's self-identification in her conversation with Maxence the weekend she travels to Nevers to visit him in anticipation of joining him permanently with her daughter, Elise. In a long exchange with Maxence, in which his open sympathy evidently confirms her decision to make the move, she gives an explanation of how, at the close of the summer at the beach, she happened to give the man called Charles a false address and of why he had at the time no address to give her, and why she could not be located in a city register because her last name was not that of her mother (who used her maiden name, and with whom she lived when she was not with a man), nor was her name that of her sisters (who had changed their names in marrying). She concludes this exchange by observing, "I'm the girl no one can find." Now this is a fair reference to Shakespeare's Paulina's line that brings Hermione as it were to life: "Turn, good lady, / Our Perdita is found." Since Paulina's line occurs in the final scene of the play, which Rohmer incorporates most of in soon showing Loic and Felicie at the play, Felicie will hear her own line almost repeated back to her as part of her transformative attendance at the play. Do we imagine that Felicie takes Paulina's line to contradict hers, or the other way around? Does she, that is, take herself there as an echo or as a shadow, a negative, of Perdita? Presumably that is under discussion in the conversation in the car ride, which we owe more attention.

Before that, we already have enough undeniable connection between Rohmer's film and Shakespeare's play to be alerted to fainter allusions between them. Take, for example, the pictures that Felicie's daughter Elise draws (five years old, plus, I suppose, a few months; the film, after the opening montage, specifies its setting as across the winter solstice to New Year's Eve) of flowers and a princess and a clown, which can be taken as references to principal motifs of Shakespeare's pastoral Act IV in Bohemia, where Perdita is queen of the annual sheep-shearing festival. And given the importance in others of Rohmer's films of the perspective in moving from place to place and back again, as if one is at home nowhere, I am prepared to take the pair of visits from Paris to Nevers as some allusion to the move and return from Shakespeare's Sicilia to Bohemia. Indeed I am prepared to consider the connection, perhaps yet fainter, of Felicie with hairdressing as a witty, citified reference to sheep-shearing, since both modes of hair cutting are associated simultaneously with festivals and with money, and represent places where the woman both is and is not in place. (In Shakespeare's festival, Perdita is an unrecognized princess playing the part of its queen.)

A more serious, no doubt, or more explicit connection between the film and the play is Loic's insistence, in the first conversation in his apartment with his intellectual friends, on the difference between religion and magic or superstition, which also recalls lines we hear in the depicted scene from *The Winter's Tale,* as Hermione obeys Paulina's instruction to show life, and Paulina instructs the onlookers, "Start not; her actions shall be as holy as / You hear my spell is lawful"—to which Leontes will respond "If this be magic, let it be an art / Lawful as eating." This oblique association of Loic with Shakespeare's Paulina, marking Loic as the friend and protector of Felicie, thus links Felicie with Hermione as well as with Perdita, a mother as well as a daughter (both of which Felicie is shown to be, unlike any woman in Shakespeare's play).

The play insists on the mother and daughter resembling each other, accented in the briefly shocking moment of incestuous desire when Perdita is presented to Leontes as the betrothed of Florizel (the son of the friend whose death Leontes had sought in his early madness) and Leontes declares that he would ask for her for himself, upon which Paulina instantly intervenes. It is more to Rohmer's point to underscore, rather than incestuousness (suggesting the prerogatives and the unsociability of absolute power), the plain fact that all mothers have begun as daughters, as necessarily as that all who are old were young. That such truths may amount to revelations seems to me remarked in the way Felicie's wonderful mother accepts the reality of Felicie's erotic life. When to Felicie's saying she prefers Maxence's roughness to Loic's sweetness, her mother replies, "Sweet men are rare," I find myself recalling the opening scenes of Felicie and Charles playing at the beach, as if these are images of her mother remembering her own youth. And the mother's acceptance of life, of a future in which she will no longer participate, is expressed in the simplicity with which she remarks, when at the end she sees her granddaughter alone on the living room sofa, having withdrawn from the power of her parents' joyful embraces, "Your mother and papa are together" and asks if she isn't glad.

A comparatively tiny, yet still incontestable, fixed point between the play and the film, and perhaps most puzzling, is the rediscovered father's (Charles's) punctual and happy impulse—having been prompted to ask "Is this my child?" and been answered by Felicie, "Doesn't she look like you?"—to sweep the child up into his arms. When Leontes asked of his five- or six-year-old son, "Art thou my boy?"—having noted, "They say [your nose] is a copy out of mine"—it expressed a sentiment, or presentiment, that sent Leontes (or else was a desperate argument meant to stave off his being sent) into his first open speech of derangement, relating passion to infection and to dreams that question what is and is not possible. What is the point of this juxtaposition of Charles and Leontes—or is it rather a juxtaposition of Felicie and Leontes, since it is she who asks the question of resemblance between father and child? That she particularly notices noses is shown in her remarking, at Nevers, the nose of a saint's effigy. Earlier we heard her comparing men's looks in conversation with her sister, saying that she agrees her nose is like Loic's and adding that she never liked her nose. (This at once plants the idea of Loic as her brother, which she will later confirm in saying that if they had met in another life they might have been brother and sister, and anticipates the idea that she wants the child to have the father's nose, not hers, hence she as if restates Leontes' question of comparison.)

The point of contrasting Charles with Leontes cannot be to emphasize Leontes' stretch of madness—how can anything emphasize it more than the suddenness and avidity of his own embracing of his madness? And it can hardly be put there to emphasize Charles's normality, since almost anyone is different from Leontes, and cannot be called normal on that account. Perhaps it is to question what would count as normal in an abnormal world, anyway a world in which we have no measure of the normal, we might even say no measure of the natural. The great question of the pastoral sequence, the longest act of the play, may be taken to be whether nature itself, or whether the entire realm of art, can either of them be taken as such measures. It is a world—the human world is one—in which anything can happen; anyone may become lost in it; anyone may be found anywhere. The opening words of Shakespeare's play are: "If you shall chance . . ."

Let us stay with the fact that it is in Felicie's mind that the contrast between Charles and Leontes is made; she would have heard Leontes' questioning of resemblance at the performance of the play we have witnessed her witnessing. So what relation are we to derive between Felicie and Leontes from recognizing that, like Charles, she takes a question bearing on the faces of father and child out of Leontes' mouth, thus momentarily impersonating him? This somewhat deranged displacement may have enough force to push to a crisis what I was calling Rohmer's "seriousness" in invoking his various ingestions, both huge and tiny fragments, of Shakespeare's play, to ask from the beginning what it is in Shakespeare's *The Winter's Tale* that has demanded Rohmer's *A Tale of Winter* as a meditation upon it.

I cited as an opening response to their connection the incontestable allusion of Felicie's "I am the girl no one can find" to Paulina's declaration "Perdita is found"; and now with the further, odder, alignment of a line of Felicie with words of Leontes, I am led to suggest—of course in retrospect, in remembering, in recounting, in reconstituting, in recognizing—that the onset of the meditation is shown in the very fact that the very opening of the film is a montage of summer playfulness on some seacoast a train ride, then a ferry ride, from Paris. (I ask nothing much right off from the knowledge that Shakespeare's tale moving by sea between Sicilia and Bohemia requires imagining that Bohemia has a seacoast, a matter of some unkind merriment or distress to Shakespeare's critics and editors for centuries.) More serious for us is that the opening montage of pleasure ends by recurring to a scene of intercourse whose conclusion motivates the film's first words, as the man says, "You're taking a risk"—making explicit the possibility of pregnancy, something the woman evidently wishes to risk, as her enigmatic, spontaneous laugh in response indicates. I understand this as a sort of materialization of the invisible intercourse that has sacked Leontes' mind ("Go, play, boy, play: thy mother plays, and I / Play too; but so disgrac'd a part, whose issue / Will hiss me to my grave."

In my essay on Shakespeare's play I make a lot of the fact that the body of the play (after the familiar Shakespearean device of a scene of prologue in which an exchange between subordinate characters prepares more of the issues of the world of the play than could be guessed) begins with the words, "Nine changes of the watery star" (that is, the moon), words that mark the fact that Hermione is nine months pregnant (she will deliver a day or two later), and simultaneously mark the time that their speaker, Polixenes, Leontes' brotherly visitor, has been present in Sicilia. It is Leontes' striking together these two facts that ignites his mind. I contend that it is the fact of Hermione's pregnancy that drives Leontes mad, which means that his jealousy of Polixenes is a cover for that madness. (As in my essay on *Othello* I contend that Othello's jealousy of Cassio is a cover for his bewilderment at Desdemona's separate, erotic responsiveness to him, to Othello.) Why it is that the pregnancy threatens Leontes, why he develops a psychic ruse to deny his role in it, I do not suppose we are given to know—perhaps it is because the birth will speak of his mortality, of one who should die after him, perhaps because it signifies his separateness from Hermione, something coming between them. (I am perhaps encouraged in taking Rohmer's preoccupations to heart just here, because of a stunning film he made a few years earlier, *The Marquise of O*, whose subject is a mysterious, as it were fatherless, pregnancy.) Leontes recovers his sanity the instant he learns that both his children are, as he believes, as good as dead.

But how would the conjunction or conjecture of pregnancies affirm a further connection between Felicie and Leontes, rather than simply between Felicie and Hermione? I do not say the conjunction with Leontes is as simple, but I point to a moment in which Felicie's pregnancy is the object of some madness of her own.

Go back to the conversation with Maxence when she visits him in Nevers in anticipation of moving there with him. In trying to explain how she can have given Charles the wrong address—really it was only the wrong town, each town with an unresonant name (like not remembering whether Leontes is the King of Sicilia or the King of Bohemia)—she recalls that she realized her error when she made the same slip "six months later on the birth-certificate forms." So she connects the slip with her pregnancy. Both may be thought to be accidents. She concludes her account to Maxence by declaring—with an explanation that excludes explanation—"I was dumb. Stark, raving dumb." Maxence responds to this in a way that shows what Felicie had described to her mother as Maxence's intelligence, resembling Charles's in being self-won, not self-conscious, but unlike Charles's in lacking refinement. Maxence says: "You can't say 'stark raving dumb.' The expression is 'stark raving mad.'" And when Felicie replies, "You see, I am inarticulate," he returns, "It could happen to anyone."

This exchange is clearly enough a preparation for the re-encounter with Charles on the bus, as Felicie, seeing him only after he has seen her, and as Elise says "Papa," picks up the thread of the same explanation, in roughly the same tone, averring that she was just dumb, nothing else, whereupon, perhaps noticing that Charles is with the woman he is seated next to, she takes Elise's hand and dashes with her off the bus, leaving Charles a confused instant in which to follow, with a parting word to his companion. The difference this time is that Felicie has given the explanation to the right person. The explanation has never worked in the past, when she always sounds as if she is saying it to herself and that she doesn't believe it. Charles is the right person because that there *is* no explanation is precisely what he needs to hear, namely that there is no impediment between them in the world, that they are free to pick up the thread where they left it.

A question arises for me here that I may seem to have been avoiding and which I must not neglect to specify. May Charles be understood to recover (let us say, by metempsychosis), the figure of Florizel in Shakespeare's play—the Prince of Bohemia, son of the man Leontes had imagined in his murderous jealousy to be his wife's lover? This would seem somehow to follow from my earlier proposal that Rohmer had transposed Shakespeare's pastoral, from its place as succeeding the tragedy or (tragedies) of the opening acts of the play, to the play's opening assertions of nature in the film, preparing the ground for a miraculous deflection of (if not tragedy, then) misadventure. My problem with drawing this implication is that the invocation of Florizel follows, let me say, too mechanically. The other transfigurations (of Loic out of Paulina, of Felicie out of Hermione and Leontes as well as out of Perdita, of the girlchild Elise out of the dead boychild Mamillius), each lend a new cast to Shakespeare's texture. (I might say that I am working with an idea that Rohmer's film proposes itself as a metempsychosis of Shakespeare's play.) The idea of Charles as Florizel merely follows from the empirical fact that he is the only man for Felicie on their summer island. He has not been shown to perceive, through his love of her, the royal Felicie in the transitory garb of a festival queen.

It may be of help to ask: Which Shakespearean *pair* does Charles/Felicie fit? Not exactly Florizel/Perdita, since Florizel does not *return* to Perdita, nor vice versa. But also not the pair Leontes/Perdita, unless Rohmer is deliberately stressing the incestuous moment in Shakespeare's narration. And not Leontes/Hermione, if I have perceived correctly that both of these participate in the figure of Felicie. Just possibly Rohmer is suggesting that Charles hints of Florizel's fleeing father Polixenes, as if holding open the question whether there had been an element of the real in the cause of Leontes' original jealousy.

Perhaps the very instability in identifying Charles's relation to Felicie's multiple metempsychoses is the cause of my wishing to describe their reencounter as I did a moment ago, insisting on the rightness of her telling Charles in effect that there is no impediment (on her side) to their, let us say, remarrying. Perhaps we can say: Charles's reference to Shakespeare's play is not to a particular *character*, but rather to a particular *relationship* to Perdita, namely that the man she would give herself to in marriage is felt by her to be, or to have been, under a prohibition from giving himself to her (a prohibition also based on misinformation about, one could say, her proper address). If we say that for her the pregnancy was the impediment, this may be understood, for example, as her fearing that it would cause the man to leave, or cause him to stay for the wrong reason. Here is this film's presentation of a central formulation I have offered of remarriage comedy, that, in contrast to classical comedy, in which a pair who are made for each other face obstacles on the path of finding each other, in remarriage comedy a pair who have found each other face obstacles in maintaining the knowledge that they are made for each other.

Have I said enough, or imagined strongly enough, to satisfy us in shadowing Shakespeare's play with Rohmer's film, where the tale lasts roughly sixteen days, through Christmas to New Year's Eve, rather than roughly sixteen years, as in Shakespeare's telling? I find, for example, that I accept the instruction and the happiness of Rohmer's depiction of a run of dumb luck—can we speak of a dumb miracle? But why isn't it *just* dumb? This option is open to us to take—as it is, more or less, in Shakespeare's conclusion.

Here what I earlier spoke of as Rohmer's raising the issue of the competition of film with theater comes to the surface. Let us ask: What is the difference proposed in Rohmer's film between a photograph's being replaced by life and a statue's coming to life? One might answer that it is the difference between the wondering whether you know that a person exists, is alive, and wondering whether you know the person's identity. The statue is not a reminder, it is not dispensable, in this granting of life, it has a (virtual) life of its own. The dispensability of the photograph is declared when Charles says that he recognized Felicie even though he had no photograph of her. But is the photograph dispensable when, as in the case of the child, it is all she has as proof of her father's identity? His photograph stands for her for his reality the way the crèche stands for her for the reality of the birth of Jesus.

The instantaneousness of still photographs stops time, they are death masks of a time; to add that motion pictures animate these masks might suggest the irreducible (if mostly ignorable) experience of magic in our exposure to photographs, still and in motion. It is a theme of my early book on film, *The World Viewed,* that if we say theater originates in religion and is never fully free of that origin, then we should say that film originates in magic. In both *The Winter's Tale* and *A Tale of Winter,* the relation of art or image to reality is portrayed, or recaptured, as miraculous, specifically as resurrection. But to say so may seem to cheapen or take for granted the value of the work of film, since its version of resurrection is achieved, let's say, automatically. (Film becomes the very picture of a dumb miracle.) But I find that Rohmer's questioning suggests that we as readily cheapen or take for granted the work of theater, the fact that it achieves its version of resurrection (maybe not automatically, but nevertheless) instantaneously, achieves let us say metempsychosis, the replacement in a body of another soul. (If we say both transformations are the province of both film and theater, then we have to specify the difference of proportion in each.) Both transformations are occurrences of our everyday. And Rohmer's great subject is the miraculousness of the everyday, the possibility and necessity of our awakening to it every day, call it the secularization of the transcendental. This makes it seem that the transcendental precedes the secular. Is this wrong? Perhaps our various arts are in disagreement, or competition, over the order of precedence.

There is no denying what Maxence says: What happened to Felicie could happen to anyone. That, however, poses a further question that may take us to a more satisfying place to stop. *What* happened to Felicie?

When Maxence stumbles onto her having as it were failed to say she was stark, raving mad—I do not suppose him to sense that that is perhaps what she *wanted* to say—and having instead said something meaningless, or anyway something that hasn't been given a meaning, namely that she was, or is, stark raving dumb, her interpretation is that she is inarticulate, which we have ample evidence that she is not. The fateful inarticulateness lay in her misspeaking her address to Charles, the thing Maxence will help her remember is called a lapsus, what Freud called a slip, an *acte manqué*—in the Standard (English) Edition of Freud's works, translated as a parapraxis. The issue here is not what motivated the slip but what it signifies as a mental state between being dumb and being mad, what it signifies that it has, with however different effects, the same consequence on her world as Leontes' madness, however motivated, had on his. Namely, it excluded from that world the one each has loved, with whom each has produced a child. (Nothing with so massive a consequence actually counts for Freud as a "slip," any more than it could count as such, I would like to add, in J. L. Austin's work on excuses, which has things as significant, in their way, to say about slips as Freud has.)

The idea of inarticulateness specifically links Felicie's sense of her condition with the inarticulateness of Leontes' derangement, as well as with Othello's decline, as he loses consciousness, into babbling, both cases I have described in terms of world-shattering skepticism, revealing itself as requiring, and desiring, the destruction of language, words having become unbearable. Felicie's sense of inarticulateness, we might say, betokens a milder form of skepticism, an expression of the everyday mistrust of the world, a sort of mistrust of existence and of what there is to say about one's existence. One might think of it as the necessity of exposure to the world as the precondition of knowing it—expressed in those slights, distractions, misgivings, contretemps, defensive silences, withdrawals, reservations, that deal little deaths through your earthly career. It happens to everyone; it is done by everyone. Why Felicie would mistrust the one by whom she becomes pregnant and to whom she was saying goodbye for a while, what madness or rage she may have for a moment felt at his intrusive and absorbing role in what was her transformation into a mother, we shall not know. She is the girl they can never find. Who is not?

But we are shown (or we eventually learn that that is what we are shown) her overcoming of her distance from this man in the presence—no less, no more—of the Nativity scene her daughter is looking at in the otherwise vastly empty church, still in Nevers. In the car ride after the performance of *The Winter's Tale*, Felicie will name to Loic this moment of her presence at the image of divine birth, or more precisely at her daughter's witnessing this image (presented as indistinguishable in itself from human birth) as her having prayed, but not as she was taught to pray as a child. She goes on to describe the experience, with Loic's help, as a meditation, one in which she was not thinking but rather was seeing her thoughts, which came to her as with a total clarity, or with the clarity of totality (she describes herself as feeling full). It is rather a denial or curtailment of Descartes's cogito argument (that I know I exist because I cannot doubt that I think); it is a meditation in which, like Descartes, she overcomes her skepticism, concluding here however by affirming her existence as independent of whether what the world calls the world (or perhaps calls God) is present or absent. She says she felt then that she was herself.

We might say that what Shakespeare's play enabled her to articulate was that she is found, by herself. And since that means, as she says, that she has found Charles within her desire, she can say further (afterward, back in Loic's apartment, as he ratifies their conversation by reading from Plato) that it does not matter whether Charles actually returns. Which is to say, it will not affect how she lives now. Or rather, as she says more precisely: she will live in a way that is not incompatible with their recovering each other.

Loic is moved to say to her in the car—in response to her acceptance of her understanding—that if he were God he would particularly cherish her. She replies: "Then God ought to give me back Charles." And when Loic then indicates that that is too much to ask, Felicie corrects the philosopher: "I am not asking God to give him back." That is to say, He simply *ought* to, it would make the world better. It ought to be better.

Felicie's interpretation of her prayer—intuiting Pascal's Wager on immortal joy and Plato's argument for the preexistence of the soul—is her way of marking the difference of Emersonian perfectionism from utilitarianism, whose calculation of pleasure is anything but Pascalian individual riskiness; and equally from Kantianism, whose universalization by the moral law she denies when, as when Loic once said to her that her words are meaningless to him (it was perhaps when she said she could understand the preexistence of the soul, that she felt that she and Charles had met in an earlier life), she replies, "I saw it; you did not." She acts neither from reason (she once remarks that she doesn't like what is plausible), nor from inclination (she speaks instead of avoiding what is counter to her convictions) nor from hope (startling Loic by saying that not everyone lives with hope, clearly not meaning that she lives with hopelessness). She exists, as her thoughts exist; she loves; she counts herself happy.

Thinking of her happy, I wonder if we have material at hand now with which to give an answer to the question I raised about her enigmatic laugh at Charles's observation, in their prologue, that she is taking a risk. Go back to my observation that Felicie's "slip" concerning her address cannot be understood as a Freudian slip. Since I still imply that her blanking out has significance, what register of significance can or must we attribute to it? At a minimum mustn't there be some sense that she does not want, or is not ready to have, Charles present with the appearance of the child, or, since she is perplexed by herself, does not want to want that?

Her blank, or contretemps, concerning her giving the wrong address, cannot directly be filled in, as if it were replacing a substitute by an original, as a Freudian slip can be, by what Freud calls, in *The Psychopathology of Everyday Life,* "a symbolic representation of a thought." An example reported by Freud is a case of someone's "mistakenly" or "accidentally" using a house key to try to enter his office at night, which becomes interpreted as meaning that the person would rather be entering his house than working at night. What might Felicie's thought have been? To arrive at an articulation of her giving a wrong address we would have to have some reason for her not wanting to be found, specifically not by the man whose child she is bearing. (I assume we have no reason to surmise, as Charles seems to have surmised when they met five years later on the bus, that she had been pregnant with someone else's child.) Don't women want to be with the father of their child, if they love him madly? We know she wants in principle to live with some man, and that she has found neither a sweet nor a bluff man to be possible. If there is meaning in her madness toward Charles it bears on why she is less ready to live with him than with his child. Why would she, in other words, wish to be the girl *he* can never find? Or is it, rather, that it is he to whom she is not prepared to give her address now? As if the woman in Rohmer's film has been confirmed by Shakespeare's play in thinking that men in general, with whom one is in love, are some kind of menace to their child at the time of its birth.

This woman is the antithesis of Lisa in *Letter from an Unknown Woman*. Felicie has no specific reason to believe the man would find the child unwelcome, a threat to his accustomed intimacy and privilege with the new mother, hence a threat to the well-being of the child. Still, Charles did raise the thought of her taking a risk. Did he mean taking a risk not simply of becoming pregnant, but at the same time, for the same reason, a risk in trusting him? Is this enough to cause some skepticism about Charles? She will answer Charles's question, on his return, about whether she has known other men, in a way that indicates that Loic and Maxence have afforded her what experience she has of men. It is not a great deal to go on.

Here is perhaps the simplest hypothesis answering the enigma of her laughter. She laughs at Charles's suggestion of risk (partly no doubt because a risk for mad happiness appeals to her, as in her Pascalian wager; but essentially) because there is no risk, since she knows she is already three months pregnant. This would explain also her detail of filling out a birth certificate six months after she and Charles parted. (There are two scenes of intercourse; my simple hypothesis requires that the earlier, in which the sound track records orgasm, dates her conceiving early in the summer, the later dates the end of summer—the sequence that follows it is of their parting, and her giving her address, after the ferry ride back to shore.)

However ordinary this young woman's tastes and accomplishments are shown to be, we have seen that she is some kind of spiritual genius, in something like Emerson's sense of demanding her uniqueness to be recognized, expressed as her "asking a lot" of men—for example, she wants them to pray for her in church "from the bottom of the heart," meaning to pray as if they *were* her; she wants them to know life from life, not from what others have said about life; she wants them masterful and submissive, intelligent and sweet; sometimes she wants to sleep next to them when she doesn't want to go home, yet does not then want to make love, in this sense wants to be a child taken care of but not even answerable to a wonderful mother (whatever happened to her father, Charles is the only man she takes home to her mother's house); and she wants them to find her without her giving her address, she wants to be *returned* to, freely, to be found as herself, loved madly.

What gives this relatively unlettered, relatively inexperienced young woman so much as the idea that there are such things to want (or to want to want)? Which I imagine comes to the question: Where do the ideas of "instinctive science," or intuitions that become philosophical tuitions, come from? Which philosophers before Wittgenstein and Emerson really care about this sense of the origin of philosophy? I think at once of moments in Descartes (proving the existence of God by means of discovering God's stamp in oneself) and in Nietzsche (understanding the significance of music by understanding the deliverances of the womb). And I think that Rohmer's sense that Plato and Pascal care about such originations is right. But they are perhaps too easy to praise in this regard: I mean too easy to praise without fully knowing whether one believes or understands them.

In a sense there are really three tales in our two texts, but one of the tales is interrupted. The interrupted tale is begun by Mamillius, Leontes' son, the announcement of whose death awakens Leontes to his folly. Near the beginning of Shakespeare's play, Mamillius begins a story that he turns to whisper into his mother's ear. His mother Hermione had asked him for a merry tale but Mamillius, asserting his independent will, replies: "A sad tale's best for winter: I have one / Of sprites and goblins." Then, as Hermione accommodatingly replies "Let's have that, good sir . . . and do your best / To fright me with your sprites: you're powerful at it," Mamillius begins: "There was a man . . . / Dwelt by a churchyard," whereupon Leontes bursts in full madness upon the scene and disarms the intimacy between mother and son. You might say that Shakespeare's tale is about why Mamillius's tale is thus interrupted; or you might say that Shakespeare completes the tale of a man who dwelt by a churchyard, since Leontes has visited Hermione's burial place every day for sixteen years, and at the same time Shakespeare has deferred to Hermione's wish for a merry tale by providing a happy ending at the grave site. You could also say that Rohmer has contested Shakespeare's completion of the tale by declaring that a woman does not know where the man may exist, an ignorance that haunts her own existence as much as any sprite or goblin, and that Rohmer responds to Hermione's readiness to be frightened, say by the almost hopeless odds in the tale, not so much against finding the man as against keeping faith in finding the man.

It is clear enough that Rohmer overcomes our epistemological sophistication with probabilities by giving a child the last words, but more systematically by trusting the infantile economy of the demand for the coincidence of fantasy and reality that film seems born to satisfy—as if our hard-won grown-up work of learning not to wish for the impossible has brought us the danger of forgetting how to believe in the possible. Call it our unnecessary and unwilling suspension of belief.

In *A Tale of Winter*—along with other of Rohmer's sorts of cinematic discovery, such as how to capture the interest in the minimal sense of an event in the world, the fact that in each instant, as Samuel Beckett puts the matter, something is taking its course, or as in Wittgenstein's *Tractatus:* "Not how the world is, but that it is, is the mystical"—Rohmer discovers the vision or interest of film in a world of strangers passing, on their individual mortal paths, and oneself as a passerby among others, each working out a stage of human fate. The vision, as I am calling it, is one in which it comes to us that no one of us need have been in precisely this time and place, coincidentally with the event or advent of precisely each of the others here and now; yet just this scene of concretion is an immortal fact for each of us, each having come from and each going to different concretions, each some part of the event of each that passes.

Emersonian transcendentalism speaks ahead to Rohmer's. From Emerson's "Self-Reliance": "Accept the place the divine Providence has found for you; the society of your contemporaries, the connection of events." Some in my hearing have taken Emerson here to be speaking conservatively, as if not, and urging us not, to disturb events; in short as if his words had been "Accept the place the *society* of your contemporaries has found for you," namely a place of conformity—even though Emerson notes a few lines later that such an acceptance would amount to our becoming "cowards fleeing before a revolution." The place the divine Providence has found for you, on the contrary, among exactly these contemporaries, a place unknown to them, would be that place from which to turn to what it is yours to find.

I add the confession that I associate the little group of three children as the concluding image of Rohmer's film with the opening image of childhood in Wittgenstein's *Philosophical Investigations*—in both of which the child reads to me, among other ways, as the witness of its elders' lives, an image of children as beneficiaries and victims of the unclear world we have to leave to them. The rest of the *Investigations* is then a record of our discovering the capacity to come specifically, concretely, patiently, to their aid in clarifying it, something not perfectly distinguishable from coming to ourselves.

THEMES OF MORAL PERFECTIONISM
IN PLATO'S *Republic*

I separate out this list of perfectionist themes derived from Plato's *Republic* not because my list claims to be uniquely definitive or exhaustive of perfectionist ideas in that text (let alone of perfectionist ideas worked out in other texts) but for two other reasons. First, it seems readily to yield a more ample and systematic set of perfectionist features than the other texts selected for these chapters, so that when a different text, as is bound to happen, contradicts one or another feature of *The Republic*'s presentation, we have at hand a convenient source from which to determine what accompanying features may account for this difference. For example, the friends in remarriage comedies, in contrast to Socrates' friends in *The Republic,* are a heterosexual married pair, not much different from each other in age (neither of them a youth), each of whom is exemplary for the other, but between whom there may be a certain inequality of education which the marriage depends upon challenging. This difference should be seen to go with a decisive difference in the mode of conversation in each work, while in both works the particular mode of conversation is of essential significance.

A second reason for using Plato's text in this way is to put my philosophical cards concerning perfectionism as fully as I can on the table. I was just suggesting, in effect, that such a question as "What *is* perfectionism (really)?" is on a par with the question "What *is* remarriage comedy (really)?" Now I claim to have given answers to these questions (in principle), in the way that I think them answerable, in drawing out their open-ended lists of features, as I am able to articulate those features. Put otherwise, if you are prompted to ask for more precision in defining the identity of the concepts of perfectionism or of remarriage comedy, I hope you will recognize that if you make the question specific (for example, "Is the appearance of a newspaper story essential to remarriage comedy?", or "Doesn't refusing the idea of a state of final perfection mean that Emersonianism is not really perfectionist?"), then

445

you have made yourself capable in principle of answering the question authoritatively. The characterization of perfectionism by further themes is not inferior to defining it by appeal to an essential property or feature, simple or complex. Discussions that undertake to match up an expanding sense of a concept with an expanding range of instances to which the concept applies and from which the concept and the instances receive their sense, yield all the intelligence there is in such questions. These discussions are not preparations for answers of a higher power, although further questions of significance should follow. In a motto from Wittgenstein's *Investigations* (§371): "Essence is expressed by grammar" (here, by genre).

In *The Republic,* given that it is taken to be among the texts that are defining for moral perfectionism, the features or themes it contributes to the concept of perfectionism, or confirms, or modifies, remain open. Obvious candidates for such themes are its ideas of:

1. a mode of conversation
2. between (older and younger) friends
3. one of whom is intellectually authoritative because
4. his life is somehow exemplary or representative of a life the other(s) are attracted to, and
5. in the attraction of which the self recognizes itself as enchained, fixated and
6. feels itself removed from reality [in various chapters I refer to the last three features together as a "crisis," characteristically presenting itself as being humbled], whereupon
7. the self finds that it can turn (convert, revolutionize itself) and
8. a process of education is undertaken, in part through
9. a discussion of education, in which
10. each self is drawn on a journey of ascent to
11. a further state of itself, where
12. the higher is determined not by natural talent but by seeking to know what you are made of and cultivating the thing you are meant to do, or to be; it is a transformation of the self which finds expression in
13. the imagination of a transformation of society into
14. something like an aristocracy where
15. what is best for society is a model for and is modeled on what is best for the individual soul, a best arrived at in

16. the view of a new reality, a realm beyond, the true world, that of the Good, sustainer of

17. the good city, of Utopia. The soul's exploration by (imitating, participating in) Socrates' imitation (narration) of philosophical exchange

18. produces an imagination of the devolution of society and rebukes the institutions of current societies and the souls that match them in terms of

19. what they regard as the necessities of life, or economy, and

20. what they conceive marriage to be good for

21. in relation to sexuality and to bearing children, the next generation; and

22. rebukes society's indiscriminate satisfactions in debased forms of culture, to begin with

23. forms of debased philosophy; arriving at the knowledge that

24. the philosophical life is the most just and happy human life, knowledge whose demonstration depends on seeing, something precisely antithetical to academic philosophy, that

25. morality is not the subject of a separate philosophical study or field, separate from the imagination of the good city in which morality imposes itself;

26. the alternative is moralism; so that

27. the burdens placed on writing in composing this conversation may be said to be the achieving of an expression public enough to show its disdain for, its refusal to participate fully in, the shameful state of current society, or rather to participate by showing society its shame, and at the same time the achieving of a promise of expression that can attract the good stranger to enter the precincts of its city of words, and accordingly

28. philosophical writing, say the field of prose, enters into competition with the field of poetry, not—though it feels otherwise—to banish all poetry from the just city but to claim for itself the privilege of the work poetry does in making things happen to the soul, so far as that work has its rights.

ACKNOWLEDGMENTS

Given the idea of preparing a course for the Moral Reasoning section of Harvard's Core Curriculum that would provide the philosophical background against which the moral encounters depicted in certain classical Hollywood films may be understood to work themselves out, it was in my discussions with James Conant, the course's first head section person, that the initial list of readings and their pairings with films were shaped. The second year the course was given, Conant offered six of its twenty-four lectures, and it was he, knowing that I would want to revive the course in order to prepare its lectures for publication, whose suggestion it was to bring the course to a concluding, more ample format at the University of Chicago. The other graduate teaching fellows over the years are as follows ("HSP" indicates head section person, the teaching fellow responsible in a given year for coordinating the work of the discussion sections and the general administration of the course): Steven Affeldt (HSP twice), Nancy Bauer (HSP), William Bracken (HSP), William Bristow, Harvey Cormier, Alice Crary, Paul Franks, Eli Friedlander, Arata Hamawaki, Joshua Leiderman, David Macarthur, Katalin Makkai, Rael Meyerowitz, Daniel Rosenberg, Sanford Shieh, Sanjay Tikku, and Charles Warren. Also, Lawrence Rhu, professor of English at the University of South Carolina, who was visiting Harvard on a fellowship in 1995–96, offered to take up a section that year. At Chicago in 2001–02, Zed Adams and Daniel Wack took over seamlessly as teaching assistants and kept the momentum of the class going through my intervals of absence as I commuted between Boston and to Chicago. Without the resourcefulness of these young teachers (a number of whom are by now notable contributors to the profession of philosophy) in conducting the discussion sections integral with the course of lectures, and in fashioning examinations and directing term papers, such a course would have been unrealizable. The weekly luncheon meetings in which the teaching staff went over progress and problems of the course have left me with memories of cooperation and instruction that are among the most precious treasures of a long lifetime of teaching. The only hesitation I have had in affording myself the pleasure of dedicating this book to the Teaching Fellows of the course came from imagining that they might be charged with shortcomings that are mine alone.

The passage on hitchhiking in *It Happened One Night* (Chapter 8) was first published in *Humanities* in 1985 (by the National Endowment for the Humanities) under the title "A Capra Moment." Portions of Chapter 10 are adapted from "What Photography Calls Thinking," a paper I gave in Graz, Austria, in 1985 and published in *Raritan* (Spring 1985) and in *Camera Austria* (1986). Portions of Chapter 12 (on *Now, Voyager*) are adapted from a talk I gave at the Freud Museum in Vienna in January 2000. The account I give of *Stella Dallas* (Chapter 14) is adapted from its presentation in my book *Contesting Tears*. An early, brief version of the material on the film *A Tale of Winter* (Chapter 23) was given at the annual meeting of the Society for Aesthetics in 1999, as part of a panel on the film with Marian Keane and William Rothman; conversations with Keane and Rothman improved my text, as did a conversation with Sandra Laugier. The list of features of Plato's *Republic* originally appeared, in somewhat different form, in the introduction to *Contesting Tears*. I took the idea of isolating the list for ready reference from the set of materials Nancy Bauer distributed to her sections. Chapter 13, on Ibsen, was revised during a period in which I was in regular e-mail conversation with the literary critic and theorist Toril Moi, whose book on Ibsen is announced and awaited. At Chicago, Avner Baz and Abraham Stone took time from their teaching and writing to attend my lectures. Remarks of theirs in the discussion periods have more than once affected what I have written here.

It was Lindsay Waters of Harvard University Press who gave me the suggestion, along with encouraging and effective advice, to think of making my Moral Perfectionism course into a book. It was then my good fortune to work with Camille Smith on the preparation of the manuscript; her stern but sympathetic editorial ear, respecting my wish to retain evidence of their classroom origin, regularly improved the pages she was dealt. To get those pages into presentable form was a task I could not have imagined possible, let alone remembered with pleasure, without the patience, the knowledge, and the computer wizardry of David Justin Hodge, who also undertook the making of the index. And I would like to add a word of thanks, thinking of the difficulties I anticipated about the look of the work, to the book's designer, Jill Breitbarth, who dispersed these misgivings in each case with graceful simplicity.

Thanks are also owed to Dean Susan Lewis and her staff at Harvard's Core Curriculum Office (in cooperation with the Harvard Film Archive) for their patience in organizing film screenings as well as appropriate venues for sections, and for indispensable direction and assistance in printing and distributing the Source Book for the course.

INDEX

conversation *(continued)*
109, 234, 362, 367; and *Gaslight,* 114; as
criticism, 140, 142; of justice, 172, 177,
186, 217, 235, 249; and *Mr. Deeds Goes to
Town,* 195; and *A Doll's House,* 254, 257,
396; and *The Lady Eve,* 309; and the idea
of *Cities of Words,* 316; and the *Republic,*
323–324; and friendship, 367; and
Aristotle, 368; clarity and, 382; and
Pygmalion, 411–412

day, and night, 151–152, 155, 161
death and resurrection, of woman, 44, 398,
421–422, 428–429
deaths, little, of everyday life, 316–317, 438
delusion, 292–293, 297–298, 325, 330
democracy, 75, 184, 207, 351; nature of, 68;
aspiration of, 78, 180, 321
Descartes, René, 205, 424–425; cogito argument, 27–28, 112, 198, 201–202, 209,
424–425, 438
desire: rights of, 182; frightened by, 206;
denied, 240; human, 349
Dewey, John, 197
Dickens, Charles, 91, 137; *Great Expectations,* 381
disappointment, 2–5, 8, 28, 371
divorce, 39, 67, 253; in remarriage comedy,
39, 421; in *The Awful Truth,* 377
Dumas, Alexander: *La Dame aux Camélias,*
271, 380–381

education, 43, 46, 82, 114, 155, 274; in the
Republic, 315; vs. indoctrination, 335; and
melodrama, 390; in remarriage comedy,
409
Eliot, George, 211
Emerson, Ralph Waldo, 19–34; "Experience,"
1, 139, 141, 162, 315–316, 389, 392; "The
American Scholar," 3, 26, 29; as a bridge,
6; "Fate," 7; repression of, 13; secret/silent
melancholy, 18, 25, 66, 97, 198; "Self-
Reliance," 18–22, 26–27, 32, 39, 49, 50–51,
139, 144, 298, 389, 442; alienated majesty,
19, 21, 33, 51, 144, 279; shame, 19, 50, 99,
110, 208, 212, 217; and philosophy, 20–21;
sound of, 20; chagrin, 24, 29–30, 49, 214;
writing of, 26; "The Poet," 28; "Are they
my poor?" 30; whim, 30, 31, 253; speaking
with necessity, 31, 214; the true man,
31–32, 140, 141, 174, 209; constitution,
139, 140, 215; "Behavior," 200; upbuilding,
213; transfiguration, 214, 215; "Where do
we find ourselves?" 332, 392; criticism of
experience, 389–390
Emersonian sentence, 22
Euripides: *Hippolytus,* 177
everyday, the, 328, 330, 333, 352

Filmer, Robert: *Patriarcha,* 55
film, 316, 400–403, 442; reading a, 116–117,
272; material conditions of, 117–118;
camera, 118, 204–205, 207, 397; medium
of, 152, 275, 277, 319, 367; Emersonian
perfectionism on, 195; cultural standing
of, 196, 226; actor over character on, 205;
and feminism, 238, 271; and opera,
311–312; effect of, 319; nature of, 397;
and total audience, 401; and photography,
402, 436
Forster, E. M.: *The Longest Journey,*
426–427
Four Weddings and a Funeral, 153
Freud, Sigmund, 4, 199, 282–300, 333; attitude toward philosophy, 237, 242, 282;
The Interpretation of Dreams, 237, 286,
290; *Introductory Lectures on Psychoanalysis,* 239, 242, 282; "On Beginning
the Treatment," 240–242; "'Civilized'
Sexual Morality and Modern Nervous Illness," 242; "Thoughts for the Times on
War and Death," 242; "Transience," 242;
"Negation," 261, 329; "Delusions and
Dreams in Jensen's *Gradiva,*" 283–292,
296–300, 390; "The Psychopathology of
Everyday Life," 286, 439; "On Psychotherapy," 286, 287, 289, 290, 293; "Three
Essays on the Theory of Sexuality," 286,
299, 310–311; "Psychical Treatment," 290;
and ego-ideals, 308; *nachträglich,* 428
Friedlander, Paul, 335
Friend, the, 27, 174
friendship, 39, 42; the erotic in, 363
Front Page, The, 346

Frye, Northrop, 44, 151; *Anatomy of
  Criticism,* 421

Gaslight, 82, 102–118, 209, 285; and vampirism, 111, 117–118, 208
gaze, 280, 312; male, 277; mother's, 279, 401
Genesis, Book of, 47, 80
genre: of remarriage comedy, 73, 150, 153,
  159; -as-medium, 150–151, 153
genres: difference between, 233–234; scale of
  time in, 233
ghosts, 28, 111, 116, 198, 202, 210
Groundhog Day, 153

Hamlet, 92, 112, 257
happiness, condition of, 381
Haralson, Eric, 406
Hawks, Howard, 346, 348
Heidegger, Martin, 129; "What Is Called
  Thinking?" 201; *Being and Time,* 258, 314,
  352; on Aristotle, 353
Herman, Barbara: *The Practice of Moral
  Judgment,* 181
His Girl Friday, 145, 340–351; perfectionist
  quest of, 349; as wedding ceremony, 350;
  as comic stoicism, 351
Hobbes, Thomas, 56–58
human: restlessness, 128, 199, 204, 218, 314;
  nervousness, 240; monstrousness,
  370–371, 393
Hume, David, 58, 127, 210; and skepticism,
  122

Ibsen, Henrik: *A Doll's House,* 1, 247–264,
  280; *Brand,* 248; *Emperor and Galilean,*
  248, 256; *Hedda Gabler,* 248; *Peer Gynt,*
  248; *Rosmersholm,* 248; *The Wild
  Duck,* 248; *An Enemy of the People,* 250;
  and melodramas of ideals, 306
imitation, 209
Imitation of Life, 271
importance: and *The Philadelphia Story,* 40,
  75; recounting of, 262; Wittgenstein on,
  299, 355
intelligible, making ourselves, 22, 24–26, 42,
  49–50, 98, 153, 165, 222, 263, 336, 381. *See
  also* moral standing

intention, 44–45
interruption, 145–146
It Happened One Night, 145–163, 183, 189
irony, dramatic, 263–264

James, Henry, 389–394, 404–407; "The
  Birthplace," 391; "The Jolly Corner," 391,
  393, 407; *The American Experience,* 393;
  The Ambassadors, 406; and Emerson,
  406–407; *The American Scene,* 407. *See
  also* "Beast in the Jungle, The"
James, William: *Varieties of Religious
  Experience,* 17
Jensen, Wilhelm: *Gradiva: A Pompeiian
  Fantasy,* 283–285, 287–289, 292, 294,
  296–300, 308
jokes, 289
Joyce, James, 202, 249
judgment, 329–330, 333, 368–369

Kant, Immanuel, 42, 43, 119–144, 170, 182,
  216; *Groundwork of the Metaphysics of
  Morals,* 121, 129, 132, 139, 140–141, 144,
  250; two standpoints, 1, 32, 129; constraint, 31–32, 139; and system, 120–121,
  127–128, 130; *Critique of Judgment,* 121,
  361; *Critique of Practical Reason,* 121;
  Critique of Pure Reason, 121, 125; judgments (analytic and synthetic), 122–125;
  judgments (synthetic *a priori*), 123; necessity, 123, 125, 130; categorical imperative,
  124, 132–135, 138, 140, 250–251, 255; categories, 124, 127; Copernican Revolution,
  125–126; and limitation, 125, 164;
  *Religion within the Limits of Reason
  Alone,* 128; moral freedom, 132; maxim,
  135–136, 141–142, 251; kingdom of ends,
  138, 141–142, 144, 164, 165, 251
Klein, Melanie, 279
knowledge, 82, 114, 127, 394; temptation to,
  80–82; male, 112; limits of, 122, 126–128;
  conditions of, 125–127, 164–165
Korsgaard, Christine, 133, 144
Kripke, Saul, 186

Lacan, Jacques, 243, 333, 403; *Freud's Papers
  on Technique, 1953–1954,* 113, 308

Index

455

Shakespeare, William *(continued)*
Night's Dream, 151; *Othello,* 424. *See also*
Winter's Tale, The
Shaw, George Bernard: *Man and Superman,*
256; *The Quintessence of Ibsenism,* 256;
and didacticism, 409, 413; *Heartbreak*
House, 409; *Saint Joan,* 409; and William
Morris, 413–414; and John Ruskin, 414.
See also Pygmalion
Shoah (Claude Lanzmann), 236
skepticism, 110, 112, 117; and Kant,
126–127; moral, 166; and Shakespeare,
424–426
sleep, 113, 370. *See also* awakening
slip *(acte manqué),* 288, 333, 353, 437, 439
social contract, theory of, 61, 348. *See also*
Locke; Rousseau
Socrates, 318
somatogram, 199–200, 205
speech: ordinary, 7; passionate, 99; action as
mode of, 135, 141, 252; and silence
197–198, 203; economy and aesthetics of,
333; justice of, 356; conditions of, 394,
411–412; proper, 412–413
standing, 125, 141, 154; for humanity, 32,
51, 140, 208, 210, 217; moral, 50, 235
Stella Dallas, 108, 116, 209, 265–281
Sturges, Preston, 305–306; *Sullivan's Travels,*
305. *See also Lady Eve, The*

Tale of Winter, A (Rohmer), 363, 421–443;
pregnancy in, 433–434, 436
tears, 77–78
theater: character and actor in, 416; and
film, 436–437
thinking, 29, 199–201, 204, 428
Thoreau, Henry David, 26, 195, 203, 225;
Walden, 20, 22–23, 157, 331; "Civil

Disobedience," 23; quiet desperation, 25,
66, 97, 198; mo(u)rning, 279
Torok, Maria: *The Wolf Man's Magic Word,*
337
tragedy, 225–226, 371

utopia, 17–18, 207, 447

Vertigo, 403
virtue ethics, 318
voice, 51–52, 69, 98, 203, 207, 209, 239, 312,
379; feminine, 77, 296; woman's, 101, 296;
lacking a, 188

Wagner, Richard: *Tannhäuser,* 311–312
walking, 329
Warshow, Robert, 286; *The Immediate*
Experience, 197
Whitman, Walt: "Song of the Open Road,"
161–162; invention of wedding ceremony,
162
Wilde, Oscar, 232
Williams, Linda: "'Something Else Besides a
Mother': *Stella Dallas* and the Maternal
Melodrama," 273, 275–276
Williams, William Carlos: *Paterson,* 313–
314
Winter's Tale, The (Shakespeare), 2, 421–437,
441–442; pregnancy in, 425
Wittgenstein, Ludwig, 114, 162, 186, 198,
214, 293, 295; and peace, 5, 128; and language games, 326; *Tractatus,* 442. *See also*
Philosophical Investigations
words, 332–333; humbled by, 19, 50, 79, 113,
144; on film, 159; city of, 225, 321, 350,
414; cure by, 294; magic of, 295; conditions for, 317; owing of, 356
writing: as allegory, 24; and suffering, 139